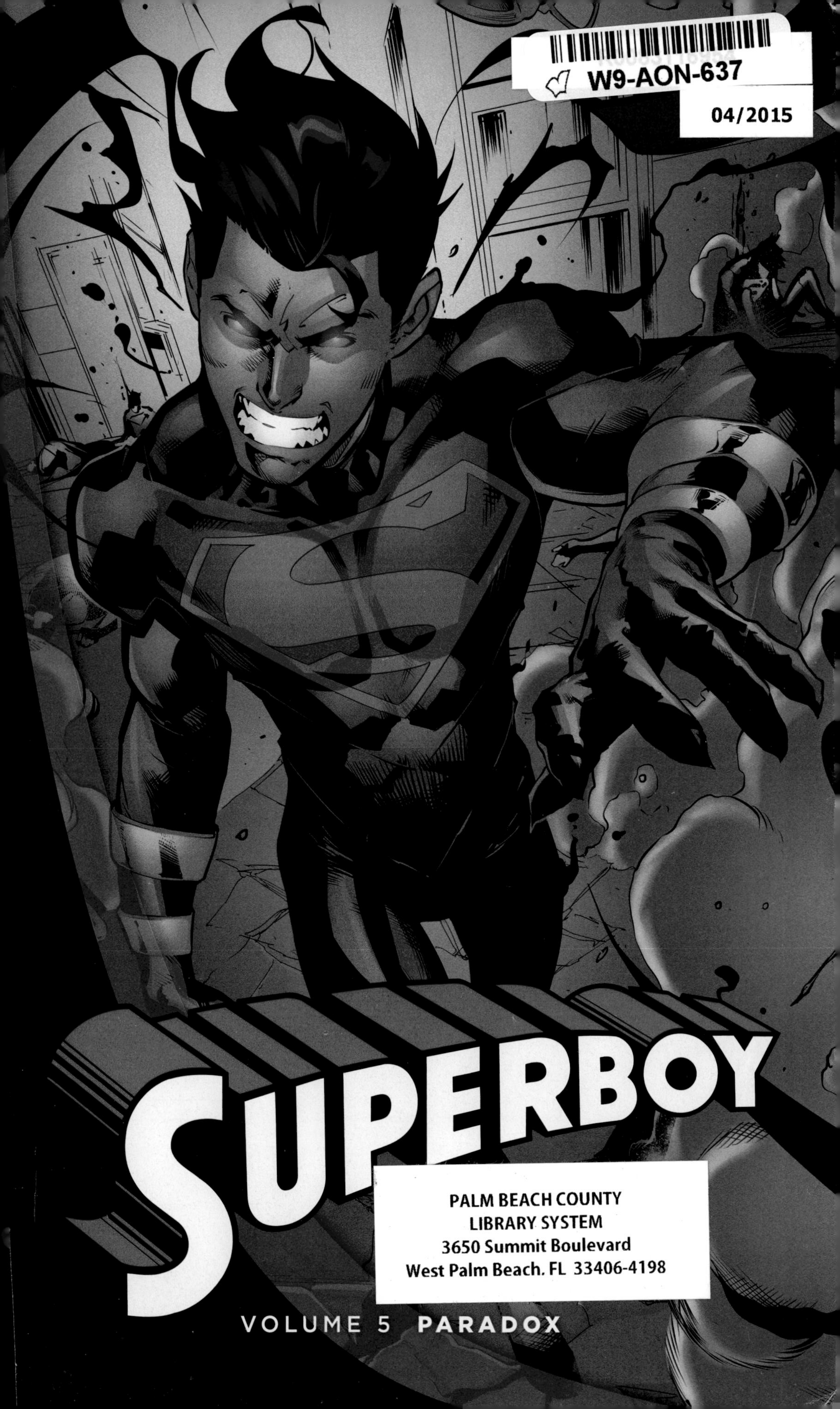
SUPERBOY
VOLUME 5 PARADOX

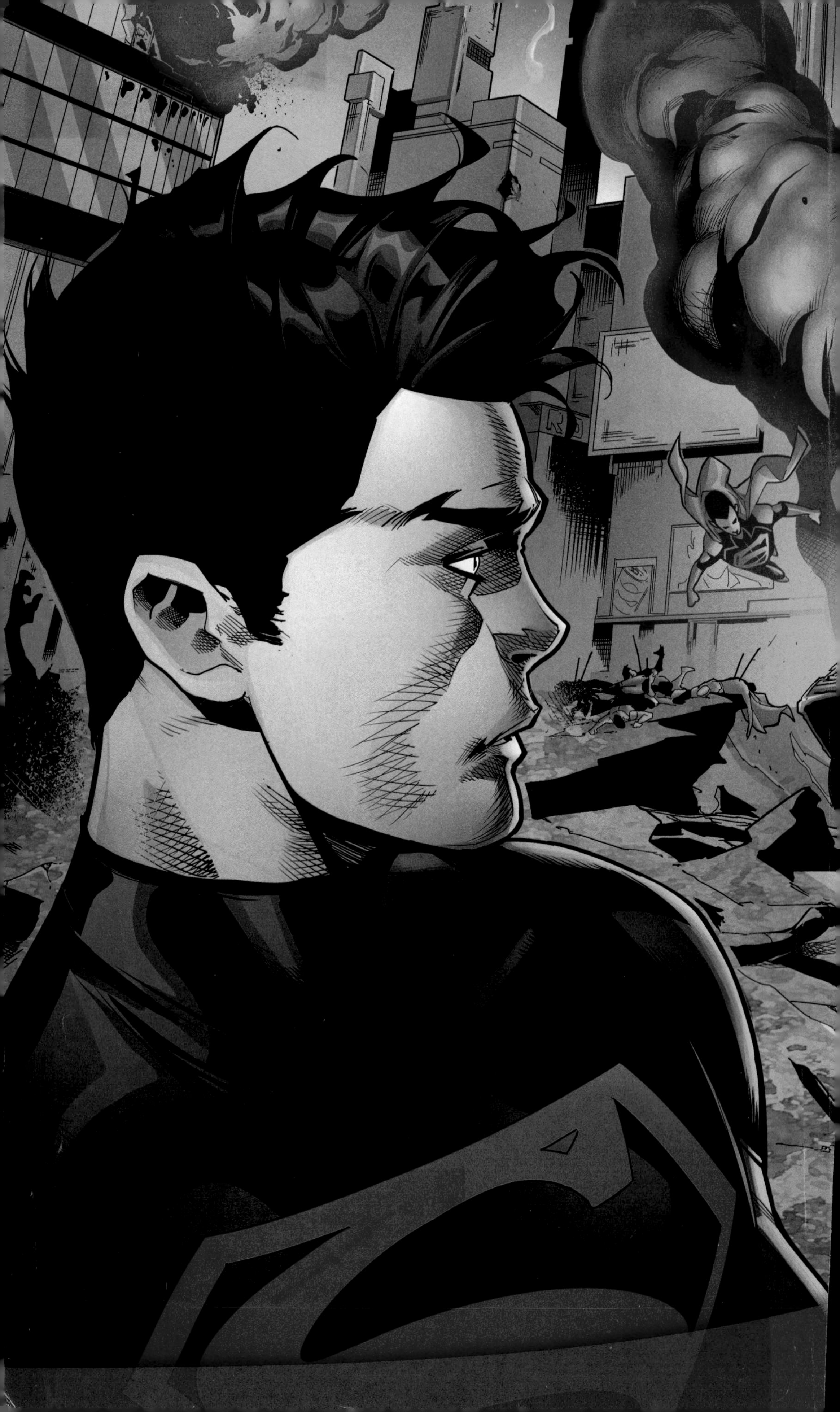

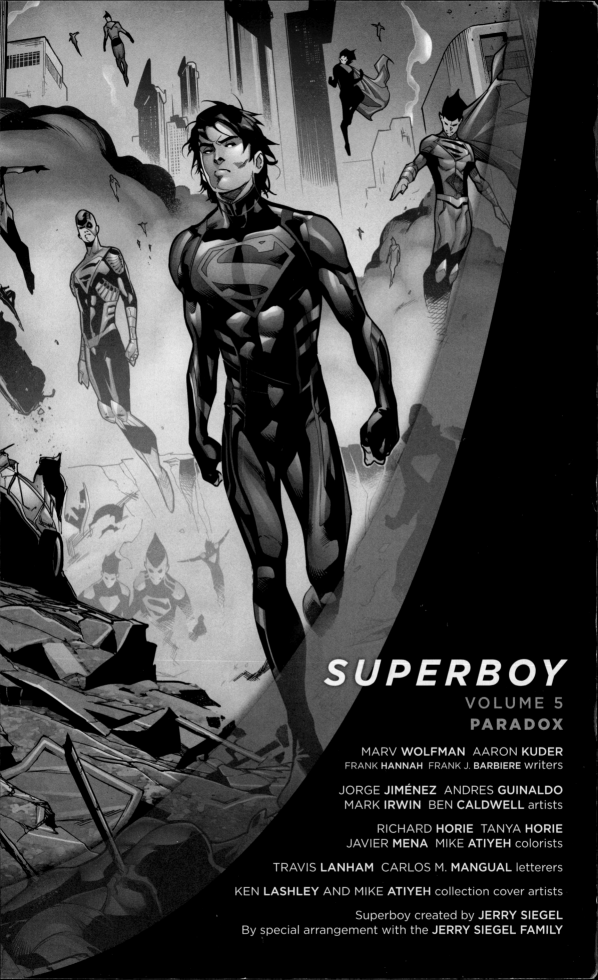

SUPERBOY
VOLUME 5
PARADOX

MARV **WOLFMAN**   AARON **KUDER**
FRANK **HANNAH**   FRANK J. **BARBIERE** writers

JORGE **JIMÉNEZ**   ANDRES **GUINALDO**
MARK **IRWIN**   BEN **CALDWELL** artists

RICHARD **HORIE**   TANYA **HORIE**
JAVIER **MENA**   MIKE **ATIYEH** colorists

TRAVIS **LANHAM**   CARLOS M. **MANGUAL** letterers

KEN **LASHLEY** AND MIKE **ATIYEH** collection cover artists

Superboy created by **JERRY SIEGEL**
By special arrangement with the **JERRY SIEGEL FAMILY**

MIKE COTTON Editor – Original Series ANTHONY MARQUES Assistant Editor – Original Series LIZ ERICKSON Editor
ROBBIN BROSTERMAN Design Director – Books ROBBIE BIEDERMAN Publication Design

BOB HARRAS Senior VP – Editor-in-Chief, DC Comics

DIANE NELSON President DAN DIDIO and JIM LEE Co-Publishers GEOFF JOHNS Chief Creative Officer
AMIT DESAI Senior VP – Marketing and Franchise Management
AMY GENKINS Senior VP – Business and Legal Affairs NAIRI GARDINER Senior VP – Finance
JEFF BOISON VP – Publishing Planning MARK CHIARELLO VP – Art Direction and Design
JOHN CUNNINGHAM VP – Marketing TERRI CUNNINGHAM VP – Editorial Administration
LARRY GANEM VP – Talent Relations and Services ALISON GILL Senior VP – Manufacturing and Operations
HANK KANALZ Senior VP – Vertigo and Integrated Publishing JAY KOGAN VP – Business and Legal Affairs, Publishing
JACK MAHAN VP – Business Affairs, Talent NICK NAPOLITANO VP – Manufacturing Administration SUE POHJA VP – Book Sales
FRED RUIZ VP – Manufacturing Operations COURTNEY SIMMONS Senior VP – Publicity BOB WAYNE Senior VP – Sales

SUPERBOY VOLUME 5: PARADOX

Published by DC Comics. Compilation Copyright © 2015 DC Comics. All Rights Reserved.

Originally published in single magazine form in SUPERBOY #26-34, SUPERBOY: FUTURES END #1 © 2014 DC Comics.
All Rights Reserved. All characters, their distinctive likenesses and related elements featured in this publication are trademarks of DC Comics.
The stories, characters and incidents featured in this publication are entirely fictional.
DC Comics does not read or accept unsolicited ideas, stories or artwork.

DC Comics, 1700 Broadway, New York, NY 10019
A Warner Bros. Entertainment Company.
Printed by RR Donnelley, Owensville, MO, USA. 12/5/14. First Printing.
ISBN: 978-1-4012-5092-8

Library of Congress Cataloging-in-Publication Data

Wolfman, Marv, author.
Superboy. Volume 5, Paradox / Marv Wolfman, writer ; Andres Guinaldo, Mark Irwin, artists.
pages cm. — (The New 52!)
Originally published in single magazine form as SUPERBOY 26-34, SUPERBOY: FUTURES END 1
ISBN 978-1-4012-5092-8 (pbk.)
1. Graphic novels. I. Guinaldo, Andres, illustrator. II. Irwin, Mark, 1969- illustrator. III. Title. IV. Title: Paradox.

PN6728.S87W65 2015
741.5'973—dc23

2014034201

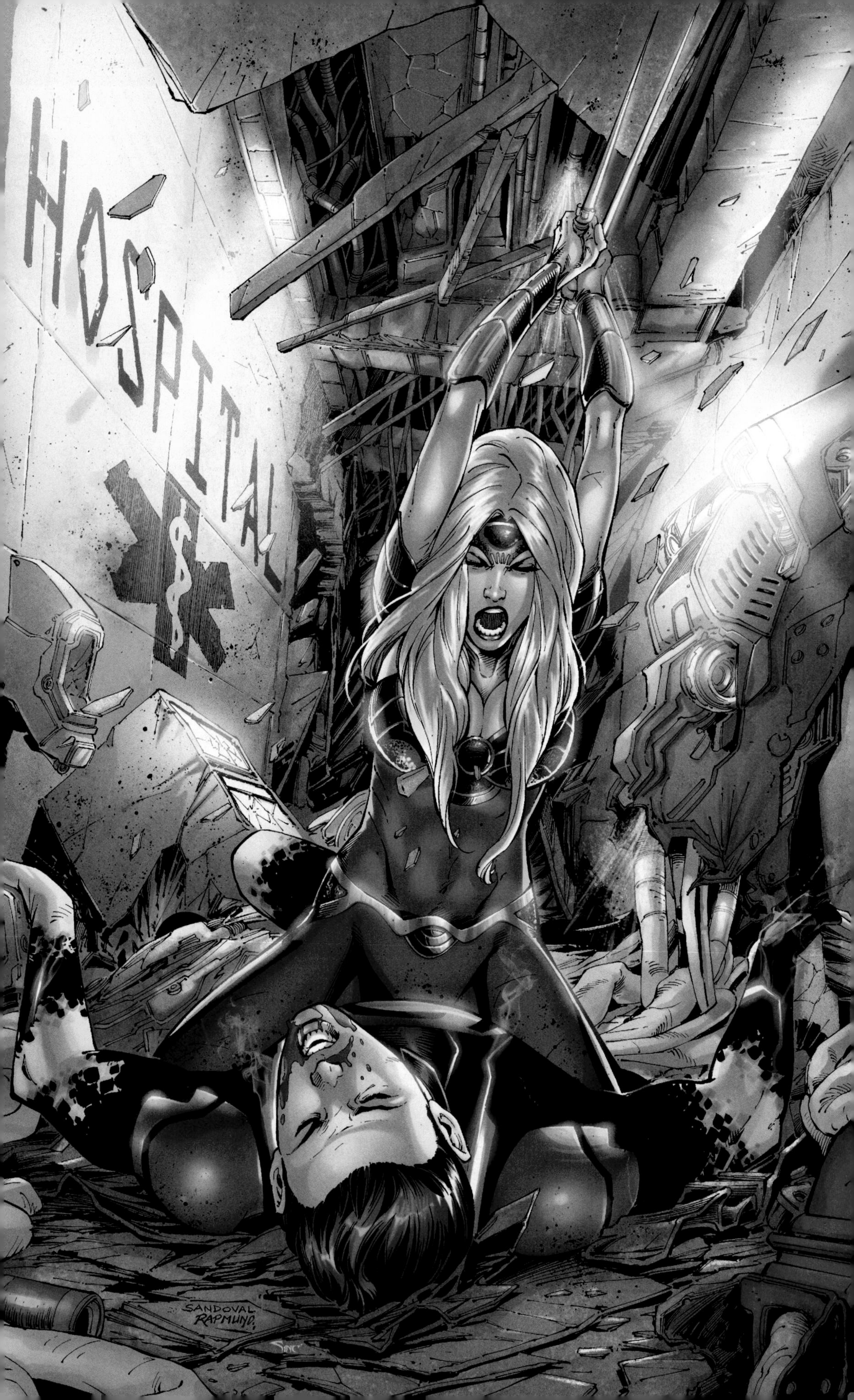
HOSPITAL
SANDOVAL
RAPMUND

TO HELL AND BACK

FRANK HANNAH and MARV WOLFMAN story MARV WOLFMAN writer ANDRES GUINALDO penciller MARK IRWIN inker JAVIER MENA colorist TRAVIS LANHAM letterer cover art by RAFAEL SANDOVAL, NORM RAPMUND and ALEX SINCLAIR

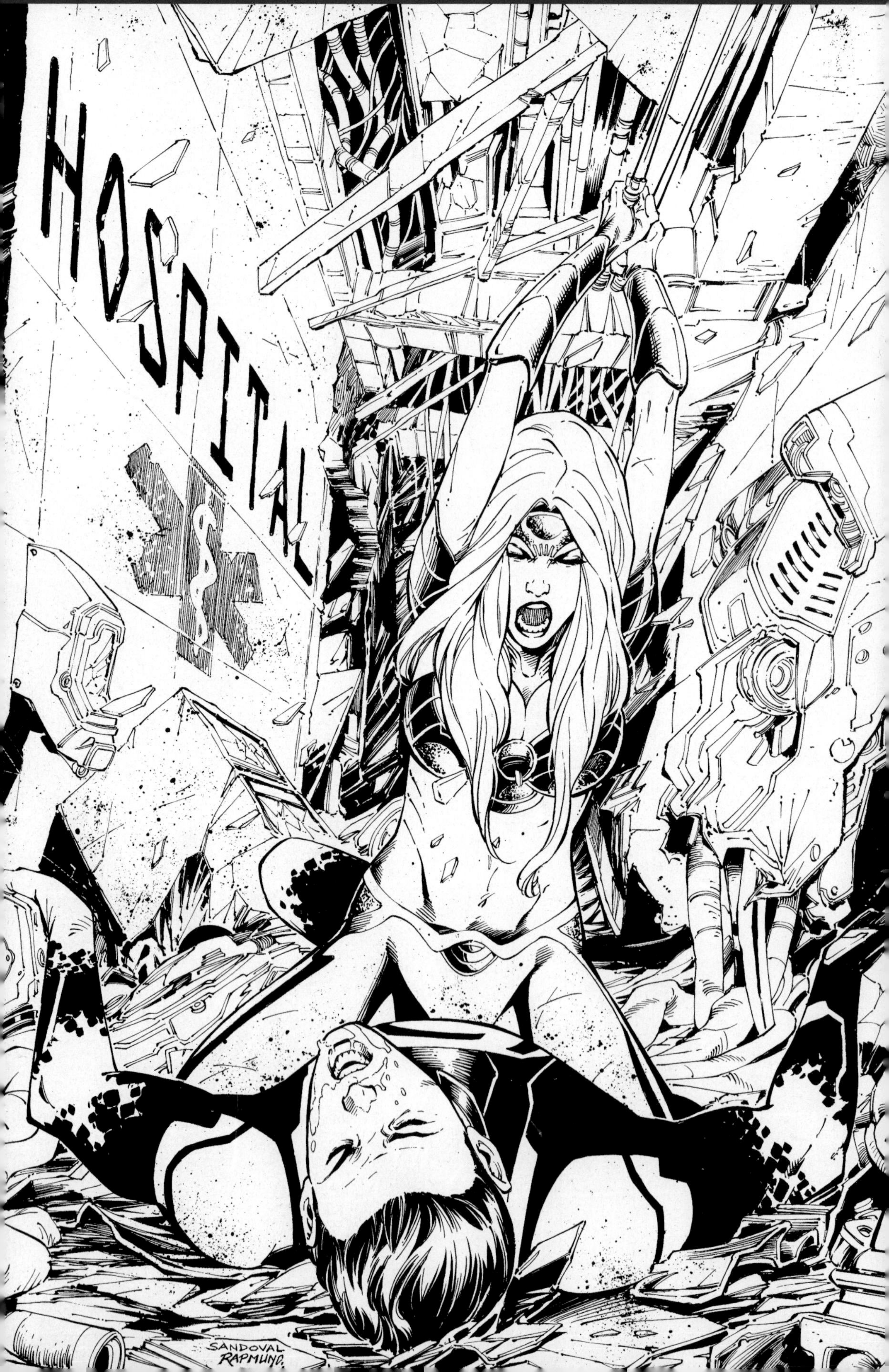

HOSPITAL
SANDOVAL
RAPMUND.

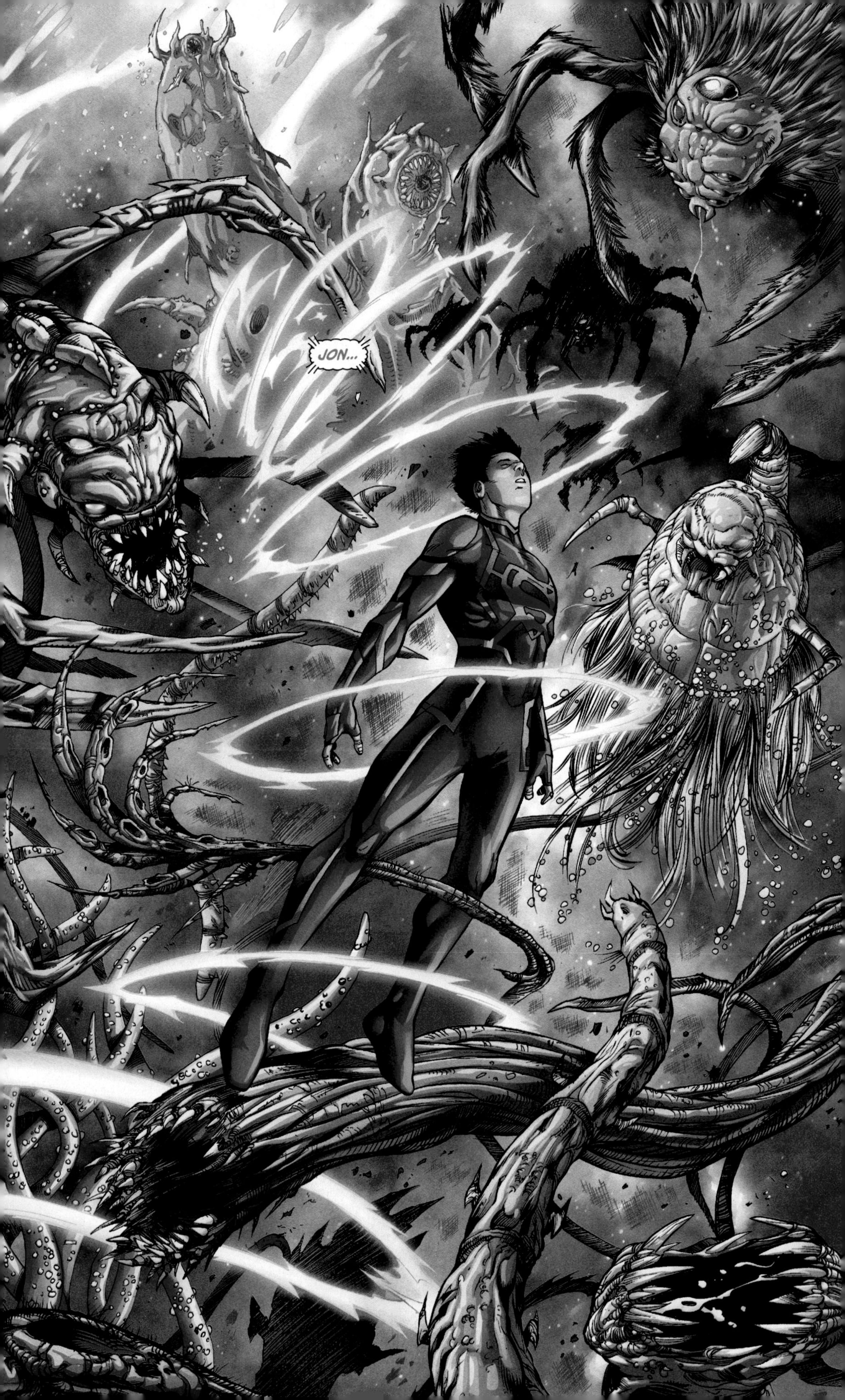
JON...

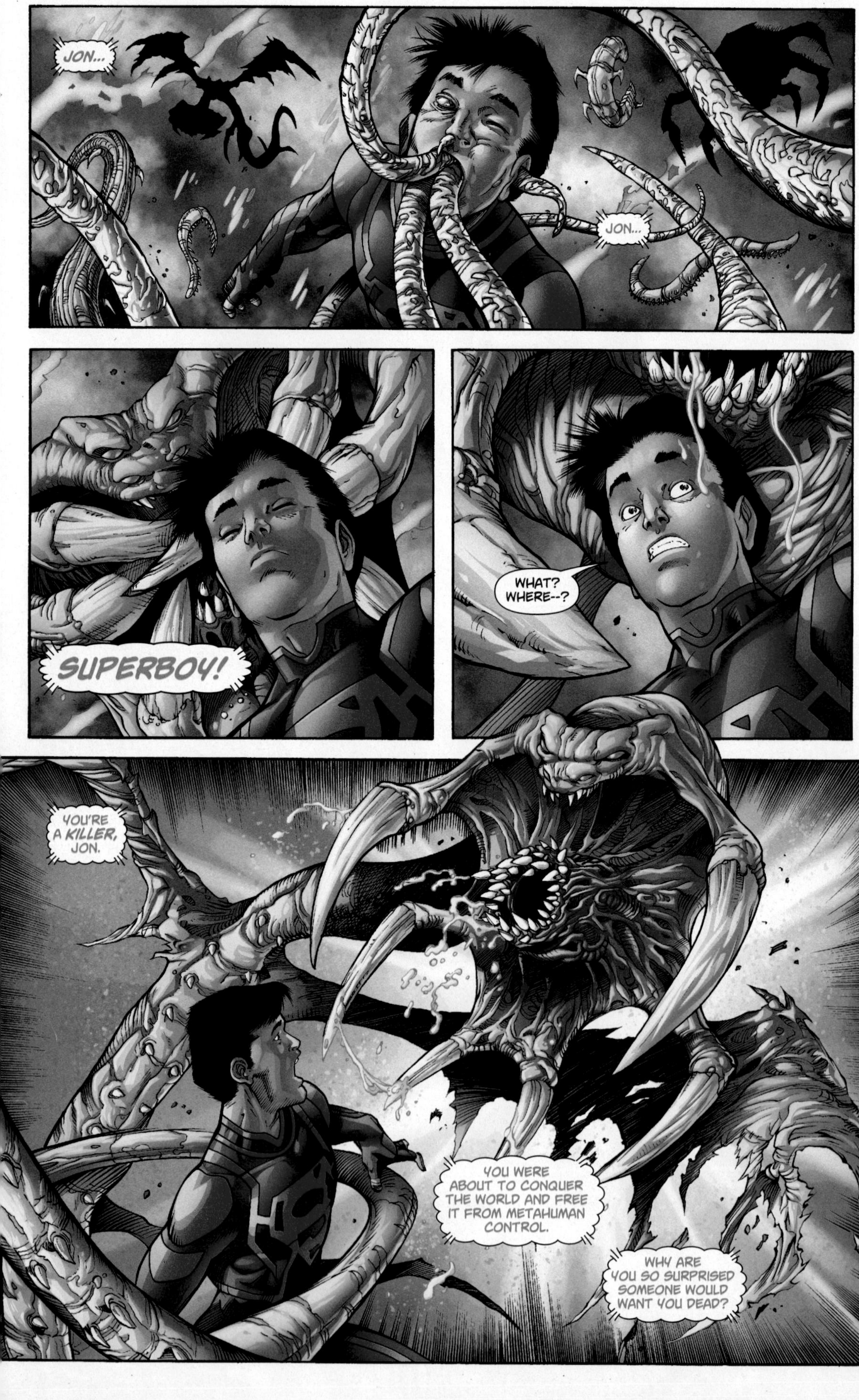
JON...
JON...
SUPERBOY!
WHAT? WHERE--?
YOU'RE A KILLER, JON.
YOU WERE ABOUT TO CONQUER THE WORLD AND FREE IT FROM METAHUMAN CONTROL.
WHY ARE YOU SO SURPRISED SOMEONE WOULD WANT YOU DEAD?

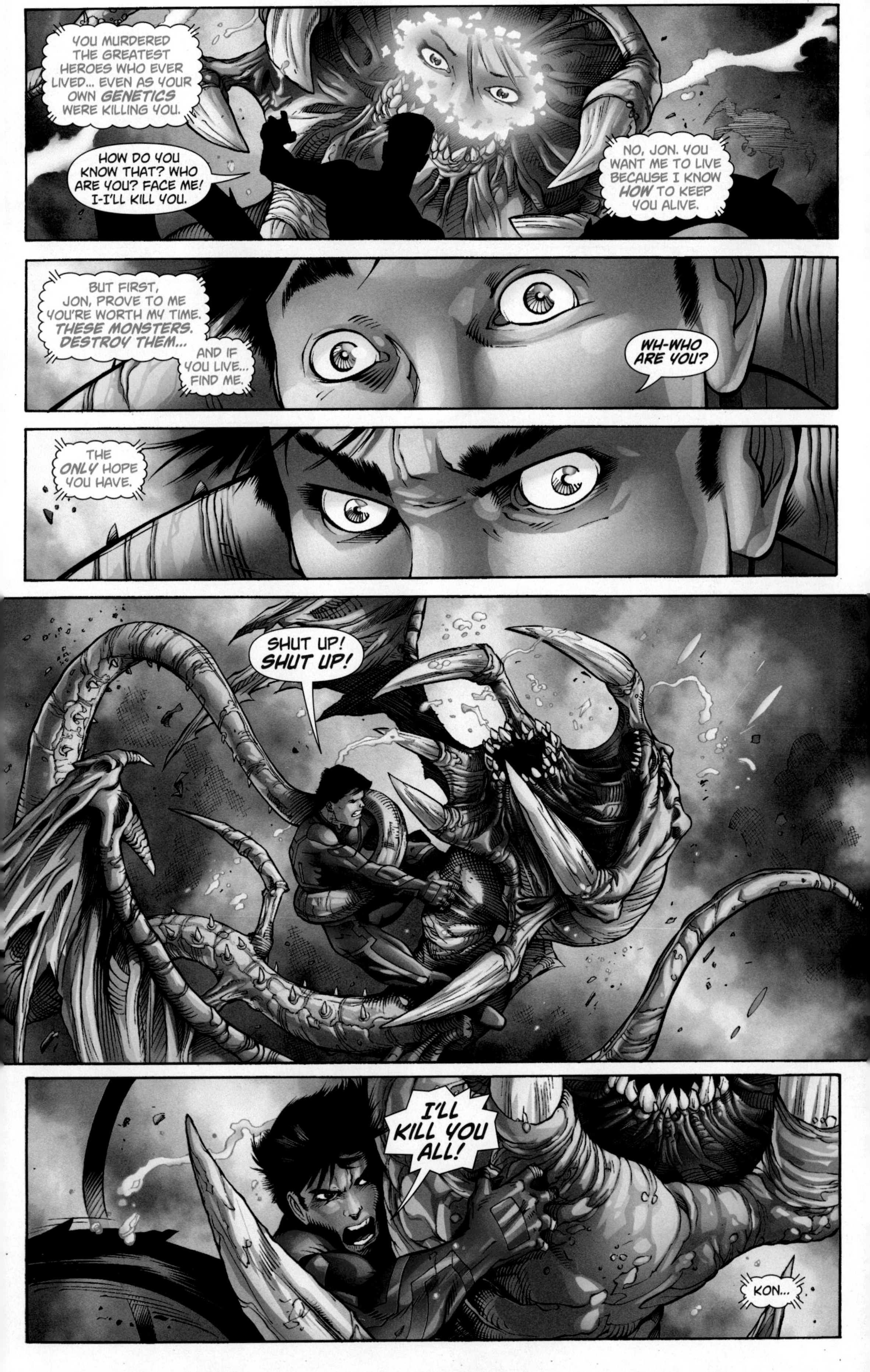
YOU MURDERED THE GREATEST HEROES WHO EVER LIVED... EVEN AS YOUR OWN GENETICS WERE KILLING YOU.
HOW DO YOU KNOW THAT? WHO ARE YOU? FACE ME! I-I'LL KILL YOU.
NO, JON. YOU WANT ME TO LIVE BECAUSE I KNOW HOW TO KEEP YOU ALIVE.
BUT FIRST, JON, PROVE TO ME YOU'RE WORTH MY TIME. THESE MONSTERS. DESTROY THEM...
AND IF YOU LIVE... FIND ME.
WH-WHO ARE YOU?
THE ONLY HOPE YOU HAVE.
SHUT UP! SHUT UP!
I'LL KILL YOU ALL!
KON...

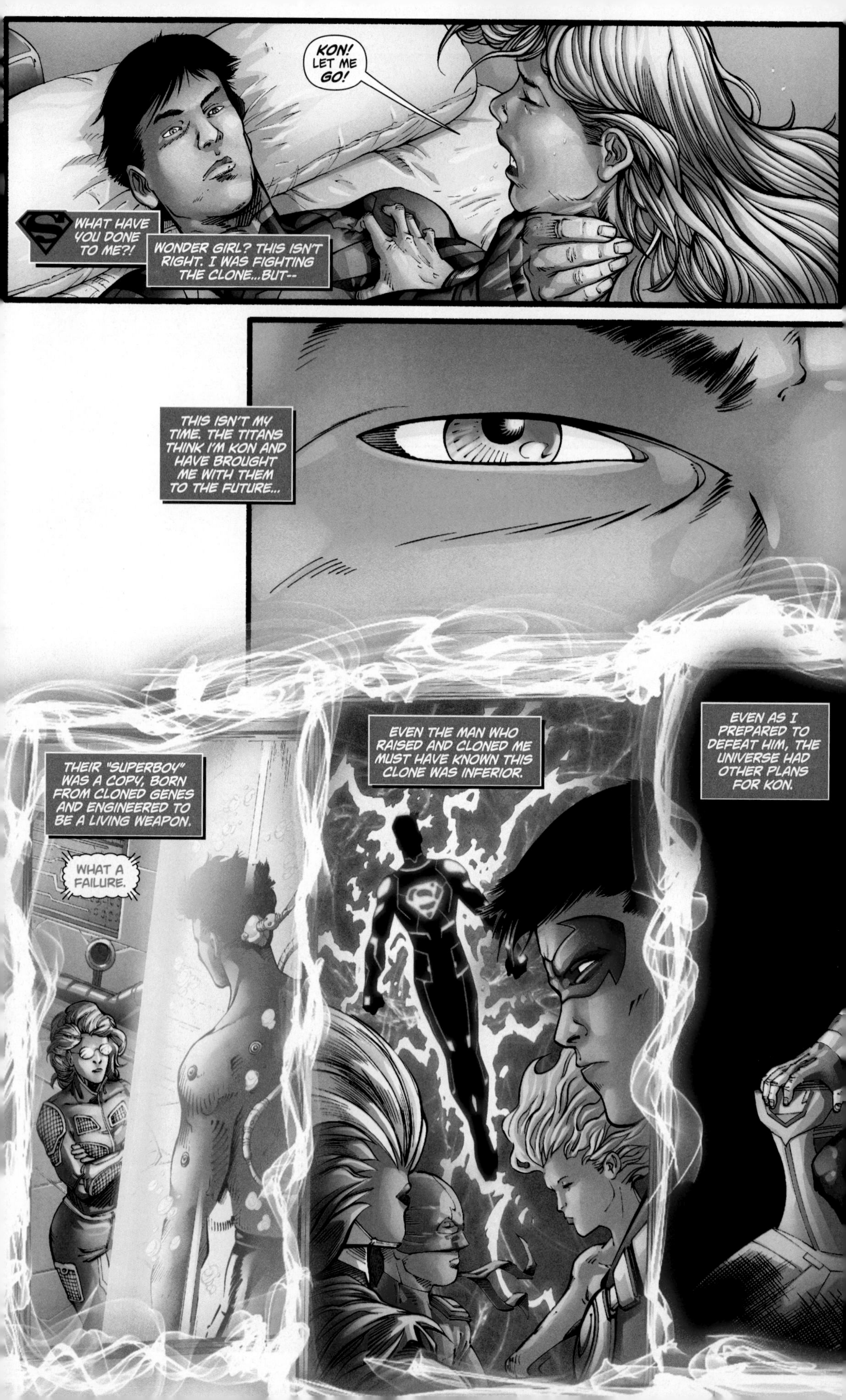
KON! LET ME GO!
WHAT HAVE YOU DONE TO ME?!
WONDER GIRL? THIS ISN'T RIGHT. I WAS FIGHTING THE CLONE...BUT--
THIS ISN'T MY TIME. THE TITANS THINK I'M KON AND HAVE BROUGHT ME WITH THEM TO THE FUTURE...
THEIR "SUPERBOY" WAS A COPY, BORN FROM CLONED GENES AND ENGINEERED TO BE A LIVING WEAPON.
WHAT A FAILURE.
EVEN THE MAN WHO RAISED AND CLONED ME MUST HAVE KNOWN THIS CLONE WAS INFERIOR.
EVEN AS I PREPARED TO DEFEAT HIM, THE UNIVERSE HAD OTHER PLANS FOR KON.

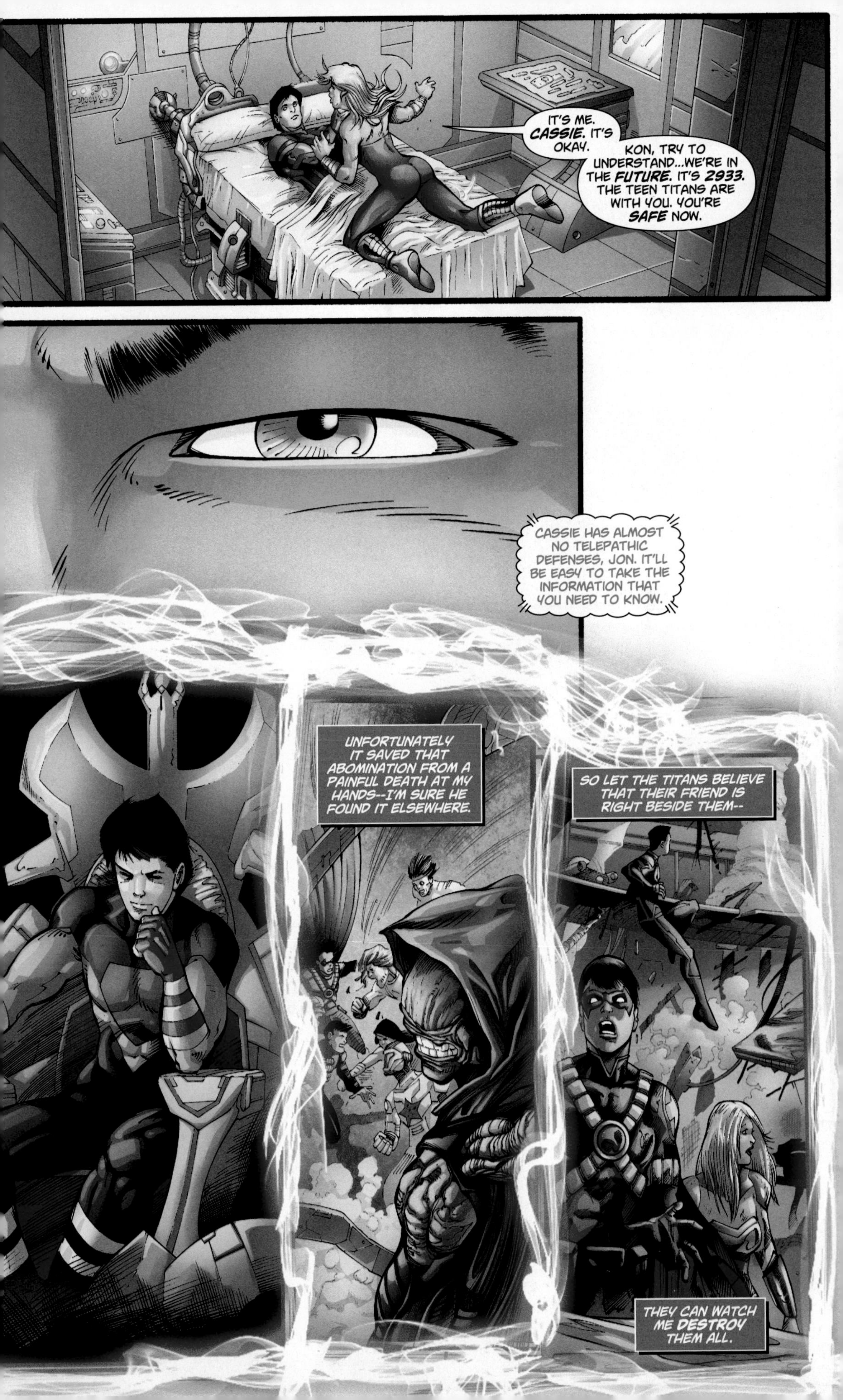

IT'S ME. CASSIE. IT'S OKAY.
KON, TRY TO UNDERSTAND...WE'RE IN THE FUTURE. IT'S 2933. THE TEEN TITANS ARE WITH YOU. YOU'RE SAFE NOW.
CASSIE HAS ALMOST NO TELEPATHIC DEFENSES, JON. IT'LL BE EASY TO TAKE THE INFORMATION THAT YOU NEED TO KNOW.
UNFORTUNATELY IT SAVED THAT ABOMINATION FROM A PAINFUL DEATH AT MY HANDS--I'M SURE HE FOUND IT ELSEWHERE.
SO LET THE TITANS BELIEVE THAT THEIR FRIEND IS RIGHT BESIDE THEM--
THEY CAN WATCH ME DESTROY THEM ALL.

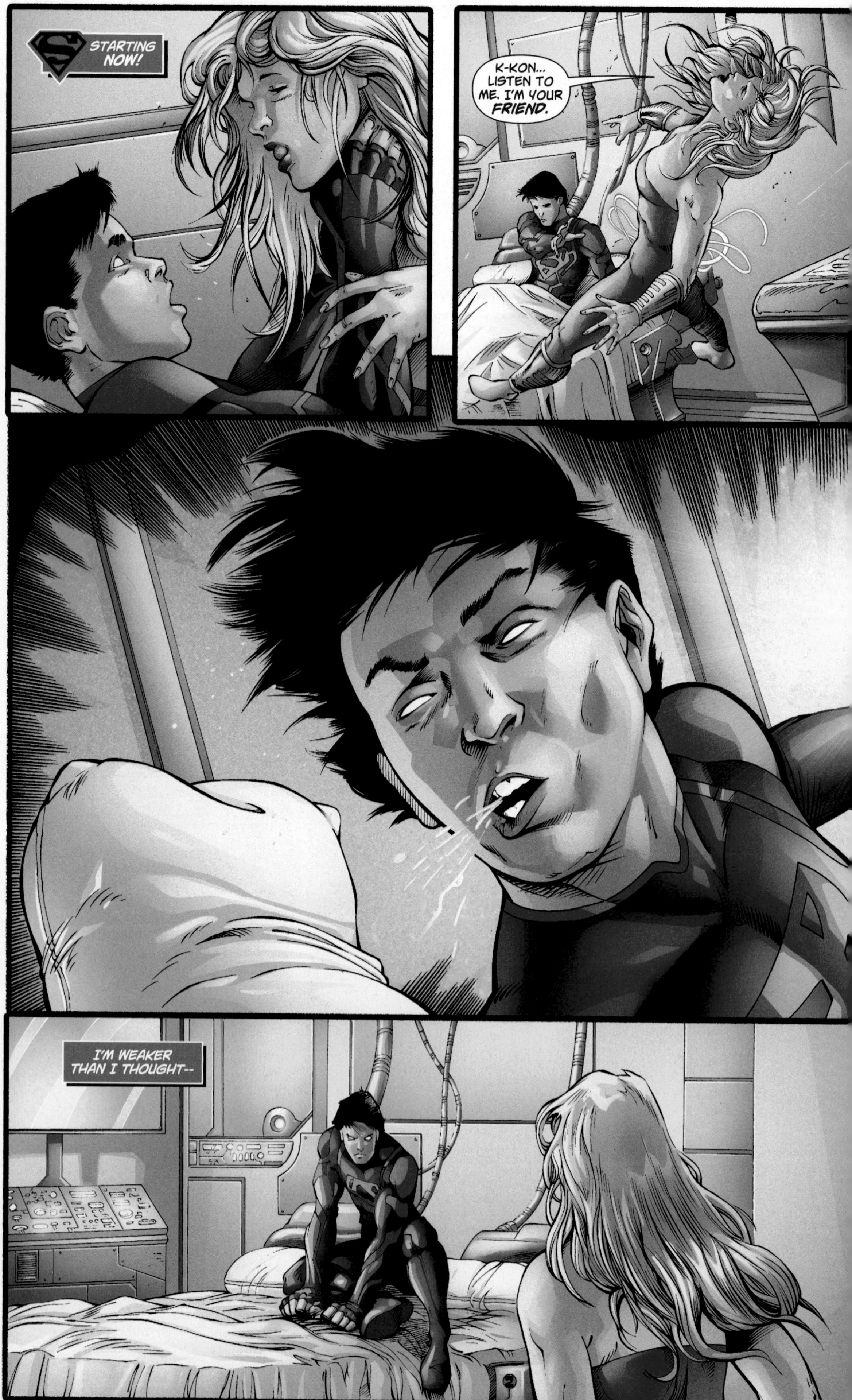
STARTING NOW!
K-KON... LISTEN TO ME. I'M YOUR FRIEND.
I'M WEAKER THAN I THOUGHT--

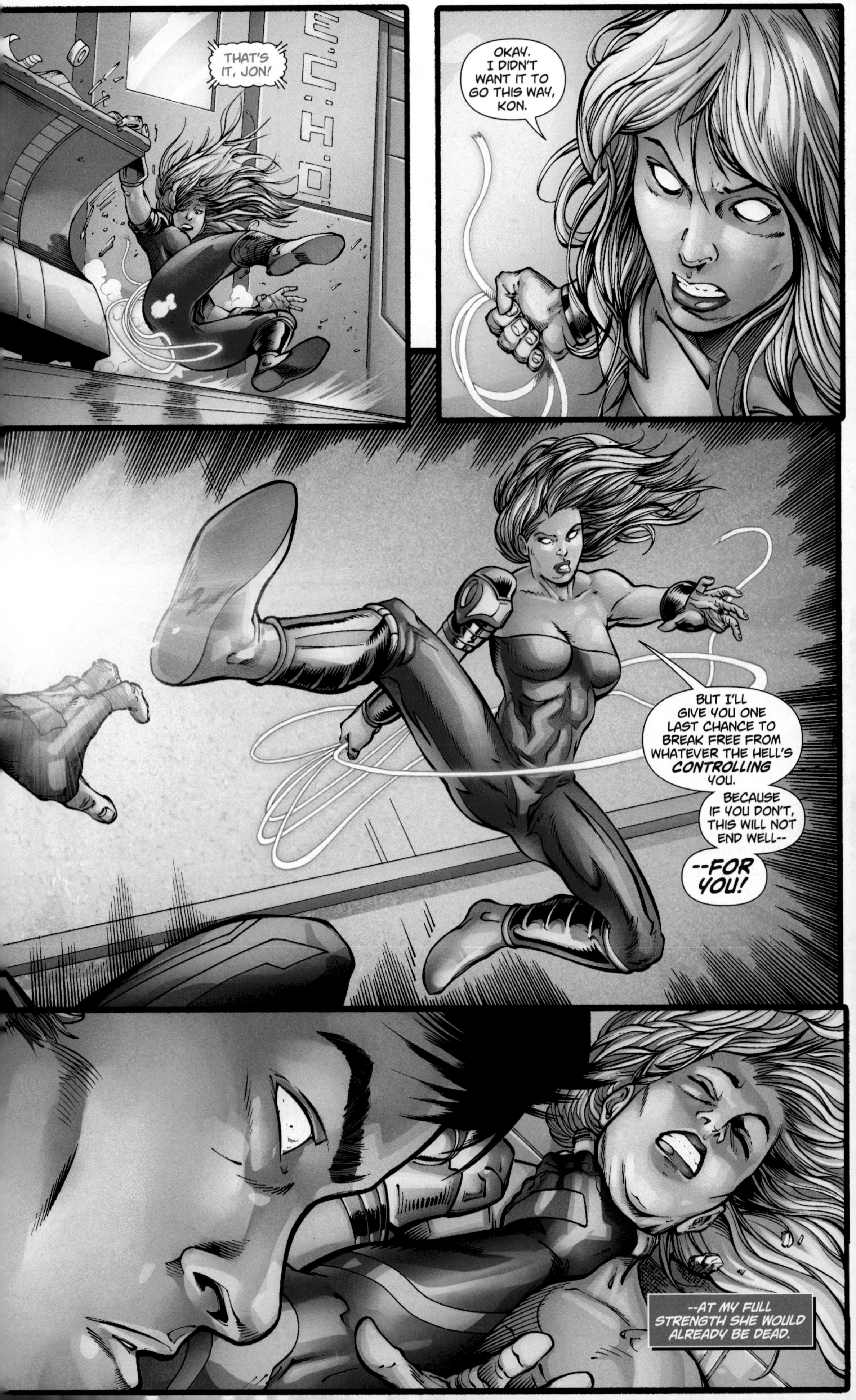
THAT'S IT, JON!
OKAY. I DIDN'T WANT IT TO GO THIS WAY, KON.
BUT I'LL GIVE YOU ONE LAST CHANCE TO BREAK FREE FROM WHATEVER THE HELL'S CONTROLLING YOU.
BECAUSE IF YOU DON'T, THIS WILL NOT END WELL--
--FOR YOU!
--AT MY FULL STRENGTH SHE WOULD ALREADY BE DEAD.
ECHO

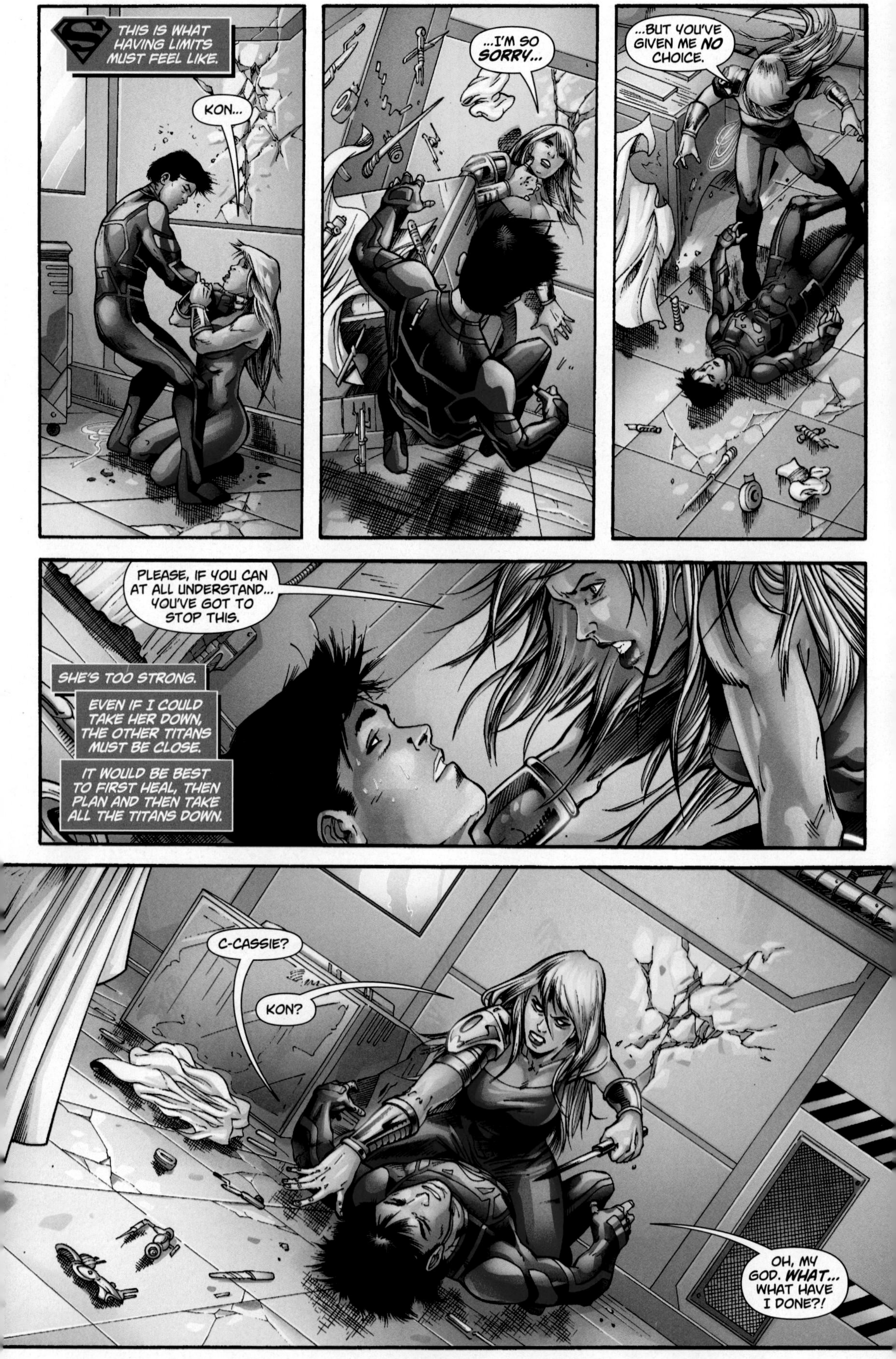

THIS IS WHAT HAVING LIMITS MUST FEEL LIKE.
KON...
...I'M SO SORRY...
...BUT YOU'VE GIVEN ME NO CHOICE.
PLEASE, IF YOU CAN AT ALL UNDERSTAND... YOU'VE GOT TO STOP THIS.
SHE'S TOO STRONG.
EVEN IF I COULD TAKE HER DOWN, THE OTHER TITANS MUST BE CLOSE.
IT WOULD BE BEST TO FIRST HEAL, THEN PLAN AND THEN TAKE ALL THE TITANS DOWN.
C-CASSIE?
KON?
OH, MY GOD. WHAT... WHAT HAVE I DONE?!

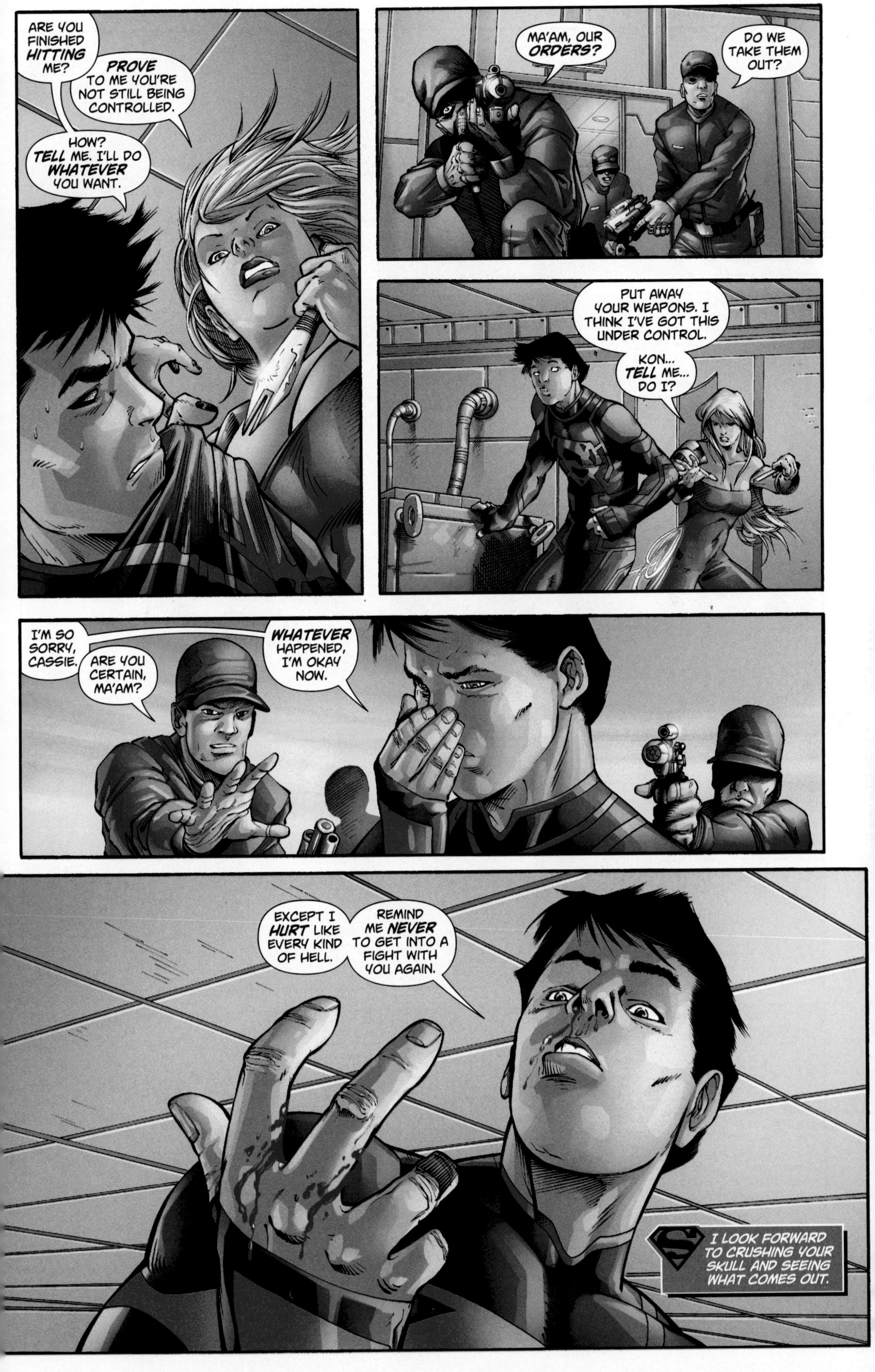
ARE YOU FINISHED HITTING ME?
PROVE TO ME YOU'RE NOT STILL BEING CONTROLLED.
HOW? TELL ME. I'LL DO WHATEVER YOU WANT.
MA'AM, OUR ORDERS?
DO WE TAKE THEM OUT?
PUT AWAY YOUR WEAPONS. I THINK I'VE GOT THIS UNDER CONTROL.
KON... TELL ME... DO I?
I'M SO SORRY, CASSIE.
ARE YOU CERTAIN, MA'AM?
WHATEVER HAPPENED, I'M OKAY NOW.
EXCEPT I HURT LIKE EVERY KIND OF HELL.
REMIND ME NEVER TO GET INTO A FIGHT WITH YOU AGAIN.
I LOOK FORWARD TO CRUSHING YOUR SKULL AND SEEING WHAT COMES OUT.

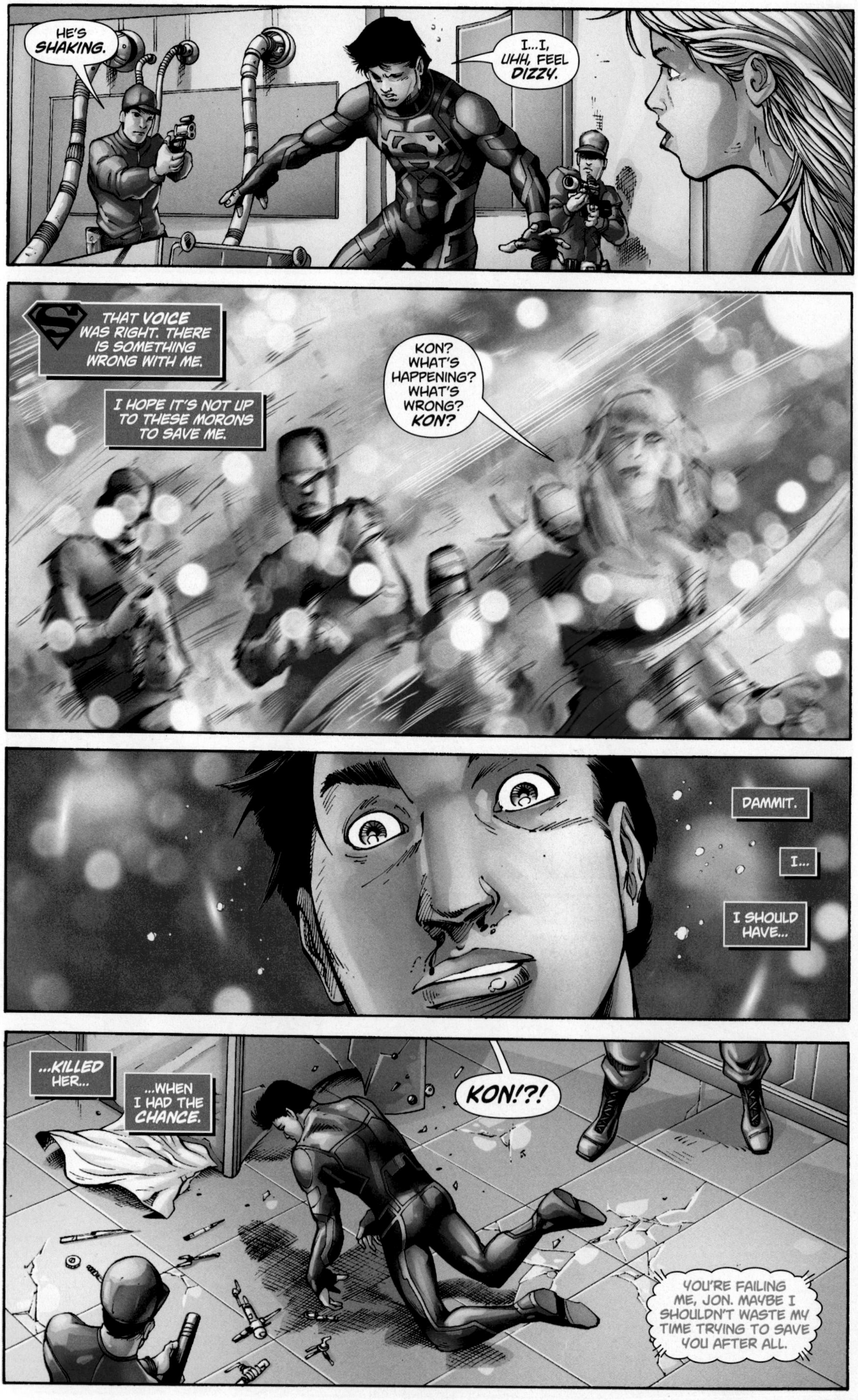
HE'S SHAKING.
I...I, UHH, FEEL DIZZY.
THAT VOICE WAS RIGHT. THERE IS SOMETHING WRONG WITH ME.
I HOPE IT'S NOT UP TO THESE MORONS TO SAVE ME.
KON? WHAT'S HAPPENING? WHAT'S WRONG? KON?
DAMMIT.
I...
I SHOULD HAVE...
...KILLED HER...
...WHEN I HAD THE CHANCE.
KON!?!
YOU'RE FAILING ME, JON. MAYBE I SHOULDN'T WASTE MY TIME TRYING TO SAVE YOU AFTER ALL.

WAKE UP, JON!

HE'S COMING TO.

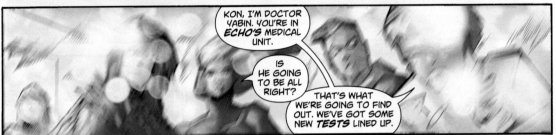

KON, I'M DOCTOR YABIN. YOU'RE IN *ECHO'S* MEDICAL UNIT.

IS HE GOING TO BE ALL RIGHT?

THAT'S WHAT WE'RE GOING TO FIND OUT. WE'VE GOT SOME NEW *TESTS* LINED UP.

IT WON'T TAKE LONG TO GET RESULTS.

THEY LOOK SO CONCERNED-- PATHETIC.

RED ROBIN.

WONDER GIRL.

ANY MISTAKES IMPERSONATING KON CAN BE EXPLAINED AWAY BY MY CONDITION.

SOLSTICE.

RAVEN.

YOU GUYS LOOK ALMOST AS BAD AS I FEEL.

HOW MUCH DO YOU *REMEMBER*, KON?

CAREFUL, JON.

I-I DON'T KNOW. NOT MUCH BESIDES CASSIE KICKING MY ASS.

IT'LL BE ALL RIGHT. YOU WEREN'T BEING YOU.

WHILE I WAS SLEEPING... YOU TOOK *TESTS?*

PRELIMINARY ONES. BUT NOW WE NEED A *FULL* ANALYSIS.

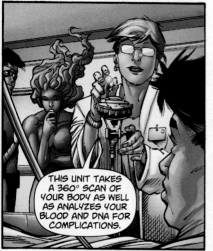

THIS UNIT TAKES A 360° SCAN OF YOUR BODY AS WELL AS ANALYZES YOUR BLOOD AND DNA FOR COMPLICATIONS.

DON'T WORRY. IT'S NON-INVASIVE AND TOTALLY PAINLE-- *WHAT?*

A LITTLE *T.K.* BLAST...

BZAKK

PAINLESS? YOU'RE *SURE* OF THAT?

THAT'S *NEVER* HAPPENED BEFORE. I SWEAR. I'LL GET *ANOTHER* ONE.

OKAY. BUT CAN WE DO IT LATER?

I AM BEYOND TIRED. I JUST WANT TO *SLEEP.*

SURE. WE'VE STILL GOT TO FIGURE OUT HOW TO FREE KID FLASH.

WE'RE ALL SO HAPPY YOU'RE FEELING BETTER, KON. WE'LL CHECK ON YOU SOON.

HMMM.

WATCH OUT FOR RAVEN, JON. SHE KNOWN MORE THAN SHE'S TELLING.

THERE WAS NO WAY IN HELL I'D LET HER TAKE *MORE* TESTS.

NOT AND RISK EXPOSING EVERYTHING I HAVE TO HIDE.

I NEED TO *ELIMINATE* THE PREVIOUS RESULTS.

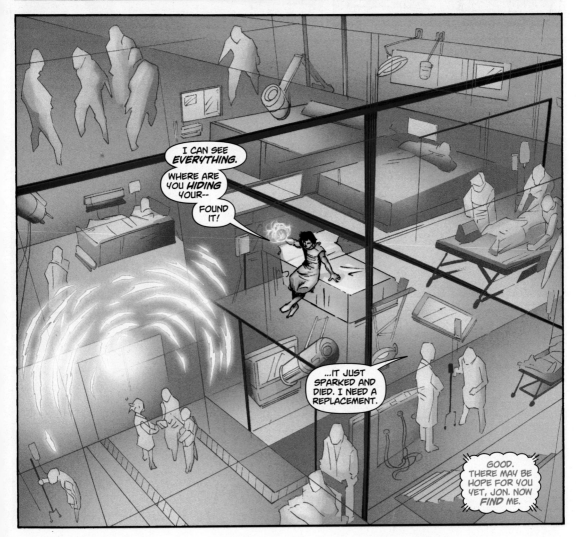

I CAN SEE *EVERYTHING.*

WHERE ARE YOU *HIDING* YOUR--

FOUND IT!

...IT JUST SPARKED AND DIED. I NEED A REPLACEMENT.

GOOD. THERE MAY BE HOPE FOR YOU YET, JON. NOW *FIND* ME.

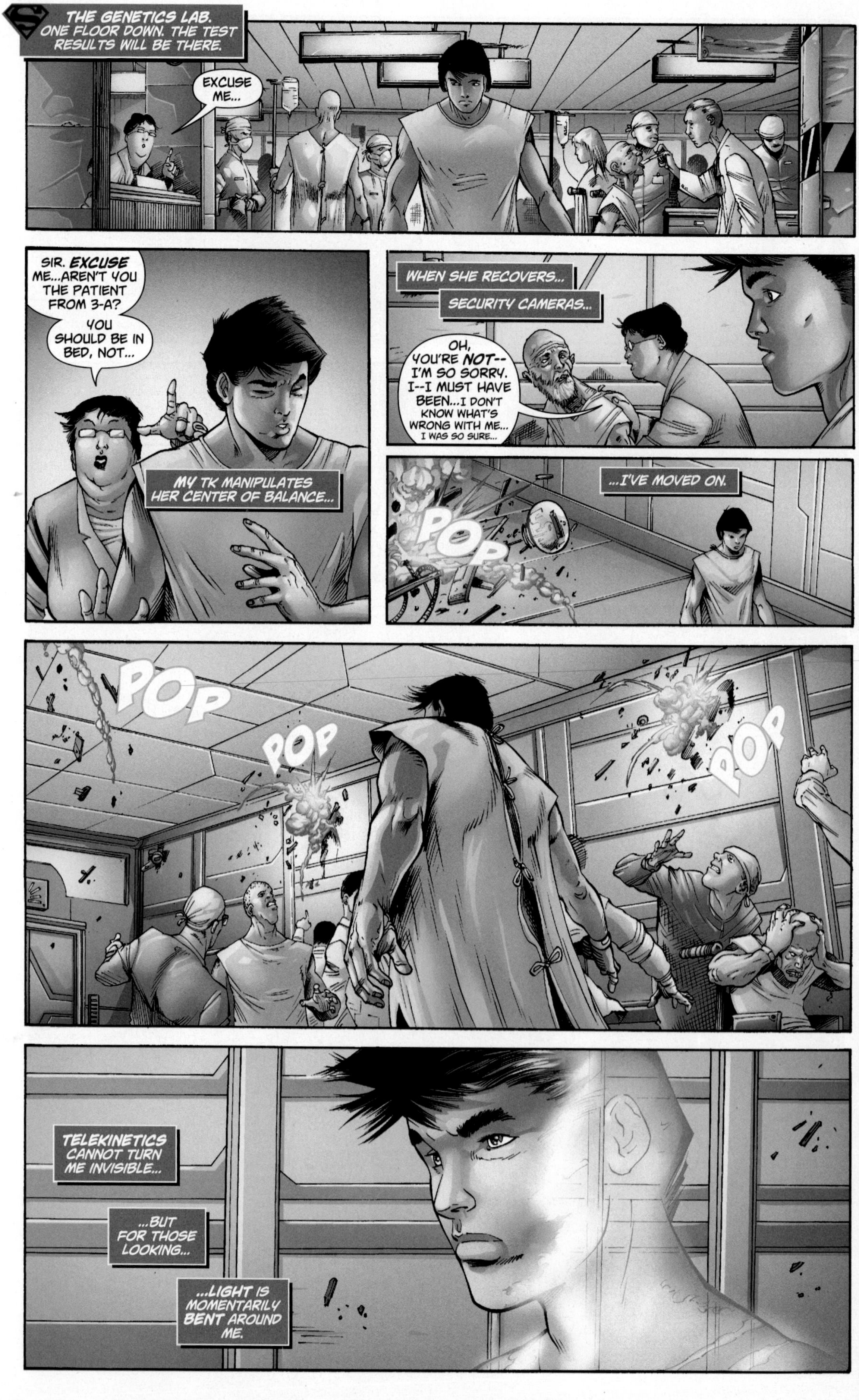
THE GENETICS LAB. ONE FLOOR DOWN. THE TEST RESULTS WILL BE THERE.
EXCUSE ME...
SIR. EXCUSE ME...AREN'T YOU THE PATIENT FROM 3-A?
YOU SHOULD BE IN BED, NOT...
MY TK MANIPULATES HER CENTER OF BALANCE...
WHEN SHE RECOVERS...
SECURITY CAMERAS...
OH, YOU'RE NOT-- I'M SO SORRY. I--I MUST HAVE BEEN...I DON'T KNOW WHAT'S WRONG WITH ME... I WAS SO SURE...
...I'VE MOVED ON.
POP
POP
POP
POP
POP
TELEKINETICS CANNOT TURN ME INVISIBLE...
...BUT FOR THOSE LOOKING...
...LIGHT IS MOMENTARILY BENT AROUND ME.

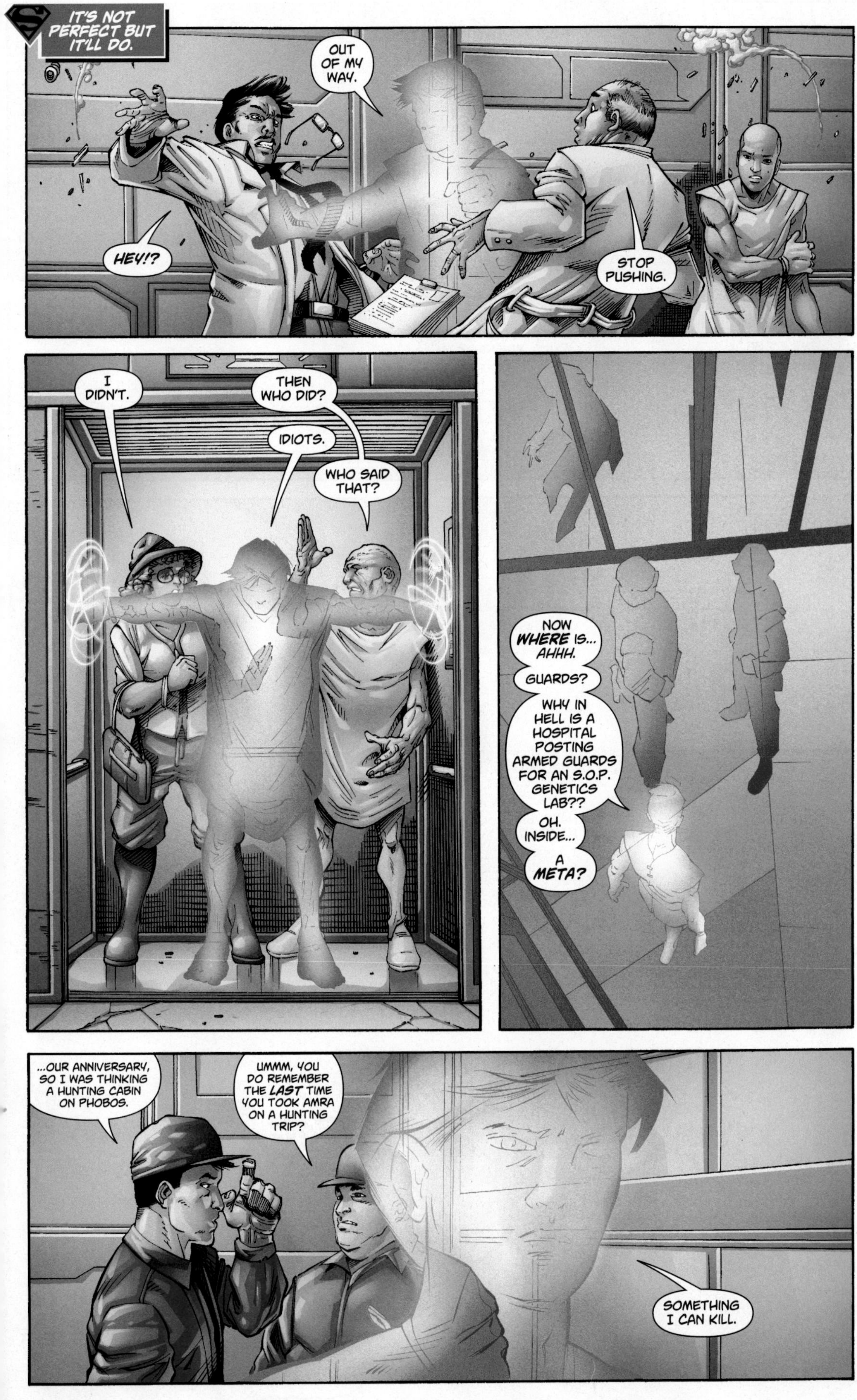

IT'S NOT PERFECT BUT IT'LL DO.
OUT OF MY WAY.
HEY!?
STOP PUSHING.
I DIDN'T.
THEN WHO DID?
IDIOTS.
WHO SAID THAT?
NOW WHERE IS... AHHH.
GUARDS?
WHY IN HELL IS A HOSPITAL POSTING ARMED GUARDS FOR AN S.O.P. GENETICS LAB??
OH. INSIDE...
A META?
...OUR ANNIVERSARY, SO I WAS THINKING A HUNTING CABIN ON PHOBOS.
UMMM, YOU DO REMEMBER THE LAST TIME YOU TOOK AMRA ON A HUNTING TRIP?
SOMETHING I CAN KILL.

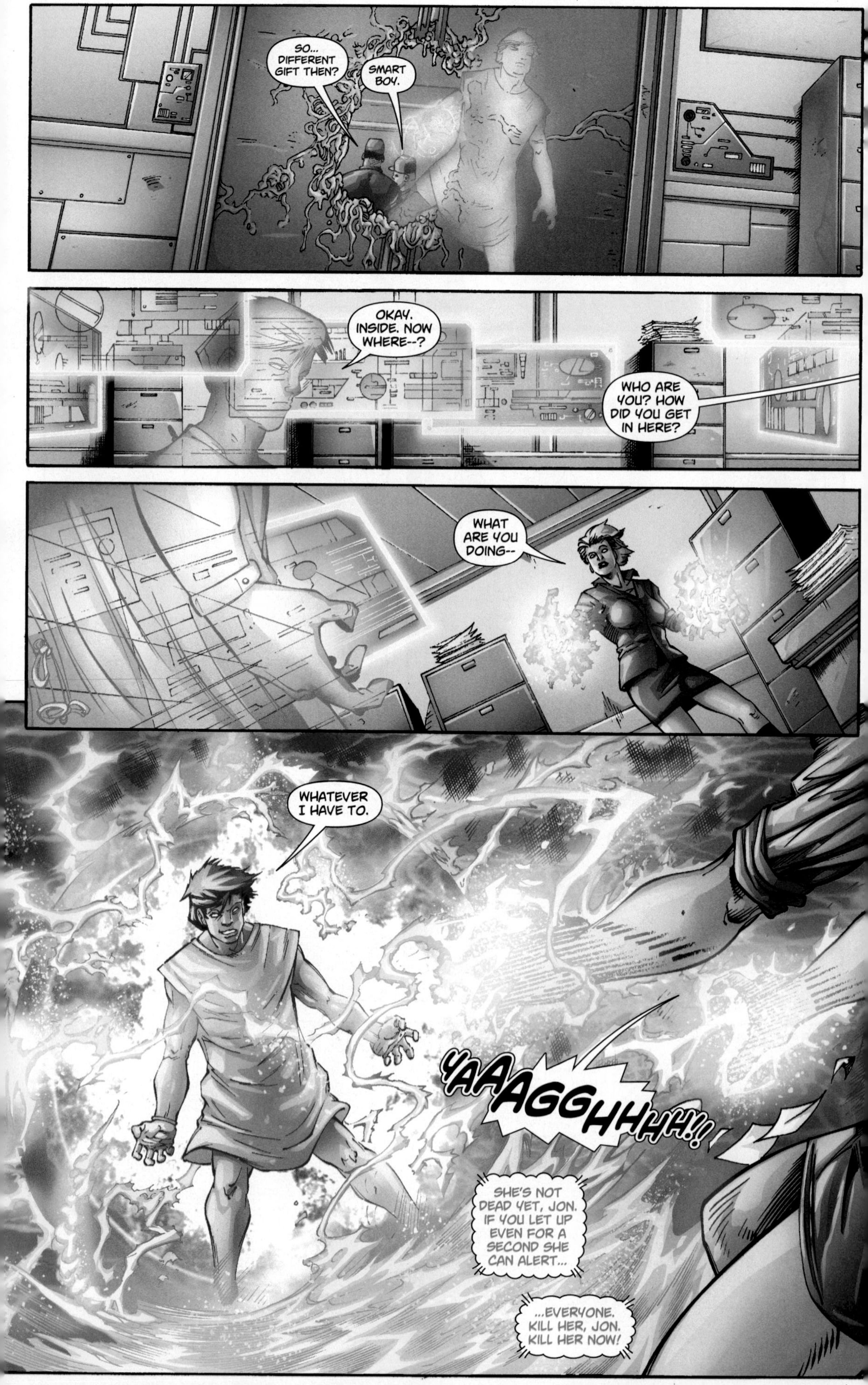
SO... DIFFERENT GIFT THEN?
SMART BOY.
OKAY. INSIDE. NOW WHERE--?
WHO ARE YOU? HOW DID YOU GET IN HERE?
WHAT ARE YOU DOING--
WHATEVER I HAVE TO.
YAAAAGGHHHHH!!
SHE'S NOT DEAD YET, JON. IF YOU LET UP EVEN FOR A SECOND SHE CAN ALERT...
...EVERYONE. KILL HER, JON. KILL HER NOW!

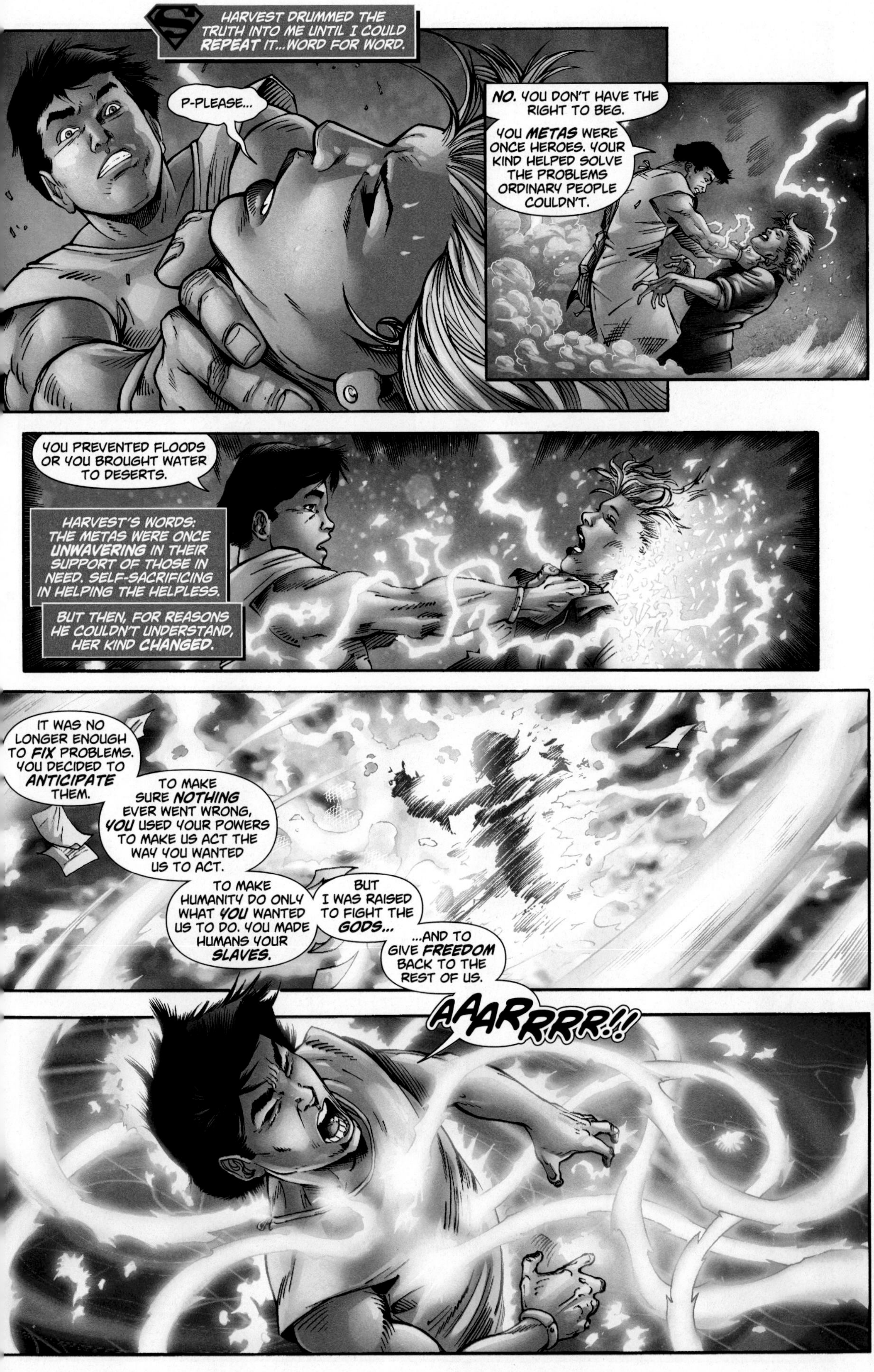
HARVEST DRUMMED THE TRUTH INTO ME UNTIL I COULD REPEAT IT...WORD FOR WORD.
P-PLEASE...
NO. YOU DON'T HAVE THE RIGHT TO BEG.
YOU METAS WERE ONCE HEROES. YOUR KIND HELPED SOLVE THE PROBLEMS ORDINARY PEOPLE COULDN'T.
YOU PREVENTED FLOODS OR YOU BROUGHT WATER TO DESERTS.
HARVEST'S WORDS: THE METAS WERE ONCE UNWAVERING IN THEIR SUPPORT OF THOSE IN NEED. SELF-SACRIFICING IN HELPING THE HELPLESS.
BUT THEN, FOR REASONS HE COULDN'T UNDERSTAND, HER KIND CHANGED.
IT WAS NO LONGER ENOUGH TO FIX PROBLEMS. YOU DECIDED TO ANTICIPATE THEM.
TO MAKE SURE NOTHING EVER WENT WRONG, YOU USED YOUR POWERS TO MAKE US ACT THE WAY YOU WANTED US TO ACT.
TO MAKE HUMANITY DO ONLY WHAT YOU WANTED US TO DO. YOU MADE HUMANS YOUR SLAVES.
BUT I WAS RAISED TO FIGHT THE GODS...
...AND TO GIVE FREEDOM BACK TO THE REST OF US.
AAARRRR!!

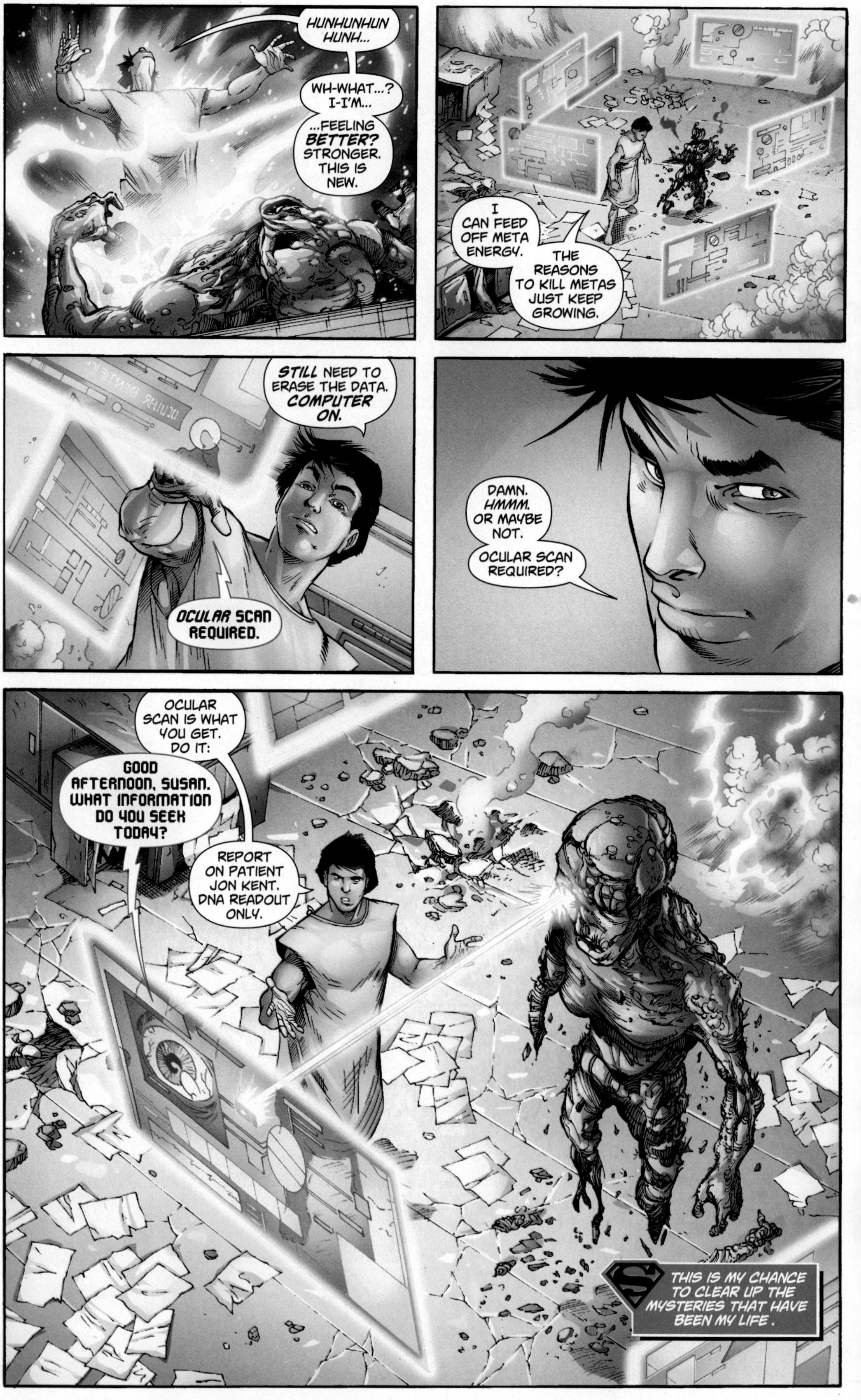
HUNHUNHUN HUNH...
WH-WHAT...? I-I'M...
...FEELING BETTER? STRONGER. THIS IS NEW.
I CAN FEED OFF META ENERGY.
THE REASONS TO KILL METAS JUST KEEP GROWING.
STILL NEED TO ERASE THE DATA. COMPUTER ON.
OCULAR SCAN REQUIRED.
DAMN. HMMM. OR MAYBE NOT.
OCULAR SCAN REQUIRED?
OCULAR SCAN IS WHAT YOU GET. DO IT:
GOOD AFTERNOON, SUSAN. WHAT INFORMATION DO YOU SEEK TODAY?
REPORT ON PATIENT JON KENT. DNA READOUT ONLY.
THIS IS MY CHANCE TO CLEAR UP THE MYSTERIES THAT HAVE BEEN MY LIFE.

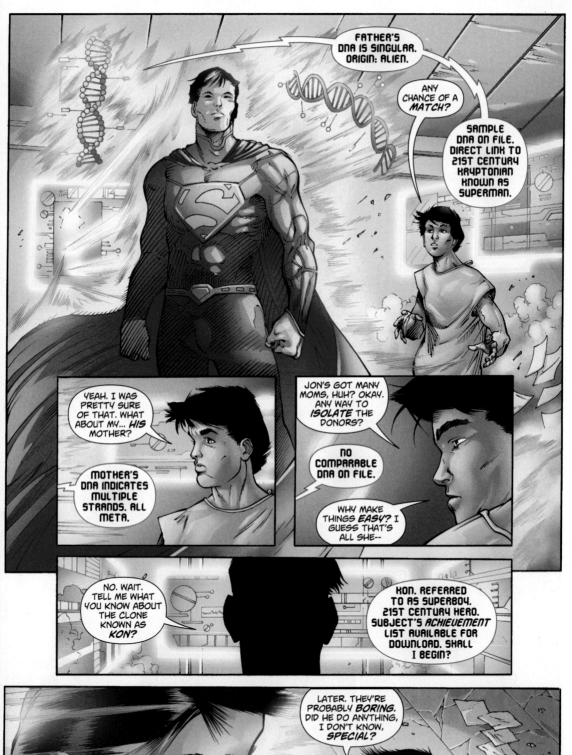

FATHER'S DNA IS SINGULAR. ORIGIN: ALIEN.

ANY CHANCE OF A *MATCH*?

SAMPLE DNA ON FILE. DIRECT LINK TO 21ST CENTURY KRYPTONIAN KNOWN AS SUPERMAN.

YEAH. I WAS PRETTY SURE OF THAT. WHAT ABOUT MY... *HIS* MOTHER?

MOTHER'S DNA INDICATES MULTIPLE STRANDS. ALL META.

JON'S GOT MANY MOMS, HUH? OKAY. ANY WAY TO *ISOLATE* THE DONORS?

NO COMPARABLE DNA ON FILE.

WHY MAKE THINGS *EASY*? I GUESS THAT'S ALL SHE--

NO. WAIT. TELL ME WHAT YOU KNOW ABOUT THE CLONE KNOWN AS *KON*?

KON. REFERRED TO AS SUPERBOY. 21ST CENTURY HERO. SUBJECT'S *ACHIEVEMENT* LIST AVAILABLE FOR DOWNLOAD. SHALL I BEGIN?

LATER. THEY'RE PROBABLY *BORING*. DID HE DO ANYTHING, I DON'T KNOW, *SPECIAL*?

GREATEST ACHIEVEMENT...

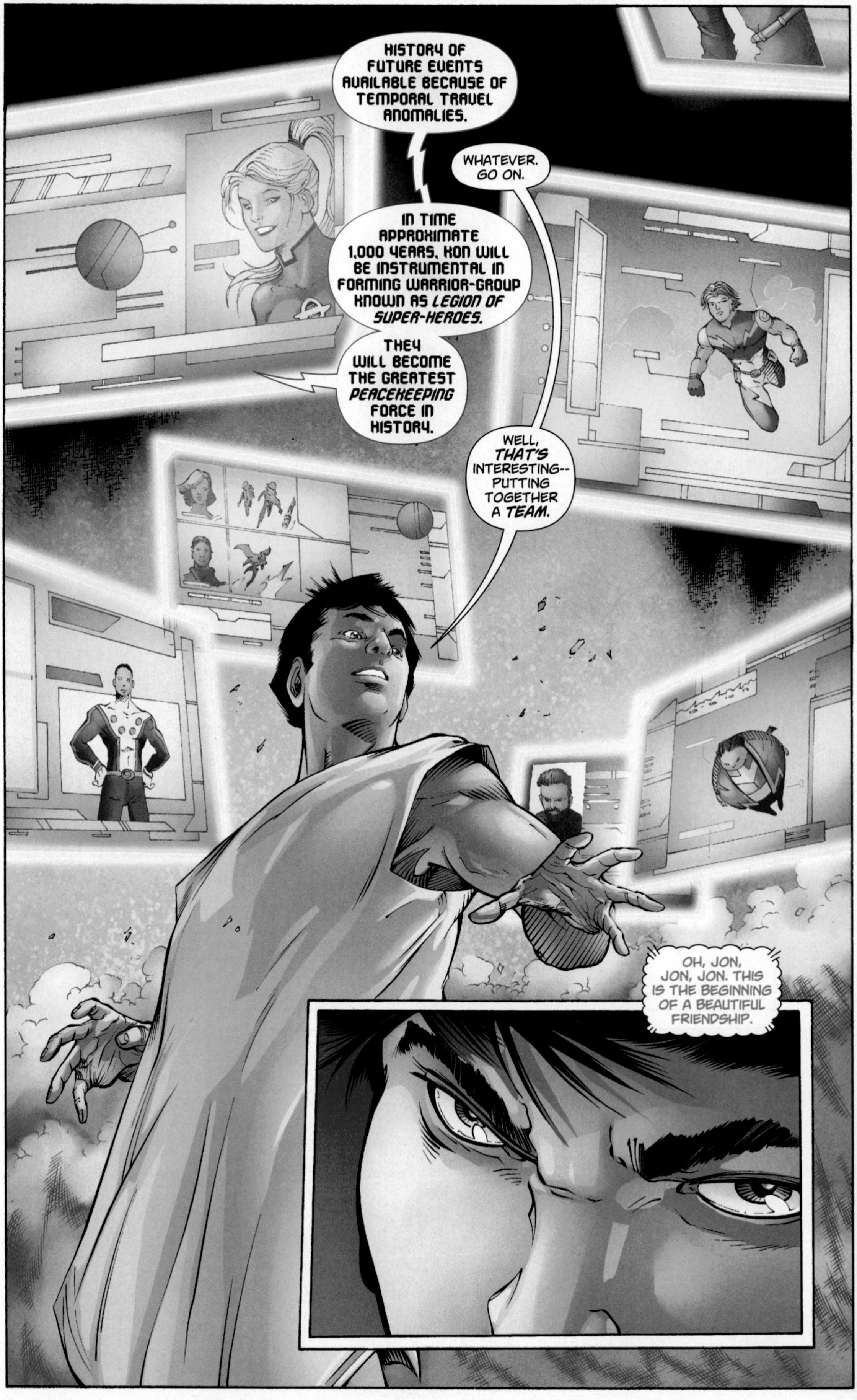
HISTORY OF FUTURE EVENTS AVAILABLE BECAUSE OF TEMPORAL TRAVEL ANOMALIES.
WHATEVER. GO ON.
IN TIME APPROXIMATE 1,000 YEARS, KON WILL BE INSTRUMENTAL IN FORMING WARRIOR-GROUP KNOWN AS *LEGION OF SUPER-HEROES.*
THEY WILL BECOME THE GREATEST *PEACEKEEPING* FORCE IN HISTORY.
WELL, *THAT'S* INTERESTING-- PUTTING TOGETHER A *TEAM.*
OH, JON, JON, JON. THIS IS THE BEGINNING OF A BEAUTIFUL FRIENDSHIP.

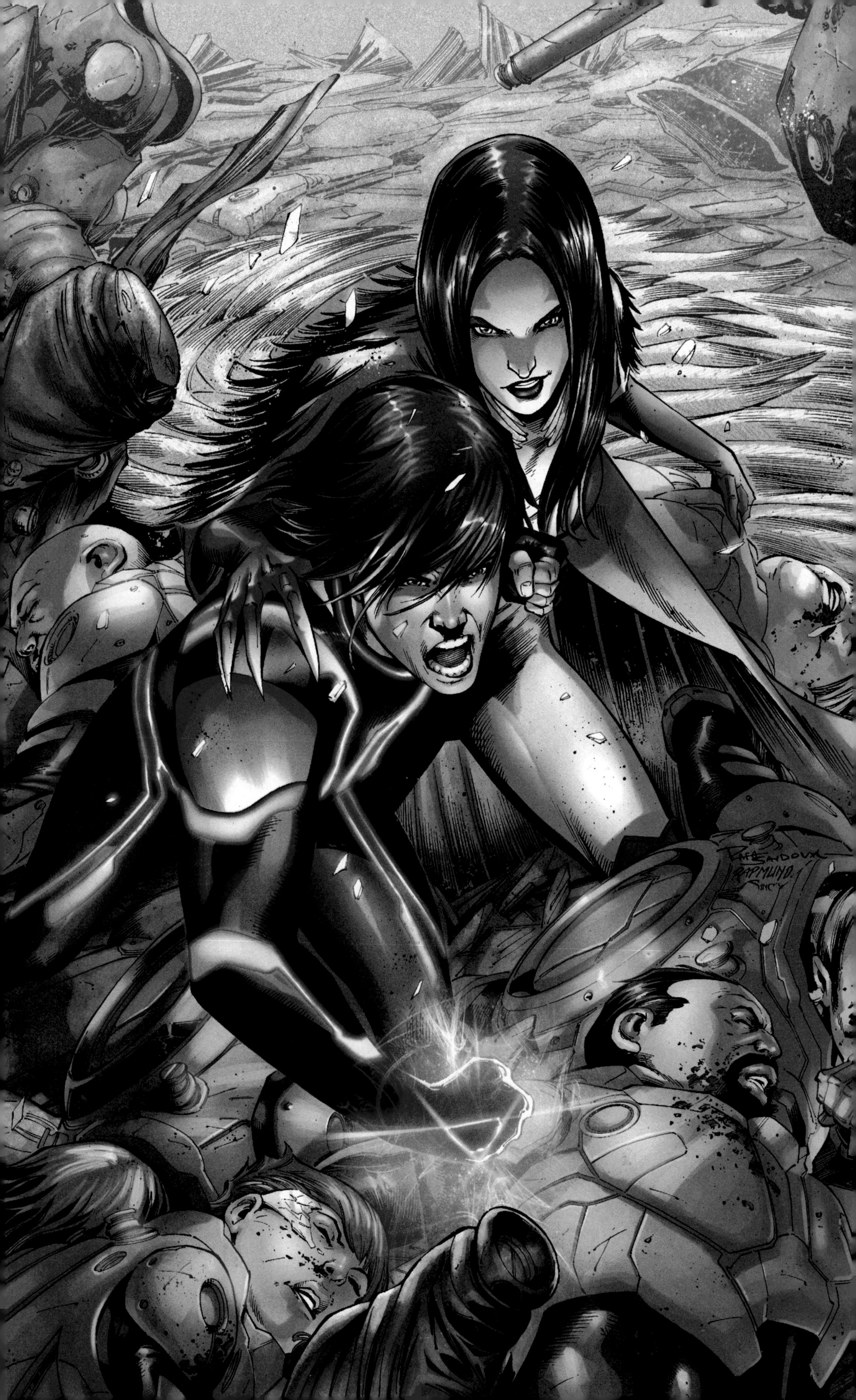

MIND GAMES

MARV WOLFMAN writer ANDRES GUINALDO penciller MARK IRWIN inker
TANYA and RICHARD HORIE colorists TRAVIS LANHAM letterer cover art by RAFAEL SANDOVAL, NORM RAPMUND and ALEX SINCLAIR

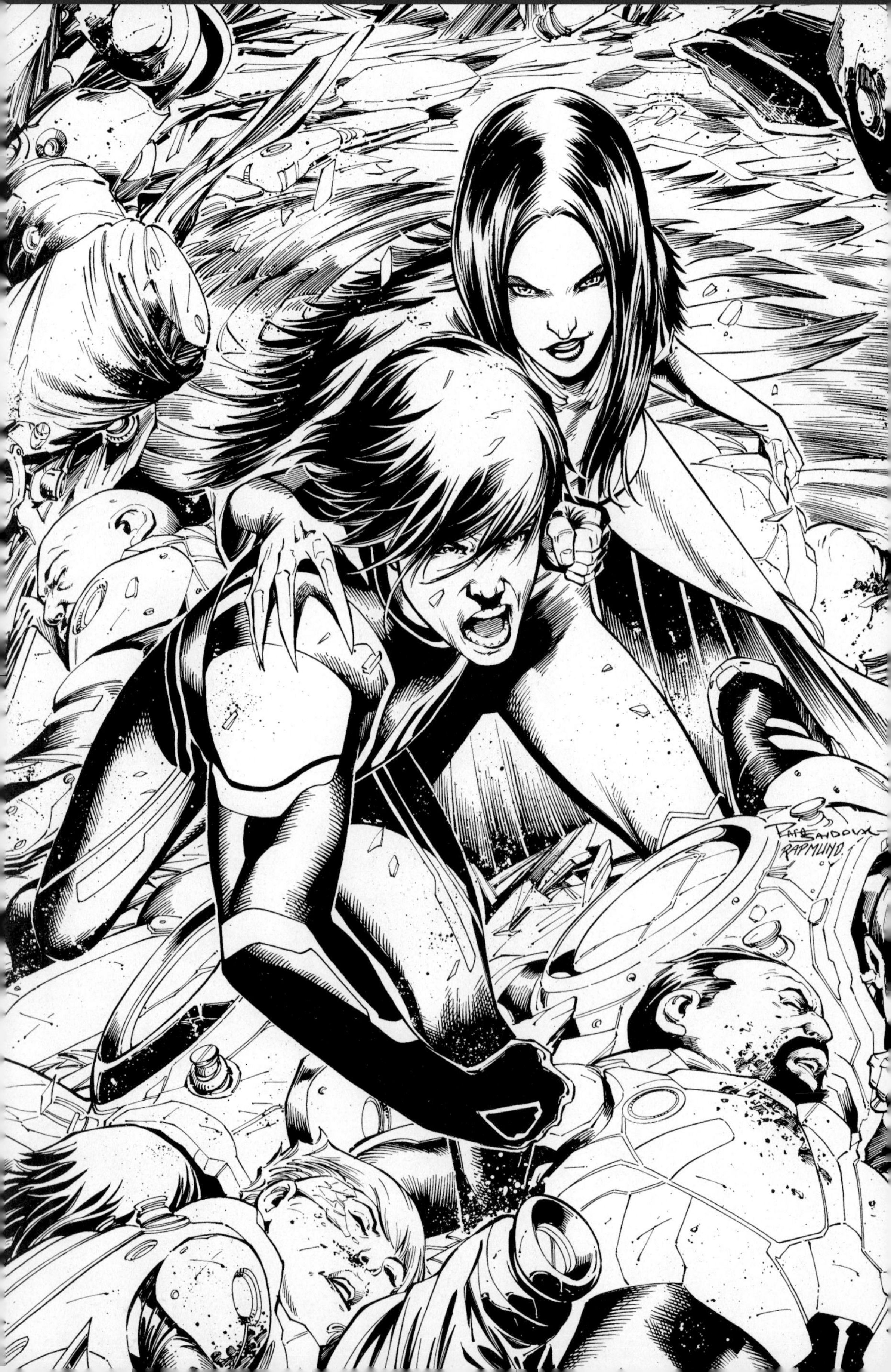
RAPMUND

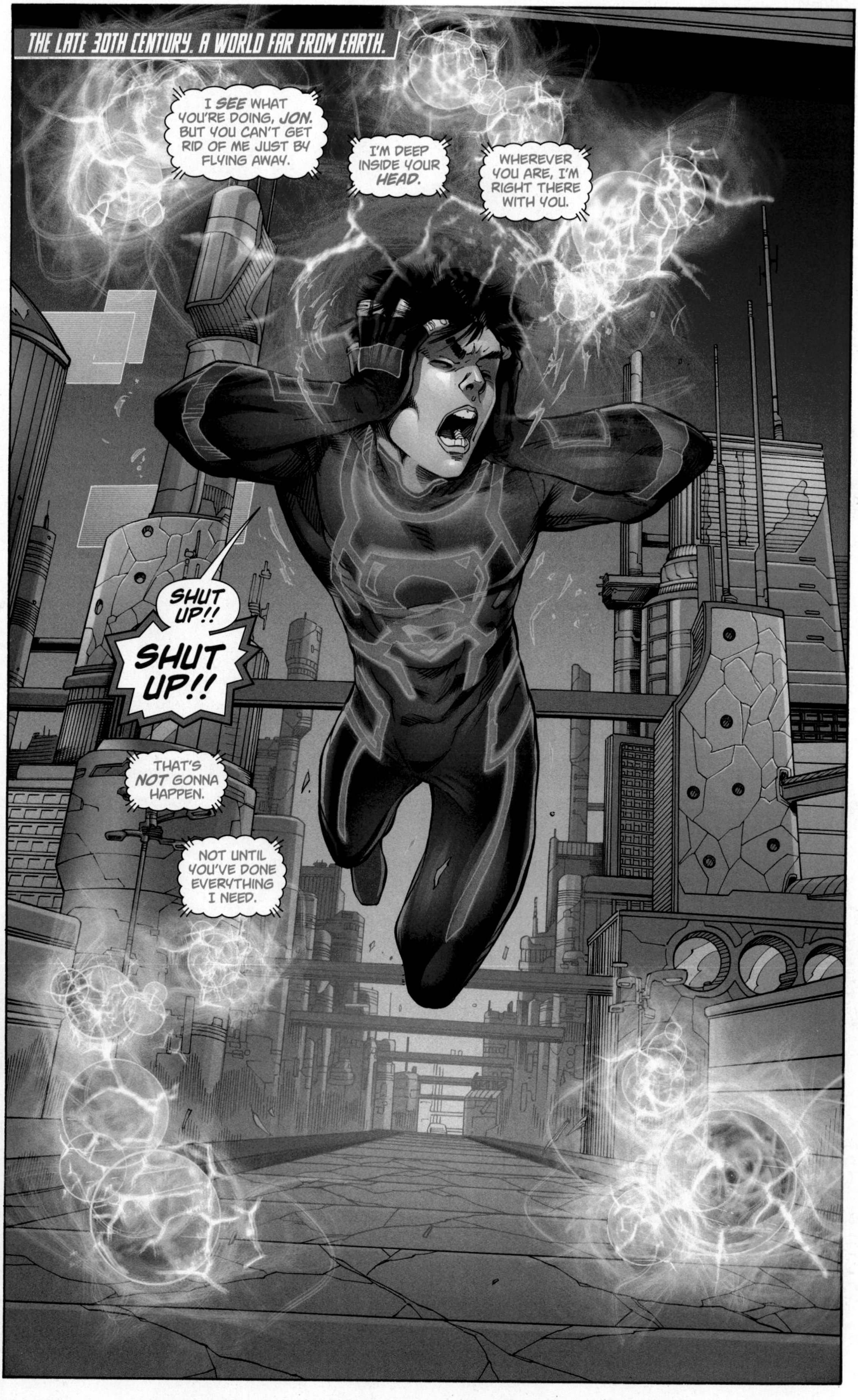
THE LATE 30TH CENTURY. A WORLD FAR FROM EARTH.
I SEE WHAT YOU'RE DOING, JON. BUT YOU CAN'T GET RID OF ME JUST BY FLYING AWAY.
I'M DEEP INSIDE YOUR HEAD.
WHEREVER YOU ARE, I'M RIGHT THERE WITH YOU.
SHUT UP!!
SHUT UP!!
THAT'S NOT GONNA HAPPEN.
NOT UNTIL YOU'VE DONE EVERYTHING I NEED.

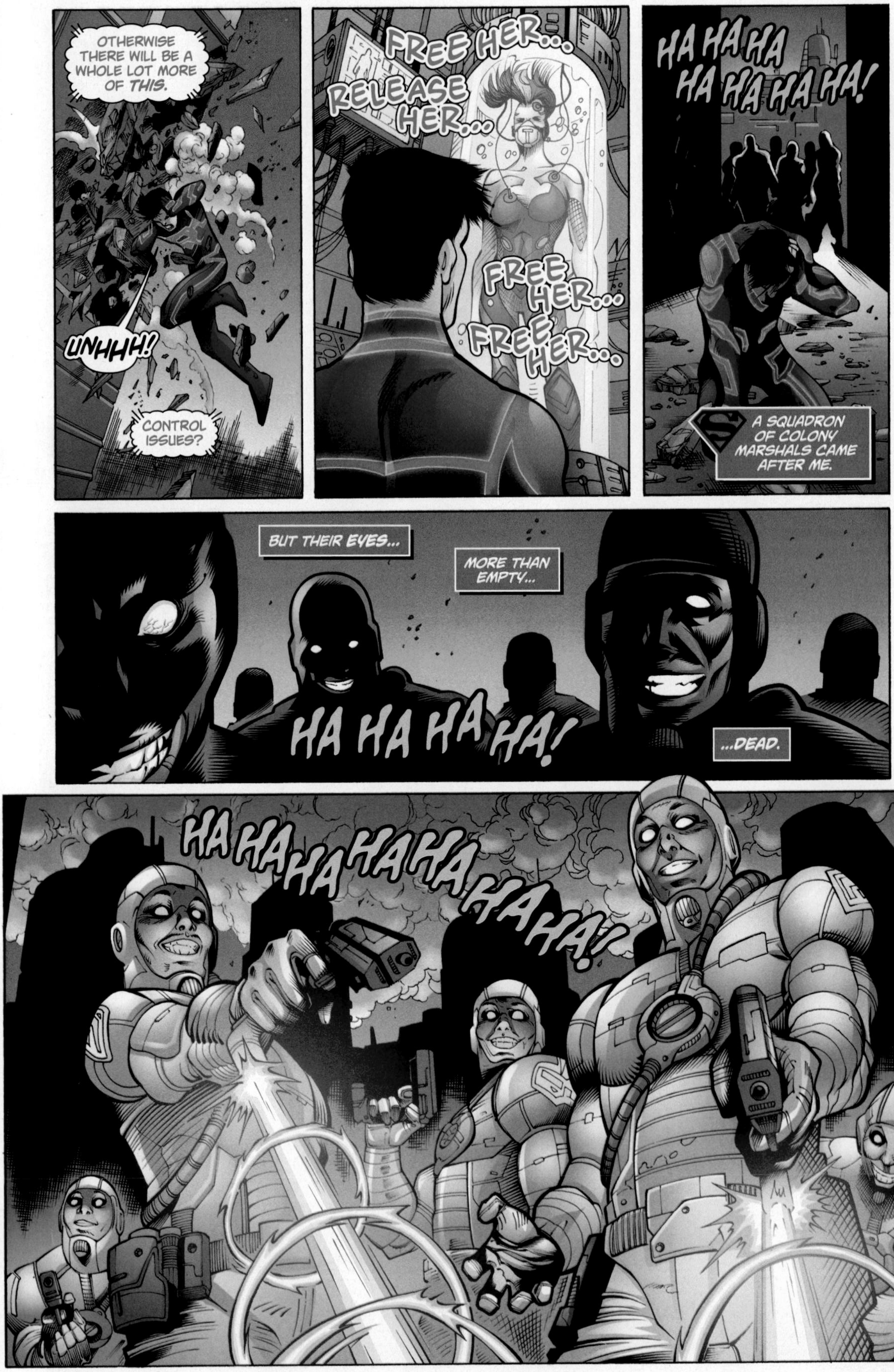
OTHERWISE THERE WILL BE A WHOLE LOT MORE OF THIS.
UNHHH!
CONTROL ISSUES?
FREE HER... RELEASE HER...
FREE HER... FREE HER...
HA HA HA HA HA HA HA HA!
A SQUADRON OF COLONY MARSHALS CAME AFTER ME.
BUT THEIR EYES...
MORE THAN EMPTY...
HA HA HA HA HA!
...DEAD.
HA HA HA HA HA HA HA HA HA HA!

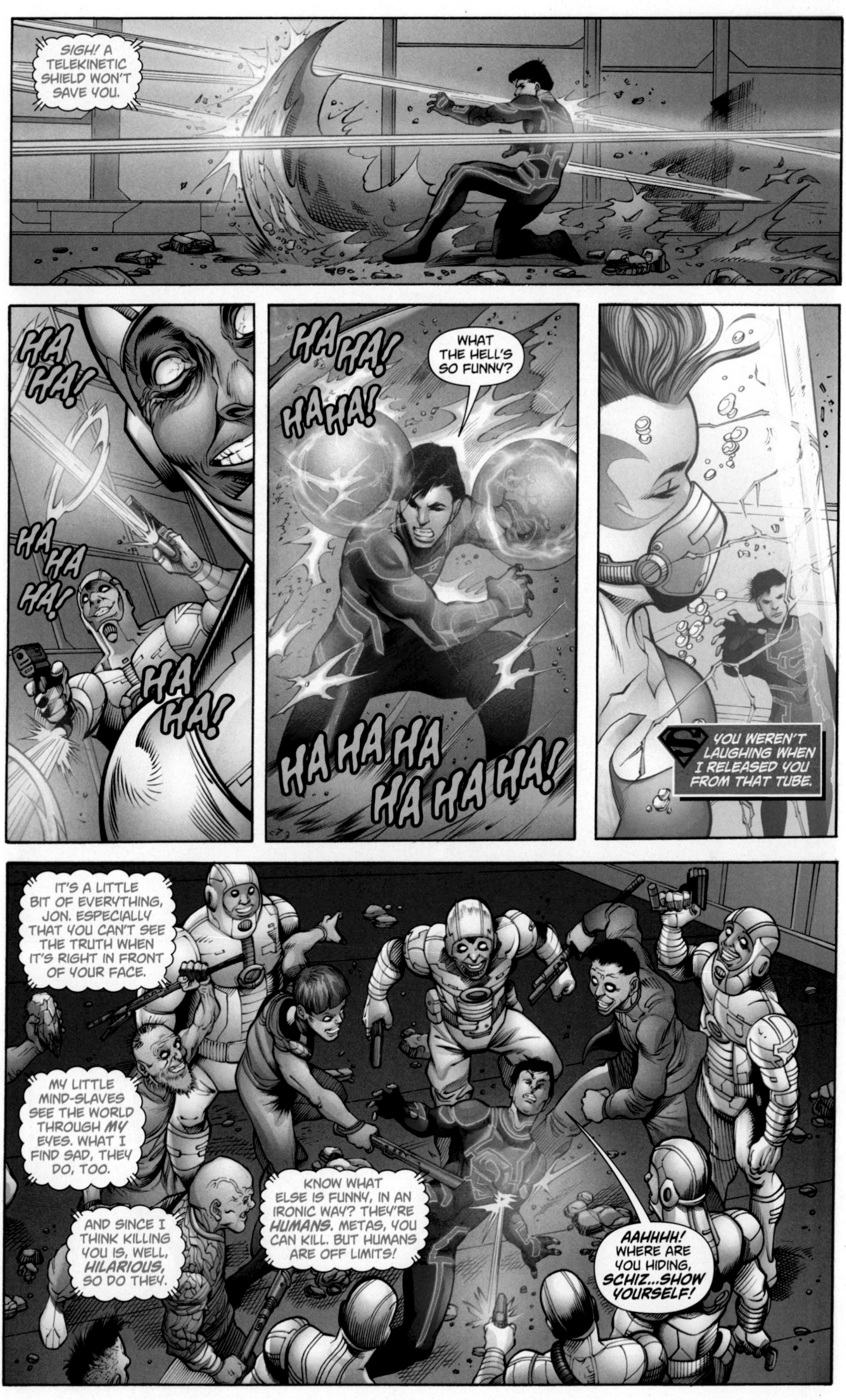

SIGH! A TELEKINETIC SHIELD WON'T SAVE YOU.
HA HA!
HA HA HA!
HA HA!
HA HA! HA HA!
WHAT THE HELL'S SO FUNNY?
HA HA HA HA HA HA!
YOU WEREN'T LAUGHING WHEN I RELEASED YOU FROM THAT TUBE.
IT'S A LITTLE BIT OF EVERYTHING, JON. ESPECIALLY THAT YOU CAN'T SEE THE TRUTH WHEN IT'S RIGHT IN FRONT OF YOUR FACE.
MY LITTLE MIND-SLAVES SEE THE WORLD THROUGH MY EYES. WHAT I FIND SAD, THEY DO, TOO.
AND SINCE I THINK KILLING YOU IS, WELL, HILARIOUS, SO DO THEY.
KNOW WHAT ELSE IS FUNNY, IN AN IRONIC WAY? THEY'RE HUMANS. METAS, YOU CAN KILL. BUT HUMANS ARE OFF LIMITS!
AAHHHH! WHERE ARE YOU HIDING, SCHIZ...SHOW YOURSELF!

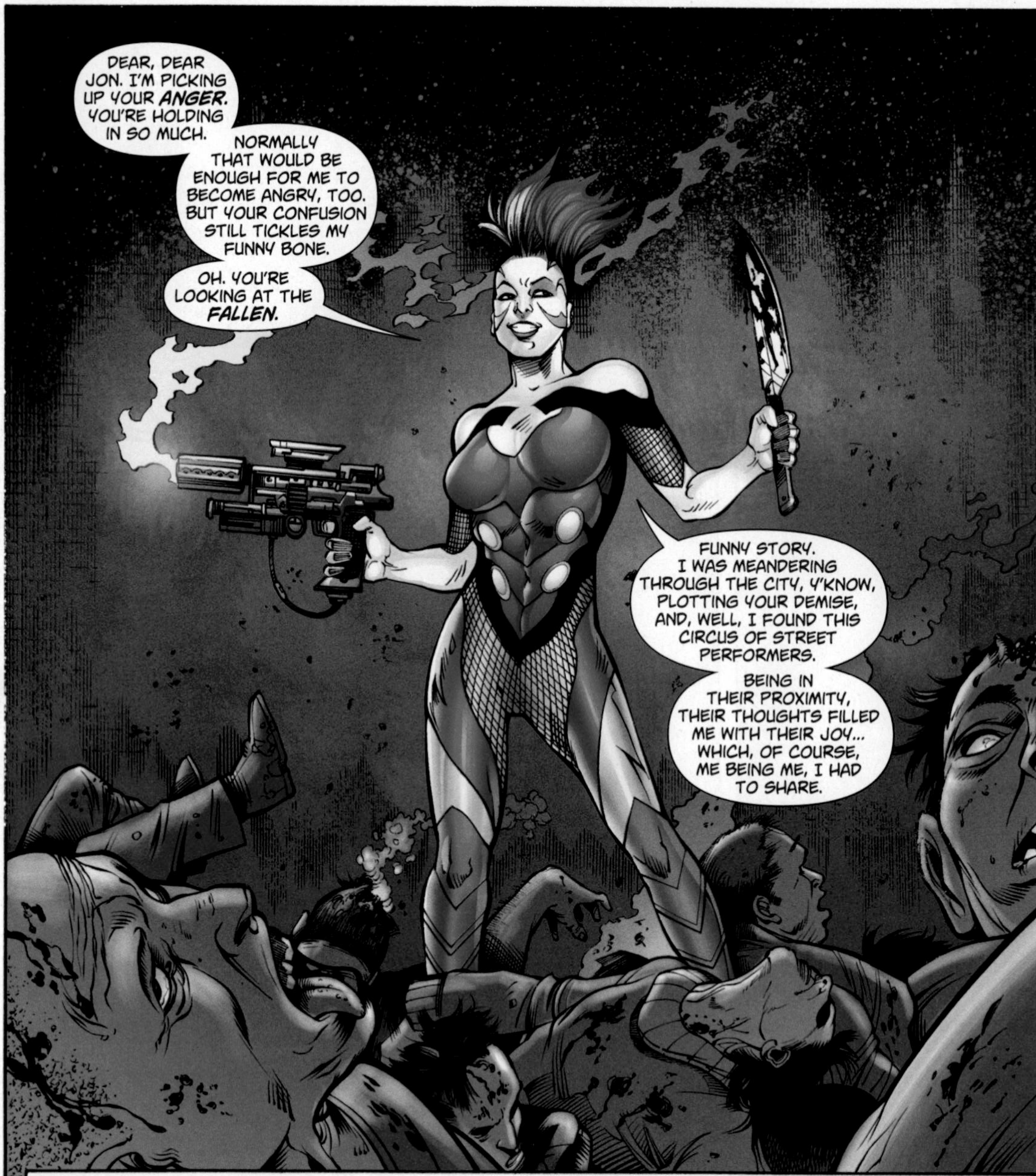
DEAR, DEAR JON. I'M PICKING UP YOUR ANGER. YOU'RE HOLDING IN SO MUCH.
NORMALLY THAT WOULD BE ENOUGH FOR ME TO BECOME ANGRY, TOO. BUT YOUR CONFUSION STILL TICKLES MY FUNNY BONE.
OH. YOU'RE LOOKING AT THE FALLEN.
FUNNY STORY. I WAS MEANDERING THROUGH THE CITY, Y'KNOW, PLOTTING YOUR DEMISE, AND, WELL, I FOUND THIS CIRCUS OF STREET PERFORMERS.
BEING IN THEIR PROXIMITY, THEIR THOUGHTS FILLED ME WITH THEIR JOY... WHICH, OF COURSE, ME BEING ME, I HAD TO SHARE.

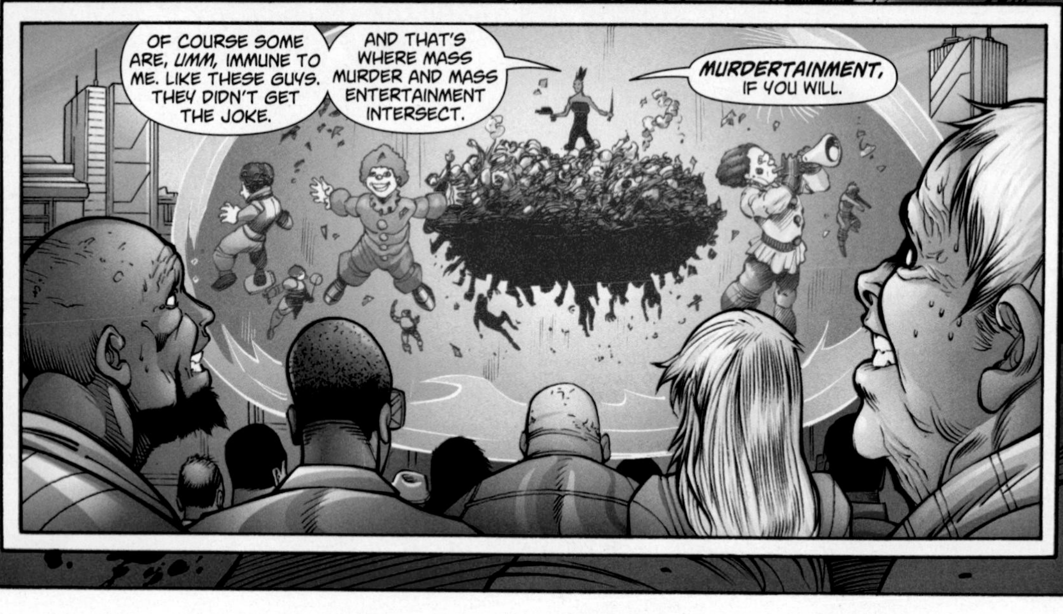
OF COURSE SOME ARE, UMM, IMMUNE TO ME. LIKE THESE GUYS. THEY DIDN'T GET THE JOKE.
AND THAT'S WHERE MASS MURDER AND MASS ENTERTAINMENT INTERSECT.
MURDERTAINMENT, IF YOU WILL.

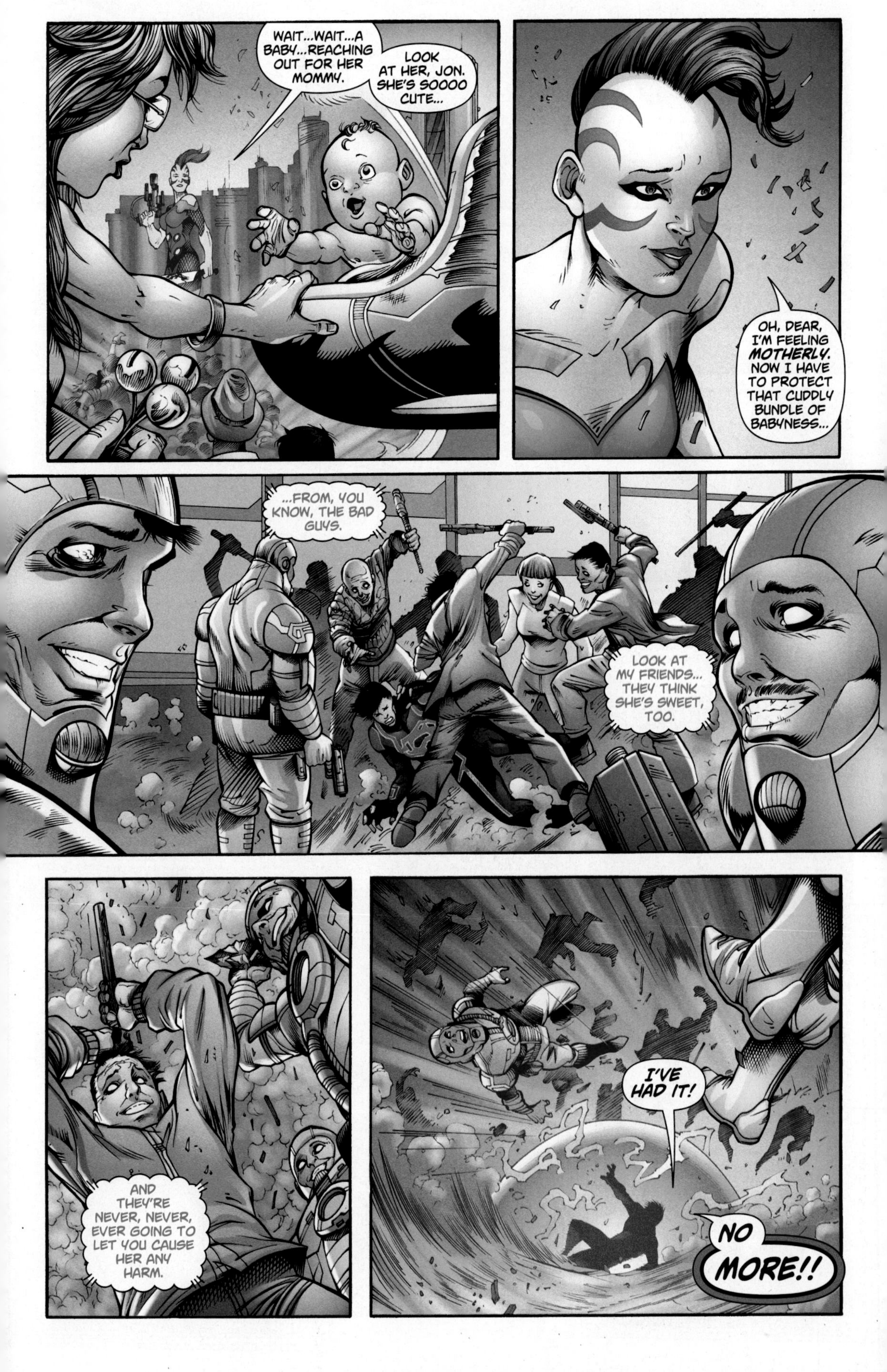
WAIT...WAIT...A BABY...REACHING OUT FOR HER MOMMY.
LOOK AT HER, JON. SHE'S SOOOO CUTE...
OH, DEAR, I'M FEELING *MOTHERLY*. NOW I HAVE TO PROTECT THAT CUDDLY BUNDLE OF BABYNESS...
...FROM, YOU KNOW, THE BAD GUYS.
LOOK AT MY FRIENDS... THEY THINK SHE'S SWEET, TOO.
AND THEY'RE NEVER, NEVER, EVER GOING TO LET YOU CAUSE HER ANY HARM.
I'VE HAD IT!
NO MORE!!

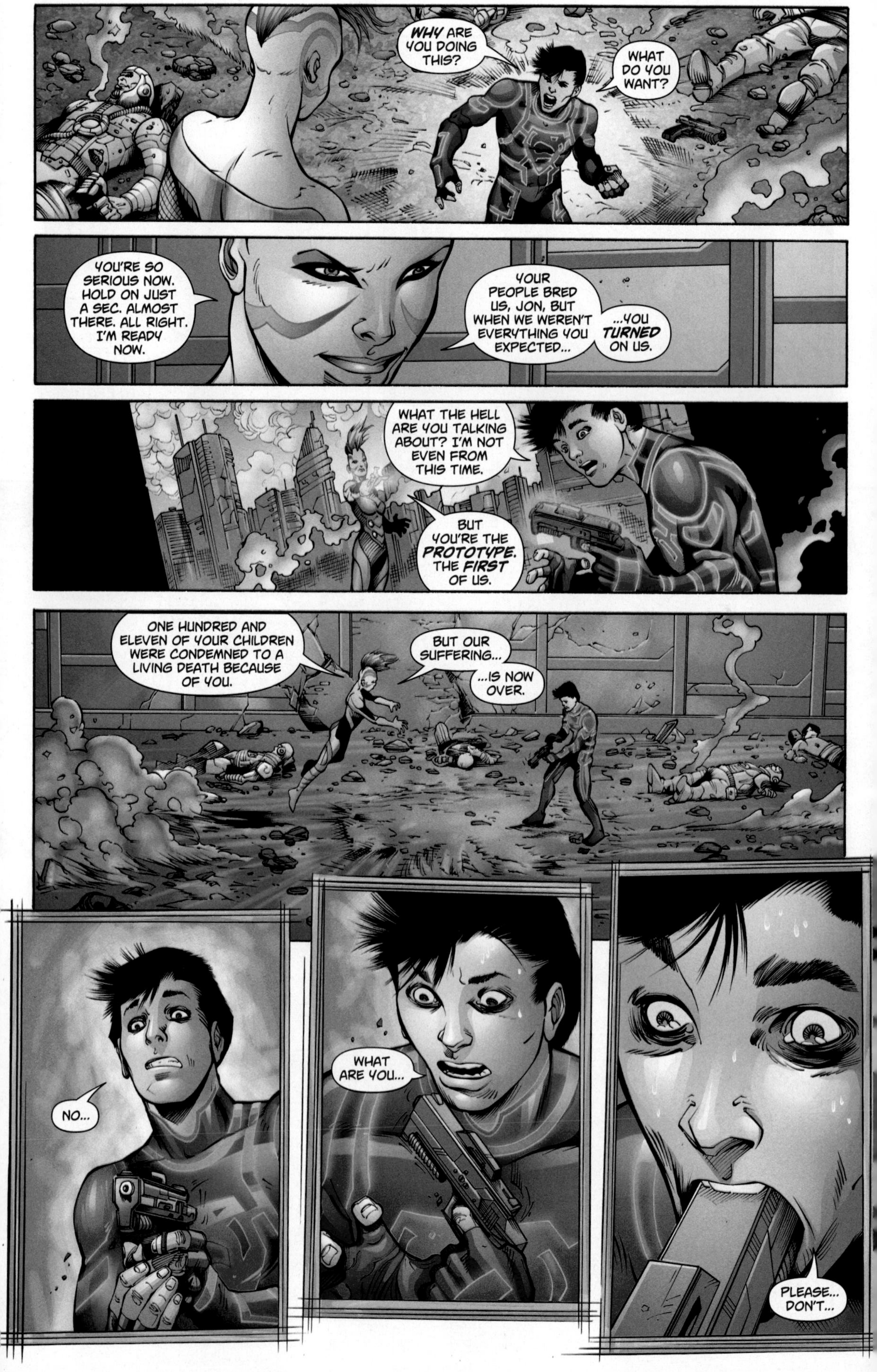
WHY ARE YOU DOING THIS?
WHAT DO YOU WANT?
YOU'RE SO SERIOUS NOW. HOLD ON JUST A SEC. ALMOST THERE. ALL RIGHT. I'M READY NOW.
YOUR PEOPLE BRED US, JON, BUT WHEN WE WEREN'T EVERYTHING YOU EXPECTED...
...YOU TURNED ON US.
WHAT THE HELL ARE YOU TALKING ABOUT? I'M NOT EVEN FROM THIS TIME.
BUT YOU'RE THE PROTOTYPE. THE FIRST OF US.
ONE HUNDRED AND ELEVEN OF YOUR CHILDREN WERE CONDEMNED TO A LIVING DEATH BECAUSE OF YOU.
BUT OUR SUFFERING...
...IS NOW OVER.
NO...
WHAT ARE YOU...
PLEASE... DON'T...

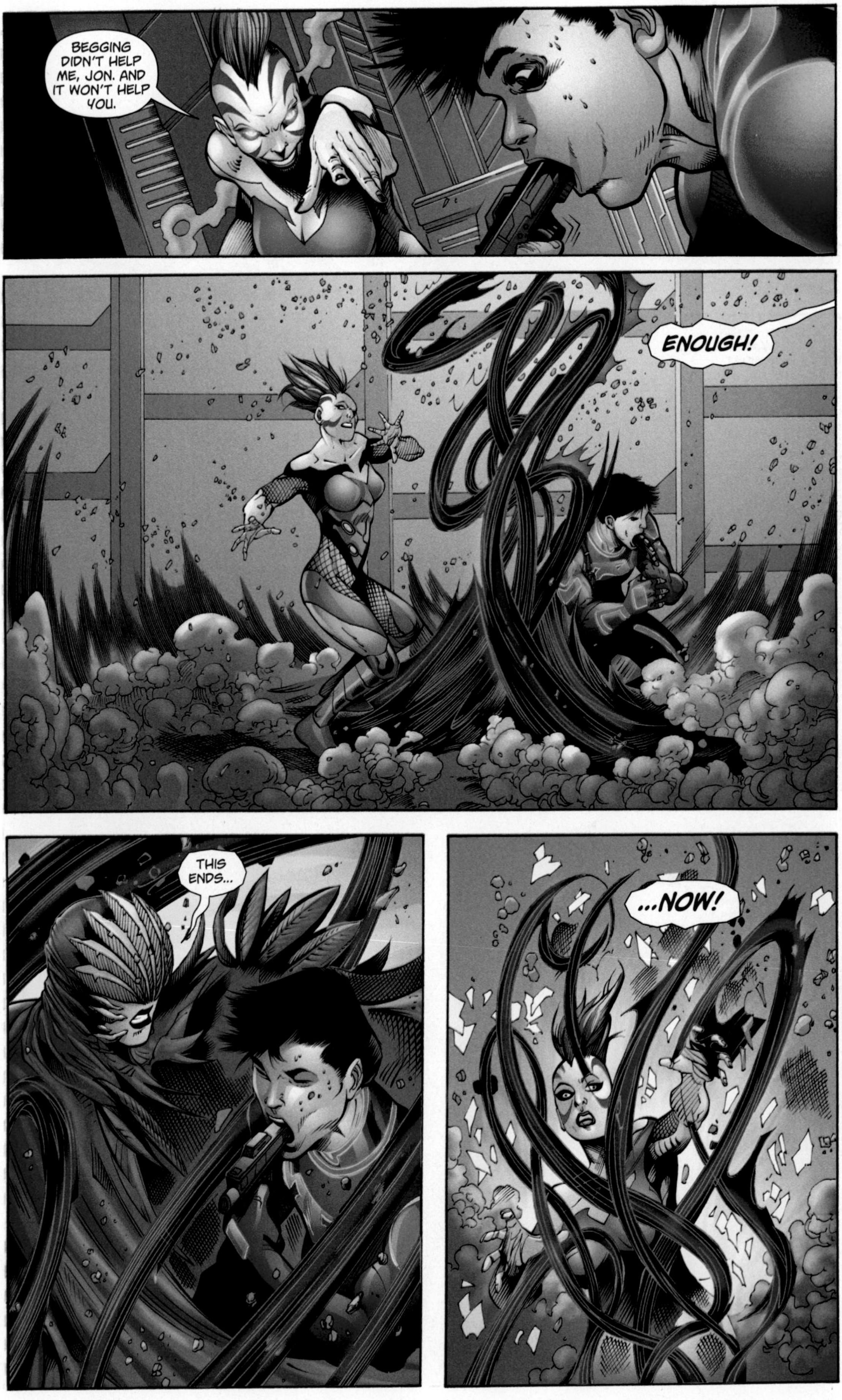
BEGGING DIDN'T HELP ME, JON. AND IT WON'T HELP YOU.
ENOUGH!
THIS ENDS...
...NOW!

WH-WH-WHERE AM I?

THE SCARLET MOUNTAINS. SEVEN THOUSAND, TWO HUNDRED MILES FROM WHERE WE WERE.

RAVEN? YOU SAVED ME.

SHHH, WE MUST FIRST HAVE YOU CALM. YOU'RE SAFE...FROM HER AND FROM YOURSELF.

I DON'T UNDERSTAND... HOW DID YOU KNOW? I MEAN, ANOTHER SECOND AND--

I SENSE PAIN. I SENSED YOURS.

BUT NOW I SENSE...A DARK CLOUD...

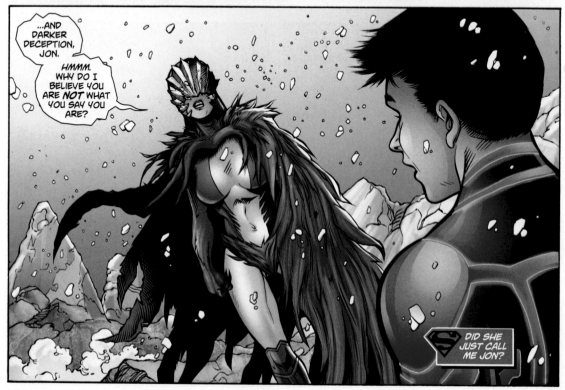

...AND DARKER DECEPTION, JON.

HMMM. WHY DO I BELIEVE YOU ARE *NOT* WHAT YOU SAY YOU ARE?

DID SHE JUST CALL ME JON?

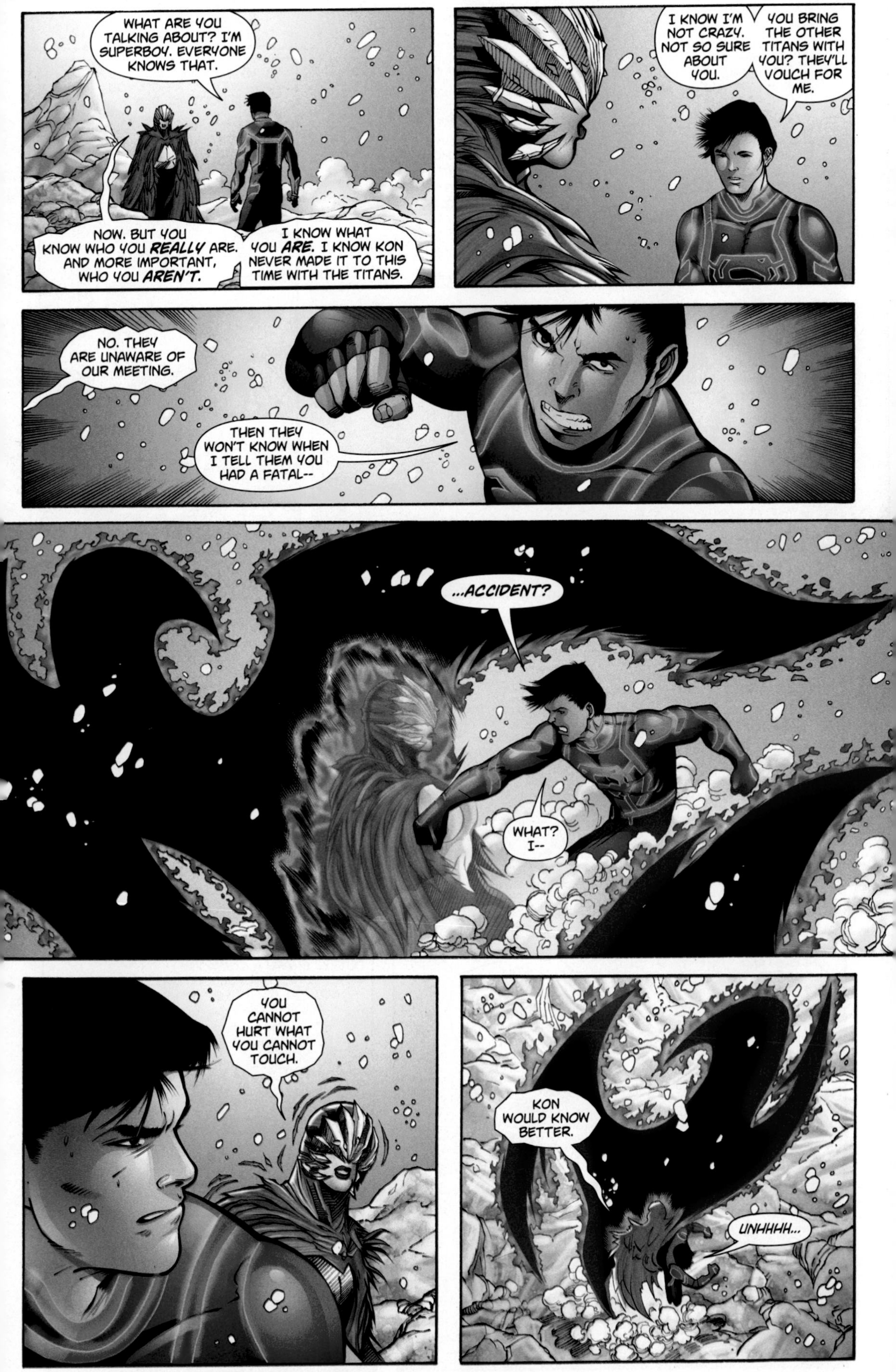
WHAT ARE YOU TALKING ABOUT? I'M SUPERBOY. EVERYONE KNOWS THAT.
NOW. BUT YOU KNOW WHO YOU REALLY ARE. AND MORE IMPORTANT, WHO YOU AREN'T.
I KNOW WHAT YOU ARE. I KNOW KON NEVER MADE IT TO THIS TIME WITH THE TITANS.
I KNOW I'M NOT CRAZY. NOT SO SURE ABOUT YOU.
YOU BRING THE OTHER TITANS WITH YOU? THEY'LL VOUCH FOR ME.
NO. THEY ARE UNAWARE OF OUR MEETING.
THEN THEY WON'T KNOW WHEN I TELL THEM YOU HAD A FATAL--
...ACCIDENT?
WHAT? I--
YOU CANNOT HURT WHAT YOU CANNOT TOUCH.
KON WOULD KNOW BETTER.
UNHHHH...

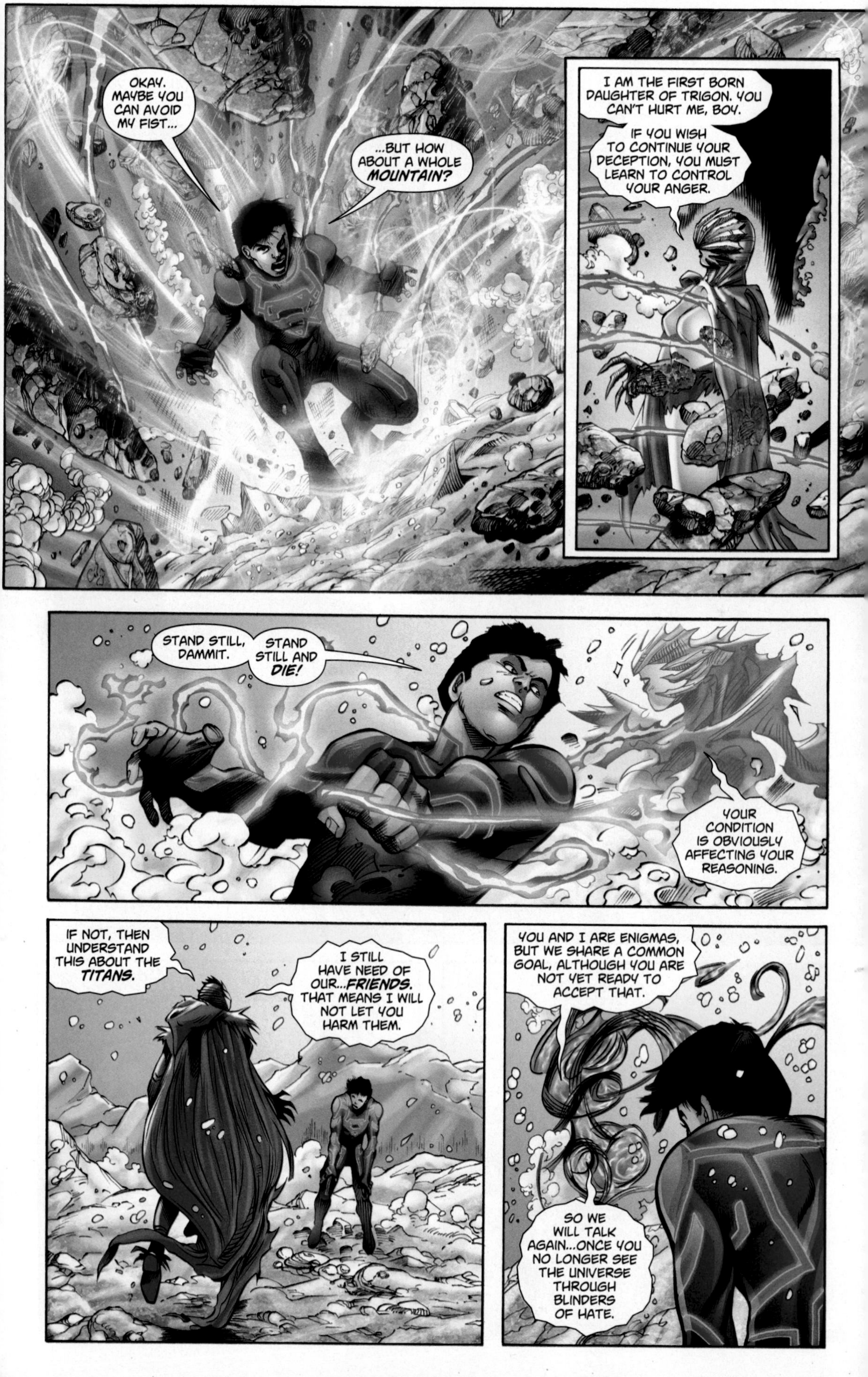
OKAY. MAYBE YOU CAN AVOID MY FIST...
...BUT HOW ABOUT A WHOLE MOUNTAIN?
I AM THE FIRST BORN DAUGHTER OF TRIGON. YOU CAN'T HURT ME, BOY.
IF YOU WISH TO CONTINUE YOUR DECEPTION, YOU MUST LEARN TO CONTROL YOUR ANGER.
STAND STILL, DAMMIT.
STAND STILL AND DIE!
YOUR CONDITION IS OBVIOUSLY AFFECTING YOUR REASONING.
IF NOT, THEN UNDERSTAND THIS ABOUT THE TITANS.
I STILL HAVE NEED OF OUR...FRIENDS. THAT MEANS I WILL NOT LET YOU HARM THEM.
YOU AND I ARE ENIGMAS, BUT WE SHARE A COMMON GOAL, ALTHOUGH YOU ARE NOT YET READY TO ACCEPT THAT.
SO WE WILL TALK AGAIN...ONCE YOU NO LONGER SEE THE UNIVERSE THROUGH BLINDERS OF HATE.

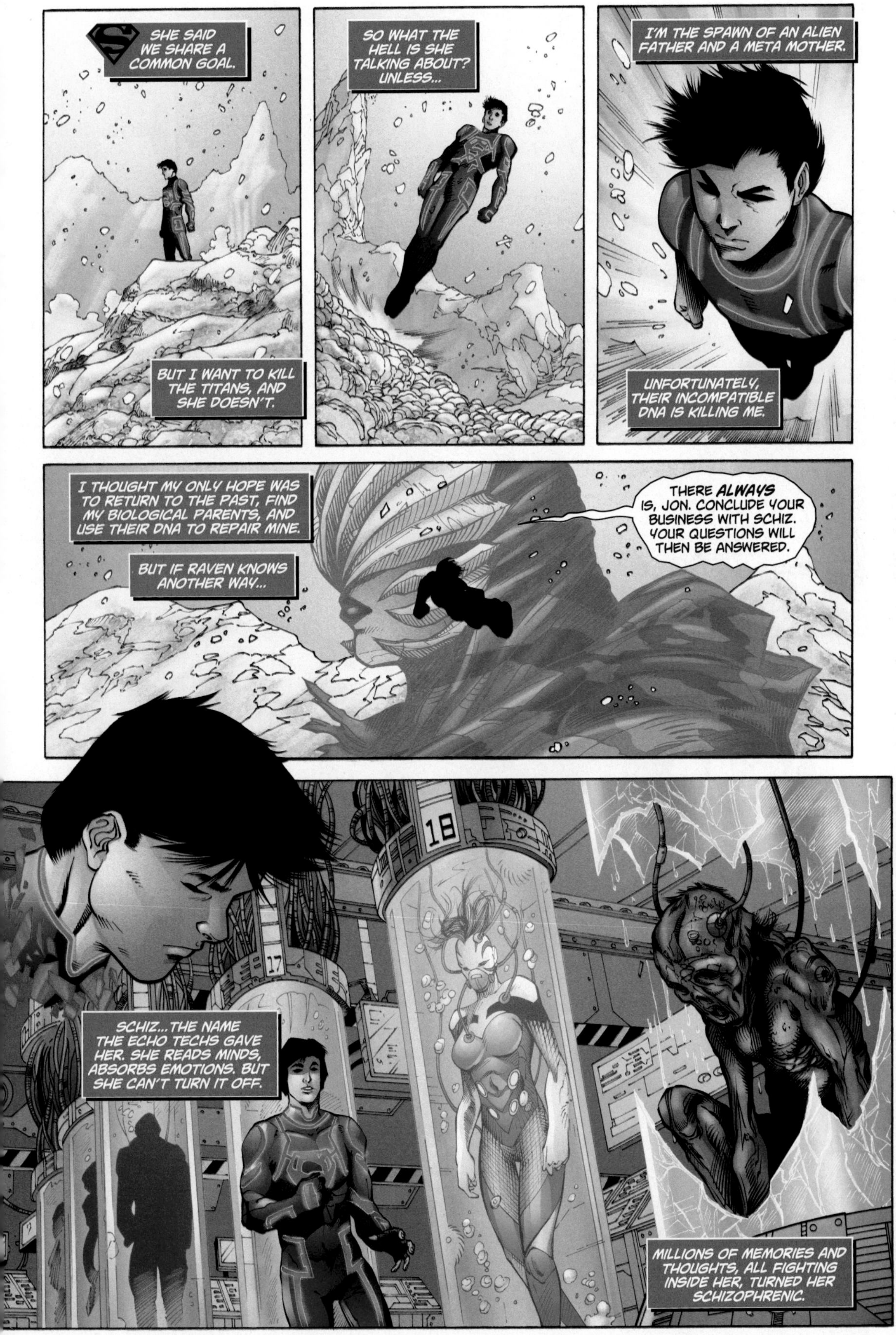
SHE SAID WE SHARE A COMMON GOAL.
BUT I WANT TO KILL THE TITANS, AND SHE DOESN'T.
SO WHAT THE HELL IS SHE TALKING ABOUT? UNLESS...
I'M THE SPAWN OF AN ALIEN FATHER AND A META MOTHER.
UNFORTUNATELY, THEIR INCOMPATIBLE DNA IS KILLING ME.
I THOUGHT MY ONLY HOPE WAS TO RETURN TO THE PAST, FIND MY BIOLOGICAL PARENTS, AND USE THEIR DNA TO REPAIR MINE.
BUT IF RAVEN KNOWS ANOTHER WAY...
THERE ALWAYS IS, JON. CONCLUDE YOUR BUSINESS WITH SCHIZ. YOUR QUESTIONS WILL THEN BE ANSWERED.
18
17
SCHIZ...THE NAME THE ECHO TECHS GAVE HER. SHE READS MINDS, ABSORBS EMOTIONS. BUT SHE CAN'T TURN IT OFF.
MILLIONS OF MEMORIES AND THOUGHTS, ALL FIGHTING INSIDE HER, TURNED HER SCHIZOPHRENIC.

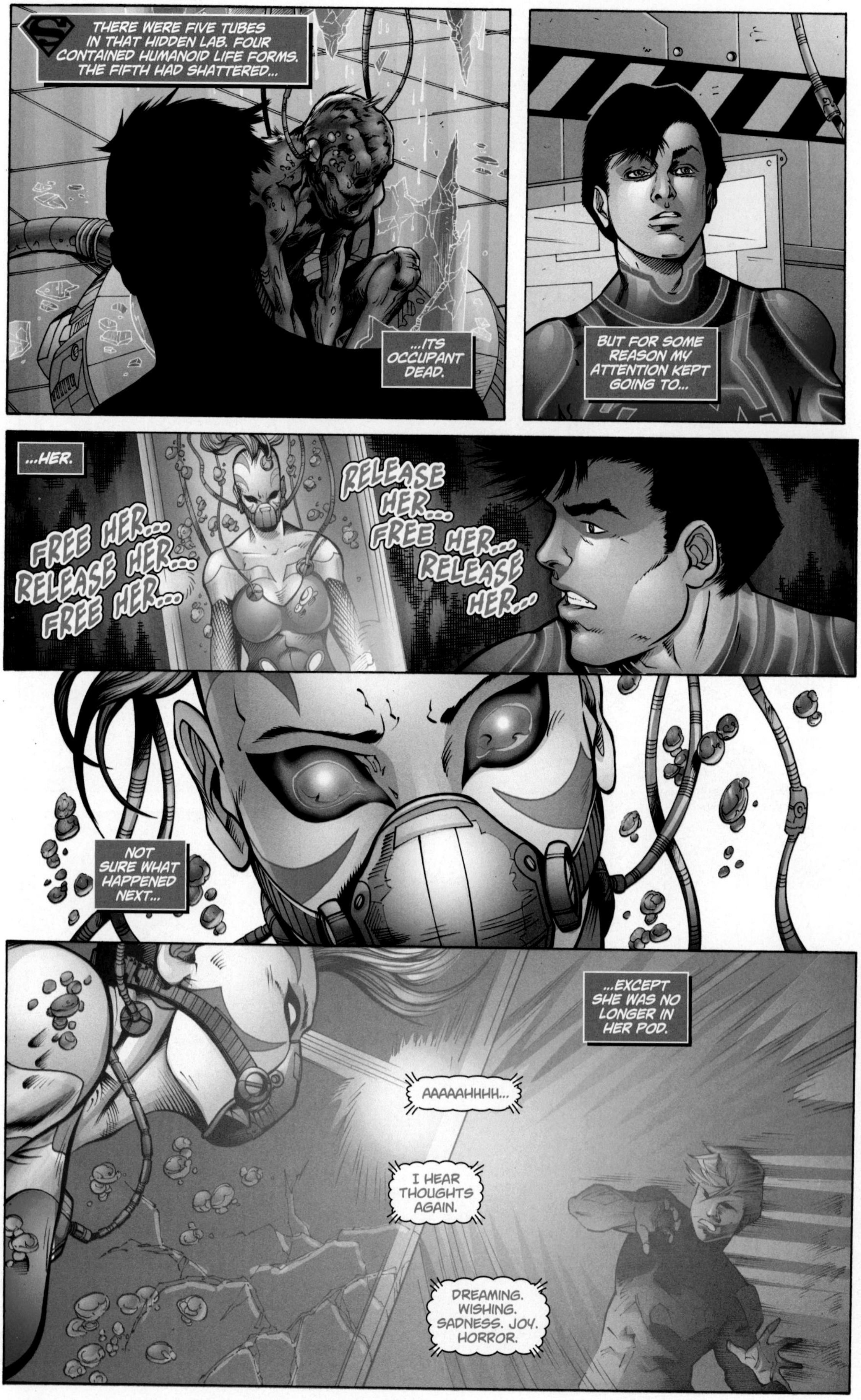
THERE WERE FIVE TUBES IN THAT HIDDEN LAB. FOUR CONTAINED HUMANOID LIFE FORMS. THE FIFTH HAD SHATTERED...
...ITS OCCUPANT DEAD.
BUT FOR SOME REASON MY ATTENTION KEPT GOING TO...
...HER.
FREE HER... RELEASE HER... FREE HER...
RELEASE HER... FREE HER... RELEASE HER...
NOT SURE WHAT HAPPENED NEXT...
...EXCEPT SHE WAS NO LONGER IN HER POD.
AAAAAHHHH...
I HEAR THOUGHTS AGAIN.
DREAMING. WISHING. SADNESS. JOY. HORROR.

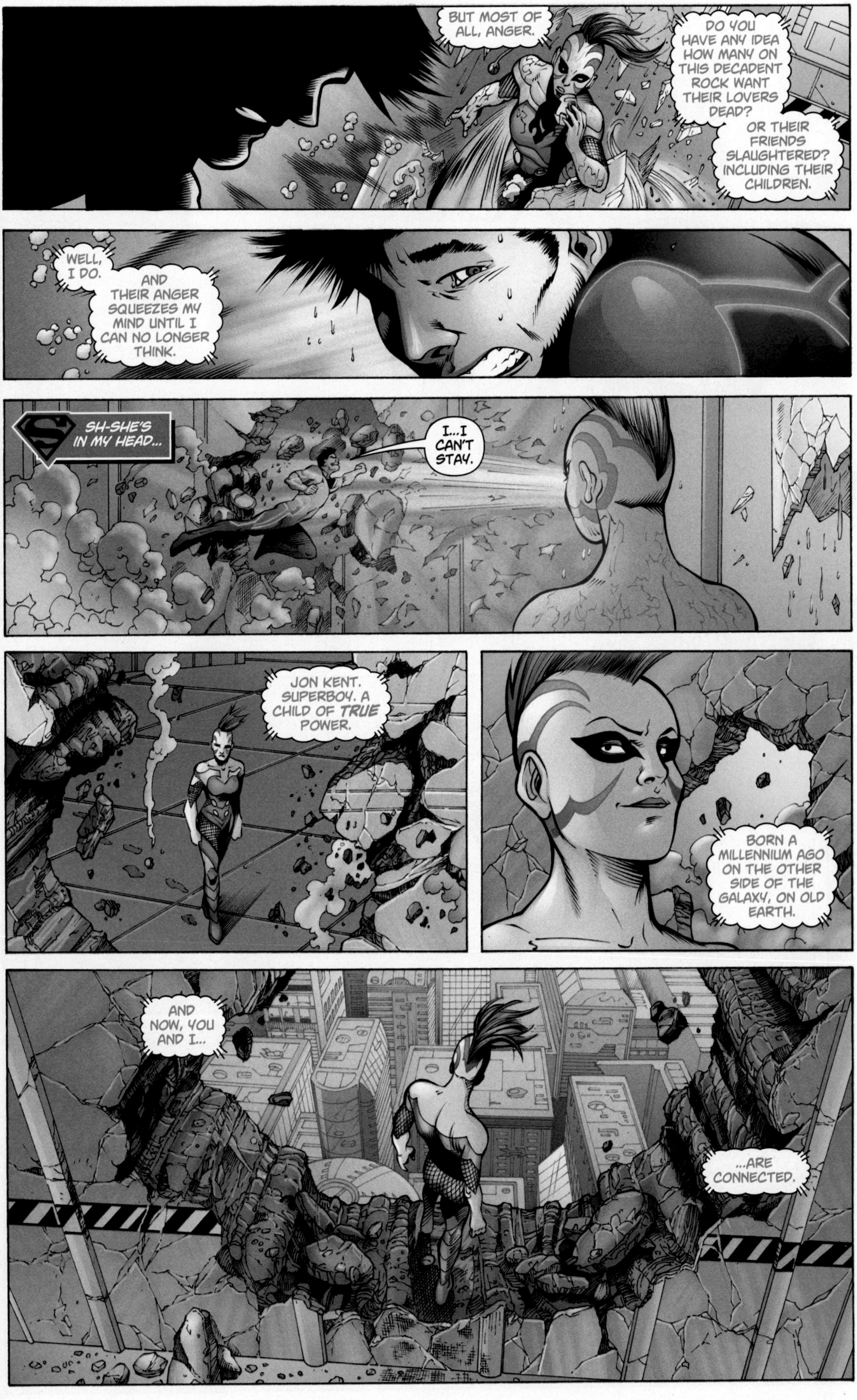
BUT MOST OF ALL, ANGER.
DO YOU HAVE ANY IDEA HOW MANY ON THIS DECADENT ROCK WANT THEIR LOVERS DEAD?
OR THEIR FRIENDS SLAUGHTERED? INCLUDING THEIR CHILDREN.
WELL, I DO.
AND THEIR ANGER SQUEEZES MY MIND UNTIL I CAN NO LONGER THINK.
SH-SHE'S IN MY HEAD...
I...I CAN'T STAY.
JON KENT. SUPERBOY. A CHILD OF TRUE POWER.
BORN A MILLENNIUM AGO ON THE OTHER SIDE OF THE GALAXY, ON OLD EARTH.
AND NOW, YOU AND I...
...ARE CONNECTED.

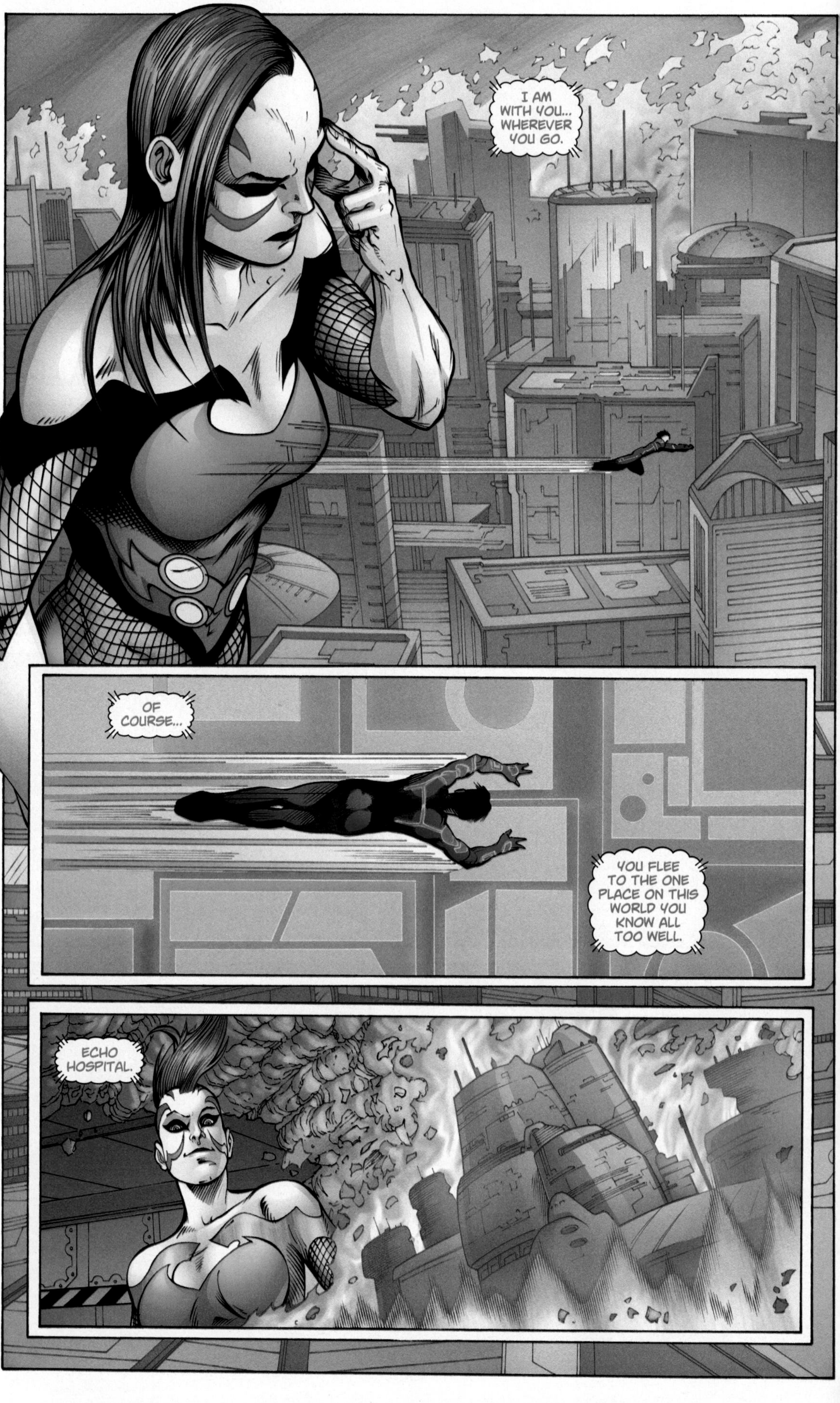
I AM WITH YOU... WHEREVER YOU GO.
OF COURSE...
YOU FLEE TO THE ONE PLACE ON THIS WORLD YOU KNOW ALL TOO WELL.
ECHO HOSPITAL.

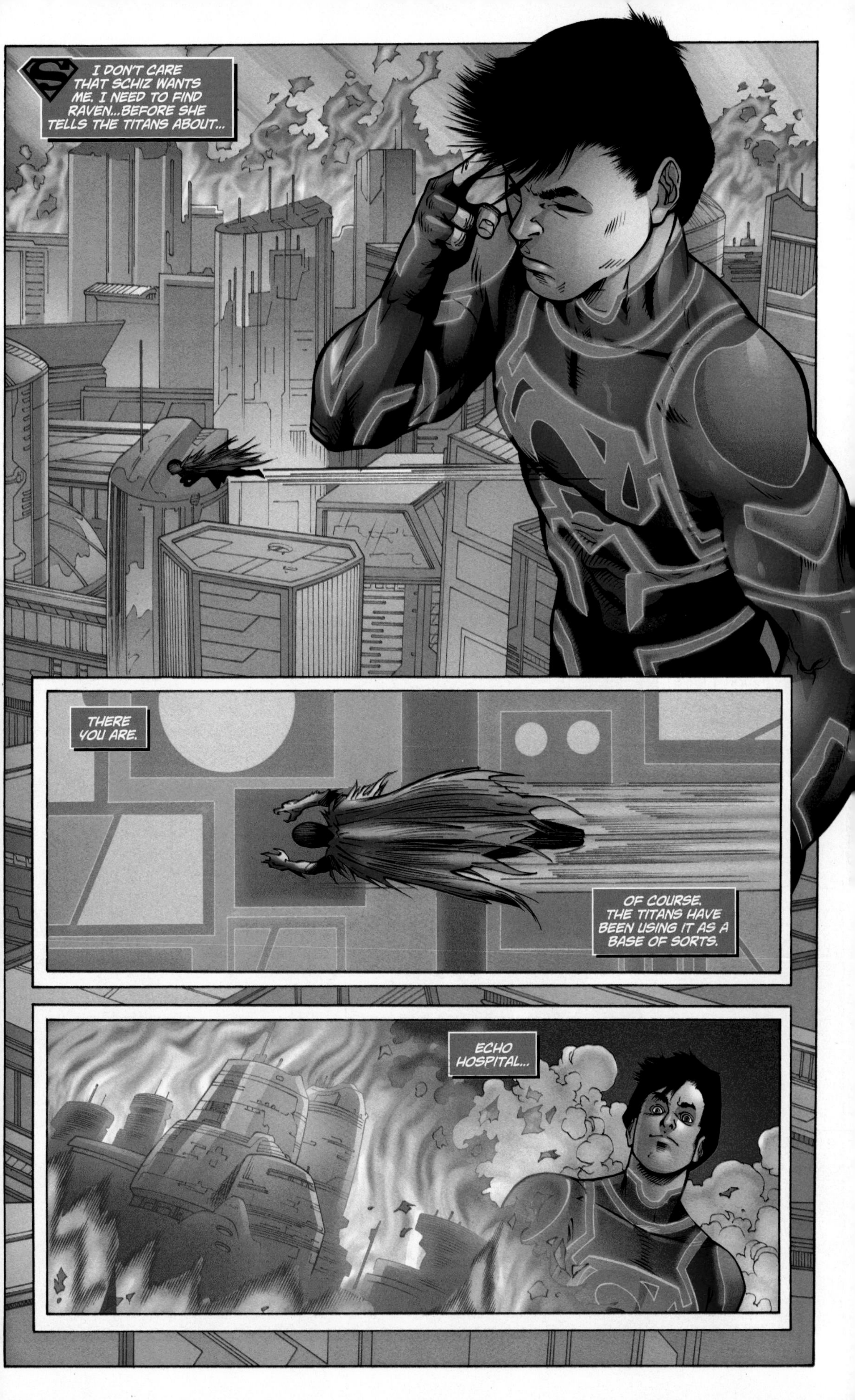
I DON'T CARE THAT SCHIZ WANTS ME. I NEED TO FIND RAVEN...BEFORE SHE TELLS THE TITANS ABOUT...
THERE YOU ARE.
OF COURSE. THE TITANS HAVE BEEN USING IT AS A BASE OF SORTS.
ECHO HOSPITAL...

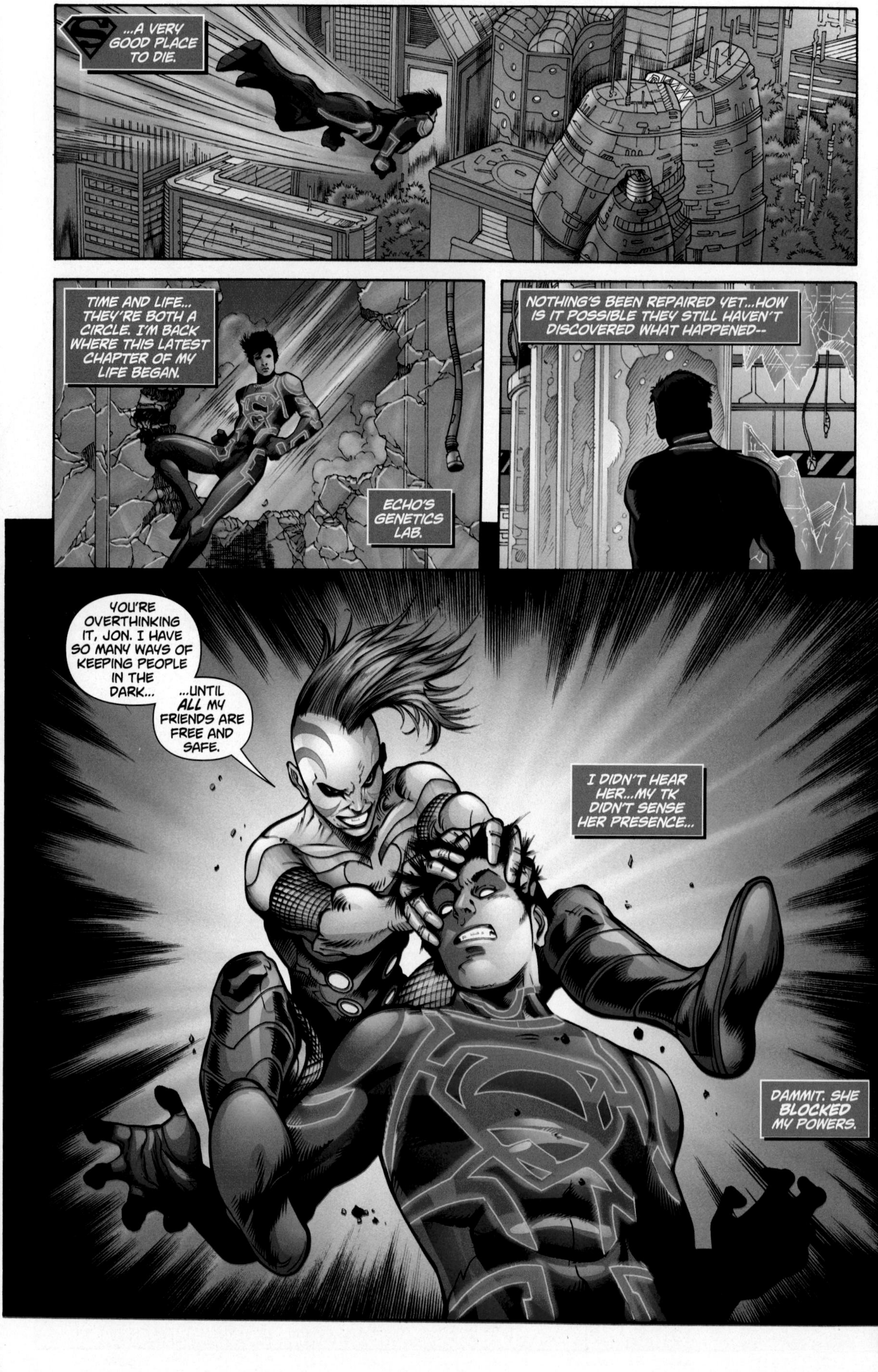
...A VERY GOOD PLACE TO DIE.
TIME AND LIFE... THEY'RE BOTH A CIRCLE. I'M BACK WHERE THIS LATEST CHAPTER OF MY LIFE BEGAN.
ECHO'S GENETICS LAB.
NOTHING'S BEEN REPAIRED YET...HOW IS IT POSSIBLE THEY STILL HAVEN'T DISCOVERED WHAT HAPPENED--
YOU'RE OVERTHINKING IT, JON. I HAVE SO MANY WAYS OF KEEPING PEOPLE IN THE DARK...
...UNTIL ALL MY FRIENDS ARE FREE AND SAFE.
I DIDN'T HEAR HER...MY TK DIDN'T SENSE HER PRESENCE...
DAMMIT. SHE BLOCKED MY POWERS.

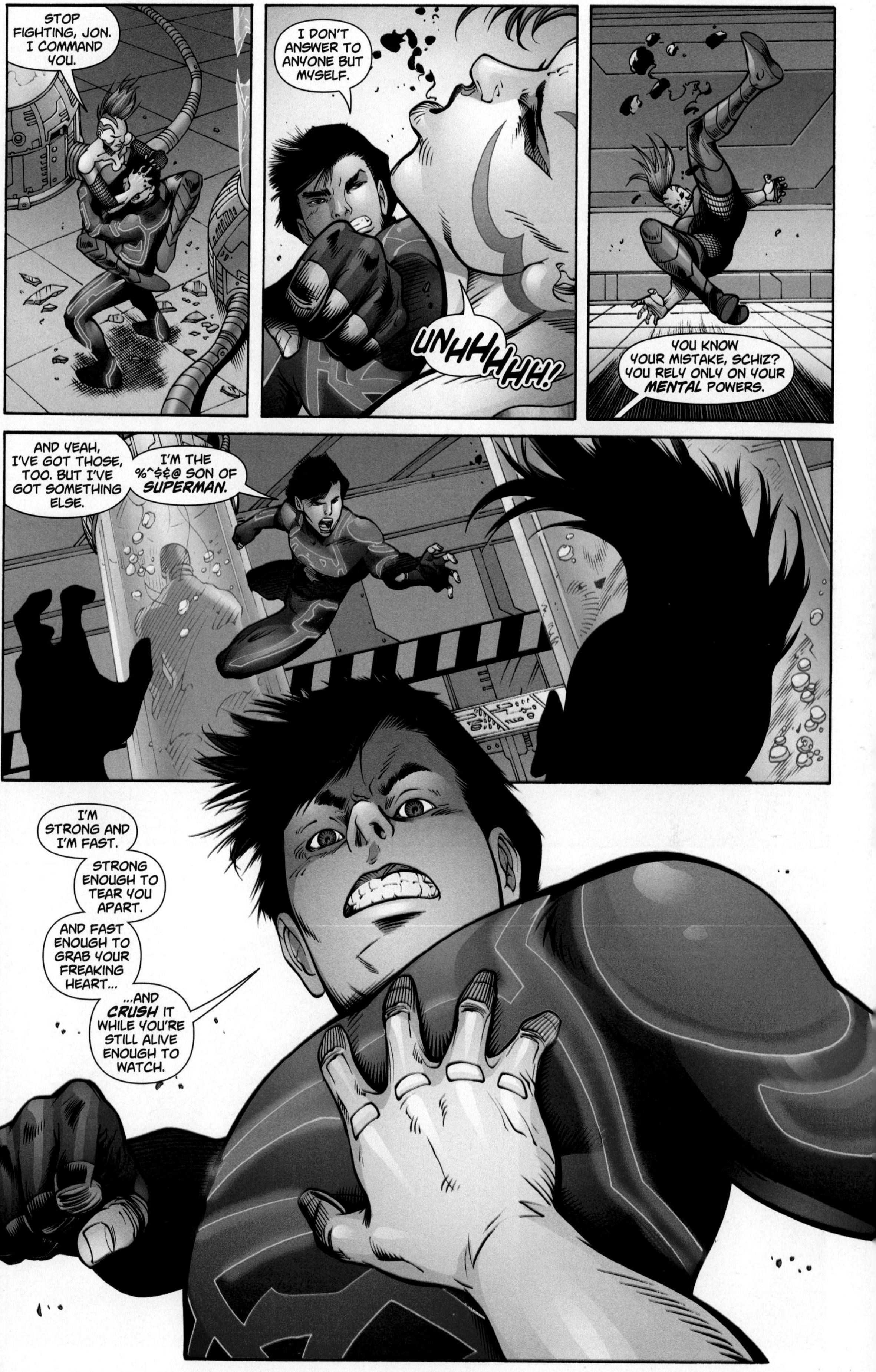

STOP FIGHTING, JON. I COMMAND YOU.
I DON'T ANSWER TO ANYONE BUT MYSELF.
UNHHHHH!
YOU KNOW YOUR MISTAKE, SCHIZ? YOU RELY ONLY ON YOUR MENTAL POWERS.
AND YEAH, I'VE GOT THOSE, TOO. BUT I'VE GOT SOMETHING ELSE.
I'M THE %^$&@ SON OF SUPERMAN.
I'M STRONG AND I'M FAST.
STRONG ENOUGH TO TEAR YOU APART.
AND FAST ENOUGH TO GRAB YOUR FREAKING HEART...
...AND CRUSH IT WHILE YOU'RE STILL ALIVE ENOUGH TO WATCH.

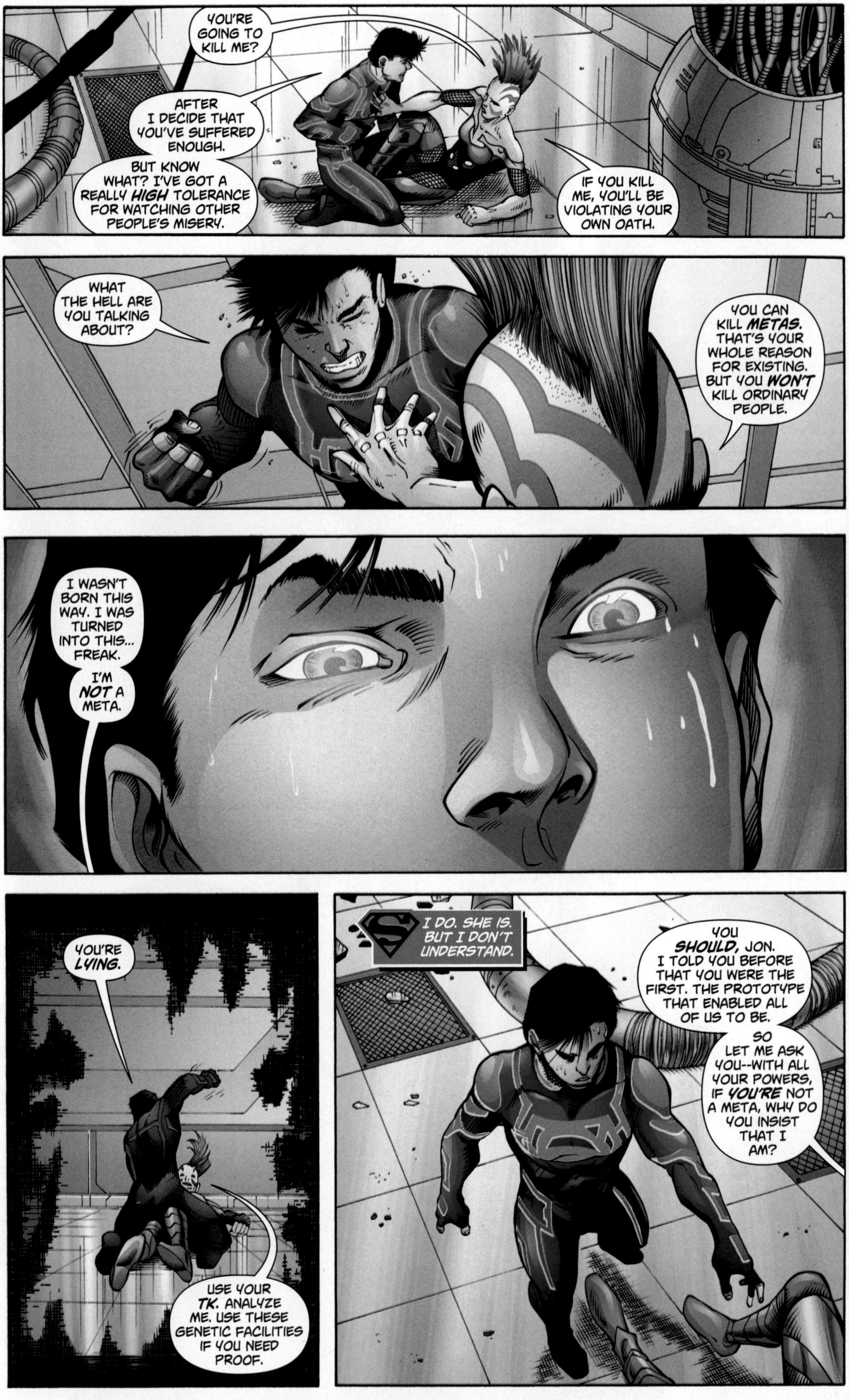
YOU'RE GOING TO KILL ME?
AFTER I DECIDE THAT YOU'VE SUFFERED ENOUGH.
BUT KNOW WHAT? I'VE GOT A REALLY HIGH TOLERANCE FOR WATCHING OTHER PEOPLE'S MISERY.
IF YOU KILL ME, YOU'LL BE VIOLATING YOUR OWN OATH.
WHAT THE HELL ARE YOU TALKING ABOUT?
YOU CAN KILL METAS. THAT'S YOUR WHOLE REASON FOR EXISTING. BUT YOU WON'T KILL ORDINARY PEOPLE.
I WASN'T BORN THIS WAY. I WAS TURNED INTO THIS... FREAK.
I'M NOT A META.
YOU'RE LYING.
USE YOUR TK. ANALYZE ME. USE THESE GENETIC FACILITIES IF YOU NEED PROOF.
I DO. SHE IS. BUT I DON'T UNDERSTAND.
YOU SHOULD, JON. I TOLD YOU BEFORE THAT YOU WERE THE FIRST. THE PROTOTYPE THAT ENABLED ALL OF US TO BE.
SO LET ME ASK YOU--WITH ALL YOUR POWERS, IF YOU'RE NOT A META, WHY DO YOU INSIST THAT I AM?

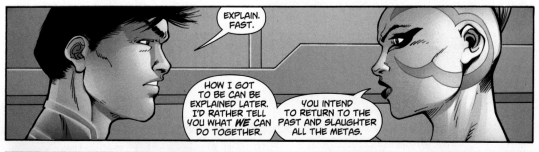

EXPLAIN. FAST.

HOW I GOT TO BE CAN BE EXPLAINED LATER. I'D RATHER TELL YOU WHAT *WE* CAN DO TOGETHER.

YOU INTEND TO RETURN TO THE PAST AND SLAUGHTER ALL THE METAS.

SO?

THERE ARE *THOUSANDS* OF THEM BACK THEN. YOU MIGHT KILL A DOZEN. IF YOU'RE LUCKY, MAYBE EVEN FIFTY...

BUT THERE'RE TOO MANY TO KILL THEM ALL... UNLESS YOU HAVE AN *ARMY*. AND I CAN PROVIDE ONE.

"THERE ARE HUNDREDS OF US, ALL WITH DIFFERENT POWERS. WE WERE BORN TO FIGHT THE METAS...

"...BUT THE NORMALS FEARED US, TOO.

"THEY HUNTED US. KILLED MANY OF US. THE REST THEY CAPTURED.

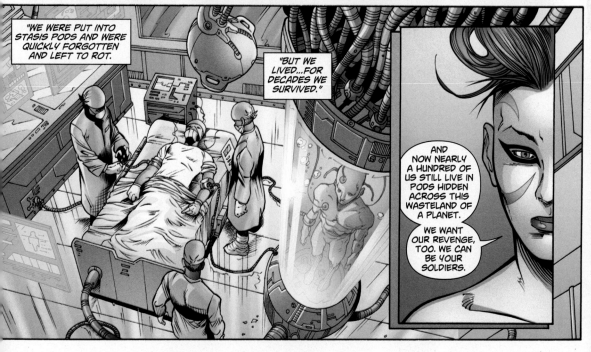

"WE WERE PUT INTO STASIS PODS AND WERE QUICKLY FORGOTTEN AND LEFT TO ROT.

"BUT WE LIVED...FOR DECADES WE SURVIVED."

AND NOW NEARLY A HUNDRED OF US STILL LIVE IN PODS HIDDEN ACROSS THIS WASTELAND OF A PLANET.

WE WANT OUR REVENGE, TOO. WE CAN BE YOUR SOLDIERS.

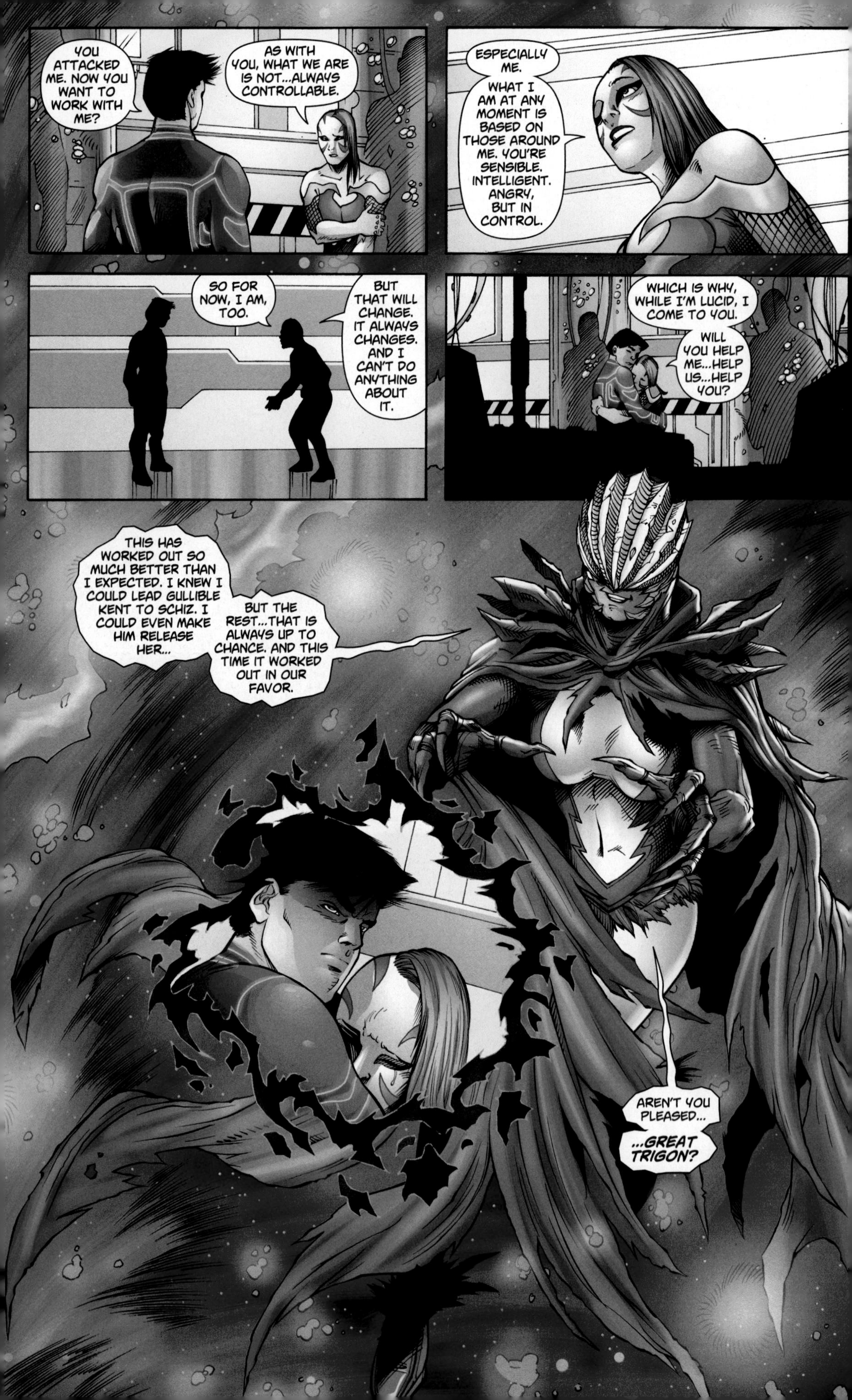
YOU ATTACKED ME. NOW YOU WANT TO WORK WITH ME?
AS WITH YOU, WHAT WE ARE IS NOT...ALWAYS CONTROLLABLE.
ESPECIALLY ME.
WHAT I AM AT ANY MOMENT IS BASED ON THOSE AROUND ME. YOU'RE SENSIBLE. INTELLIGENT. ANGRY, BUT IN CONTROL.
SO FOR NOW, I AM, TOO.
BUT THAT WILL CHANGE. IT ALWAYS CHANGES. AND I CAN'T DO ANYTHING ABOUT IT.
WHICH IS WHY, WHILE I'M LUCID, I COME TO YOU.
WILL YOU HELP ME...HELP US...HELP YOU?
THIS HAS WORKED OUT SO MUCH BETTER THAN I EXPECTED. I KNEW I COULD LEAD GULLIBLE KENT TO SCHIZ. I COULD EVEN MAKE HIM RELEASE HER...
BUT THE REST...THAT IS ALWAYS UP TO CHANCE. AND THIS TIME IT WORKED OUT IN OUR FAVOR.
AREN'T YOU PLEASED...
...GREAT TRIGON?

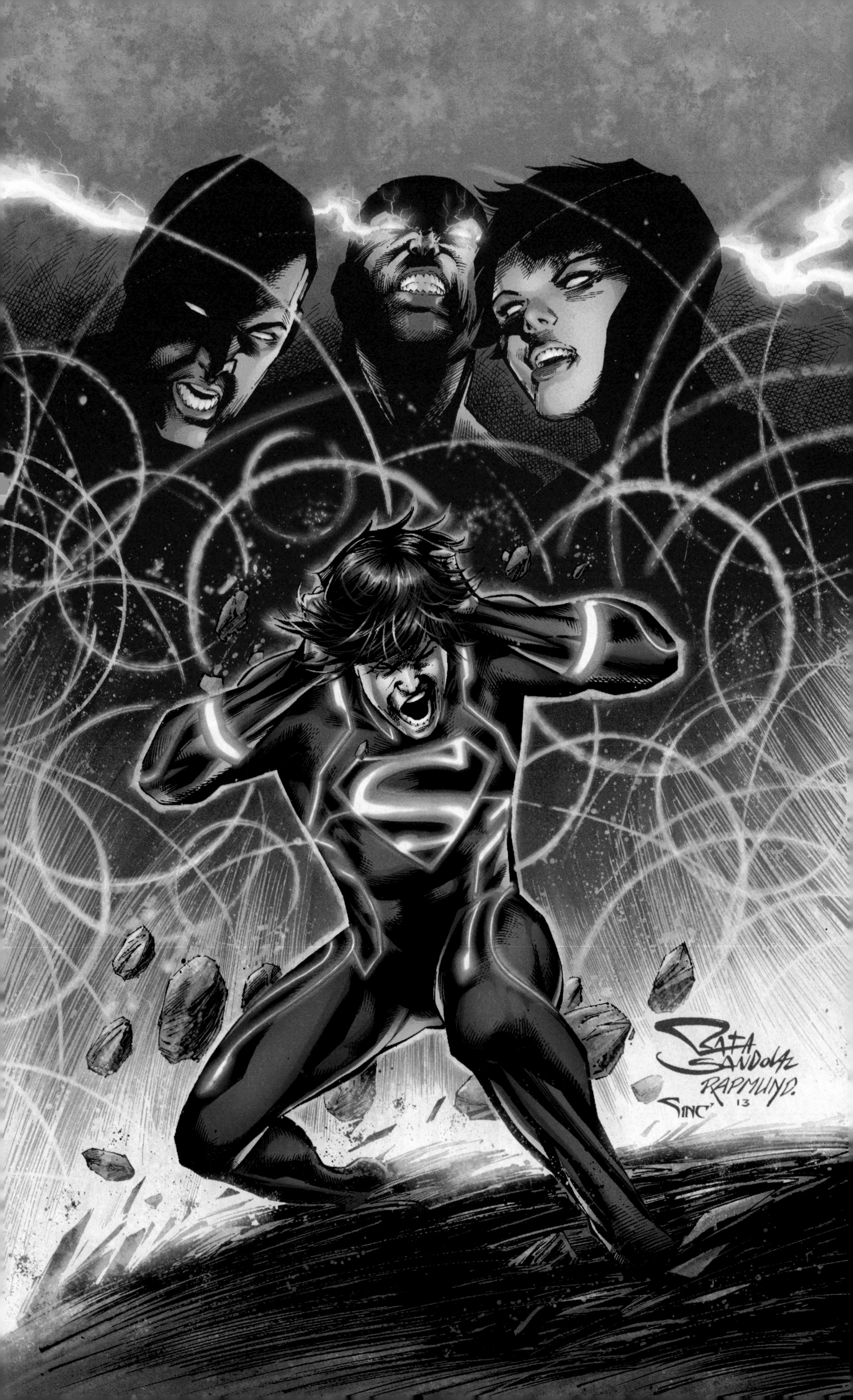

LOST SOULS

MARV WOLFMAN writer **ANDRES GUINALDO** penciller **MARK IRWIN** Inker
TANYA and **RICHARD HORIE** colorists **TRAVIS LANHAM** letterer cover art by **RAFAEL SANDOVAL, NORM RAPMUND** and **ALEX SINCLAIR**

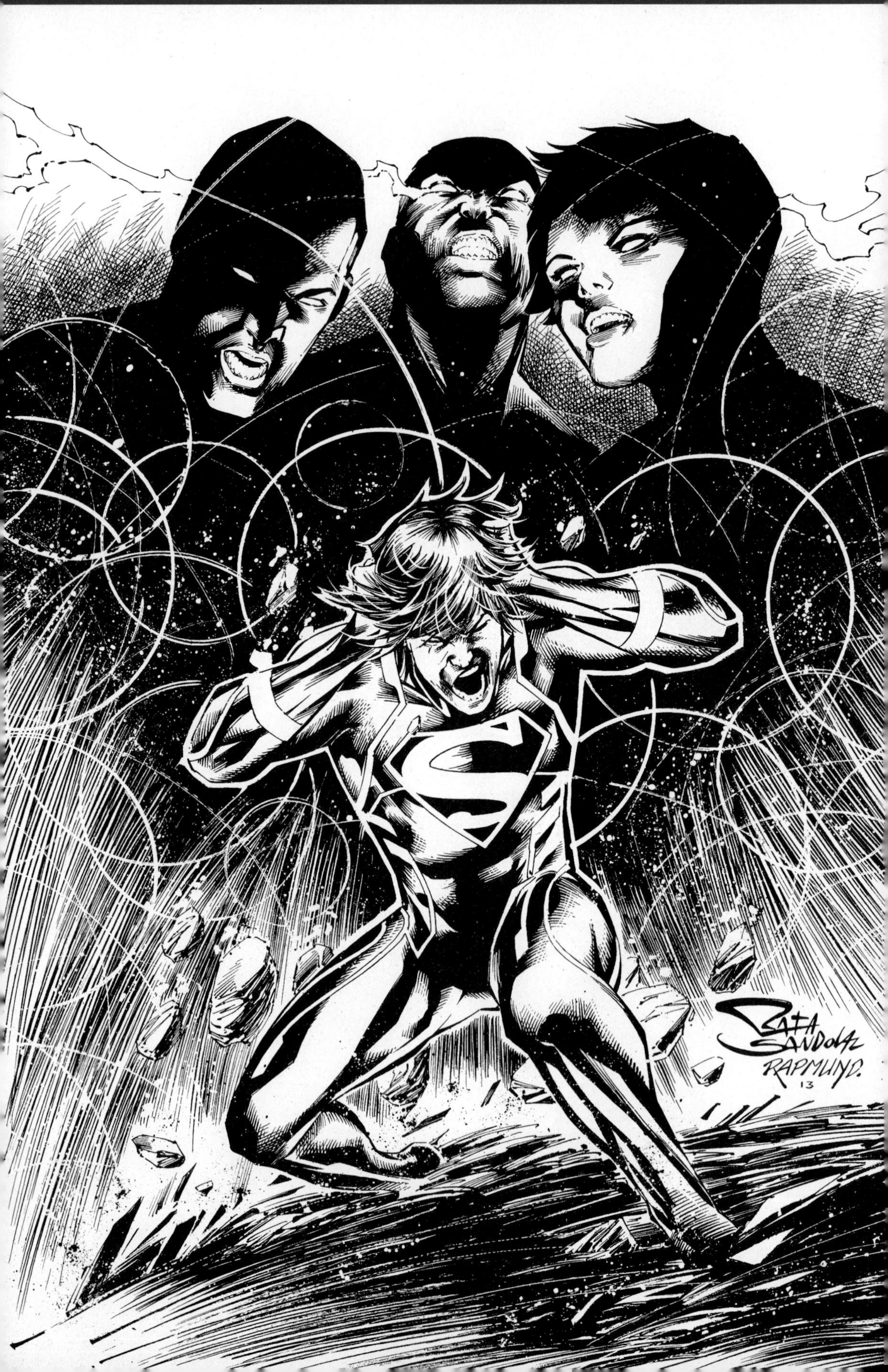

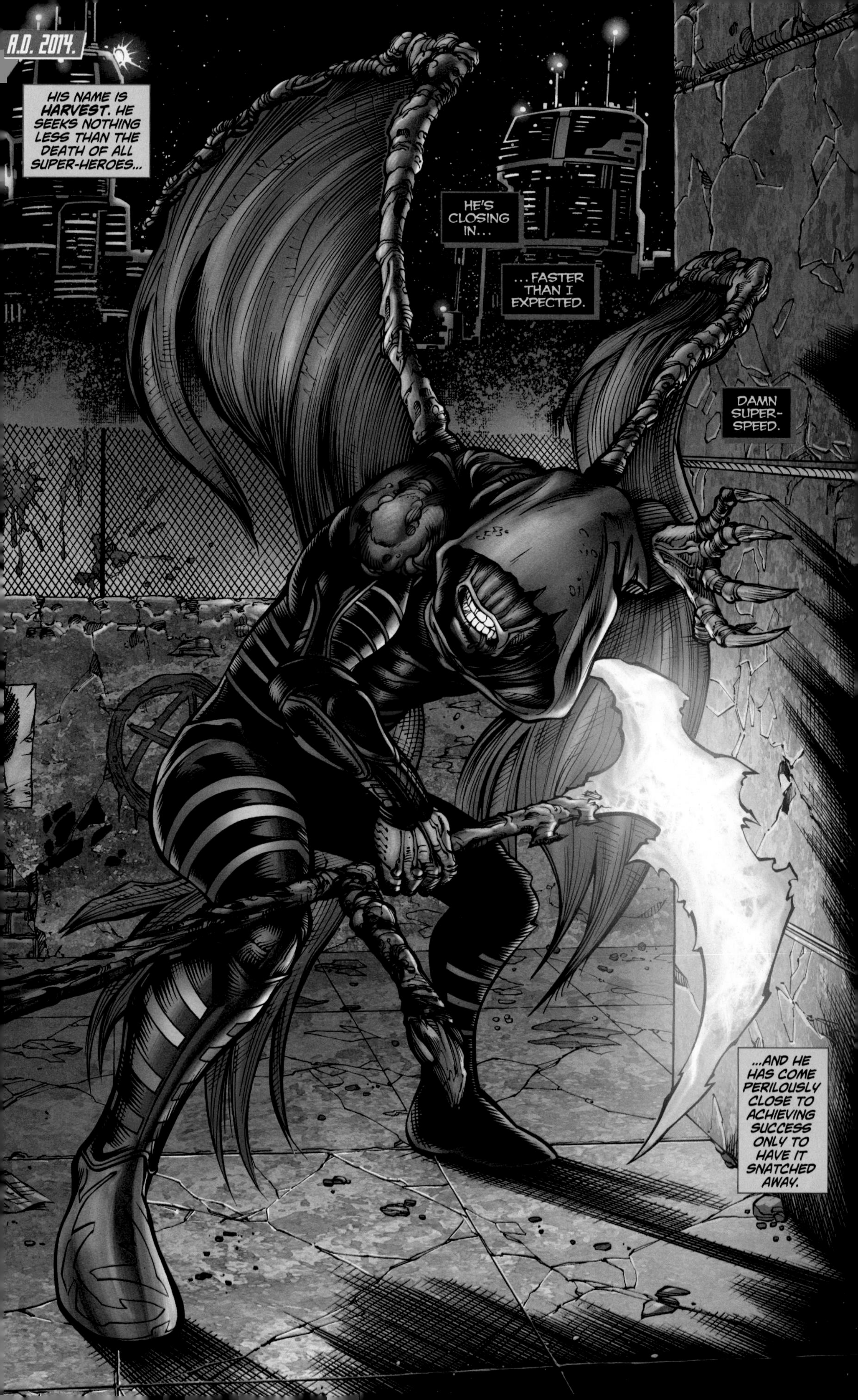
A.D. 2014.
HIS NAME IS HARVEST. HE SEEKS NOTHING LESS THAN THE DEATH OF ALL SUPER-HEROES...
HE'S CLOSING IN...
...FASTER THAN I EXPECTED.
DAMN SUPER-SPEED.
...AND HE HAS COME PERILOUSLY CLOSE TO ACHIEVING SUCCESS ONLY TO HAVE IT SNATCHED AWAY.

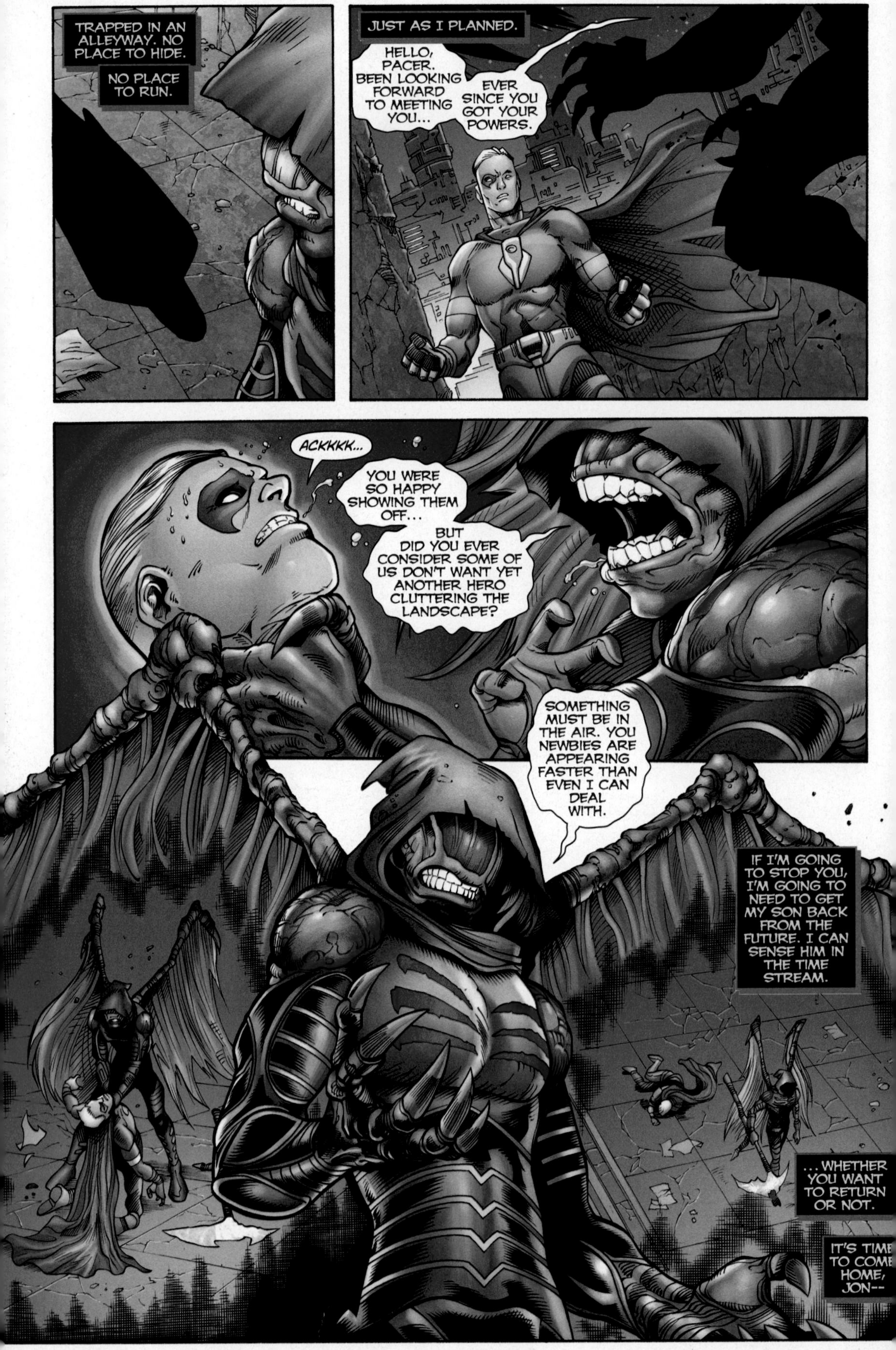
TRAPPED IN AN ALLEYWAY. NO PLACE TO HIDE.
NO PLACE TO RUN.
JUST AS I PLANNED.
HELLO, PACER. BEEN LOOKING FORWARD TO MEETING YOU...
EVER SINCE YOU GOT YOUR POWERS.
ACKKKK...
YOU WERE SO HAPPY SHOWING THEM OFF...
BUT DID YOU EVER CONSIDER SOME OF US DON'T WANT YET ANOTHER HERO CLUTTERING THE LANDSCAPE?
SOMETHING MUST BE IN THE AIR. YOU NEWBIES ARE APPEARING FASTER THAN EVEN I CAN DEAL WITH.
IF I'M GOING TO STOP YOU, I'M GOING TO NEED TO GET MY SON BACK FROM THE FUTURE. I CAN SENSE HIM IN THE TIME STREAM.
...WHETHER YOU WANT TO RETURN OR NOT.
IT'S TIME TO COME HOME, JON--

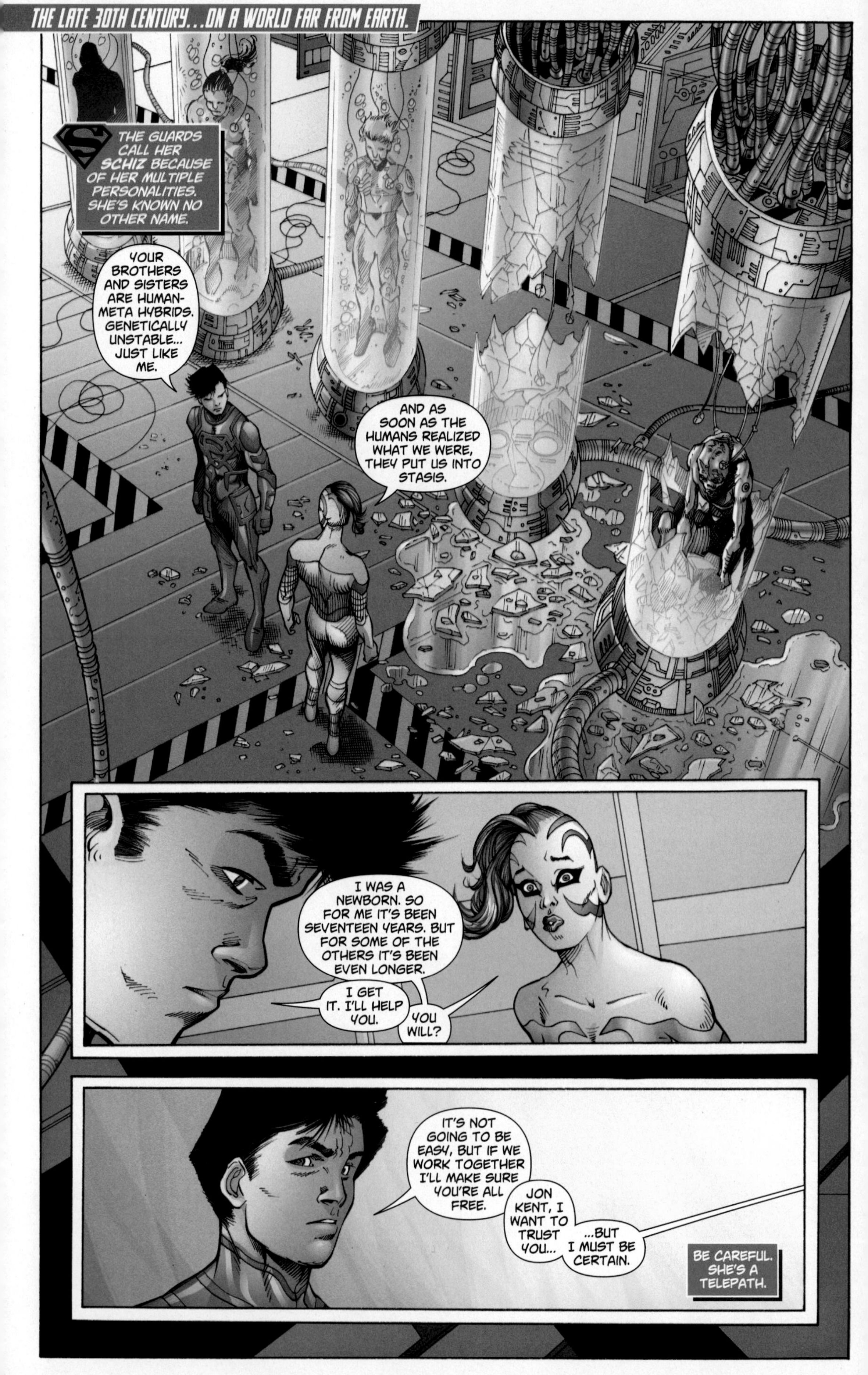
THE LATE 30TH CENTURY...ON A WORLD FAR FROM EARTH.
THE GUARDS CALL HER SCHIZ BECAUSE OF HER MULTIPLE PERSONALITIES. SHE'S KNOWN NO OTHER NAME.
YOUR BROTHERS AND SISTERS ARE HUMAN-META HYBRIDS. GENETICALLY UNSTABLE... JUST LIKE ME.
AND AS SOON AS THE HUMANS REALIZED WHAT WE WERE, THEY PUT US INTO STASIS.
I WAS A NEWBORN. SO FOR ME IT'S BEEN SEVENTEEN YEARS. BUT FOR SOME OF THE OTHERS IT'S BEEN EVEN LONGER.
I GET IT. I'LL HELP YOU.
YOU WILL?
IT'S NOT GOING TO BE EASY, BUT IF WE WORK TOGETHER I'LL MAKE SURE YOU'RE ALL FREE.
JON KENT, I WANT TO TRUST YOU...
...BUT I MUST BE CERTAIN.
BE CAREFUL. SHE'S A TELEPATH.

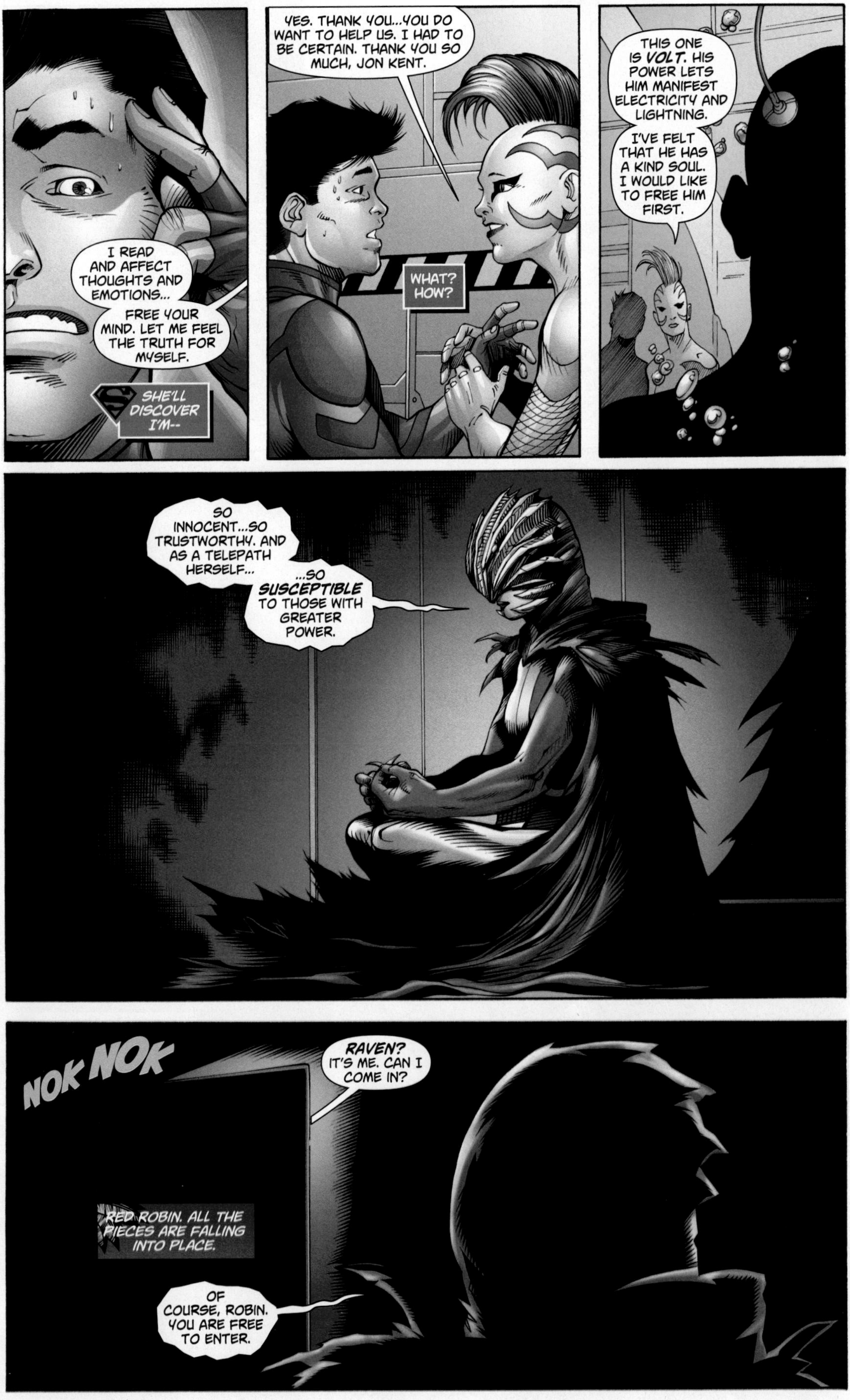
I READ AND AFFECT THOUGHTS AND EMOTIONS...
FREE YOUR MIND. LET ME FEEL THE TRUTH FOR MYSELF.
SHE'LL DISCOVER I'M--
YES. THANK YOU...YOU DO WANT TO HELP US. I HAD TO BE CERTAIN. THANK YOU SO MUCH, JON KENT.
WHAT? HOW?
THIS ONE IS VOLT. HIS POWER LETS HIM MANIFEST ELECTRICITY AND LIGHTNING.
I'VE FELT THAT HE HAS A KIND SOUL. I WOULD LIKE TO FREE HIM FIRST.
SO INNOCENT...SO TRUSTWORTHY. AND AS A TELEPATH HERSELF...
...SO SUSCEPTIBLE TO THOSE WITH GREATER POWER.
NOK NOK
RAVEN? IT'S ME. CAN I COME IN?
RED ROBIN. ALL THE PIECES ARE FALLING INTO PLACE.
OF COURSE, ROBIN. YOU ARE FREE TO ENTER.

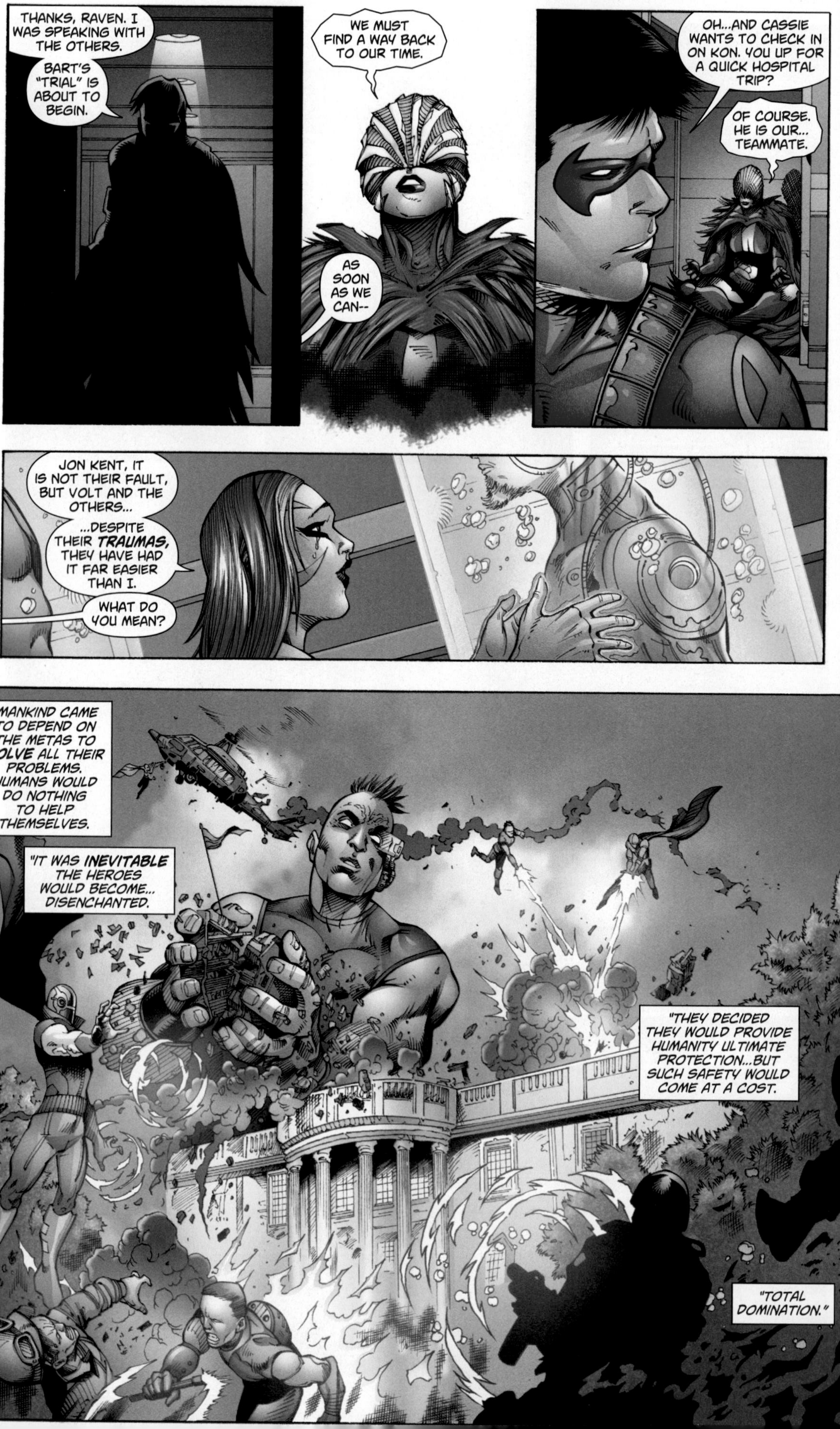
THANKS, RAVEN. I WAS SPEAKING WITH THE OTHERS.
BART'S "TRIAL" IS ABOUT TO BEGIN.
WE MUST FIND A WAY BACK TO OUR TIME.
AS SOON AS WE CAN--
OH...AND CASSIE WANTS TO CHECK IN ON KON. YOU UP FOR A QUICK HOSPITAL TRIP?
OF COURSE. HE IS OUR... TEAMMATE.
JON KENT, IT IS NOT THEIR FAULT, BUT VOLT AND THE OTHERS...
...DESPITE THEIR TRAUMAS, THEY HAVE HAD IT FAR EASIER THAN I.
WHAT DO YOU MEAN?
"MANKIND CAME TO DEPEND ON THE METAS TO SOLVE ALL THEIR PROBLEMS. HUMANS WOULD DO NOTHING TO HELP THEMSELVES.
"IT WAS INEVITABLE THE HEROES WOULD BECOME... DISENCHANTED.
"THEY DECIDED THEY WOULD PROVIDE HUMANITY ULTIMATE PROTECTION...BUT SUCH SAFETY WOULD COME AT A COST.
"TOTAL DOMINATION."

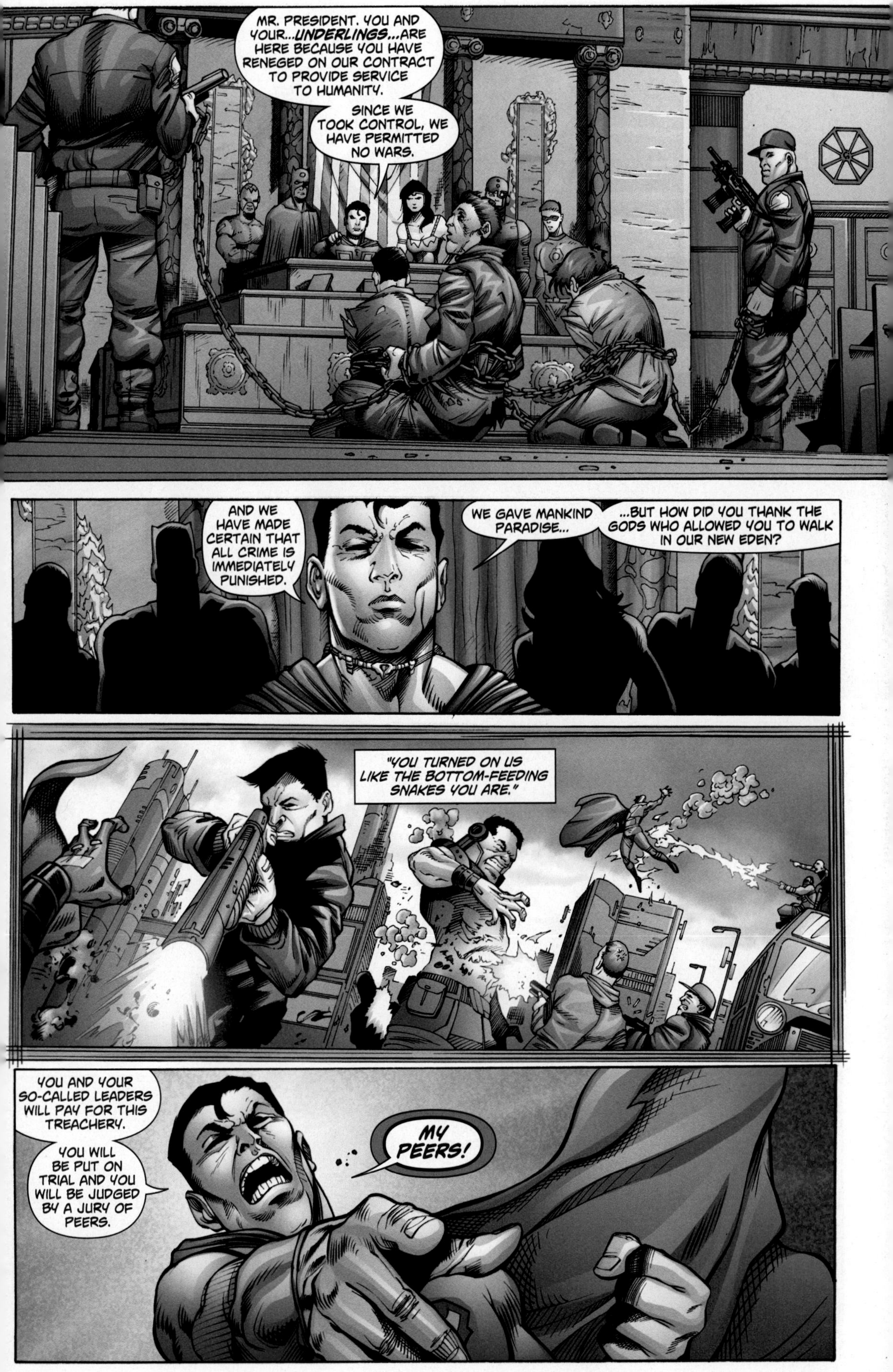

MR. PRESIDENT. YOU AND YOUR...*UNDERLINGS*...ARE HERE BECAUSE YOU HAVE RENEGED ON OUR CONTRACT TO PROVIDE SERVICE TO HUMANITY.
SINCE WE TOOK CONTROL, WE HAVE PERMITTED NO WARS.
AND WE HAVE MADE CERTAIN THAT ALL CRIME IS IMMEDIATELY PUNISHED.
WE GAVE MANKIND PARADISE...
...BUT HOW DID YOU THANK THE GODS WHO ALLOWED YOU TO WALK IN OUR NEW EDEN?
"YOU TURNED ON US LIKE THE BOTTOM-FEEDING SNAKES YOU ARE."
YOU AND YOUR SO-CALLED LEADERS WILL PAY FOR THIS TREACHERY.
YOU WILL BE PUT ON TRIAL AND YOU WILL BE JUDGED BY A JURY OF PEERS.
MY PEERS!

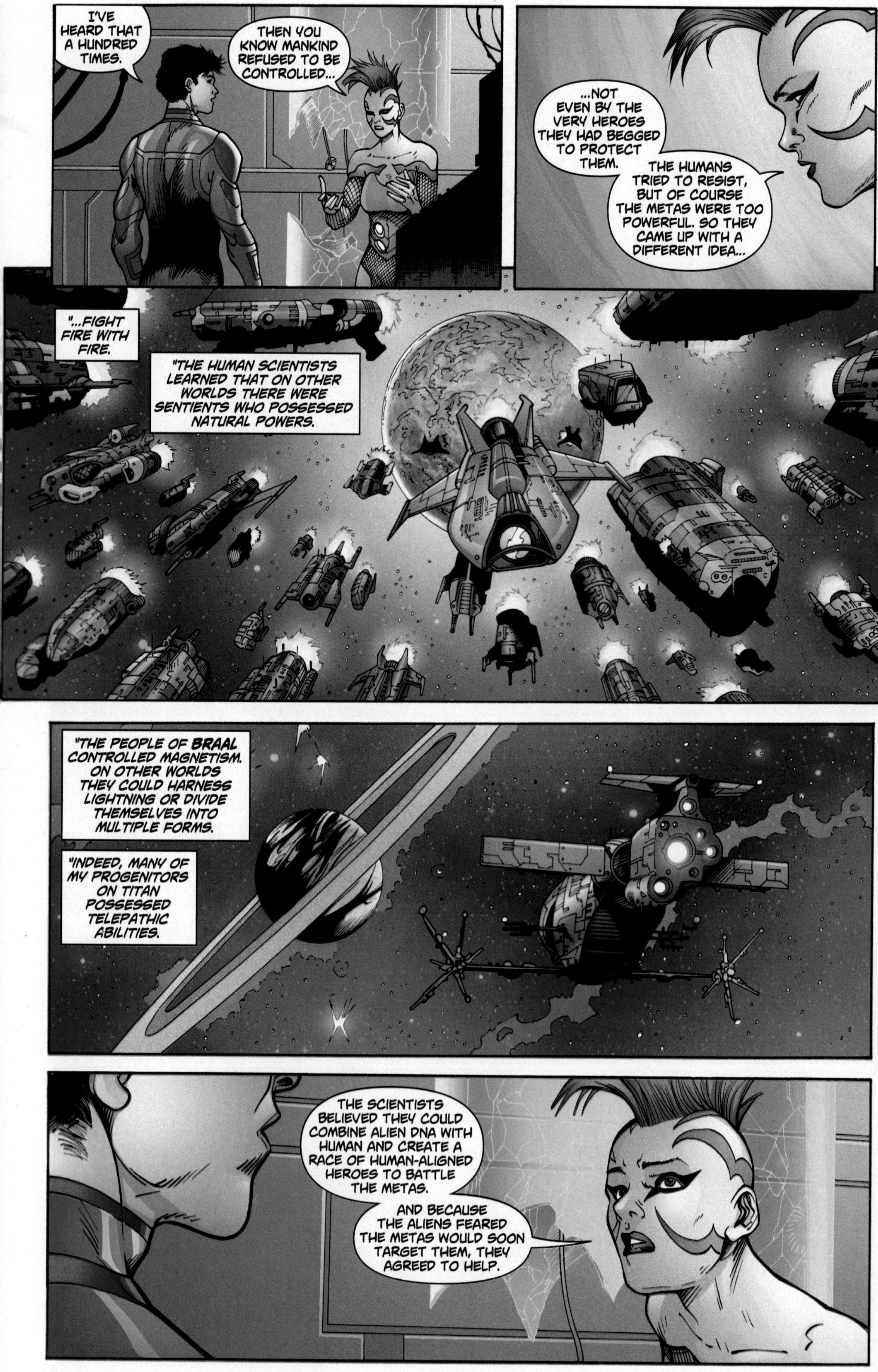
I'VE HEARD THAT A HUNDRED TIMES.
THEN YOU KNOW MANKIND REFUSED TO BE CONTROLLED...
...NOT EVEN BY THE VERY HEROES THEY HAD BEGGED TO PROTECT THEM.
THE HUMANS TRIED TO RESIST, BUT OF COURSE THE METAS WERE TOO POWERFUL. SO THEY CAME UP WITH A DIFFERENT IDEA...
"...FIGHT FIRE WITH FIRE.
"THE HUMAN SCIENTISTS LEARNED THAT ON OTHER WORLDS THERE WERE SENTIENTS WHO POSSESSED NATURAL POWERS.
"THE PEOPLE OF BRAAL CONTROLLED MAGNETISM. ON OTHER WORLDS THEY COULD HARNESS LIGHTNING OR DIVIDE THEMSELVES INTO MULTIPLE FORMS.
"INDEED, MANY OF MY PROGENITORS ON TITAN POSSESSED TELEPATHIC ABILITIES.
THE SCIENTISTS BELIEVED THEY COULD COMBINE ALIEN DNA WITH HUMAN AND CREATE A RACE OF HUMAN-ALIGNED HEROES TO BATTLE THE METAS.
AND BECAUSE THE ALIENS FEARED THE METAS WOULD SOON TARGET THEM, THEY AGREED TO HELP.

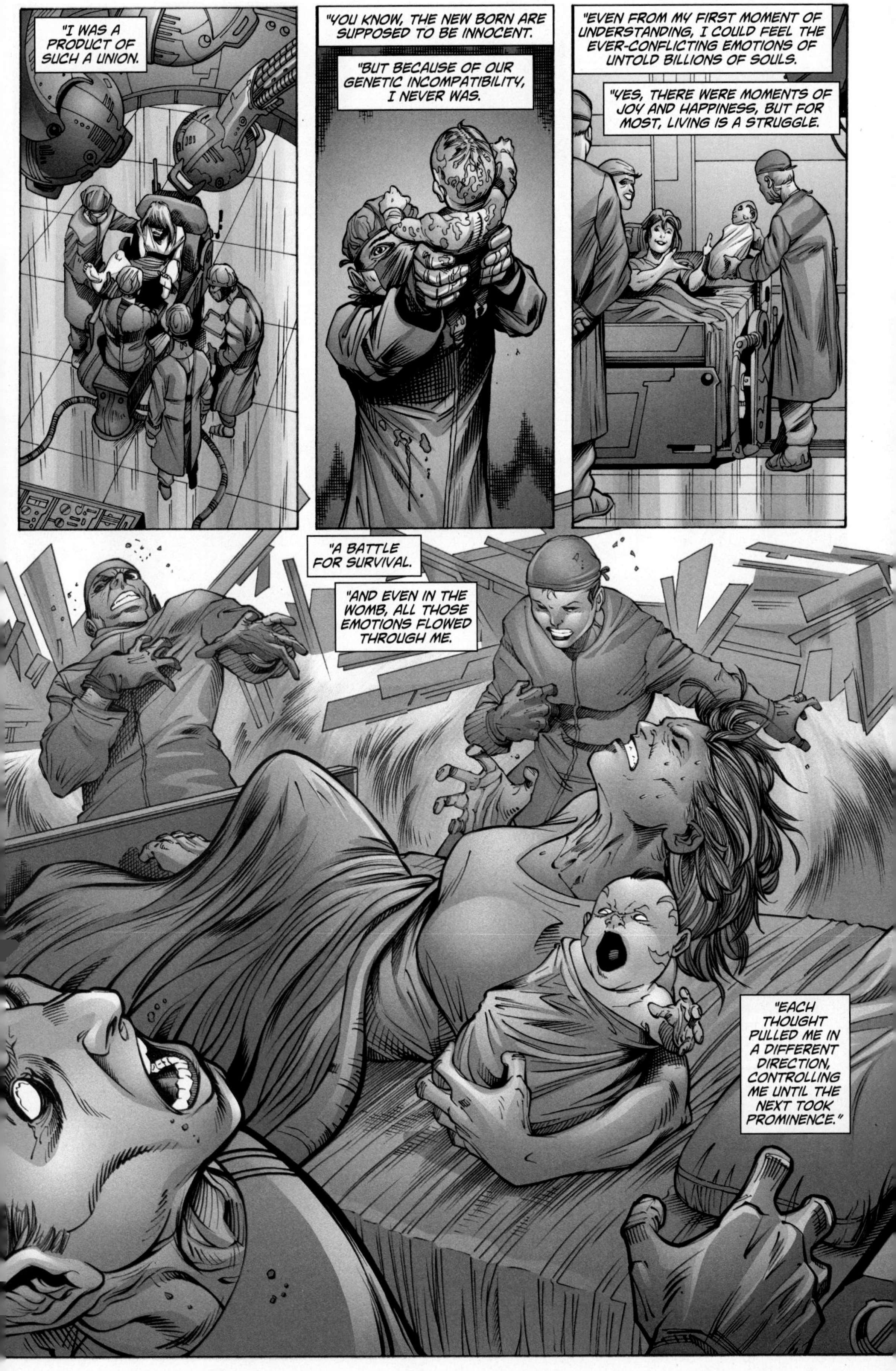
"I WAS A PRODUCT OF SUCH A UNION.
"YOU KNOW, THE NEW BORN ARE SUPPOSED TO BE INNOCENT.
"BUT BECAUSE OF OUR GENETIC INCOMPATIBILITY, I NEVER WAS.
"EVEN FROM MY FIRST MOMENT OF UNDERSTANDING, I COULD FEEL THE EVER-CONFLICTING EMOTIONS OF UNTOLD BILLIONS OF SOULS.
"YES, THERE WERE MOMENTS OF JOY AND HAPPINESS, BUT FOR MOST, LIVING IS A STRUGGLE.
"A BATTLE FOR SURVIVAL.
"AND EVEN IN THE WOMB, ALL THOSE EMOTIONS FLOWED THROUGH ME.
"EACH THOUGHT PULLED ME IN A DIFFERENT DIRECTION, CONTROLLING ME UNTIL THE NEXT TOOK PROMINENCE."

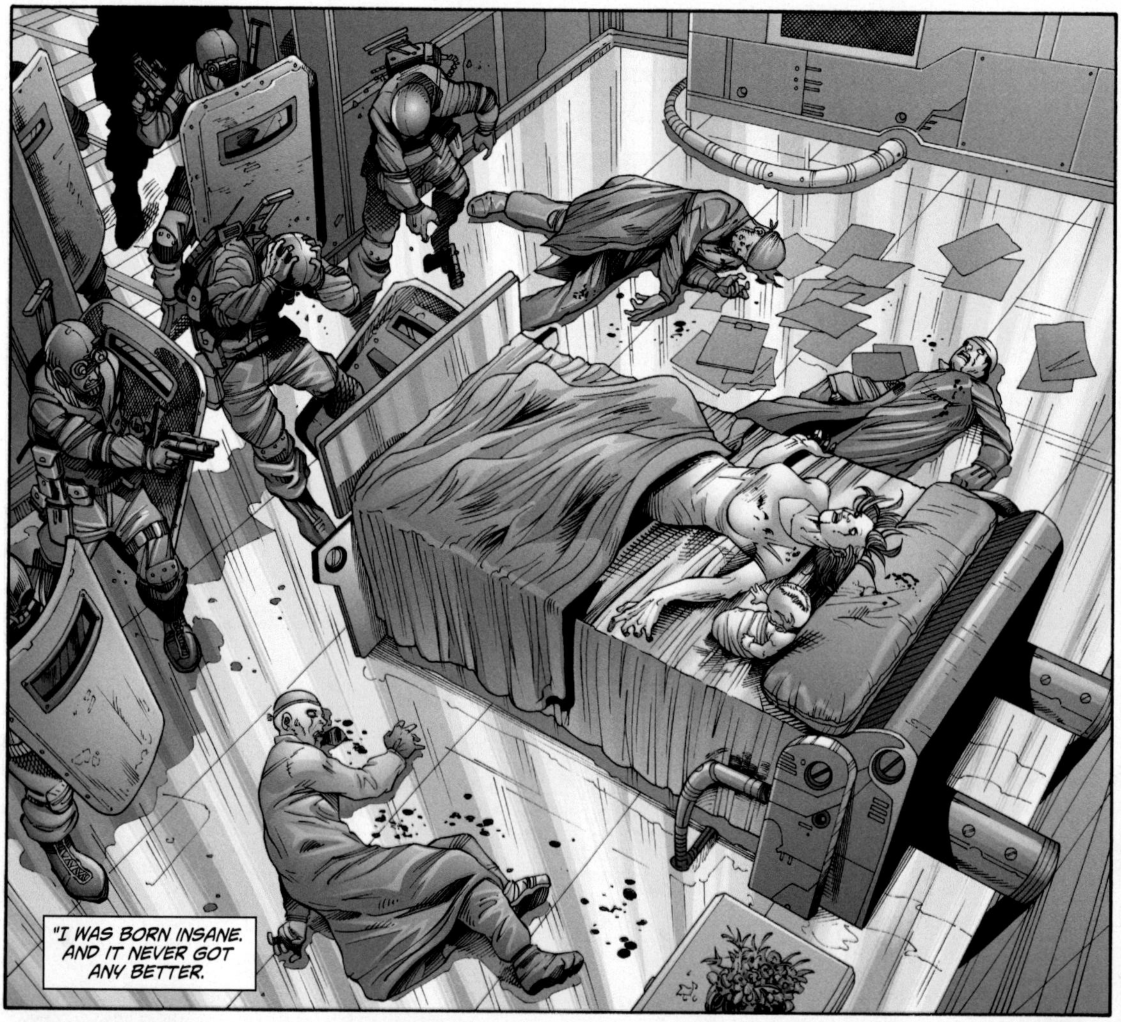
"I WAS BORN INSANE. AND IT NEVER GOT ANY BETTER.

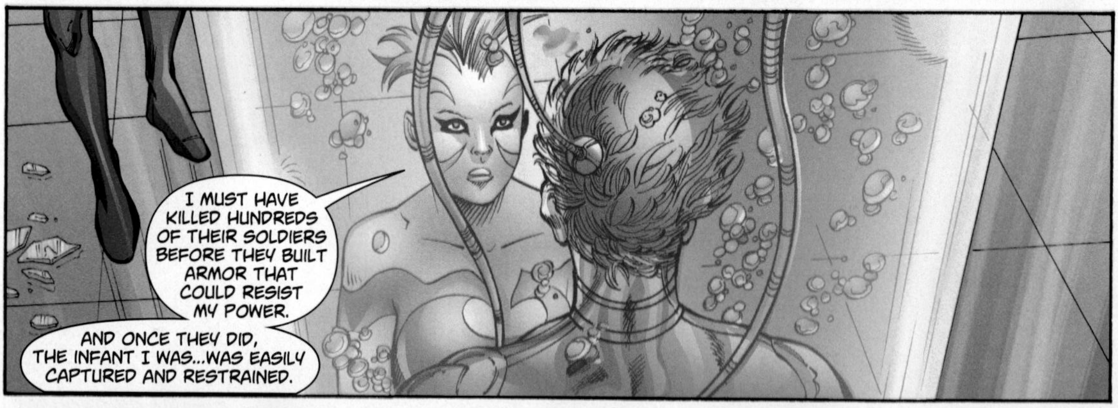
I MUST HAVE KILLED HUNDREDS OF THEIR SOLDIERS BEFORE THEY BUILT ARMOR THAT COULD RESIST MY POWER.
AND ONCE THEY DID, THE INFANT I WAS...WAS EASILY CAPTURED AND RESTRAINED.

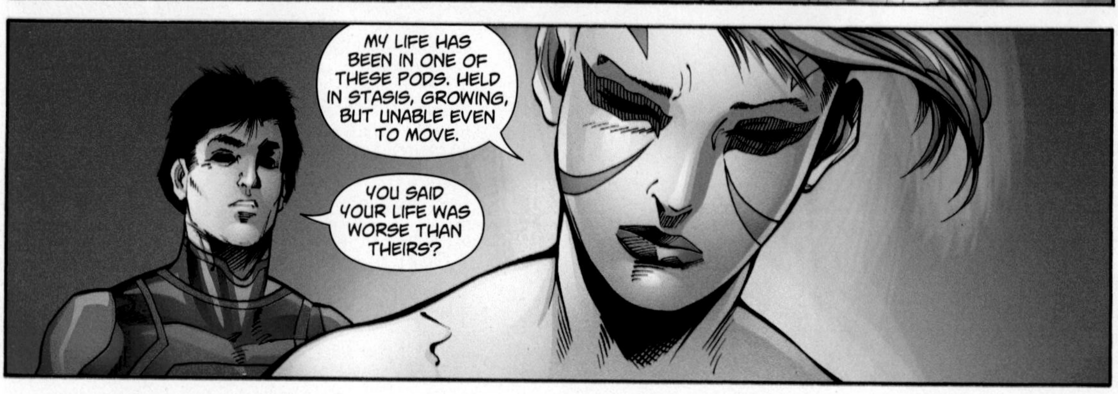
MY LIFE HAS BEEN IN ONE OF THESE PODS. HELD IN STASIS, GROWING, BUT UNABLE EVEN TO MOVE.
YOU SAID YOUR LIFE WAS WORSE THAN THEIRS?

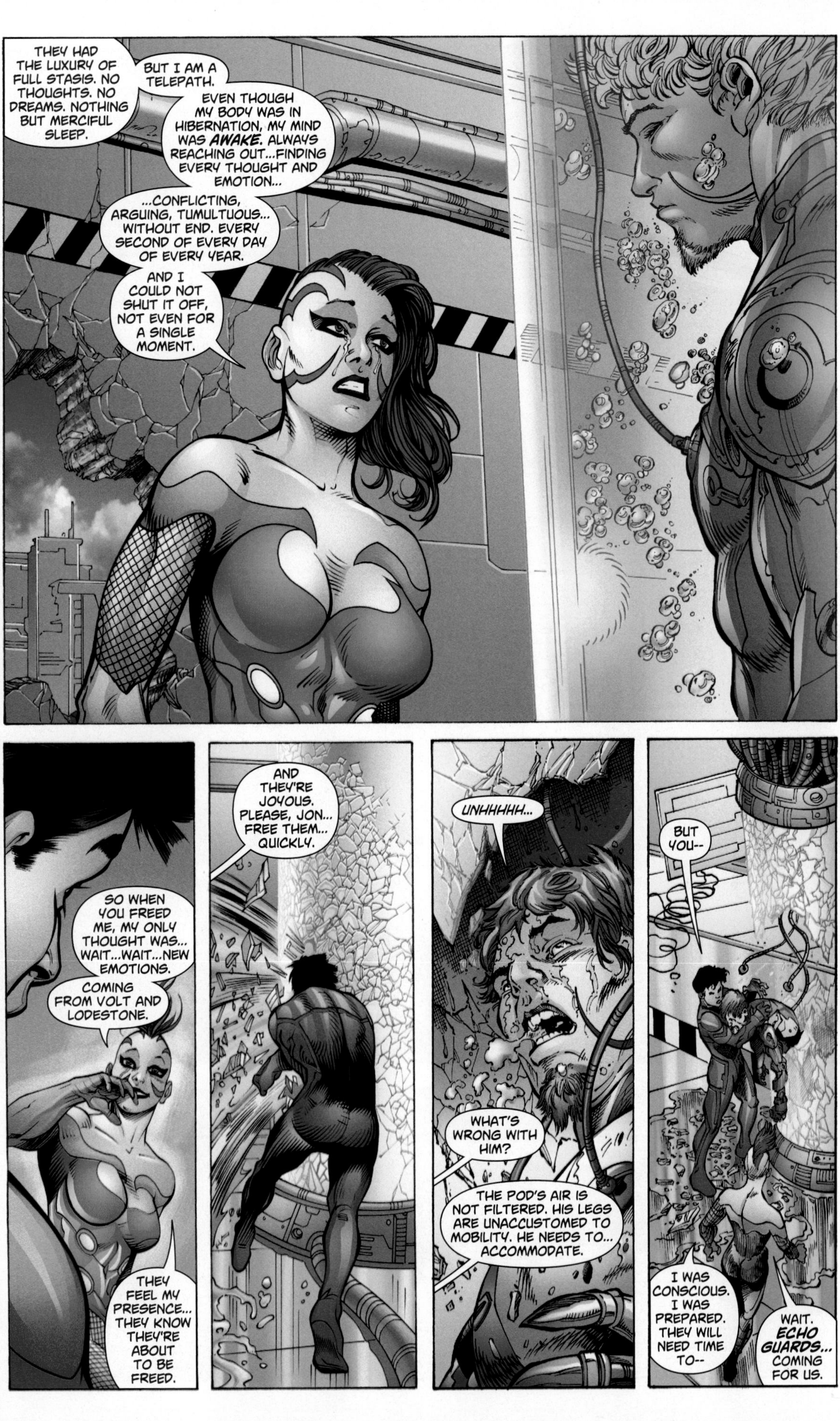
THEY HAD THE LUXURY OF FULL STASIS. NO THOUGHTS. NO DREAMS. NOTHING BUT MERCIFUL SLEEP.
BUT I AM A TELEPATH.
EVEN THOUGH MY BODY WAS IN HIBERNATION, MY MIND WAS AWAKE. ALWAYS REACHING OUT...FINDING EVERY THOUGHT AND EMOTION...
...CONFLICTING, ARGUING, TUMULTUOUS... WITHOUT END. EVERY SECOND OF EVERY DAY OF EVERY YEAR.
AND I COULD NOT SHUT IT OFF, NOT EVEN FOR A SINGLE MOMENT.
SO WHEN YOU FREED ME, MY ONLY THOUGHT WAS... WAIT...WAIT...NEW EMOTIONS.
COMING FROM VOLT AND LODESTONE.
THEY FEEL MY PRESENCE... THEY KNOW THEY'RE ABOUT TO BE FREED.
AND THEY'RE JOYOUS. PLEASE, JON... FREE THEM... QUICKLY.
UNHHHHH...
WHAT'S WRONG WITH HIM?
THE POD'S AIR IS NOT FILTERED. HIS LEGS ARE UNACCUSTOMED TO MOBILITY. HE NEEDS TO... ACCOMMODATE.
BUT YOU--
I WAS CONSCIOUS. I WAS PREPARED. THEY WILL NEED TIME TO--
WAIT. ECHO GUARDS... COMING FOR US.

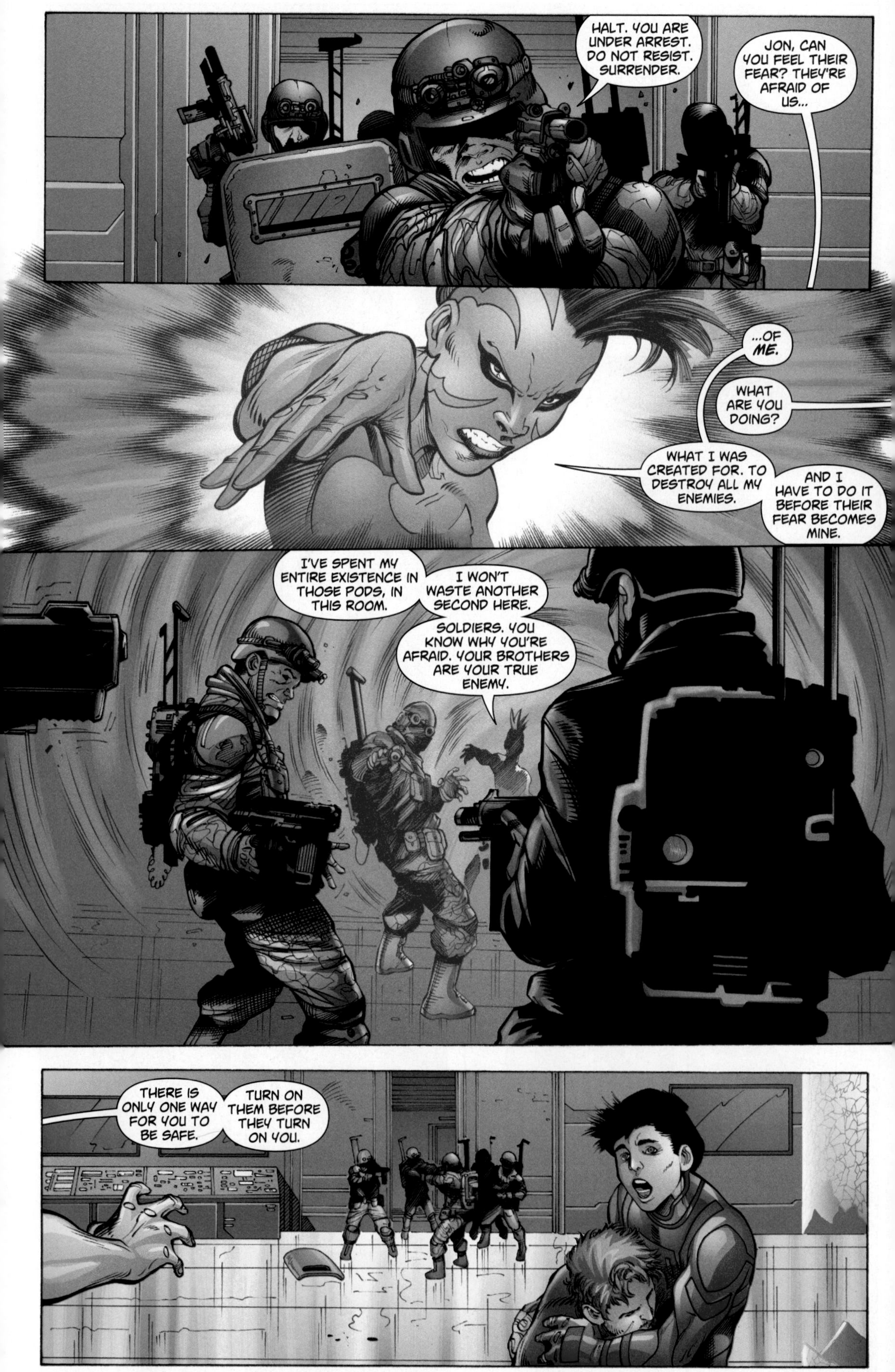
HALT. YOU ARE UNDER ARREST. DO NOT RESIST. SURRENDER.
JON, CAN YOU FEEL THEIR FEAR? THEY'RE AFRAID OF US...
...OF *ME.*
WHAT ARE YOU DOING?
WHAT I WAS CREATED FOR. TO DESTROY ALL MY ENEMIES.
AND I HAVE TO DO IT BEFORE THEIR FEAR BECOMES MINE.
I'VE SPENT MY ENTIRE EXISTENCE IN THOSE PODS, IN THIS ROOM.
I WON'T WASTE ANOTHER SECOND HERE.
SOLDIERS. YOU KNOW WHY YOU'RE AFRAID. YOUR BROTHERS ARE YOUR TRUE ENEMY.
THERE IS ONLY ONE WAY FOR YOU TO BE SAFE.
TURN ON THEM BEFORE THEY TURN ON YOU.

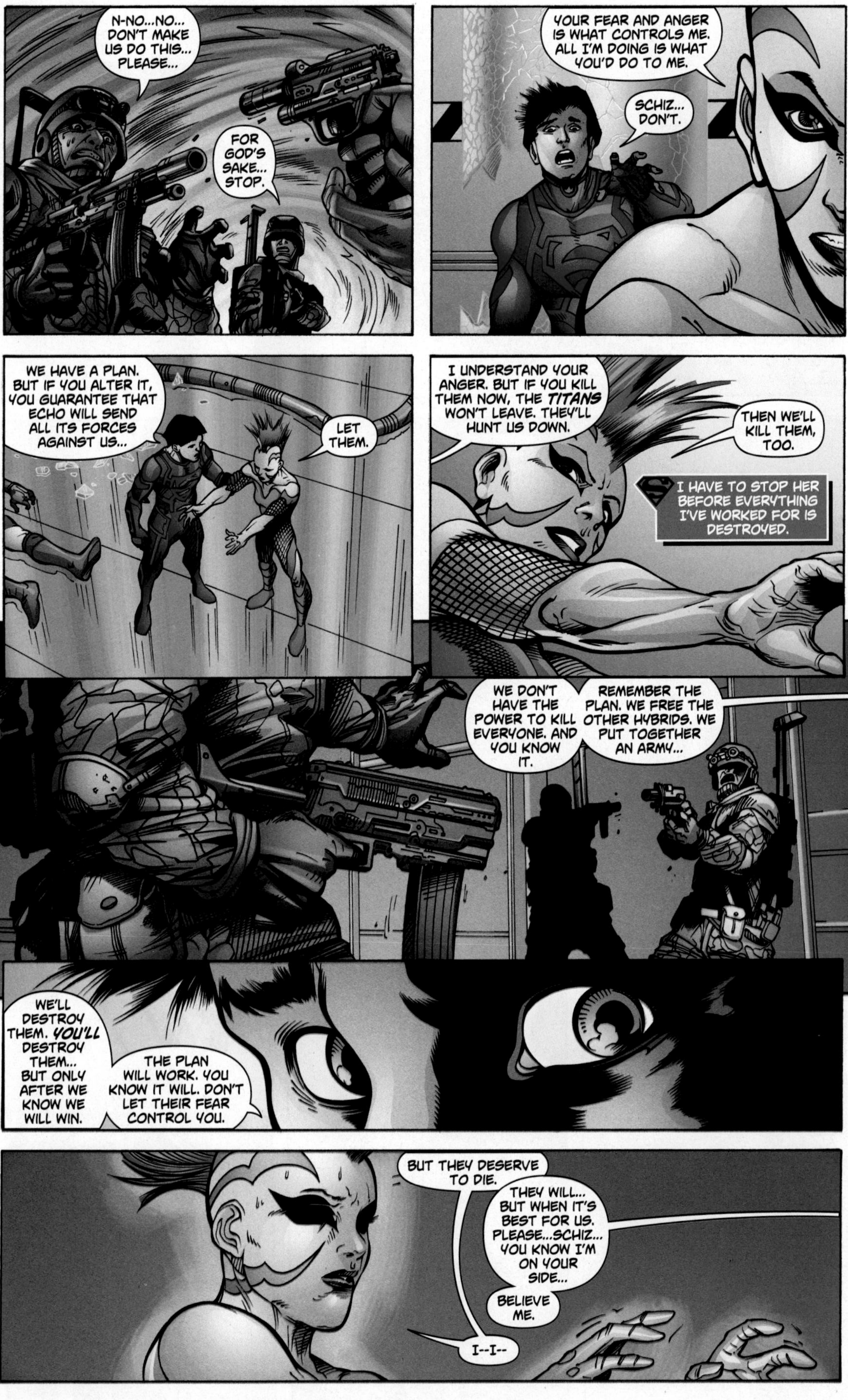
N-NO...NO... DON'T MAKE US DO THIS... PLEASE...
FOR GOD'S SAKE... STOP.
YOUR FEAR AND ANGER IS WHAT CONTROLS ME. ALL I'M DOING IS WHAT YOU'D DO TO ME.
SCHIZ... DON'T.
WE HAVE A PLAN. BUT IF YOU ALTER IT, YOU GUARANTEE THAT ECHO WILL SEND ALL ITS FORCES AGAINST US...
LET THEM.
I UNDERSTAND YOUR ANGER. BUT IF YOU KILL THEM NOW, THE TITANS WON'T LEAVE. THEY'LL HUNT US DOWN.
THEN WE'LL KILL THEM, TOO.
I HAVE TO STOP HER BEFORE EVERYTHING I'VE WORKED FOR IS DESTROYED.
WE DON'T HAVE THE POWER TO KILL EVERYONE. AND YOU KNOW IT.
REMEMBER THE PLAN. WE FREE THE OTHER HYBRIDS. WE PUT TOGETHER AN ARMY...
WE'LL DESTROY THEM. YOU'LL DESTROY THEM... BUT ONLY AFTER WE KNOW WE WILL WIN.
THE PLAN WILL WORK. YOU KNOW IT WILL. DON'T LET THEIR FEAR CONTROL YOU.
BUT THEY DESERVE TO DIE.
THEY WILL... BUT WHEN IT'S BEST FOR US. PLEASE...SCHIZ... YOU KNOW I'M ON YOUR SIDE...
BELIEVE ME.
I--I--

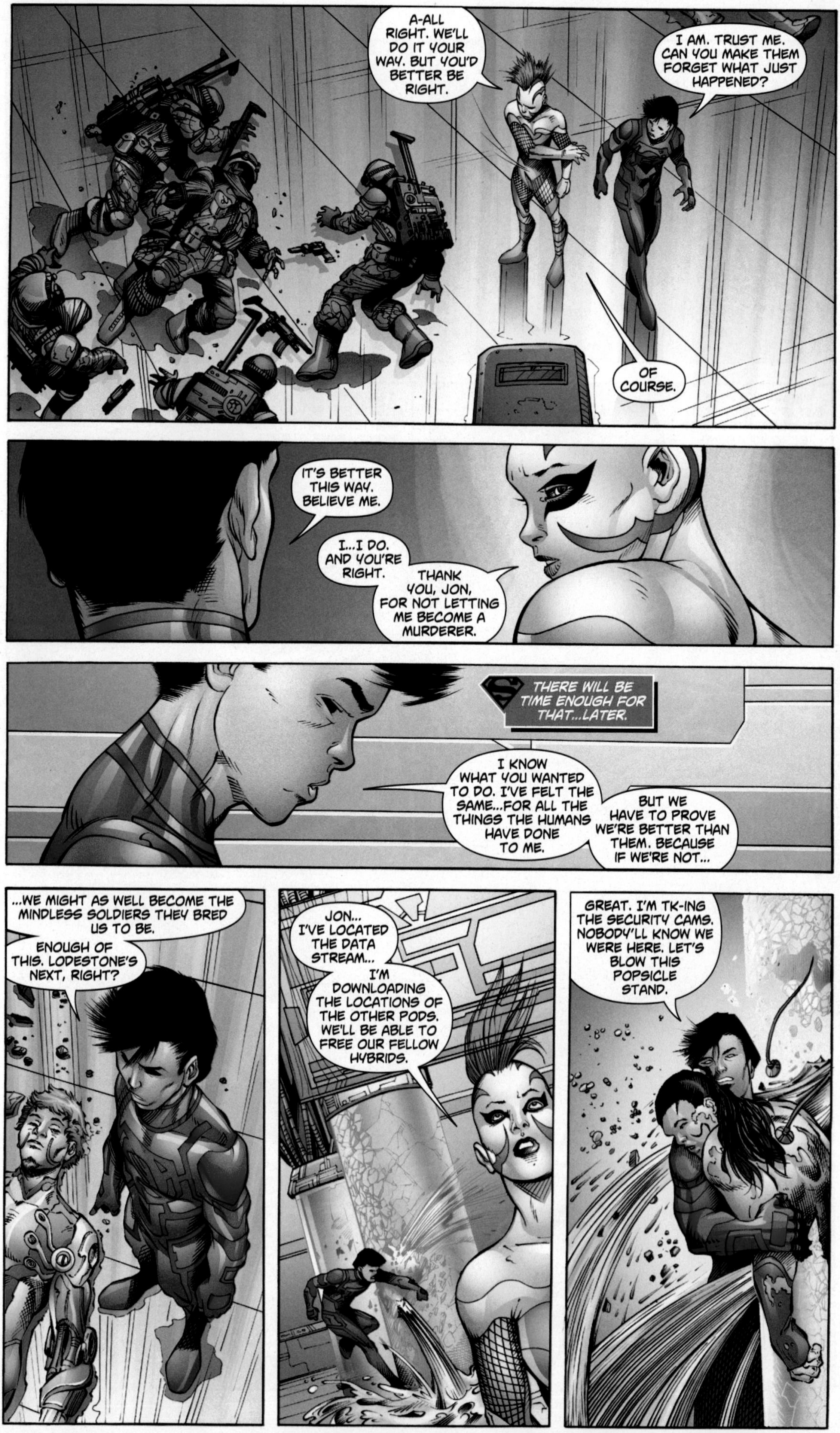
A-ALL RIGHT. WE'LL DO IT YOUR WAY. BUT YOU'D BETTER BE RIGHT.
I AM. TRUST ME. CAN YOU MAKE THEM FORGET WHAT JUST HAPPENED?
OF COURSE.
IT'S BETTER THIS WAY. BELIEVE ME.
I...I DO. AND YOU'RE RIGHT.
THANK YOU, JON, FOR NOT LETTING ME BECOME A MURDERER.
THERE WILL BE TIME ENOUGH FOR THAT...LATER.
I KNOW WHAT YOU WANTED TO DO. I'VE FELT THE SAME...FOR ALL THE THINGS THE HUMANS HAVE DONE TO ME.
BUT WE HAVE TO PROVE WE'RE BETTER THAN THEM. BECAUSE IF WE'RE NOT...
...WE MIGHT AS WELL BECOME THE MINDLESS SOLDIERS THEY BRED US TO BE.
ENOUGH OF THIS. LODESTONE'S NEXT, RIGHT?
JON... I'VE LOCATED THE DATA STREAM...
I'M DOWNLOADING THE LOCATIONS OF THE OTHER PODS. WE'LL BE ABLE TO FREE OUR FELLOW HYBRIDS.
GREAT. I'M TK-ING THE SECURITY CAMS. NOBODY'LL KNOW WE WERE HERE. LET'S BLOW THIS POPSICLE STAND.

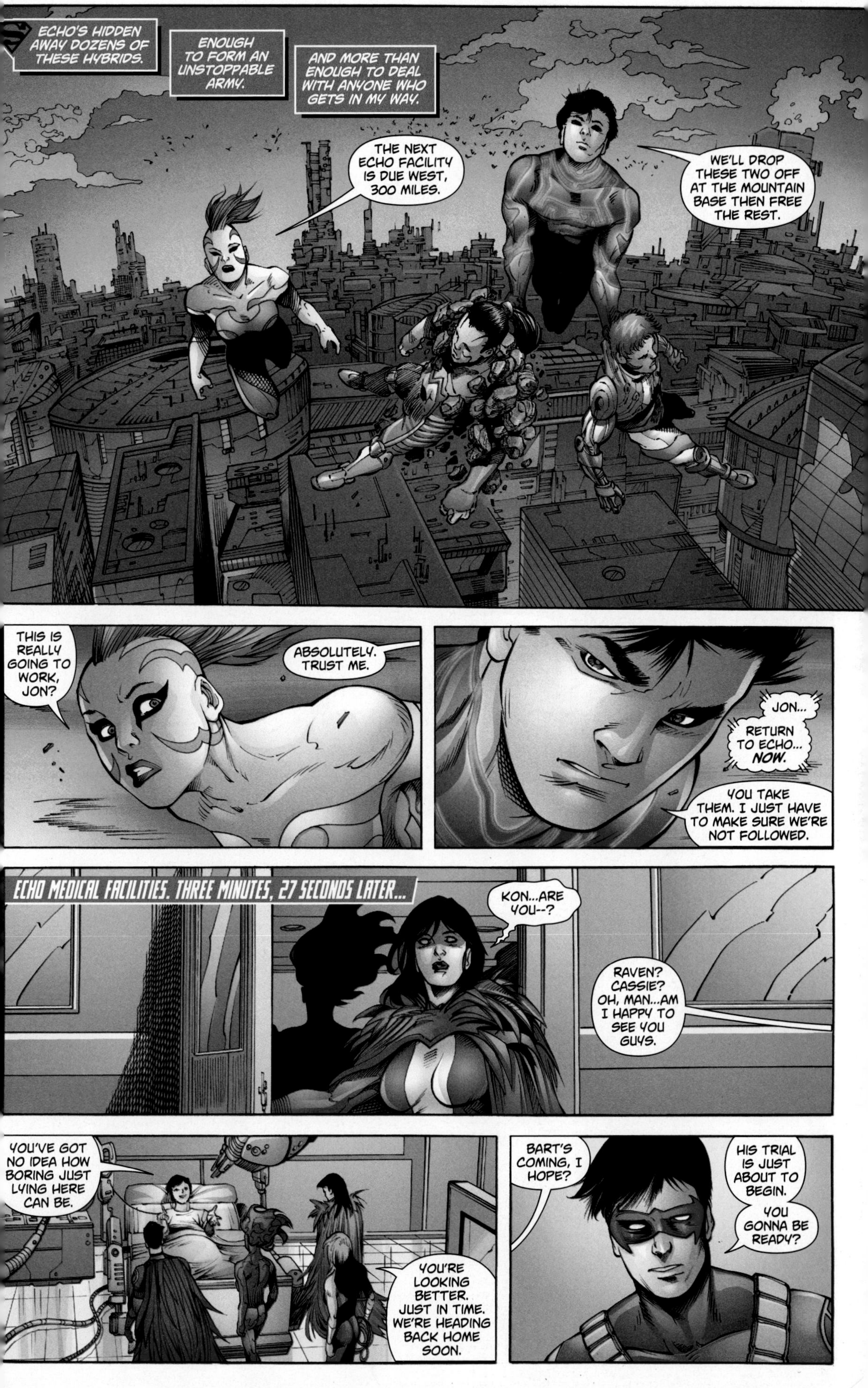
ECHO'S HIDDEN AWAY DOZENS OF THESE HYBRIDS.
ENOUGH TO FORM AN UNSTOPPABLE ARMY.
AND MORE THAN ENOUGH TO DEAL WITH ANYONE WHO GETS IN MY WAY.
THE NEXT ECHO FACILITY IS DUE WEST, 300 MILES.
WE'LL DROP THESE TWO OFF AT THE MOUNTAIN BASE THEN FREE THE REST.
THIS IS REALLY GOING TO WORK, JON?
ABSOLUTELY. TRUST ME.
JON...
RETURN TO ECHO... NOW.
YOU TAKE THEM. I JUST HAVE TO MAKE SURE WE'RE NOT FOLLOWED.
ECHO MEDICAL FACILITIES. THREE MINUTES, 27 SECONDS LATER...
KON...ARE YOU--?
RAVEN? CASSIE? OH, MAN...AM I HAPPY TO SEE YOU GUYS.
YOU'VE GOT NO IDEA HOW BORING JUST LYING HERE CAN BE.
YOU'RE LOOKING BETTER. JUST IN TIME. WE'RE HEADING BACK HOME SOON.
BART'S COMING, I HOPE?
HIS TRIAL IS JUST ABOUT TO BEGIN.
YOU GONNA BE READY?

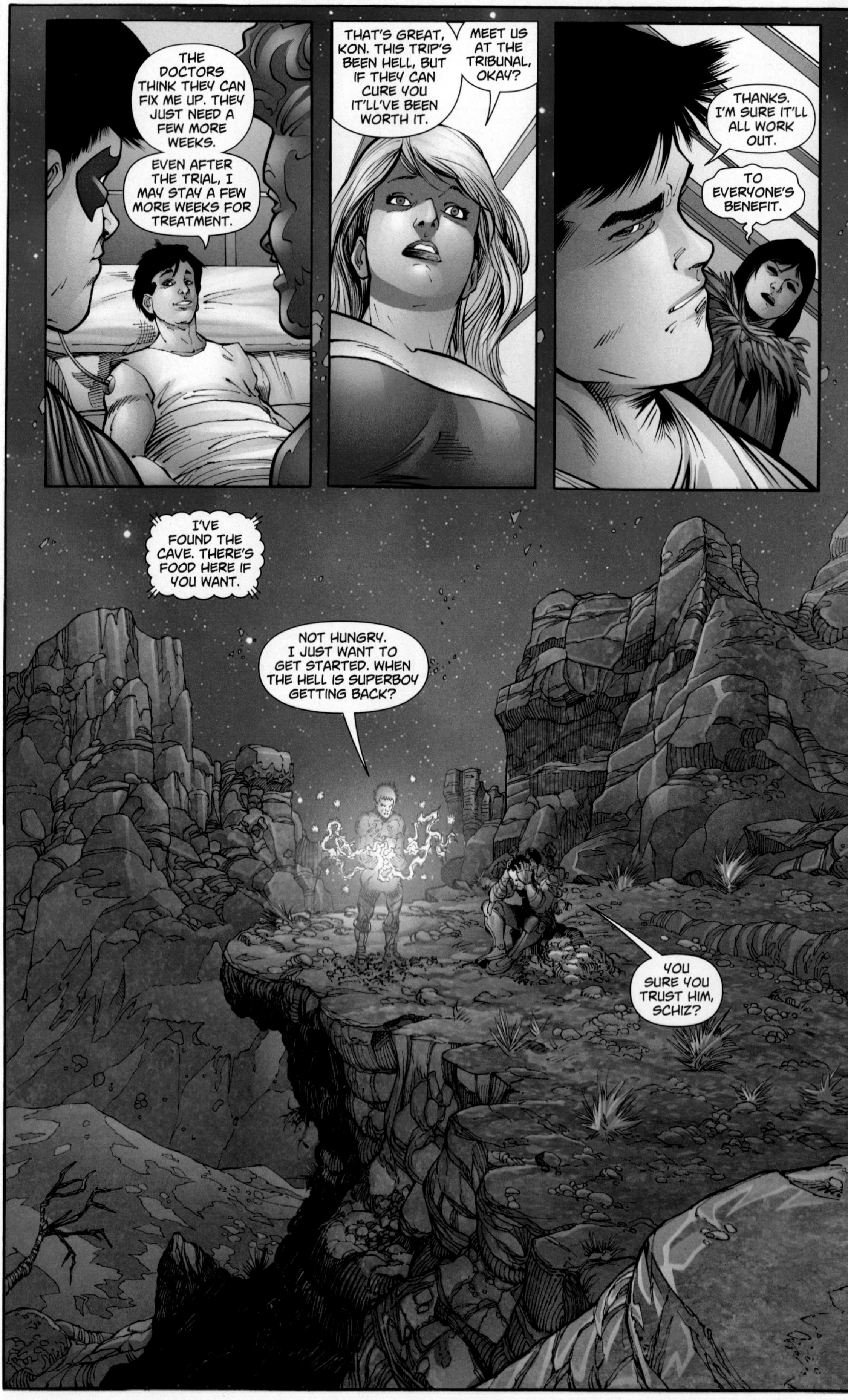
THE DOCTORS THINK THEY CAN FIX ME UP. THEY JUST NEED A FEW MORE WEEKS.
EVEN AFTER THE TRIAL, I MAY STAY A FEW MORE WEEKS FOR TREATMENT.
THAT'S GREAT, KON. THIS TRIP'S BEEN HELL, BUT IF THEY CAN CURE YOU IT'LL'VE BEEN WORTH IT.
MEET US AT THE TRIBUNAL, OKAY?
THANKS. I'M SURE IT'LL ALL WORK OUT.
TO EVERYONE'S BENEFIT.
I'VE FOUND THE CAVE. THERE'S FOOD HERE IF YOU WANT.
NOT HUNGRY. I JUST WANT TO GET STARTED. WHEN THE HELL IS SUPERBOY GETTING BACK?
YOU SURE YOU TRUST HIM, SCHIZ?

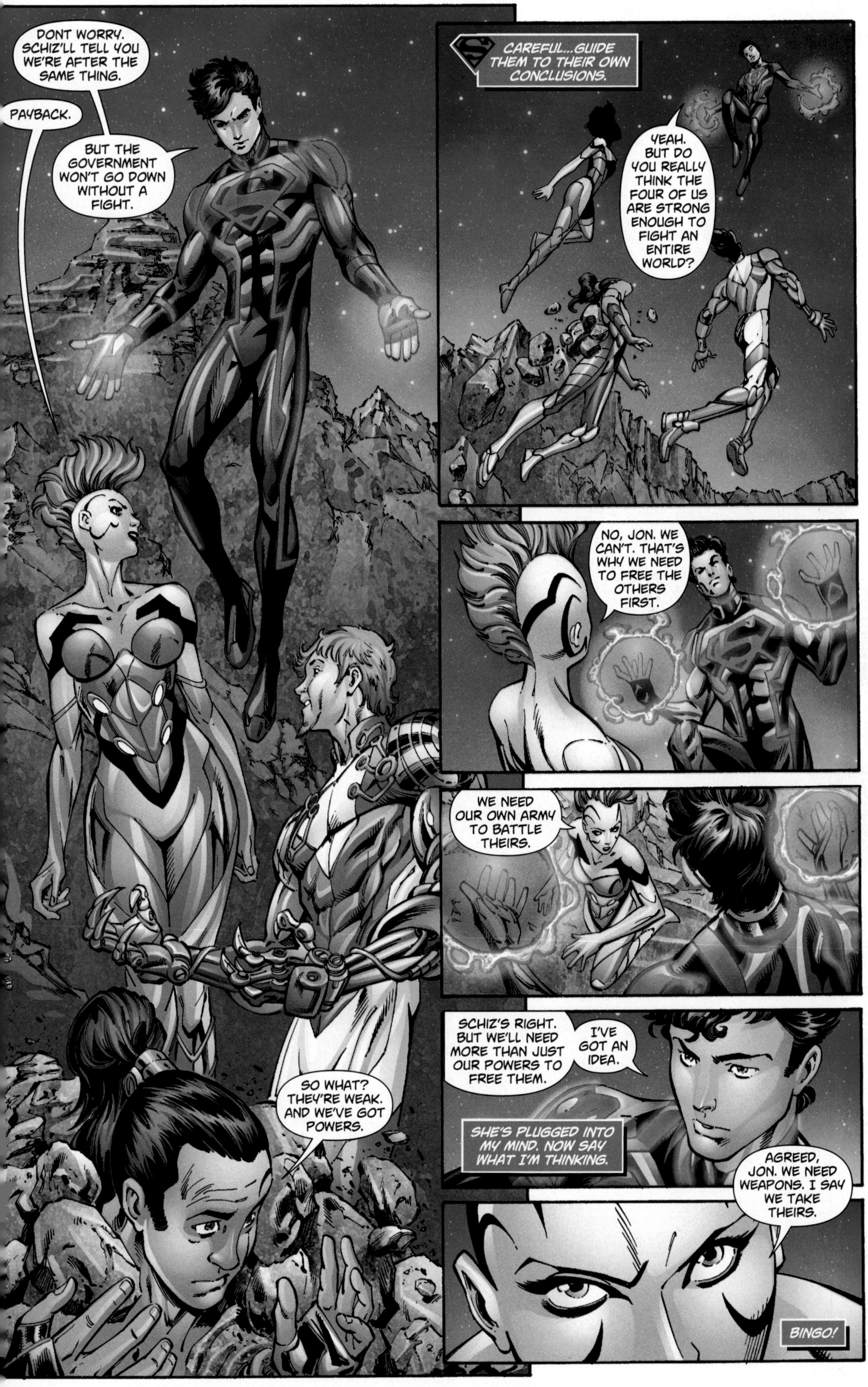
DONT WORRY. SCHIZ'LL TELL YOU WE'RE AFTER THE SAME THING.
PAYBACK.
BUT THE GOVERNMENT WON'T GO DOWN WITHOUT A FIGHT.
SO WHAT? THEY'RE WEAK. AND WE'VE GOT POWERS.
CAREFUL...GUIDE THEM TO THEIR OWN CONCLUSIONS.
YEAH. BUT DO YOU REALLY THINK THE FOUR OF US ARE STRONG ENOUGH TO FIGHT AN ENTIRE WORLD?
NO, JON. WE CAN'T. THAT'S WHY WE NEED TO FREE THE OTHERS FIRST.
WE NEED OUR OWN ARMY TO BATTLE THEIRS.
SCHIZ'S RIGHT. BUT WE'LL NEED MORE THAN JUST OUR POWERS TO FREE THEM.
I'VE GOT AN IDEA.
SHE'S PLUGGED INTO MY MIND. NOW SAY WHAT I'M THINKING.
AGREED, JON. WE NEED WEAPONS. I SAY WE TAKE THEIRS.
BINGO!

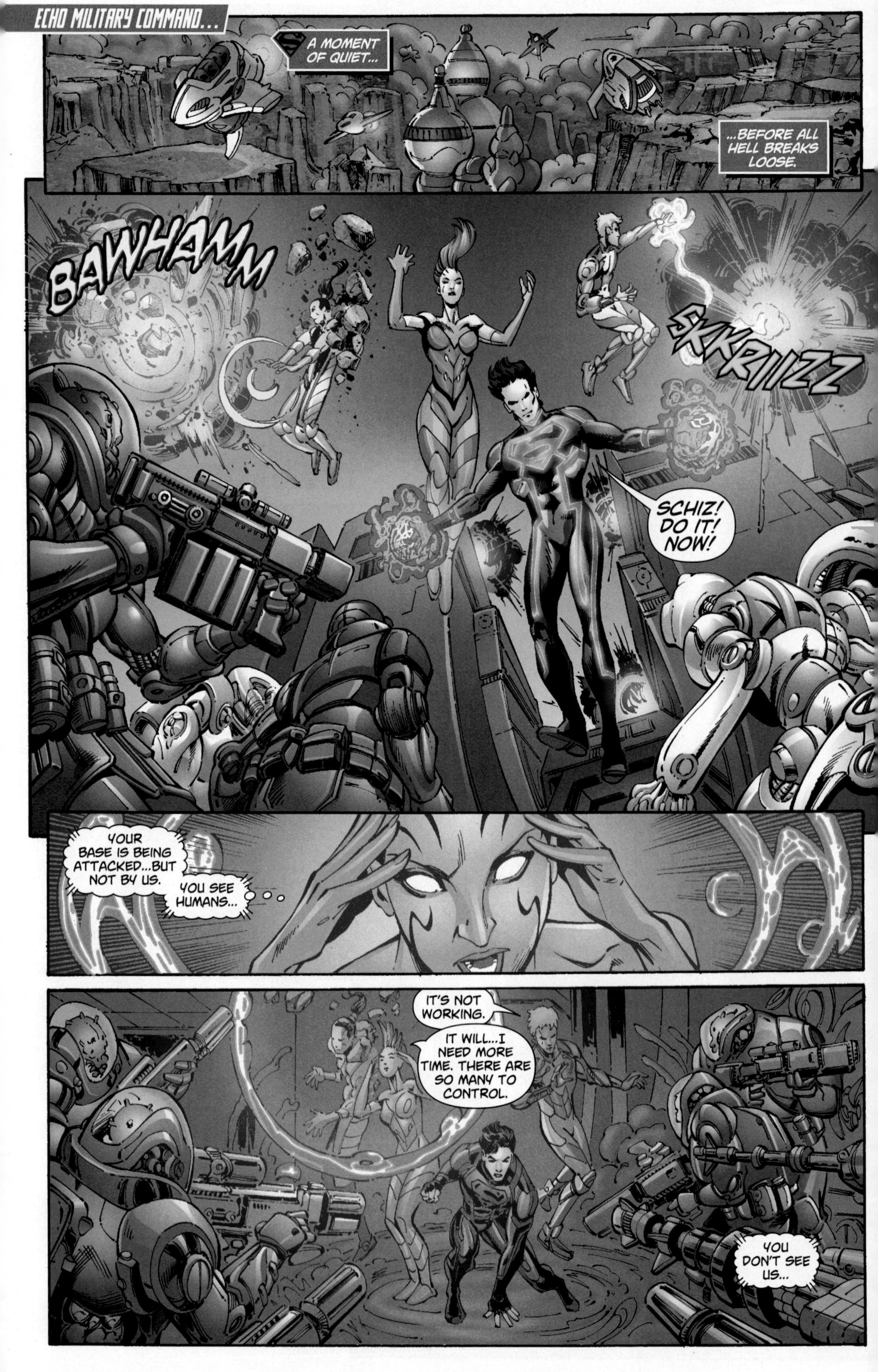
ECHO MILITARY COMMAND...
A MOMENT OF QUIET...
...BEFORE ALL HELL BREAKS LOOSE.
BAWHAMM
SKKRIIZZ
SCHIZ! DO IT! NOW!
YOUR BASE IS BEING ATTACKED...BUT NOT BY US.
YOU SEE HUMANS...
IT'S NOT WORKING.
IT WILL...I NEED MORE TIME. THERE ARE SO MANY TO CONTROL.
YOU DON'T SEE US...

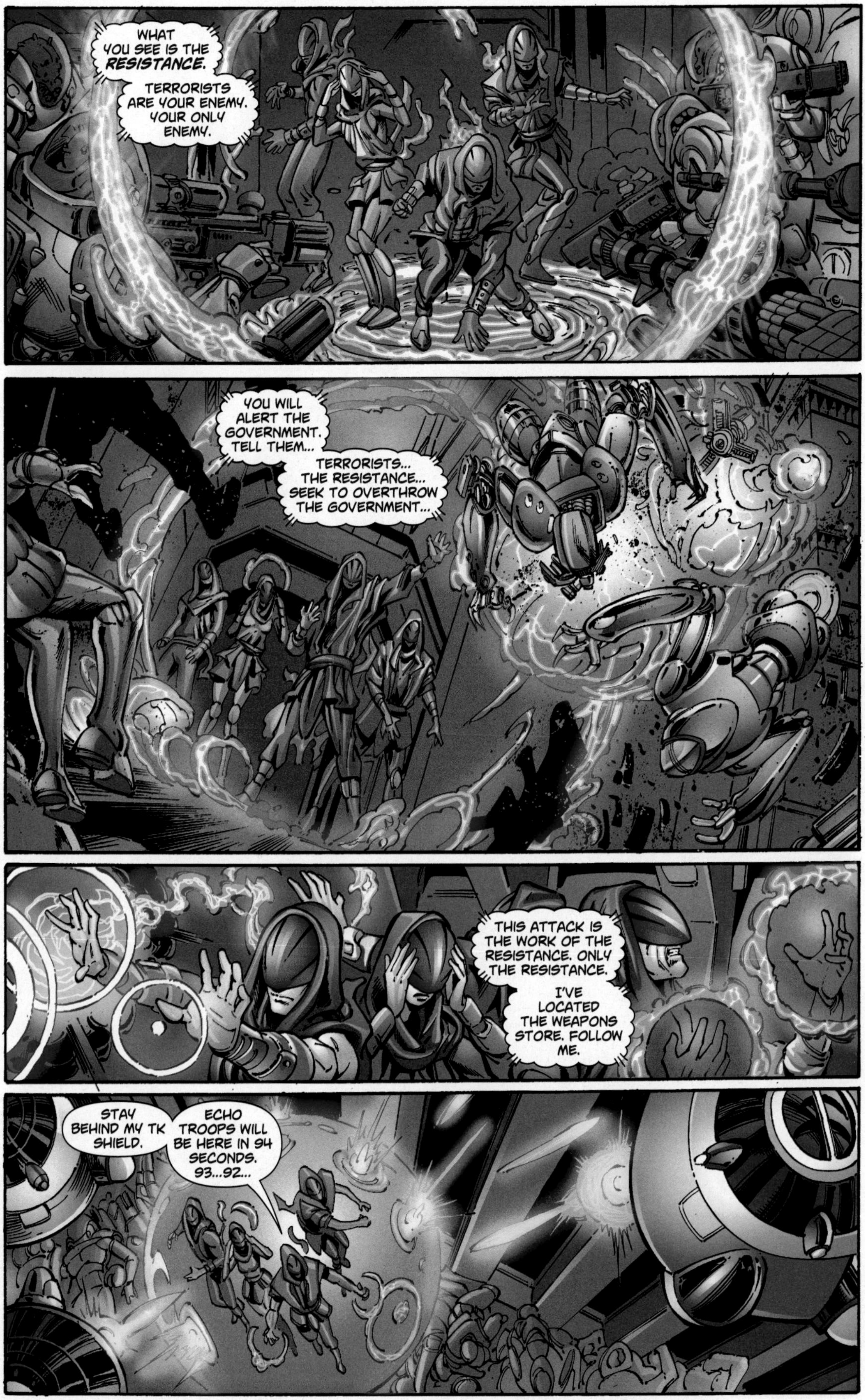
WHAT YOU SEE IS THE RESISTANCE.
TERRORISTS ARE YOUR ENEMY. YOUR ONLY ENEMY.
YOU WILL ALERT THE GOVERNMENT. TELL THEM...
TERRORISTS... THE RESISTANCE... SEEK TO OVERTHROW THE GOVERNMENT...
THIS ATTACK IS THE WORK OF THE RESISTANCE. ONLY THE RESISTANCE.
I'VE LOCATED THE WEAPONS STORE. FOLLOW ME.
STAY BEHIND MY TK SHIELD.
ECHO TROOPS WILL BE HERE IN 94 SECONDS. 93...92...

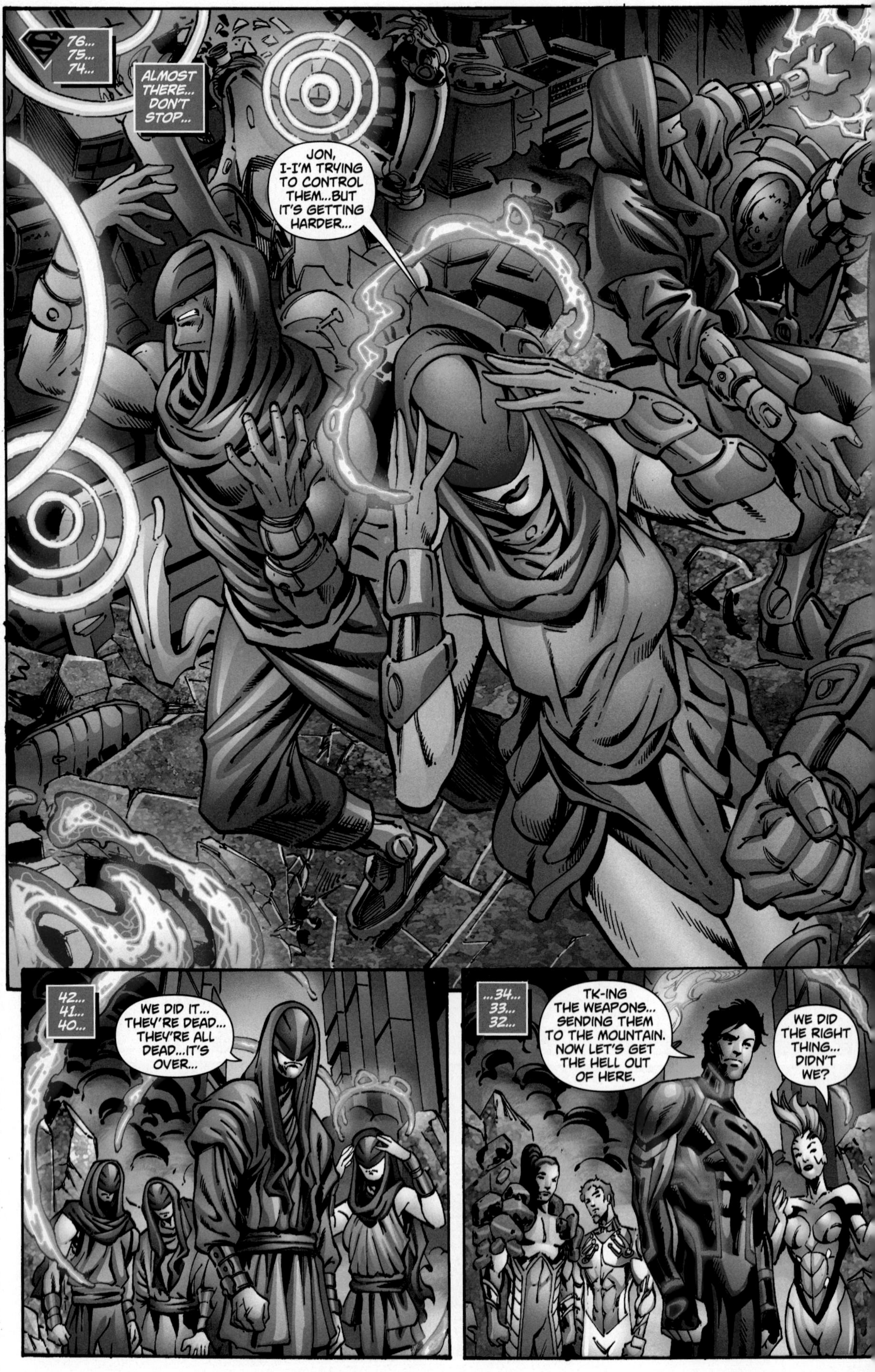

76...
75...
74...
ALMOST THERE... DON'T STOP...
JON, I-I'M TRYING TO CONTROL THEM...BUT IT'S GETTING HARDER...
42...
41...
40...
WE DID IT... THEY'RE DEAD... THEY'RE ALL DEAD...IT'S OVER...
...34...
33...
32...
TK-ING THE WEAPONS... SENDING THEM TO THE MOUNTAIN. NOW LET'S GET THE HELL OUT OF HERE.
WE DID THE RIGHT THING... DIDN'T WE?

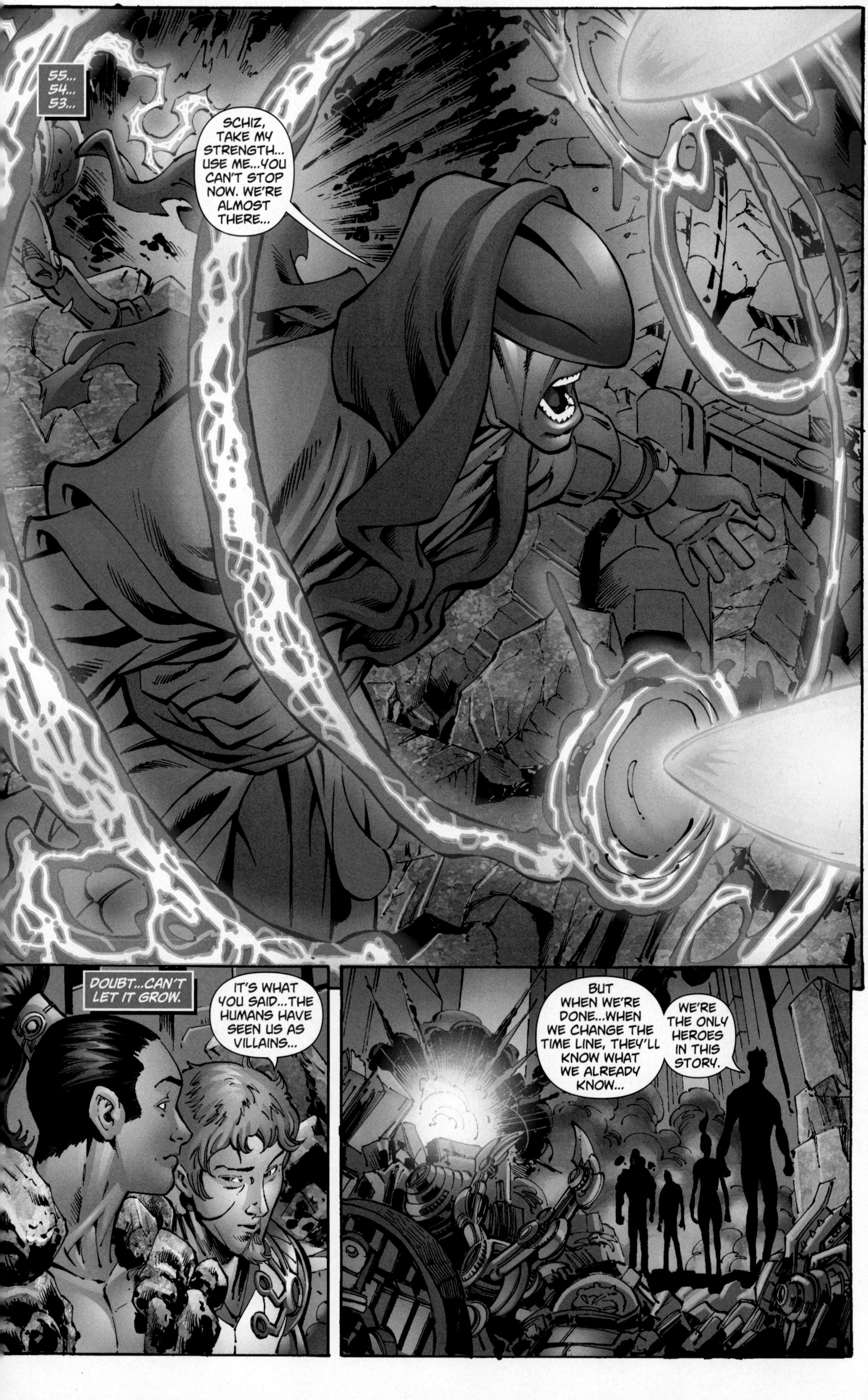

55...
54...
53...
SCHIZ, TAKE MY STRENGTH... USE ME...YOU CAN'T STOP NOW. WE'RE ALMOST THERE...
DOUBT...CAN'T LET IT GROW.
IT'S WHAT YOU SAID...THE HUMANS HAVE SEEN US AS VILLAINS...
BUT WHEN WE'RE DONE...WHEN WE CHANGE THE TIME LINE, THEY'LL KNOW WHAT WE ALREADY KNOW...
WE'RE THE ONLY HEROES IN THIS STORY.

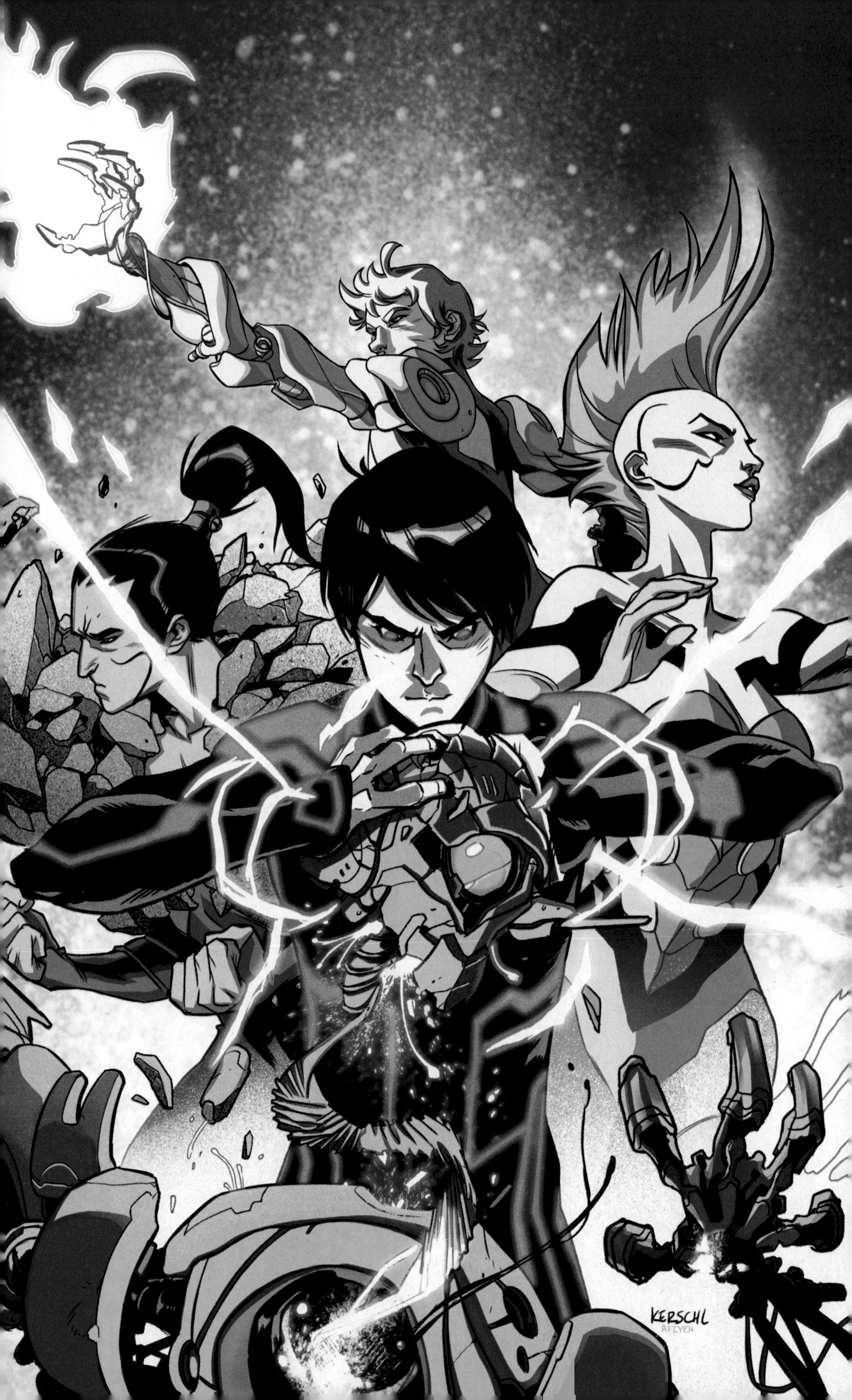
KERSCHL

HOMEWARD BOUND

MARV WOLFMAN writer **ANDRES GUINALDO** penciller **MARK IRWIN** inker
TANYA and **RICHARD HORIE** colorists **TRAVIS LANHAM** letterer cover art by **KARL KERSCHL** and **MIKE ATIYEH**

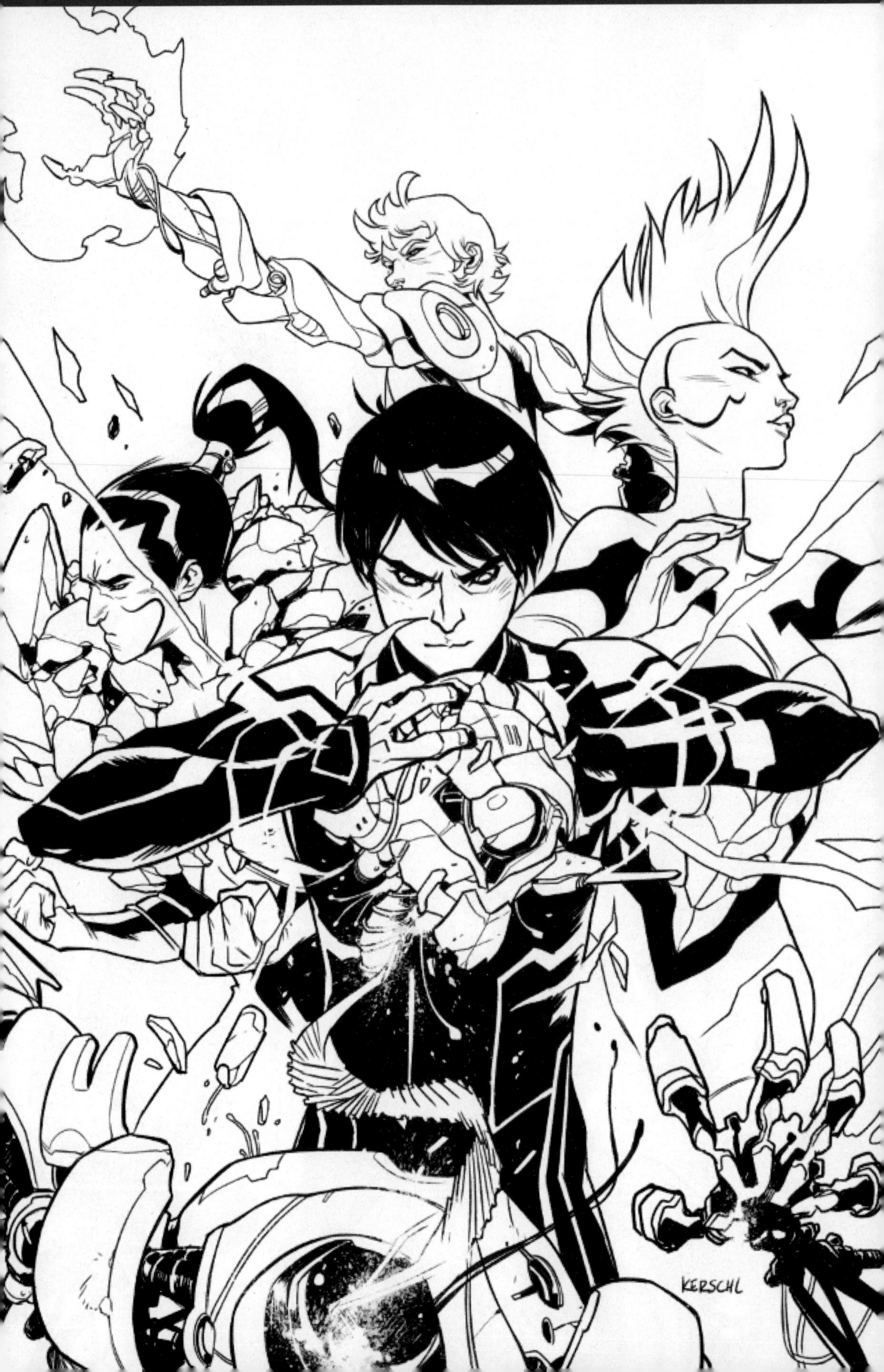
KERSCHL

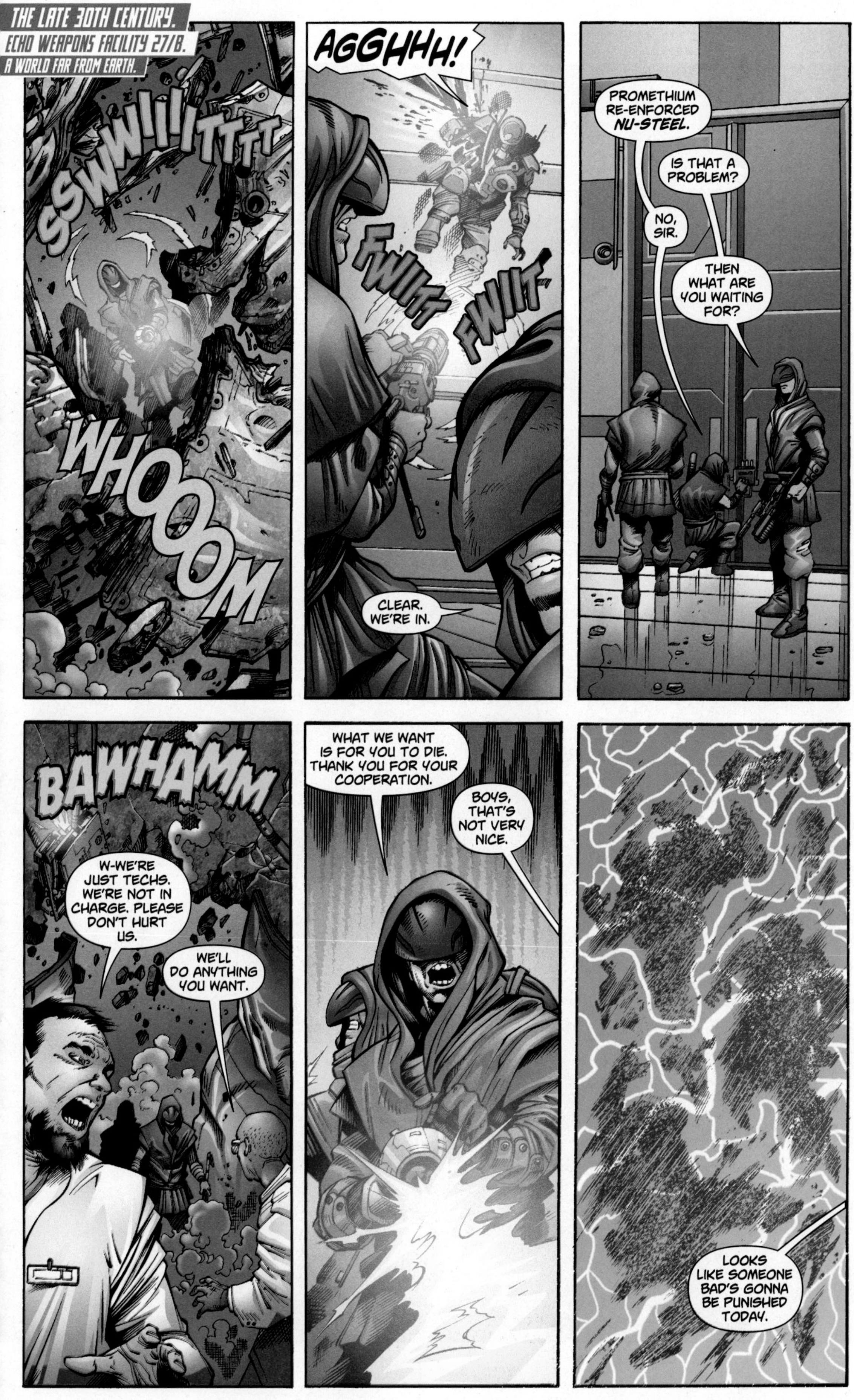
THE LATE 30TH CENTURY.
ECHO WEAPONS FACILITY 27/B.
A WORLD FAR FROM EARTH.
SSWIIIITTTT
WHOOOOM
AGGHHH!
FWIKT
FWIIT
CLEAR. WE'RE IN.
PROMETHIUM RE-ENFORCED NU-STEEL.
IS THAT A PROBLEM?
NO, SIR.
THEN WHAT ARE YOU WAITING FOR?
BAWHAMM
W-WE'RE JUST TECHS. WE'RE NOT IN CHARGE. PLEASE DON'T HURT US.
WE'LL DO ANYTHING YOU WANT.
WHAT WE WANT IS FOR YOU TO DIE. THANK YOU FOR YOUR COOPERATION.
BOYS, THAT'S NOT VERY NICE.
LOOKS LIKE SOMEONE BAD'S GONNA BE PUNISHED TODAY.

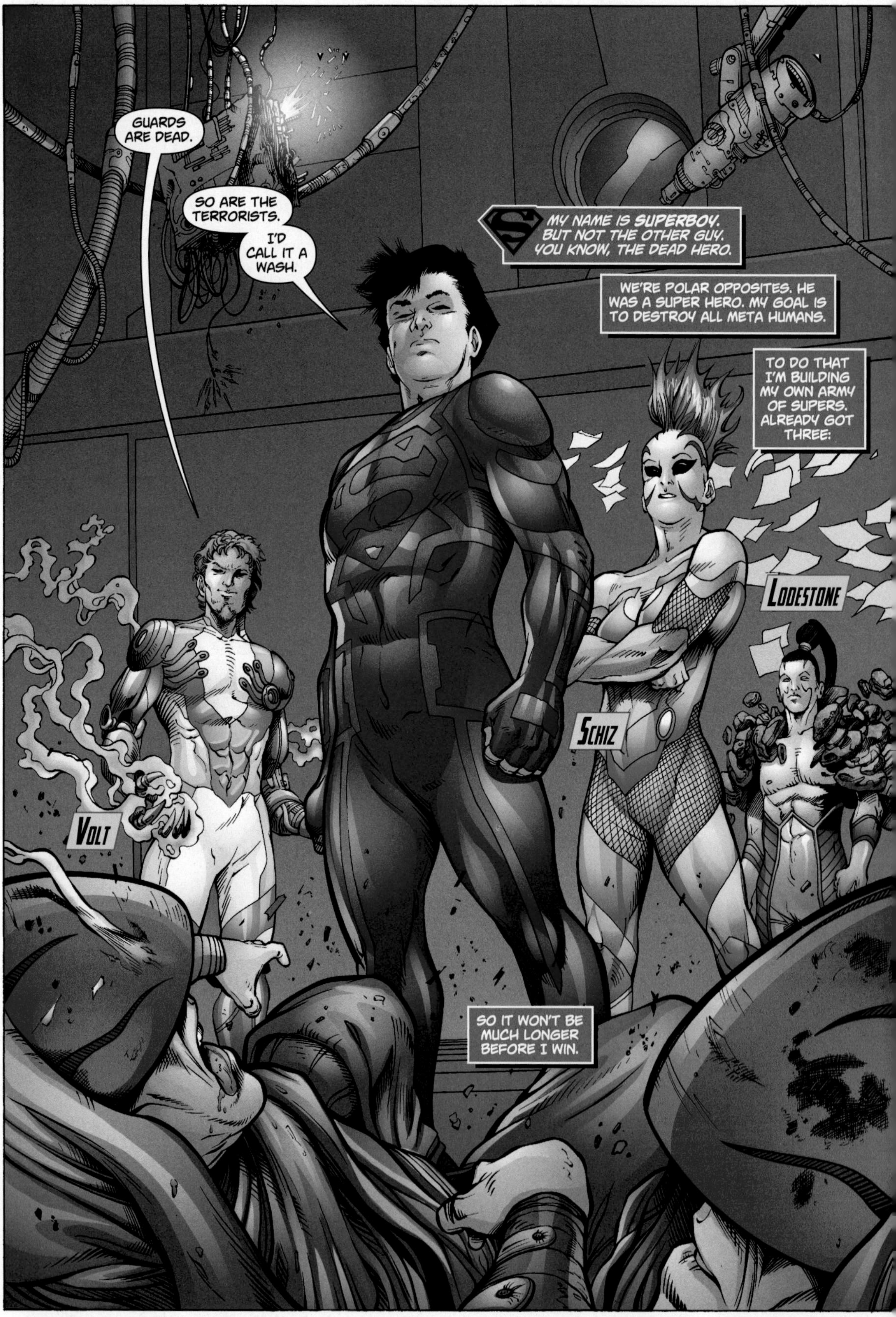
GUARDS ARE DEAD.
SO ARE THE TERRORISTS.
I'D CALL IT A WASH.
MY NAME IS SUPERBOY. BUT NOT THE OTHER GUY. YOU KNOW, THE DEAD HERO.
WE'RE POLAR OPPOSITES. HE WAS A SUPER HERO. MY GOAL IS TO DESTROY ALL META HUMANS.
TO DO THAT I'M BUILDING MY OWN ARMY OF SUPERS. ALREADY GOT THREE:
LODESTONE
SCHIZ
VOLT
SO IT WON'T BE MUCH LONGER BEFORE I WIN.

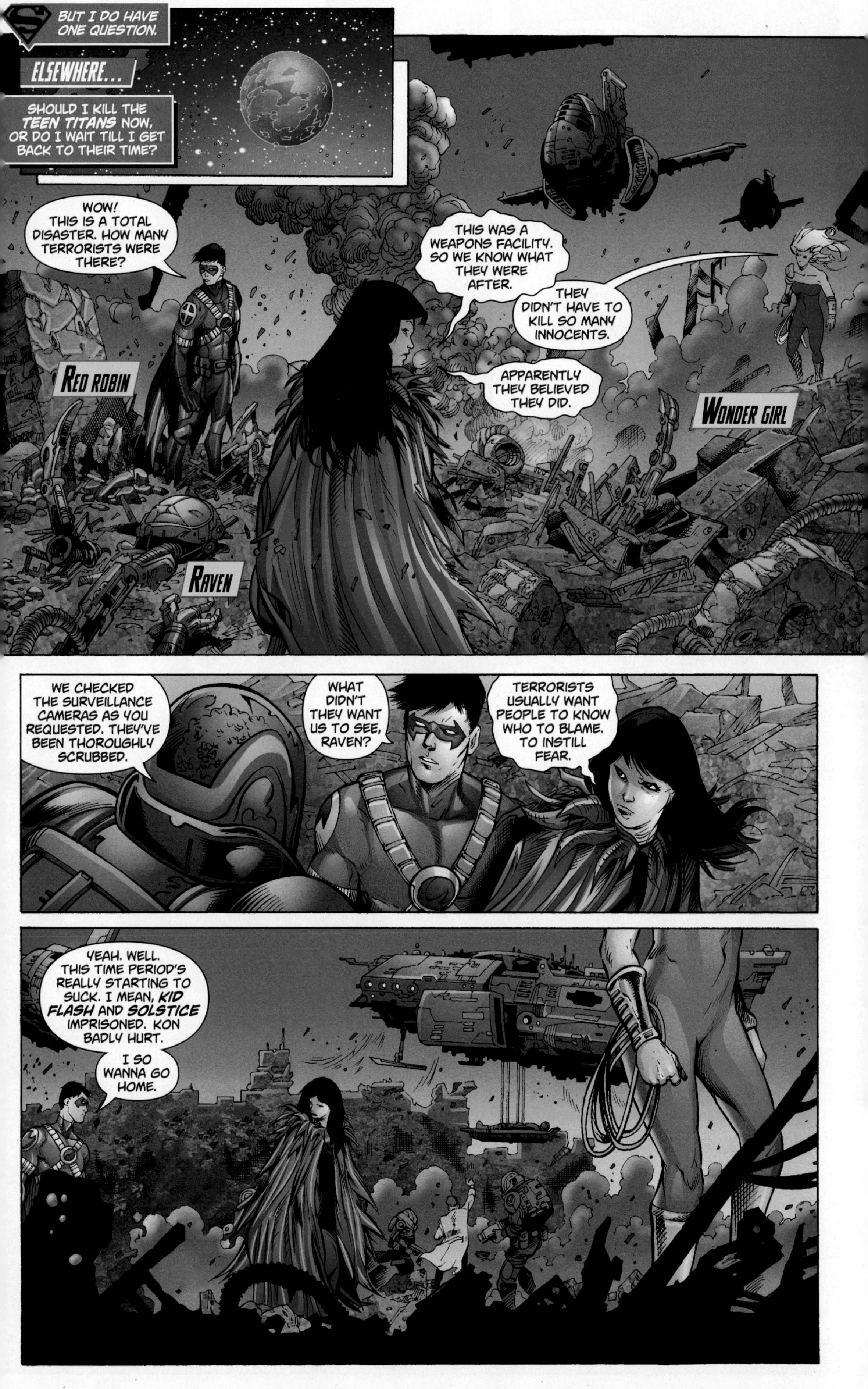

BUT I DO HAVE ONE QUESTION.
ELSEWHERE...
SHOULD I KILL THE TEEN TITANS NOW, OR DO I WAIT TILL I GET BACK TO THEIR TIME?
WOW! THIS IS A TOTAL DISASTER. HOW MANY TERRORISTS WERE THERE?
THIS WAS A WEAPONS FACILITY. SO WE KNOW WHAT THEY WERE AFTER.
THEY DIDN'T HAVE TO KILL SO MANY INNOCENTS.
APPARENTLY THEY BELIEVED THEY DID.
RED ROBIN
WONDER GIRL
RAVEN
WE CHECKED THE SURVEILLANCE CAMERAS AS YOU REQUESTED. THEY'VE BEEN THOROUGHLY SCRUBBED.
WHAT DIDN'T THEY WANT US TO SEE, RAVEN?
TERRORISTS USUALLY WANT PEOPLE TO KNOW WHO TO BLAME. TO INSTILL FEAR.
YEAH. WELL. THIS TIME PERIOD'S REALLY STARTING TO SUCK. I MEAN, KID FLASH AND SOLSTICE IMPRISONED. KON BADLY HURT.
I SO WANNA GO HOME.

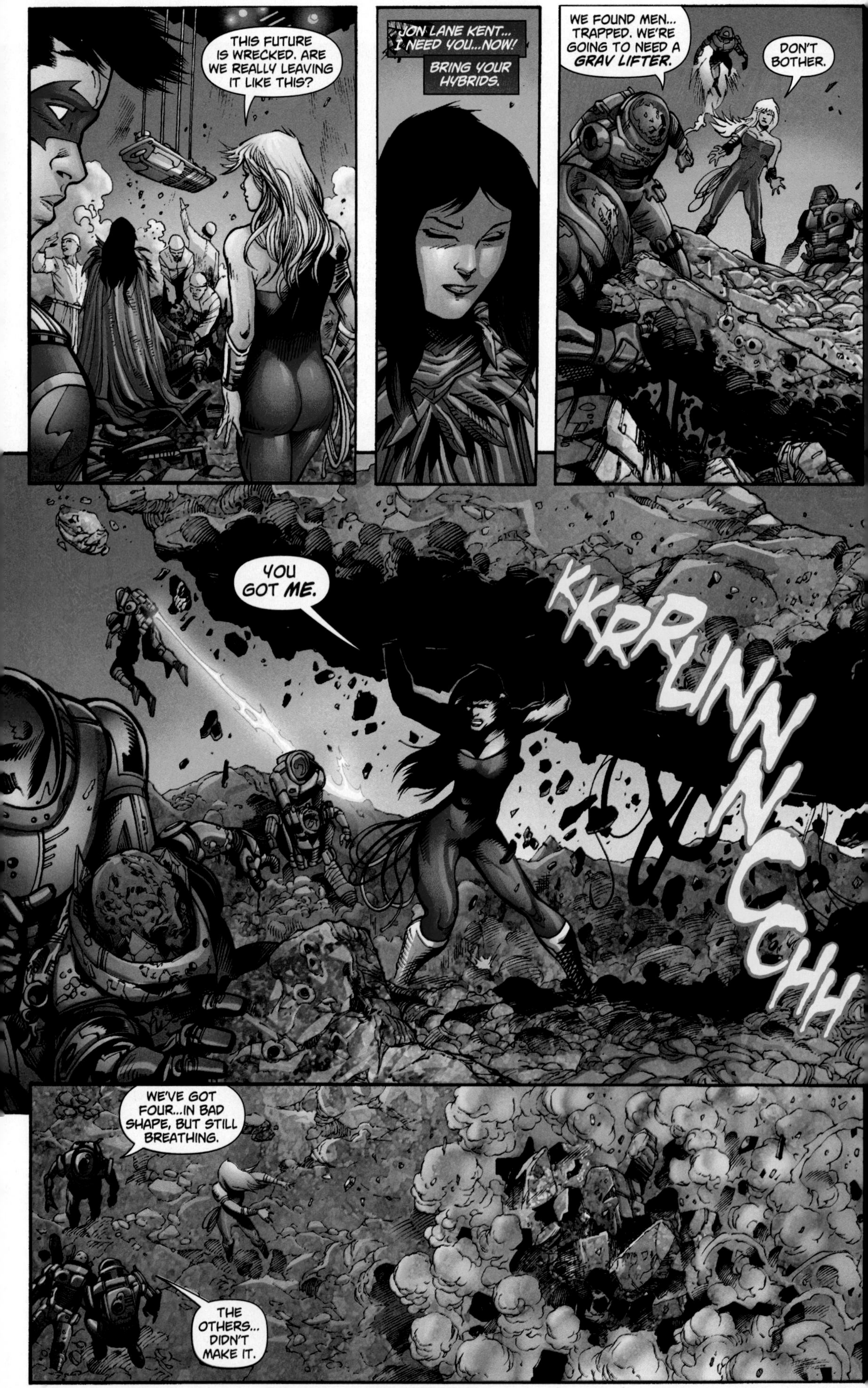
THIS FUTURE IS WRECKED. ARE WE REALLY LEAVING IT LIKE THIS?
JON LANE KENT... I NEED YOU...NOW!
BRING YOUR HYBRIDS.
WE FOUND MEN... TRAPPED. WE'RE GOING TO NEED A GRAV LIFTER.
DON'T BOTHER.
YOU GOT ME.
KKRRUNNNCHH
WE'VE GOT FOUR...IN BAD SHAPE, BUT STILL BREATHING.
THE OTHERS... DIDN'T MAKE IT.

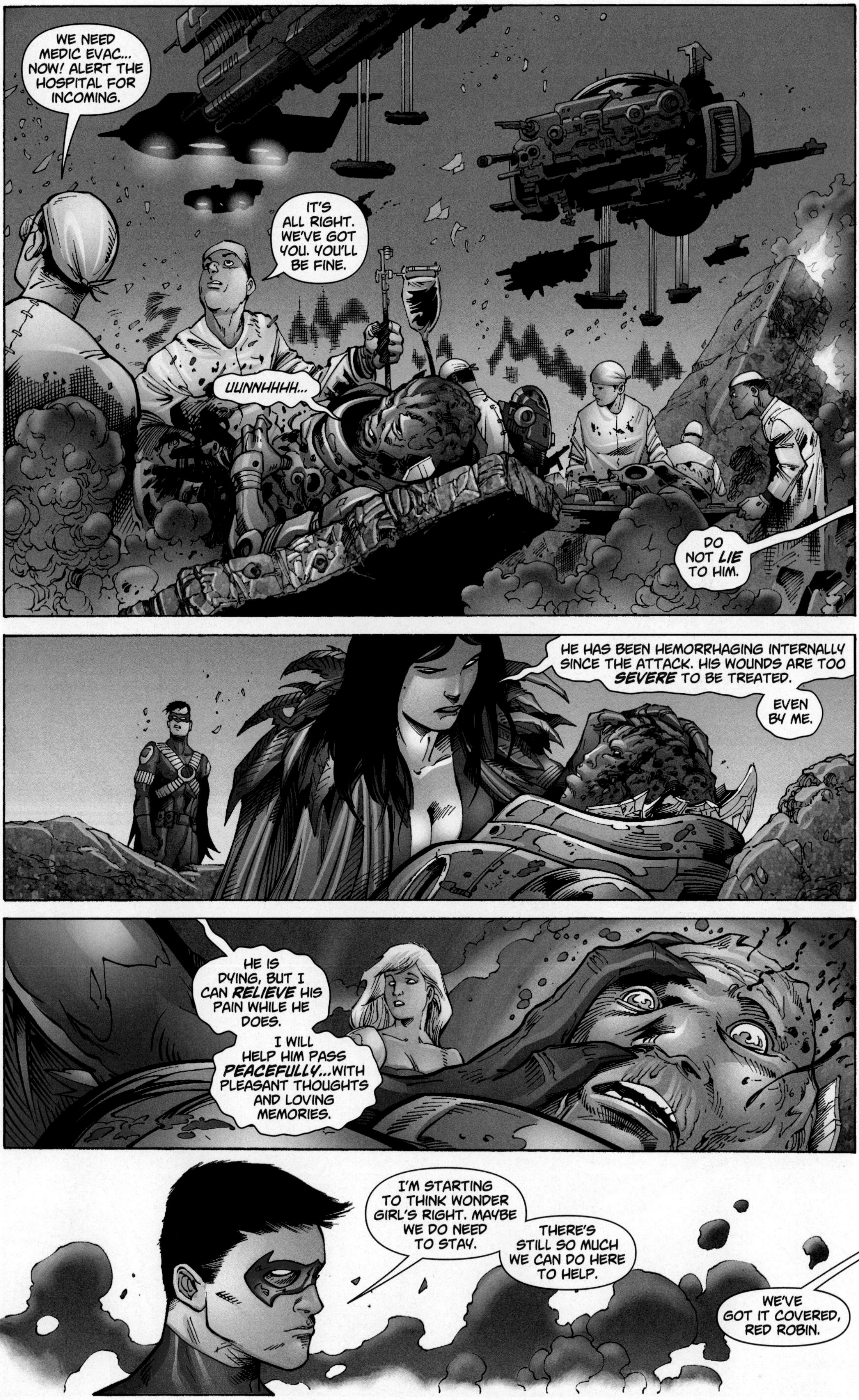
WE NEED MEDIC EVAC... NOW! ALERT THE HOSPITAL FOR INCOMING.
IT'S ALL RIGHT. WE'VE GOT YOU. YOU'LL BE FINE.
UUNNHHHH...
DO NOT LIE TO HIM.
HE HAS BEEN HEMORRHAGING INTERNALLY SINCE THE ATTACK. HIS WOUNDS ARE TOO SEVERE TO BE TREATED.
EVEN BY ME.
HE IS DYING, BUT I CAN RELIEVE HIS PAIN WHILE HE DOES.
I WILL HELP HIM PASS PEACEFULLY...WITH PLEASANT THOUGHTS AND LOVING MEMORIES.
I'M STARTING TO THINK WONDER GIRL'S RIGHT. MAYBE WE DO NEED TO STAY.
THERE'S STILL SO MUCH WE CAN DO HERE TO HELP.
WE'VE GOT IT COVERED, RED ROBIN.

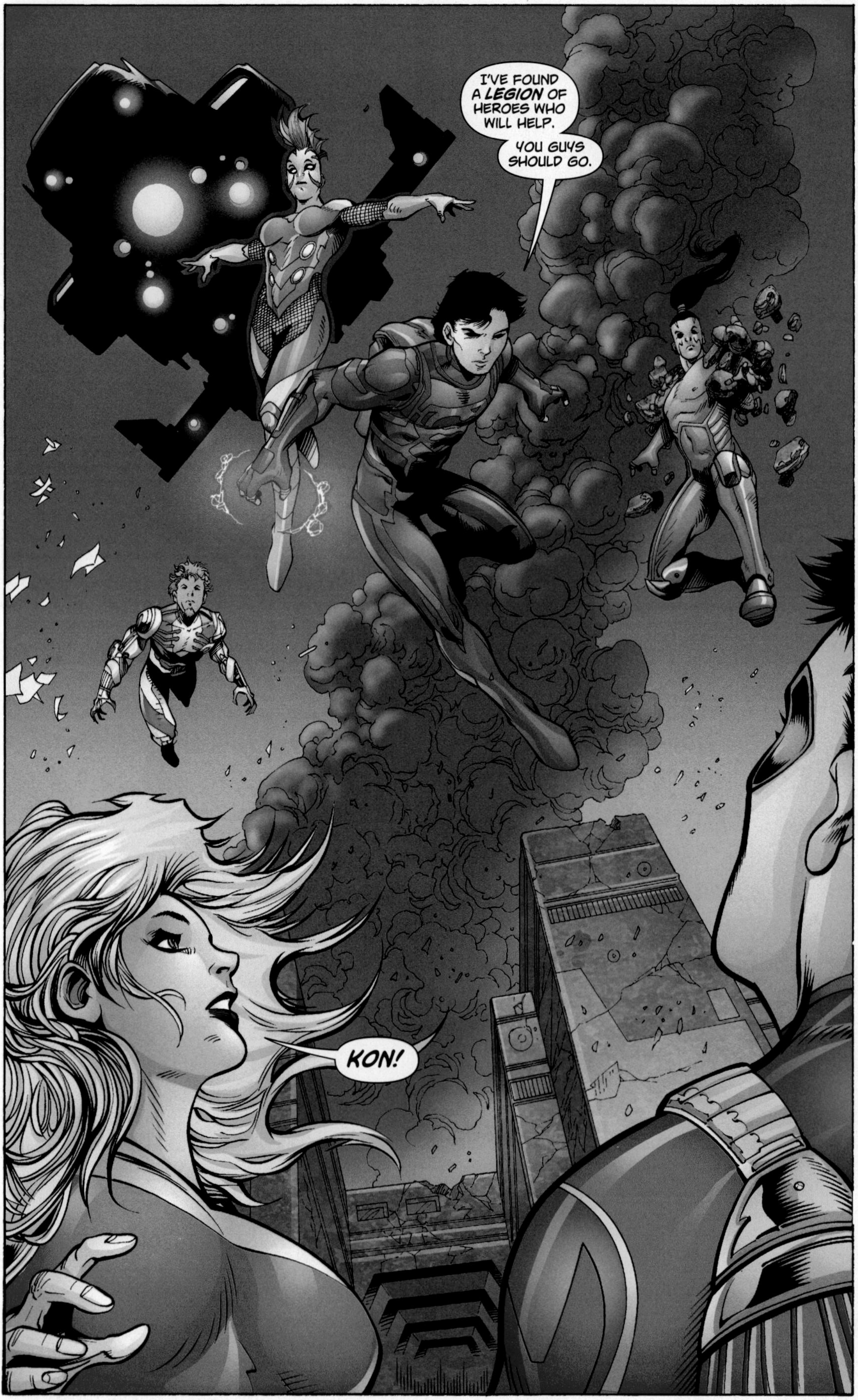
I'VE FOUND A LEGION OF HEROES WHO WILL HELP.
YOU GUYS SHOULD GO.
KON!

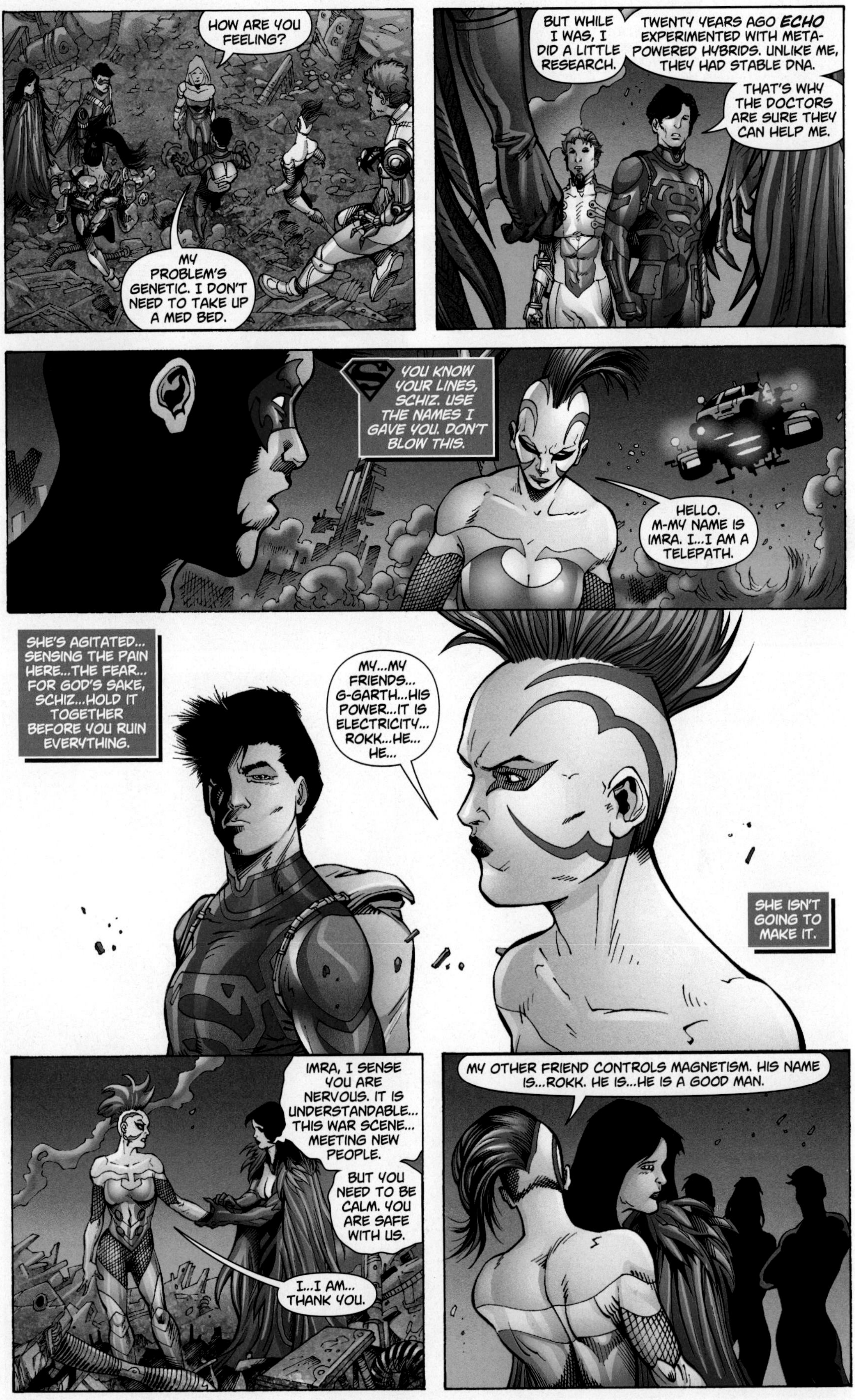
HOW ARE YOU FEELING?
MY PROBLEM'S GENETIC. I DON'T NEED TO TAKE UP A MED BED.
BUT WHILE I WAS, I DID A LITTLE RESEARCH.
TWENTY YEARS AGO ECHO EXPERIMENTED WITH META-POWERED HYBRIDS. UNLIKE ME, THEY HAD STABLE DNA.
THAT'S WHY THE DOCTORS ARE SURE THEY CAN HELP ME.
YOU KNOW YOUR LINES, SCHIZ. USE THE NAMES I GAVE YOU. DON'T BLOW THIS.
HELLO. M-MY NAME IS IMRA. I...I AM A TELEPATH.
SHE'S AGITATED... SENSING THE PAIN HERE...THE FEAR... FOR GOD'S SAKE, SCHIZ...HOLD IT TOGETHER BEFORE YOU RUIN EVERYTHING.
MY...MY FRIENDS... G-GARTH...HIS POWER...IT IS ELECTRICITY... ROKK...HE... HE...
SHE ISN'T GOING TO MAKE IT.
IMRA, I SENSE YOU ARE NERVOUS. IT IS UNDERSTANDABLE... THIS WAR SCENE... MEETING NEW PEOPLE.
BUT YOU NEED TO BE CALM. YOU ARE SAFE WITH US.
I...I AM... THANK YOU.
MY OTHER FRIEND CONTROLS MAGNETISM. HIS NAME IS...ROKK. HE IS...HE IS A GOOD MAN.

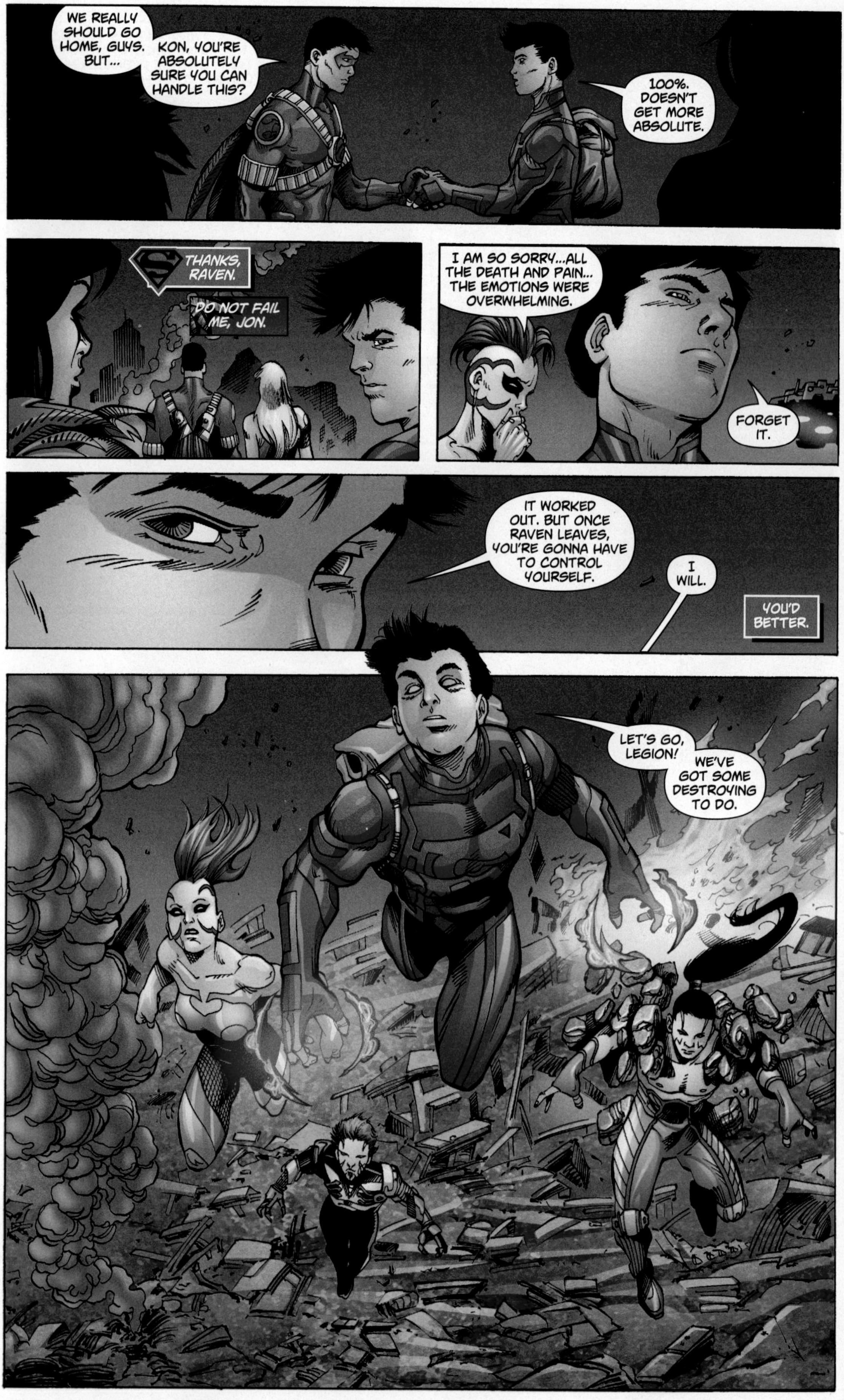
WE REALLY SHOULD GO HOME, GUYS. BUT...
KON, YOU'RE ABSOLUTELY SURE YOU CAN HANDLE THIS?
100%. DOESN'T GET MORE ABSOLUTE.
THANKS, RAVEN.
DO NOT FAIL ME, JON.
I AM SO SORRY...ALL THE DEATH AND PAIN... THE EMOTIONS WERE OVERWHELMING.
FORGET IT.
IT WORKED OUT. BUT ONCE RAVEN LEAVES, YOU'RE GONNA HAVE TO CONTROL YOURSELF.
I WILL.
YOU'D BETTER.
LET'S GO, LEGION!
WE'VE GOT SOME DESTROYING TO DO.

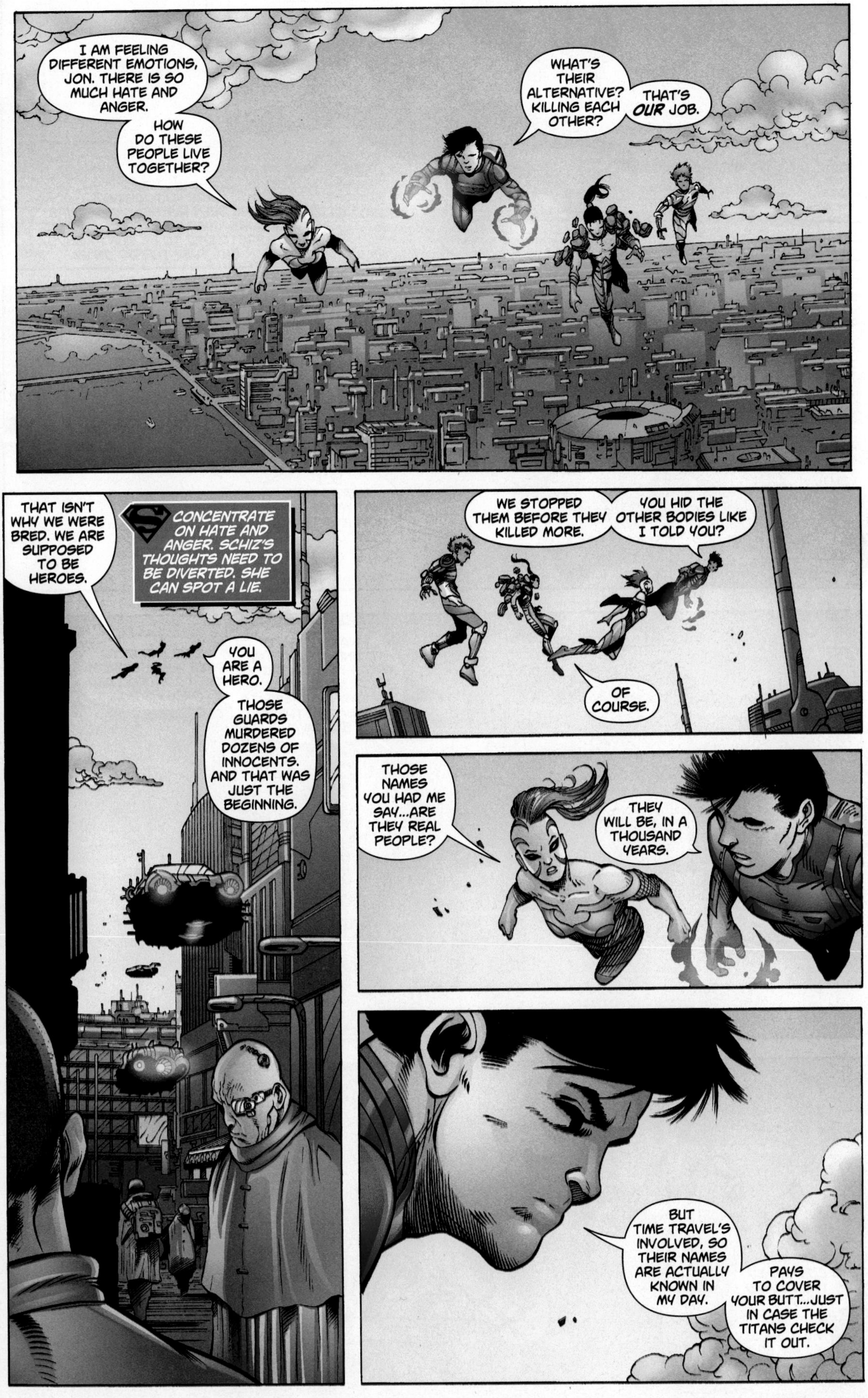
I AM FEELING DIFFERENT EMOTIONS, JON. THERE IS SO MUCH HATE AND ANGER.
HOW DO THESE PEOPLE LIVE TOGETHER?
WHAT'S THEIR ALTERNATIVE? KILLING EACH OTHER?
THAT'S OUR JOB.
THAT ISN'T WHY WE WERE BRED. WE ARE SUPPOSED TO BE HEROES.
CONCENTRATE ON HATE AND ANGER. SCHIZ'S THOUGHTS NEED TO BE DIVERTED. SHE CAN SPOT A LIE.
YOU ARE A HERO.
THOSE GUARDS MURDERED DOZENS OF INNOCENTS. AND THAT WAS JUST THE BEGINNING.
WE STOPPED THEM BEFORE THEY KILLED MORE.
YOU HID THE OTHER BODIES LIKE I TOLD YOU?
OF COURSE.
THOSE NAMES YOU HAD ME SAY...ARE THEY REAL PEOPLE?
THEY WILL BE, IN A THOUSAND YEARS.
BUT TIME TRAVEL'S INVOLVED, SO THEIR NAMES ARE ACTUALLY KNOWN IN MY DAY.
PAYS TO COVER YOUR BUTT...JUST IN CASE THE TITANS CHECK IT OUT.

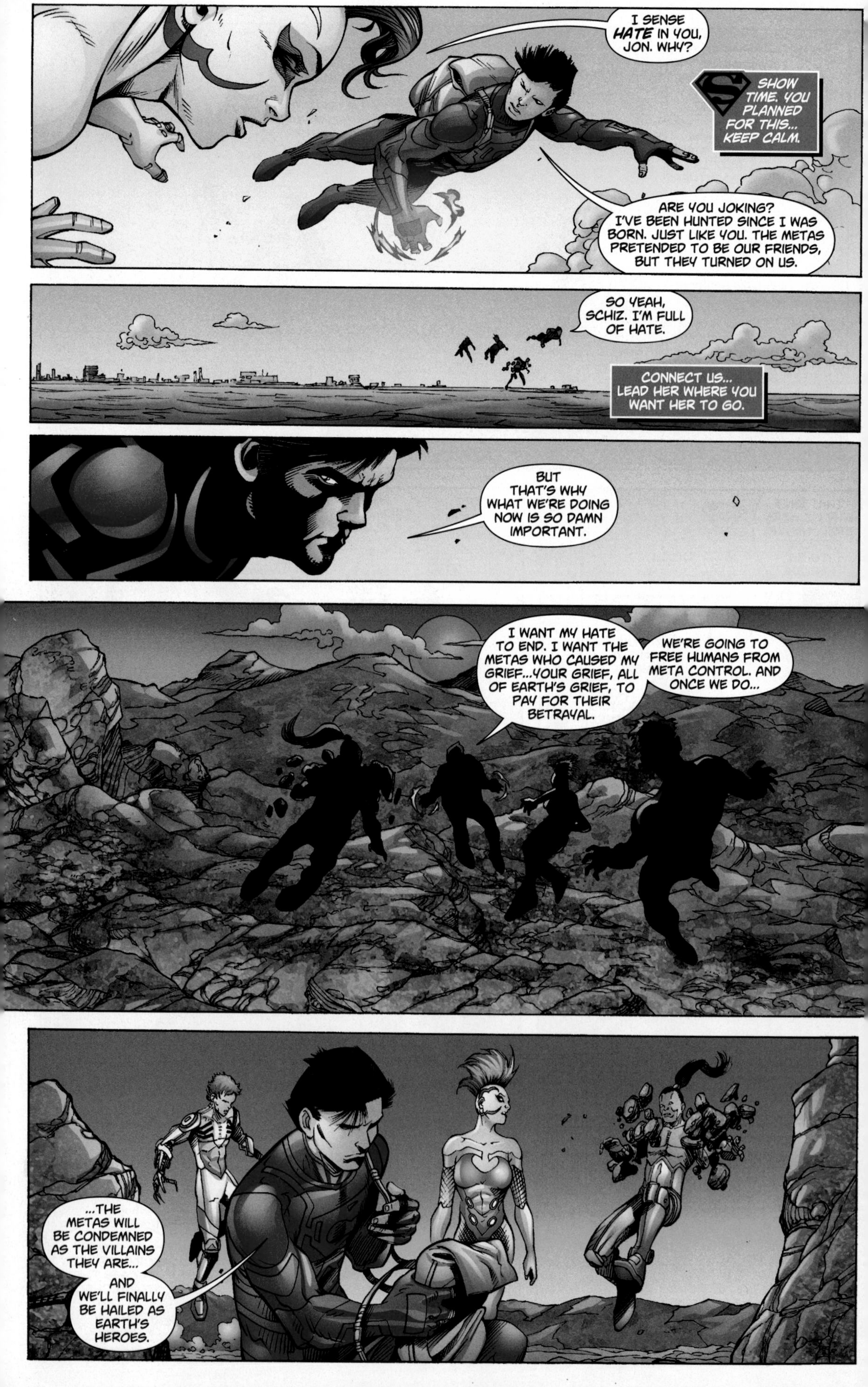
I SENSE HATE IN YOU, JON. WHY?
SHOW TIME. YOU PLANNED FOR THIS... KEEP CALM.
ARE YOU JOKING? I'VE BEEN HUNTED SINCE I WAS BORN. JUST LIKE YOU. THE METAS PRETENDED TO BE OUR FRIENDS, BUT THEY TURNED ON US.
SO YEAH, SCHIZ. I'M FULL OF HATE.
CONNECT US... LEAD HER WHERE YOU WANT HER TO GO.
BUT THAT'S WHY WHAT WE'RE DOING NOW IS SO DAMN IMPORTANT.
I WANT MY HATE TO END. I WANT THE METAS WHO CAUSED MY GRIEF...YOUR GRIEF, ALL OF EARTH'S GRIEF, TO PAY FOR THEIR BETRAYAL.
WE'RE GOING TO FREE HUMANS FROM META CONTROL. AND ONCE WE DO...
...THE METAS WILL BE CONDEMNED AS THE VILLAINS THEY ARE...
AND WE'LL FINALLY BE HAILED AS EARTH'S HEROES.

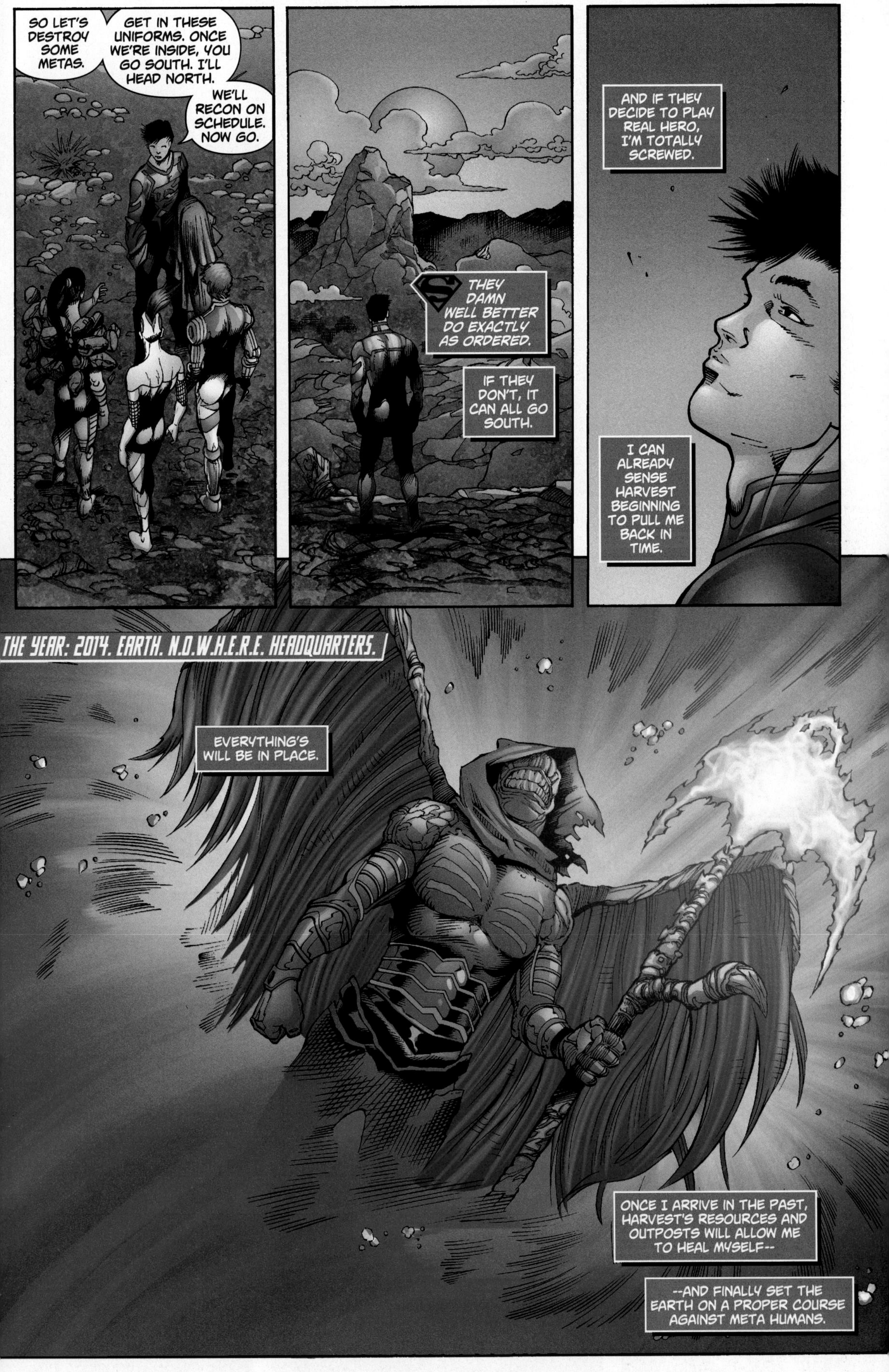

SO LET'S DESTROY SOME METAS.
GET IN THESE UNIFORMS. ONCE WE'RE INSIDE, YOU GO SOUTH. I'LL HEAD NORTH.
WE'LL RECON ON SCHEDULE. NOW GO.
THEY DAMN WELL BETTER DO EXACTLY AS ORDERED.
IF THEY DON'T, IT CAN ALL GO SOUTH.
AND IF THEY DECIDE TO PLAY REAL HERO, I'M TOTALLY SCREWED.
I CAN ALREADY SENSE HARVEST BEGINNING TO PULL ME BACK IN TIME.
THE YEAR: 2014. EARTH. N.O.W.H.E.R.E. HEADQUARTERS.
EVERYTHING'S WILL BE IN PLACE.
ONCE I ARRIVE IN THE PAST, HARVEST'S RESOURCES AND OUTPOSTS WILL ALLOW ME TO HEAL MYSELF--
--AND FINALLY SET THE EARTH ON A PROPER COURSE AGAINST META HUMANS.

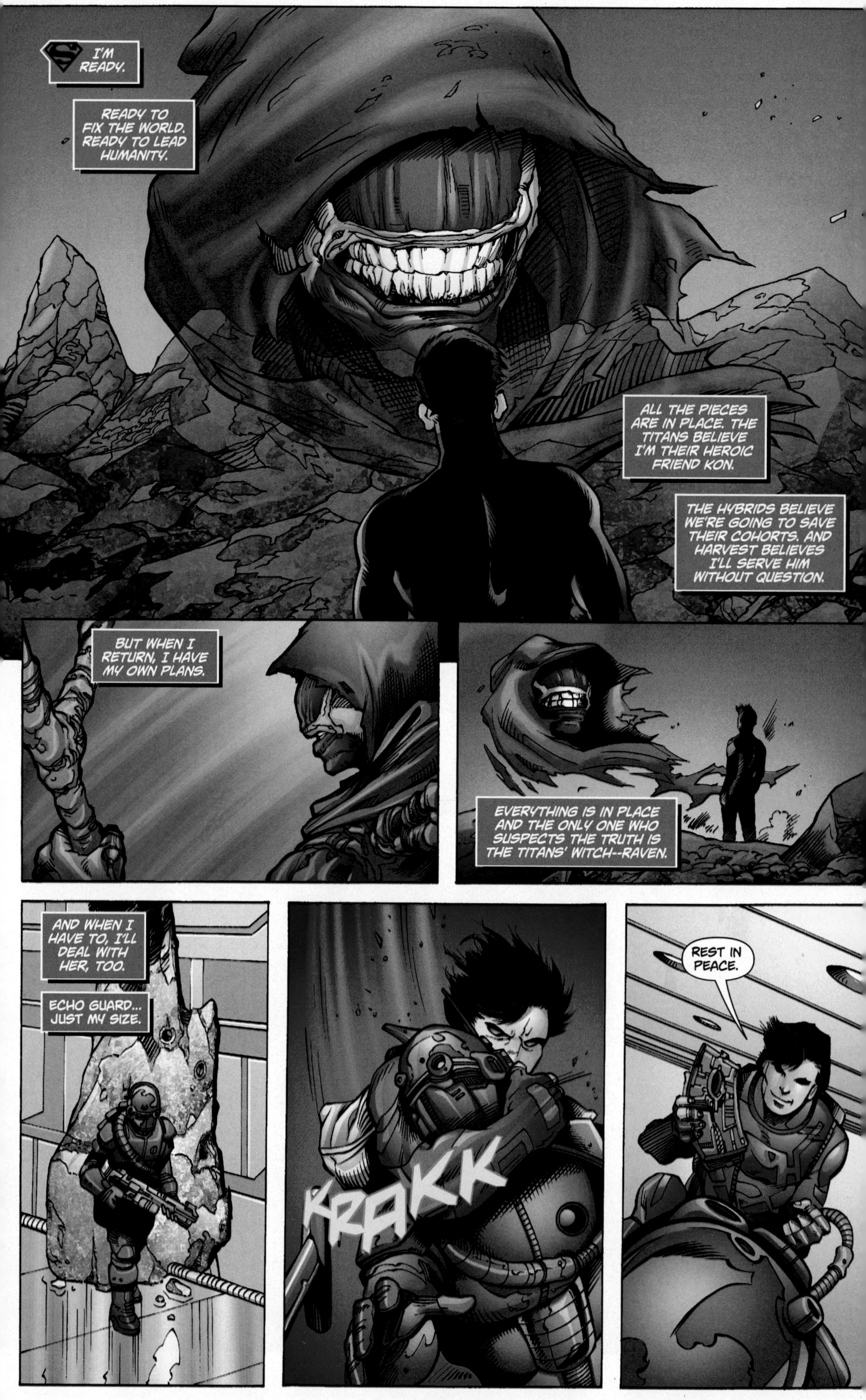
I'M READY.
READY TO FIX THE WORLD. READY TO LEAD HUMANITY.
ALL THE PIECES ARE IN PLACE. THE TITANS BELIEVE I'M THEIR HEROIC FRIEND KON.
THE HYBRIDS BELIEVE WE'RE GOING TO SAVE THEIR COHORTS. AND HARVEST BELIEVES I'LL SERVE HIM WITHOUT QUESTION.
BUT WHEN I RETURN, I HAVE MY OWN PLANS.
EVERYTHING IS IN PLACE AND THE ONLY ONE WHO SUSPECTS THE TRUTH IS THE TITANS' WITCH--RAVEN.
AND WHEN I HAVE TO, I'LL DEAL WITH HER, TOO.
ECHO GUARD... JUST MY SIZE.
KRAKK
REST IN PEACE.

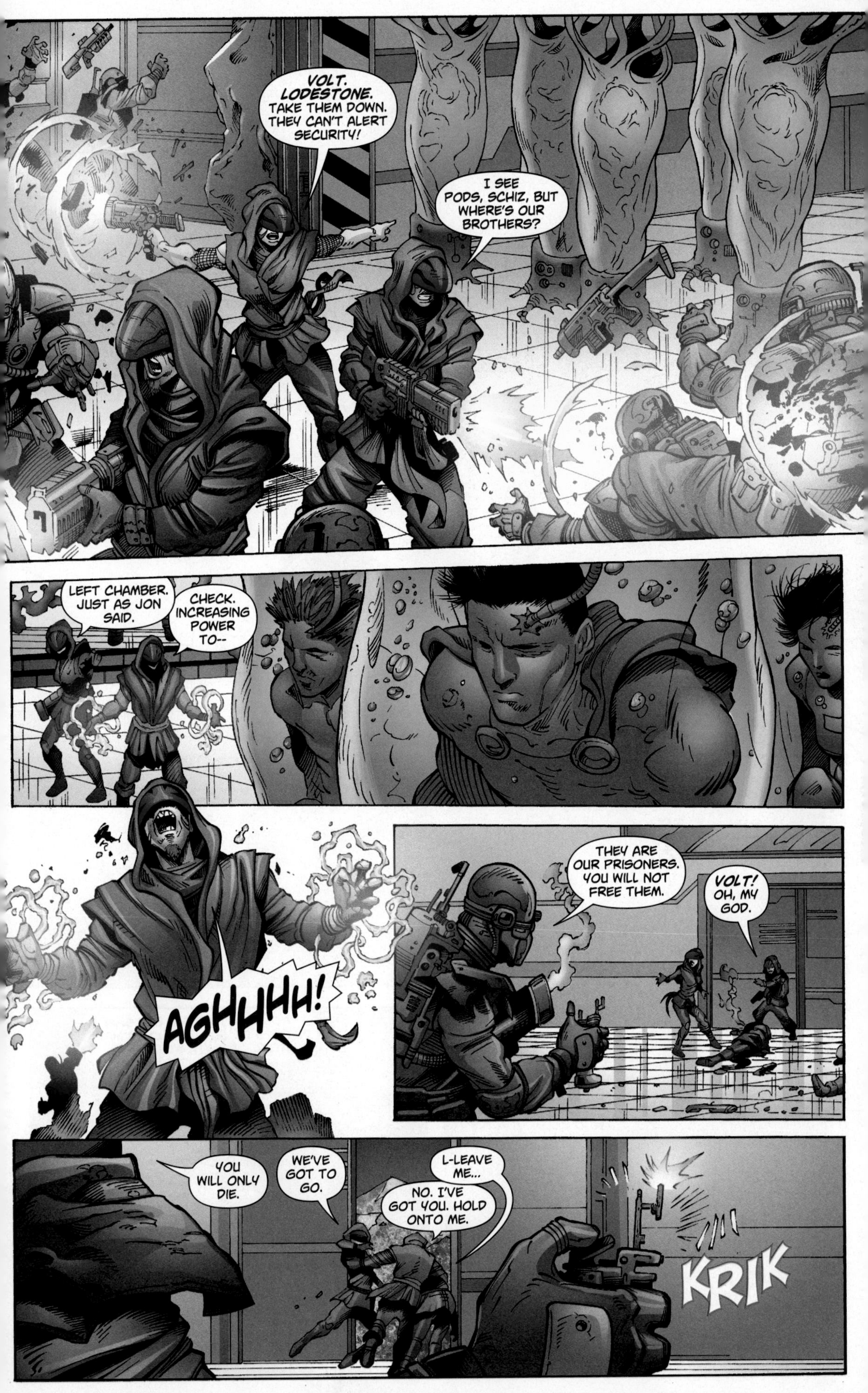

VOLT. LODESTONE. TAKE THEM DOWN. THEY CAN'T ALERT SECURITY!
I SEE PODS, SCHIZ, BUT WHERE'S OUR BROTHERS?
LEFT CHAMBER. JUST AS JON SAID.
CHECK. INCREASING POWER TO--
AGHHHH!
THEY ARE OUR PRISONERS. YOU WILL NOT FREE THEM.
VOLT! OH, MY GOD.
YOU WILL ONLY DIE.
WE'VE GOT TO GO.
L-LEAVE ME...
NO. I'VE GOT YOU. HOLD ONTO ME.
KRIK

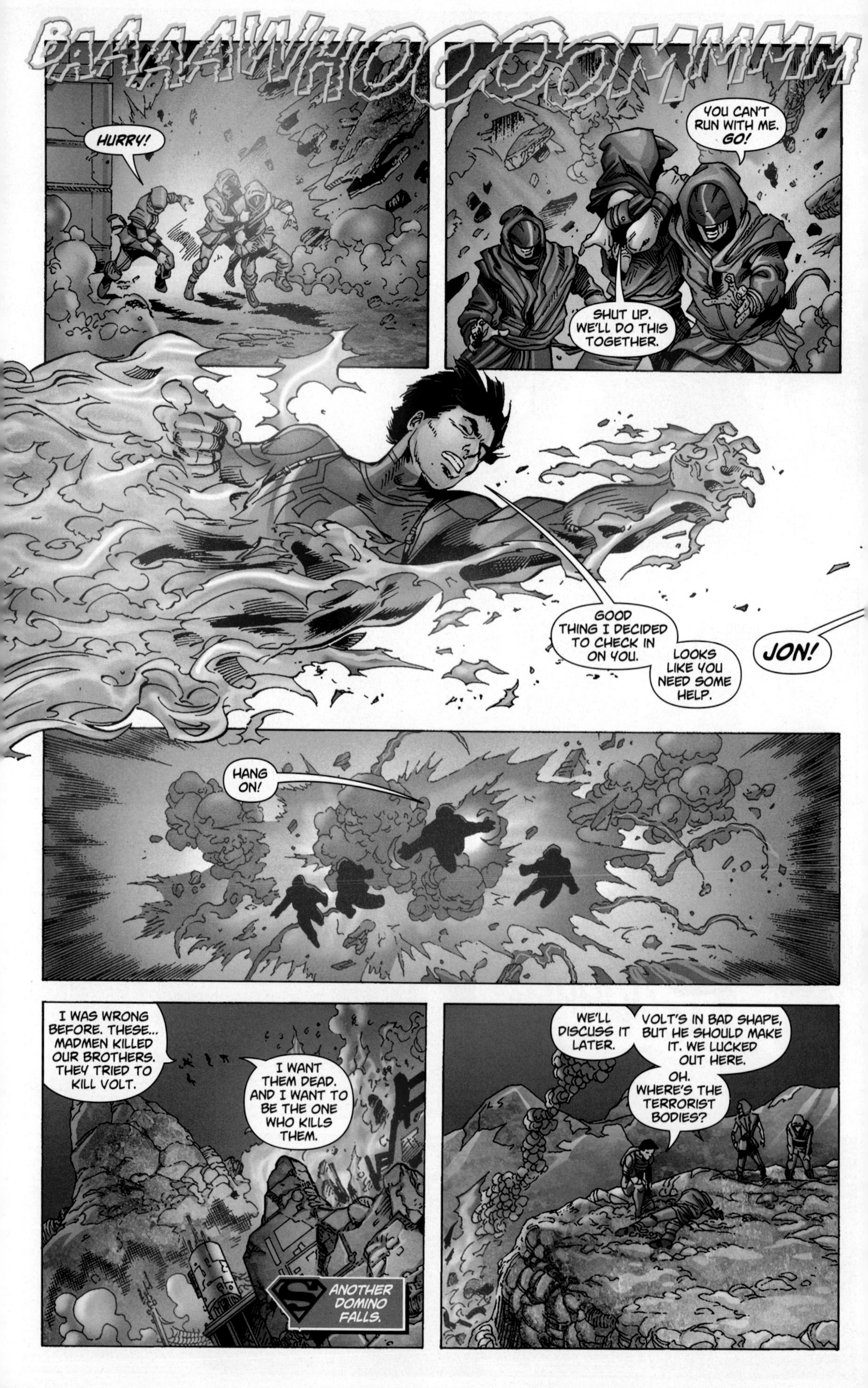
BAAAAWHOOOOOMMMM
HURRY!
YOU CAN'T RUN WITH ME. GO!
SHUT UP. WE'LL DO THIS TOGETHER.
GOOD THING I DECIDED TO CHECK IN ON YOU.
LOOKS LIKE YOU NEED SOME HELP.
JON!
HANG ON!
I WAS WRONG BEFORE. THESE... MADMEN KILLED OUR BROTHERS. THEY TRIED TO KILL VOLT.
I WANT THEM DEAD. AND I WANT TO BE THE ONE WHO KILLS THEM.
ANOTHER DOMINO FALLS.
WE'LL DISCUSS IT LATER.
VOLT'S IN BAD SHAPE, BUT HE SHOULD MAKE IT. WE LUCKED OUT HERE.
OH. WHERE'S THE TERRORIST BODIES?

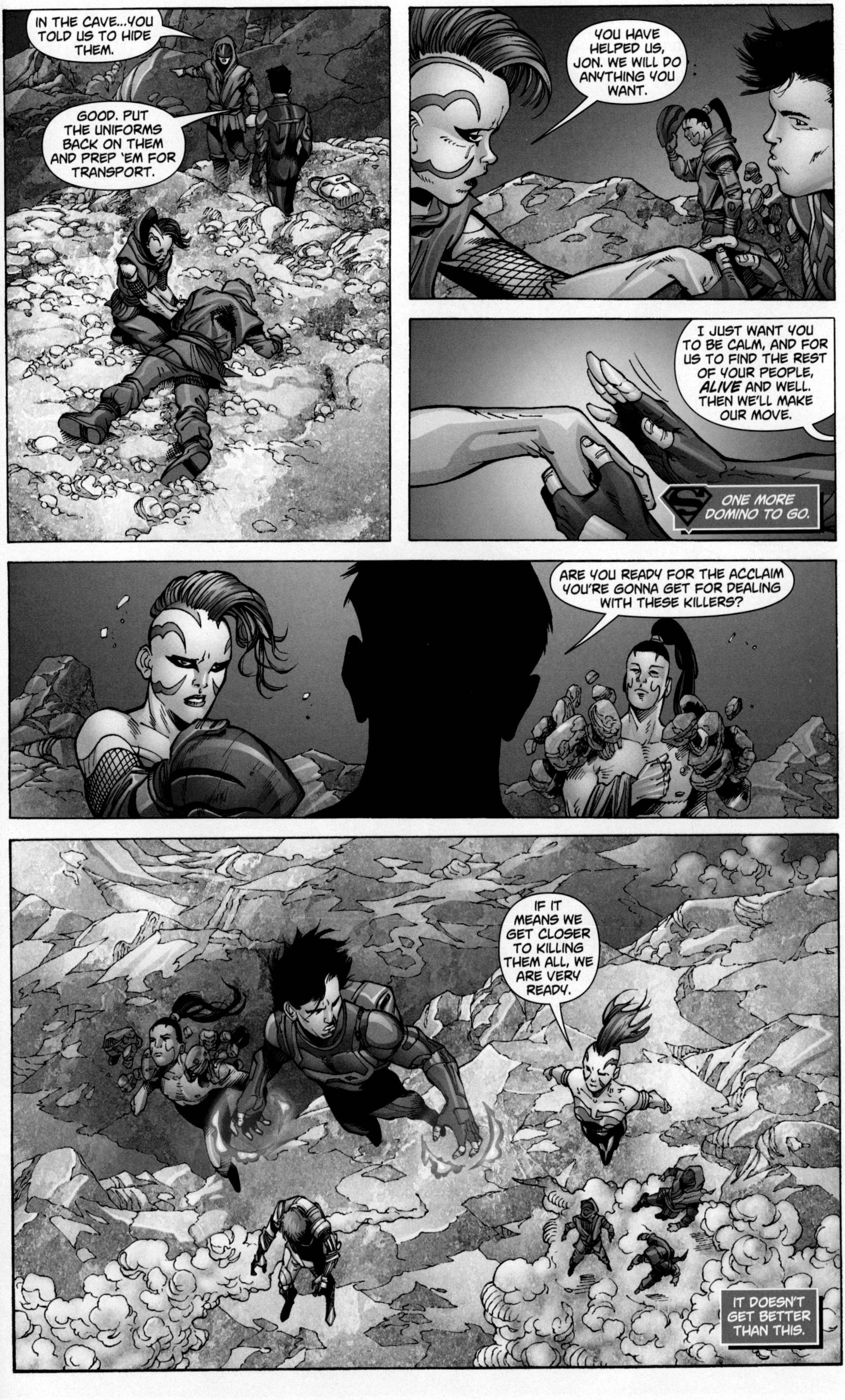
IN THE CAVE...YOU TOLD US TO HIDE THEM.
GOOD. PUT THE UNIFORMS BACK ON THEM AND PREP 'EM FOR TRANSPORT.
YOU HAVE HELPED US, JON. WE WILL DO ANYTHING YOU WANT.
I JUST WANT YOU TO BE CALM, AND FOR US TO FIND THE REST OF YOUR PEOPLE, *ALIVE* AND WELL. THEN WE'LL MAKE OUR MOVE.
ONE MORE DOMINO TO GO.
ARE YOU READY FOR THE ACCLAIM YOU'RE GONNA GET FOR DEALING WITH THESE KILLERS?
IF IT MEANS WE GET CLOSER TO KILLING THEM ALL, WE ARE VERY READY.
IT DOESN'T GET BETTER THAN THIS.

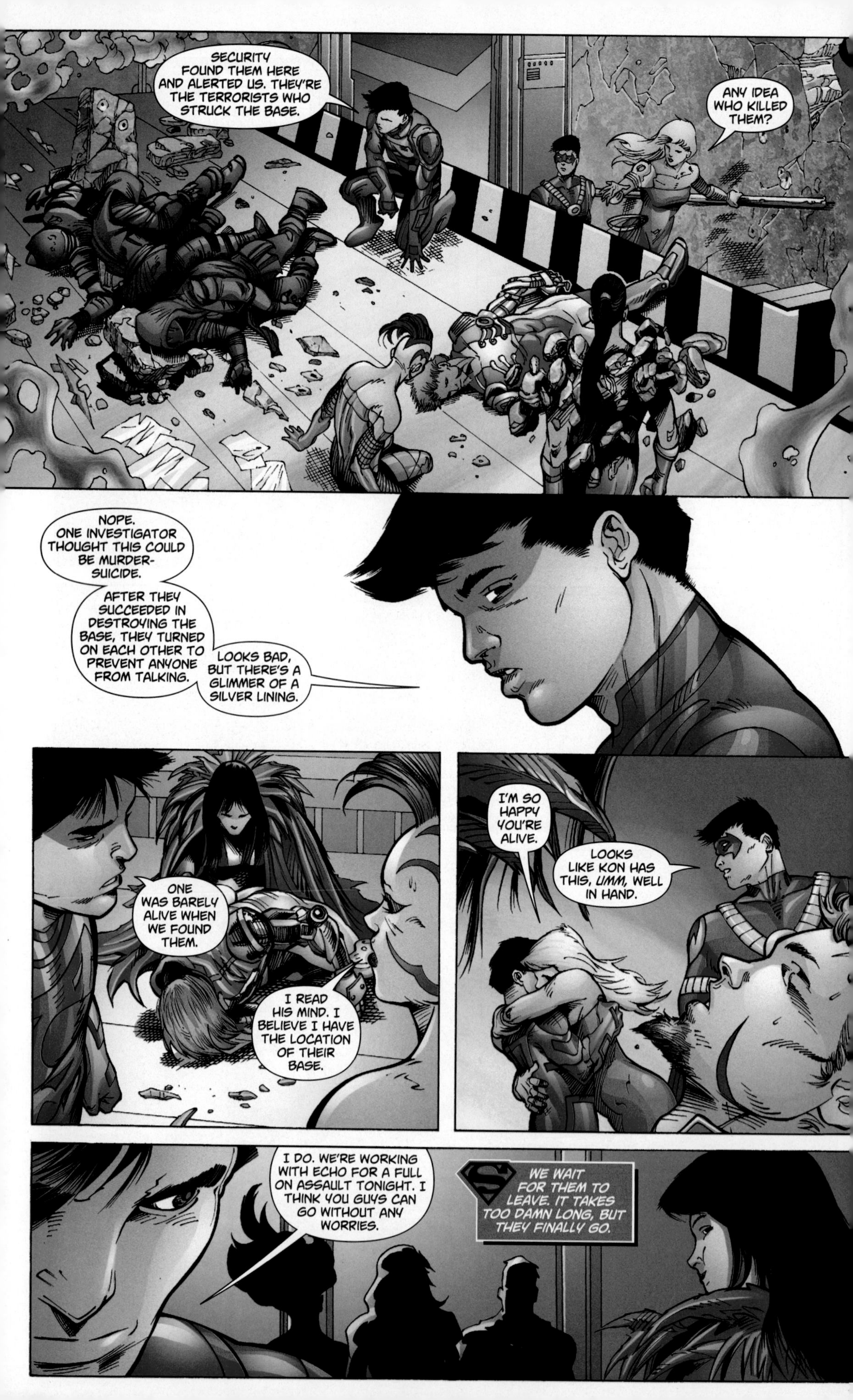
SECURITY FOUND THEM HERE AND ALERTED US. THEY'RE THE TERRORISTS WHO STRUCK THE BASE.
ANY IDEA WHO KILLED THEM?
NOPE. ONE INVESTIGATOR THOUGHT THIS COULD BE MURDER-SUICIDE.
AFTER THEY SUCCEEDED IN DESTROYING THE BASE, THEY TURNED ON EACH OTHER TO PREVENT ANYONE FROM TALKING.
LOOKS BAD, BUT THERE'S A GLIMMER OF A SILVER LINING.
ONE WAS BARELY ALIVE WHEN WE FOUND THEM.
I READ HIS MIND. I BELIEVE I HAVE THE LOCATION OF THEIR BASE.
I'M SO HAPPY YOU'RE ALIVE.
LOOKS LIKE KON HAS THIS, UMM, WELL IN HAND.
I DO. WE'RE WORKING WITH ECHO FOR A FULL ON ASSAULT TONIGHT. I THINK YOU GUYS CAN GO WITHOUT ANY WORRIES.
WE WAIT FOR THEM TO LEAVE. IT TAKES TOO DAMN LONG, BUT THEY FINALLY GO.

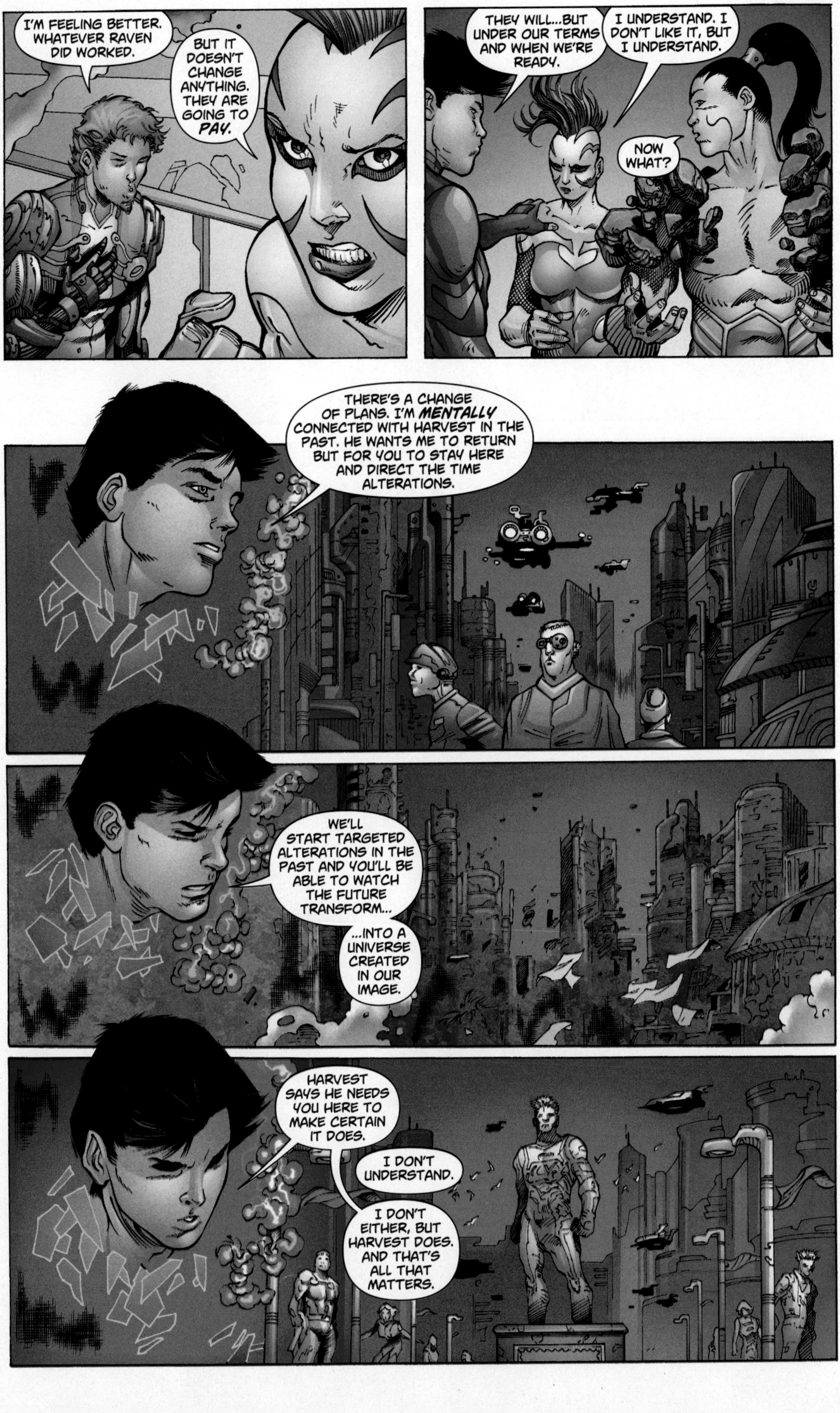
I'M FEELING BETTER. WHATEVER RAVEN DID WORKED.
BUT IT DOESN'T CHANGE ANYTHING. THEY ARE GOING TO PAY.
THEY WILL...BUT UNDER OUR TERMS AND WHEN WE'RE READY.
I UNDERSTAND. I DON'T LIKE IT, BUT I UNDERSTAND.
NOW WHAT?
THERE'S A CHANGE OF PLANS. I'M MENTALLY CONNECTED WITH HARVEST IN THE PAST. HE WANTS ME TO RETURN BUT FOR YOU TO STAY HERE AND DIRECT THE TIME ALTERATIONS.
WE'LL START TARGETED ALTERATIONS IN THE PAST AND YOU'LL BE ABLE TO WATCH THE FUTURE TRANSFORM...
...INTO A UNIVERSE CREATED IN OUR IMAGE.
HARVEST SAYS HE NEEDS YOU HERE TO MAKE CERTAIN IT DOES.
I DON'T UNDERSTAND.
I DON'T EITHER, BUT HARVEST DOES. AND THAT'S ALL THAT MATTERS.

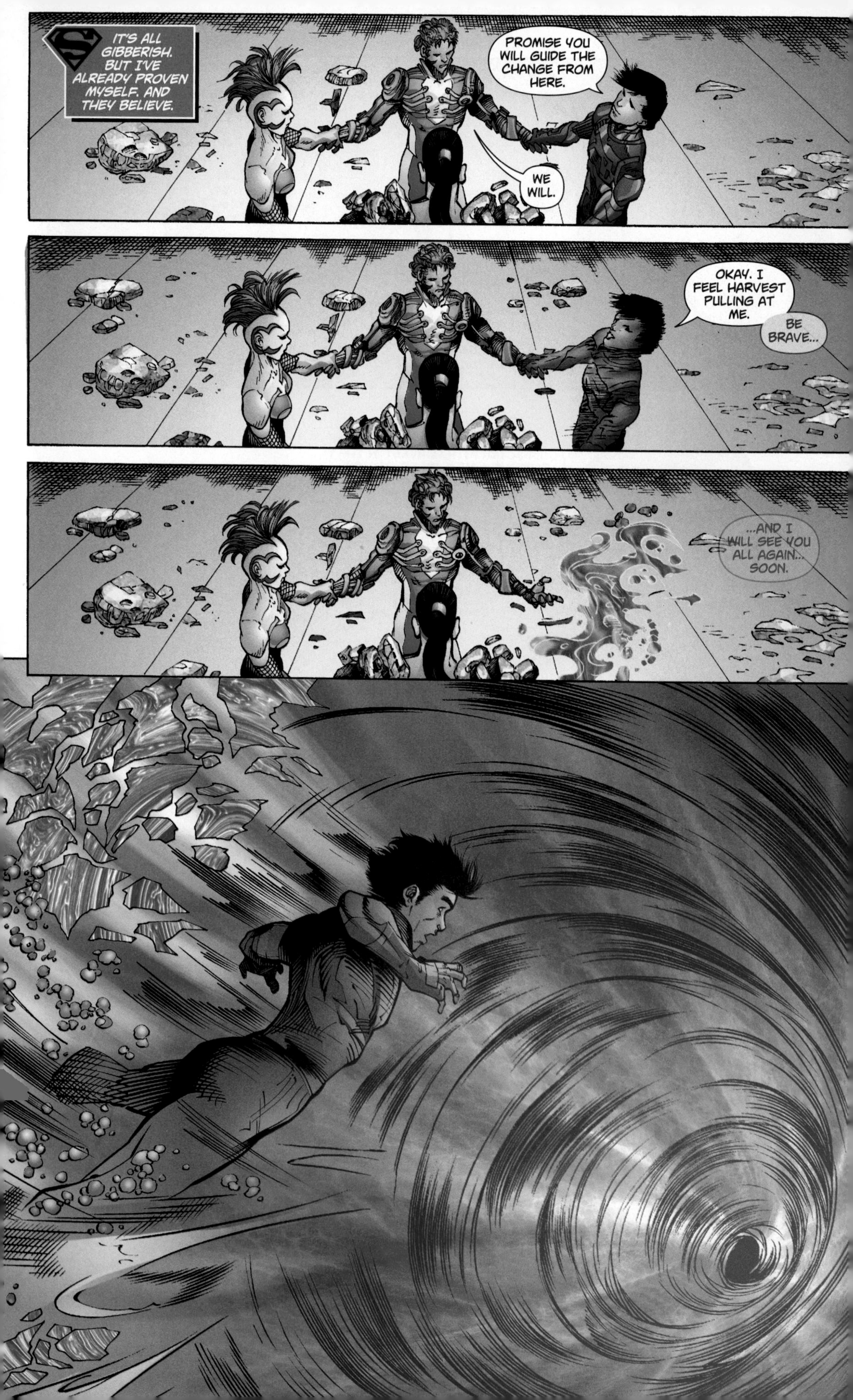
IT'S ALL GIBBERISH. BUT I'VE ALREADY PROVEN MYSELF. AND THEY BELIEVE.
PROMISE YOU WILL GUIDE THE CHANGE FROM HERE.
WE WILL.
OKAY. I FEEL HARVEST PULLING AT ME.
BE BRAVE...
...AND I WILL SEE YOU ALL AGAIN... SOON.

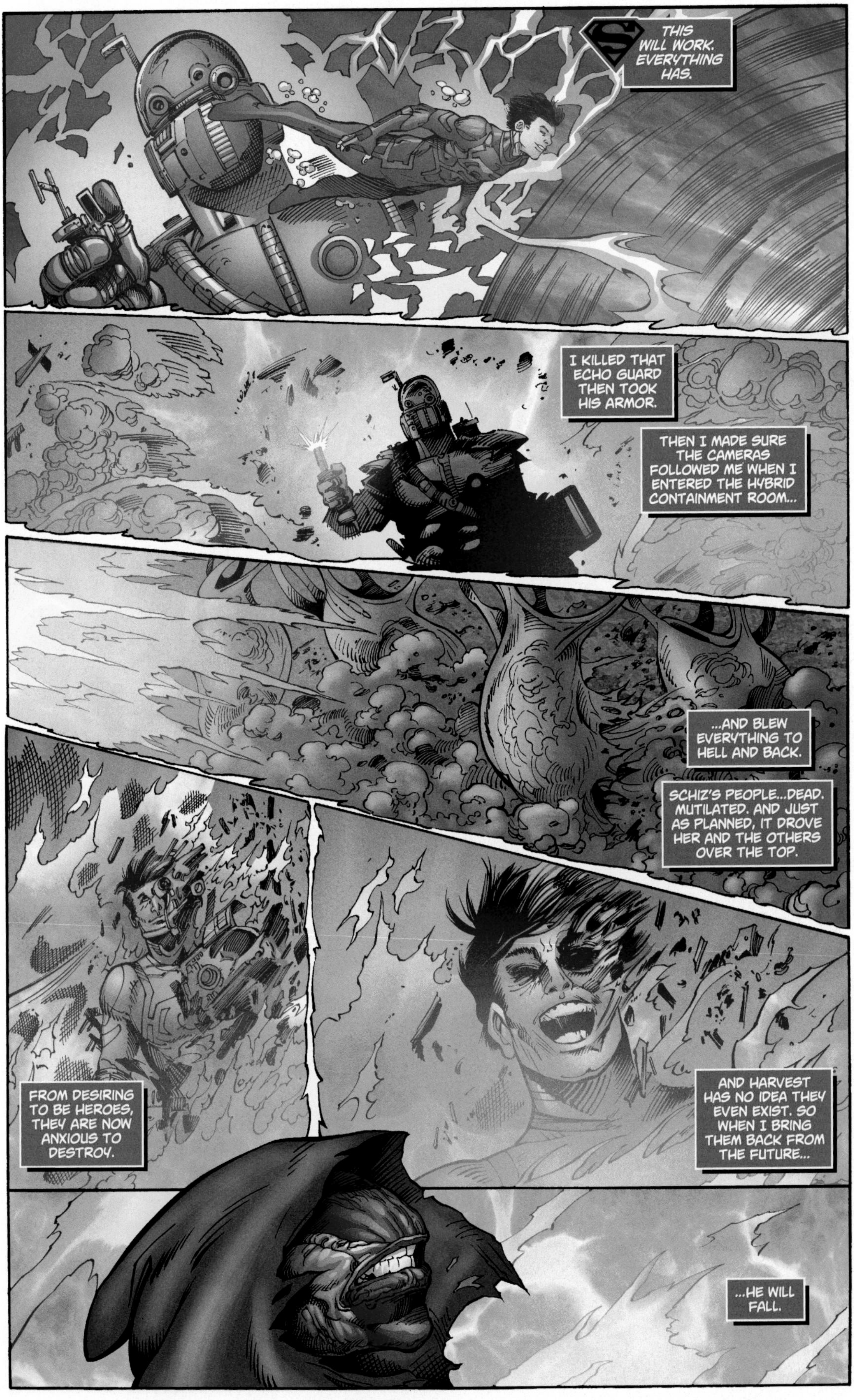
THIS WILL WORK. EVERYTHING HAS.
I KILLED THAT ECHO GUARD THEN TOOK HIS ARMOR.
THEN I MADE SURE THE CAMERAS FOLLOWED ME WHEN I ENTERED THE HYBRID CONTAINMENT ROOM...
...AND BLEW EVERYTHING TO HELL AND BACK.
SCHIZ'S PEOPLE...DEAD. MUTILATED. AND JUST AS PLANNED, IT DROVE HER AND THE OTHERS OVER THE TOP.
FROM DESIRING TO BE HEROES, THEY ARE NOW ANXIOUS TO DESTROY.
AND HARVEST HAS NO IDEA THEY EVEN EXIST. SO WHEN I BRING THEM BACK FROM THE FUTURE...
...HE WILL FALL.

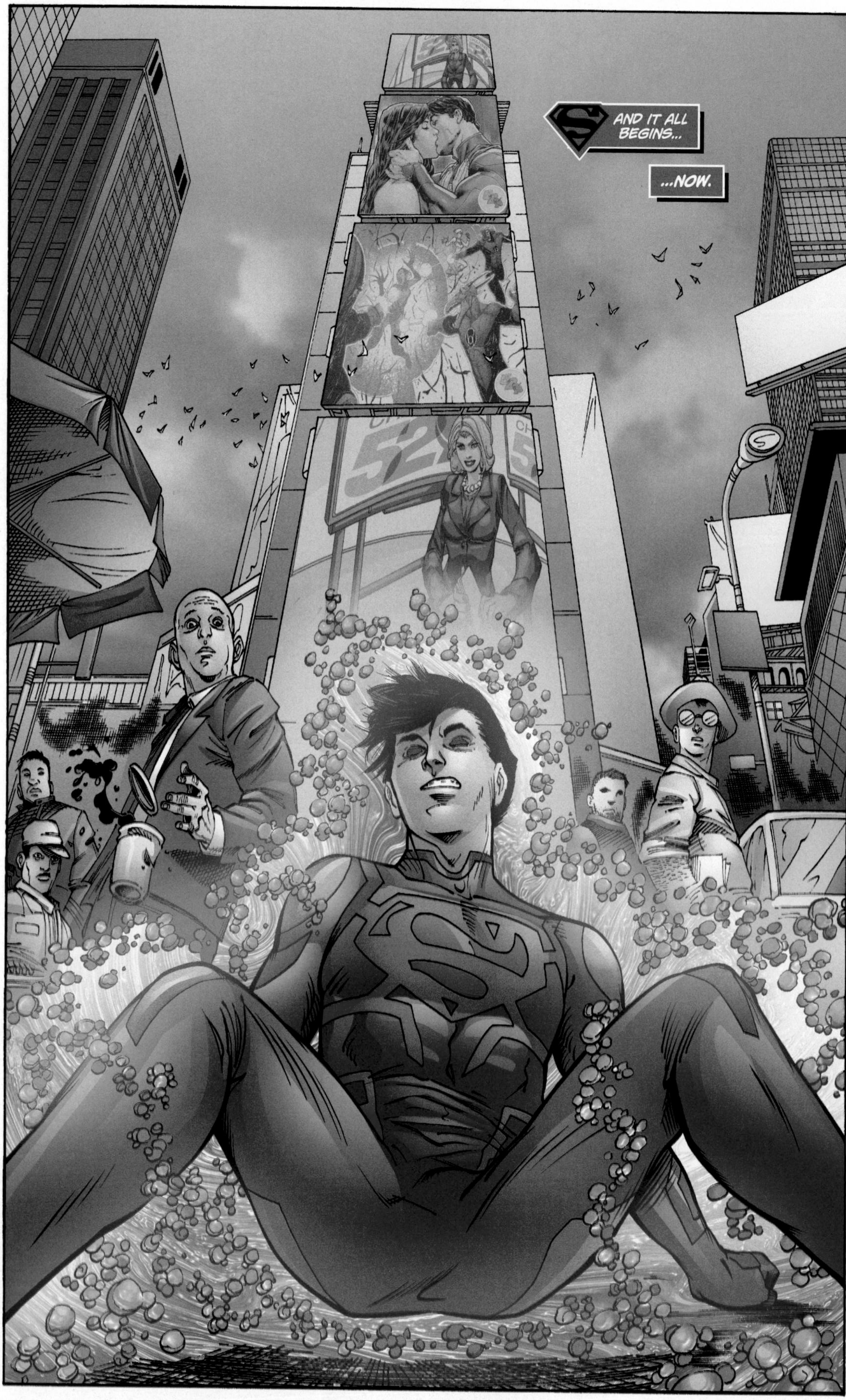
AND IT ALL BEGINS...
...NOW.

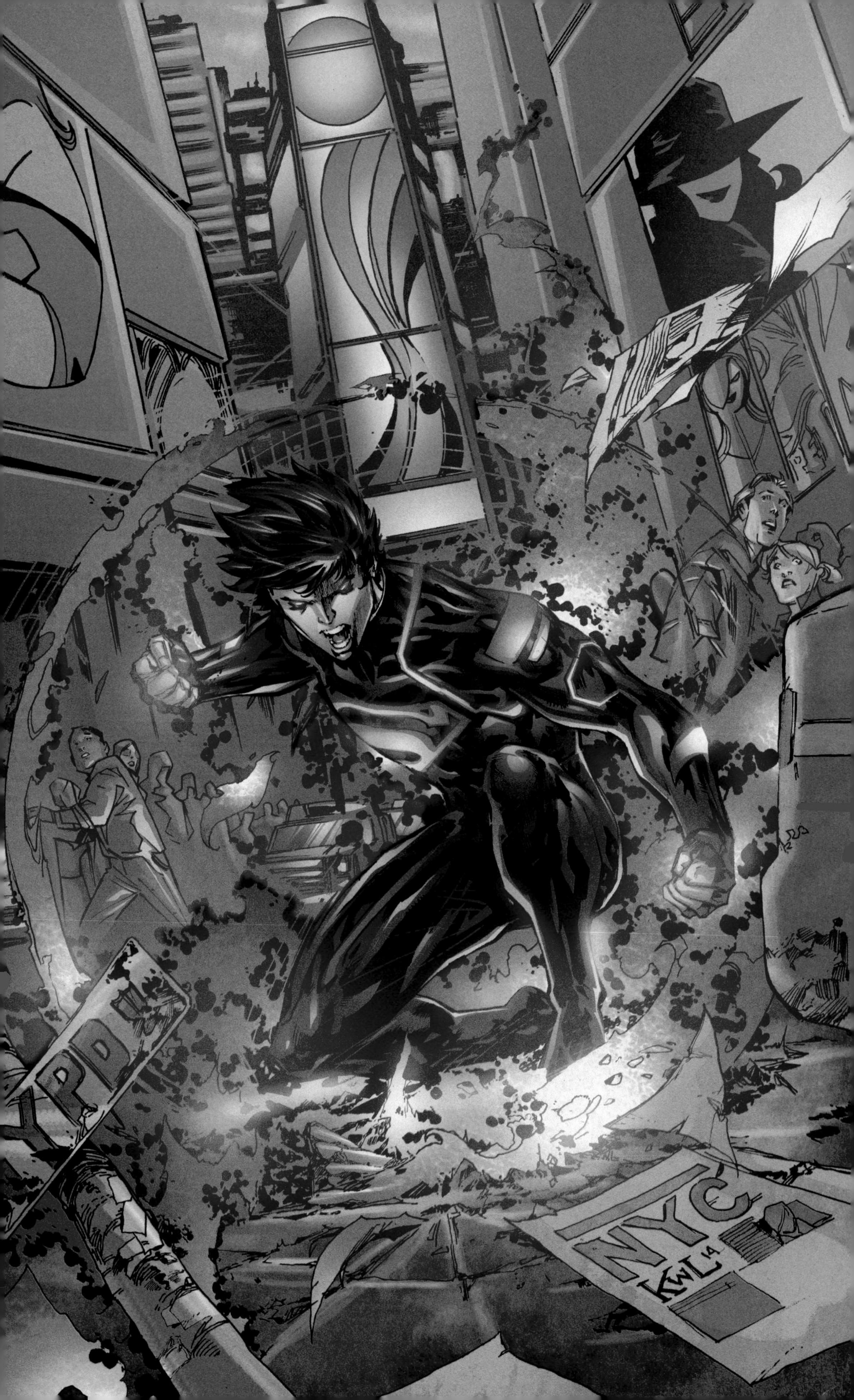
NYC

FORGET THE PAST

AARON KUDER writer **JORGE JIMÉNEZ** artist **TANYA** and **RICHARD HORIE** colorists
CARLOS M. MANGUAL letterer cover art by **KEN LASHLEY** and **MIKE ATIYEH**

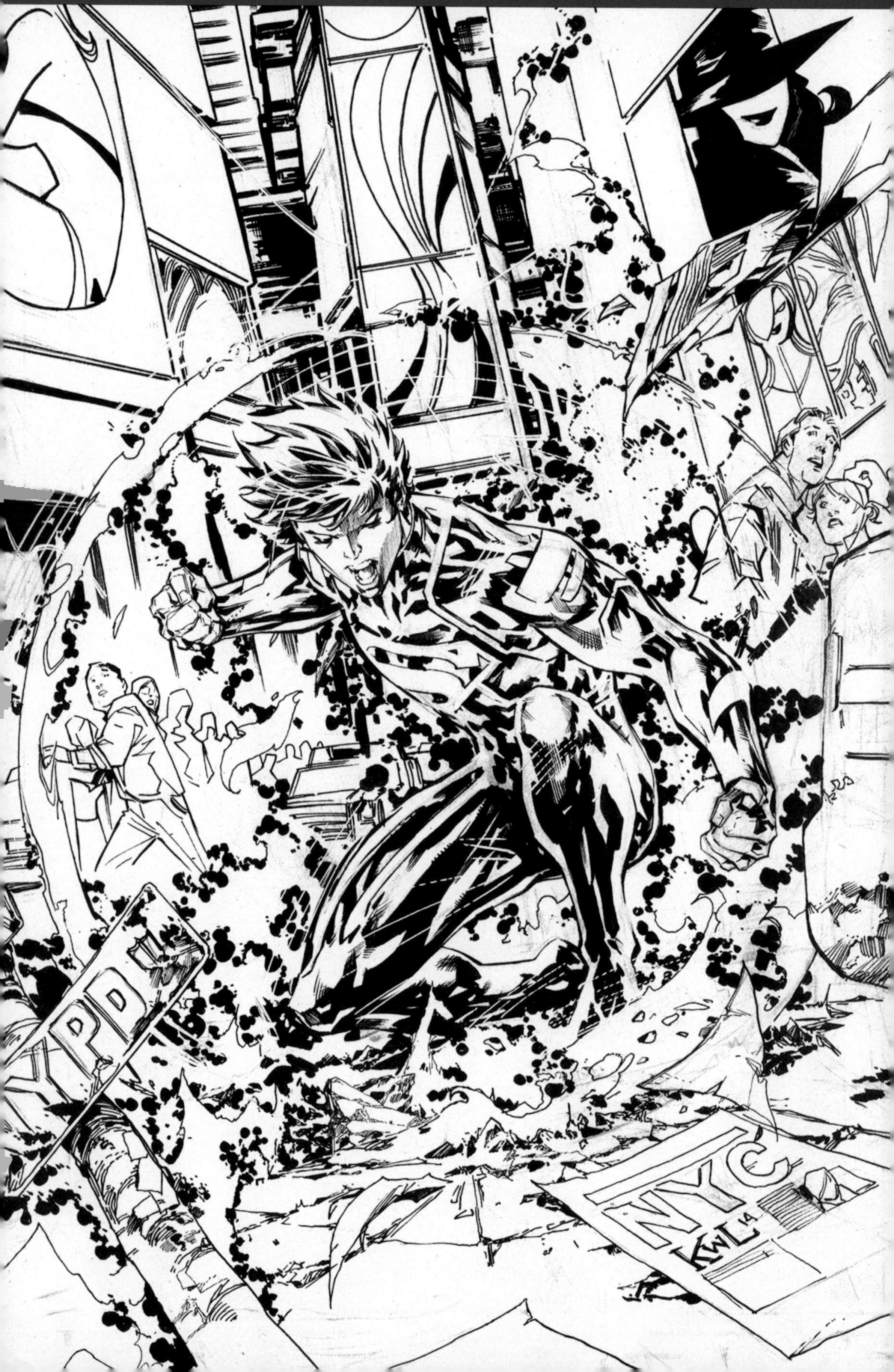
NYPD
NYC
KWL '14

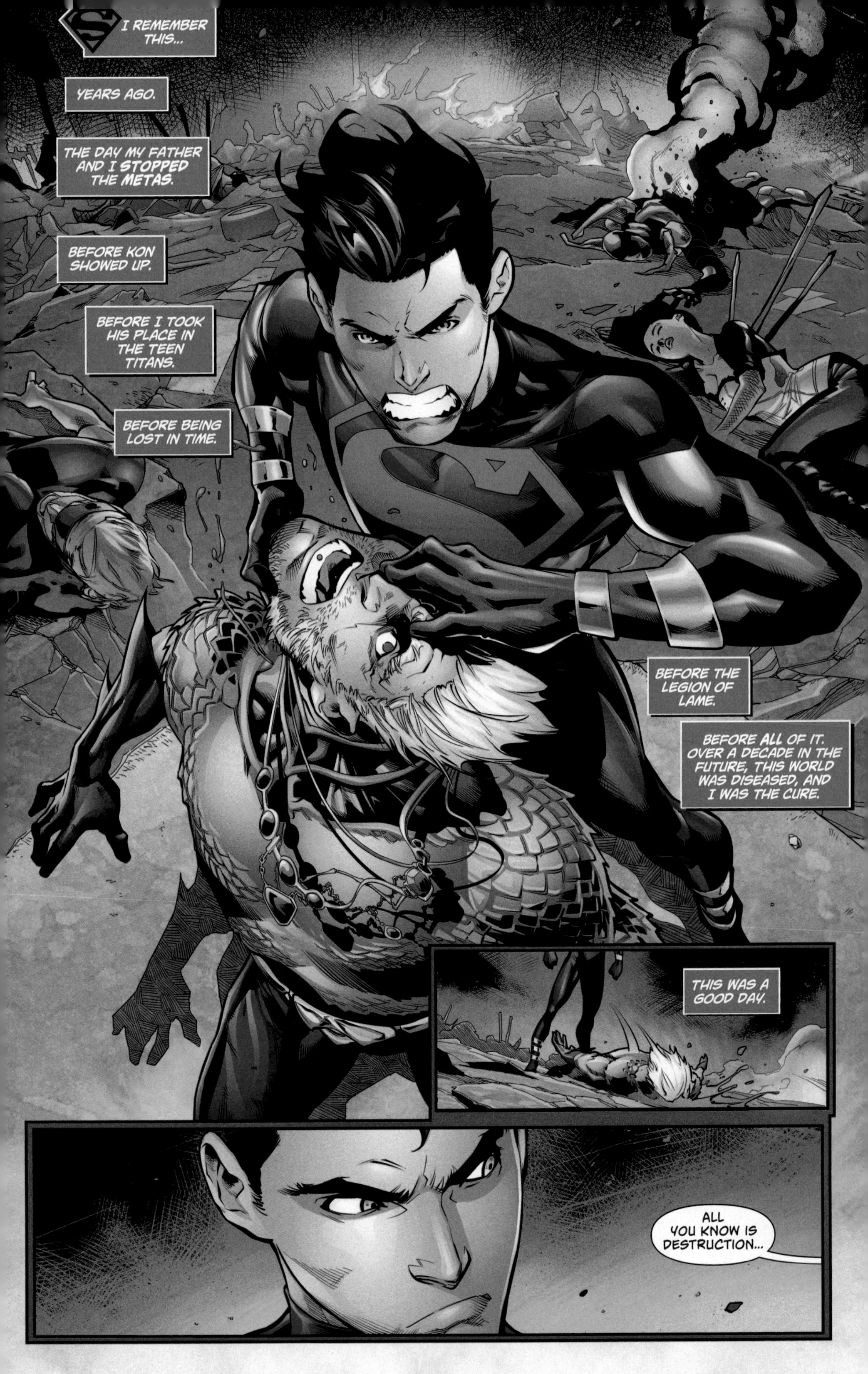
I REMEMBER THIS...
YEARS AGO.
THE DAY MY FATHER AND I STOPPED THE METAS.
BEFORE KON SHOWED UP.
BEFORE I TOOK HIS PLACE IN THE TEEN TITANS.
BEFORE BEING LOST IN TIME.
BEFORE THE LEGION OF LAME.
BEFORE ALL OF IT. OVER A DECADE IN THE FUTURE, THIS WORLD WAS DISEASED, AND I WAS THE CURE.
THIS WAS A GOOD DAY.
ALL YOU KNOW IS DESTRUCTION...

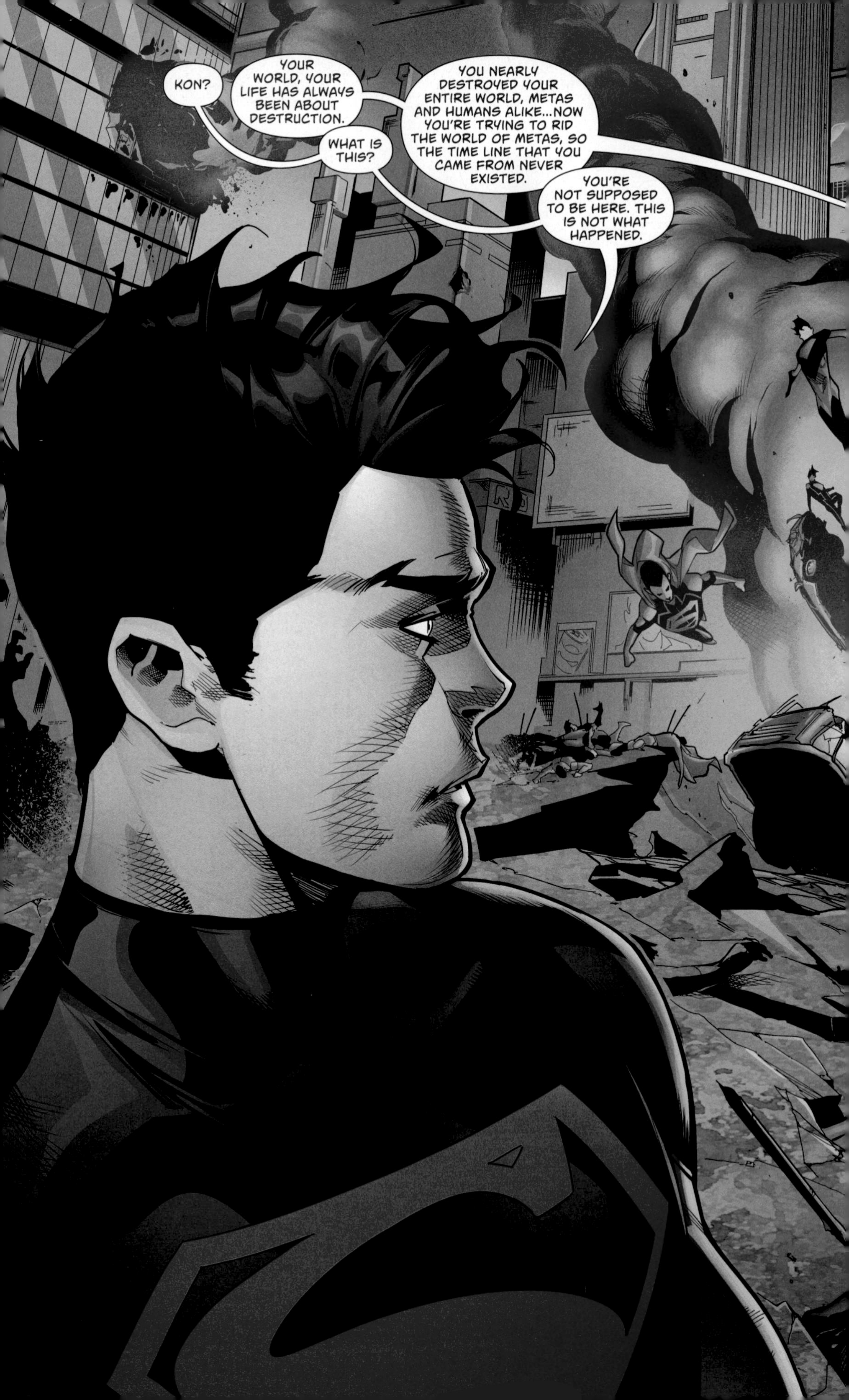
KON?
YOUR WORLD, YOUR LIFE HAS ALWAYS BEEN ABOUT DESTRUCTION.
WHAT IS THIS?
YOU NEARLY DESTROYED YOUR ENTIRE WORLD, METAS AND HUMANS ALIKE...NOW YOU'RE TRYING TO RID THE WORLD OF METAS, SO THE TIME LINE THAT YOU CAME FROM NEVER EXISTED.
YOU'RE NOT SUPPOSED TO BE HERE. THIS IS NOT WHAT HAPPENED.

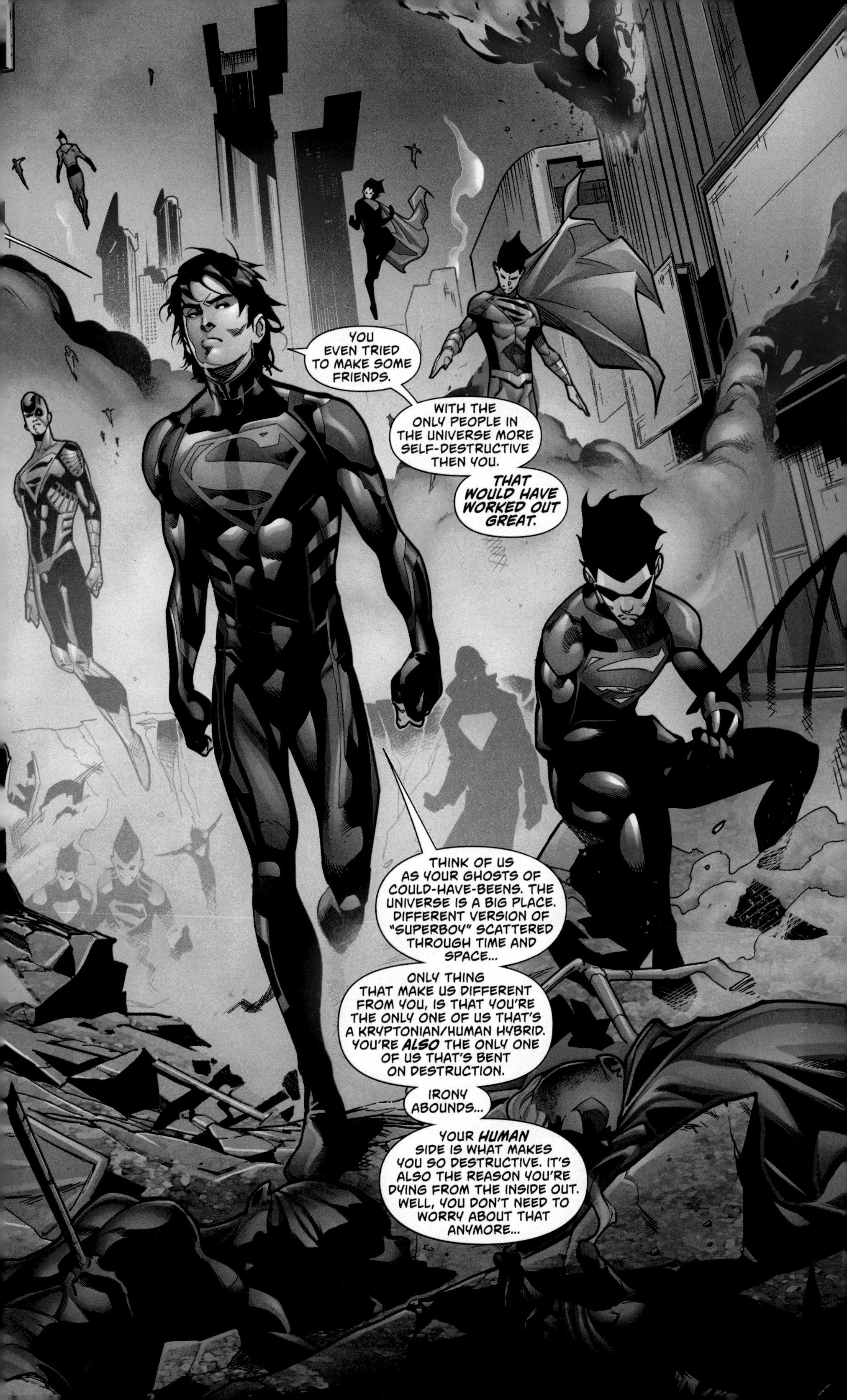
YOU EVEN TRIED TO MAKE SOME FRIENDS.
WITH THE ONLY PEOPLE IN THE UNIVERSE MORE SELF-DESTRUCTIVE THEN YOU.
THAT WOULD HAVE WORKED OUT GREAT.
THINK OF US AS YOUR GHOSTS OF COULD-HAVE-BEENS. THE UNIVERSE IS A BIG PLACE. DIFFERENT VERSION OF "SUPERBOY" SCATTERED THROUGH TIME AND SPACE...
ONLY THING THAT MAKE US DIFFERENT FROM YOU, IS THAT YOU'RE THE ONLY ONE OF US THAT'S A KRYPTONIAN/HUMAN HYBRID. YOU'RE ALSO THE ONLY ONE OF US THAT'S BENT ON DESTRUCTION.
IRONY ABOUNDS...
YOUR HUMAN SIDE IS WHAT MAKES YOU SO DESTRUCTIVE. IT'S ALSO THE REASON YOU'RE DYING FROM THE INSIDE OUT. WELL, YOU DON'T NEED TO WORRY ABOUT THAT ANYMORE...

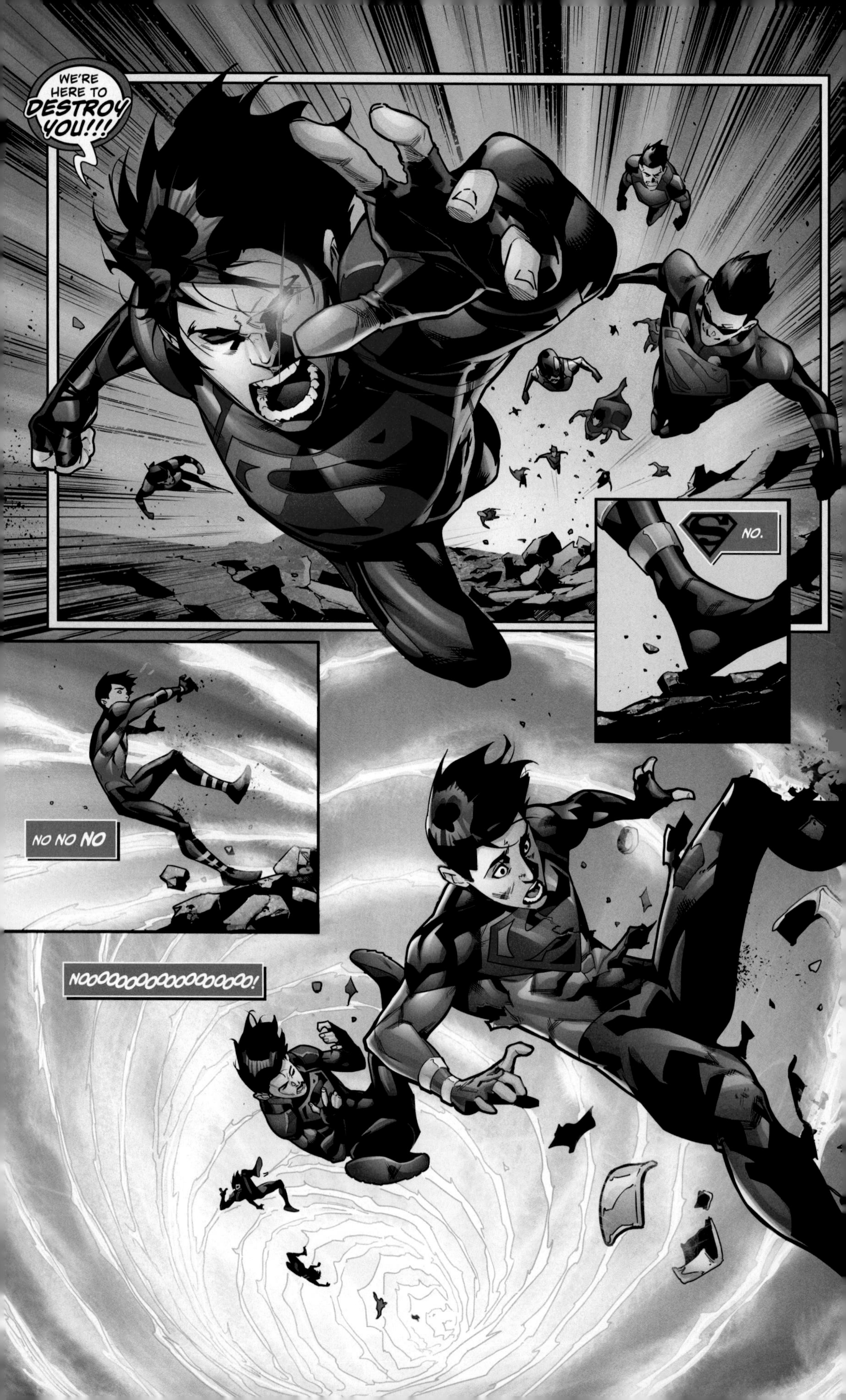
WE'RE HERE TO DESTROY YOU!!!
NO.
NO NO NO
NOOOOOOOOOOOOOOOOO!

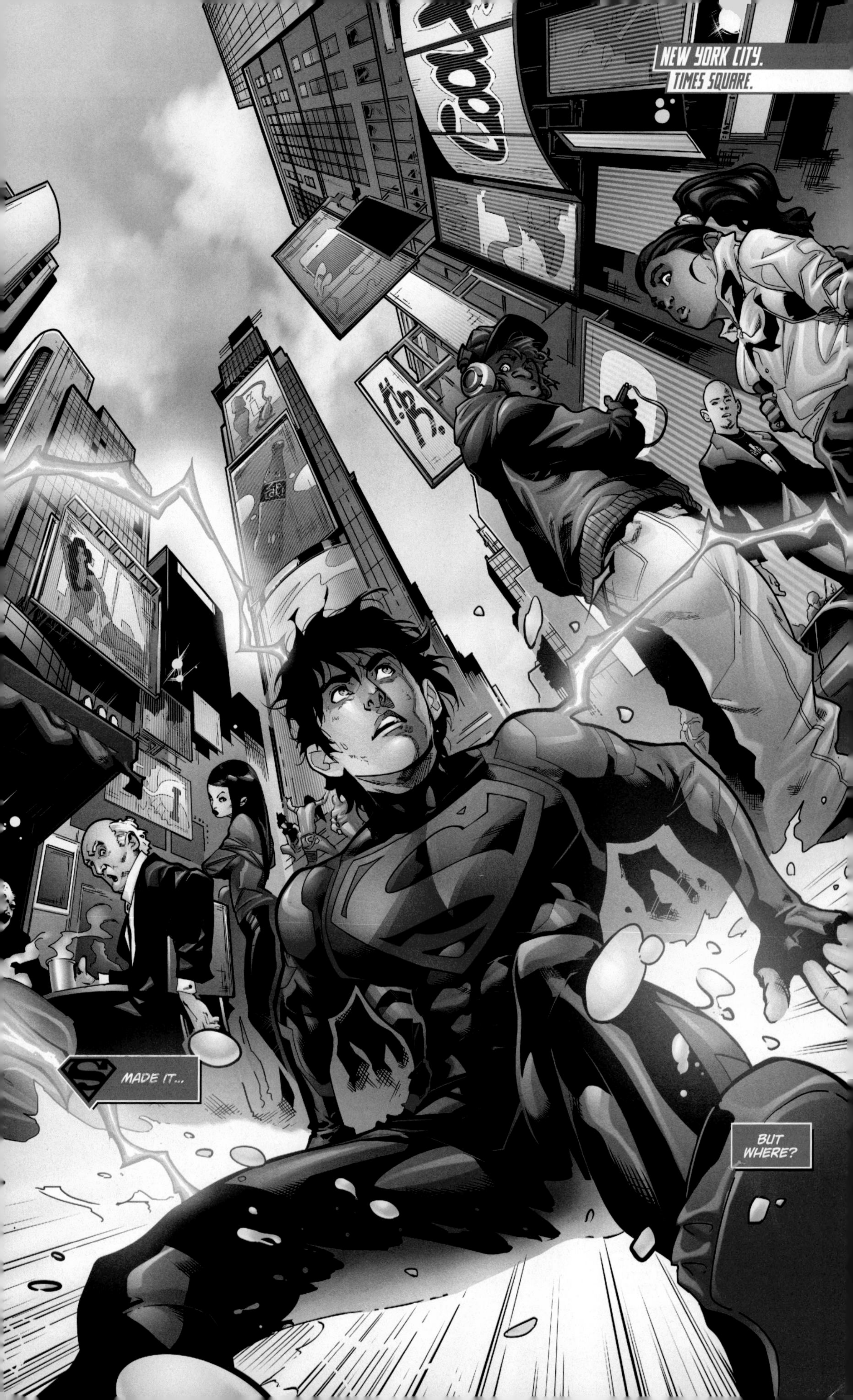
NEW YORK CITY.
TIMES SQUARE.
MADE IT...
BUT WHERE?

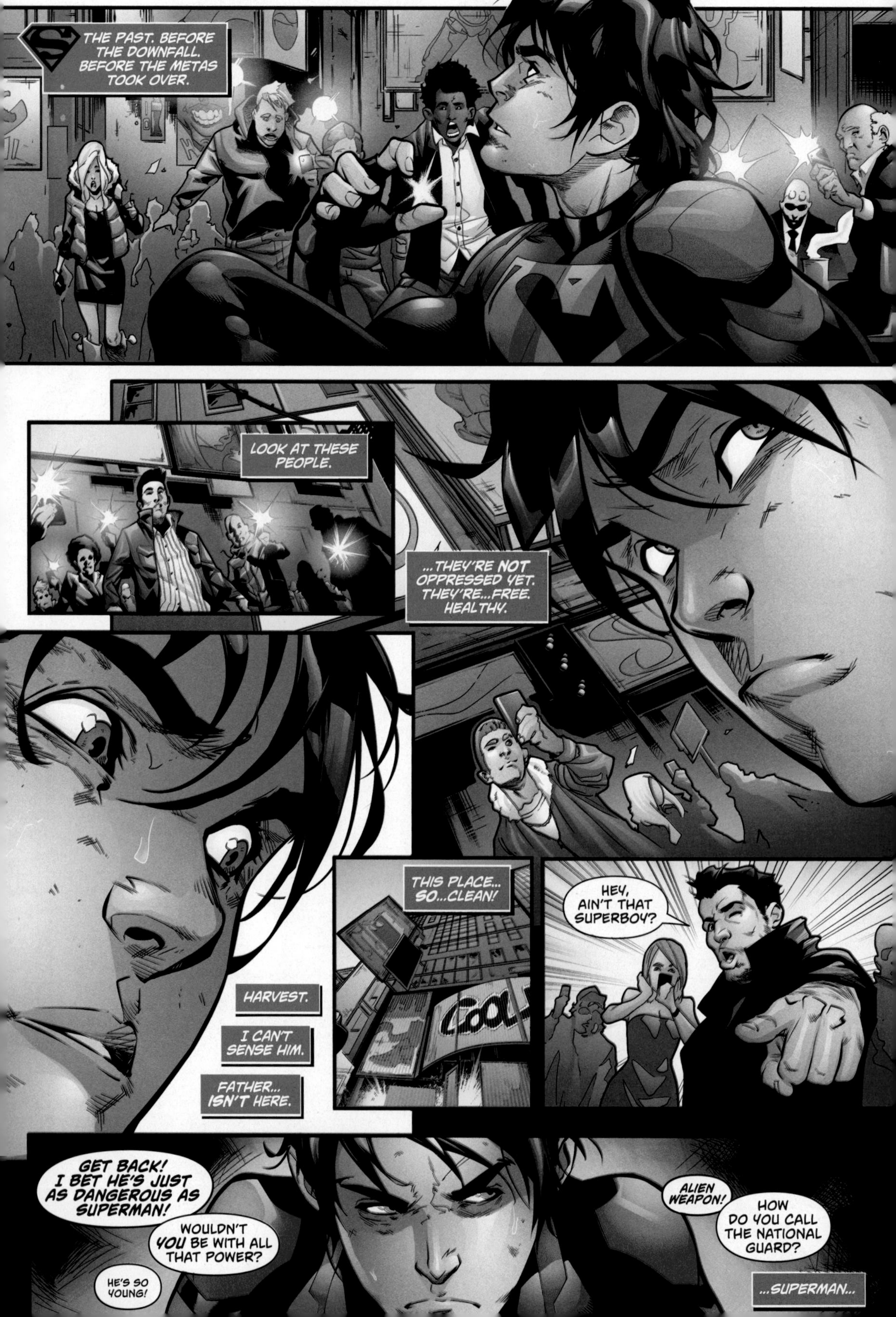
THE PAST. BEFORE THE DOWNFALL. BEFORE THE METAS TOOK OVER.
LOOK AT THESE PEOPLE.
...THEY'RE NOT OPPRESSED YET. THEY'RE...FREE. HEALTHY.
HARVEST.
I CAN'T SENSE HIM.
FATHER... ISN'T HERE.
THIS PLACE... SO...CLEAN!
HEY, AIN'T THAT SUPERBOY?
GET BACK! I BET HE'S JUST AS DANGEROUS AS SUPERMAN!
WOULDN'T YOU BE WITH ALL THAT POWER?
HE'S SO YOUNG!
ALIEN WEAPON!
HOW DO YOU CALL THE NATIONAL GUARD?
...SUPERMAN...

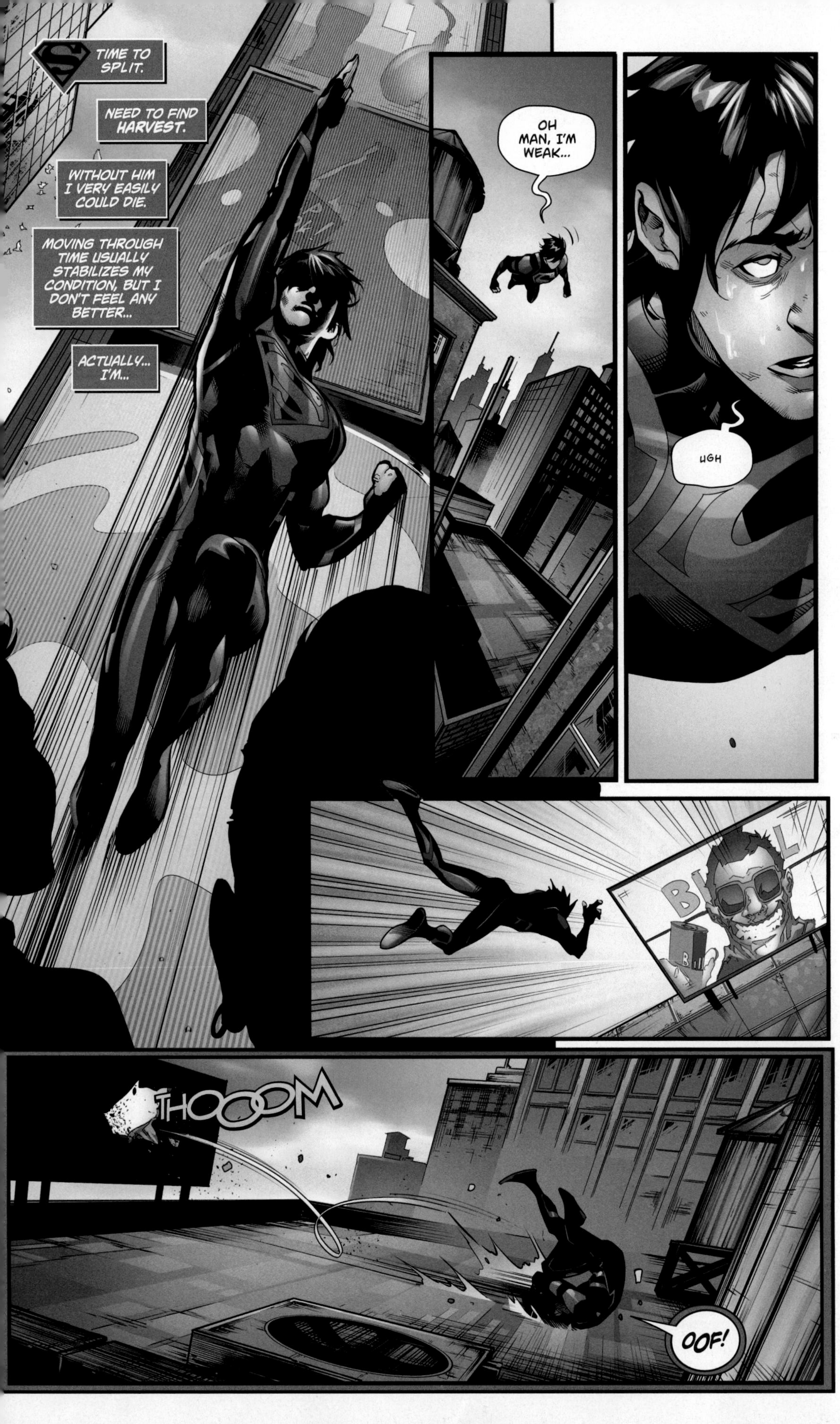

TIME TO SPLIT.
NEED TO FIND HARVEST.
WITHOUT HIM I VERY EASILY COULD DIE.
MOVING THROUGH TIME USUALLY STABILIZES MY CONDITION, BUT I DON'T FEEL ANY BETTER...
ACTUALLY... I'M...
OH MAN, I'M WEAK...
UGH
THOOOM
OOF!

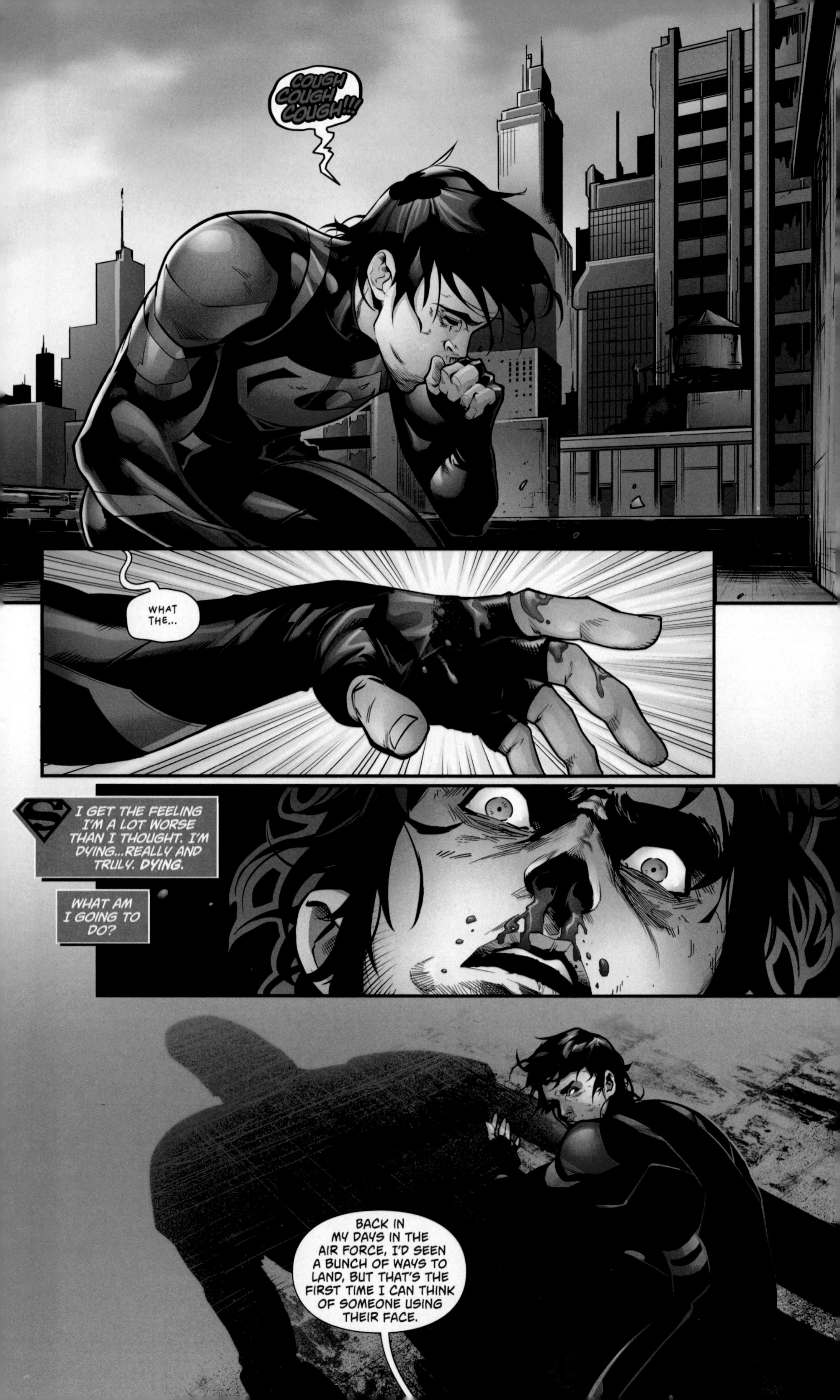
COUGH COUGH COUGH!!!
WHAT THE...
I GET THE FEELING I'M A LOT WORSE THAN I THOUGHT. I'M DYING...REALLY AND TRULY. DYING.
WHAT AM I GOING TO DO?
BACK IN MY DAYS IN THE AIR FORCE, I'D SEEN A BUNCH OF WAYS TO LAND, BUT THAT'S THE FIRST TIME I CAN THINK OF SOMEONE USING THEIR FACE.

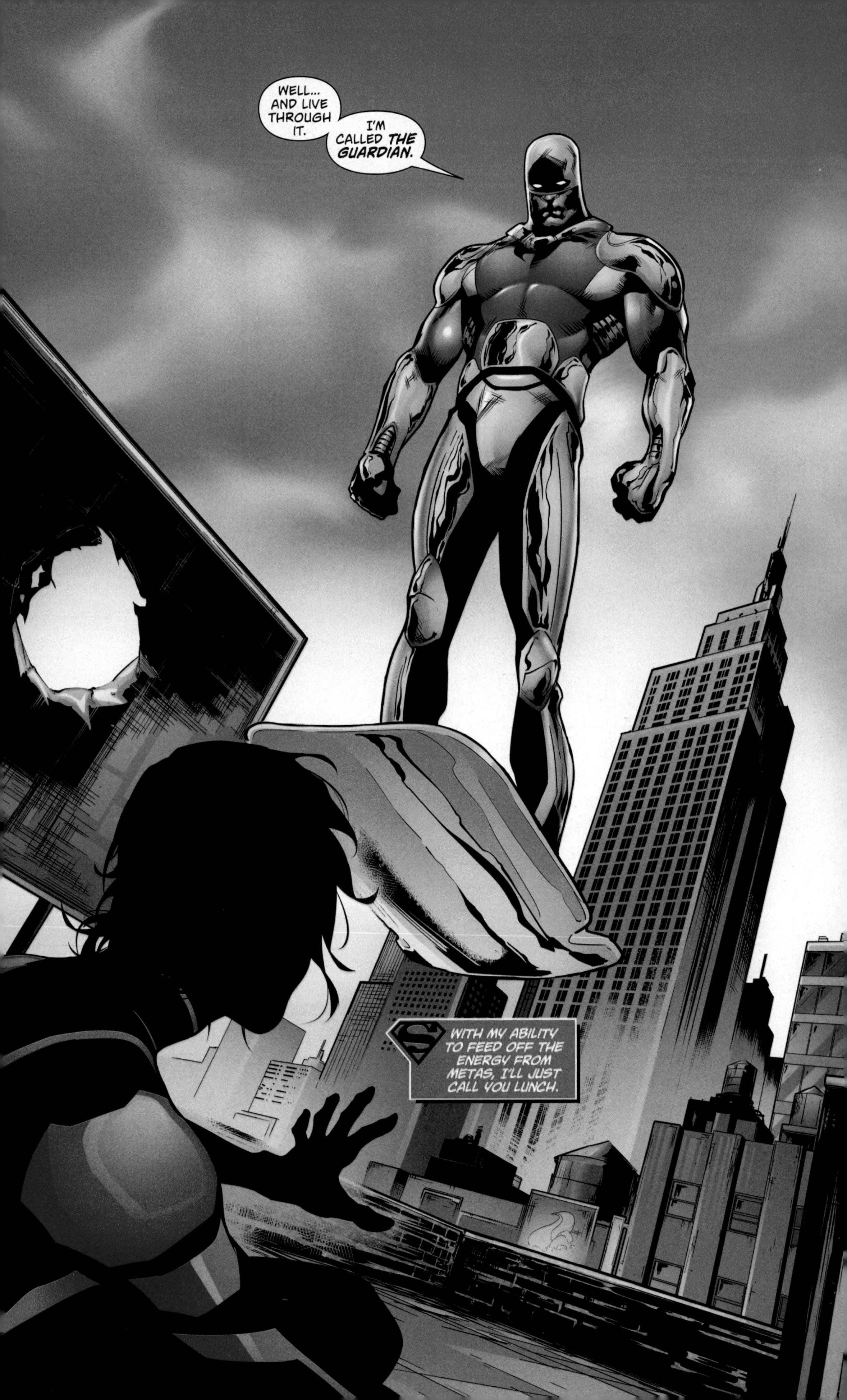
WELL... AND LIVE THROUGH IT.
I'M CALLED THE GUARDIAN.
WITH MY ABILITY TO FEED OFF THE ENERGY FROM METAS, I'LL JUST CALL YOU LUNCH.

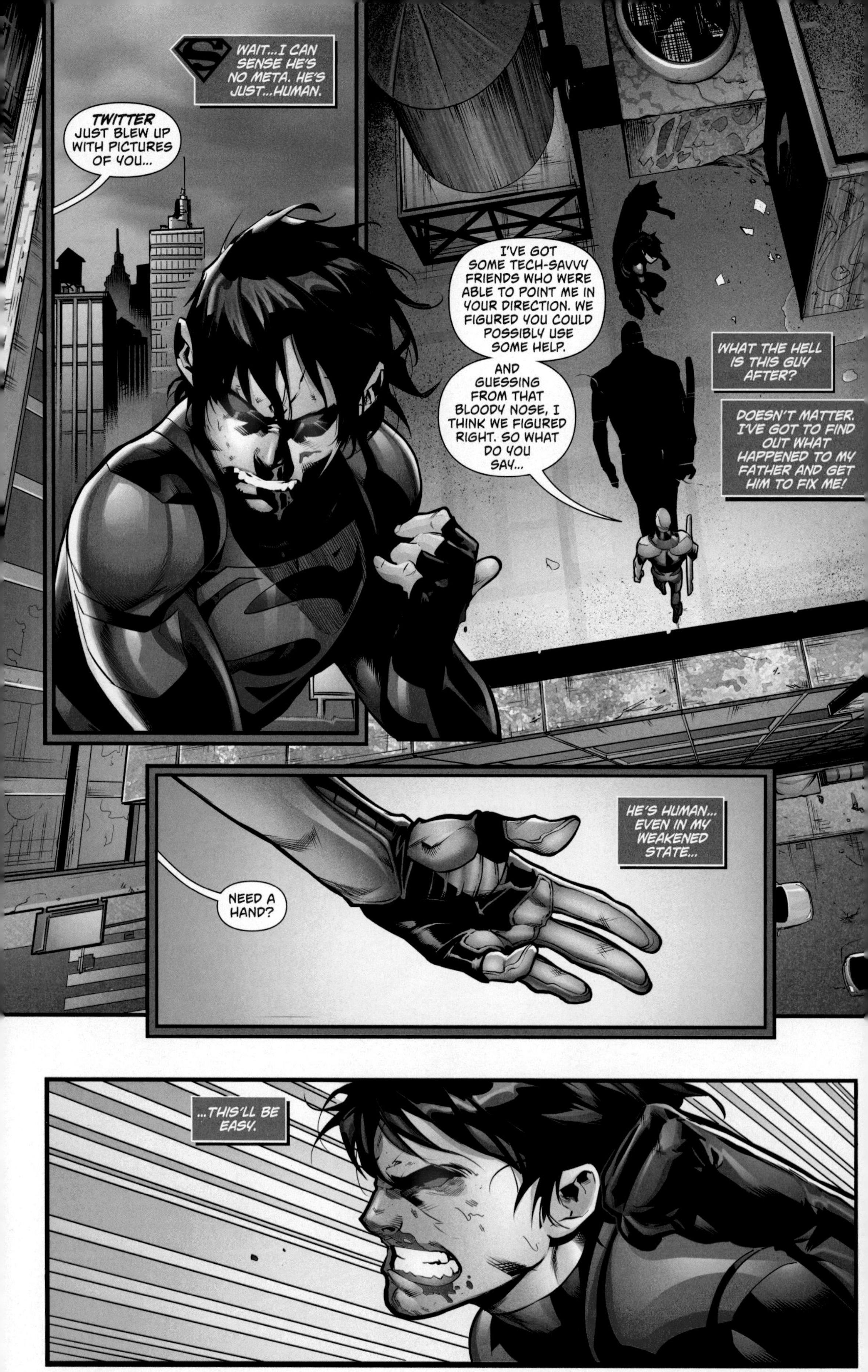
WAIT...I CAN SENSE HE'S NO META. HE'S JUST...HUMAN.
TWITTER JUST BLEW UP WITH PICTURES OF YOU...
I'VE GOT SOME TECH-SAVVY FRIENDS WHO WERE ABLE TO POINT ME IN YOUR DIRECTION. WE FIGURED YOU COULD POSSIBLY USE SOME HELP.
AND GUESSING FROM THAT BLOODY NOSE, I THINK WE FIGURED RIGHT. SO WHAT DO YOU SAY...
WHAT THE HELL IS THIS GUY AFTER?
DOESN'T MATTER. I'VE GOT TO FIND OUT WHAT HAPPENED TO MY FATHER AND GET HIM TO FIX ME!
NEED A HAND?
HE'S HUMAN... EVEN IN MY WEAKENED STATE...
...THIS'LL BE EASY.

CHILL, DUDE.

YOU REALLY DON'T LOOK SO GOOD.

DAMN.

CHURP-ZIT

BASE, THIS IS GUARDIAN-01, YOU READ ME? OVER.

LOUD AND CLEAR, G-1. EVERYTHING COOL?

BEEP-DEP

MADE CONTACT WITH THE MAGICALLY APPEARING SUPERBOY. HE'S OUT COLD NOW, I'M GOING TO BRING HIM.

HE'S GOT SOME MINOR BLEEDING FROM HIS NOSE, THOUGH IT COULD MEAN SOME SORT OF WORSE HEMORRHAGE...BETTER HAVE A MED-UNIT READY TO MEET US...

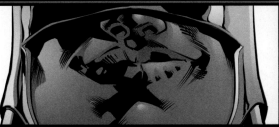

THIS KID SEEMS MESSED UP FROM HEAD TO TOE...BUT MOSTLY IN THE HEAD.

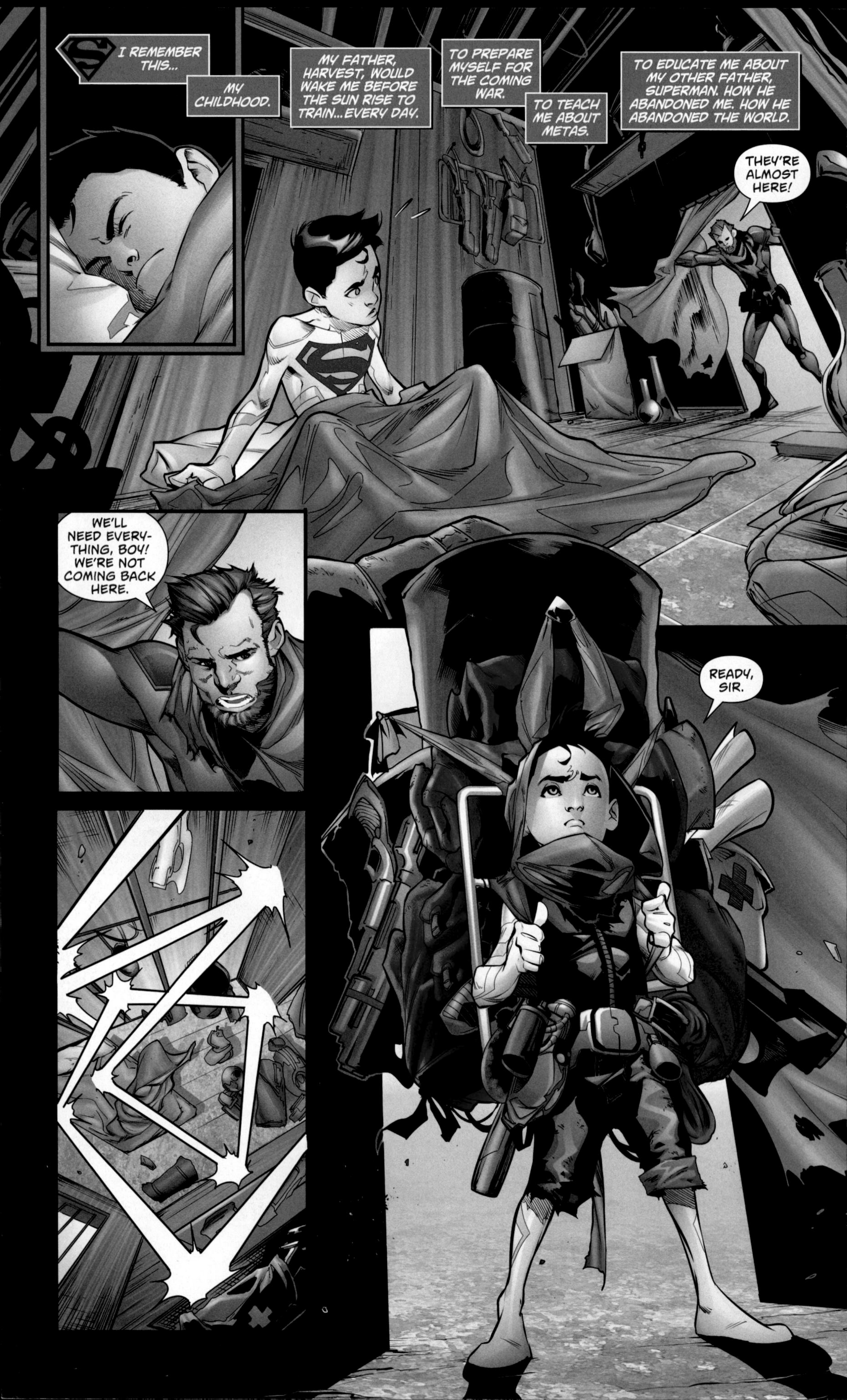

I REMEMBER THIS...
MY CHILDHOOD.
MY FATHER, HARVEST, WOULD WAKE ME BEFORE THE SUN RISE TO TRAIN...EVERY DAY.
TO PREPARE MYSELF FOR THE COMING WAR.
TO TEACH ME ABOUT METAS.
TO EDUCATE ME ABOUT MY OTHER FATHER, SUPERMAN. HOW HE ABANDONED ME. HOW HE ABANDONED THE WORLD.
THEY'RE ALMOST HERE!
WE'LL NEED EVERYTHING, BOY! WE'RE NOT COMING BACK HERE.
READY, SIR.

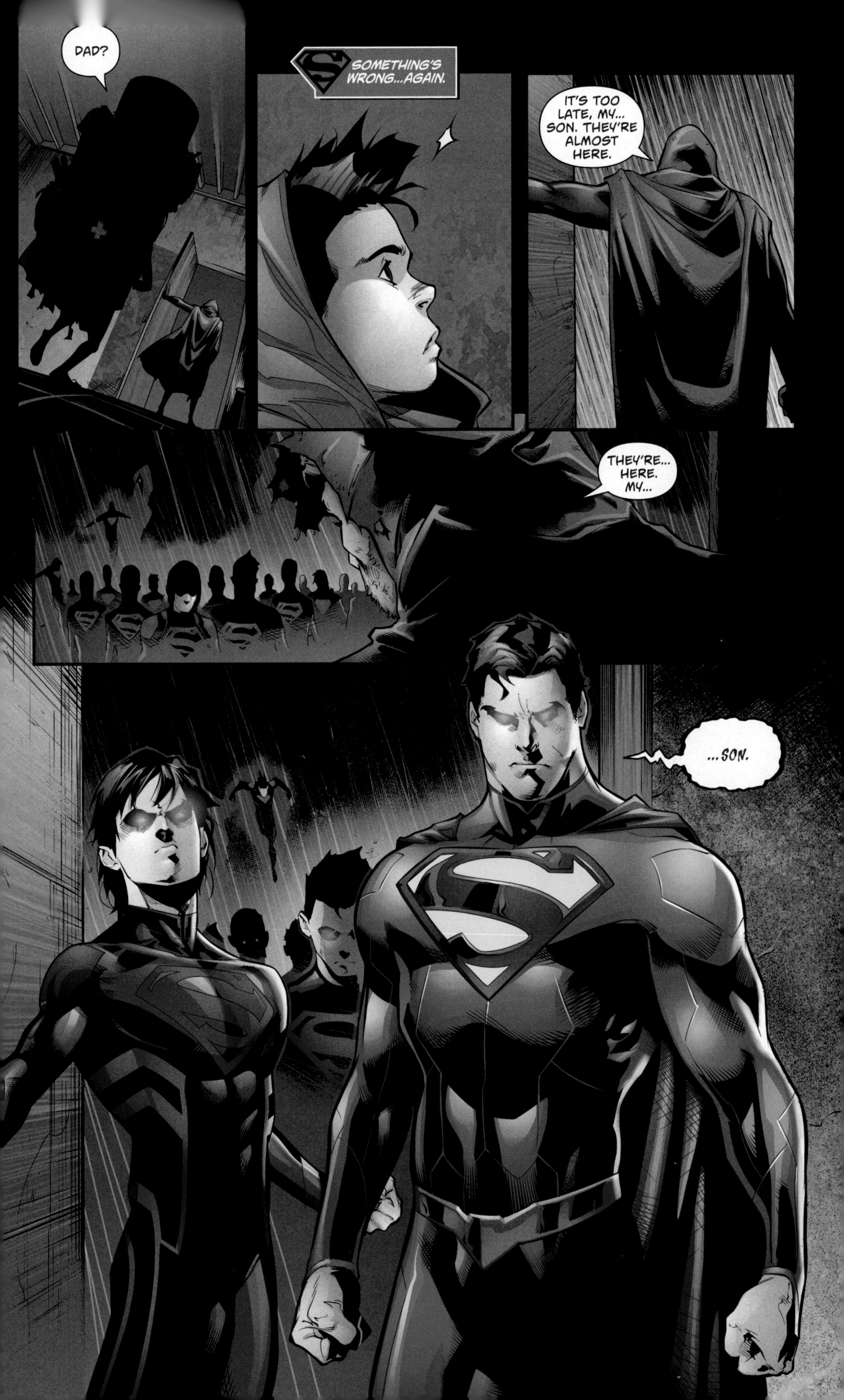
DAD?
SOMETHING'S WRONG...AGAIN.
IT'S TOO LATE, MY... SON. THEY'RE ALMOST HERE.
THEY'RE... HERE. MY...
...SON.

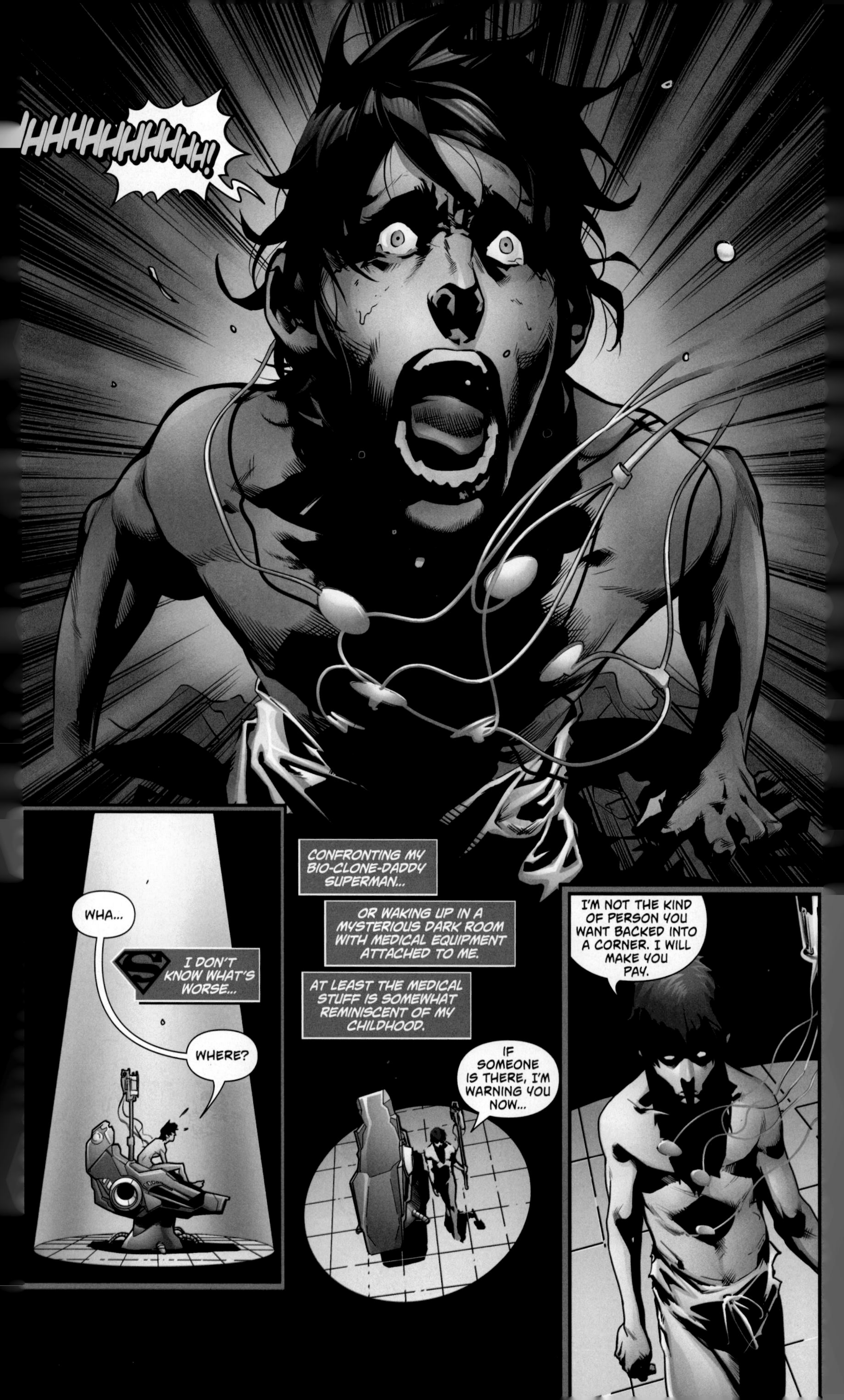
HHHHHHHHHHH!
WHA...
I DON'T KNOW WHAT'S WORSE...
CONFRONTING MY BIO-CLONE-DADDY SUPERMAN...
OR WAKING UP IN A MYSTERIOUS DARK ROOM WITH MEDICAL EQUIPMENT ATTACHED TO ME.
AT LEAST THE MEDICAL STUFF IS SOMEWHAT REMINISCENT OF MY CHILDHOOD.
WHERE?
IF SOMEONE IS THERE, I'M WARNING YOU NOW...
I'M NOT THE KIND OF PERSON YOU WANT BACKED INTO A CORNER. I WILL MAKE YOU PAY.

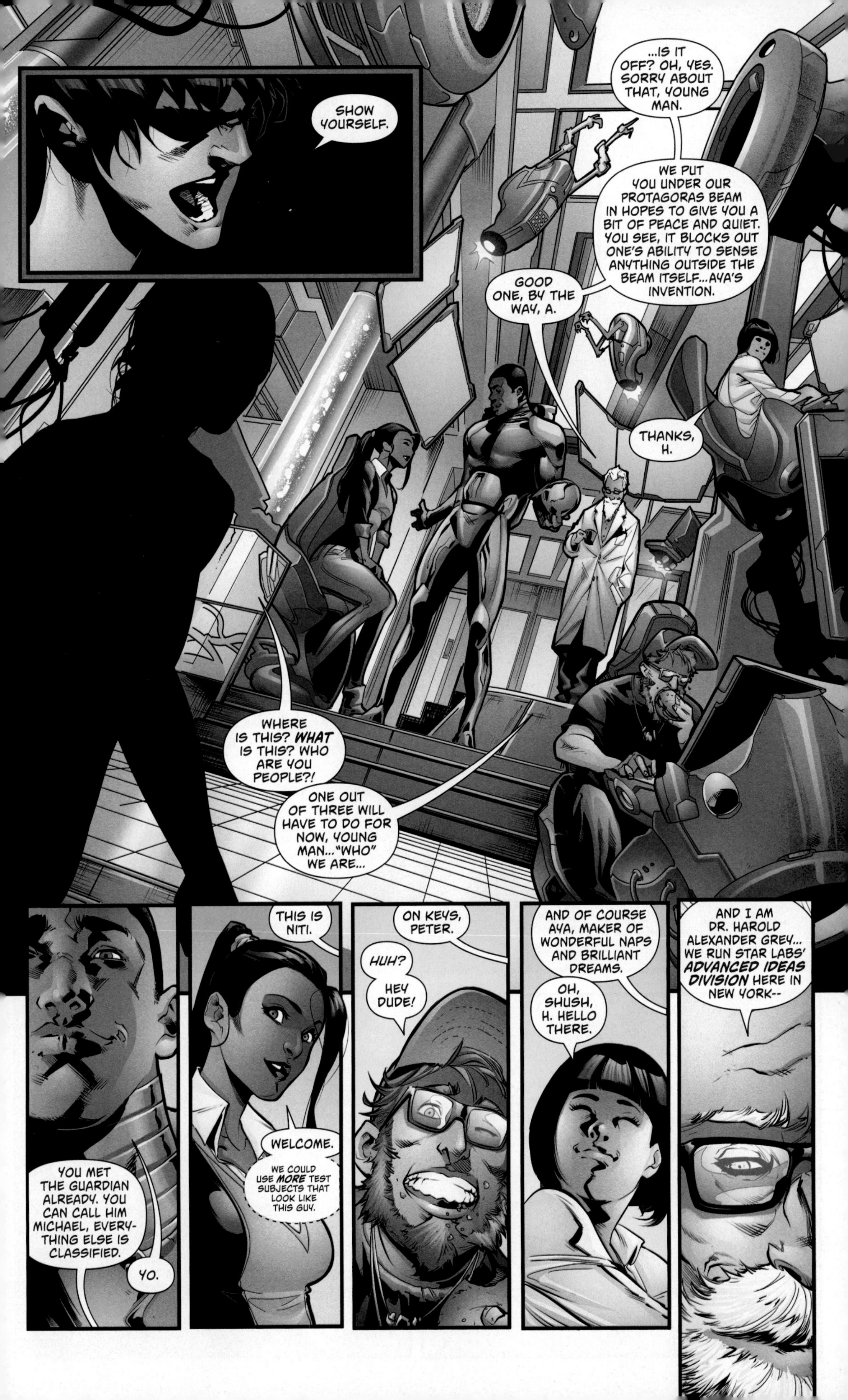
SHOW YOURSELF.
...IS IT OFF? OH, YES. SORRY ABOUT THAT, YOUNG MAN.
WE PUT YOU UNDER OUR PROTAGORAS BEAM IN HOPES TO GIVE YOU A BIT OF PEACE AND QUIET. YOU SEE, IT BLOCKS OUT ONE'S ABILITY TO SENSE ANYTHING OUTSIDE THE BEAM ITSELF...AYA'S INVENTION.
GOOD ONE, BY THE WAY, A.
THANKS, H.
WHERE IS THIS? *WHAT* IS THIS? WHO ARE YOU PEOPLE?!
ONE OUT OF THREE WILL HAVE TO DO FOR NOW, YOUNG MAN... "WHO" WE ARE...
YOU MET THE GUARDIAN ALREADY. YOU CAN CALL HIM MICHAEL, EVERY-THING ELSE IS CLASSIFIED.
YO.
THIS IS NITI.
WELCOME.
WE COULD USE *MORE* TEST SUBJECTS THAT LOOK LIKE THIS GUY.
ON KEYS, PETER.
HUH?
HEY DUDE!
AND OF COURSE AYA, MAKER OF WONDERFUL NAPS AND BRILLIANT DREAMS.
OH, SHUSH, H. HELLO THERE.
AND I AM DR. HAROLD ALEXANDER GREY... WE RUN STAR LABS' *ADVANCED IDEAS DIVISION* HERE IN NEW YORK--

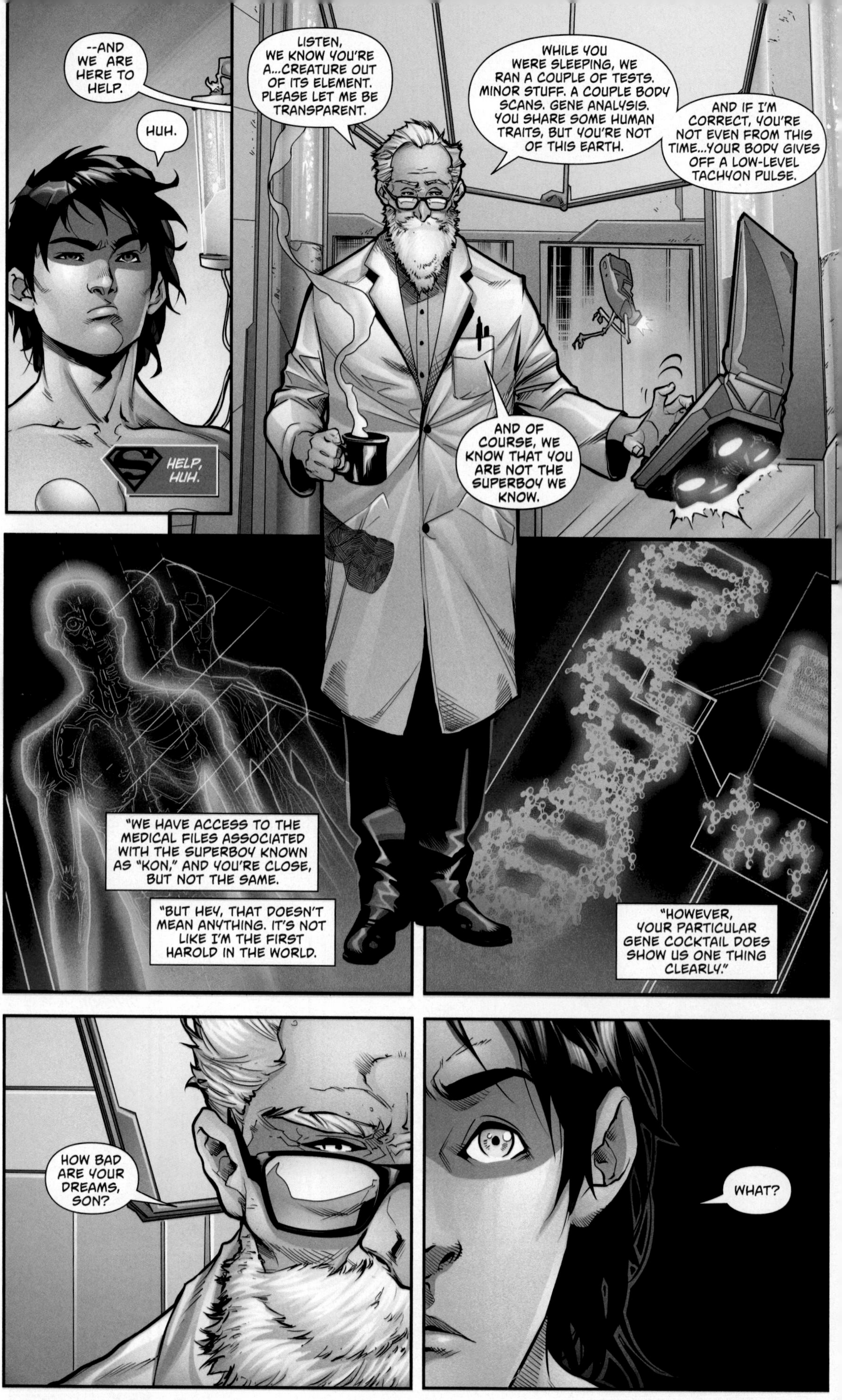
--AND WE ARE HERE TO HELP.
HUH.
HELP, HUH.
LISTEN, WE KNOW YOU'RE A...CREATURE OUT OF ITS ELEMENT. PLEASE LET ME BE TRANSPARENT.
WHILE YOU WERE SLEEPING, WE RAN A COUPLE OF TESTS. MINOR STUFF. A COUPLE BODY SCANS. GENE ANALYSIS. YOU SHARE SOME HUMAN TRAITS, BUT YOU'RE NOT OF THIS EARTH.
AND IF I'M CORRECT, YOU'RE NOT EVEN FROM THIS TIME...YOUR BODY GIVES OFF A LOW-LEVEL TACHYON PULSE.
AND OF COURSE, WE KNOW THAT YOU ARE NOT THE SUPERBOY WE KNOW.
"WE HAVE ACCESS TO THE MEDICAL FILES ASSOCIATED WITH THE SUPERBOY KNOWN AS "KON," AND YOU'RE CLOSE, BUT NOT THE SAME.
"BUT HEY, THAT DOESN'T MEAN ANYTHING. IT'S NOT LIKE I'M THE FIRST HAROLD IN THE WORLD.
"HOWEVER, YOUR PARTICULAR GENE COCKTAIL DOES SHOW US ONE THING CLEARLY."
HOW BAD ARE YOUR DREAMS, SON?
WHAT?

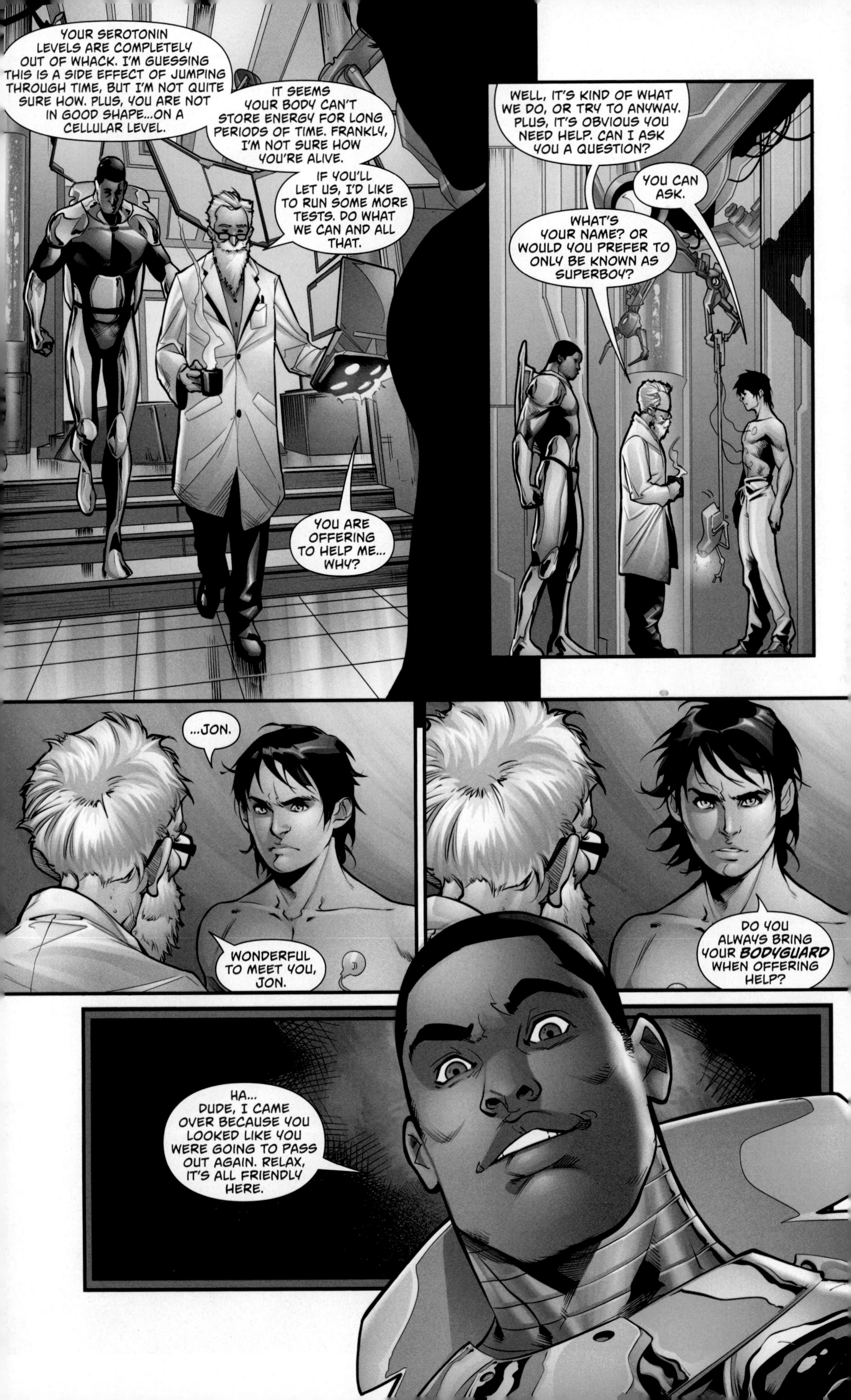
YOUR SEROTONIN LEVELS ARE COMPLETELY OUT OF WHACK. I'M GUESSING THIS IS A SIDE EFFECT OF JUMPING THROUGH TIME, BUT I'M NOT QUITE SURE HOW. PLUS, YOU ARE NOT IN GOOD SHAPE...ON A CELLULAR LEVEL.
IT SEEMS YOUR BODY CAN'T STORE ENERGY FOR LONG PERIODS OF TIME. FRANKLY, I'M NOT SURE HOW YOU'RE ALIVE.
IF YOU'LL LET US, I'D LIKE TO RUN SOME MORE TESTS. DO WHAT WE CAN AND ALL THAT.
YOU ARE OFFERING TO HELP ME... WHY?
WELL, IT'S KIND OF WHAT WE DO, OR TRY TO ANYWAY. PLUS, IT'S OBVIOUS YOU NEED HELP. CAN I ASK YOU A QUESTION?
YOU CAN ASK.
WHAT'S YOUR NAME? OR WOULD YOU PREFER TO ONLY BE KNOWN AS SUPERBOY?
...JON.
WONDERFUL TO MEET YOU, JON.
DO YOU ALWAYS BRING YOUR BODYGUARD WHEN OFFERING HELP?
HA... DUDE, I CAME OVER BECAUSE YOU LOOKED LIKE YOU WERE GOING TO PASS OUT AGAIN. RELAX, IT'S ALL FRIENDLY HERE.

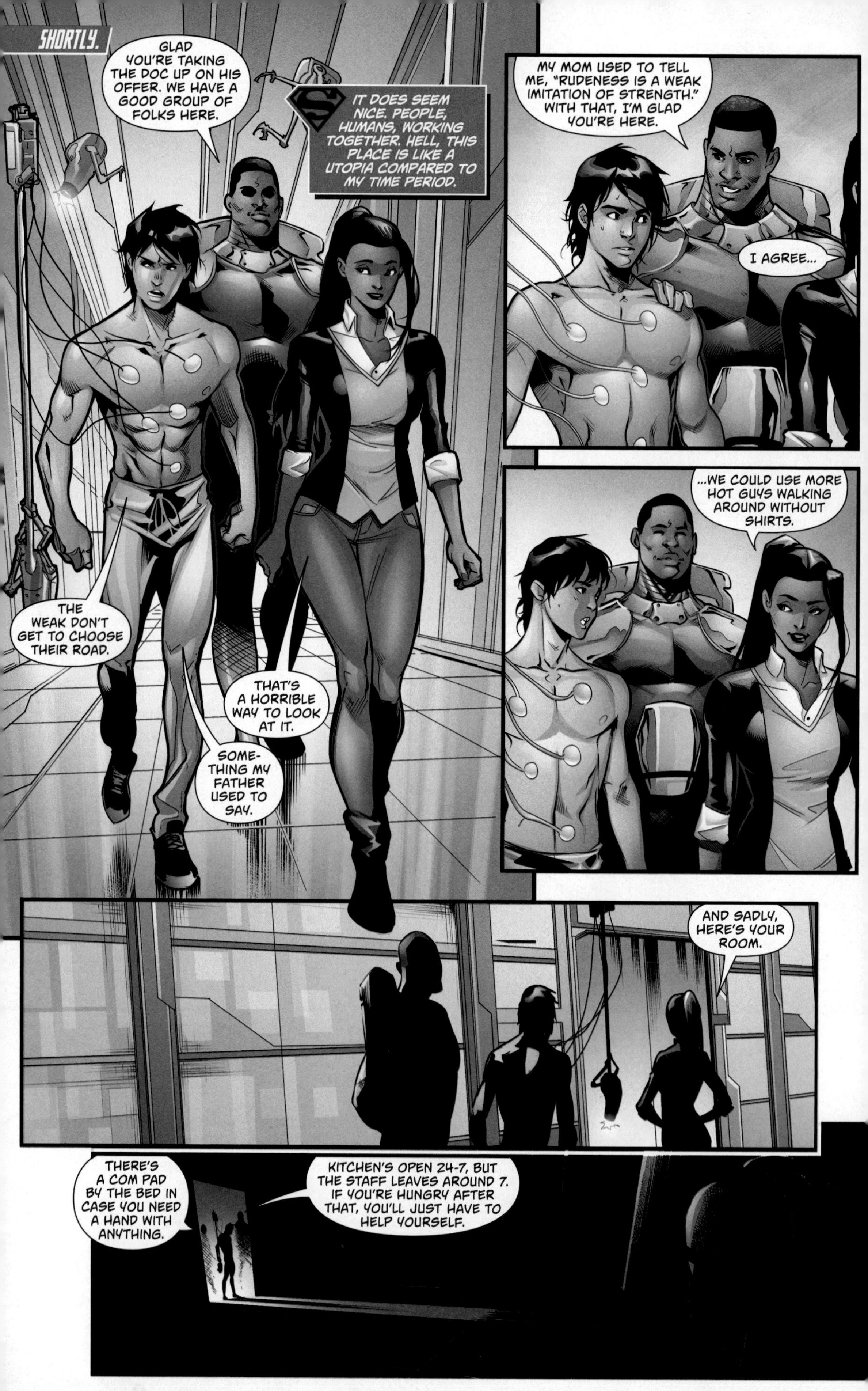
SHORTLY.
GLAD YOU'RE TAKING THE DOC UP ON HIS OFFER. WE HAVE A GOOD GROUP OF FOLKS HERE.
IT DOES SEEM NICE. PEOPLE, HUMANS, WORKING TOGETHER. HELL, THIS PLACE IS LIKE A UTOPIA COMPARED TO MY TIME PERIOD.
THE WEAK DON'T GET TO CHOOSE THEIR ROAD.
THAT'S A HORRIBLE WAY TO LOOK AT IT.
SOME-THING MY FATHER USED TO SAY.
MY MOM USED TO TELL ME, "RUDENESS IS A WEAK IMITATION OF STRENGTH." WITH THAT, I'M GLAD YOU'RE HERE.
I AGREE...
...WE COULD USE MORE HOT GUYS WALKING AROUND WITHOUT SHIRTS.
AND SADLY, HERE'S YOUR ROOM.
THERE'S A COM PAD BY THE BED IN CASE YOU NEED A HAND WITH ANYTHING.
KITCHEN'S OPEN 24-7, BUT THE STAFF LEAVES AROUND 7. IF YOU'RE HUNGRY AFTER THAT, YOU'LL JUST HAVE TO HELP YOURSELF.

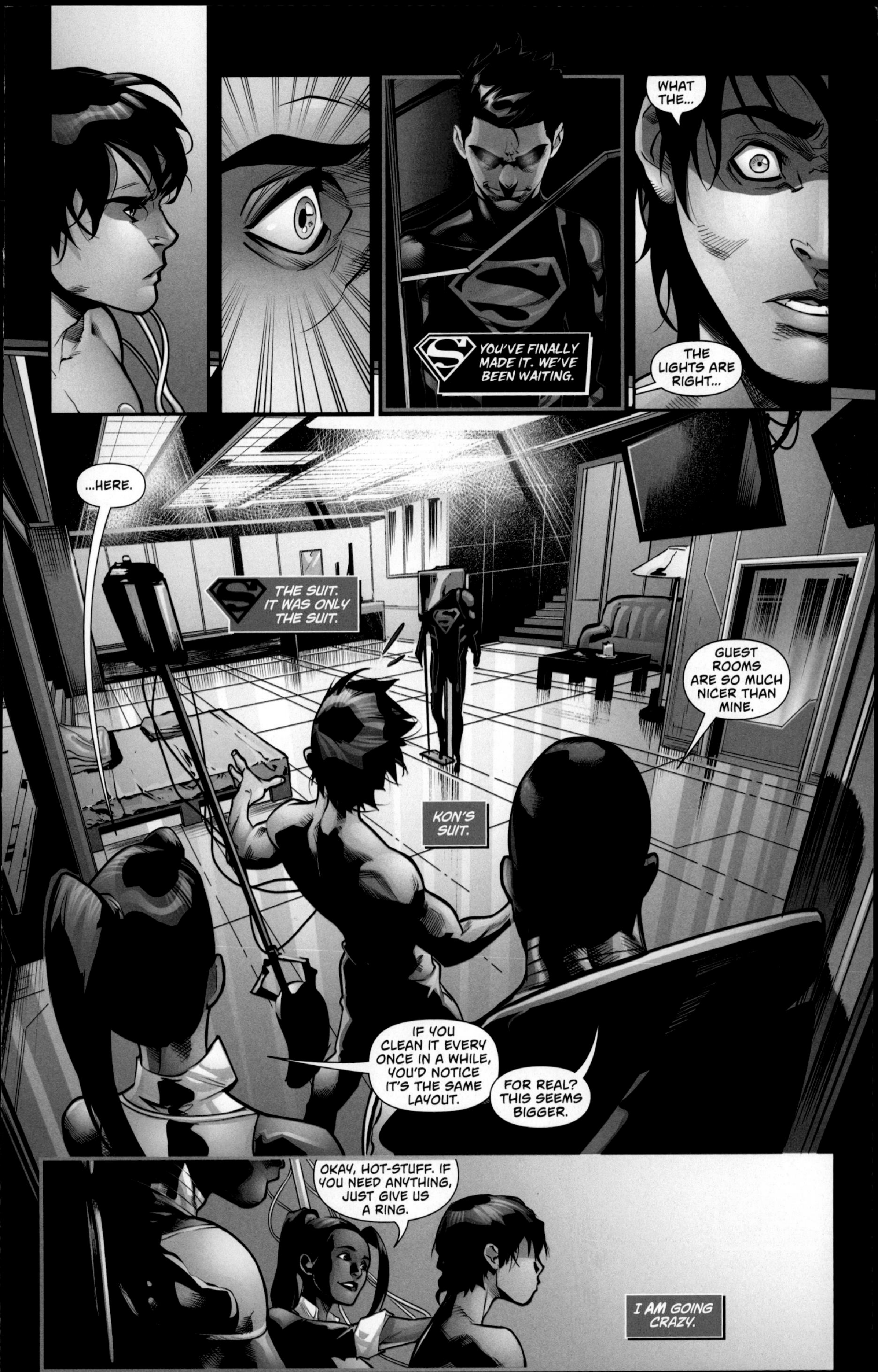
WHAT THE...
YOU'VE FINALLY MADE IT. WE'VE BEEN WAITING.
THE LIGHTS ARE RIGHT...
...HERE.
THE SUIT. IT WAS ONLY THE SUIT.
GUEST ROOMS ARE SO MUCH NICER THAN MINE.
KON'S SUIT.
IF YOU CLEAN IT EVERY ONCE IN A WHILE, YOU'D NOTICE IT'S THE SAME LAYOUT.
FOR REAL? THIS SEEMS BIGGER.
OKAY, HOT-STUFF. IF YOU NEED ANYTHING, JUST GIVE US A RING.
I AM GOING CRAZY.

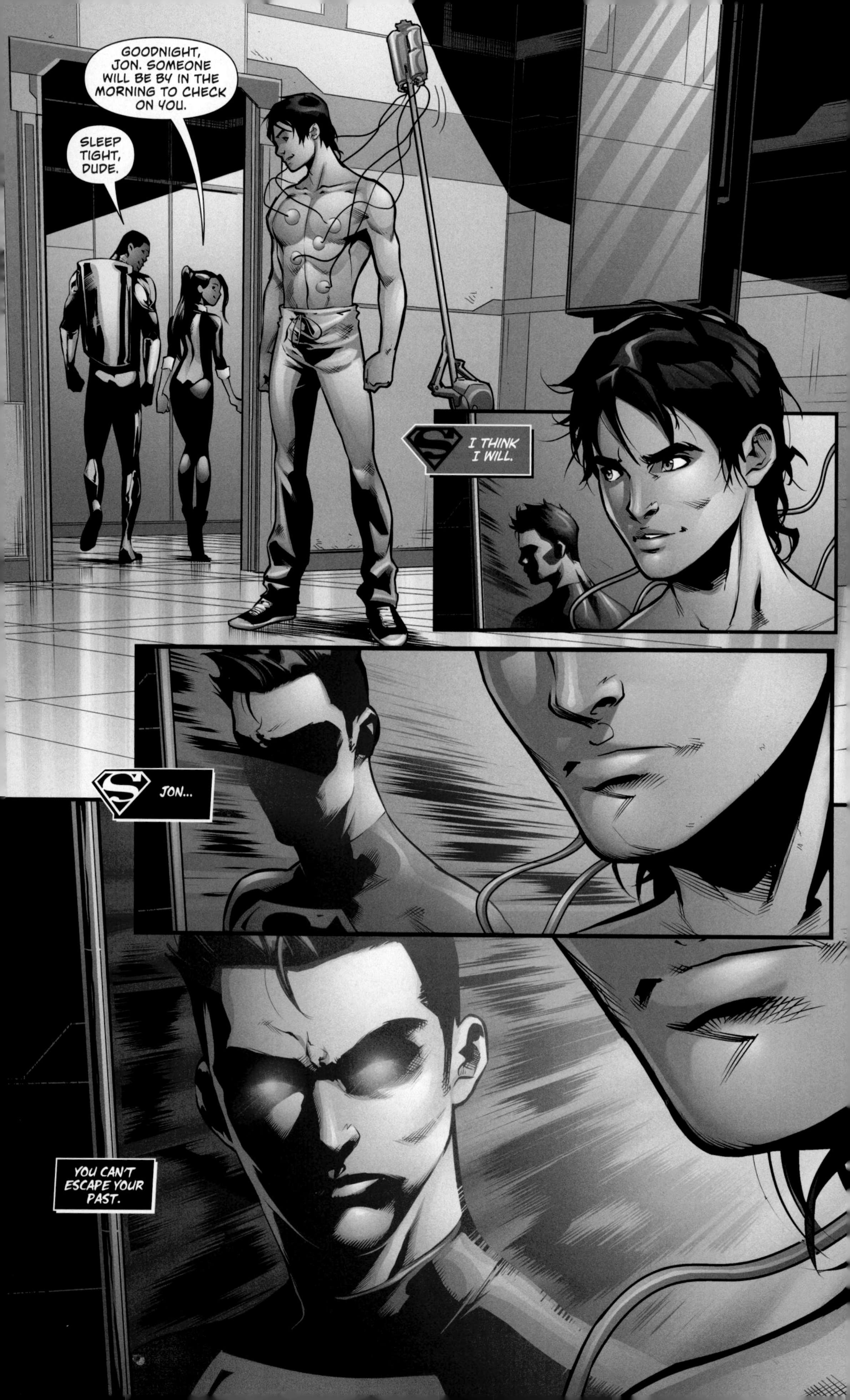
GOODNIGHT, JON. SOMEONE WILL BE BY IN THE MORNING TO CHECK ON YOU.
SLEEP TIGHT, DUDE.
I THINK I WILL.
JON...
YOU CAN'T ESCAPE YOUR PAST.

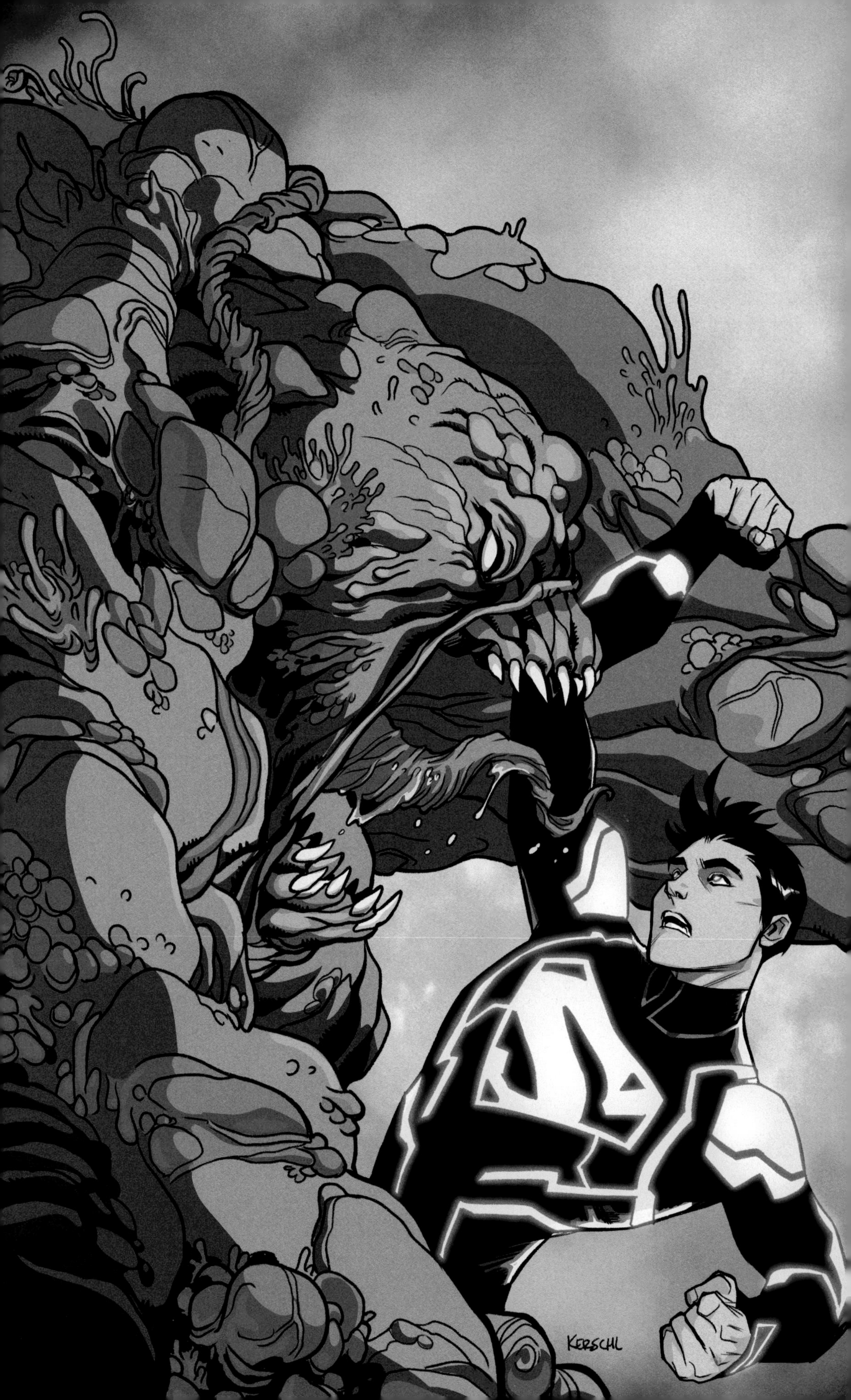
KERSCHL

DELIVERY

AARON KUDER writer **JORGE JIMÉNEZ** artist **TANYA** and **RICHARD HORIE** colorists
CARLOS M. MANGUAL letterer cover art by **KARL KERSCHL** and **MIKE ATIYEH**

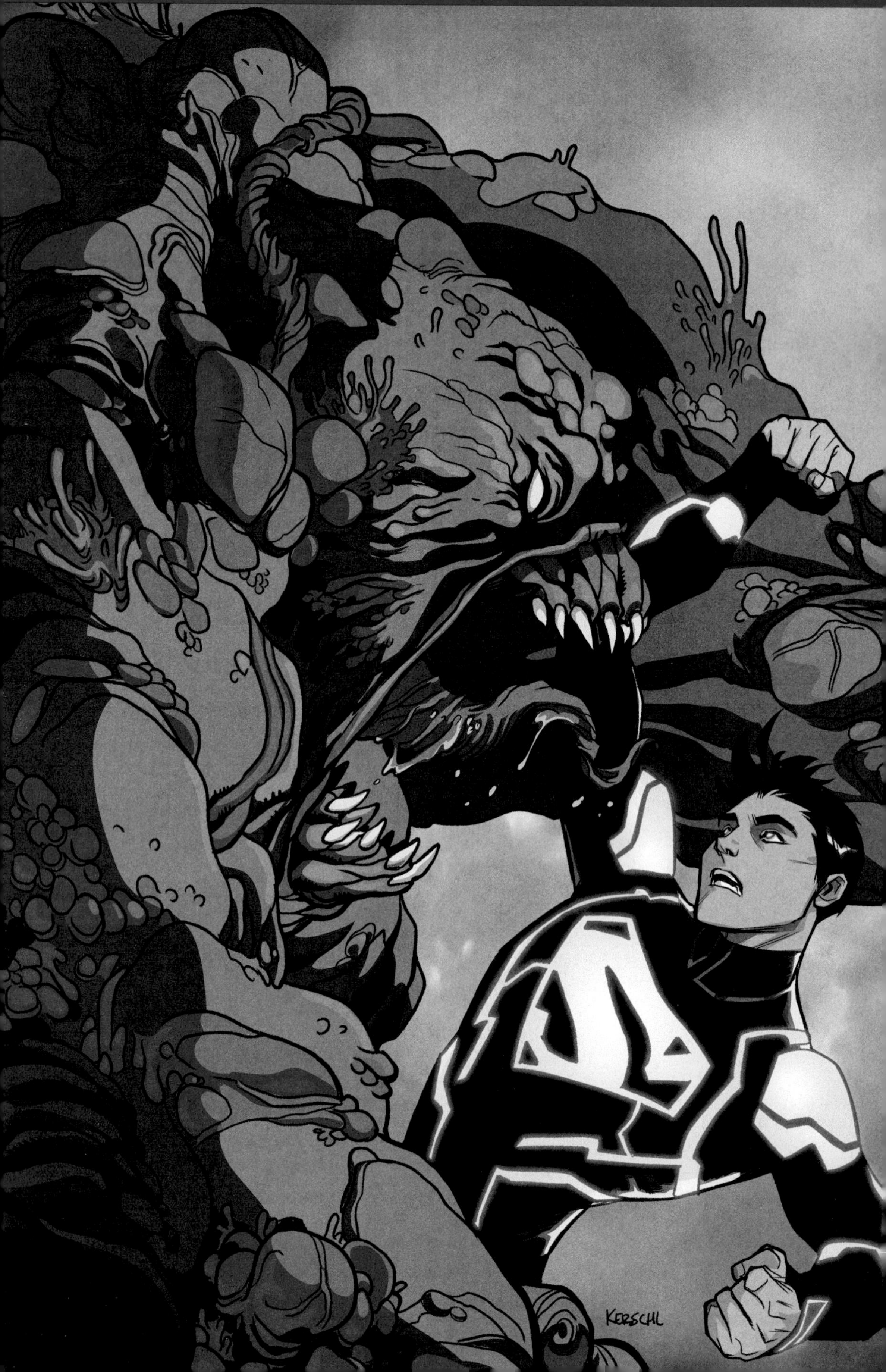
KERSCHL

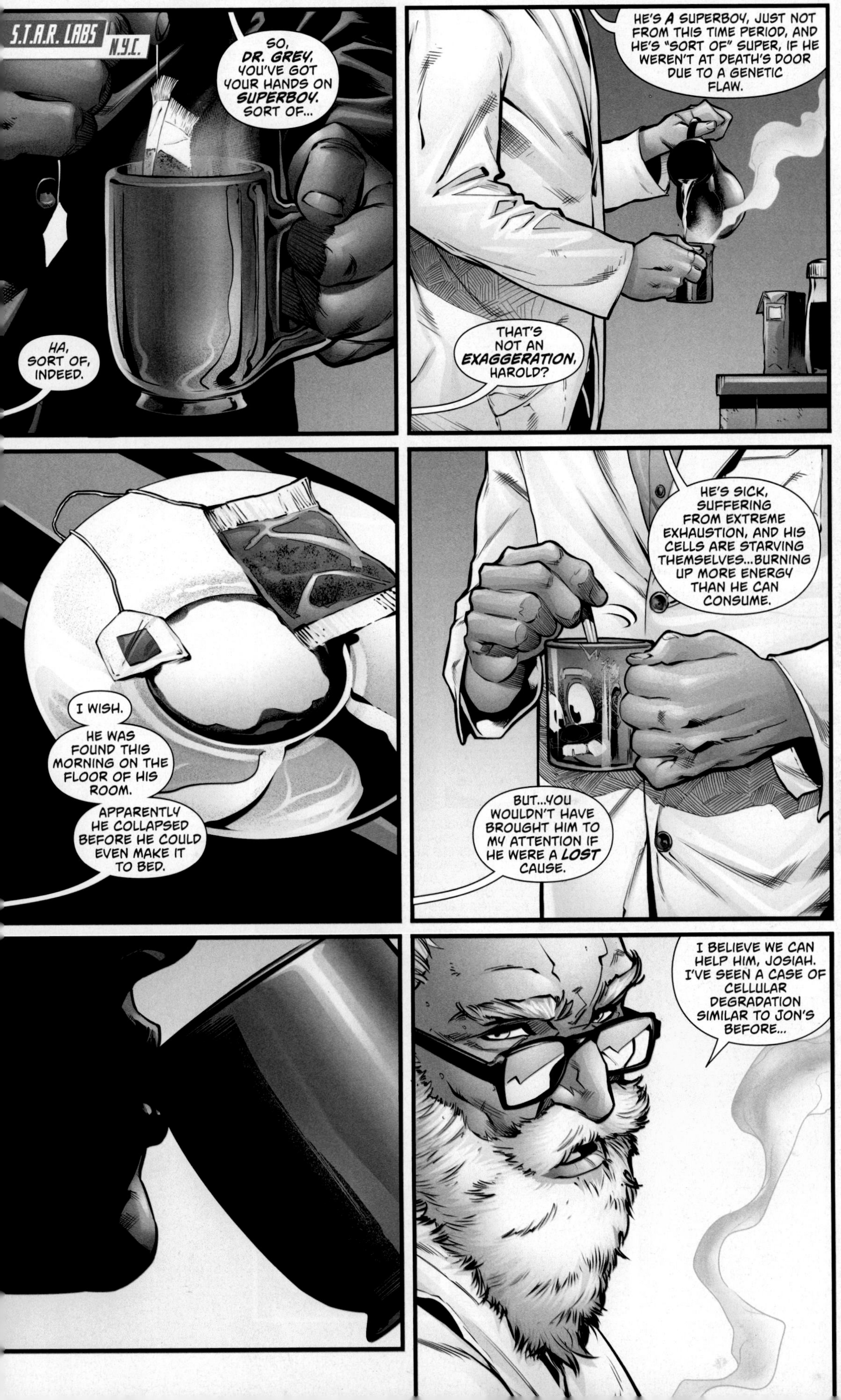
S.T.A.R. LABS
N.Y.C.
SO, DR. GREY, YOU'VE GOT YOUR HANDS ON SUPERBOY. SORT OF...
HA, SORT OF, INDEED.
HE'S A SUPERBOY, JUST NOT FROM THIS TIME PERIOD, AND HE'S "SORT OF" SUPER, IF HE WEREN'T AT DEATH'S DOOR DUE TO A GENETIC FLAW.
THAT'S NOT AN EXAGGERATION, HAROLD?
I WISH.
HE WAS FOUND THIS MORNING ON THE FLOOR OF HIS ROOM.
APPARENTLY HE COLLAPSED BEFORE HE COULD EVEN MAKE IT TO BED.
HE'S SICK, SUFFERING FROM EXTREME EXHAUSTION, AND HIS CELLS ARE STARVING THEMSELVES...BURNING UP MORE ENERGY THAN HE CAN CONSUME.
BUT...YOU WOULDN'T HAVE BROUGHT HIM TO MY ATTENTION IF HE WERE A LOST CAUSE.
I BELIEVE WE CAN HELP HIM, JOSIAH. I'VE SEEN A CASE OF CELLULAR DEGRADATION SIMILAR TO JON'S BEFORE...

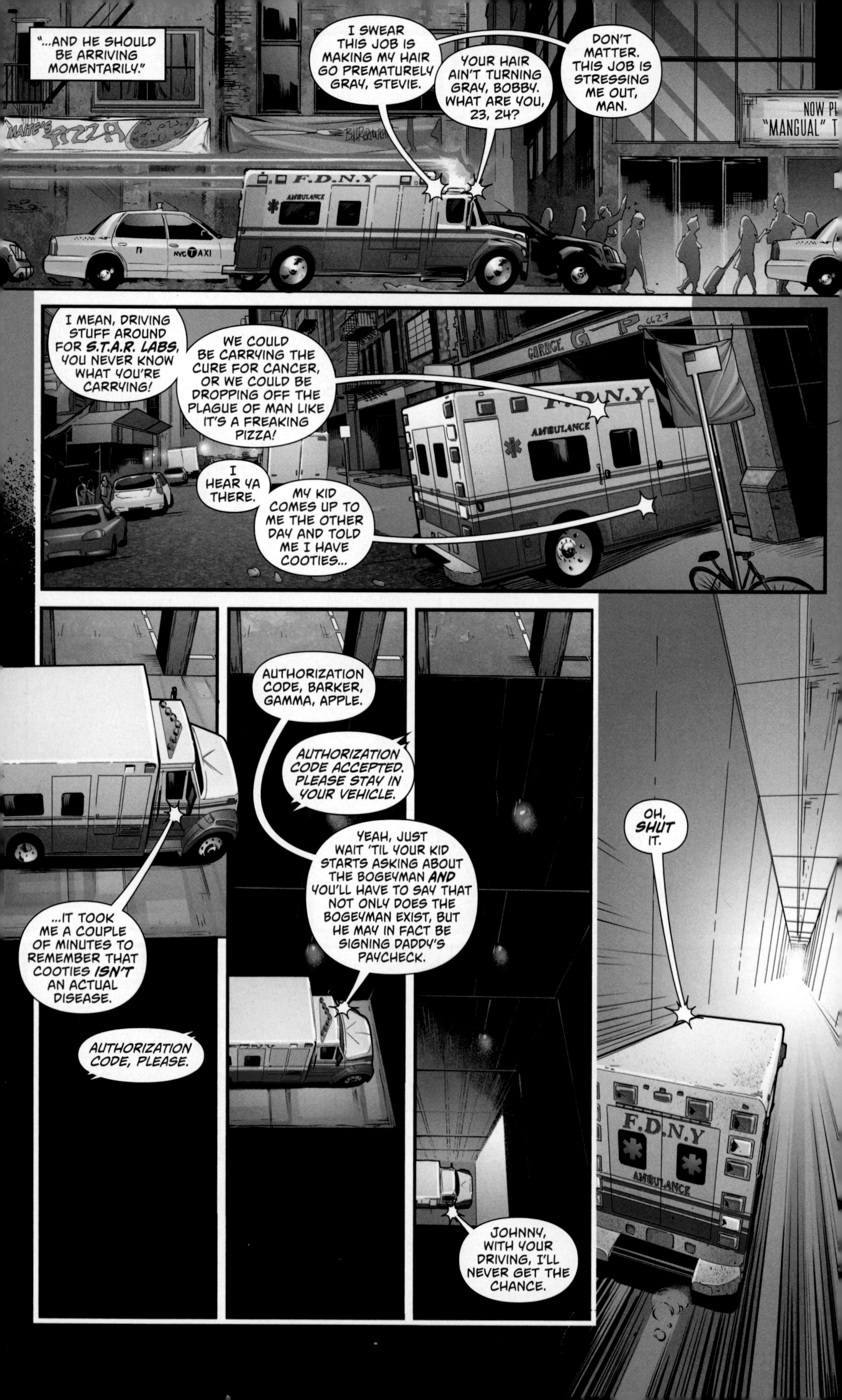

"...AND HE SHOULD BE ARRIVING MOMENTARILY."
MAITE'S PIZZA
I SWEAR THIS JOB IS MAKING MY HAIR GO PREMATURELY GRAY, STEVIE.
YOUR HAIR AIN'T TURNING GRAY, BOBBY. WHAT ARE YOU, 23, 24?
DON'T MATTER. THIS JOB IS STRESSING ME OUT, MAN.
NOW P
"MANGUAL" T
F.D.N.Y
AMBULANCE
NYC TAXI
I MEAN, DRIVING STUFF AROUND FOR S.T.A.R. LABS, YOU NEVER KNOW WHAT YOU'RE CARRYING!
WE COULD BE CARRYING THE CURE FOR CANCER, OR WE COULD BE DROPPING OFF THE PLAGUE OF MAN LIKE IT'S A FREAKING PIZZA!
I HEAR YA THERE.
MY KID COMES UP TO ME THE OTHER DAY AND TOLD ME I HAVE COOTIES...
GARAGE
...IT TOOK ME A COUPLE OF MINUTES TO REMEMBER THAT COOTIES ISN'T AN ACTUAL DISEASE.
AUTHORIZATION CODE, PLEASE.
AUTHORIZATION CODE, BARKER, GAMMA, APPLE.
AUTHORIZATION CODE ACCEPTED. PLEASE STAY IN YOUR VEHICLE.
YEAH, JUST WAIT 'TIL YOUR KID STARTS ASKING ABOUT THE BOGEYMAN AND YOU'LL HAVE TO SAY THAT NOT ONLY DOES THE BOGEYMAN EXIST, BUT HE MAY IN FACT BE SIGNING DADDY'S PAYCHECK.
JOHNNY, WITH YOUR DRIVING, I'LL NEVER GET THE CHANCE.
OH, SHUT IT.
F.D.N.Y
AMBULANCE

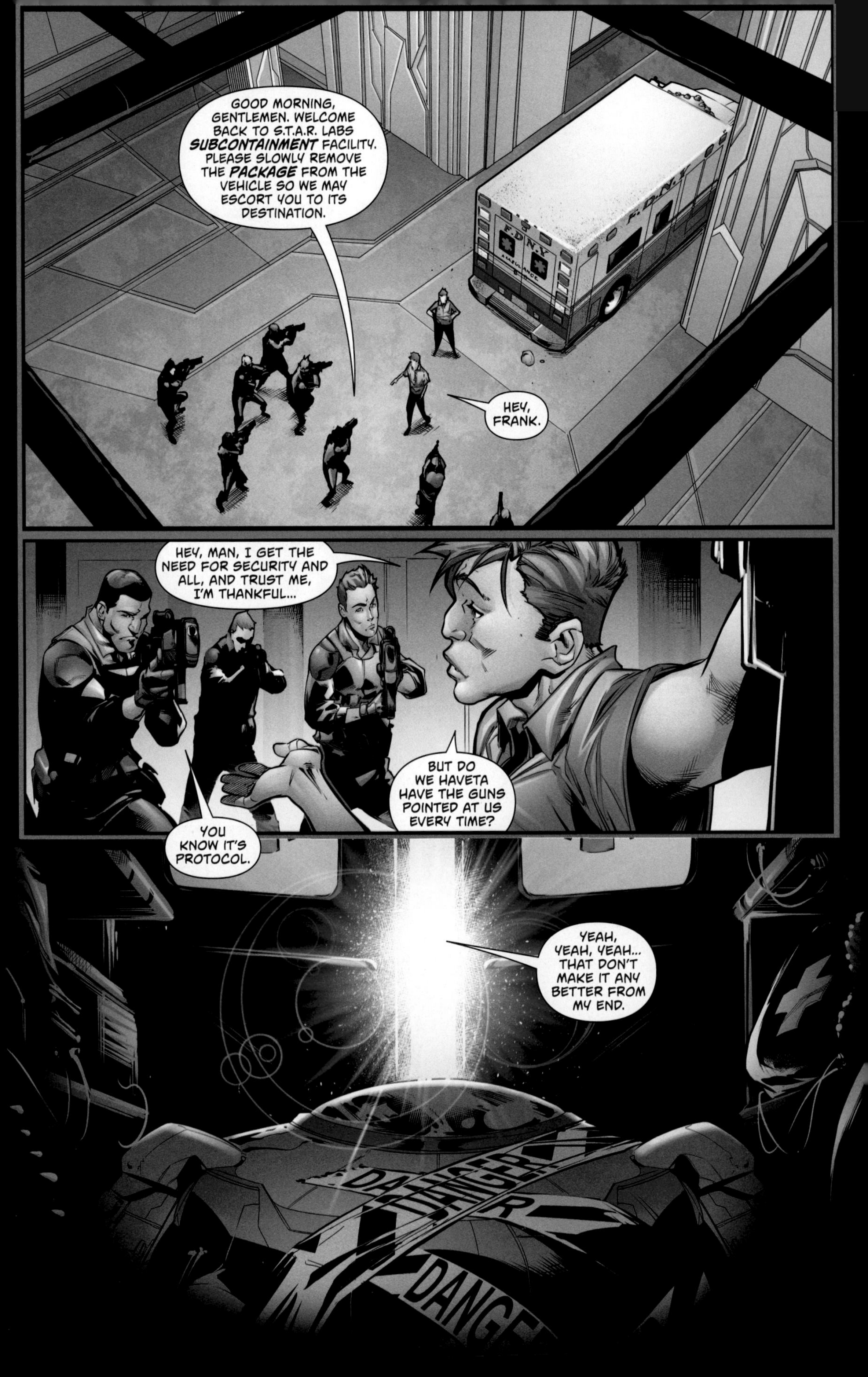
GOOD MORNING, GENTLEMEN. WELCOME BACK TO S.T.A.R. LABS SUBCONTAINMENT FACILITY. PLEASE SLOWLY REMOVE THE PACKAGE FROM THE VEHICLE SO WE MAY ESCORT YOU TO ITS DESTINATION.
HEY, FRANK.
HEY, MAN, I GET THE NEED FOR SECURITY AND ALL, AND TRUST ME, I'M THANKFUL...
BUT DO WE HAVETA HAVE THE GUNS POINTED AT US EVERY TIME?
YOU KNOW IT'S PROTOCOL.
YEAH, YEAH, YEAH... THAT DON'T MAKE IT ANY BETTER FROM MY END.
DANGER
DANGER

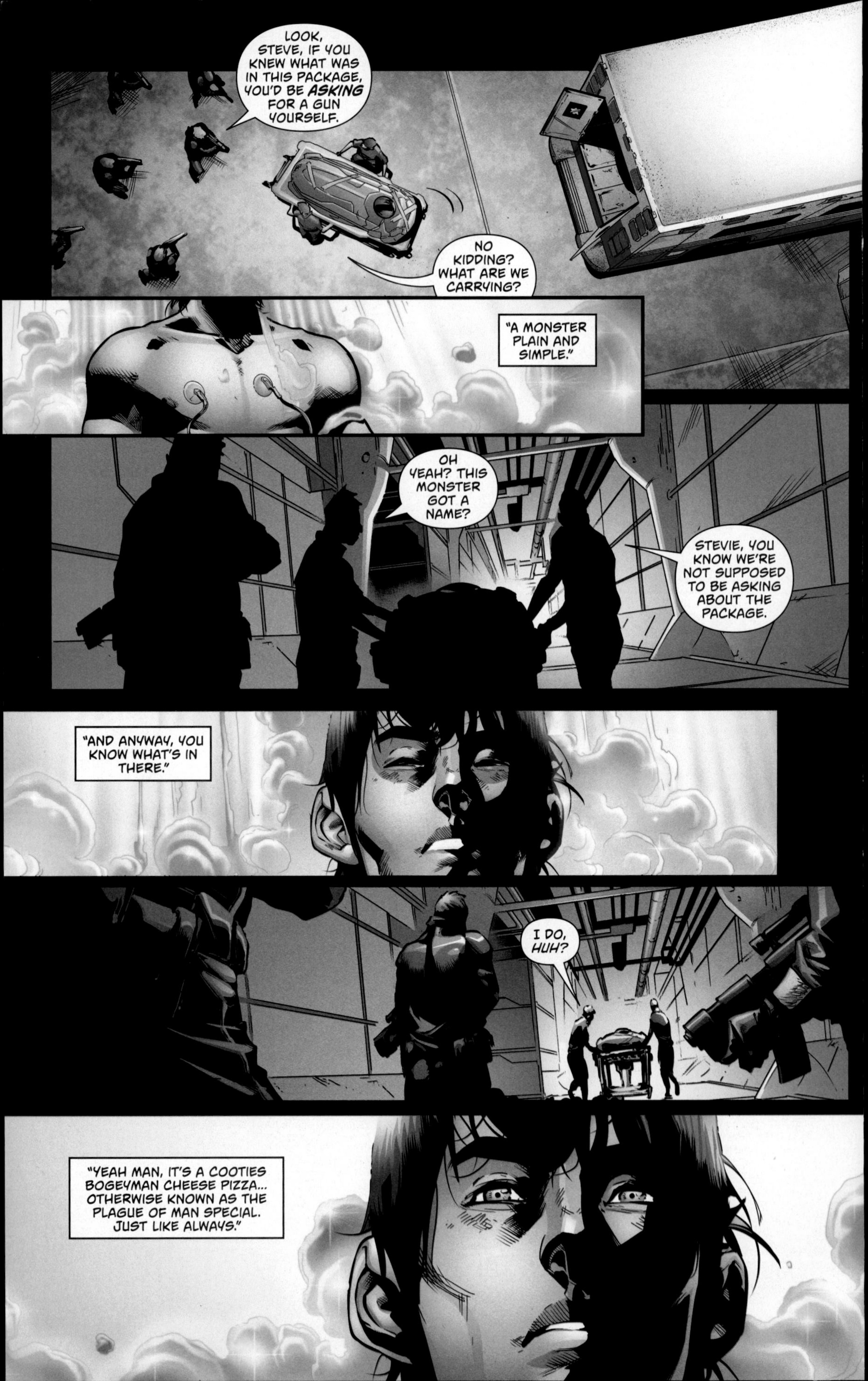
LOOK, STEVE, IF YOU KNEW WHAT WAS IN THIS PACKAGE, YOU'D BE ASKING FOR A GUN YOURSELF.
NO KIDDING? WHAT ARE WE CARRYING?
"A MONSTER PLAIN AND SIMPLE."
OH YEAH? THIS MONSTER GOT A NAME?
STEVIE, YOU KNOW WE'RE NOT SUPPOSED TO BE ASKING ABOUT THE PACKAGE.
"AND ANYWAY, YOU KNOW WHAT'S IN THERE."
I DO, HUH?
"YEAH MAN, IT'S A COOTIES BOGEYMAN CHEESE PIZZA... OTHERWISE KNOWN AS THE PLAGUE OF MAN SPECIAL. JUST LIKE ALWAYS."

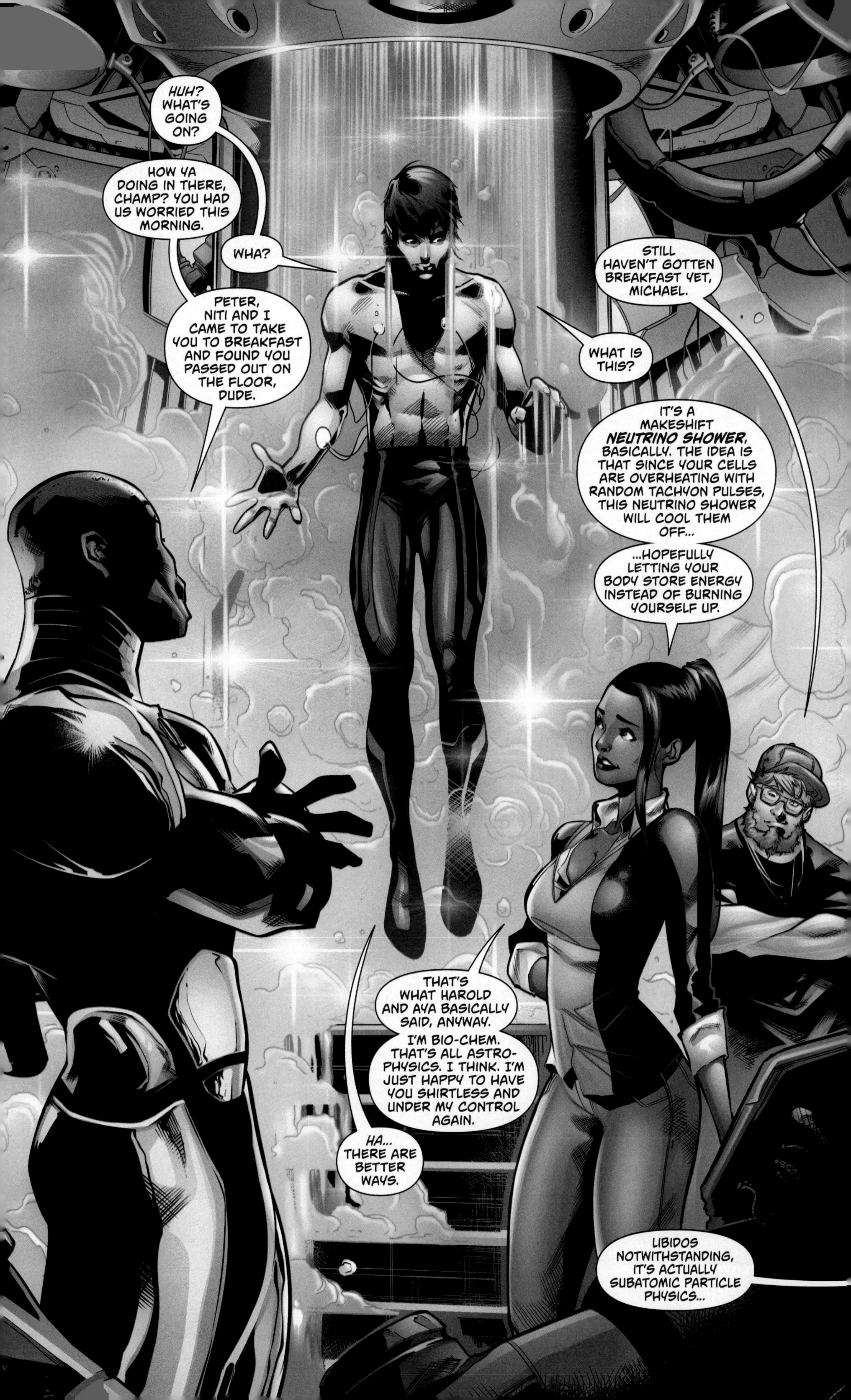
HUH? WHAT'S GOING ON?
HOW YA DOING IN THERE, CHAMP? YOU HAD US WORRIED THIS MORNING.
WHA?
PETER, NITI AND I CAME TO TAKE YOU TO BREAKFAST AND FOUND YOU PASSED OUT ON THE FLOOR, DUDE.
STILL HAVEN'T GOTTEN BREAKFAST YET, MICHAEL.
WHAT IS THIS?
IT'S A MAKESHIFT NEUTRINO SHOWER, BASICALLY. THE IDEA IS THAT SINCE YOUR CELLS ARE OVERHEATING WITH RANDOM TACHYON PULSES, THIS NEUTRINO SHOWER WILL COOL THEM OFF...
...HOPEFULLY LETTING YOUR BODY STORE ENERGY INSTEAD OF BURNING YOURSELF UP.
THAT'S WHAT HAROLD AND AYA BASICALLY SAID, ANYWAY.
I'M BIO-CHEM. THAT'S ALL ASTRO-PHYSICS. I THINK. I'M JUST HAPPY TO HAVE YOU SHIRTLESS AND UNDER MY CONTROL AGAIN.
HA... THERE ARE BETTER WAYS.
LIBIDOS NOTWITHSTANDING, IT'S ACTUALLY SUBATOMIC PARTICLE PHYSICS...

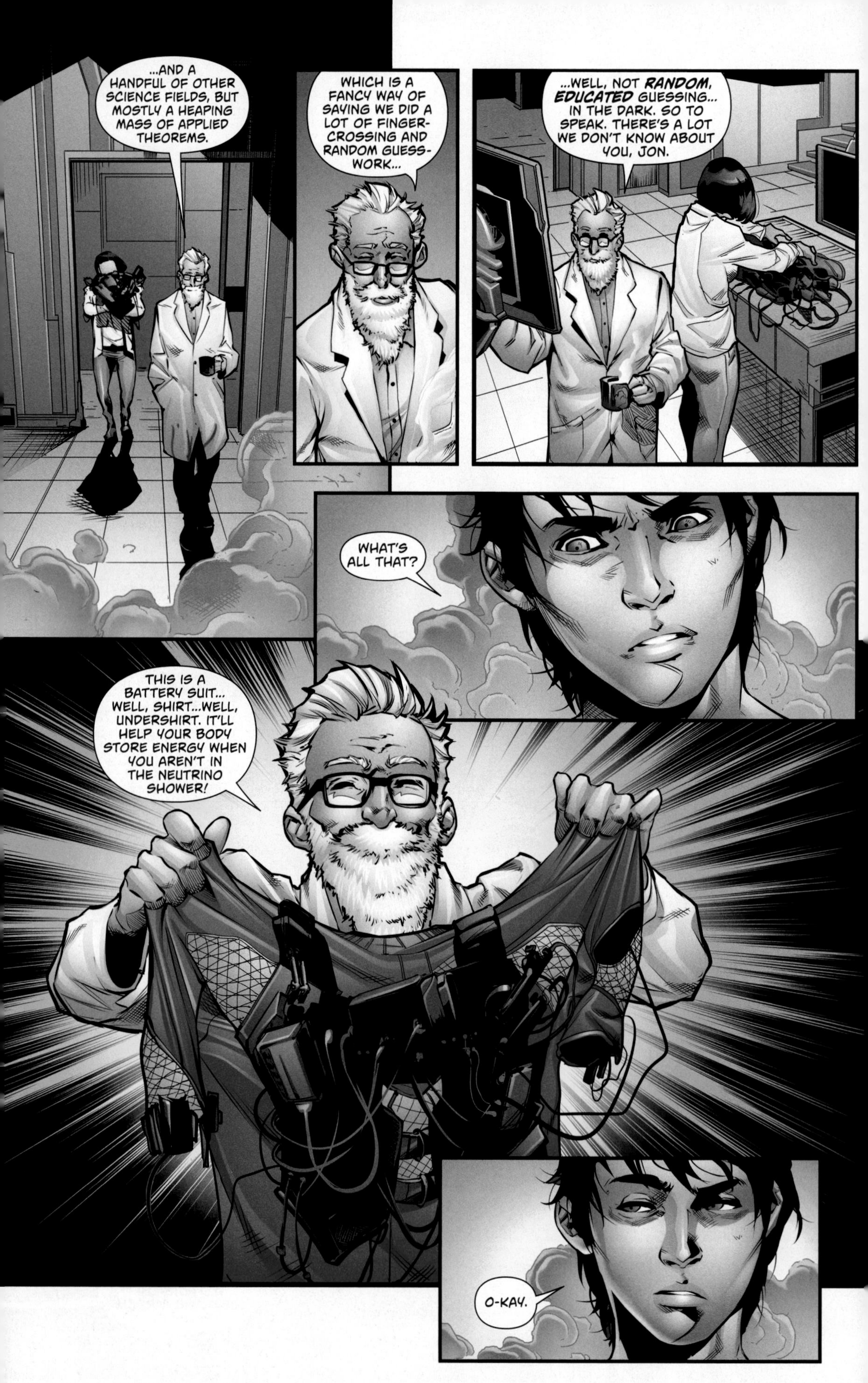
...AND A HANDFUL OF OTHER SCIENCE FIELDS, BUT MOSTLY A HEAPING MASS OF APPLIED THEOREMS.
WHICH IS A FANCY WAY OF SAYING WE DID A LOT OF FINGER-CROSSING AND RANDOM GUESS-WORK...
...WELL, NOT RANDOM, EDUCATED GUESSING... IN THE DARK. SO TO SPEAK. THERE'S A LOT WE DON'T KNOW ABOUT YOU, JON.
WHAT'S ALL THAT?
THIS IS A BATTERY SUIT... WELL, SHIRT...WELL, UNDERSHIRT. IT'LL HELP YOUR BODY STORE ENERGY WHEN YOU AREN'T IN THE NEUTRINO SHOWER!
O-KAY.

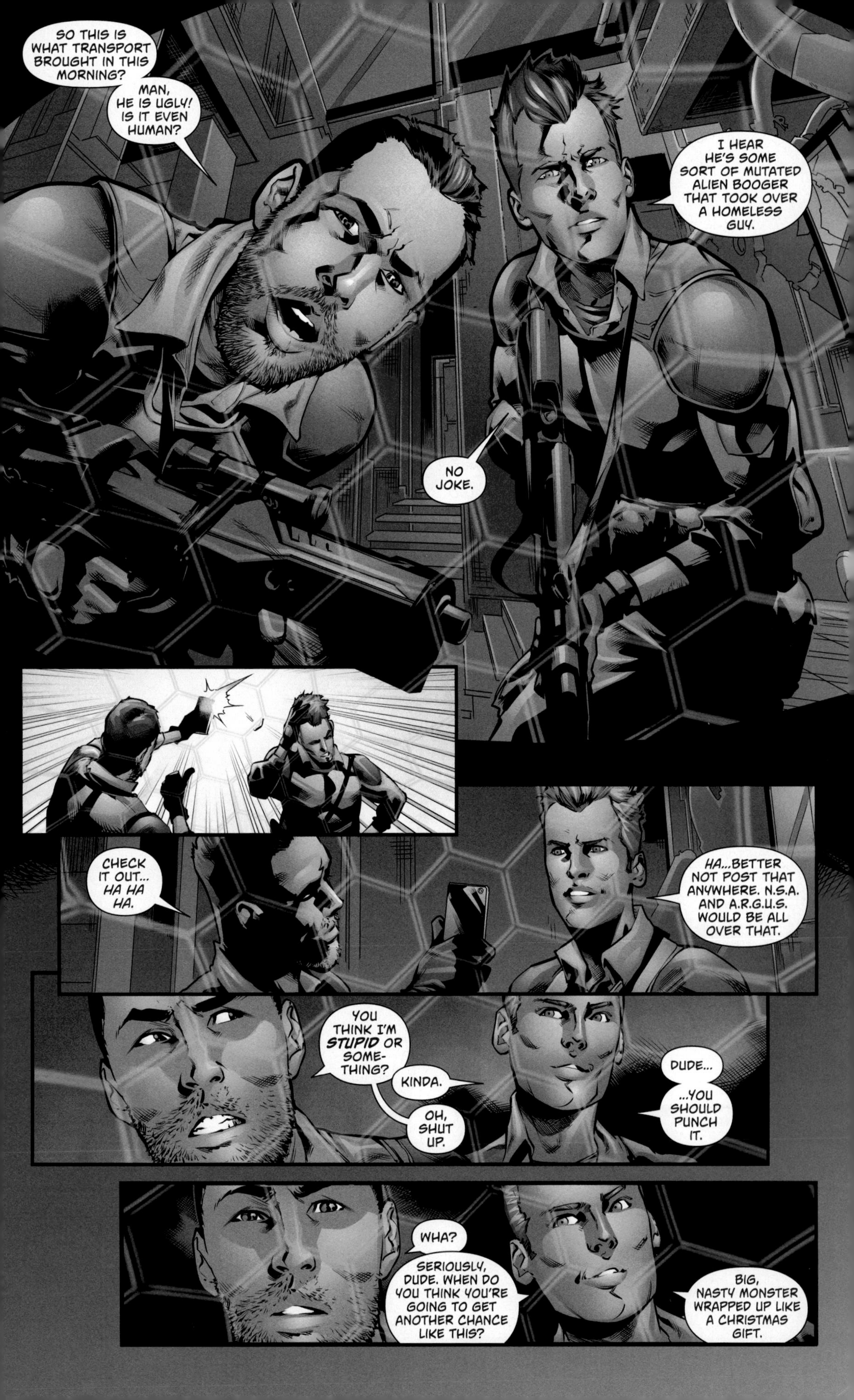
SO THIS IS WHAT TRANSPORT BROUGHT IN THIS MORNING?
MAN, HE IS UGLY! IS IT EVEN HUMAN?
I HEAR HE'S SOME SORT OF MUTATED ALIEN BOOGER THAT TOOK OVER A HOMELESS GUY.
NO JOKE.
CHECK IT OUT... HA HA HA.
HA...BETTER NOT POST THAT ANYWHERE. N.S.A. AND A.R.G.U.S. WOULD BE ALL OVER THAT.
YOU THINK I'M STUPID OR SOME-THING?
KINDA.
OH, SHUT UP.
DUDE...
...YOU SHOULD PUNCH IT.
WHA?
SERIOUSLY, DUDE. WHEN DO YOU THINK YOU'RE GOING TO GET ANOTHER CHANCE LIKE THIS?
BIG, NASTY MONSTER WRAPPED UP LIKE A CHRISTMAS GIFT.

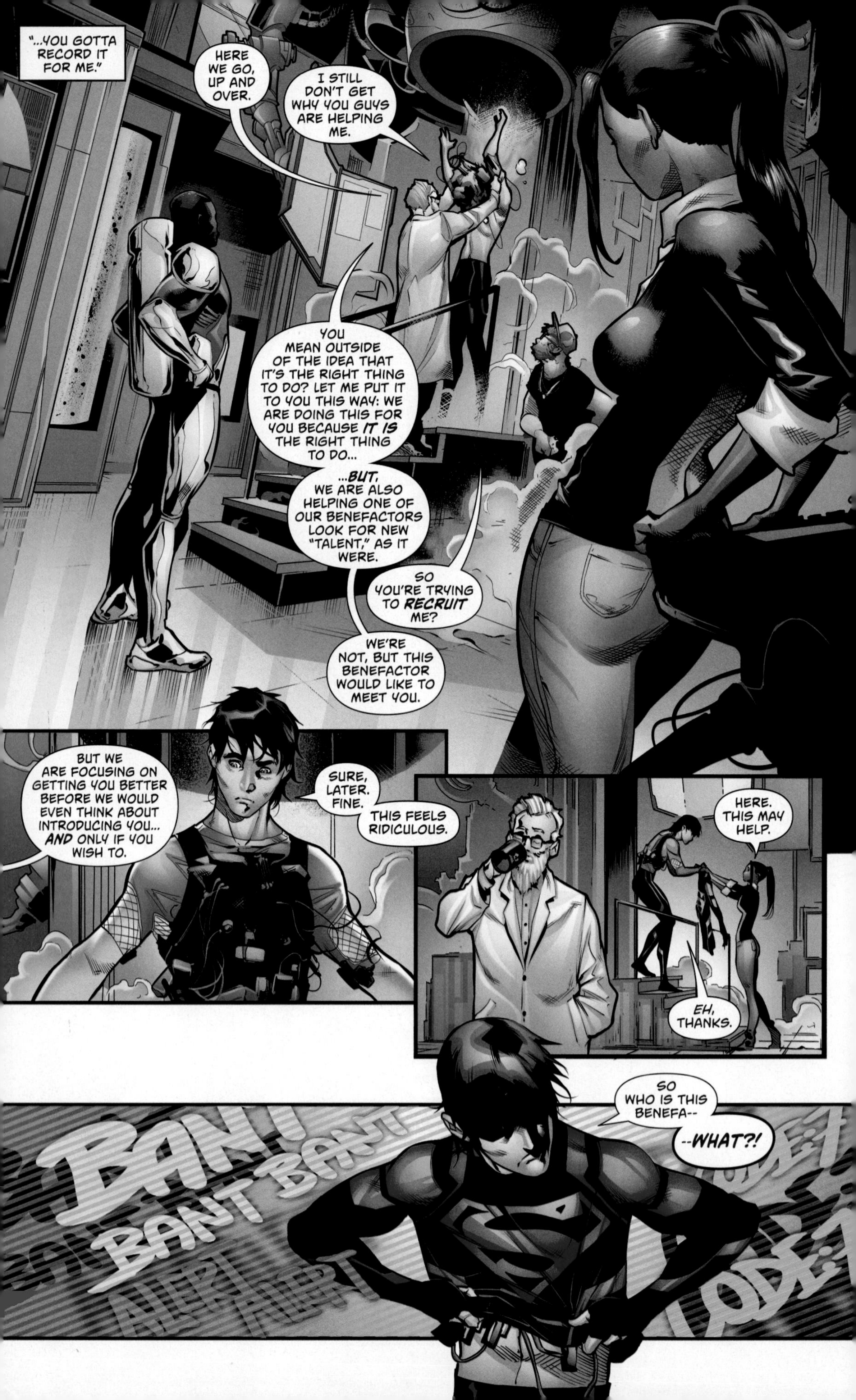
"...YOU GOTTA RECORD IT FOR ME."
HERE WE GO, UP AND OVER.
I STILL DON'T GET WHY YOU GUYS ARE HELPING ME.
YOU MEAN OUTSIDE OF THE IDEA THAT IT'S THE RIGHT THING TO DO? LET ME PUT IT TO YOU THIS WAY: WE ARE DOING THIS FOR YOU BECAUSE IT IS THE RIGHT THING TO DO...
...BUT, WE ARE ALSO HELPING ONE OF OUR BENEFACTORS LOOK FOR NEW "TALENT," AS IT WERE.
SO YOU'RE TRYING TO RECRUIT ME?
WE'RE NOT, BUT THIS BENEFACTOR WOULD LIKE TO MEET YOU.
BUT WE ARE FOCUSING ON GETTING YOU BETTER BEFORE WE WOULD EVEN THINK ABOUT INTRODUCING YOU... AND ONLY IF YOU WISH TO.
SURE, LATER. FINE.
THIS FEELS RIDICULOUS.
HERE. THIS MAY HELP.
EH, THANKS.
SO WHO IS THIS BENEFA--
--WHAT?!
BANT
BANT BANT BANT

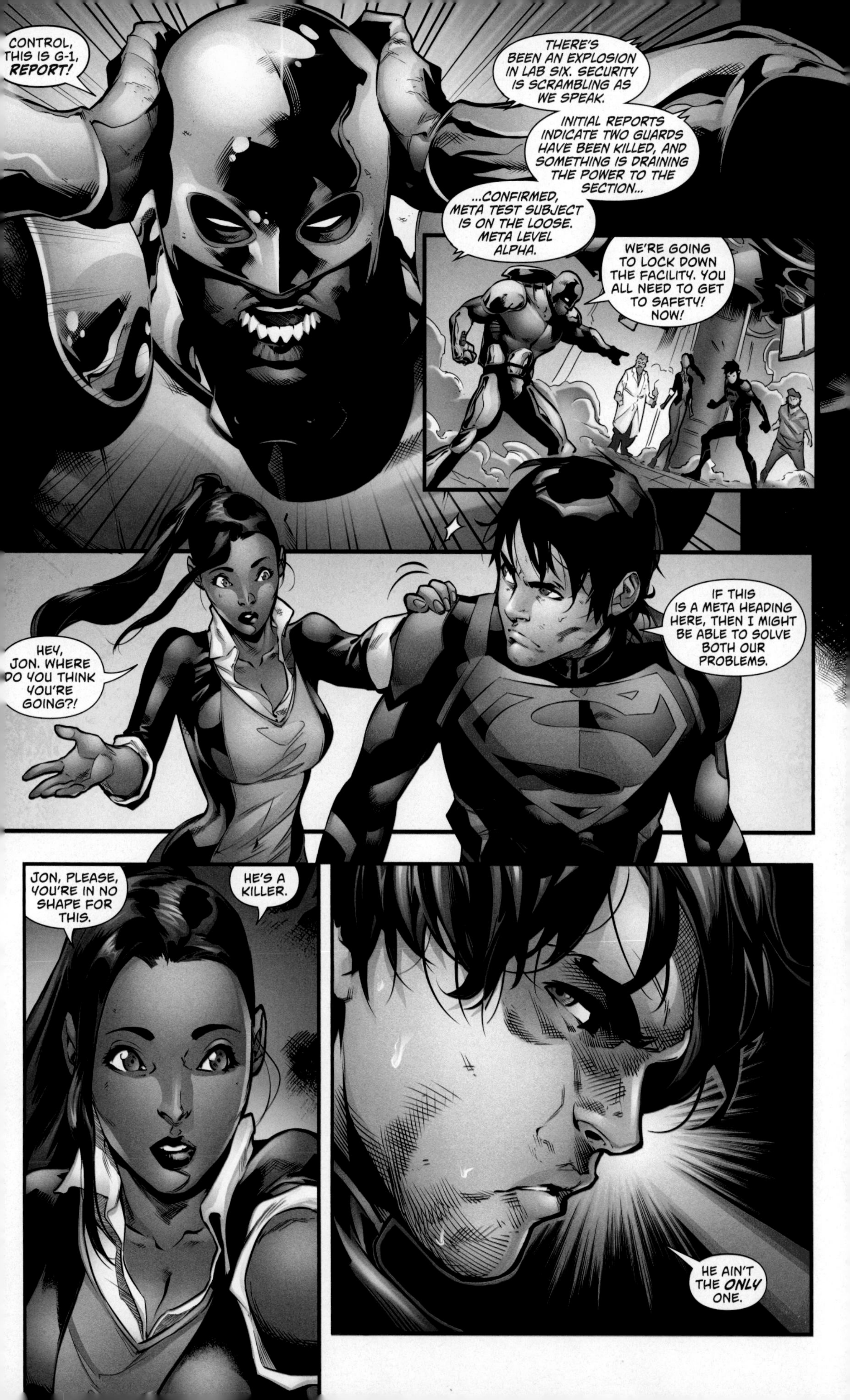
CONTROL, THIS IS G-1, **REPORT!**
THERE'S BEEN AN EXPLOSION IN LAB SIX. SECURITY IS SCRAMBLING AS WE SPEAK.
INITIAL REPORTS INDICATE TWO GUARDS HAVE BEEN KILLED, AND SOMETHING IS DRAINING THE POWER TO THE SECTION...
...CONFIRMED, META TEST SUBJECT IS ON THE LOOSE. META LEVEL ALPHA.
WE'RE GOING TO LOCK DOWN THE FACILITY. YOU ALL NEED TO GET TO SAFETY! NOW!
HEY, JON. WHERE DO YOU THINK YOU'RE GOING?!
IF THIS IS A META HEADING HERE, THEN I MIGHT BE ABLE TO SOLVE BOTH OUR PROBLEMS.
JON, PLEASE, YOU'RE IN NO SHAPE FOR THIS.
HE'S A KILLER.
HE AIN'T THE ***ONLY*** ONE.

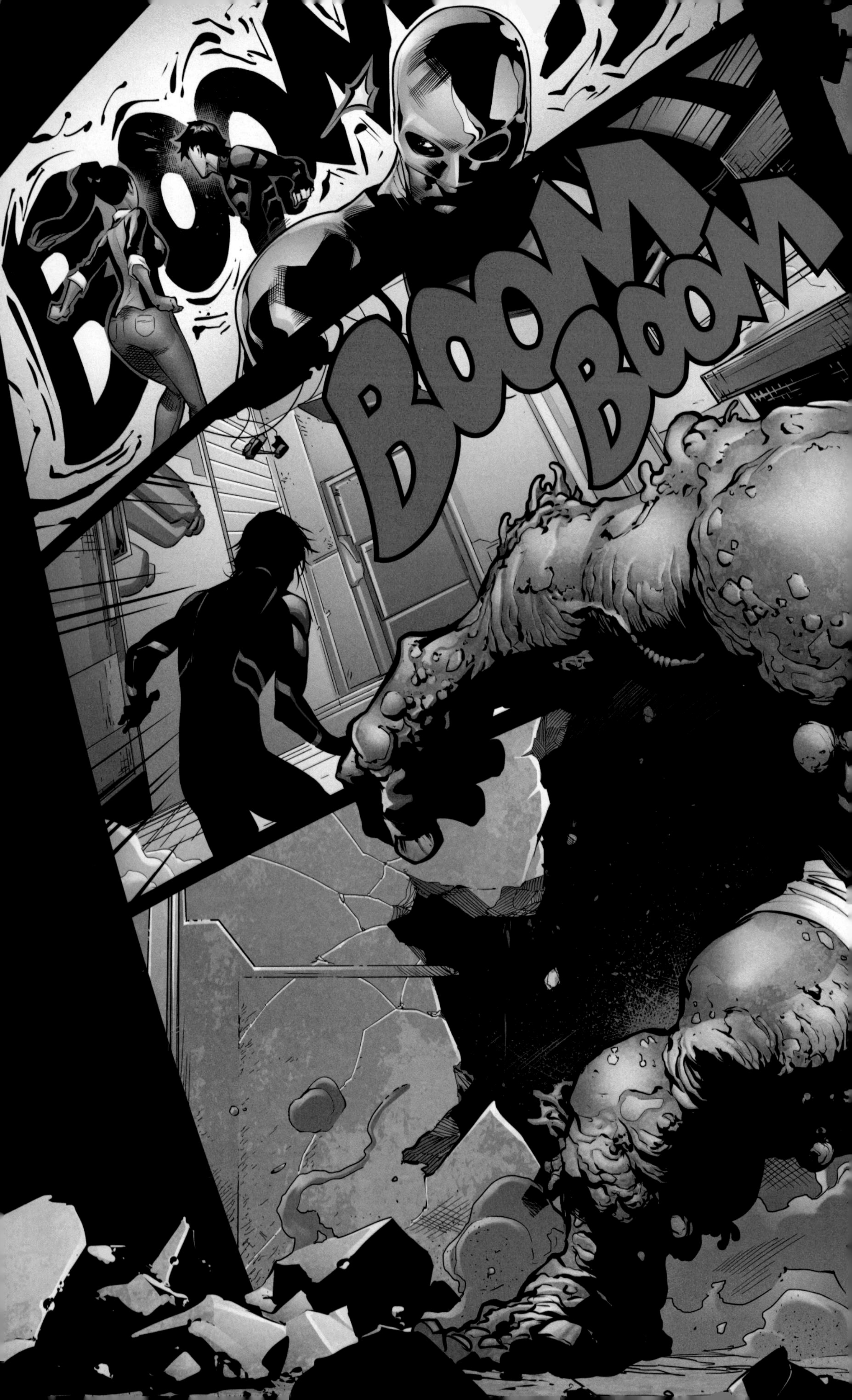
BOOM
BOOM

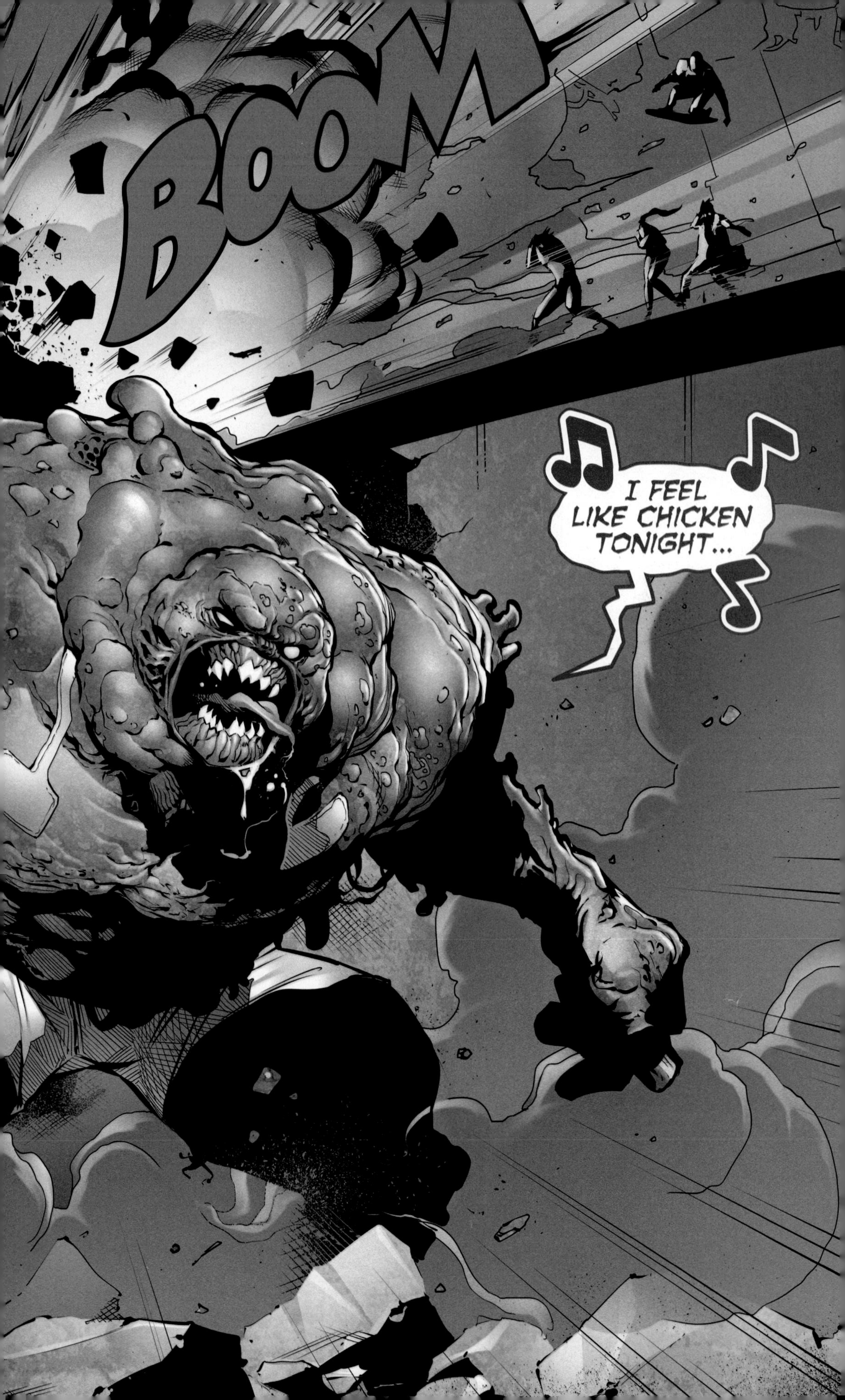
BOOM
I FEEL LIKE CHICKEN TONIGHT...

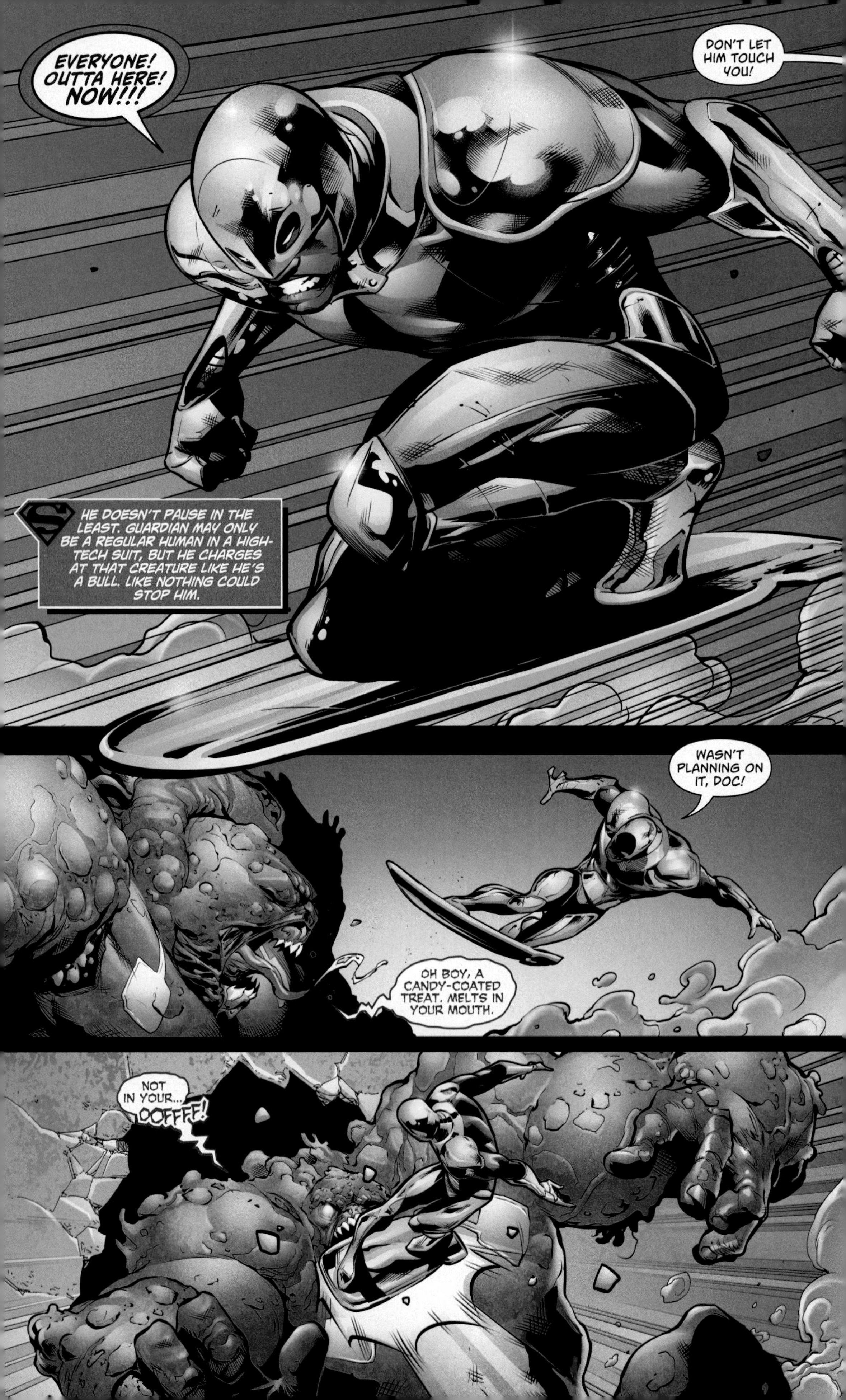
EVERYONE! OUTTA HERE! NOW!!!
DON'T LET HIM TOUCH YOU!
HE DOESN'T PAUSE IN THE LEAST. GUARDIAN MAY ONLY BE A REGULAR HUMAN IN A HIGH-TECH SUIT, BUT HE CHARGES AT THAT CREATURE LIKE HE'S A BULL. LIKE NOTHING COULD STOP HIM.
WASN'T PLANNING ON IT, DOC!
OH BOY, A CANDY-COATED TREAT. MELTS IN YOUR MOUTH.
NOT IN YOUR...
OOFFFF!

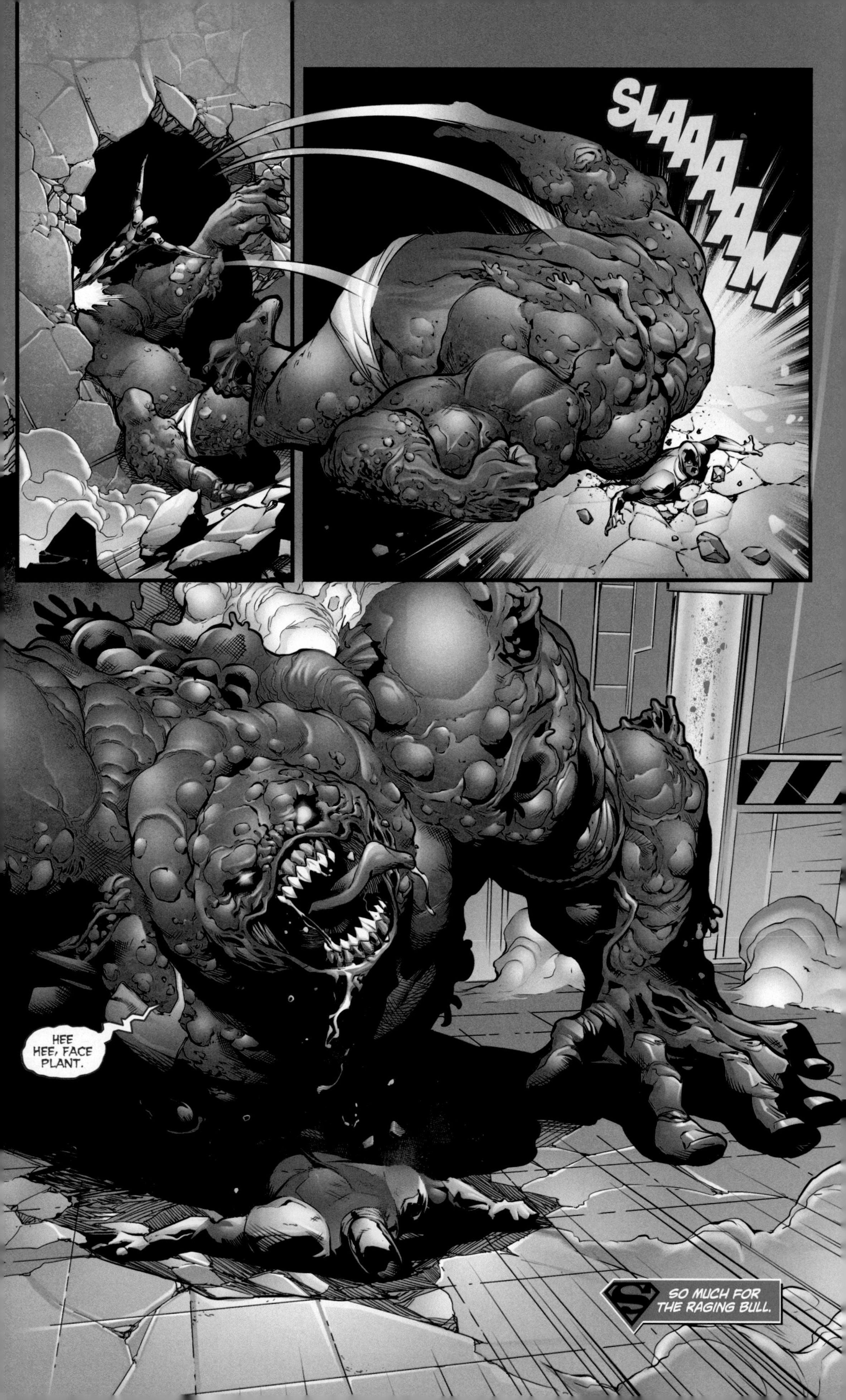
SLAAAAAM
HEE HEE, FACE PLANT.
SO MUCH FOR THE RAGING BULL.

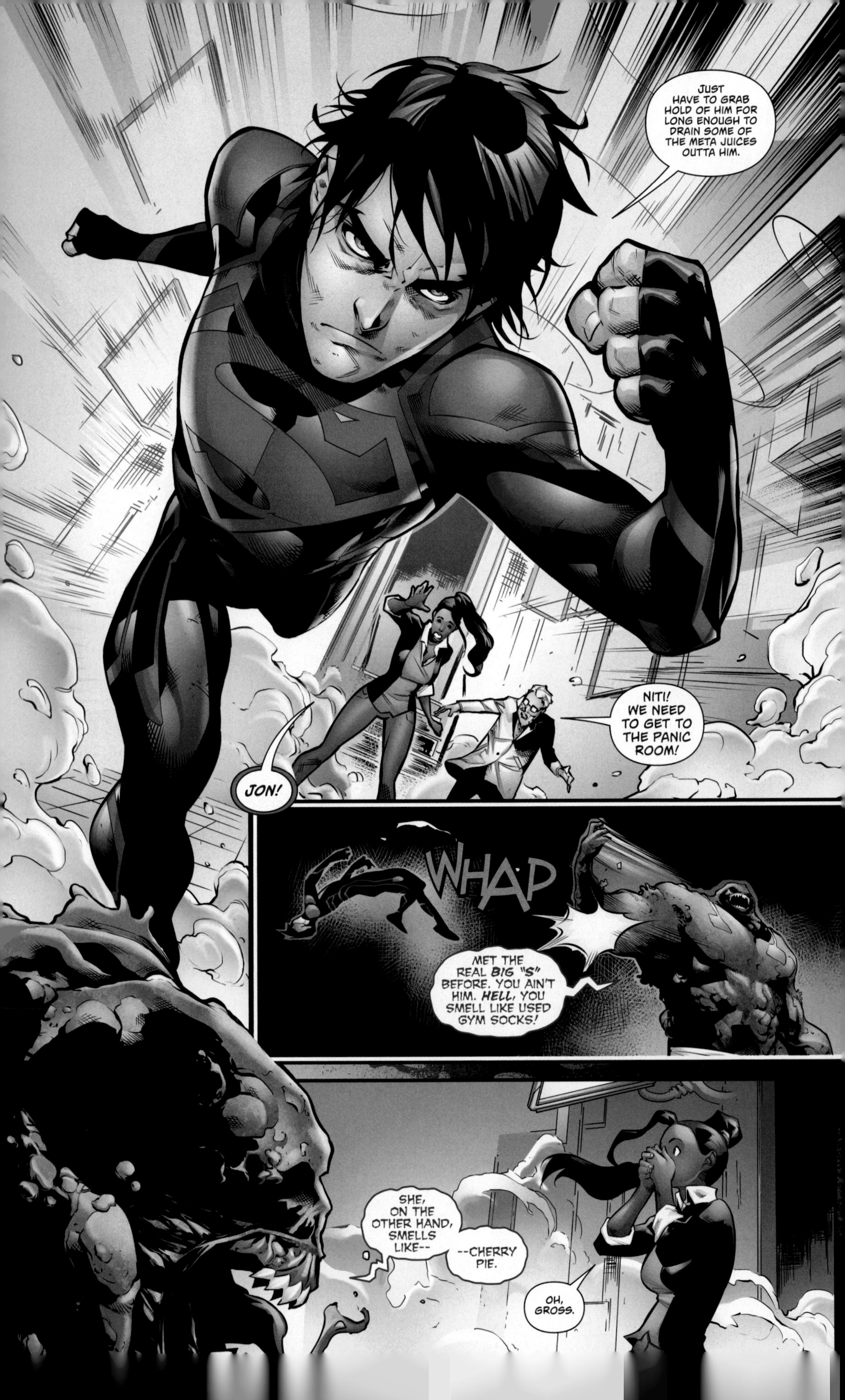
JUST HAVE TO GRAB HOLD OF HIM FOR LONG ENOUGH TO DRAIN SOME OF THE META JUICES OUTTA HIM.
NITI! WE NEED TO GET TO THE PANIC ROOM!
JON!
WHAP
MET THE REAL BIG "S" BEFORE. YOU AIN'T HIM. HELL, YOU SMELL LIKE USED GYM SOCKS!
SHE, ON THE OTHER HAND, SMELLS LIKE--
--CHERRY PIE.
OH, GROSS.

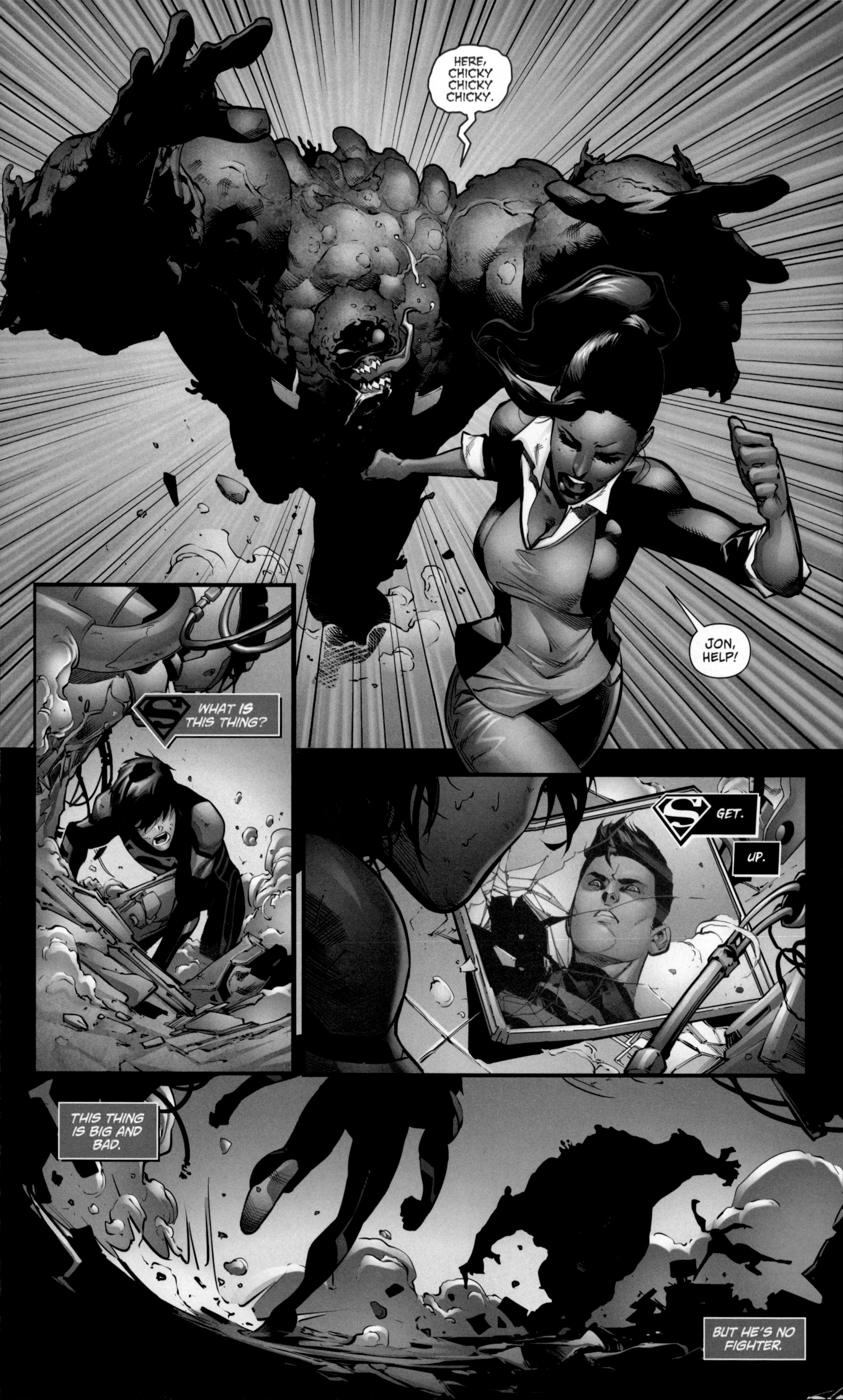
HERE, CHICKY CHICKY CHICKY.
JON, HELP!
WHAT IS THIS THING?
GET.
UP.
THIS THING IS BIG AND BAD.
BUT HE'S NO FIGHTER.

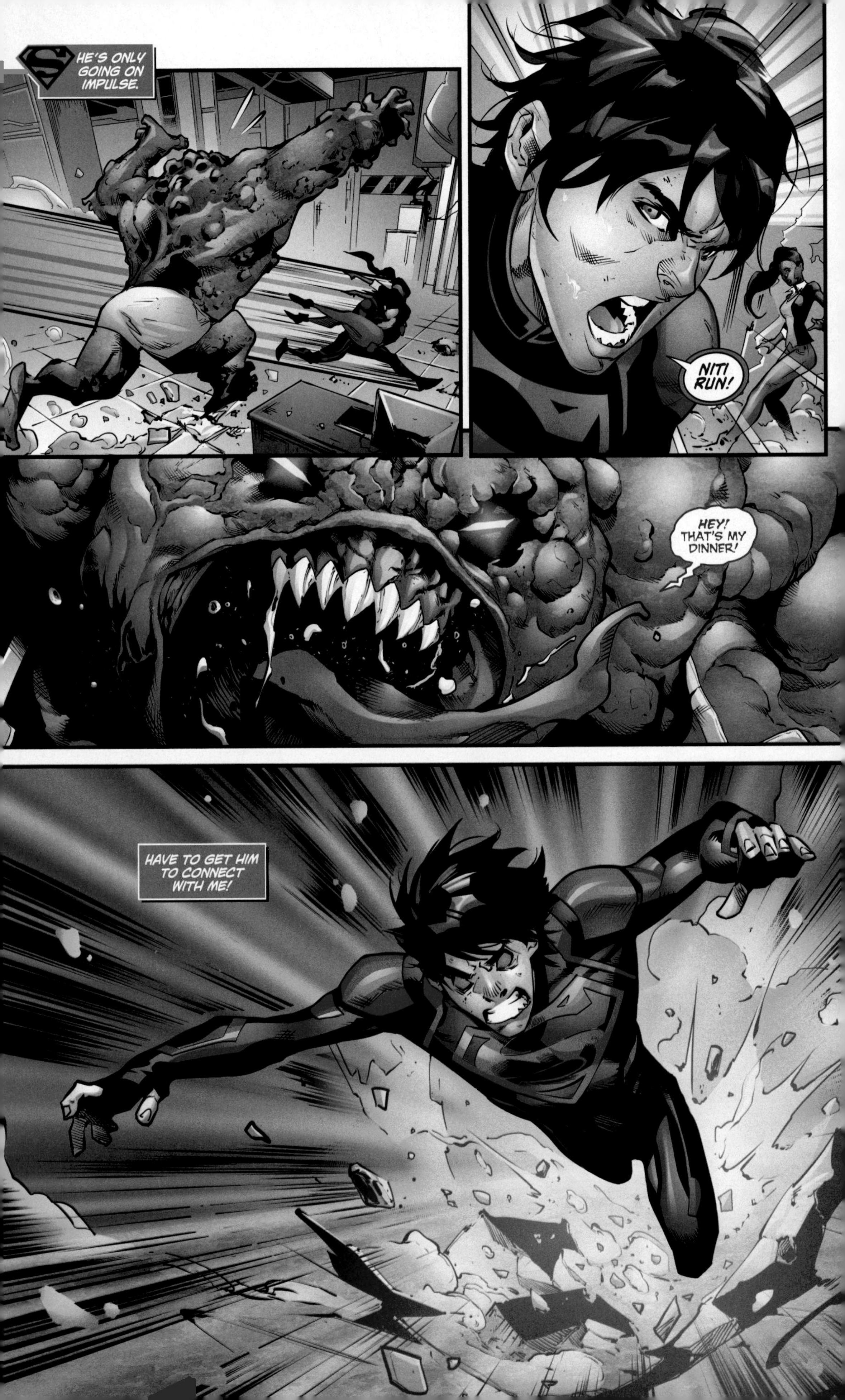
HE'S ONLY GOING ON IMPULSE.
NITI RUN!
HEY! THAT'S MY DINNER!
HAVE TO GET HIM TO CONNECT WITH ME!

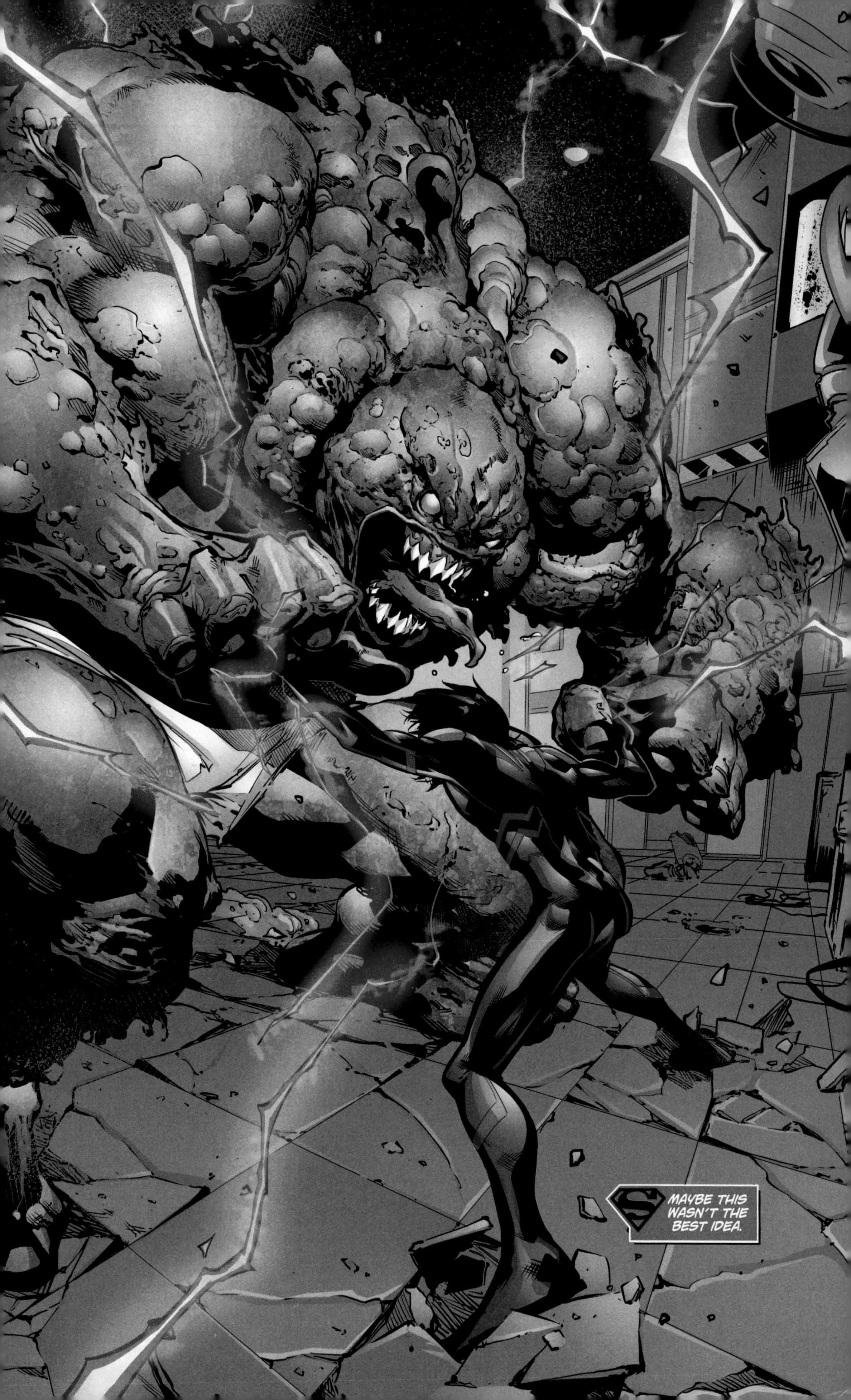
MAYBE THIS WASN'T THE BEST IDEA.

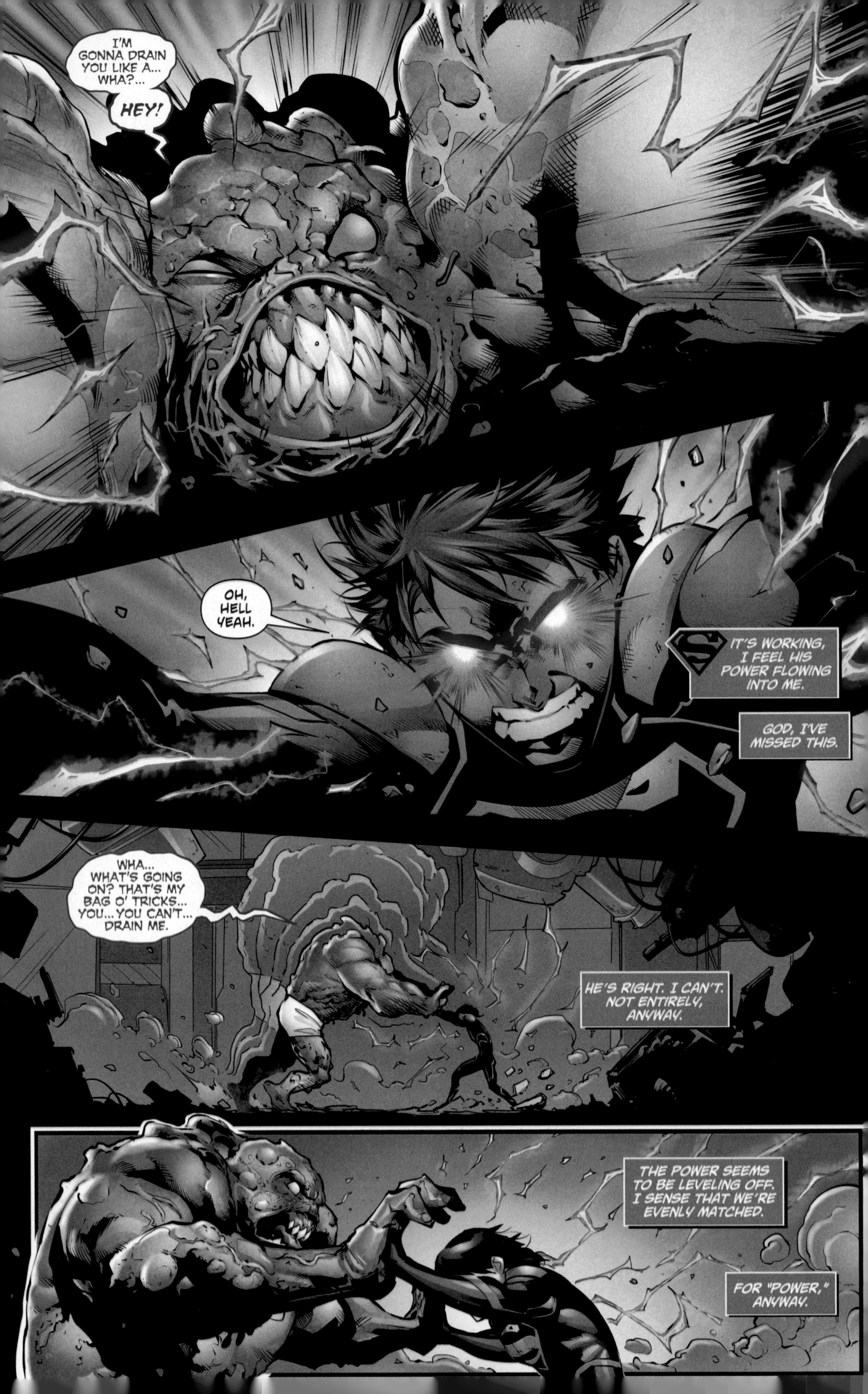
I'M GONNA DRAIN YOU LIKE A... WHA?...
HEY!
OH, HELL YEAH.
IT'S WORKING, I FEEL HIS POWER FLOWING INTO ME.
GOD, I'VE MISSED THIS.
WHA... WHAT'S GOING ON? THAT'S MY BAG O' TRICKS... YOU...YOU CAN'T... DRAIN ME.
HE'S RIGHT. I CAN'T. NOT ENTIRELY, ANYWAY.
THE POWER SEEMS TO BE LEVELING OFF. I SENSE THAT WE'RE EVENLY MATCHED.
FOR "POWER," ANYWAY.

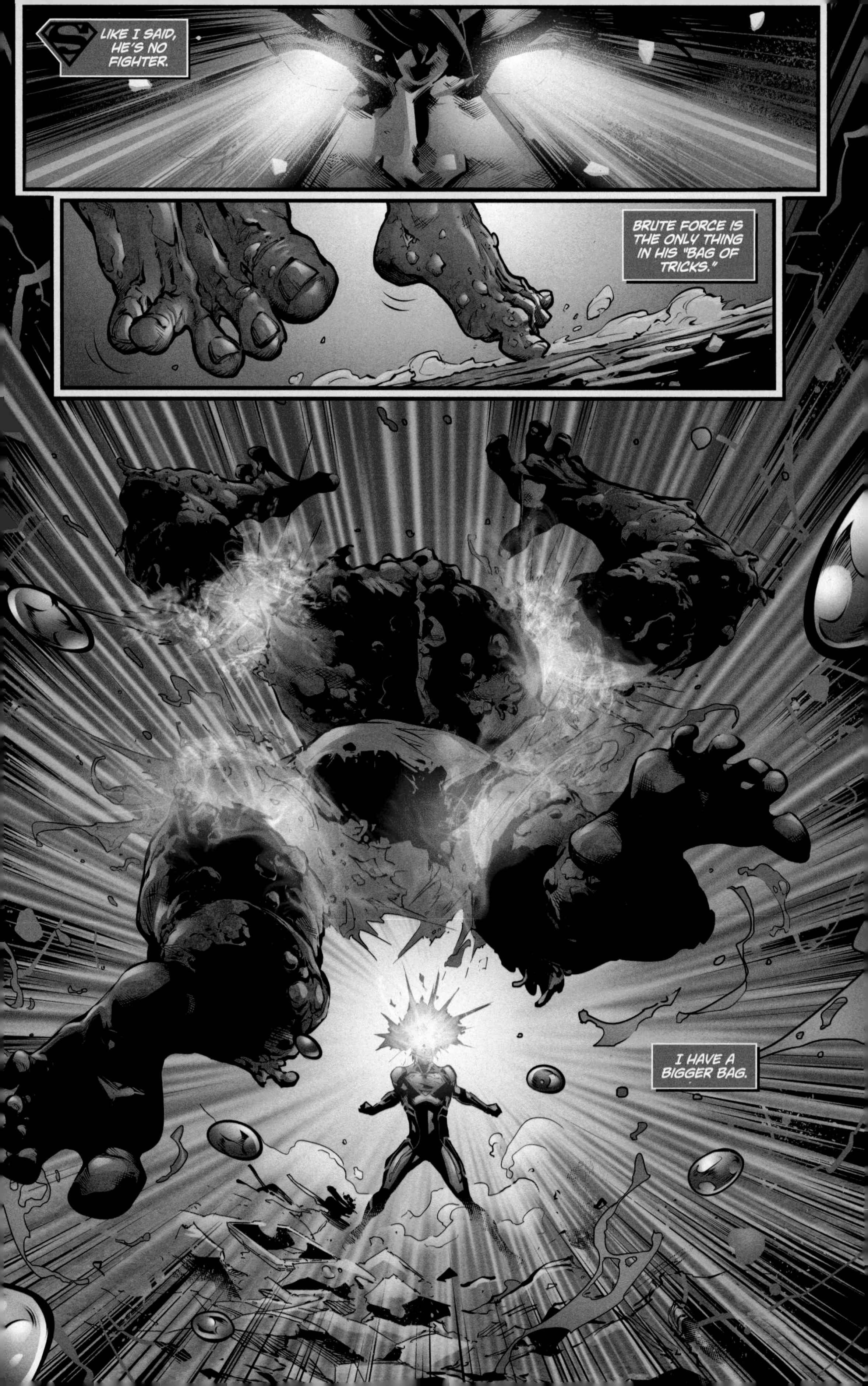
LIKE I SAID, HE'S NO FIGHTER.
BRUTE FORCE IS THE ONLY THING IN HIS "BAG OF TRICKS."
I HAVE A BIGGER BAG.

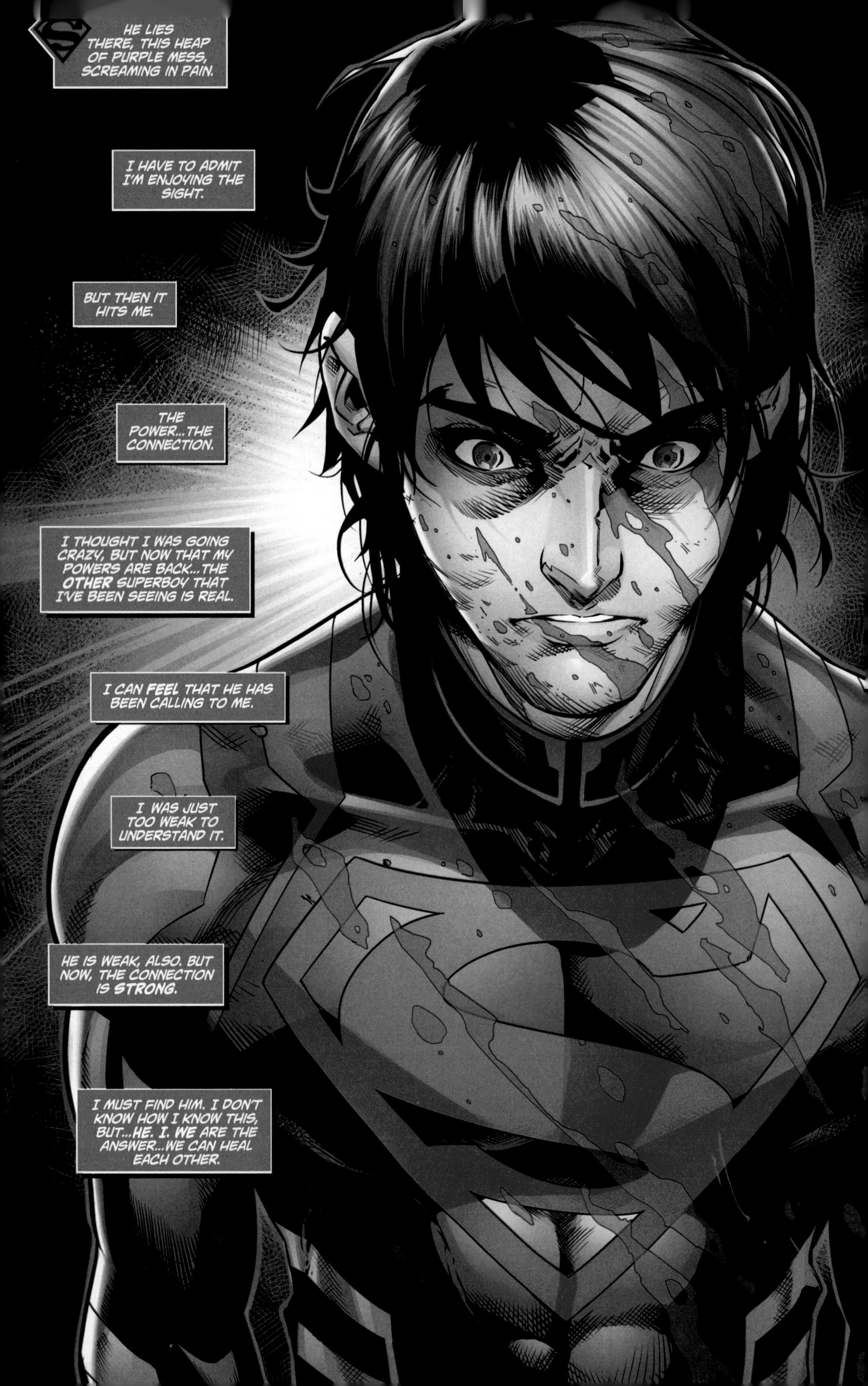
HE LIES THERE, THIS HEAP OF PURPLE MESS, SCREAMING IN PAIN.
I HAVE TO ADMIT I'M ENJOYING THE SIGHT.
BUT THEN IT HITS ME.
THE POWER...THE CONNECTION.
I THOUGHT I WAS GOING CRAZY, BUT NOW THAT MY POWERS ARE BACK...THE OTHER SUPERBOY THAT I'VE BEEN SEEING IS REAL.
I CAN FEEL THAT HE HAS BEEN CALLING TO ME.
I WAS JUST TOO WEAK TO UNDERSTAND IT.
HE IS WEAK, ALSO. BUT NOW, THE CONNECTION IS STRONG.
I MUST FIND HIM. I DON'T KNOW HOW I KNOW THIS, BUT...HE. I. WE ARE THE ANSWER...WE CAN HEAL EACH OTHER.

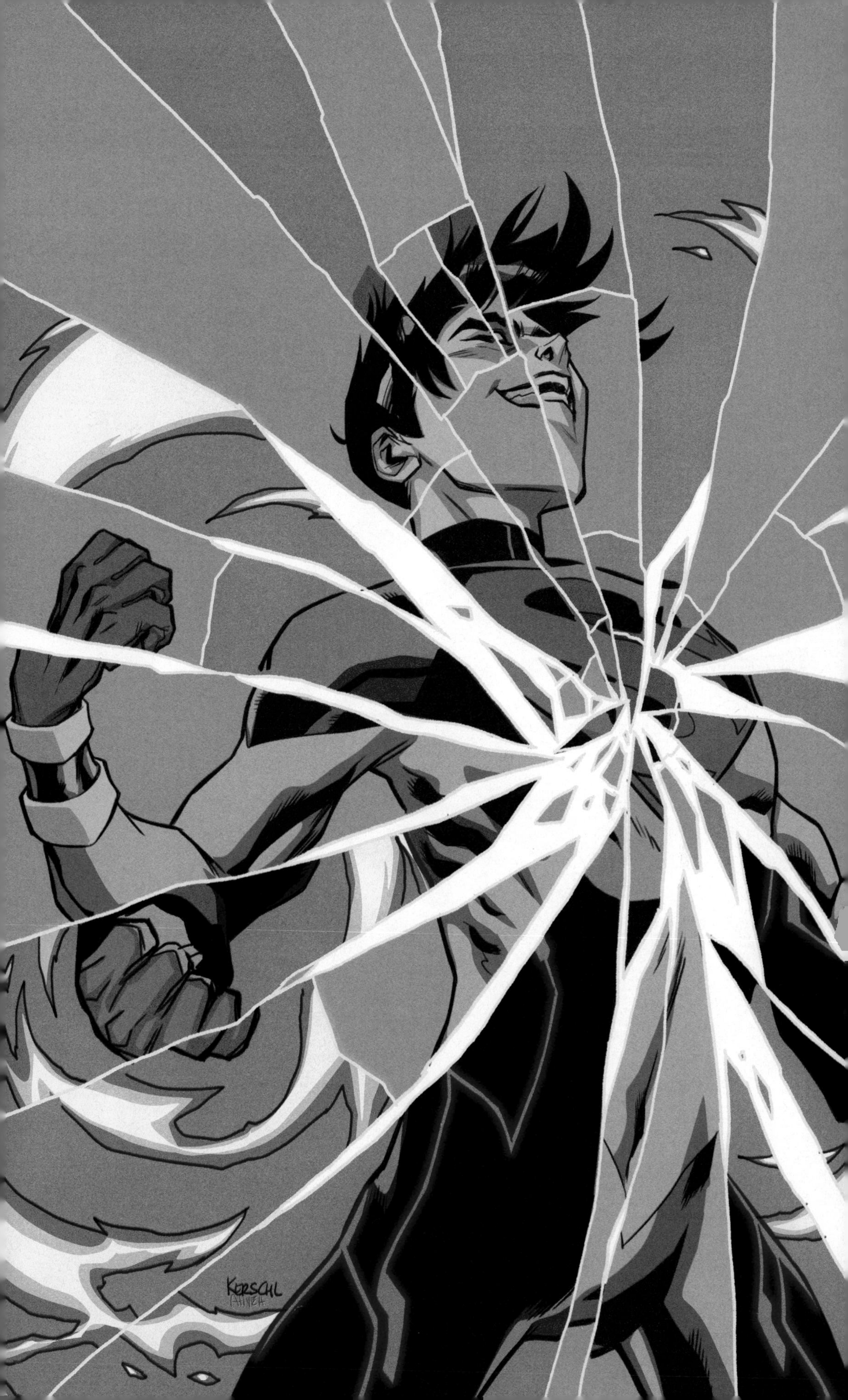
KERSCHL

HAPPENINGS

AARON KUDER writer **JORGE JIMÉNEZ** artist **TANYA** and **RICHARD HORIE** colorists
CARLOS M. MANGUAL letterer cover art by **KARL KERSCHL** and **MIKE ATIYEH**

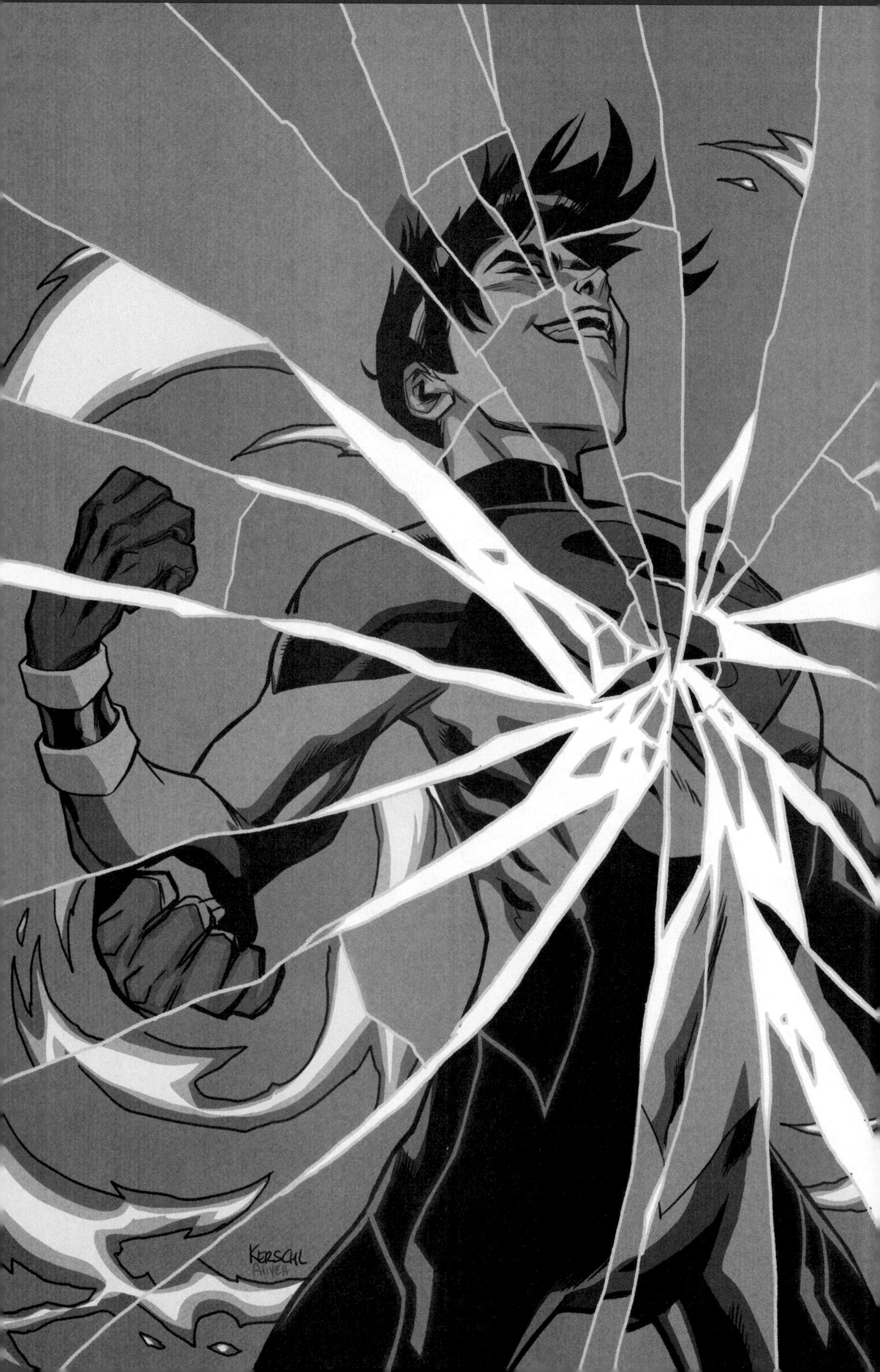

KERSCHL
ATIYEH

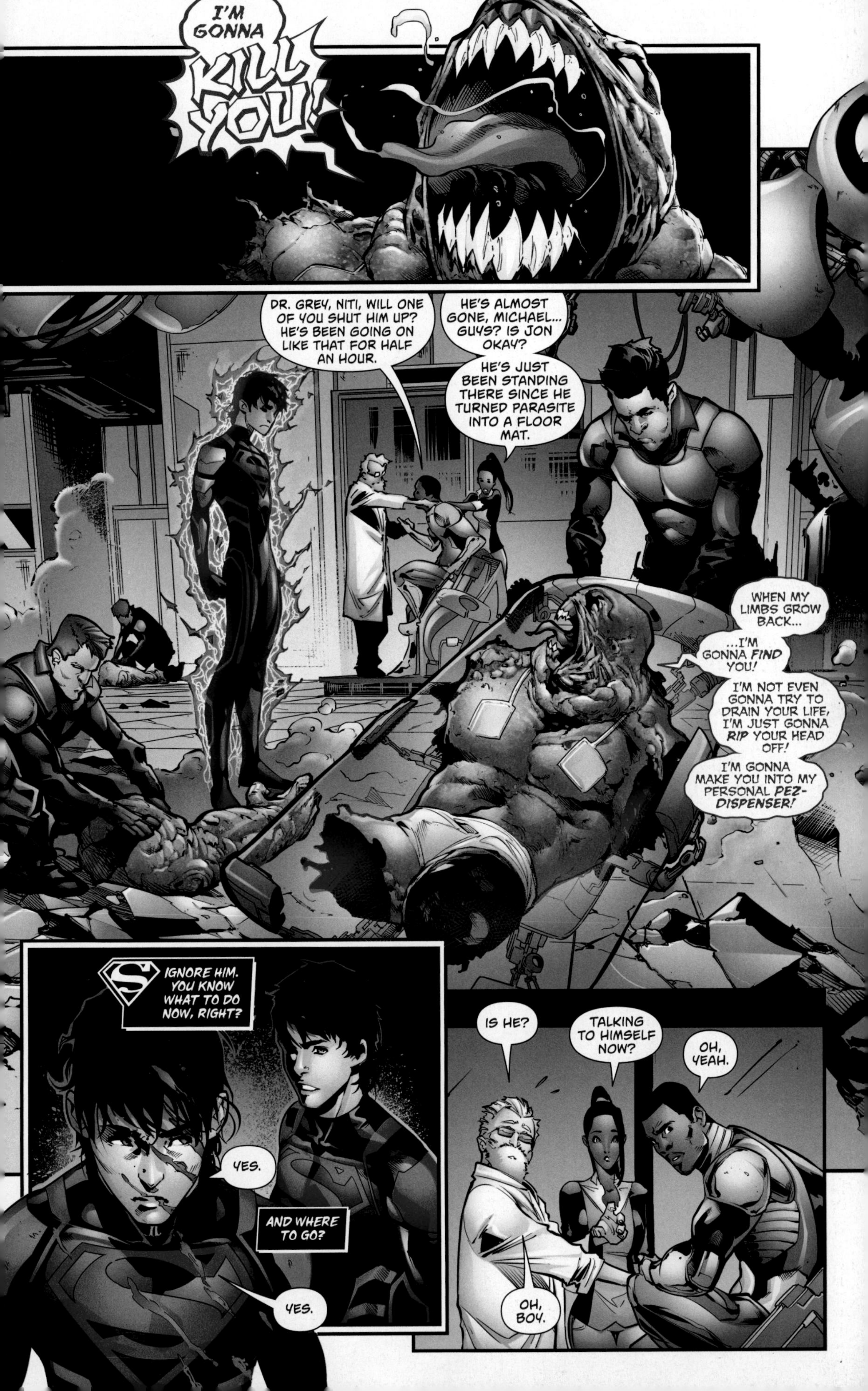

I'M GONNA KILL YOU!
DR. GREY, NITI, WILL ONE OF YOU SHUT HIM UP? HE'S BEEN GOING ON LIKE THAT FOR HALF AN HOUR.
HE'S ALMOST GONE, MICHAEL... GUYS? IS JON OKAY?
HE'S JUST BEEN STANDING THERE SINCE HE TURNED PARASITE INTO A FLOOR MAT.
WHEN MY LIMBS GROW BACK...
...I'M GONNA FIND YOU!
I'M NOT EVEN GONNA TRY TO DRAIN YOUR LIFE, I'M JUST GONNA RIP YOUR HEAD OFF!
I'M GONNA MAKE YOU INTO MY PERSONAL PEZ-DISPENSER!
IGNORE HIM. YOU KNOW WHAT TO DO NOW, RIGHT?
YES.
AND WHERE TO GO?
YES.
IS HE?
TALKING TO HIMSELF NOW?
OH, YEAH.
OH, BOY.

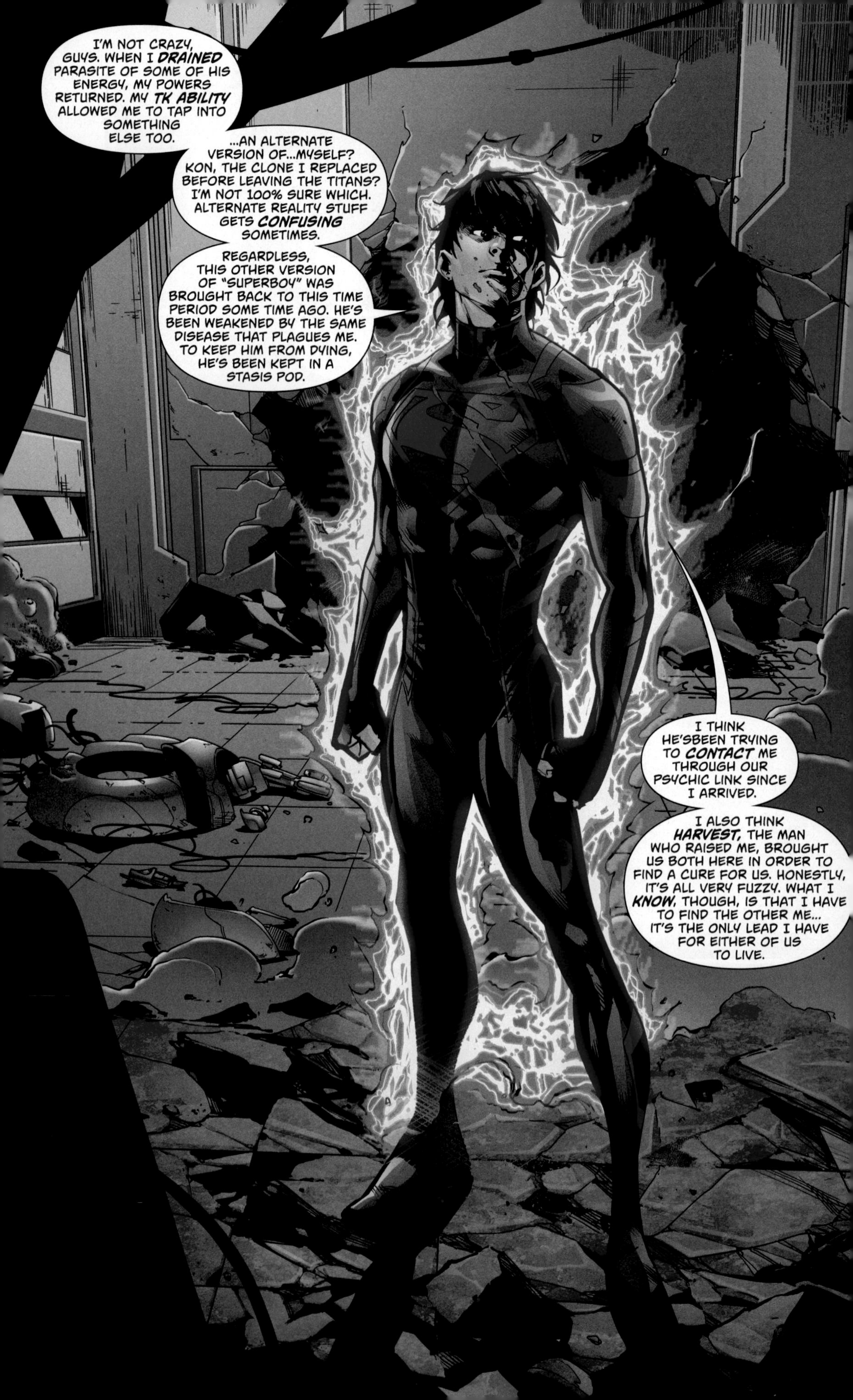
I'M NOT CRAZY, GUYS. WHEN I DRAINED PARASITE OF SOME OF HIS ENERGY, MY POWERS RETURNED. MY TK ABILITY ALLOWED ME TO TAP INTO SOMETHING ELSE TOO.
...AN ALTERNATE VERSION OF...MYSELF? KON, THE CLONE I REPLACED BEFORE LEAVING THE TITANS? I'M NOT 100% SURE WHICH. ALTERNATE REALITY STUFF GETS CONFUSING SOMETIMES.
REGARDLESS, THIS OTHER VERSION OF "SUPERBOY" WAS BROUGHT BACK TO THIS TIME PERIOD SOME TIME AGO. HE'S BEEN WEAKENED BY THE SAME DISEASE THAT PLAGUES ME. TO KEEP HIM FROM DYING, HE'S BEEN KEPT IN A STASIS POD.
I THINK HE'SBEEN TRYING TO CONTACT ME THROUGH OUR PSYCHIC LINK SINCE I ARRIVED.
I ALSO THINK HARVEST, THE MAN WHO RAISED ME, BROUGHT US BOTH HERE IN ORDER TO FIND A CURE FOR US. HONESTLY, IT'S ALL VERY FUZZY. WHAT I KNOW, THOUGH, IS THAT I HAVE TO FIND THE OTHER ME... IT'S THE ONLY LEAD I HAVE FOR EITHER OF US TO LIVE.

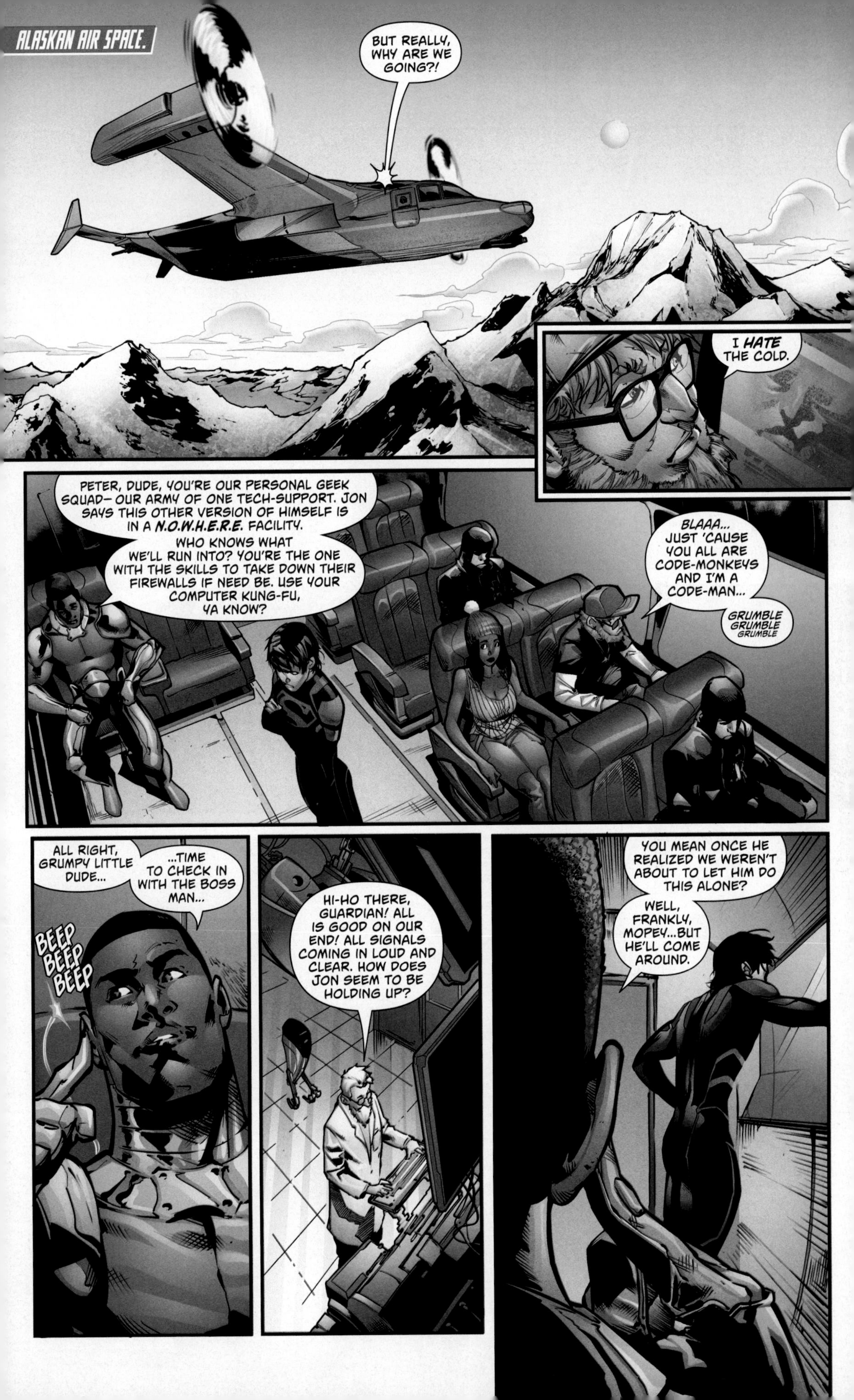
ALASKAN AIR SPACE.
BUT REALLY, WHY ARE WE GOING?!
I HATE THE COLD.
PETER, DUDE, YOU'RE OUR PERSONAL GEEK SQUAD— OUR ARMY OF ONE TECH-SUPPORT. JON SAYS THIS OTHER VERSION OF HIMSELF IS IN A N.O.W.H.E.R.E. FACILITY.
WHO KNOWS WHAT WE'LL RUN INTO? YOU'RE THE ONE WITH THE SKILLS TO TAKE DOWN THEIR FIREWALLS IF NEED BE. USE YOUR COMPUTER KUNG-FU, YA KNOW?
BLAAA... JUST 'CAUSE YOU ALL ARE CODE-MONKEYS AND I'M A CODE-MAN...
GRUMBLE GRUMBLE GRUMBLE
ALL RIGHT, GRUMPY LITTLE DUDE...
...TIME TO CHECK IN WITH THE BOSS MAN...
BEEP BEEP BEEP
HI-HO THERE, GUARDIAN! ALL IS GOOD ON OUR END! ALL SIGNALS COMING IN LOUD AND CLEAR. HOW DOES JON SEEM TO BE HOLDING UP?
YOU MEAN ONCE HE REALIZED WE WEREN'T ABOUT TO LET HIM DO THIS ALONE?
WELL, FRANKLY, MOPEY...BUT HE'LL COME AROUND.

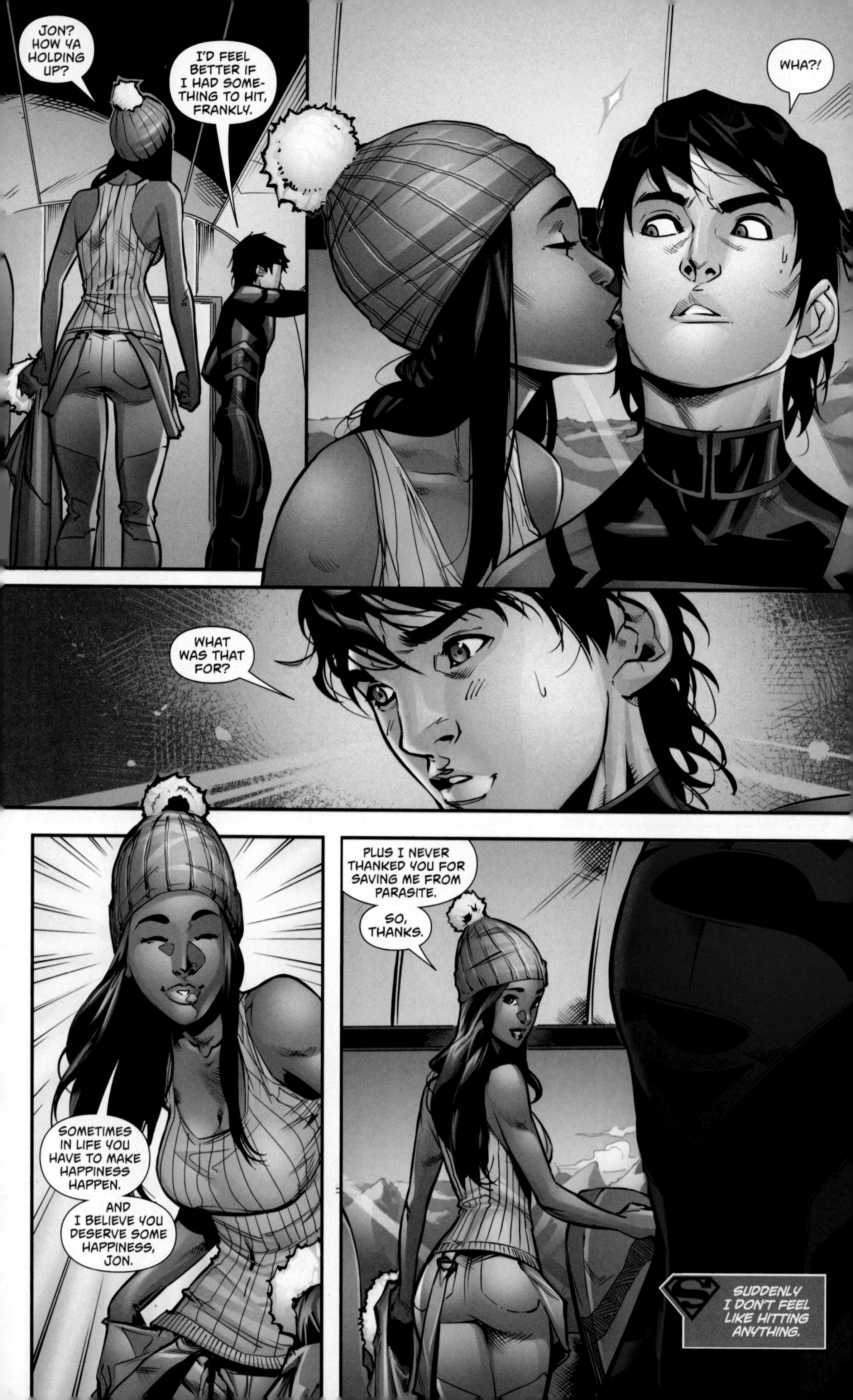
JON? HOW YA HOLDING UP?
I'D FEEL BETTER IF I HAD SOME-THING TO HIT, FRANKLY.
WHA?!
WHAT WAS THAT FOR?
SOMETIMES IN LIFE YOU HAVE TO MAKE HAPPINESS HAPPEN.
AND I BELIEVE YOU DESERVE SOME HAPPINESS, JON.
PLUS I NEVER THANKED YOU FOR SAVING ME FROM PARASITE.
SO, THANKS.
SUDDENLY I DON'T FEEL LIKE HITTING ANYTHING.

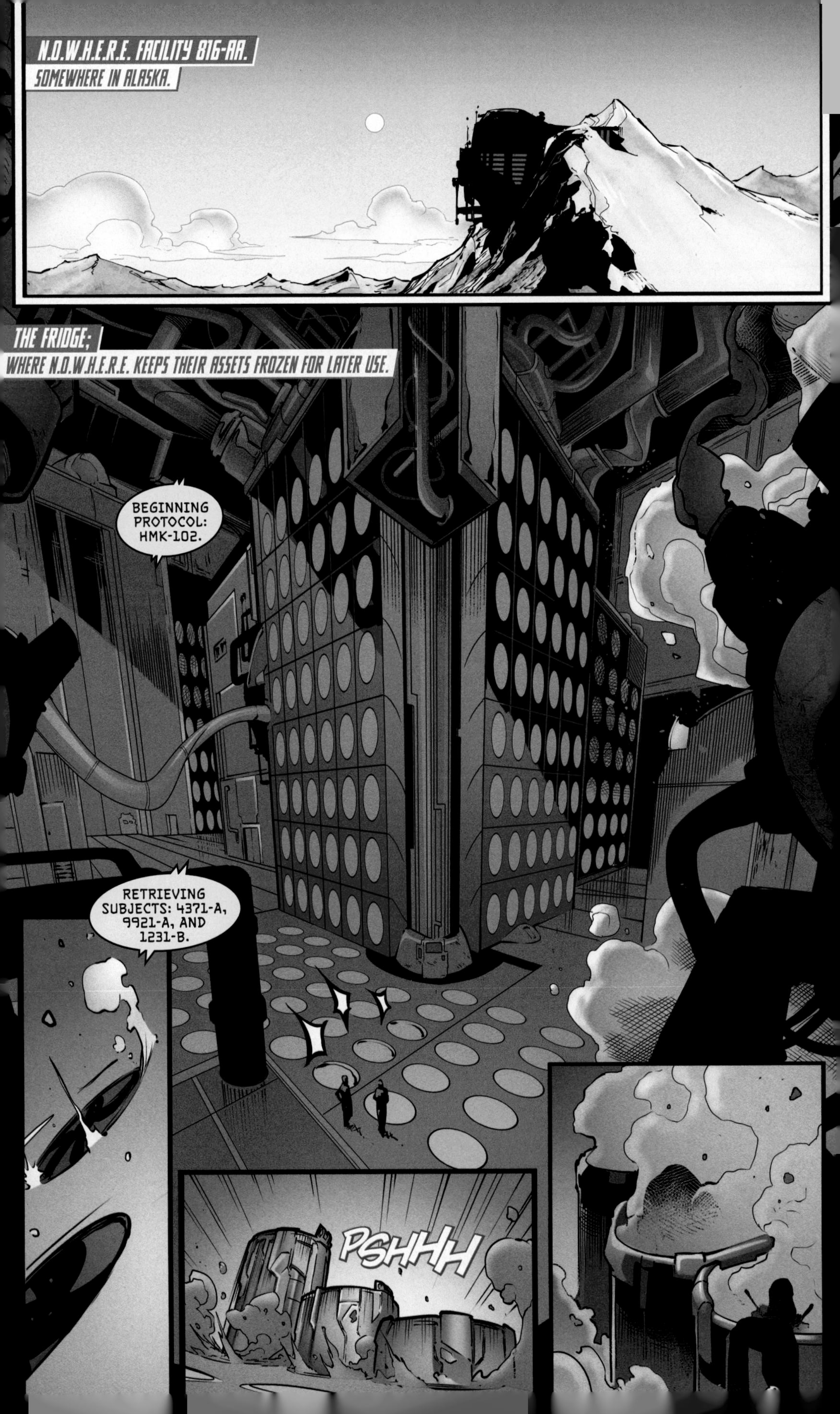
N.O.W.H.E.R.E. FACILITY 816-AA.
SOMEWHERE IN ALASKA.
THE FRIDGE;
WHERE N.O.W.H.E.R.E. KEEPS THEIR ASSETS FROZEN FOR LATER USE.
BEGINNING PROTOCOL: HMK-102.
RETRIEVING SUBJECTS: 4371-A, 9921-A, AND 1231-B.
PSHHH

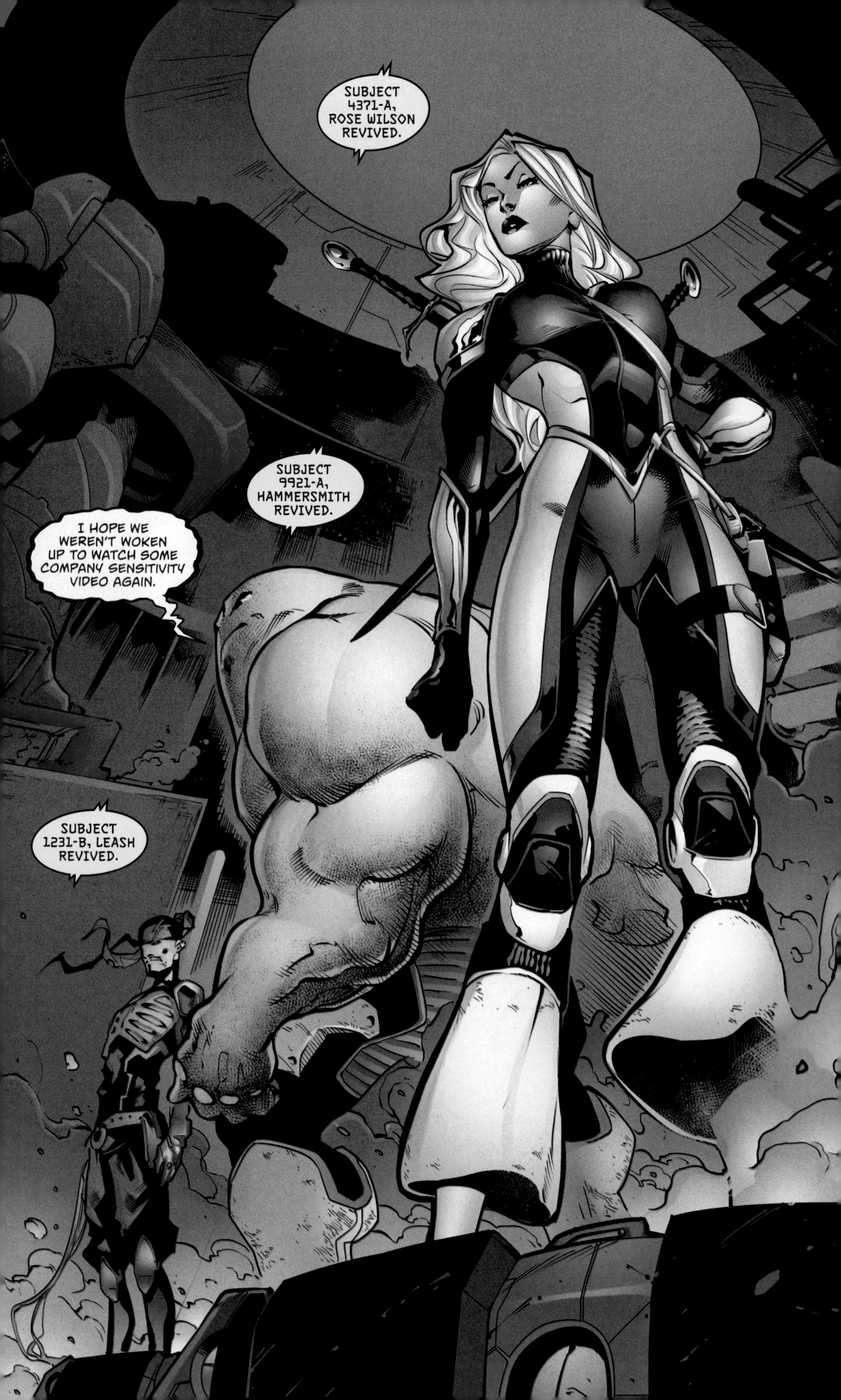
SUBJECT 4371-A, ROSE WILSON REVIVED.
SUBJECT 9921-A, HAMMERSMITH REVIVED.
I HOPE WE WEREN'T WOKEN UP TO WATCH SOME COMPANY SENSITIVITY VIDEO AGAIN.
SUBJECT 1231-B, LEASH REVIVED.

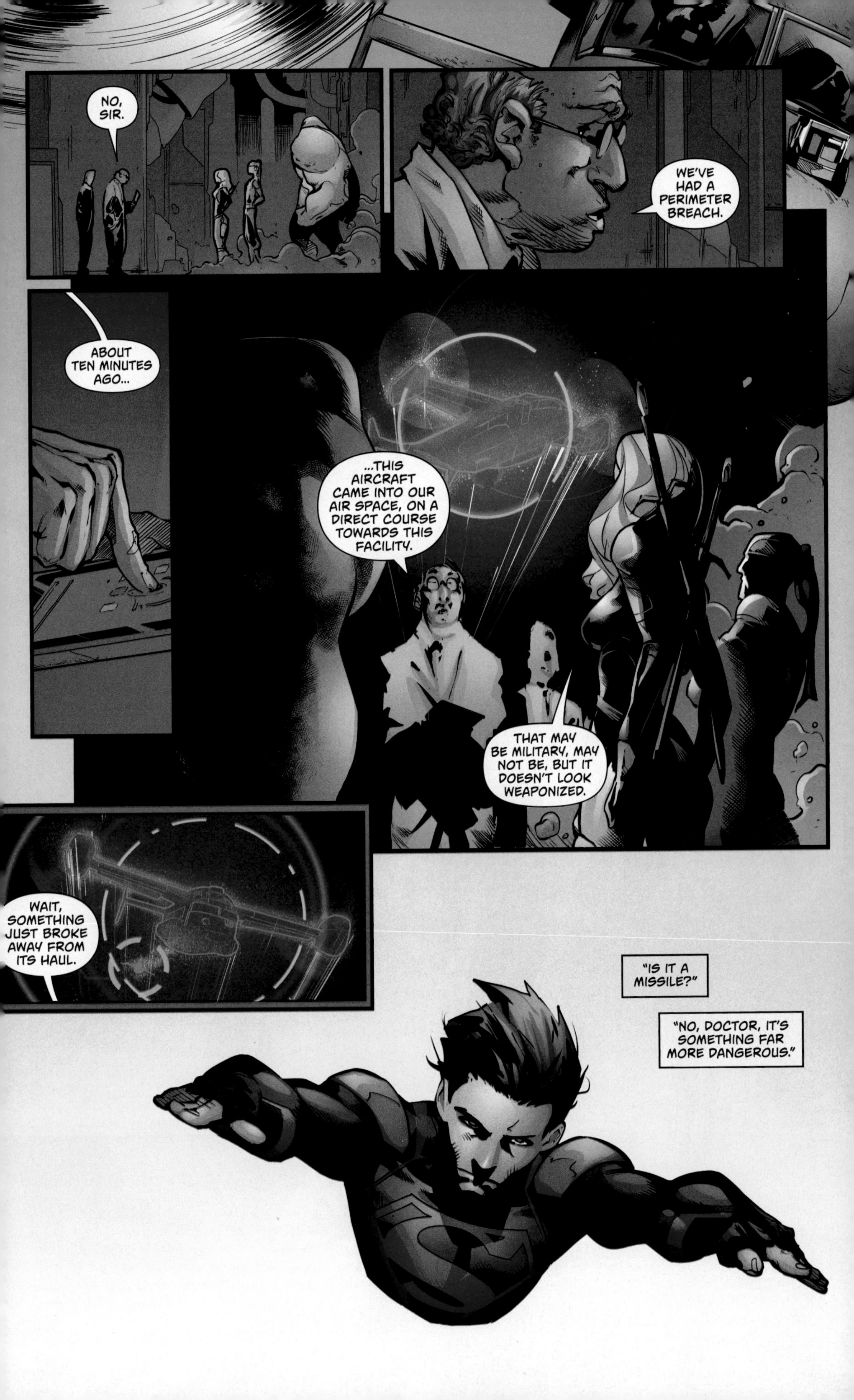
NO, SIR.
WE'VE HAD A PERIMETER BREACH.
ABOUT TEN MINUTES AGO...
...THIS AIRCRAFT CAME INTO OUR AIR SPACE, ON A DIRECT COURSE TOWARDS THIS FACILITY.
THAT MAY BE MILITARY, MAY NOT BE, BUT IT DOESN'T LOOK WEAPONIZED.
WAIT, SOMETHING JUST BROKE AWAY FROM ITS HAUL.
"IS IT A MISSILE?"
"NO, DOCTOR, IT'S SOMETHING FAR MORE DANGEROUS."

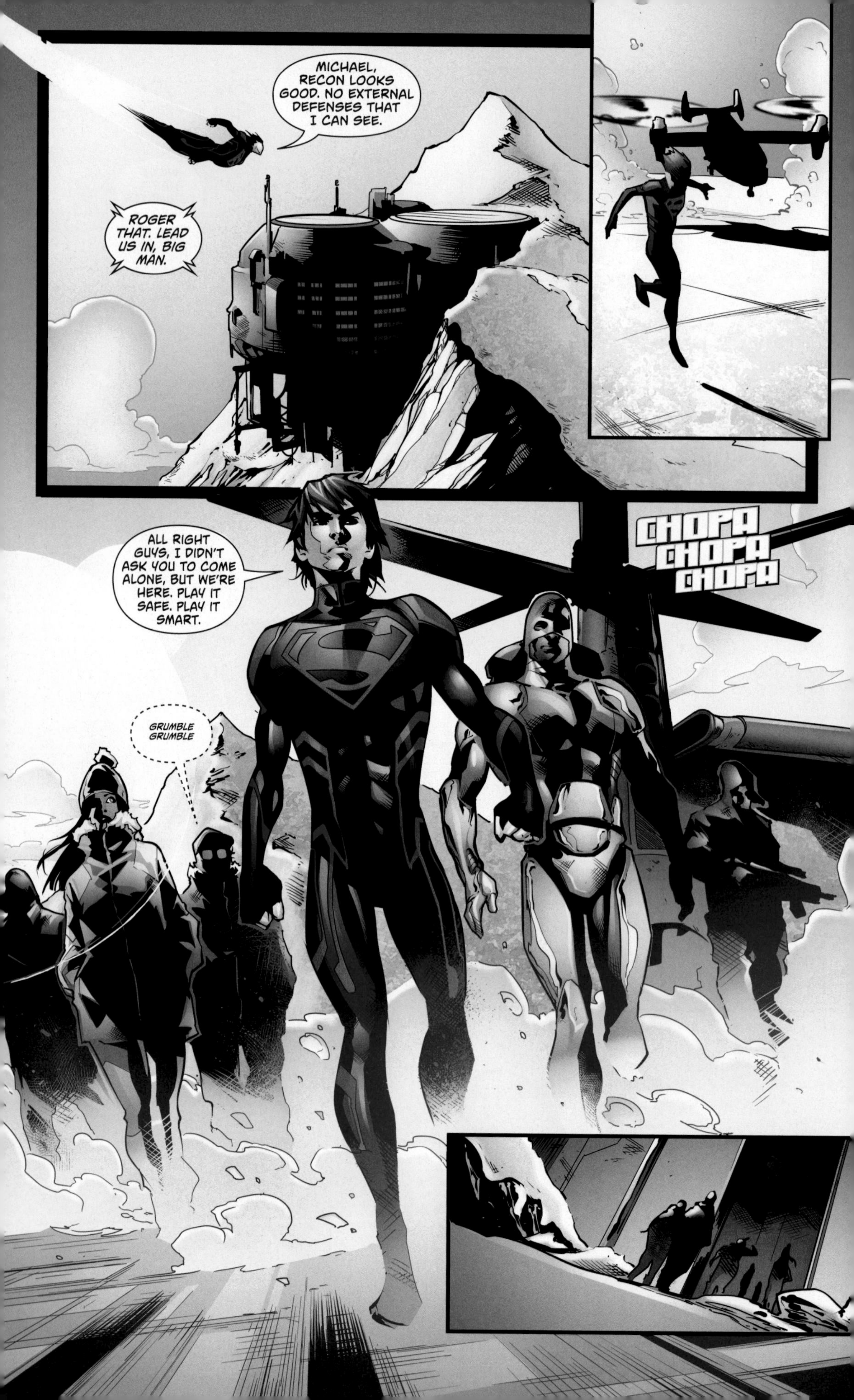
MICHAEL, RECON LOOKS GOOD. NO EXTERNAL DEFENSES THAT I CAN SEE.
ROGER THAT. LEAD US IN, BIG MAN.
ALL RIGHT GUYS, I DIDN'T ASK YOU TO COME ALONE, BUT WE'RE HERE. PLAY IT SAFE. PLAY IT SMART.
CHOPA CHOPA CHOPA
GRUMBLE GRUMBLE

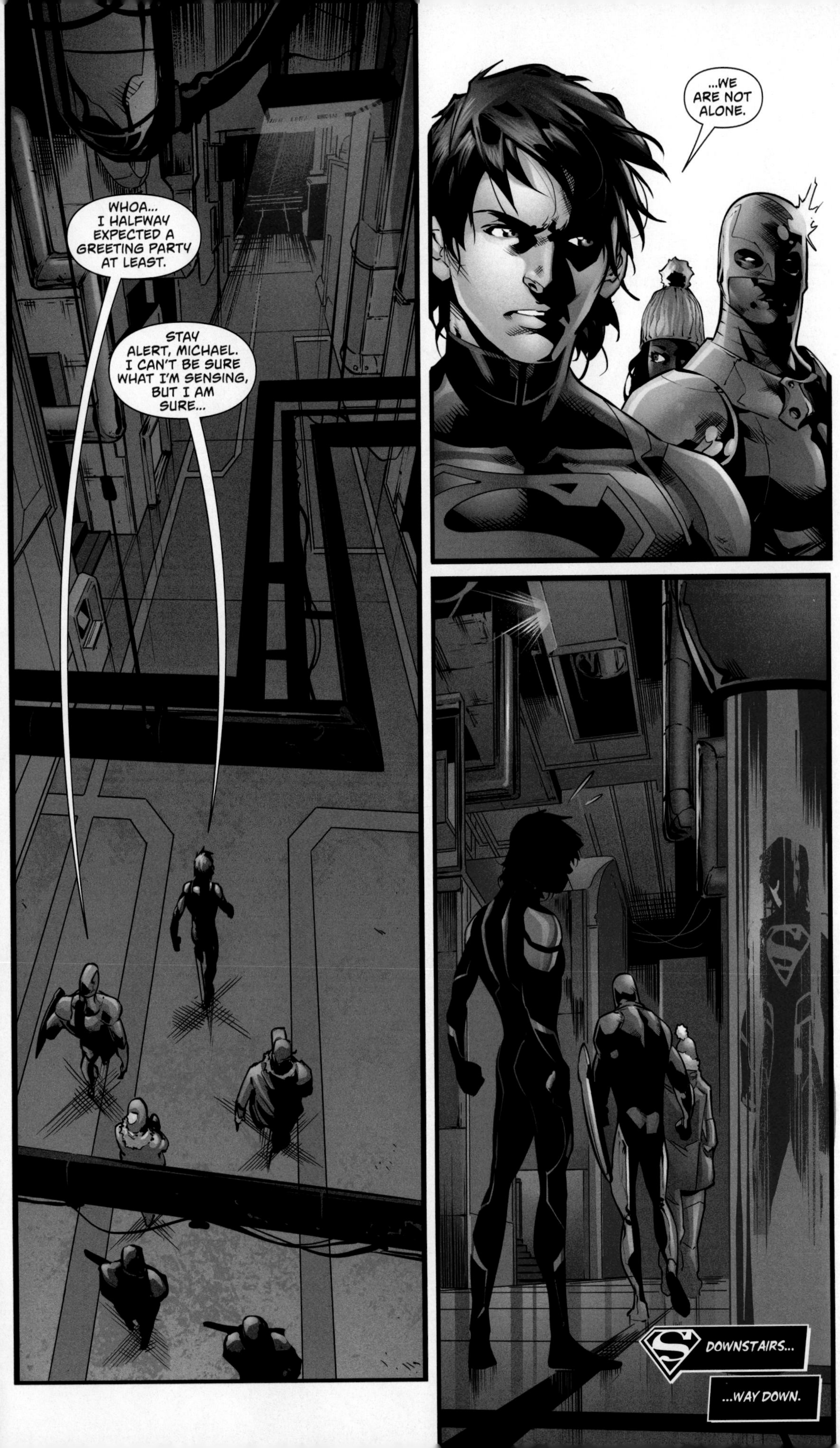
WHOA... I HALFWAY EXPECTED A GREETING PARTY AT LEAST.
STAY ALERT, MICHAEL. I CAN'T BE SURE WHAT I'M SENSING, BUT I AM SURE...
...WE ARE NOT ALONE.
DOWNSTAIRS...
...WAY DOWN.

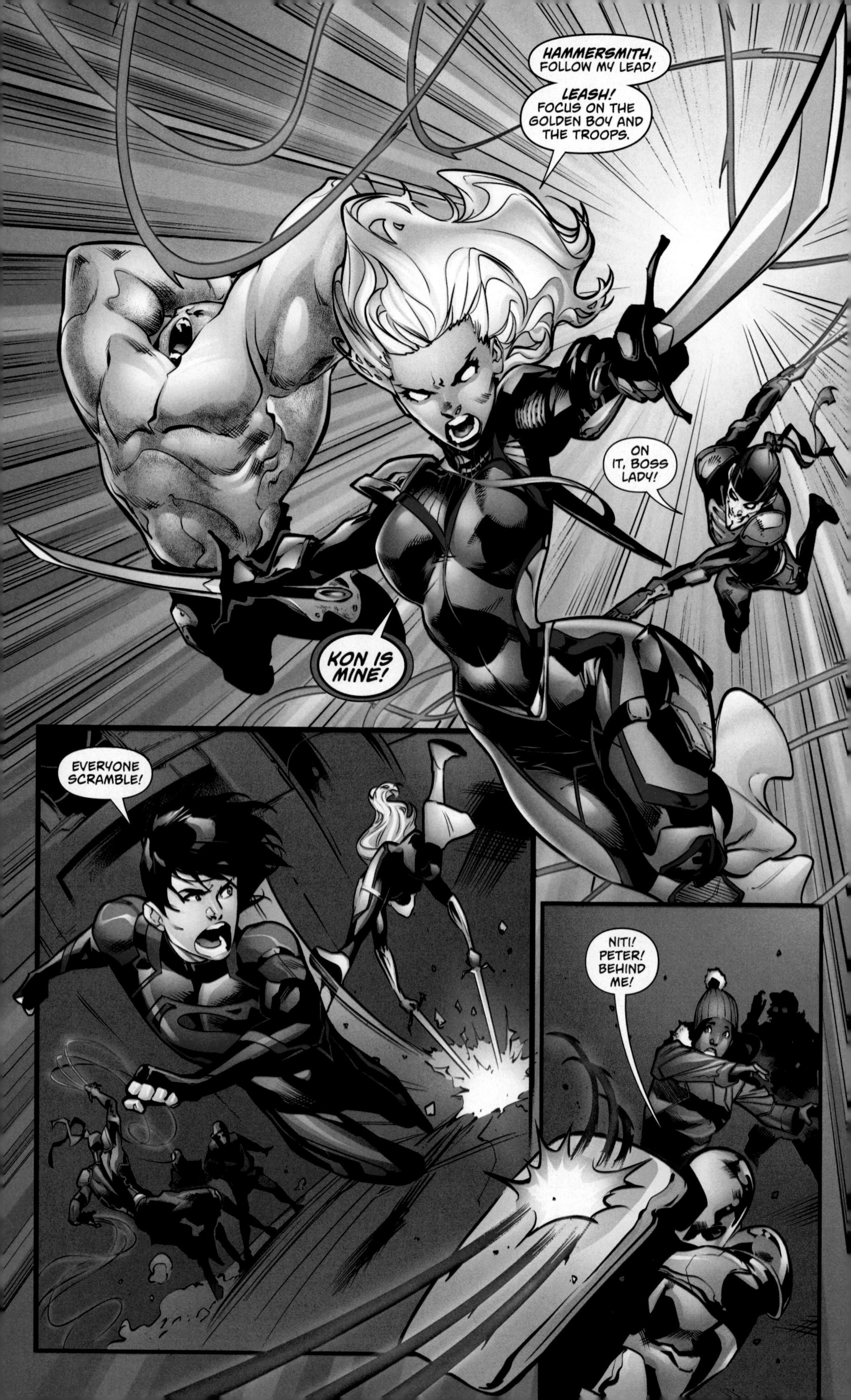
HAMMERSMITH, FOLLOW MY LEAD!
LEASH! FOCUS ON THE GOLDEN BOY AND THE TROOPS.
ON IT, BOSS LADY!
KON IS MINE!
EVERYONE SCRAMBLE!
NITI! PETER! BEHIND ME!

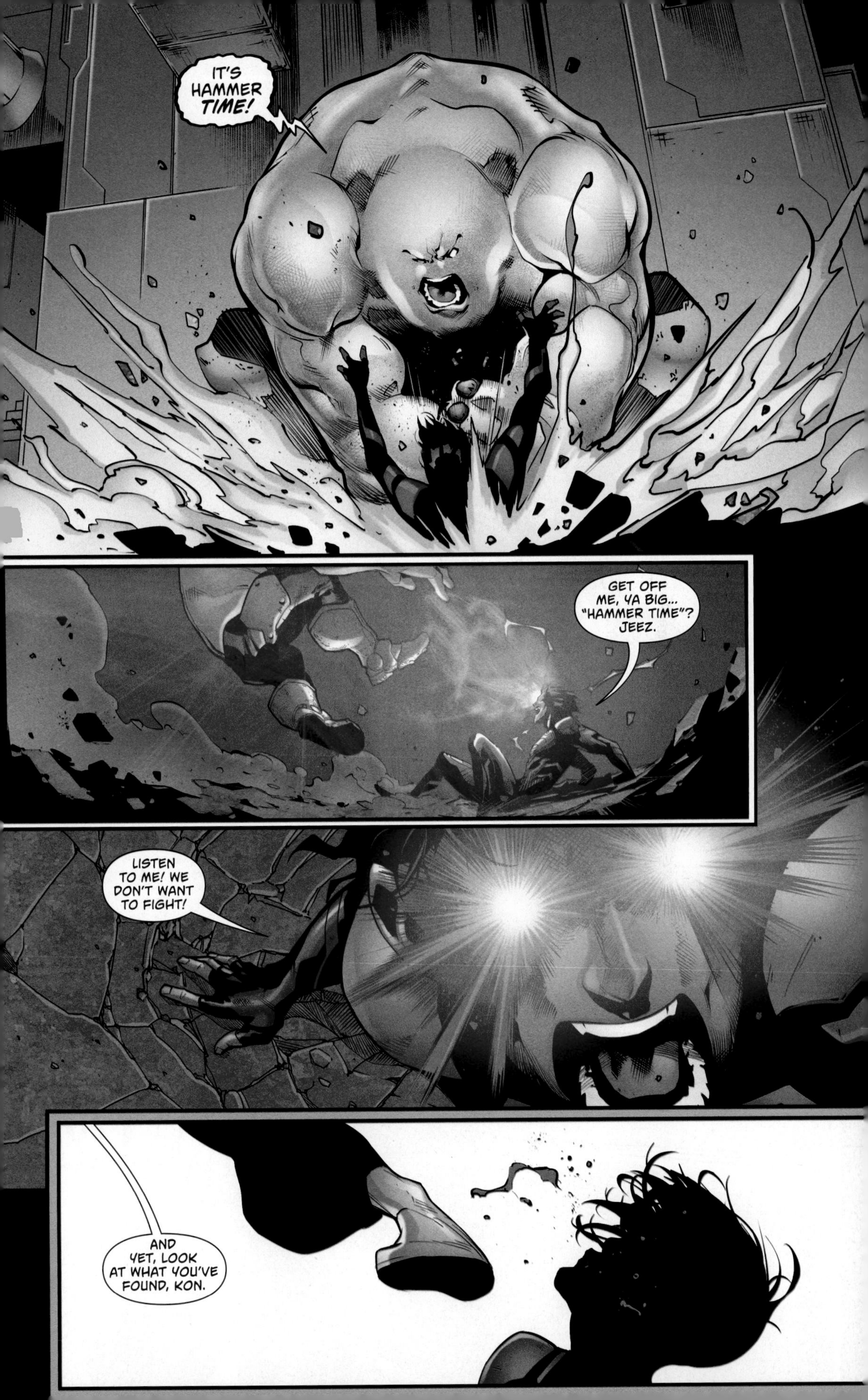
IT'S HAMMER TIME!
GET OFF ME, YA BIG... "HAMMER TIME"? JEEZ.
LISTEN TO ME! WE DON'T WANT TO FIGHT!
AND YET, LOOK AT WHAT YOU'VE FOUND, KON.

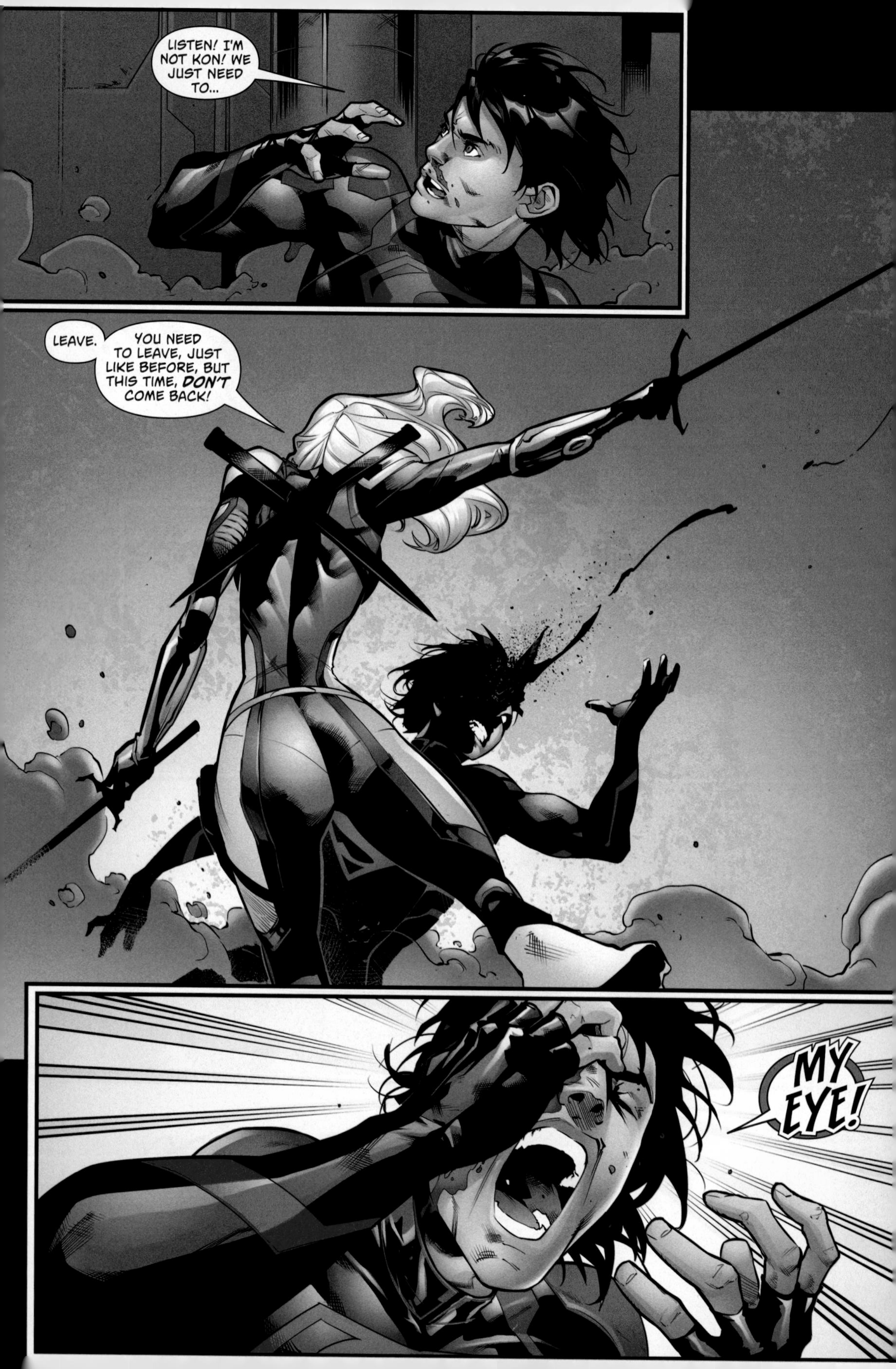
LISTEN! I'M NOT KON! WE JUST NEED TO...
LEAVE.
YOU NEED TO LEAVE, JUST LIKE BEFORE, BUT THIS TIME, *DON'T* COME BACK!
MY EYE!

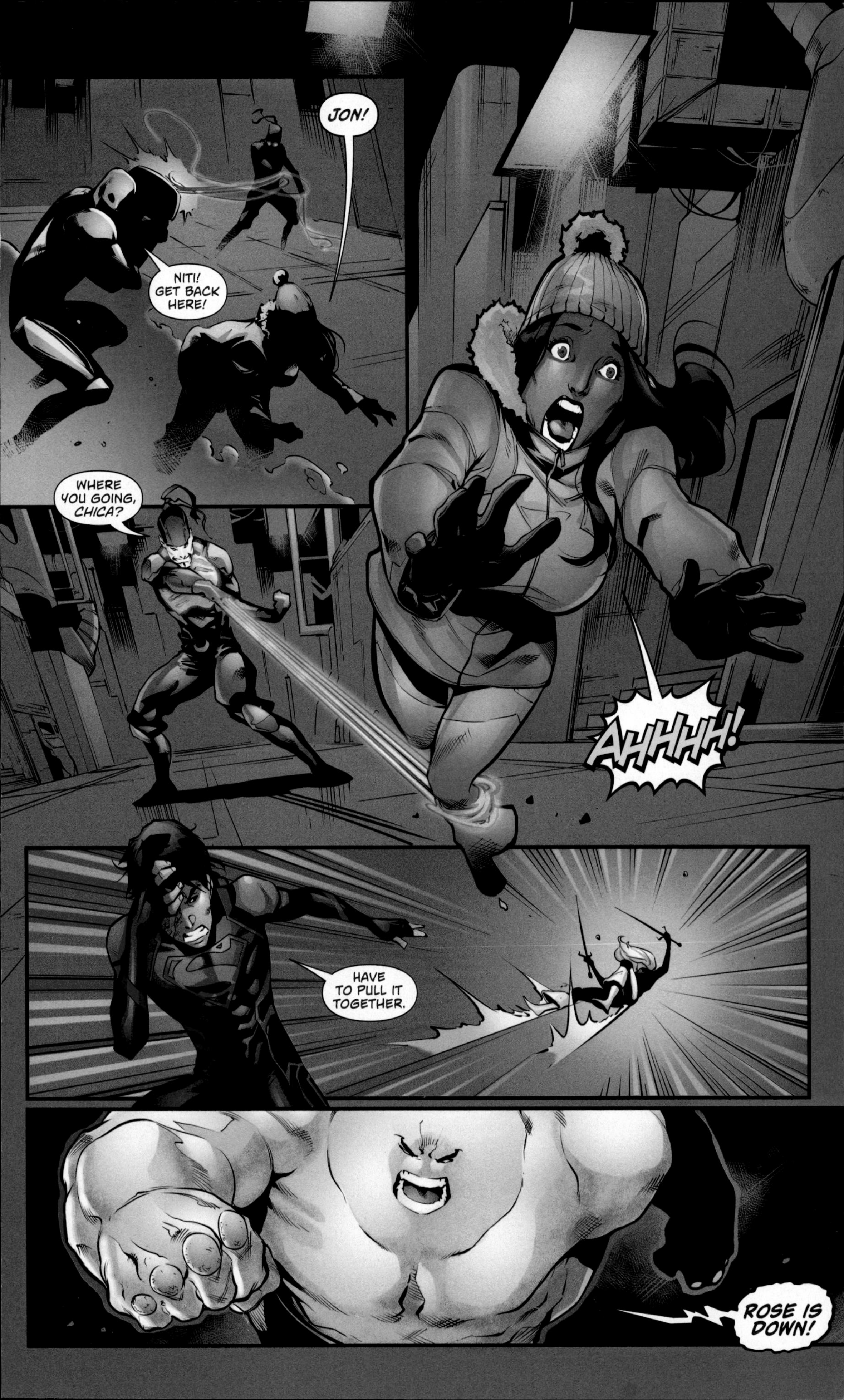
JON!
NITI! GET BACK HERE!
WHERE YOU GOING, CHICA?
AHHHH!
HAVE TO PULL IT TOGETHER.
ROSE IS DOWN!

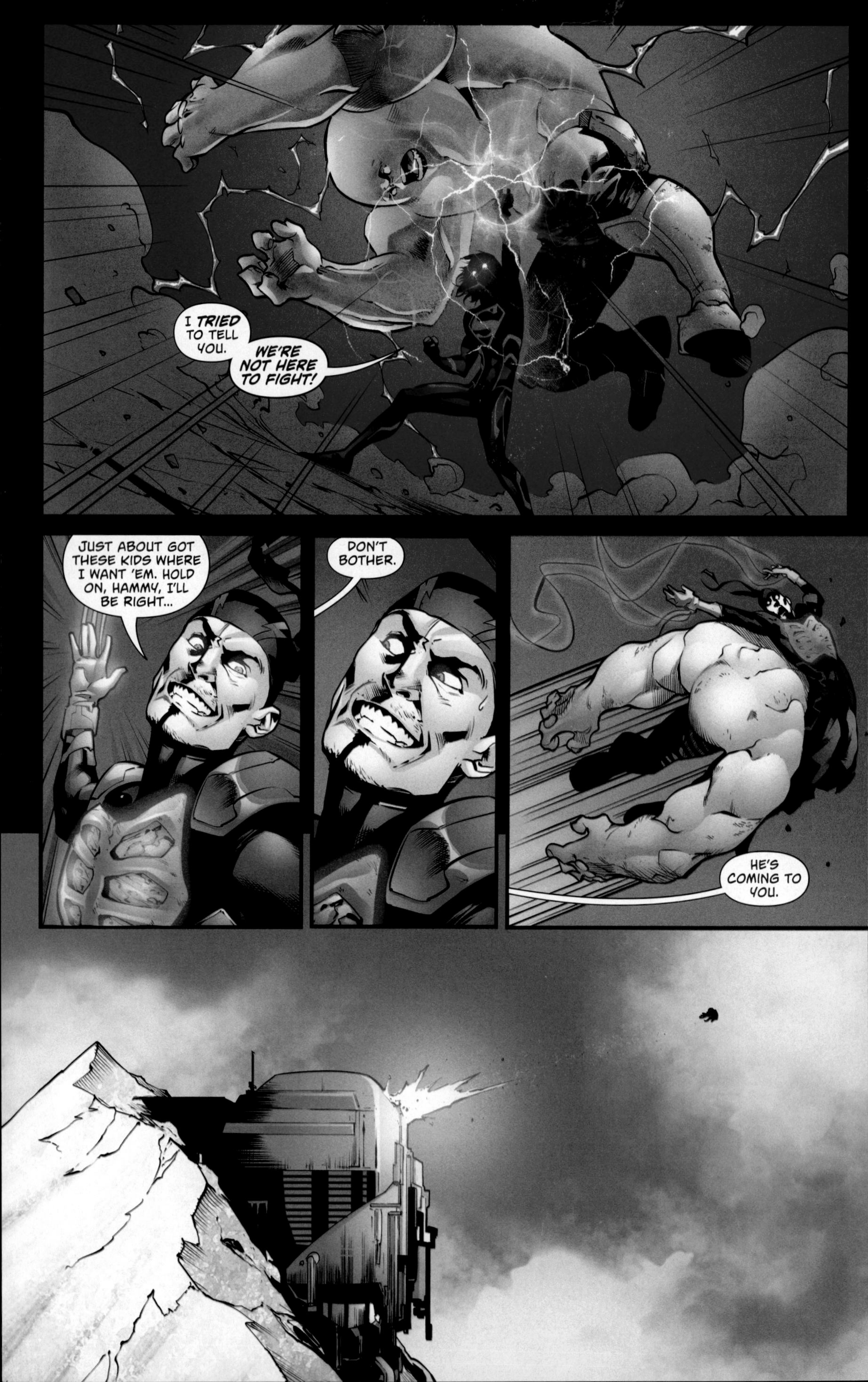
I TRIED TO TELL YOU.
WE'RE NOT HERE TO FIGHT!
JUST ABOUT GOT THESE KIDS WHERE I WANT 'EM. HOLD ON, HAMMY, I'LL BE RIGHT...
DON'T BOTHER.
HE'S COMING TO YOU.

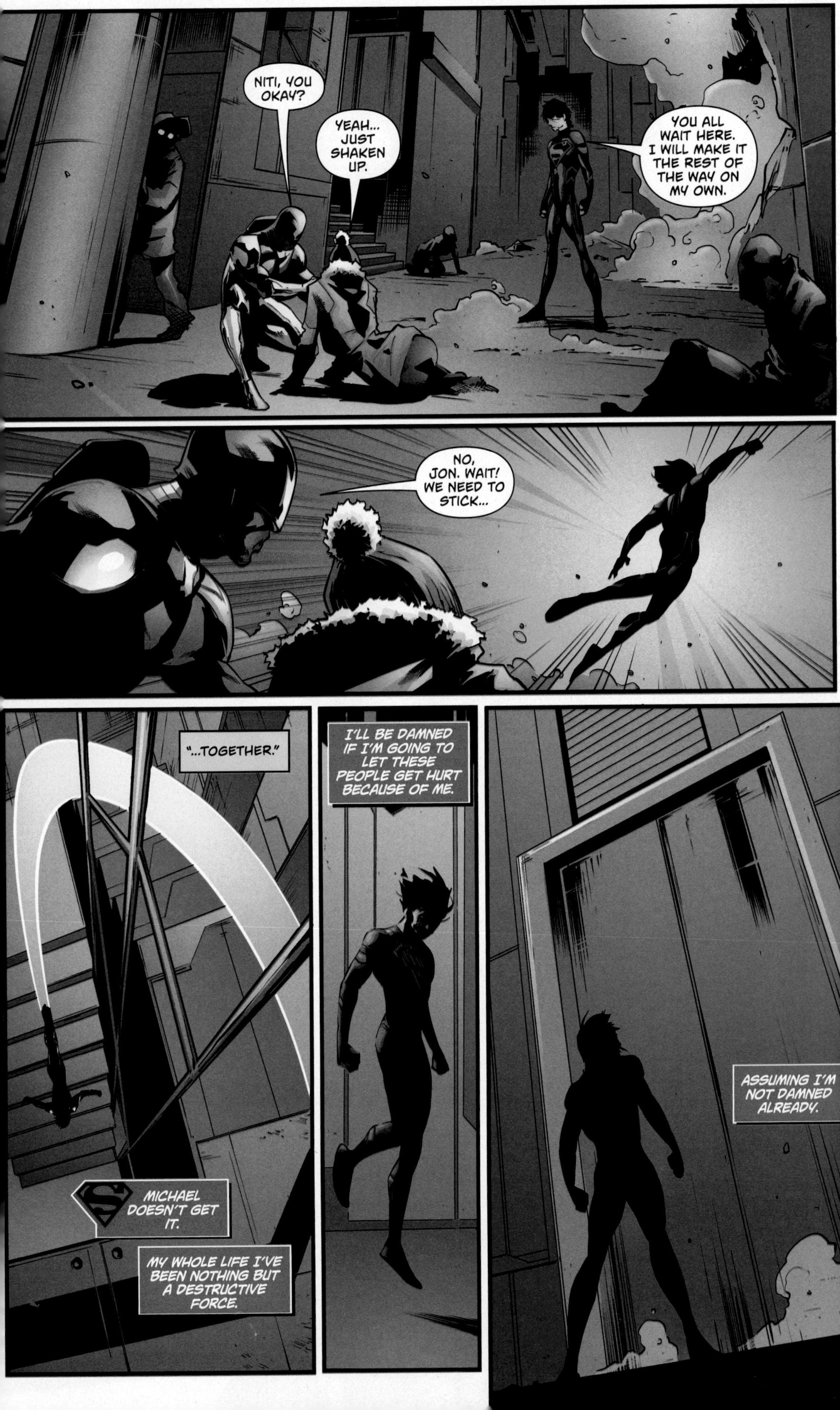
NITI, YOU OKAY?
YEAH... JUST SHAKEN UP.
YOU ALL WAIT HERE. I WILL MAKE IT THE REST OF THE WAY ON MY OWN.
NO, JON. WAIT! WE NEED TO STICK...
"...TOGETHER."
MICHAEL DOESN'T GET IT.
MY WHOLE LIFE I'VE BEEN NOTHING BUT A DESTRUCTIVE FORCE.
I'LL BE DAMNED IF I'M GOING TO LET THESE PEOPLE GET HURT BECAUSE OF ME.
ASSUMING I'M NOT DAMNED ALREADY.

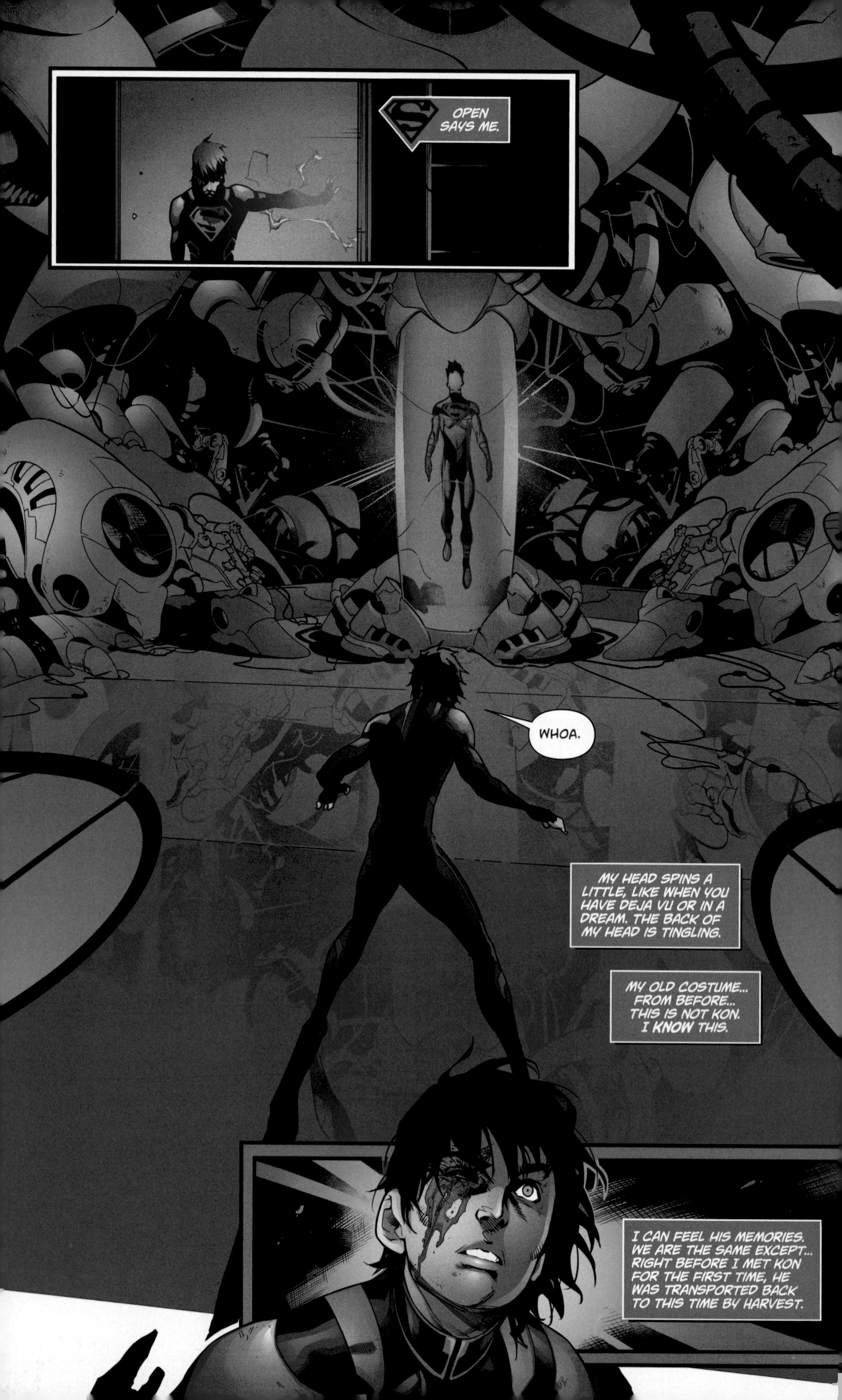
OPEN SAYS ME.
WHOA.
MY HEAD SPINS A LITTLE, LIKE WHEN YOU HAVE DEJA VU OR IN A DREAM. THE BACK OF MY HEAD IS TINGLING.
MY OLD COSTUME... FROM BEFORE... THIS IS NOT KON. I KNOW THIS.
I CAN FEEL HIS MEMORIES. WE ARE THE SAME EXCEPT... RIGHT BEFORE I MET KON FOR THE FIRST TIME, HE WAS TRANSPORTED BACK TO THIS TIME BY HARVEST.

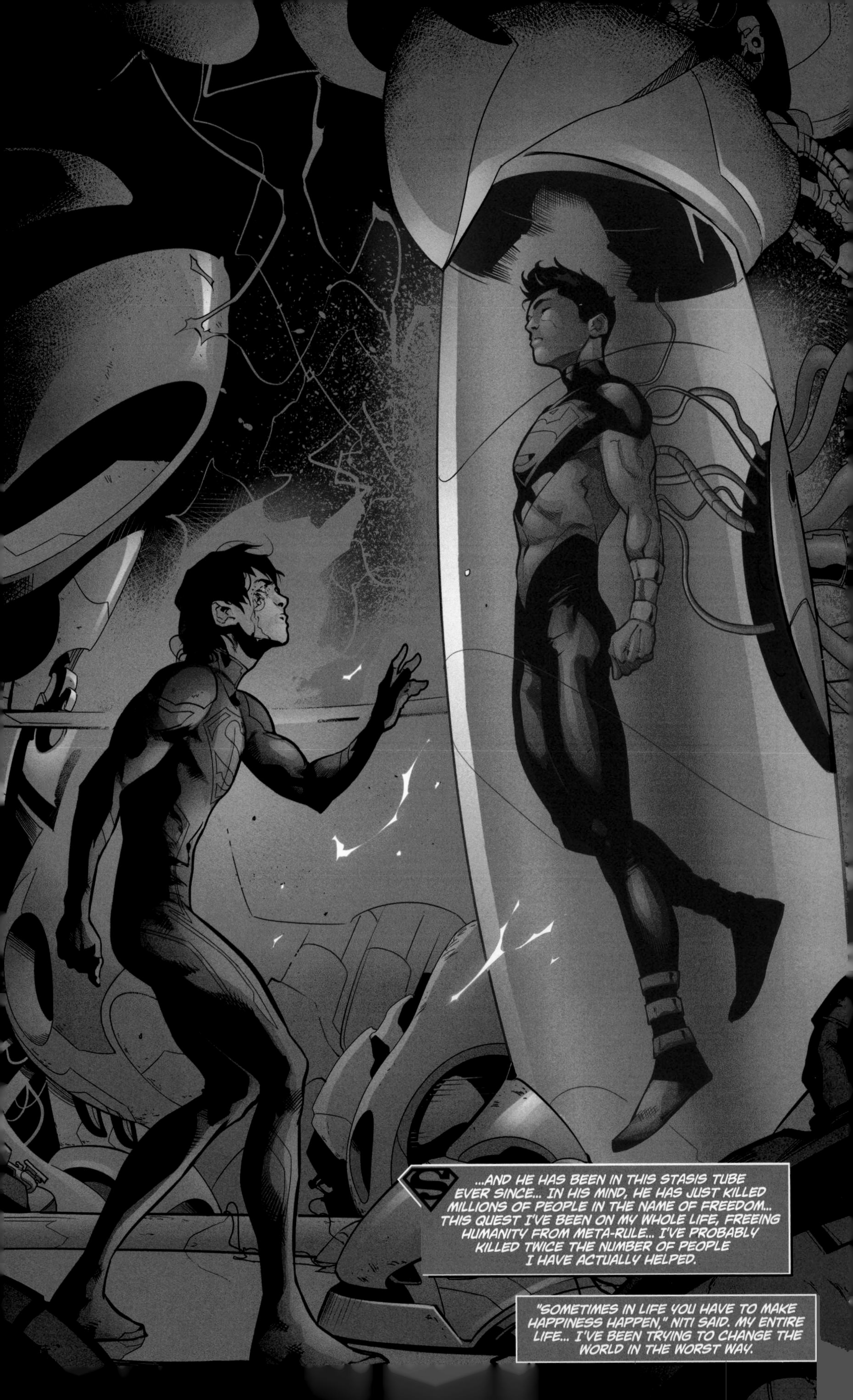
...AND HE HAS BEEN IN THIS STASIS TUBE EVER SINCE... IN HIS MIND, HE HAS JUST KILLED MILLIONS OF PEOPLE IN THE NAME OF FREEDOM... THIS QUEST I'VE BEEN ON MY WHOLE LIFE, FREEING HUMANITY FROM META-RULE... I'VE PROBABLY KILLED TWICE THE NUMBER OF PEOPLE I HAVE ACTUALLY HELPED.
"SOMETIMES IN LIFE YOU HAVE TO MAKE HAPPINESS HAPPEN," NITI SAID. MY ENTIRE LIFE... I'VE BEEN TRYING TO CHANGE THE WORLD IN THE WORST WAY.

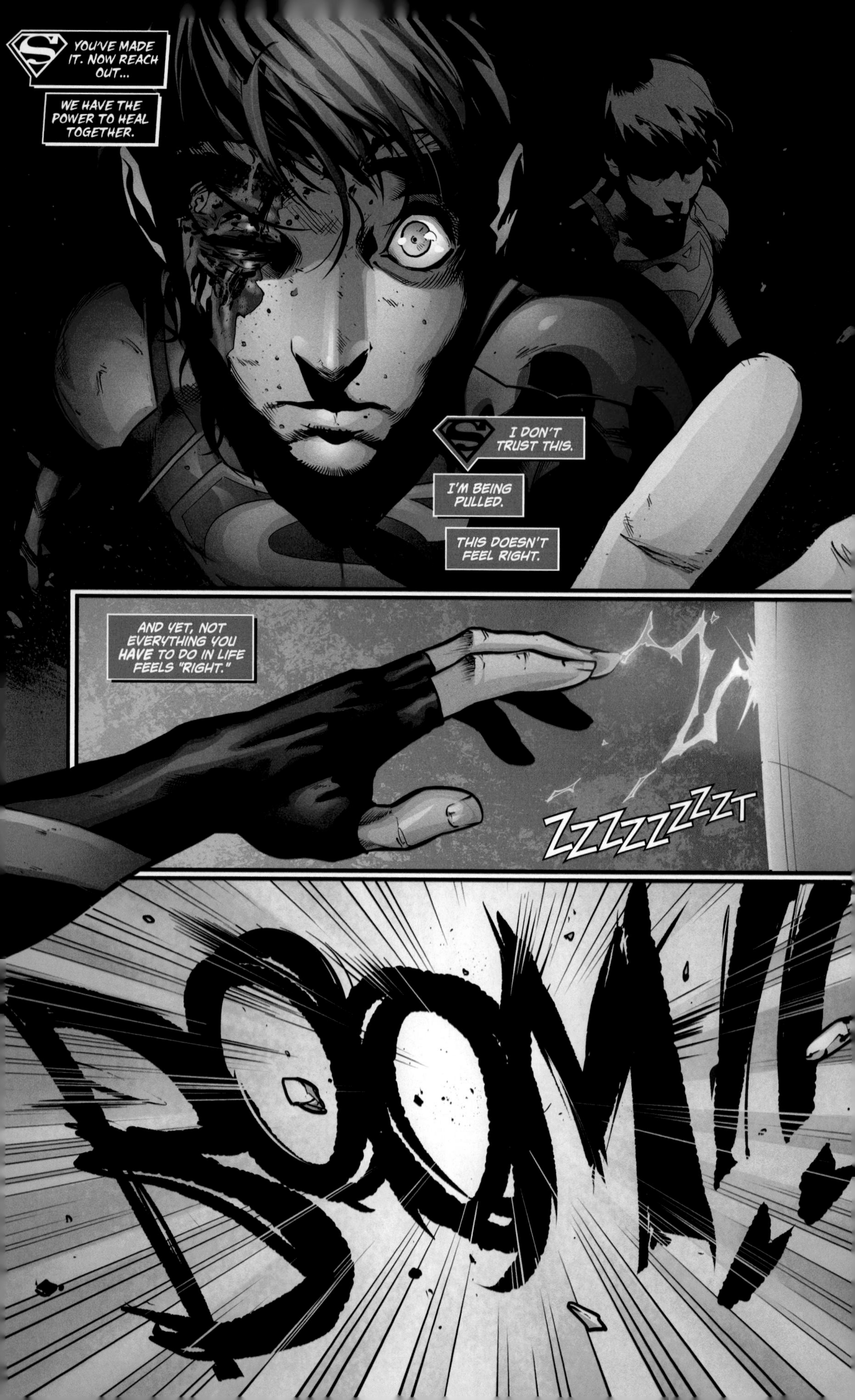

YOU'VE MADE IT. NOW REACH OUT...
WE HAVE THE POWER TO HEAL TOGETHER.
I DON'T TRUST THIS.
I'M BEING PULLED.
THIS DOESN'T FEEL RIGHT.
AND YET, NOT EVERYTHING YOU HAVE TO DO IN LIFE FEELS "RIGHT."
ZZZZZZZZZT
BOOM!!

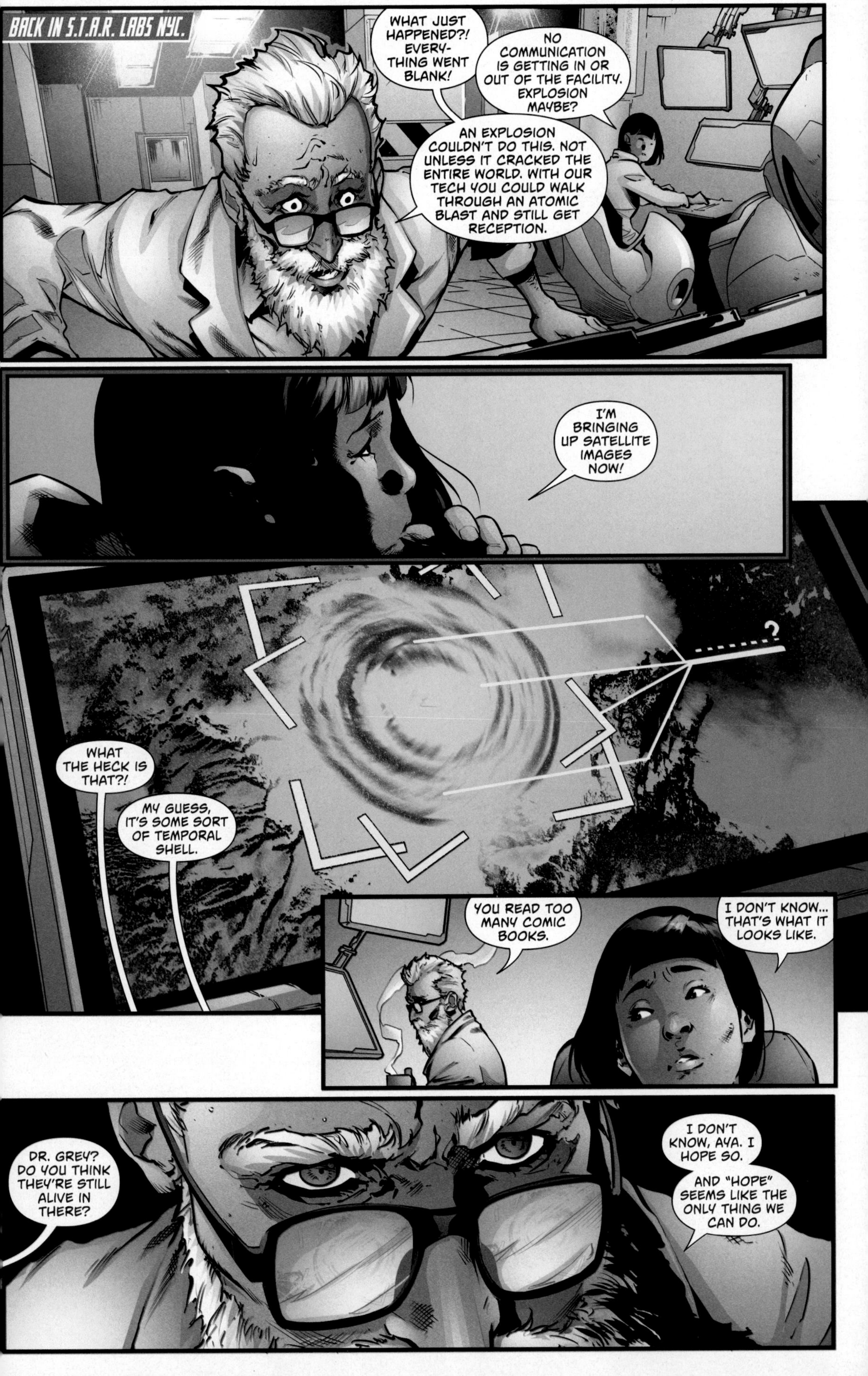
BACK IN S.T.A.R. LABS NYC.
WHAT JUST HAPPENED?! EVERY-THING WENT BLANK!
NO COMMUNICATION IS GETTING IN OR OUT OF THE FACILITY. EXPLOSION MAYBE?
AN EXPLOSION COULDN'T DO THIS. NOT UNLESS IT CRACKED THE ENTIRE WORLD. WITH OUR TECH YOU COULD WALK THROUGH AN ATOMIC BLAST AND STILL GET RECEPTION.
I'M BRINGING UP SATELLITE IMAGES NOW!
?
WHAT THE HECK IS THAT?!
MY GUESS, IT'S SOME SORT OF TEMPORAL SHELL.
YOU READ TOO MANY COMIC BOOKS.
I DON'T KNOW... THAT'S WHAT IT LOOKS LIKE.
DR. GREY? DO YOU THINK THEY'RE STILL ALIVE IN THERE?
I DON'T KNOW, AYA. I HOPE SO.
AND "HOPE" SEEMS LIKE THE ONLY THING WE CAN DO.

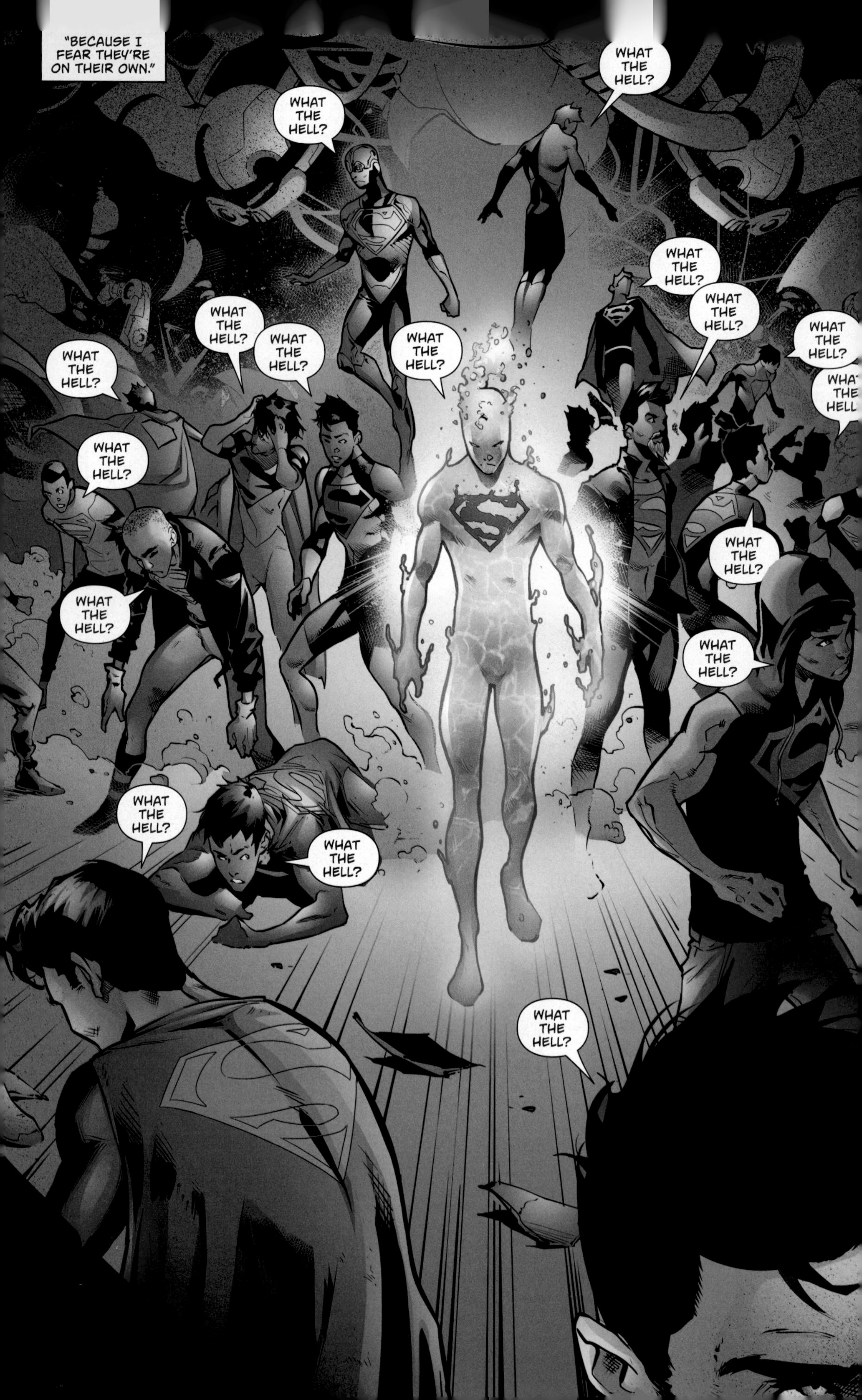
"BECAUSE I FEAR THEY'RE ON THEIR OWN."
WHAT THE HELL?
WHAT THE HELL?
WHAT THE HELL?
WHAT THE HELL?
WHAT THE HELL?
WHAT THE HELL?
WHAT THE HELL?
WHAT THE HELL?
WHAT THE HELL?
WHA THE HELL
WHAT THE HELL?
WHAT THE HELL?
WHAT THE HELL?
WHAT THE HELL?
WHAT THE HELL?
WHAT THE HELL?
WHAT THE HELL?

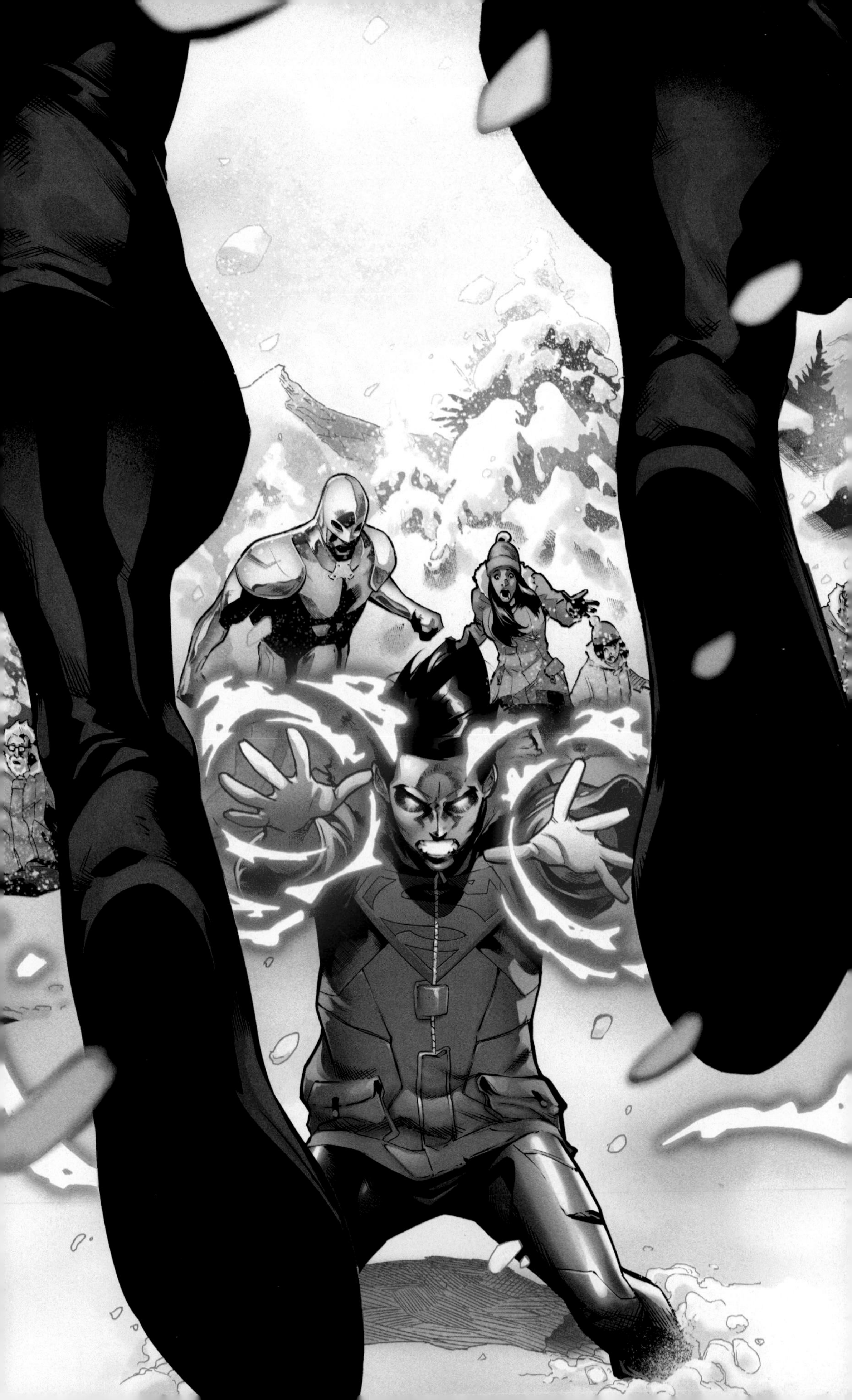

PARADOX

AARON KUDER writer JORGE JIMÉNEZ artist TANYA and RICHARD HORIE colorists
CARLOS M. MANGUAL letterer cover art by JORGE JIMÉNEZ and MIKE ATIYEH

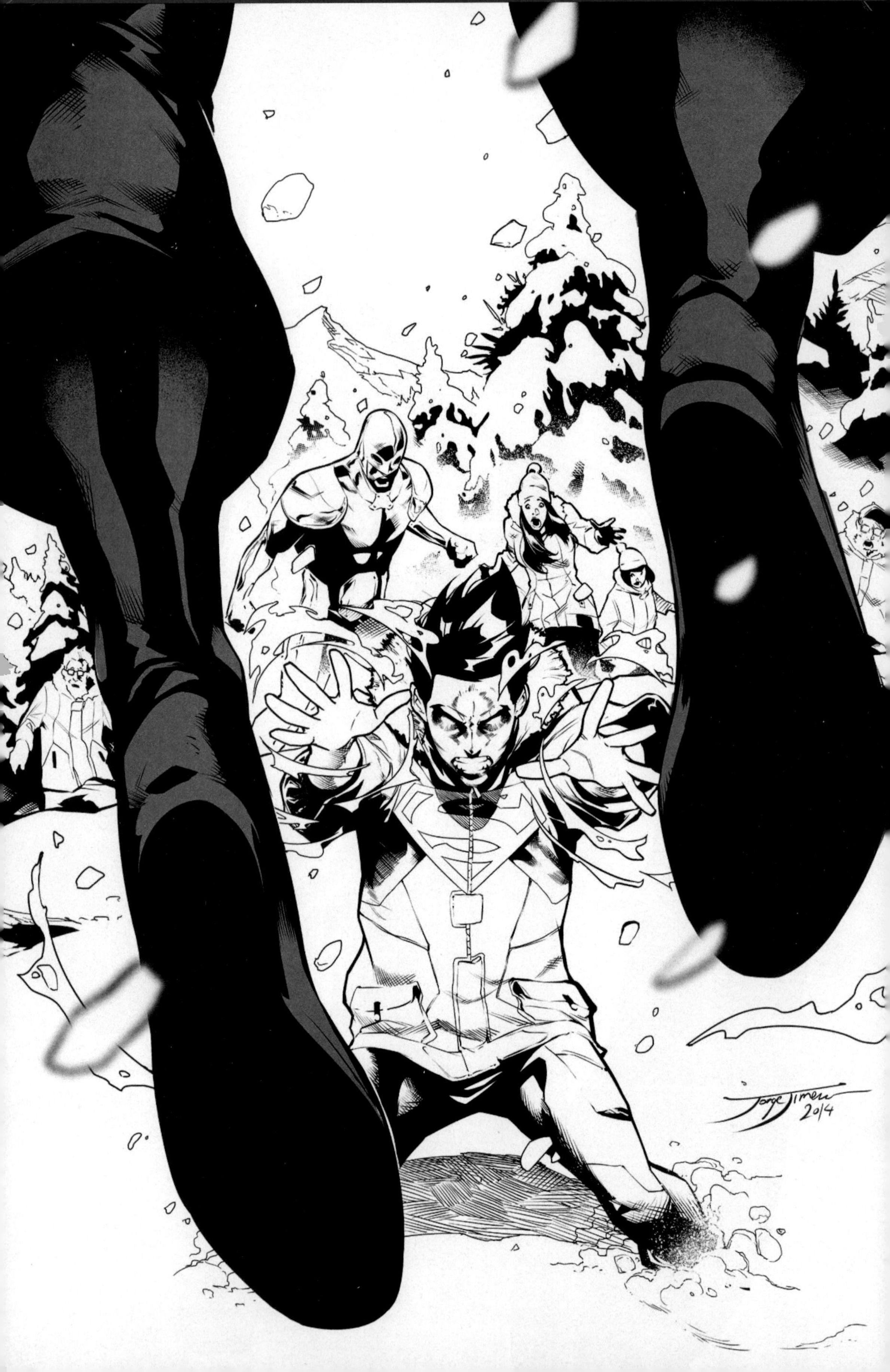

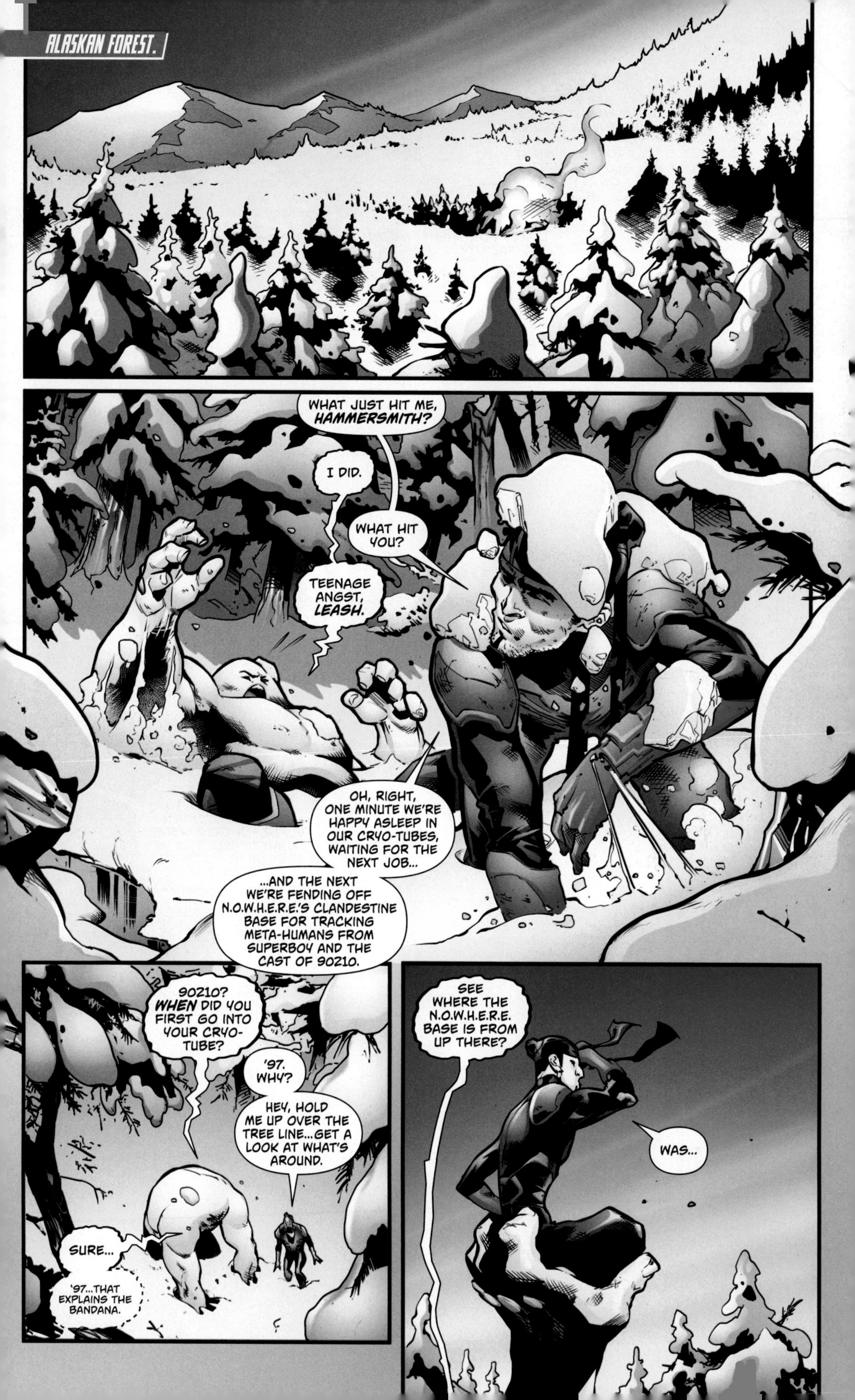
ALASKAN FOREST.
WHAT JUST HIT ME, HAMMERSMITH?
I DID.
WHAT HIT YOU?
TEENAGE ANGST, LEASH.
OH, RIGHT, ONE MINUTE WE'RE HAPPY ASLEEP IN OUR CRYO-TUBES, WAITING FOR THE NEXT JOB...
...AND THE NEXT WE'RE FENDING OFF N.O.W.H.E.R.E.'S CLANDESTINE BASE FOR TRACKING META-HUMANS FROM SUPERBOY AND THE CAST OF 90210.
90210? WHEN DID YOU FIRST GO INTO YOUR CRYO-TUBE?
'97. WHY?
HEY, HOLD ME UP OVER THE TREE LINE...GET A LOOK AT WHAT'S AROUND.
SURE...
'97...THAT EXPLAINS THE BANDANA.
SEE WHERE THE N.O.W.H.E.R.E. BASE IS FROM UP THERE?
WAS...

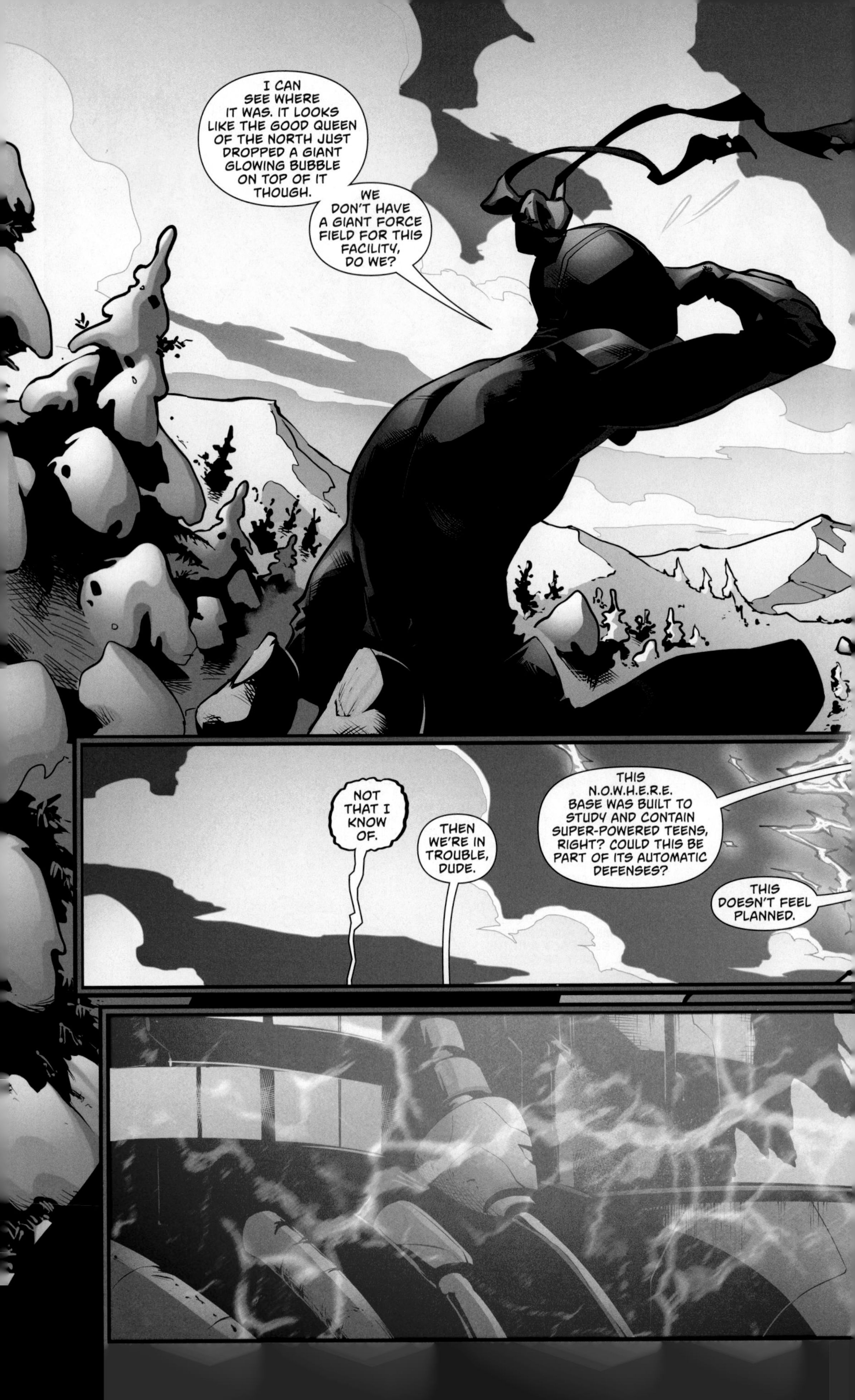

I CAN SEE WHERE IT WAS. IT LOOKS LIKE THE GOOD QUEEN OF THE NORTH JUST DROPPED A GIANT GLOWING BUBBLE ON TOP OF IT THOUGH.
WE DON'T HAVE A GIANT FORCE FIELD FOR THIS FACILITY, DO WE?
NOT THAT I KNOW OF.
THEN WE'RE IN TROUBLE, DUDE.
THIS N.O.W.H.E.R.E. BASE WAS BUILT TO STUDY AND CONTAIN SUPER-POWERED TEENS, RIGHT? COULD THIS BE PART OF ITS AUTOMATIC DEFENSES?
THIS DOESN'T FEEL PLANNED.

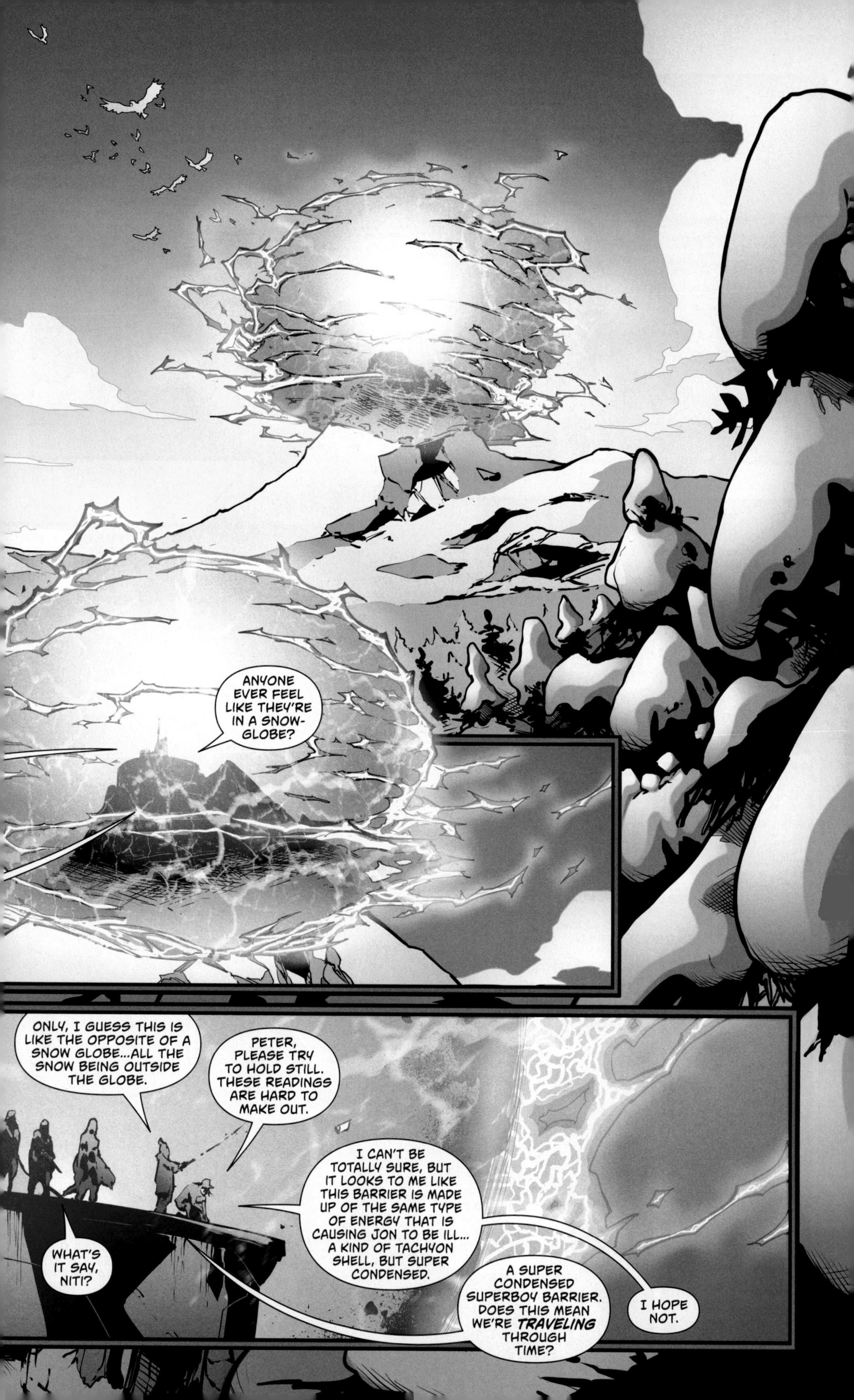
ANYONE EVER FEEL LIKE THEY'RE IN A SNOW-GLOBE?
ONLY, I GUESS THIS IS LIKE THE OPPOSITE OF A SNOW GLOBE...ALL THE SNOW BEING OUTSIDE THE GLOBE.
PETER, PLEASE TRY TO HOLD STILL. THESE READINGS ARE HARD TO MAKE OUT.
WHAT'S IT SAY, NITI?
I CAN'T BE TOTALLY SURE, BUT IT LOOKS TO ME LIKE THIS BARRIER IS MADE UP OF THE SAME TYPE OF ENERGY THAT IS CAUSING JON TO BE ILL... A KIND OF TACHYON SHELL, BUT SUPER CONDENSED.
A SUPER CONDENSED SUPERBOY BARRIER. DOES THIS MEAN WE'RE *TRAVELING* THROUGH TIME?
I HOPE NOT.

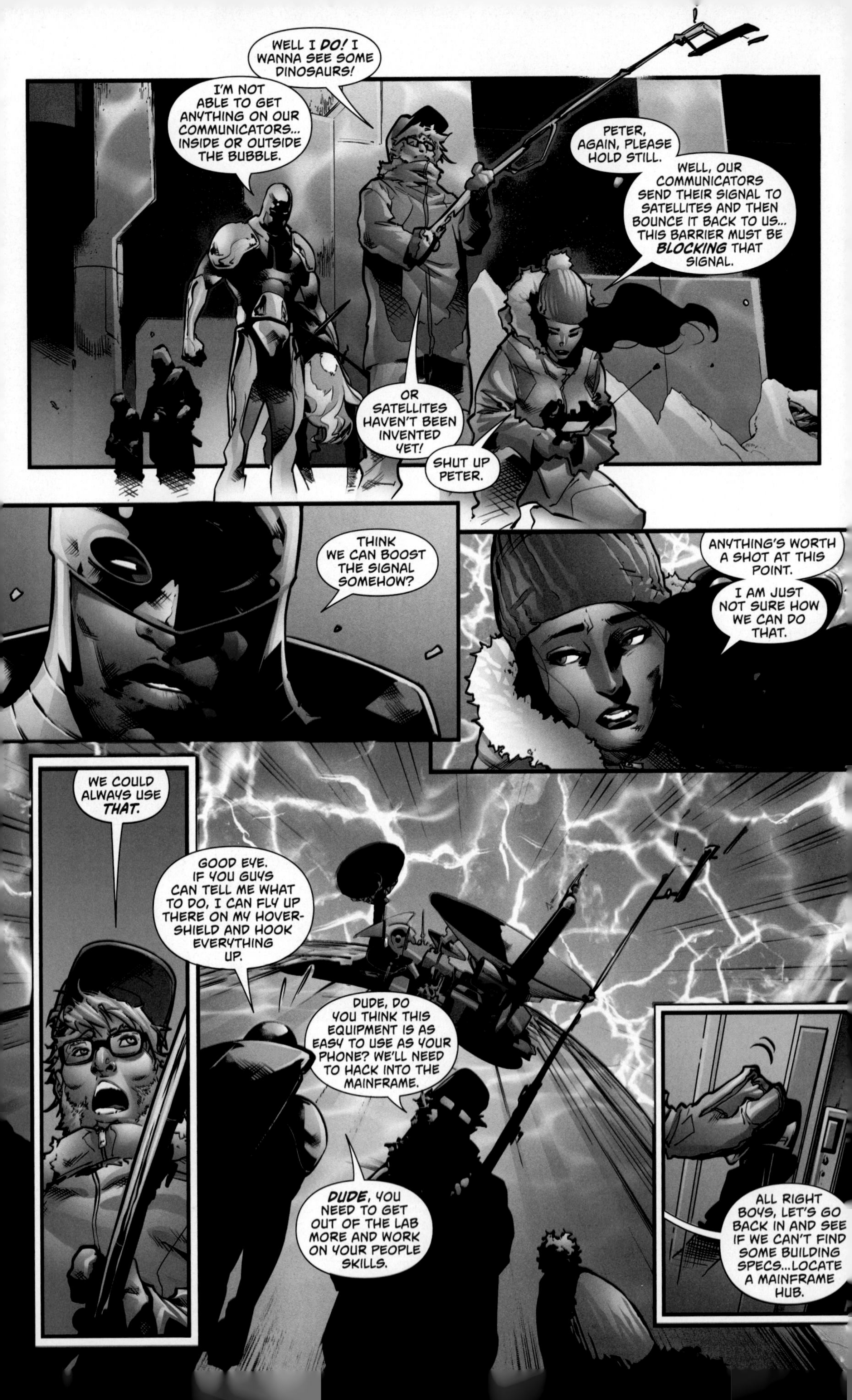
WELL I DO! I WANNA SEE SOME DINOSAURS!
I'M NOT ABLE TO GET ANYTHING ON OUR COMMUNICATORS... INSIDE OR OUTSIDE THE BUBBLE.
PETER, AGAIN, PLEASE HOLD STILL.
WELL, OUR COMMUNICATORS SEND THEIR SIGNAL TO SATELLITES AND THEN BOUNCE IT BACK TO US... THIS BARRIER MUST BE BLOCKING THAT SIGNAL.
OR SATELLITES HAVEN'T BEEN INVENTED YET!
SHUT UP PETER.
THINK WE CAN BOOST THE SIGNAL SOMEHOW?
ANYTHING'S WORTH A SHOT AT THIS POINT.
I AM JUST NOT SURE HOW WE CAN DO THAT.
WE COULD ALWAYS USE THAT.
GOOD EYE. IF YOU GUYS CAN TELL ME WHAT TO DO, I CAN FLY UP THERE ON MY HOVER-SHIELD AND HOOK EVERYTHING UP.
DUDE, DO YOU THINK THIS EQUIPMENT IS AS EASY TO USE AS YOUR PHONE? WE'LL NEED TO HACK INTO THE MAINFRAME.
DUDE, YOU NEED TO GET OUT OF THE LAB MORE AND WORK ON YOUR PEOPLE SKILLS.
ALL RIGHT BOYS, LET'S GO BACK IN AND SEE IF WE CAN'T FIND SOME BUILDING SPECS...LOCATE A MAINFRAME HUB.

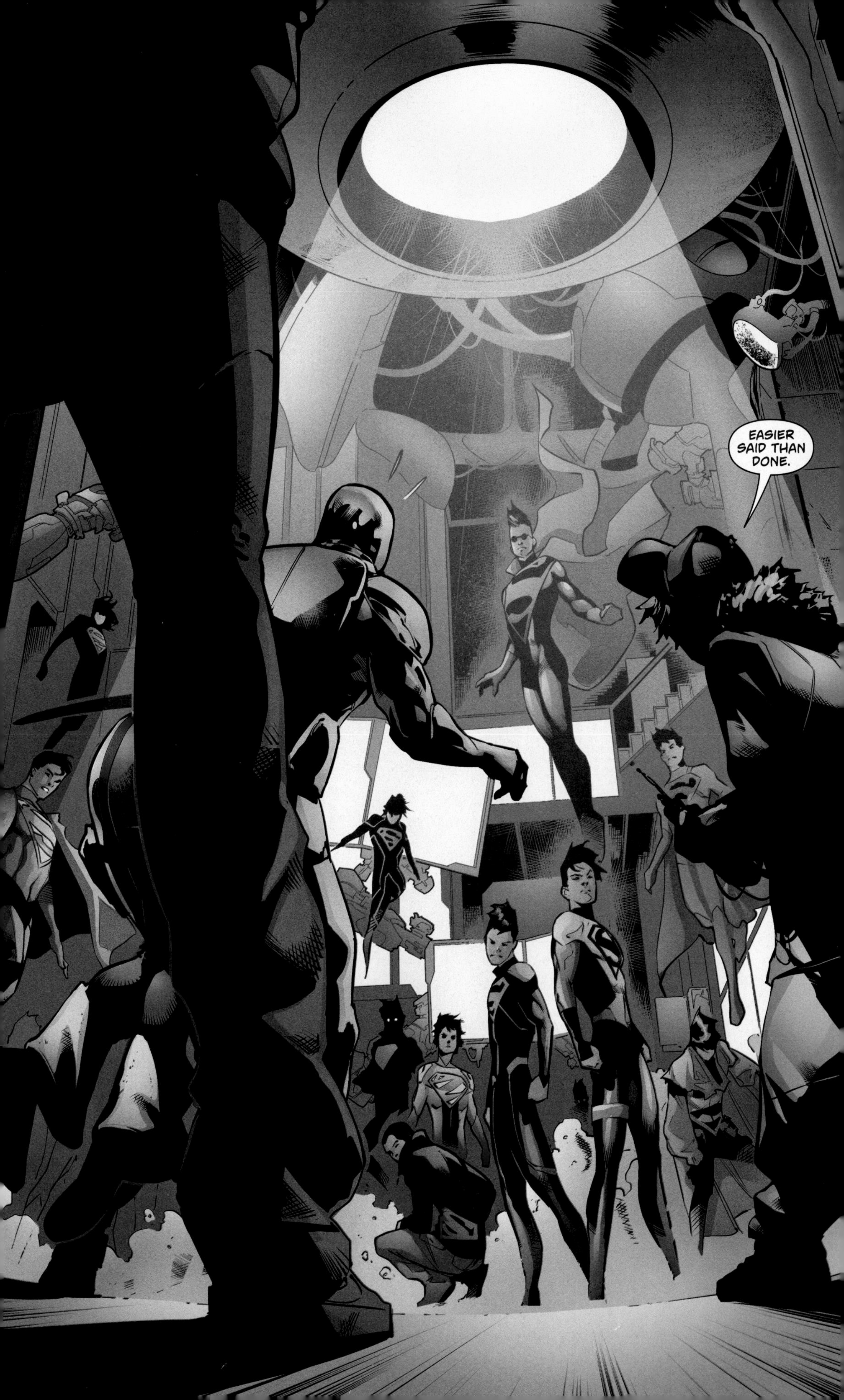
EASIER SAID THAN DONE.

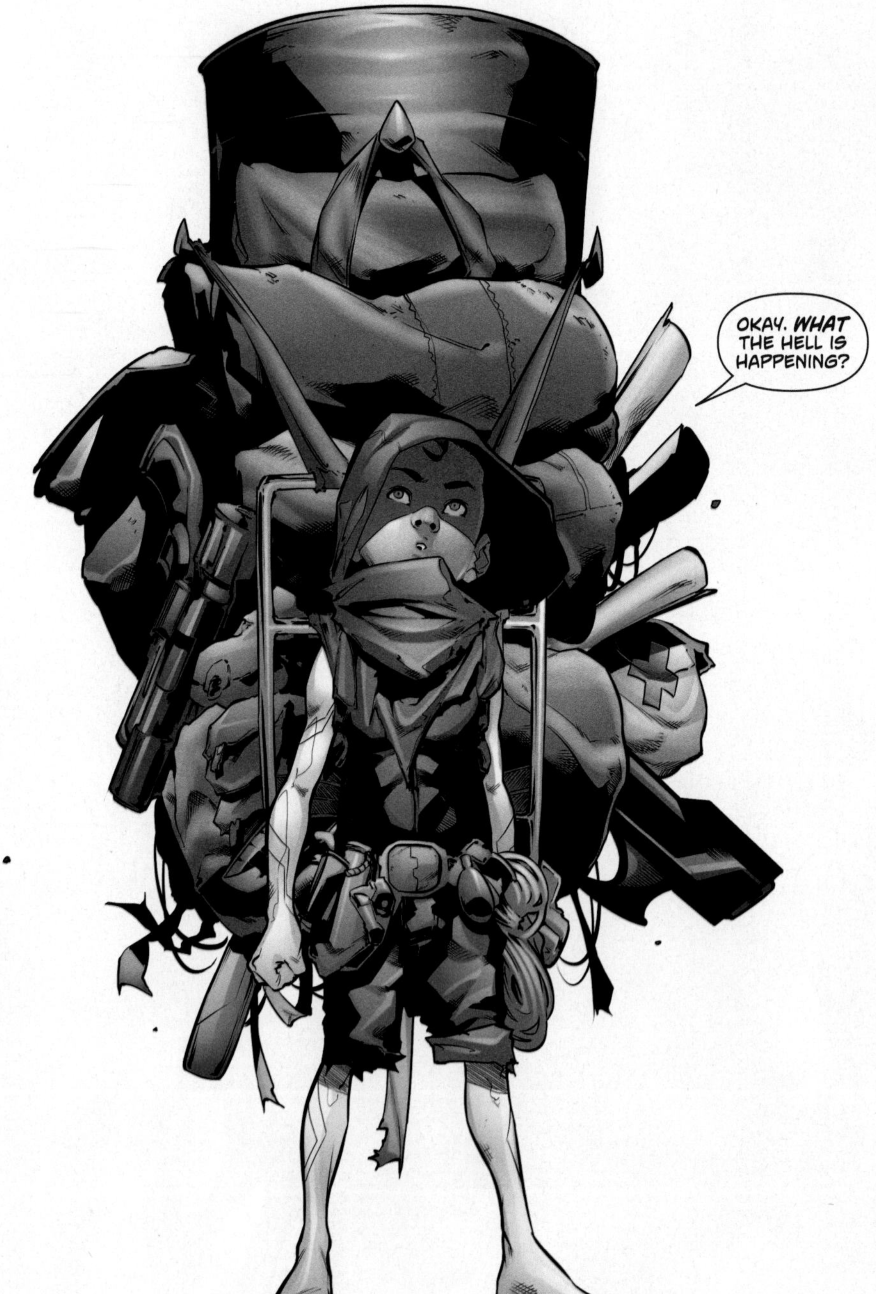
OKAY. WHAT THE HELL IS HAPPENING?

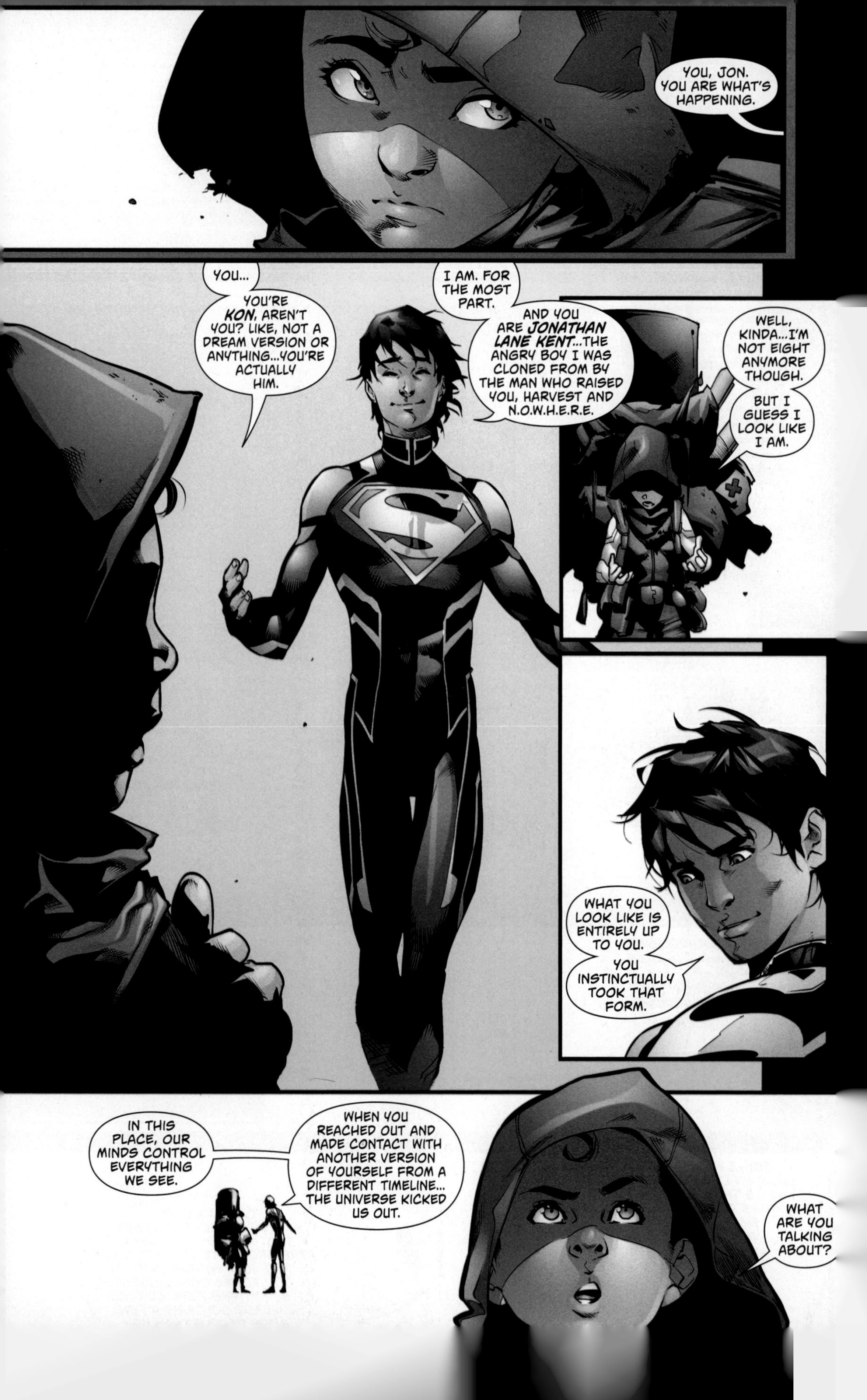
YOU, JON. YOU ARE WHAT'S HAPPENING.
YOU...
YOU'RE KON, AREN'T YOU? LIKE, NOT A DREAM VERSION OR ANYTHING...YOU'RE ACTUALLY HIM.
I AM. FOR THE MOST PART.
AND YOU ARE JONATHAN LANE KENT...THE ANGRY BOY I WAS CLONED FROM BY THE MAN WHO RAISED YOU, HARVEST AND N.O.W.H.E.R.E.
WELL, KINDA...I'M NOT EIGHT ANYMORE THOUGH.
BUT I GUESS I LOOK LIKE I AM.
WHAT YOU LOOK LIKE IS ENTIRELY UP TO YOU.
YOU INSTINCTUALLY TOOK THAT FORM.
IN THIS PLACE, OUR MINDS CONTROL EVERYTHING WE SEE.
WHEN YOU REACHED OUT AND MADE CONTACT WITH ANOTHER VERSION OF YOURSELF FROM A DIFFERENT TIMELINE... THE UNIVERSE KICKED US OUT.
WHAT ARE YOU TALKING ABOUT?

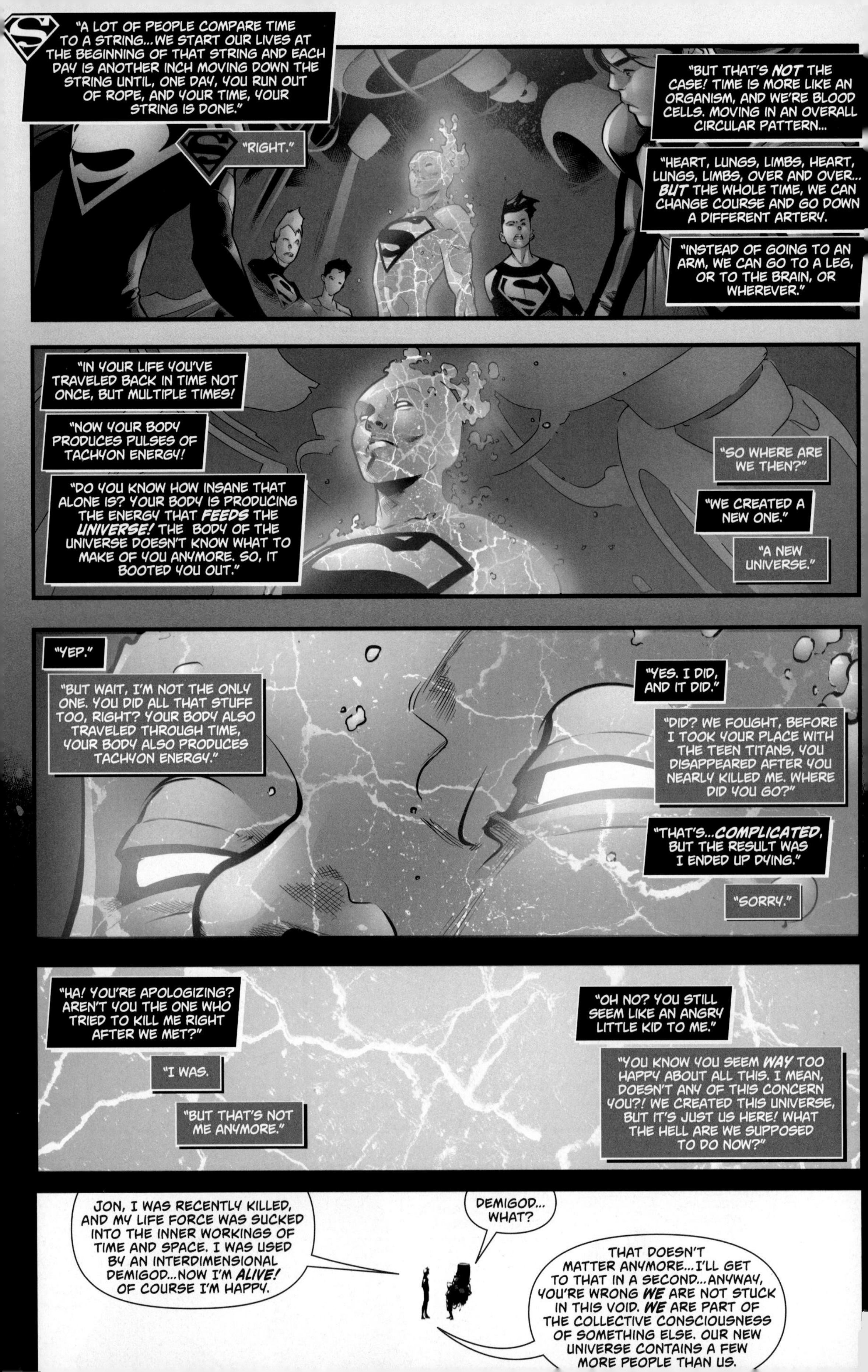
"A LOT OF PEOPLE COMPARE TIME TO A STRING...WE START OUR LIVES AT THE BEGINNING OF THAT STRING AND EACH DAY IS ANOTHER INCH MOVING DOWN THE STRING UNTIL, ONE DAY, YOU RUN OUT OF ROPE, AND YOUR TIME, YOUR STRING IS DONE."
"RIGHT."
"BUT THAT'S *NOT* THE CASE! TIME IS MORE LIKE AN ORGANISM, AND WE'RE BLOOD CELLS. MOVING IN AN OVERALL CIRCULAR PATTERN...
"HEART, LUNGS, LIMBS, HEART, LUNGS, LIMBS, OVER AND OVER... *BUT* THE WHOLE TIME, WE CAN CHANGE COURSE AND GO DOWN A DIFFERENT ARTERY.
"INSTEAD OF GOING TO AN ARM, WE CAN GO TO A LEG, OR TO THE BRAIN, OR WHEREVER."
"IN YOUR LIFE YOU'VE TRAVELED BACK IN TIME NOT ONCE, BUT MULTIPLE TIMES!
"NOW YOUR BODY PRODUCES PULSES OF TACHYON ENERGY!
"DO YOU KNOW HOW INSANE THAT ALONE IS? YOUR BODY IS PRODUCING THE ENERGY THAT *FEEDS* THE *UNIVERSE!* THE BODY OF THE UNIVERSE DOESN'T KNOW WHAT TO MAKE OF YOU ANYMORE. SO, IT BOOTED YOU OUT."
"SO WHERE ARE WE THEN?"
"WE CREATED A NEW ONE."
"A NEW UNIVERSE."
"YEP."
"BUT WAIT, I'M NOT THE ONLY ONE. YOU DID ALL THAT STUFF TOO, RIGHT? YOUR BODY ALSO TRAVELED THROUGH TIME, YOUR BODY ALSO PRODUCES TACHYON ENERGY."
"YES. I DID, AND IT DID."
"DID? WE FOUGHT, BEFORE I TOOK YOUR PLACE WITH THE TEEN TITANS, YOU DISAPPEARED AFTER YOU NEARLY KILLED ME. WHERE DID YOU GO?"
"THAT'S...*COMPLICATED*, BUT THE RESULT WAS I ENDED UP DYING."
"SORRY."
"HA! YOU'RE APOLOGIZING? AREN'T YOU THE ONE WHO TRIED TO KILL ME RIGHT AFTER WE MET?"
"I WAS.
"BUT THAT'S NOT ME ANYMORE."
"OH NO? YOU STILL SEEM LIKE AN ANGRY LITTLE KID TO ME."
"YOU KNOW YOU SEEM *WAY* TOO HAPPY ABOUT ALL THIS. I MEAN, DOESN'T ANY OF THIS CONCERN YOU?! WE CREATED THIS UNIVERSE, BUT IT'S JUST US HERE! WHAT THE HELL ARE WE SUPPOSED TO DO NOW?"
JON, I WAS RECENTLY KILLED, AND MY LIFE FORCE WAS SUCKED INTO THE INNER WORKINGS OF TIME AND SPACE. I WAS USED BY AN INTERDIMENSIONAL DEMIGOD...NOW I'M *ALIVE!* OF COURSE I'M HAPPY.
DEMIGOD... WHAT?
THAT DOESN'T MATTER ANYMORE...I'LL GET TO THAT IN A SECOND...ANYWAY, YOU'RE WRONG *WE* ARE NOT STUCK IN THIS VOID. *WE* ARE PART OF THE COLLECTIVE CONSCIOUSNESS OF SOMETHING ELSE. OUR NEW UNIVERSE CONTAINS A FEW MORE PEOPLE THAN US.

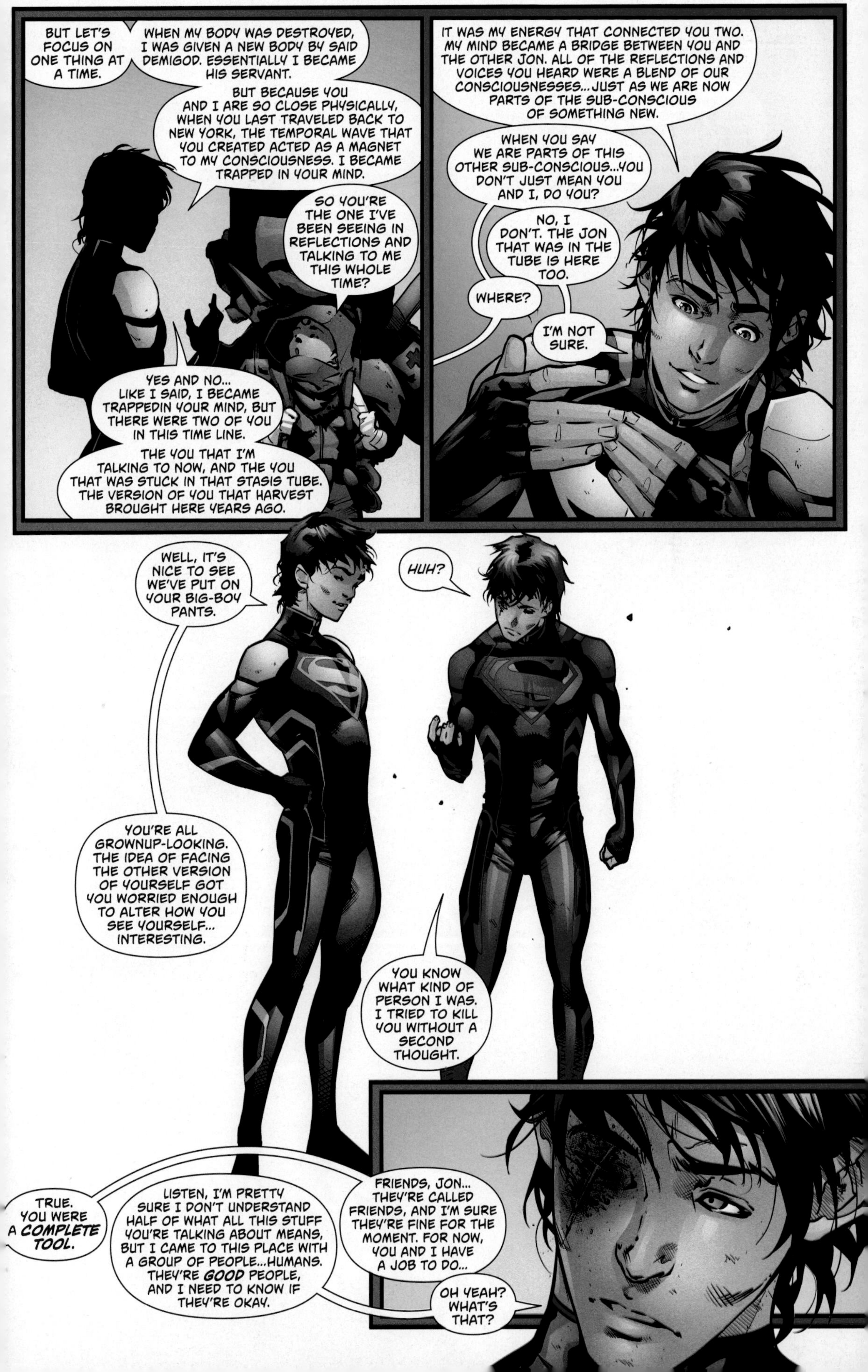
BUT LET'S FOCUS ON ONE THING AT A TIME.
WHEN MY BODY WAS DESTROYED, I WAS GIVEN A NEW BODY BY SAID DEMIGOD. ESSENTIALLY I BECAME HIS SERVANT.
BUT BECAUSE YOU AND I ARE SO CLOSE PHYSICALLY, WHEN YOU LAST TRAVELED BACK TO NEW YORK, THE TEMPORAL WAVE THAT YOU CREATED ACTED AS A MAGNET TO MY CONSCIOUSNESS. I BECAME TRAPPED IN YOUR MIND.
SO YOU'RE THE ONE I'VE BEEN SEEING IN REFLECTIONS AND TALKING TO ME THIS WHOLE TIME?
YES AND NO... LIKE I SAID, I BECAME TRAPPEDIN YOUR MIND, BUT THERE WERE TWO OF YOU IN THIS TIME LINE.
THE YOU THAT I'M TALKING TO NOW, AND THE YOU THAT WAS STUCK IN THAT STASIS TUBE. THE VERSION OF YOU THAT HARVEST BROUGHT HERE YEARS AGO.
IT WAS MY ENERGY THAT CONNECTED YOU TWO. MY MIND BECAME A BRIDGE BETWEEN YOU AND THE OTHER JON. ALL OF THE REFLECTIONS AND VOICES YOU HEARD WERE A BLEND OF OUR CONSCIOUSNESSES... JUST AS WE ARE NOW PARTS OF THE SUB-CONSCIOUS OF SOMETHING NEW.
WHEN YOU SAY WE ARE PARTS OF THIS OTHER SUB-CONSCIOUS...YOU DON'T JUST MEAN YOU AND I, DO YOU?
NO, I DON'T. THE JON THAT WAS IN THE TUBE IS HERE TOO.
WHERE?
I'M NOT SURE.
WELL, IT'S NICE TO SEE WE'VE PUT ON YOUR BIG-BOY PANTS.
HUH?
YOU'RE ALL GROWNUP-LOOKING. THE IDEA OF FACING THE OTHER VERSION OF YOURSELF GOT YOU WORRIED ENOUGH TO ALTER HOW YOU SEE YOURSELF... INTERESTING.
YOU KNOW WHAT KIND OF PERSON I WAS. I TRIED TO KILL YOU WITHOUT A SECOND THOUGHT.
TRUE. YOU WERE A **COMPLETE TOOL.**
LISTEN, I'M PRETTY SURE I DON'T UNDERSTAND HALF OF WHAT ALL THIS STUFF YOU'RE TALKING ABOUT MEANS, BUT I CAME TO THIS PLACE WITH A GROUP OF PEOPLE...HUMANS. THEY'RE **GOOD** PEOPLE, AND I NEED TO KNOW IF THEY'RE OKAY.
FRIENDS, JON... THEY'RE CALLED FRIENDS, AND I'M SURE THEY'RE FINE FOR THE MOMENT. FOR NOW, YOU AND I HAVE A JOB TO DO...
OH YEAH? WHAT'S THAT?

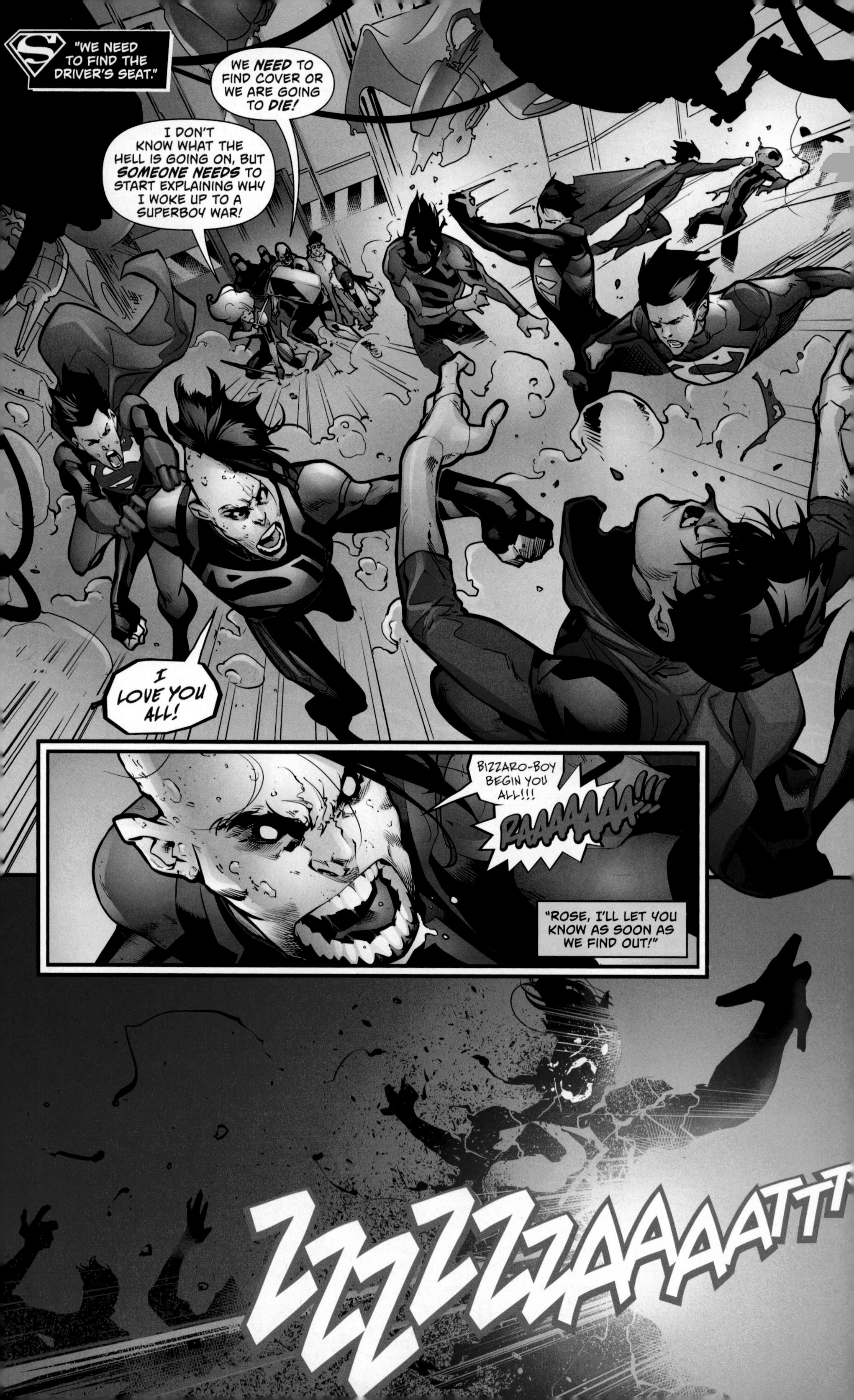

"WE NEED TO FIND THE DRIVER'S SEAT."
WE NEED TO FIND COVER OR WE ARE GOING TO DIE!
I DON'T KNOW WHAT THE HELL IS GOING ON, BUT SOMEONE NEEDS TO START EXPLAINING WHY I WOKE UP TO A SUPERBOY WAR!
I LOVE YOU ALL!
BIZZARO-BOY BEGIN YOU ALL!!!
RAAAAAAA!!!
"ROSE, I'LL LET YOU KNOW AS SOON AS WE FIND OUT!"
ZZZZZZAAAAATTT

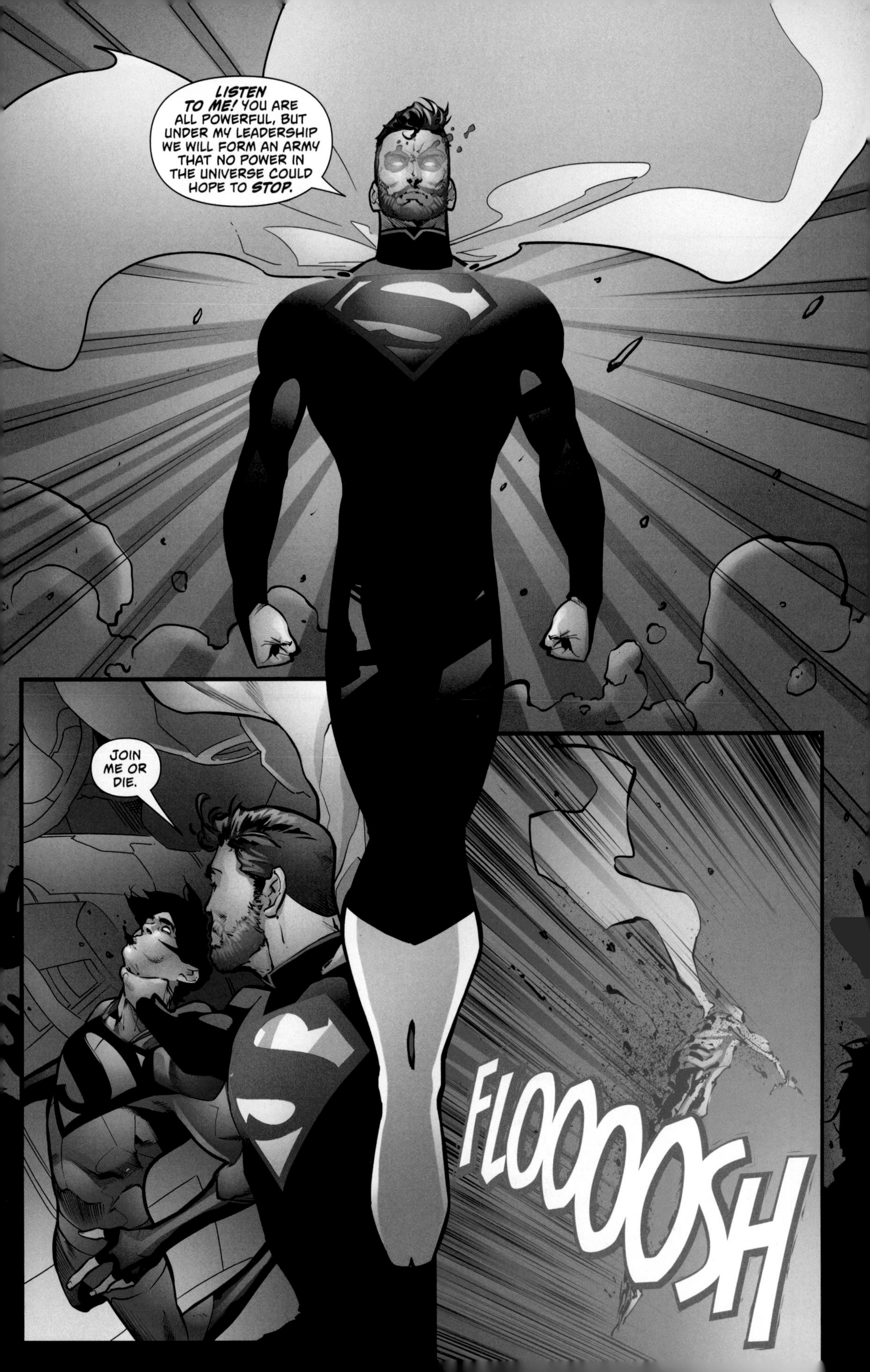
LISTEN TO ME! YOU ARE ALL POWERFUL, BUT UNDER MY LEADERSHIP WE WILL FORM AN ARMY THAT NO POWER IN THE UNIVERSE COULD HOPE TO STOP.
JOIN ME OR DIE.
FLOOOOSH

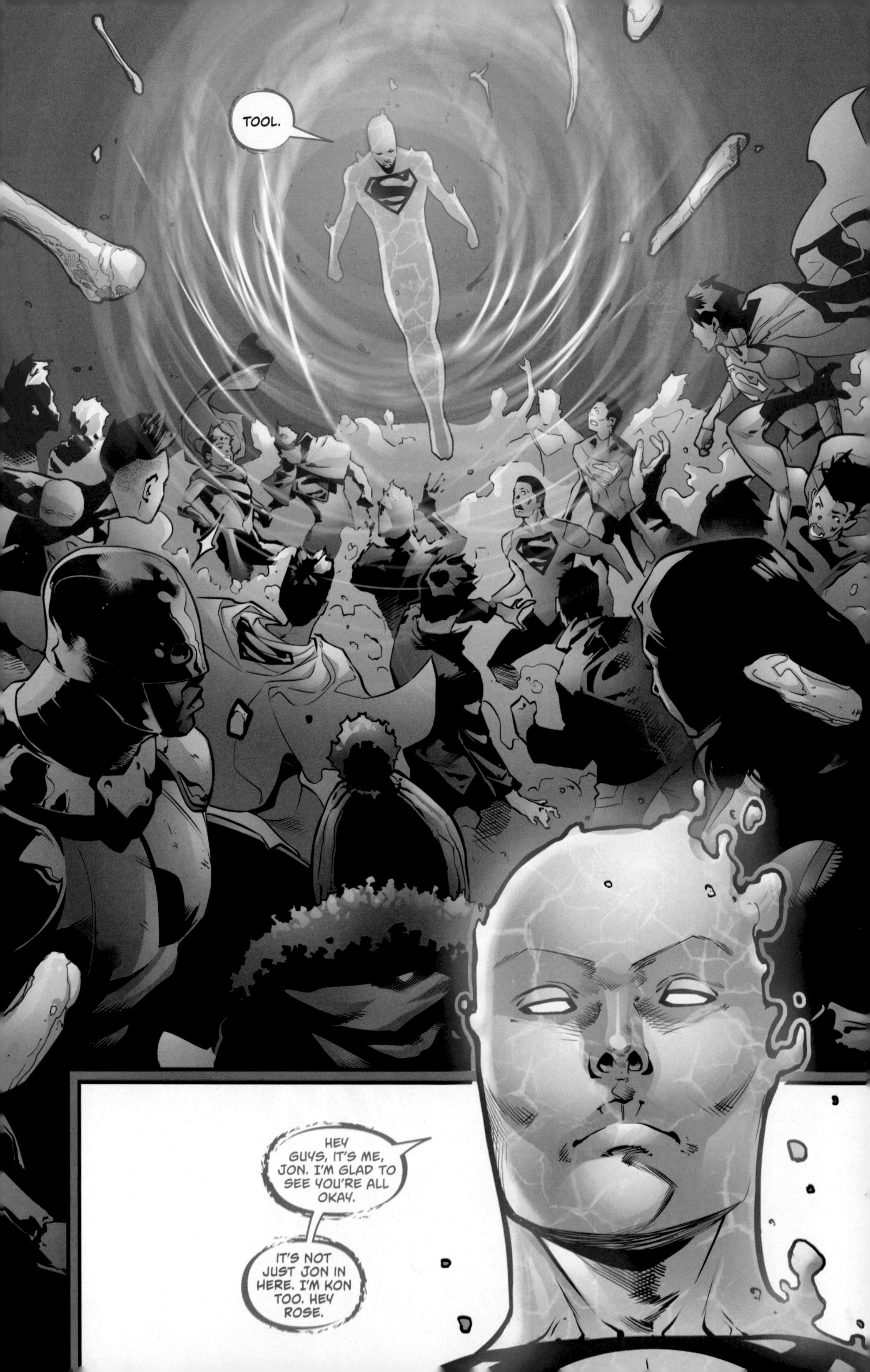
TOOL.
HEY GUYS, IT'S ME, JON. I'M GLAD TO SEE YOU'RE ALL OKAY.
IT'S NOT JUST JON IN HERE. I'M KON TOO. HEY ROSE.

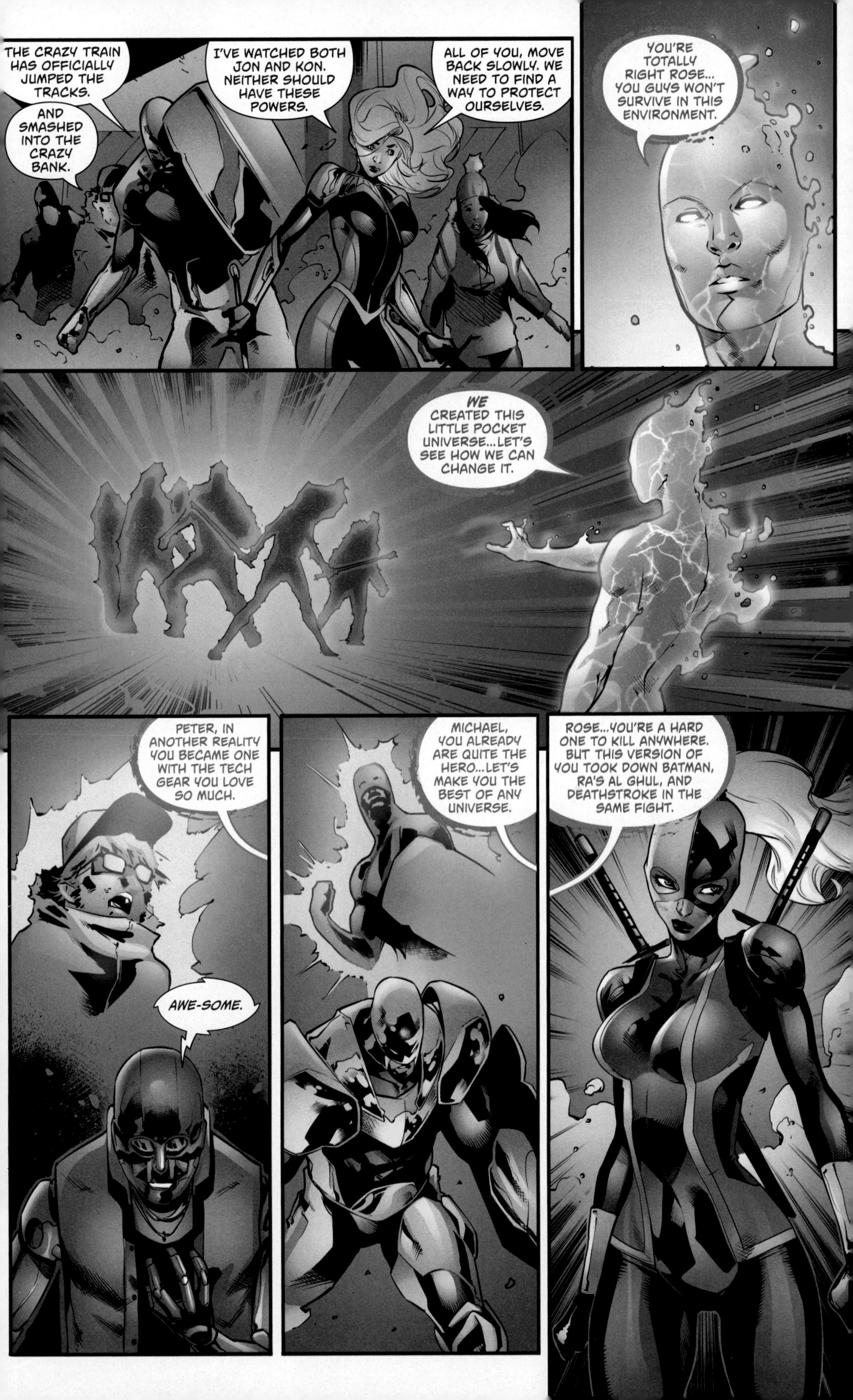
THE CRAZY TRAIN HAS OFFICIALLY JUMPED THE TRACKS.
AND SMASHED INTO THE CRAZY BANK.
I'VE WATCHED BOTH JON AND KON. NEITHER SHOULD HAVE THESE POWERS.
ALL OF YOU, MOVE BACK SLOWLY. WE NEED TO FIND A WAY TO PROTECT OURSELVES.
YOU'RE TOTALLY RIGHT ROSE... YOU GUYS WON'T SURVIVE IN THIS ENVIRONMENT.
WE CREATED THIS LITTLE POCKET UNIVERSE...LET'S SEE HOW WE CAN CHANGE IT.
PETER, IN ANOTHER REALITY YOU BECAME ONE WITH THE TECH GEAR YOU LOVE SO MUCH.
AWE-SOME.
MICHAEL, YOU ALREADY ARE QUITE THE HERO...LET'S MAKE YOU THE BEST OF ANY UNIVERSE.
ROSE...YOU'RE A HARD ONE TO KILL ANYWHERE. BUT THIS VERSION OF YOU TOOK DOWN BATMAN, RA'S AL GHUL, AND DEATHSTROKE IN THE SAME FIGHT.

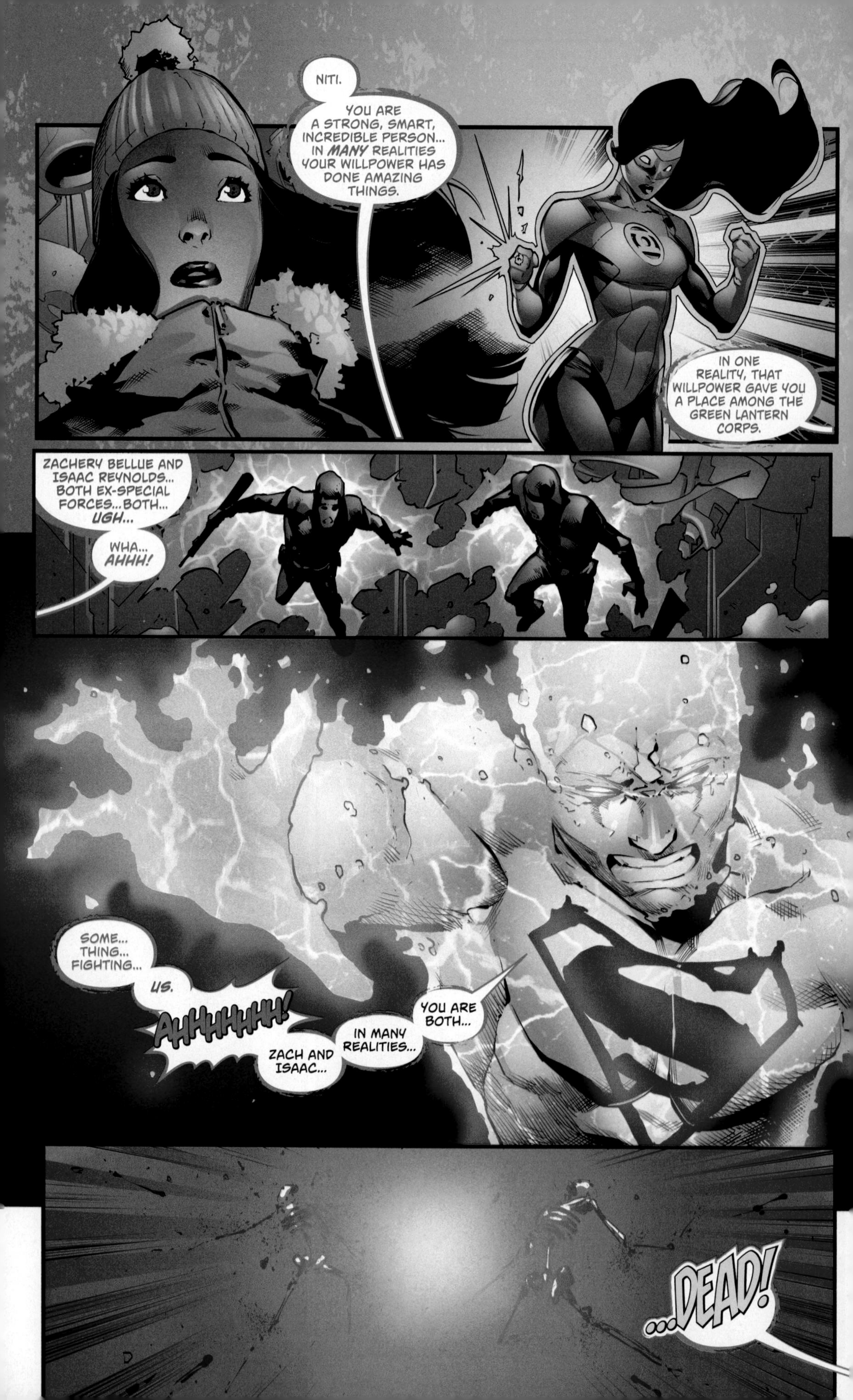
NITI.
YOU ARE A STRONG, SMART, INCREDIBLE PERSON... IN MANY REALITIES YOUR WILLPOWER HAS DONE AMAZING THINGS.
IN ONE REALITY, THAT WILLPOWER GAVE YOU A PLACE AMONG THE GREEN LANTERN CORPS.
ZACHERY BELLUE AND ISAAC REYNOLDS... BOTH EX-SPECIAL FORCES...BOTH... UGH...
WHA... AHHH!
SOME... THING... FIGHTING...
US.
AHHHHHHH!
ZACH AND ISAAC...
IN MANY REALITIES...
YOU ARE BOTH...
...DEAD!

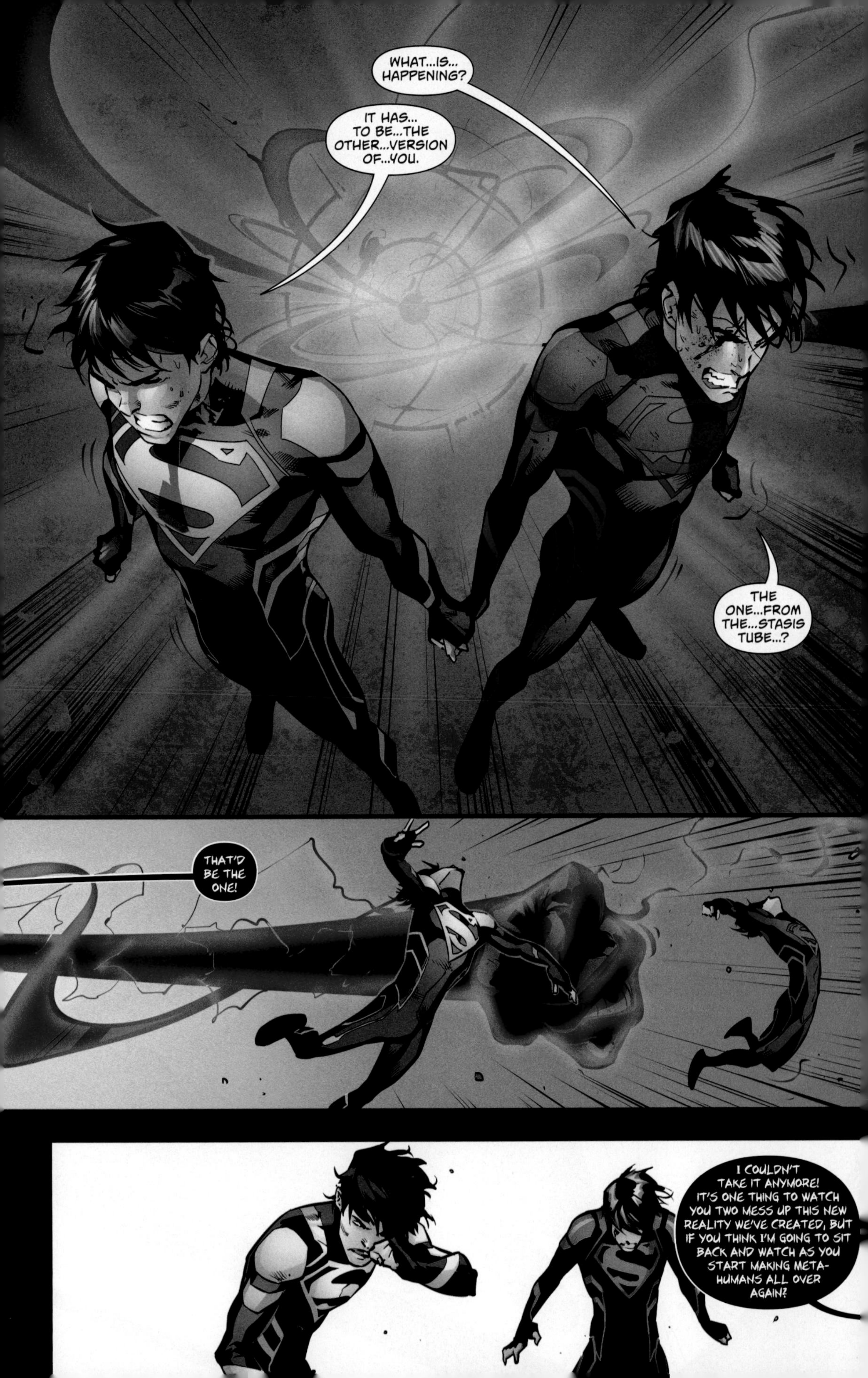
WHAT...IS... HAPPENING?
IT HAS... TO BE...THE OTHER...VERSION OF...YOU.
THE ONE...FROM THE...STASIS TUBE...?
THAT'D BE THE ONE!
I COULDN'T TAKE IT ANYMORE! IT'S ONE THING TO WATCH YOU TWO MESS UP THIS NEW REALITY WE'VE CREATED, BUT IF YOU THINK I'M GOING TO SIT BACK AND WATCH AS YOU START MAKING META-HUMANS ALL OVER AGAIN?

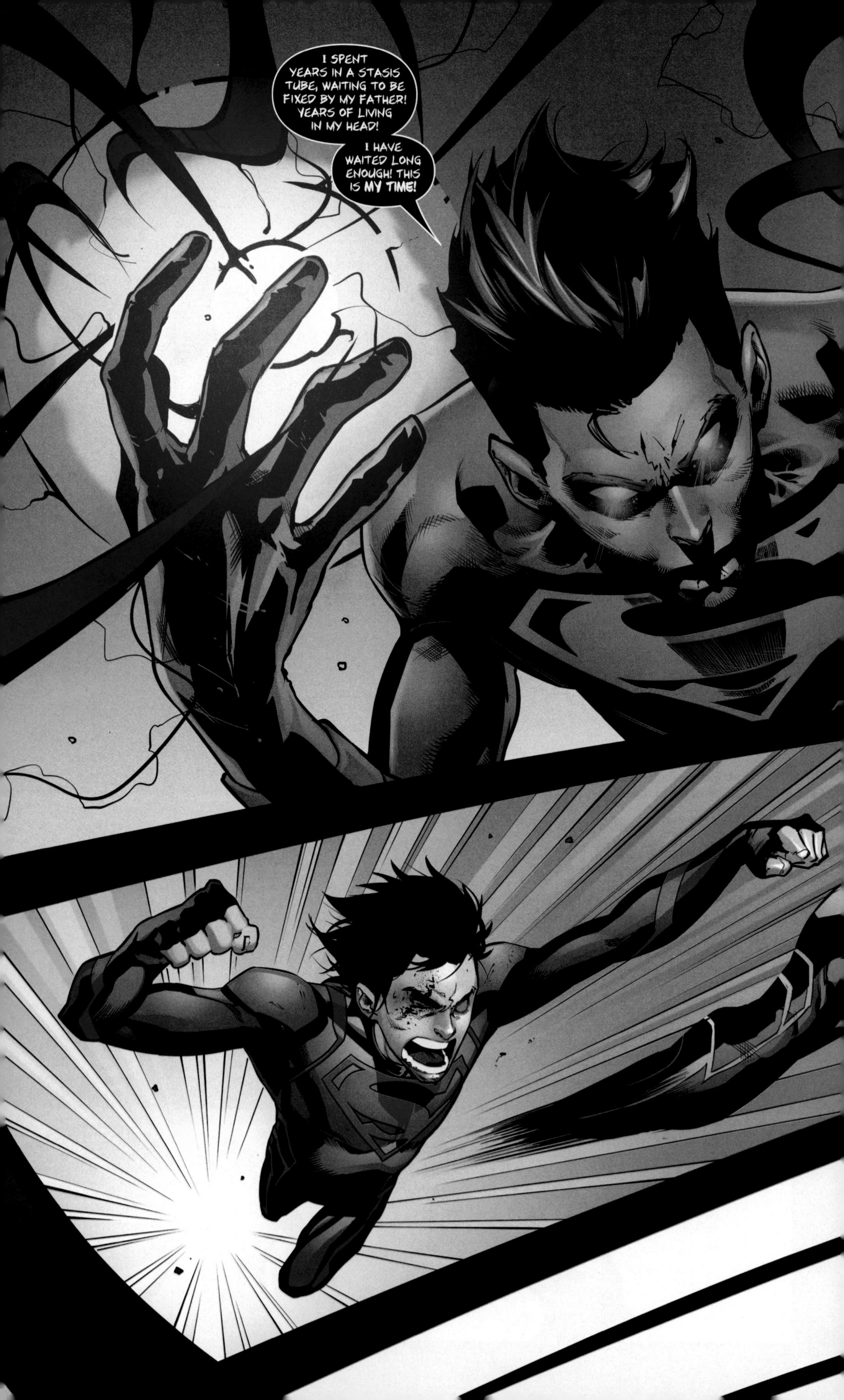
I SPENT YEARS IN A STASIS TUBE, WAITING TO BE FIXED BY MY FATHER! YEARS OF LIVING IN MY HEAD!
I HAVE WAITED LONG ENOUGH! THIS IS MY TIME!

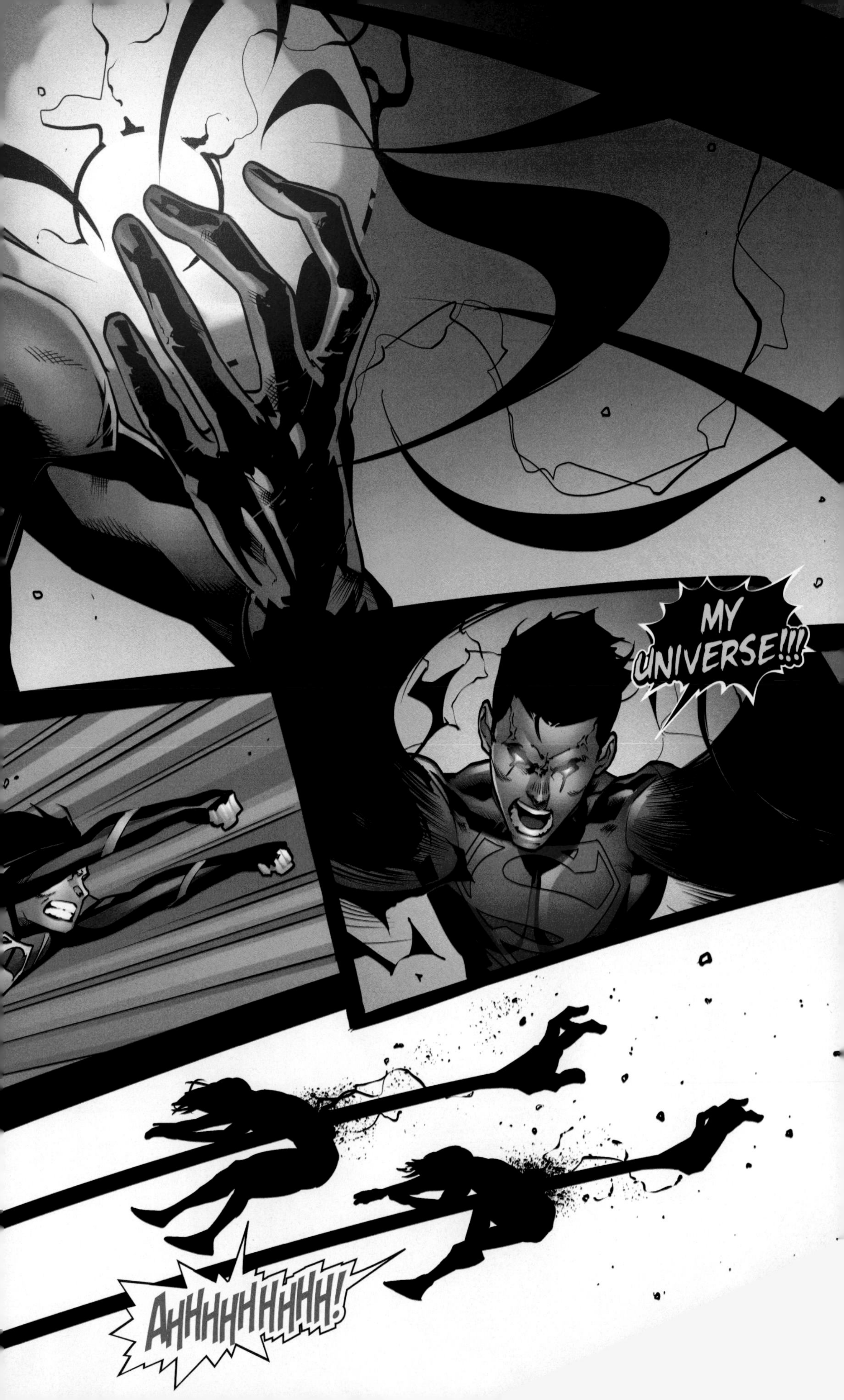
MY UNIVERSE!!!
AHHHHHHHHH!

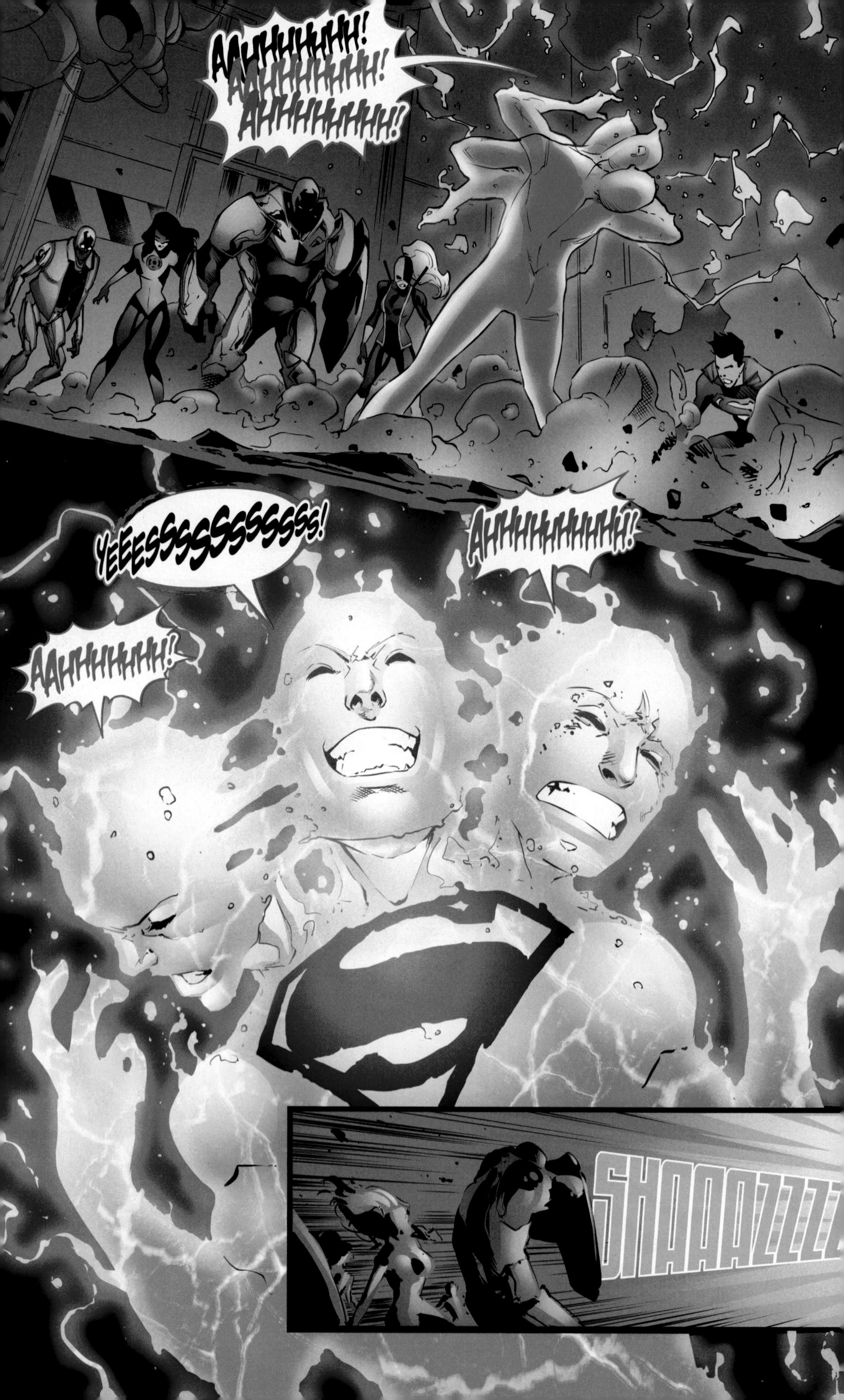
AAHHHHHHH!
AAHHHHHHH!
AHHHHHHHH!
YEEESSSSSSSSSSS!
AHHHHHHHHHH!
AAHHHHHHH!
SHAAAZZZZ

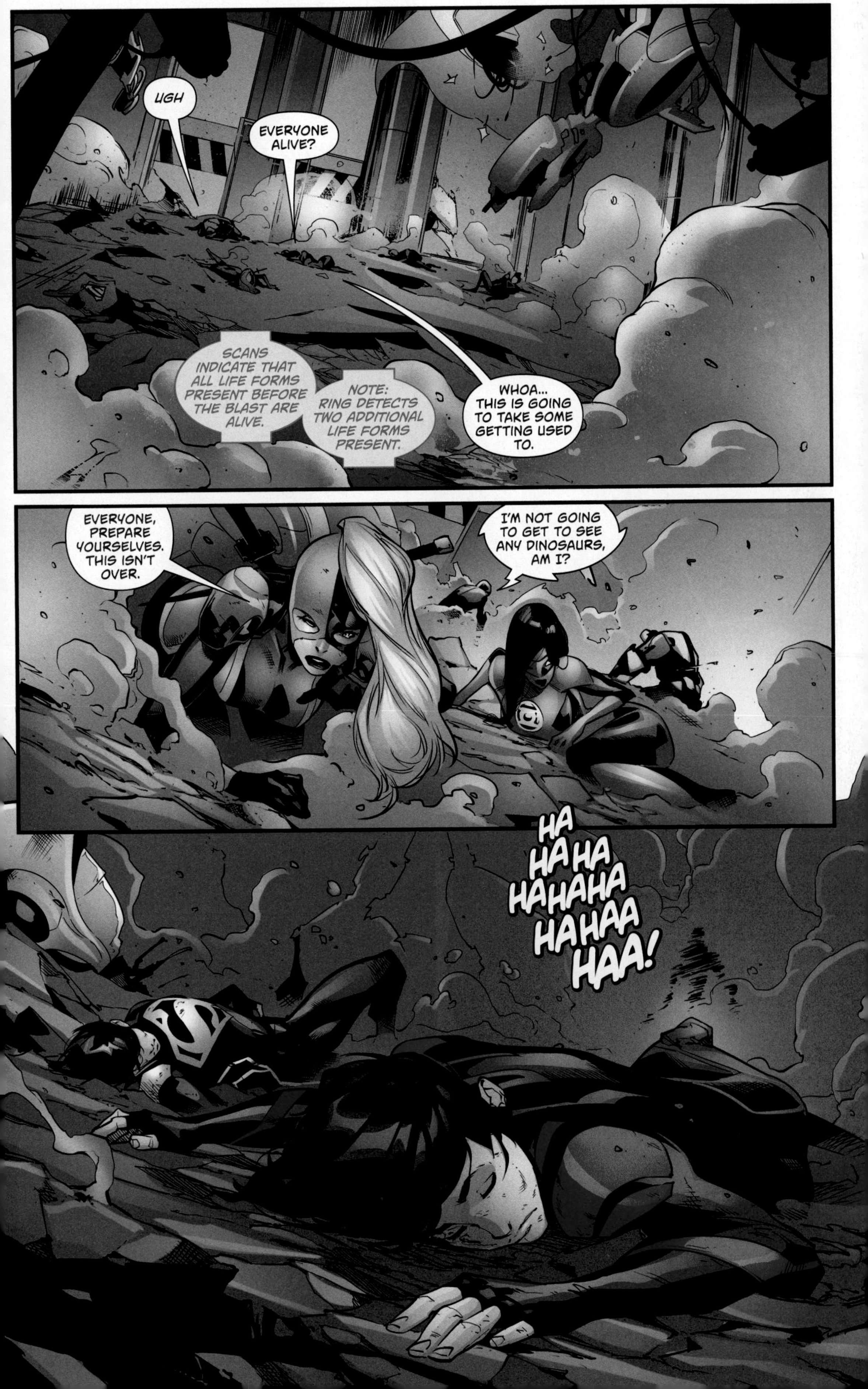
UGH
EVERYONE ALIVE?
SCANS INDICATE THAT ALL LIFE FORMS PRESENT BEFORE THE BLAST ARE ALIVE.
NOTE: RING DETECTS TWO ADDITIONAL LIFE FORMS PRESENT.
WHOA... THIS IS GOING TO TAKE SOME GETTING USED TO.
EVERYONE, PREPARE YOURSELVES. THIS ISN'T OVER.
I'M NOT GOING TO GET TO SEE ANY DINOSAURS, AM I?
HA HA HA HAHAHA HAHAA HAA!

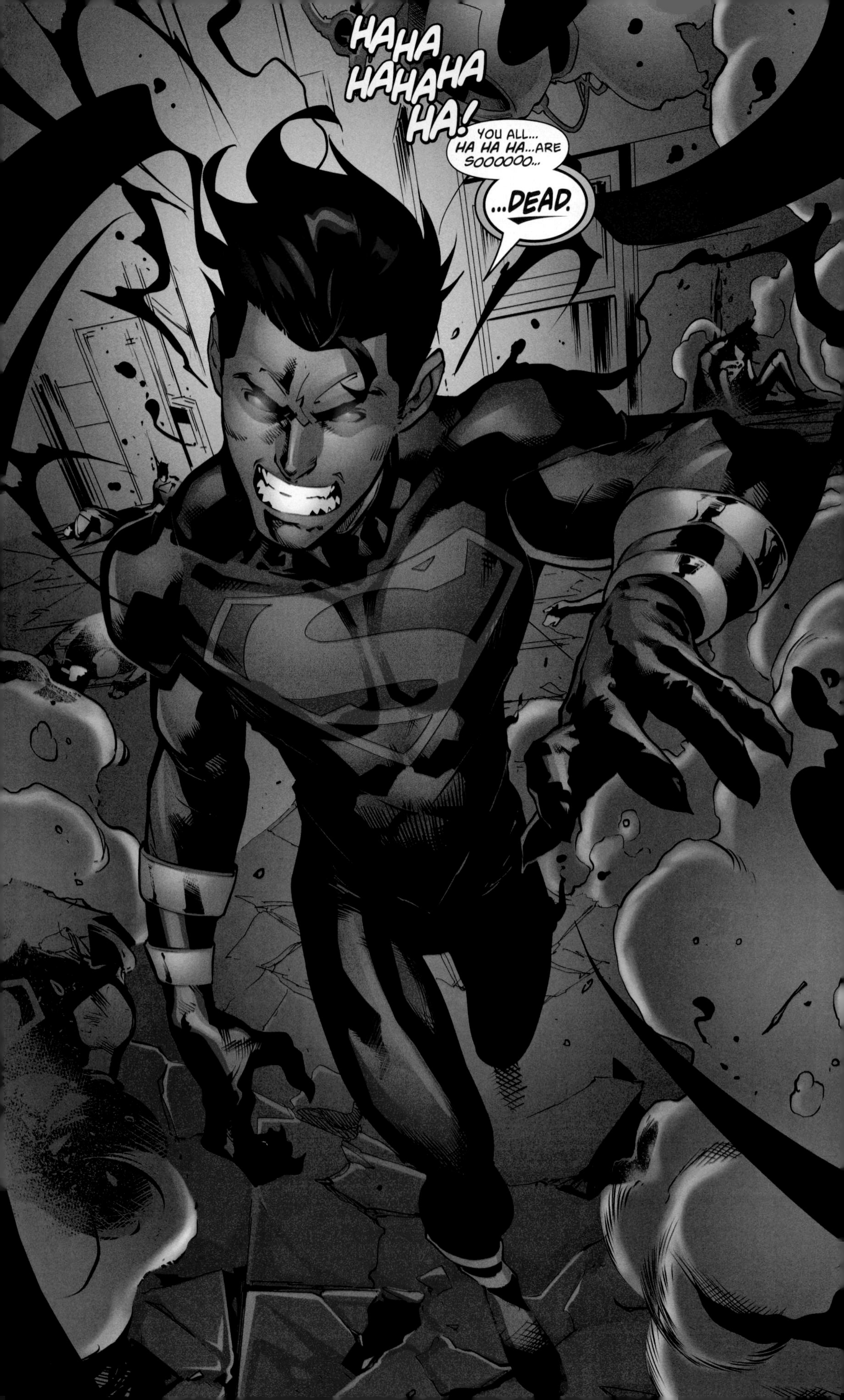
HAHA HAHAHA HA!
YOU ALL... HA HA HA...ARE SOOOOOO...
...DEAD.

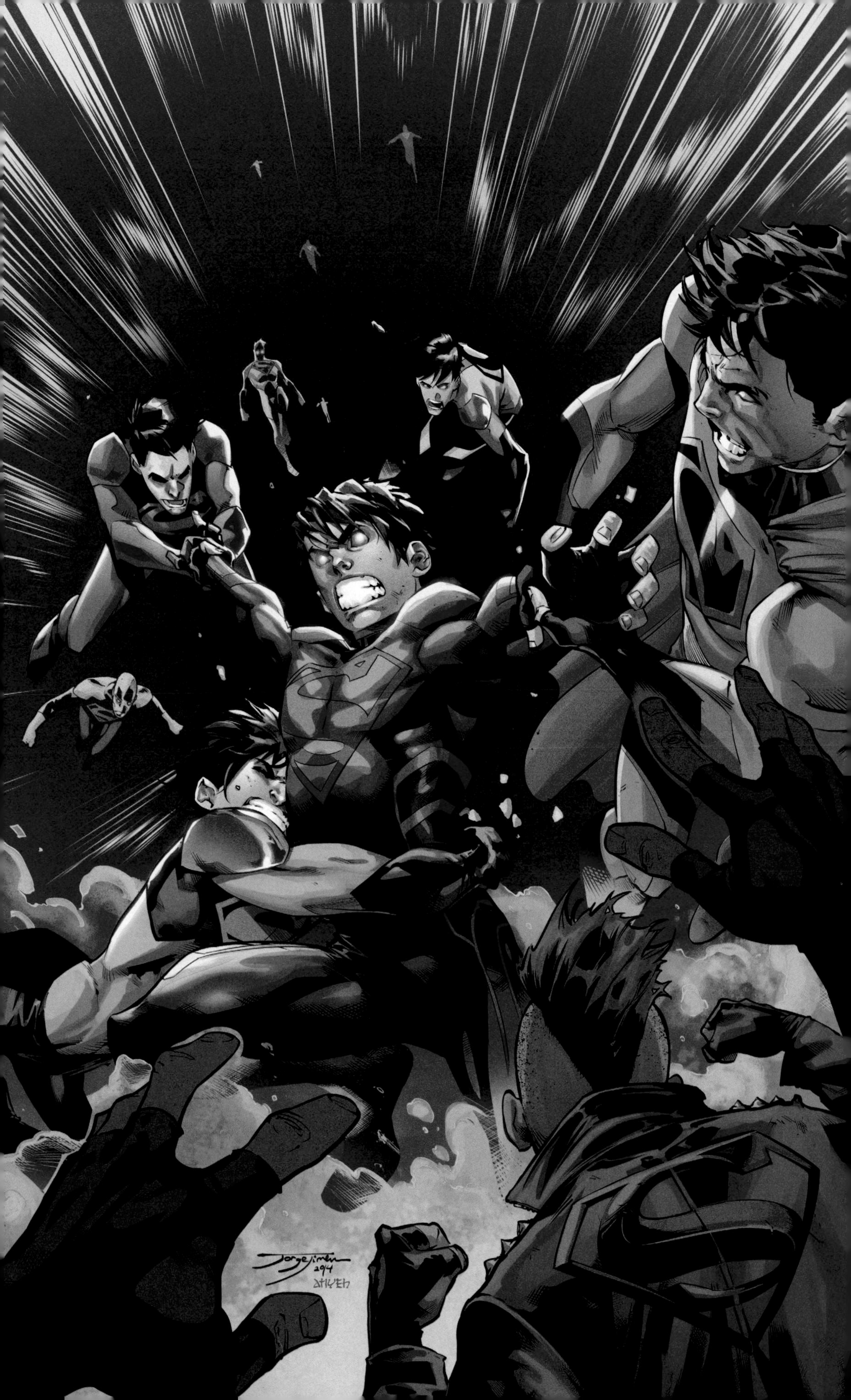

KNOW THY SELF

AARON KUDER writer **JORGE JIMÉNEZ** artist **TANYA** and **RICHARD HORIE** colorists
CARLOS M. MANGUAL letterer cover art by **JORGE JIMÉNEZ** and **MIKE ATIYEH**

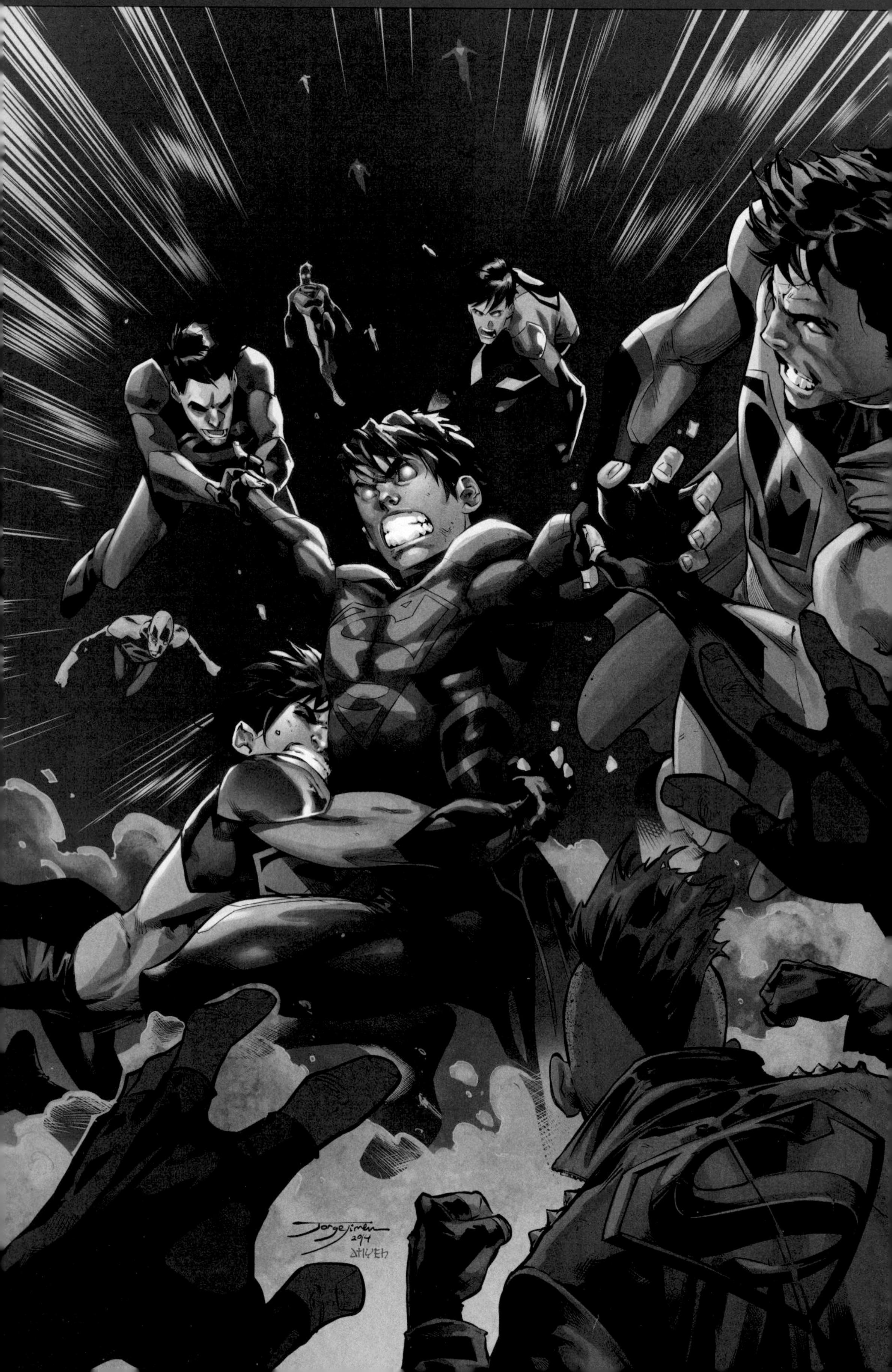

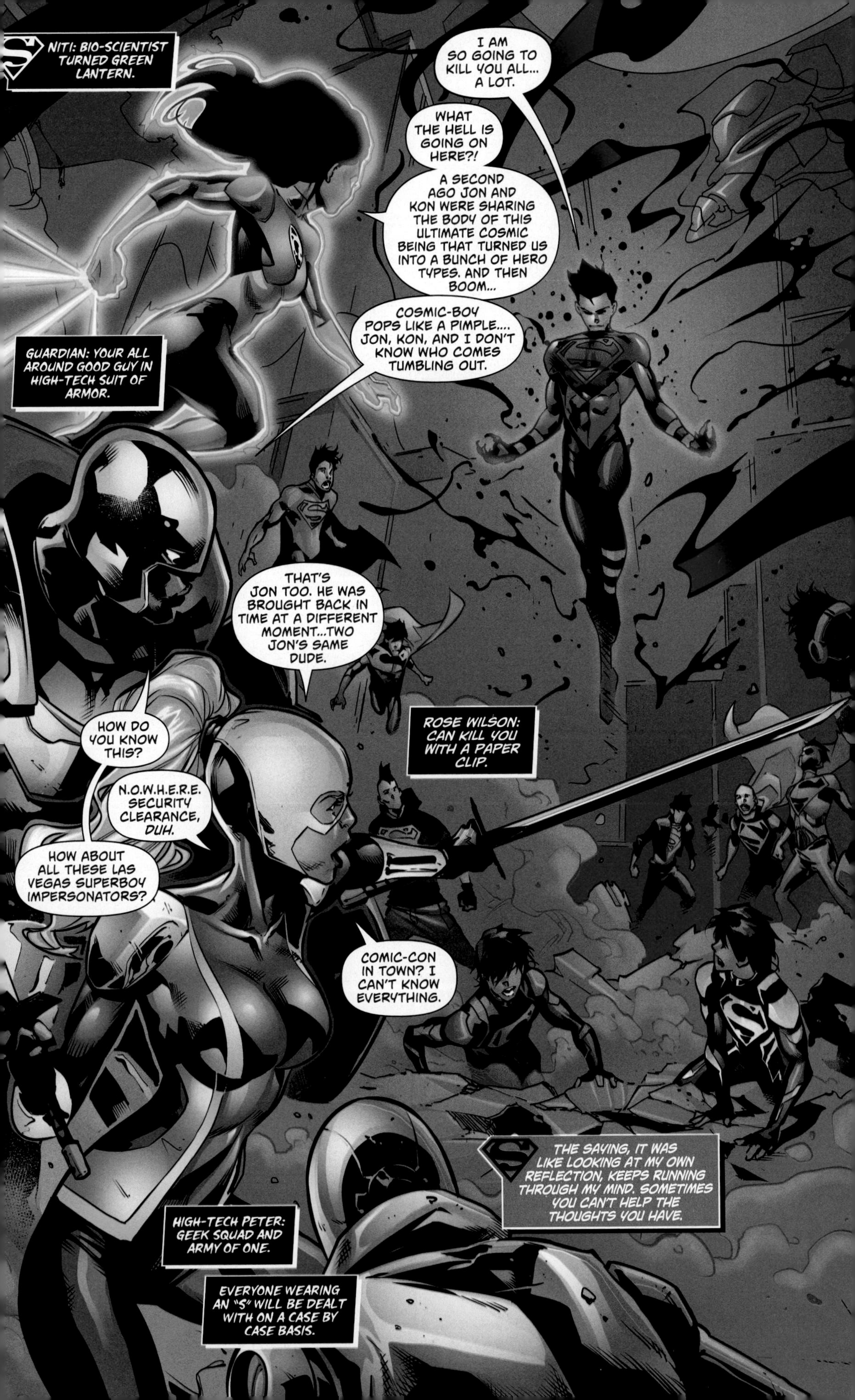
NITI: BIO-SCIENTIST TURNED GREEN LANTERN.
I AM SO GOING TO KILL YOU ALL... A LOT.
WHAT THE HELL IS GOING ON HERE?!
A SECOND AGO JON AND KON WERE SHARING THE BODY OF THIS ULTIMATE COSMIC BEING THAT TURNED US INTO A BUNCH OF HERO TYPES. AND THEN BOOM...
COSMIC-BOY POPS LIKE A PIMPLE.... JON, KON, AND I DON'T KNOW WHO COMES TUMBLING OUT.
GUARDIAN: YOUR ALL AROUND GOOD GUY IN HIGH-TECH SUIT OF ARMOR.
THAT'S JON TOO. HE WAS BROUGHT BACK IN TIME AT A DIFFERENT MOMENT...TWO JON'S SAME DUDE.
HOW DO YOU KNOW THIS?
N.O.W.H.E.R.E. SECURITY CLEARANCE, DUH.
HOW ABOUT ALL THESE LAS VEGAS SUPERBOY IMPERSONATORS?
ROSE WILSON: CAN KILL YOU WITH A PAPER CLIP.
COMIC-CON IN TOWN? I CAN'T KNOW EVERYTHING.
THE SAYING, IT WAS LIKE LOOKING AT MY OWN REFLECTION, KEEPS RUNNING THROUGH MY MIND. SOMETIMES YOU CAN'T HELP THE THOUGHTS YOU HAVE.
HIGH-TECH PETER: GEEK SQUAD AND ARMY OF ONE.
EVERYONE WEARING AN "S" WILL BE DEALT WITH ON A CASE BY CASE BASIS.

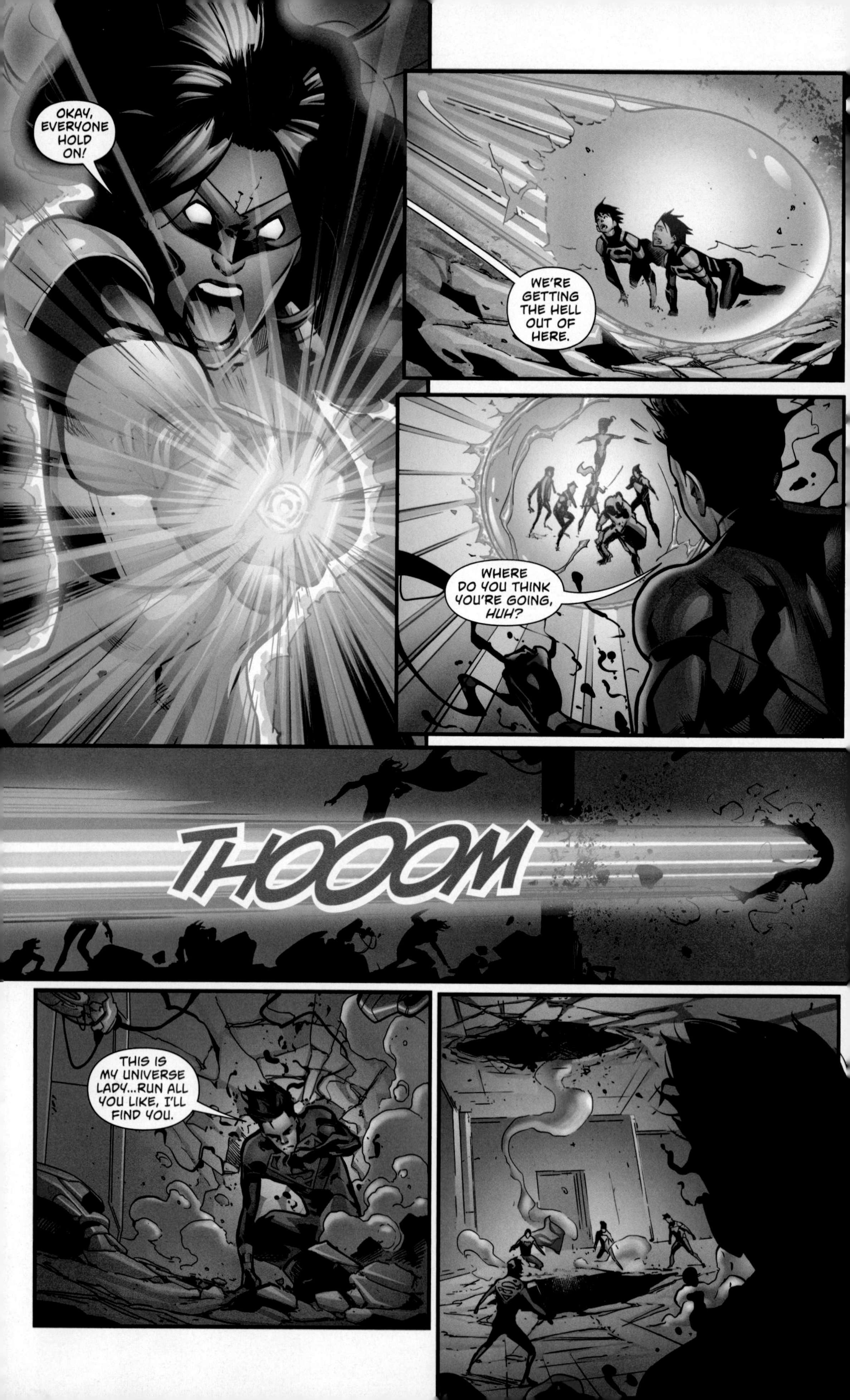
OKAY, EVERYONE HOLD ON!
WE'RE GETTING THE HELL OUT OF HERE.
WHERE DO YOU THINK YOU'RE GOING, HUH?
THOOOM
THIS IS MY UNIVERSE LADY...RUN ALL YOU LIKE, I'LL FIND YOU.

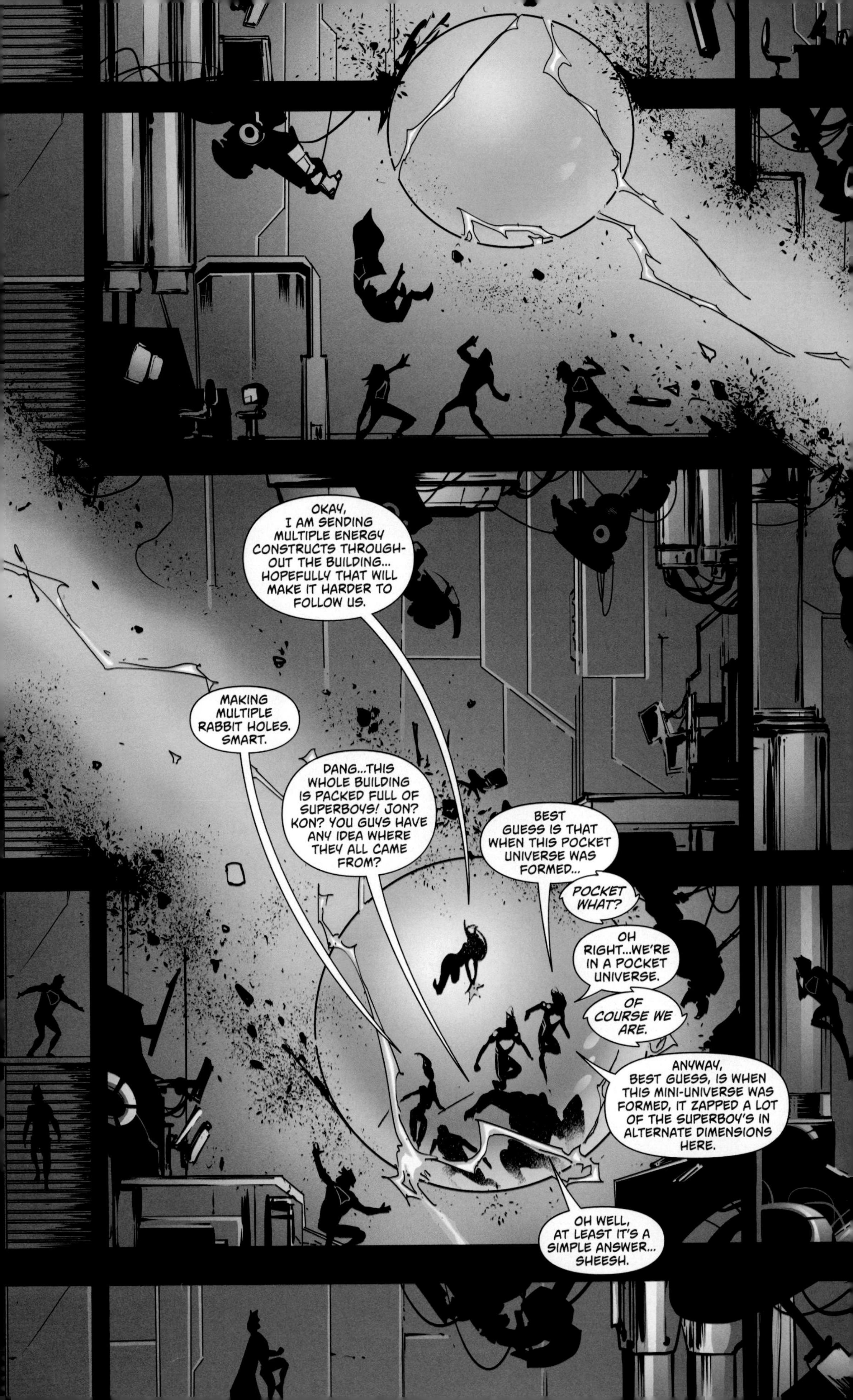
OKAY, I AM SENDING MULTIPLE ENERGY CONSTRUCTS THROUGH-OUT THE BUILDING... HOPEFULLY THAT WILL MAKE IT HARDER TO FOLLOW US.
MAKING MULTIPLE RABBIT HOLES. SMART.
DANG...THIS WHOLE BUILDING IS PACKED FULL OF SUPERBOYS! JON? KON? YOU GUYS HAVE ANY IDEA WHERE THEY ALL CAME FROM?
BEST GUESS IS THAT WHEN THIS POCKET UNIVERSE WAS FORMED...
POCKET WHAT?
OH RIGHT...WE'RE IN A POCKET UNIVERSE.
OF COURSE WE ARE.
ANYWAY, BEST GUESS, IS WHEN THIS MINI-UNIVERSE WAS FORMED, IT ZAPPED A LOT OF THE SUPERBOY'S IN ALTERNATE DIMENSIONS HERE.
OH WELL, AT LEAST IT'S A SIMPLE ANSWER... SHEESH.

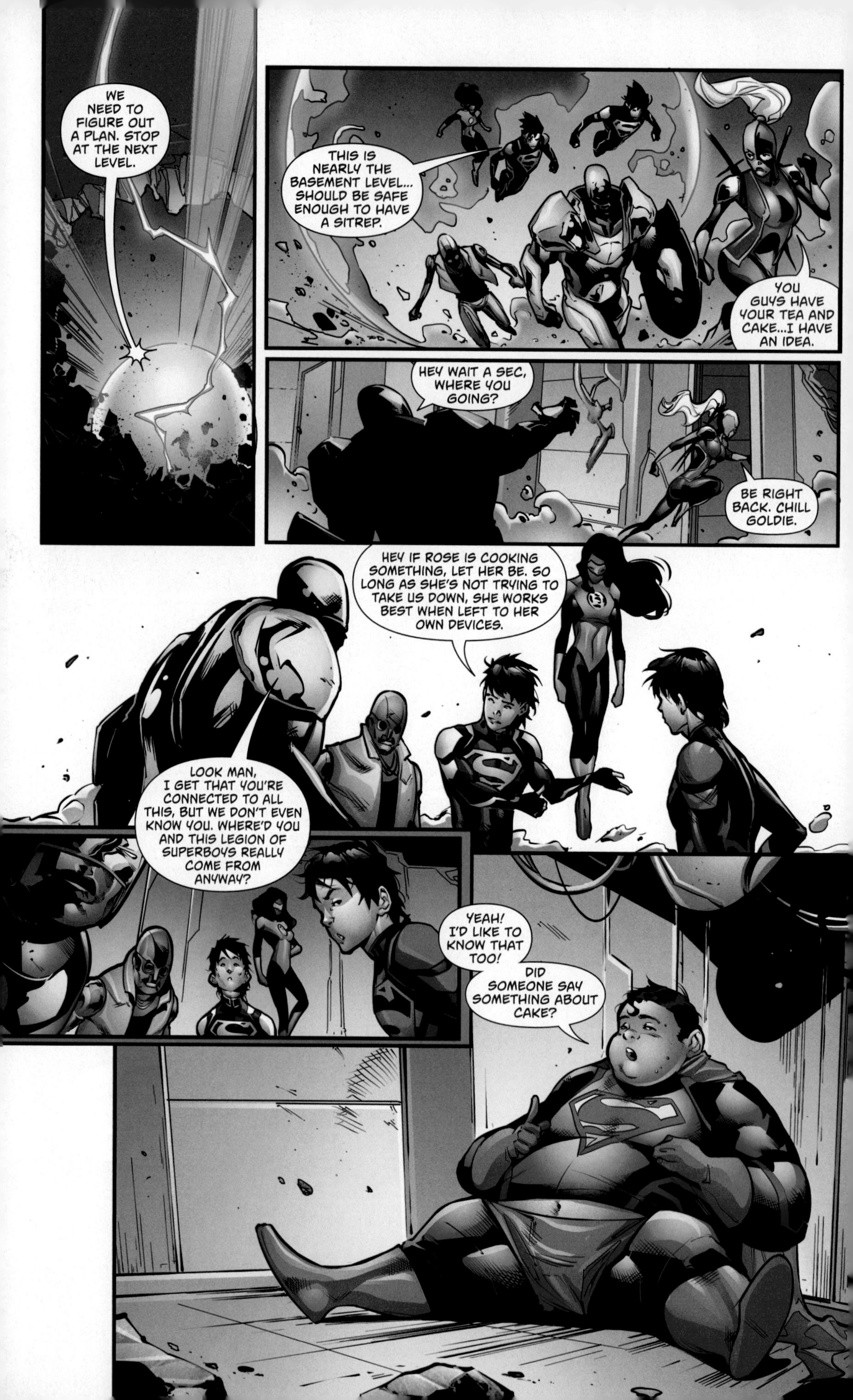
WE NEED TO FIGURE OUT A PLAN. STOP AT THE NEXT LEVEL.
THIS IS NEARLY THE BASEMENT LEVEL... SHOULD BE SAFE ENOUGH TO HAVE A SITREP.
YOU GUYS HAVE YOUR TEA AND CAKE...I HAVE AN IDEA.
HEY WAIT A SEC, WHERE YOU GOING?
BE RIGHT BACK. CHILL GOLDIE.
HEY IF ROSE IS COOKING SOMETHING, LET HER BE. SO LONG AS SHE'S NOT TRYING TO TAKE US DOWN, SHE WORKS BEST WHEN LEFT TO HER OWN DEVICES.
LOOK MAN, I GET THAT YOU'RE CONNECTED TO ALL THIS, BUT WE DON'T EVEN KNOW YOU. WHERE'D YOU AND THIS LEGION OF SUPERBOYS REALLY COME FROM ANYWAY?
YEAH! I'D LIKE TO KNOW THAT TOO!
DID SOMEONE SAY SOMETHING ABOUT CAKE?

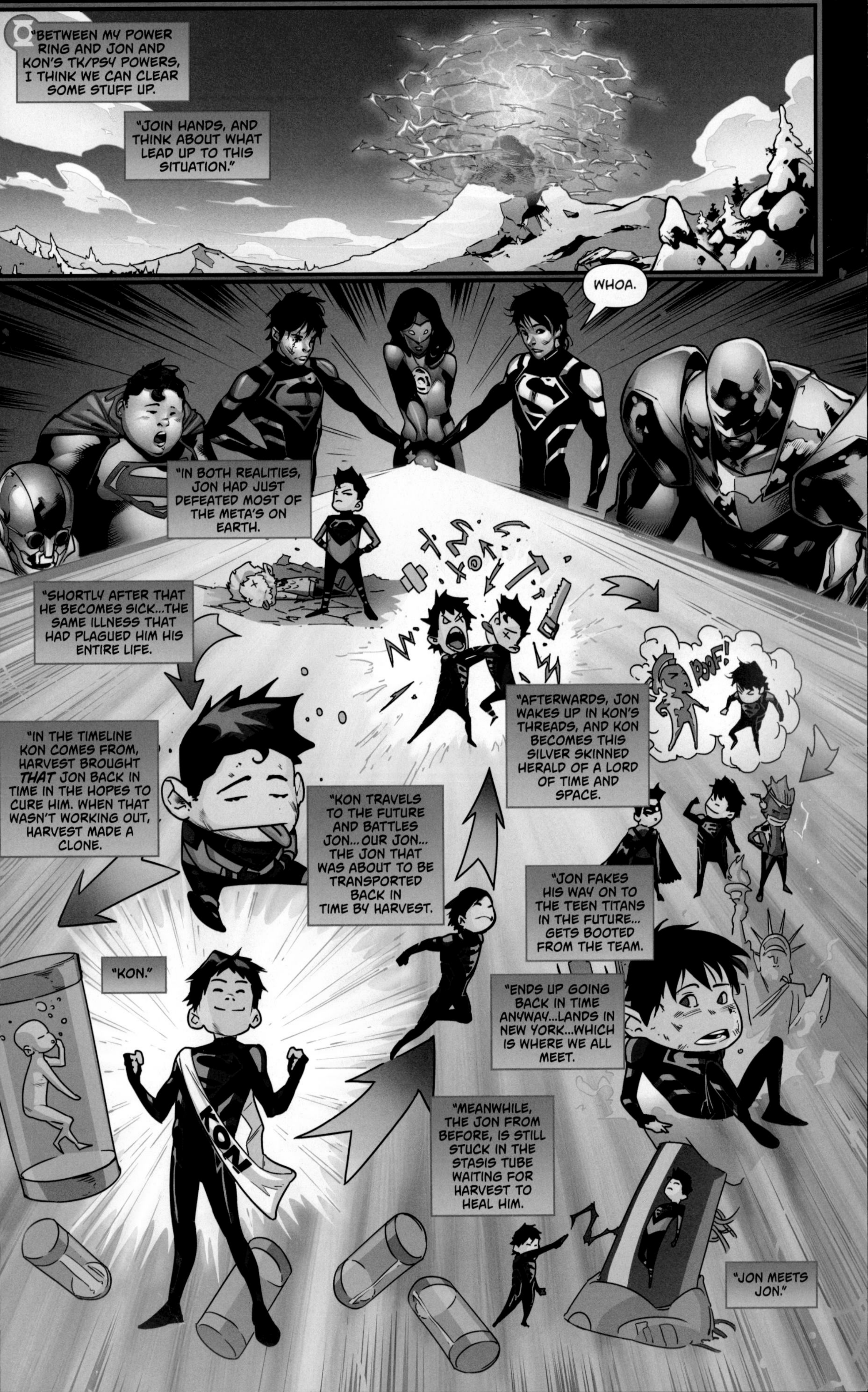
"BETWEEN MY POWER RING AND JON AND KON'S TK/PSY POWERS, I THINK WE CAN CLEAR SOME STUFF UP.
"JOIN HANDS, AND THINK ABOUT WHAT LEAD UP TO THIS SITUATION."
WHOA.
"IN BOTH REALITIES, JON HAD JUST DEFEATED MOST OF THE META'S ON EARTH.
"SHORTLY AFTER THAT HE BECOMES SICK...THE SAME ILLNESS THAT HAD PLAGUED HIM HIS ENTIRE LIFE.
"IN THE TIMELINE KON COMES FROM, HARVEST BROUGHT *THAT* JON BACK IN TIME IN THE HOPES TO CURE HIM. WHEN THAT WASN'T WORKING OUT, HARVEST MADE A CLONE.
"KON TRAVELS TO THE FUTURE AND BATTLES JON...OUR JON... THE JON THAT WAS ABOUT TO BE TRANSPORTED BACK IN TIME BY HARVEST.
"AFTERWARDS, JON WAKES UP IN KON'S THREADS, AND KON BECOMES THIS SILVER SKINNED HERALD OF A LORD OF TIME AND SPACE.
POOF!
"JON FAKES HIS WAY ON TO THE TEEN TITANS IN THE FUTURE... GETS BOOTED FROM THE TEAM.
"KON."
KON
"ENDS UP GOING BACK IN TIME ANYWAY...LANDS IN NEW YORK...WHICH IS WHERE WE ALL MEET.
"MEANWHILE, THE JON FROM BEFORE, IS STILL STUCK IN THE STASIS TUBE WAITING FOR HARVEST TO HEAL HIM.
"JON MEETS JON."

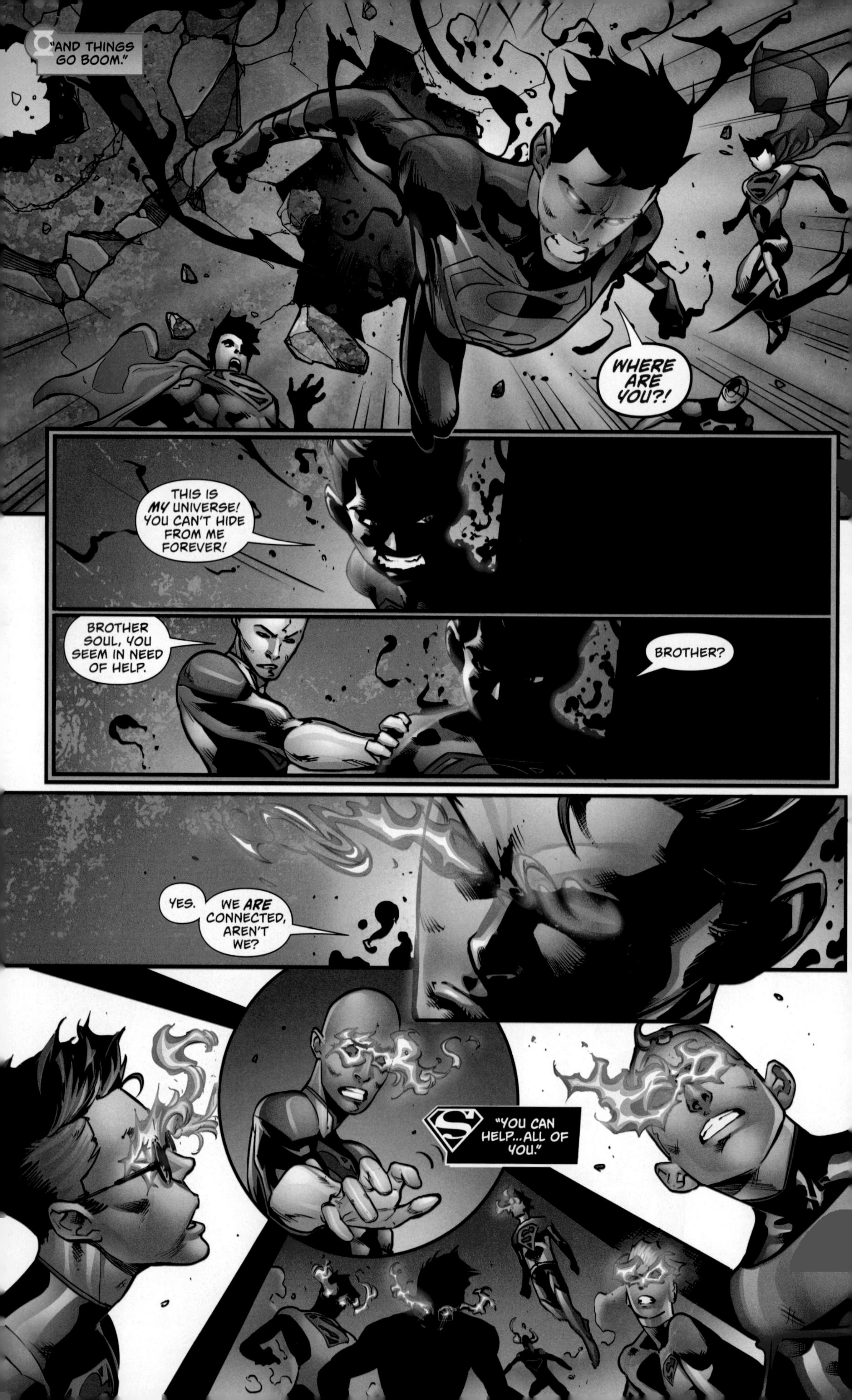
"AND THINGS GO BOOM."
WHERE ARE YOU?!
THIS IS MY UNIVERSE! YOU CAN'T HIDE FROM ME FOREVER!
BROTHER SOUL, YOU SEEM IN NEED OF HELP.
BROTHER?
YES.
WE ARE CONNECTED, AREN'T WE?
"YOU CAN HELP...ALL OF YOU."

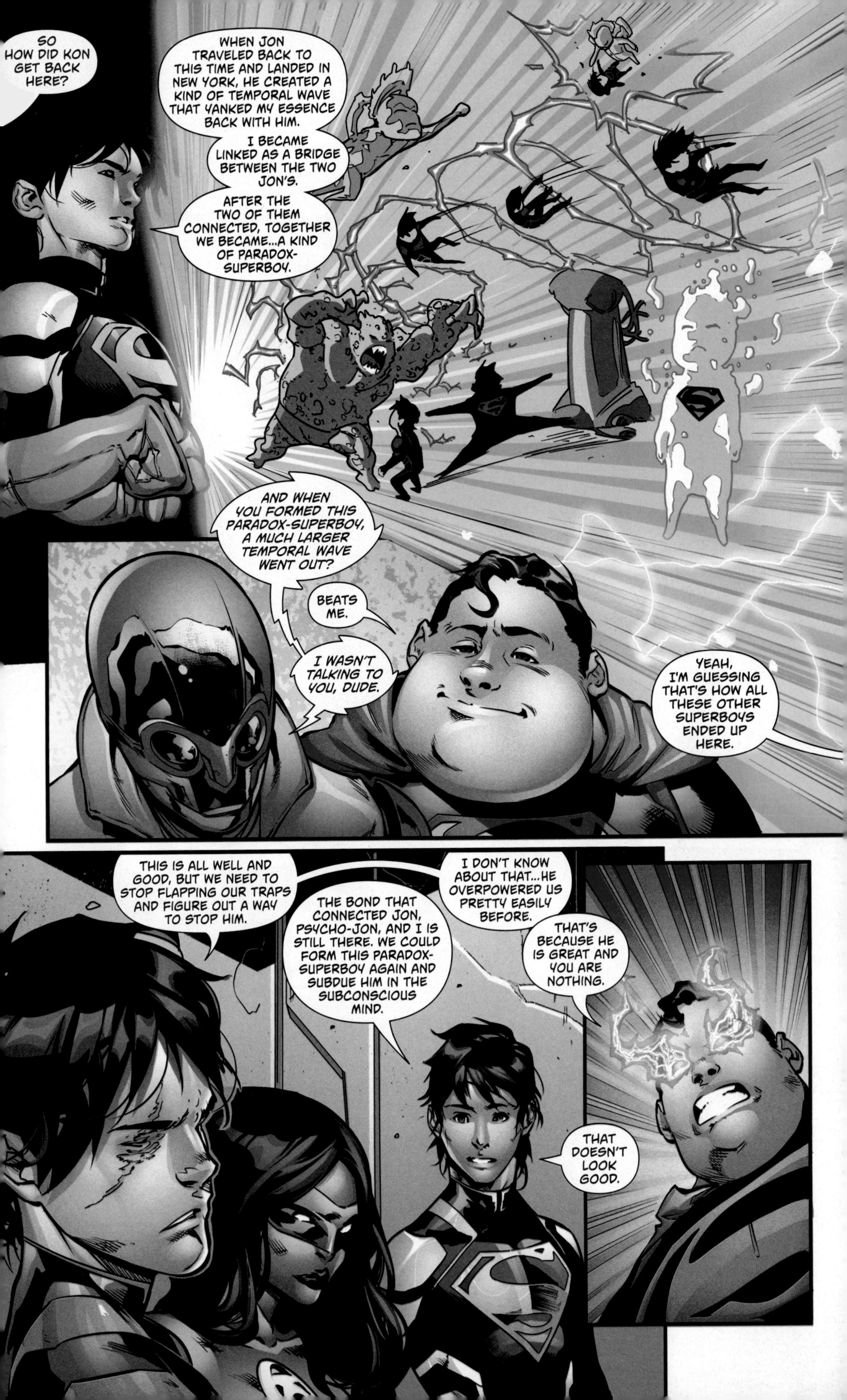

SO HOW DID KON GET BACK HERE?
WHEN JON TRAVELED BACK TO THIS TIME AND LANDED IN NEW YORK, HE CREATED A KIND OF TEMPORAL WAVE THAT YANKED MY ESSENCE BACK WITH HIM.
I BECAME LINKED AS A BRIDGE BETWEEN THE TWO JON'S.
AFTER THE TWO OF THEM CONNECTED, TOGETHER WE BECAME...A KIND OF PARADOX-SUPERBOY.
AND WHEN YOU FORMED THIS PARADOX-SUPERBOY, A MUCH LARGER TEMPORAL WAVE WENT OUT?
BEATS ME.
I WASN'T TALKING TO YOU, DUDE.
YEAH, I'M GUESSING THAT'S HOW ALL THESE OTHER SUPERBOYS ENDED UP HERE.
THIS IS ALL WELL AND GOOD, BUT WE NEED TO STOP FLAPPING OUR TRAPS AND FIGURE OUT A WAY TO STOP HIM.
I DON'T KNOW ABOUT THAT...HE OVERPOWERED US PRETTY EASILY BEFORE.
THE BOND THAT CONNECTED JON, PSYCHO-JON, AND I IS STILL THERE. WE COULD FORM THIS PARADOX-SUPERBOY AGAIN AND SUBDUE HIM IN THE SUBCONSCIOUS MIND.
THAT'S BECAUSE HE IS GREAT AND YOU ARE NOTHING.
THAT DOESN'T LOOK GOOD.

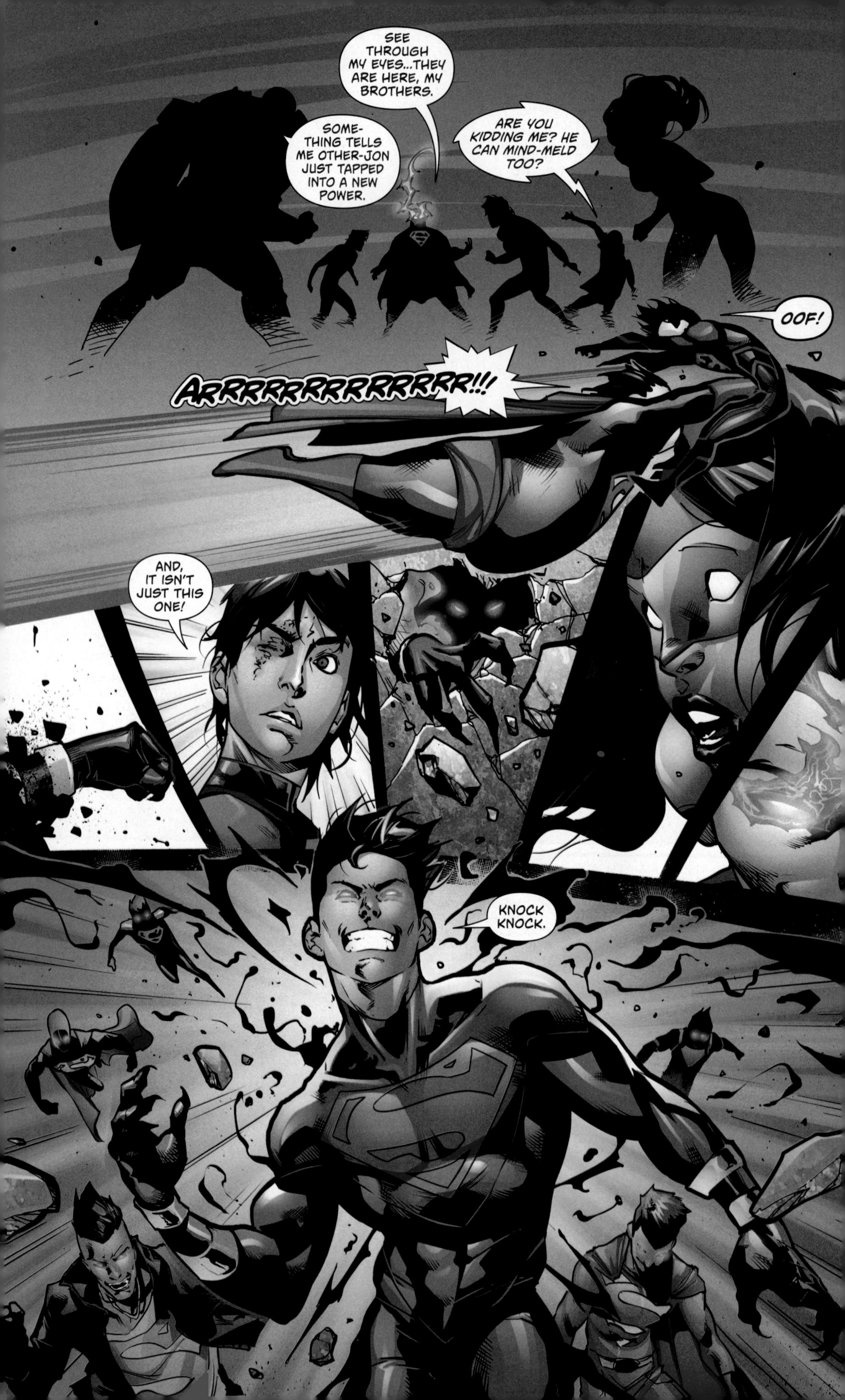
SEE THROUGH MY EYES...THEY ARE HERE, MY BROTHERS.
SOME-THING TELLS ME OTHER-JON JUST TAPPED INTO A NEW POWER.
ARE YOU KIDDING ME? HE CAN MIND-MELD TOO?
OOF!
ARRRRRRRRRRRRR!!!
AND, IT ISN'T JUST THIS ONE!
KNOCK KNOCK.

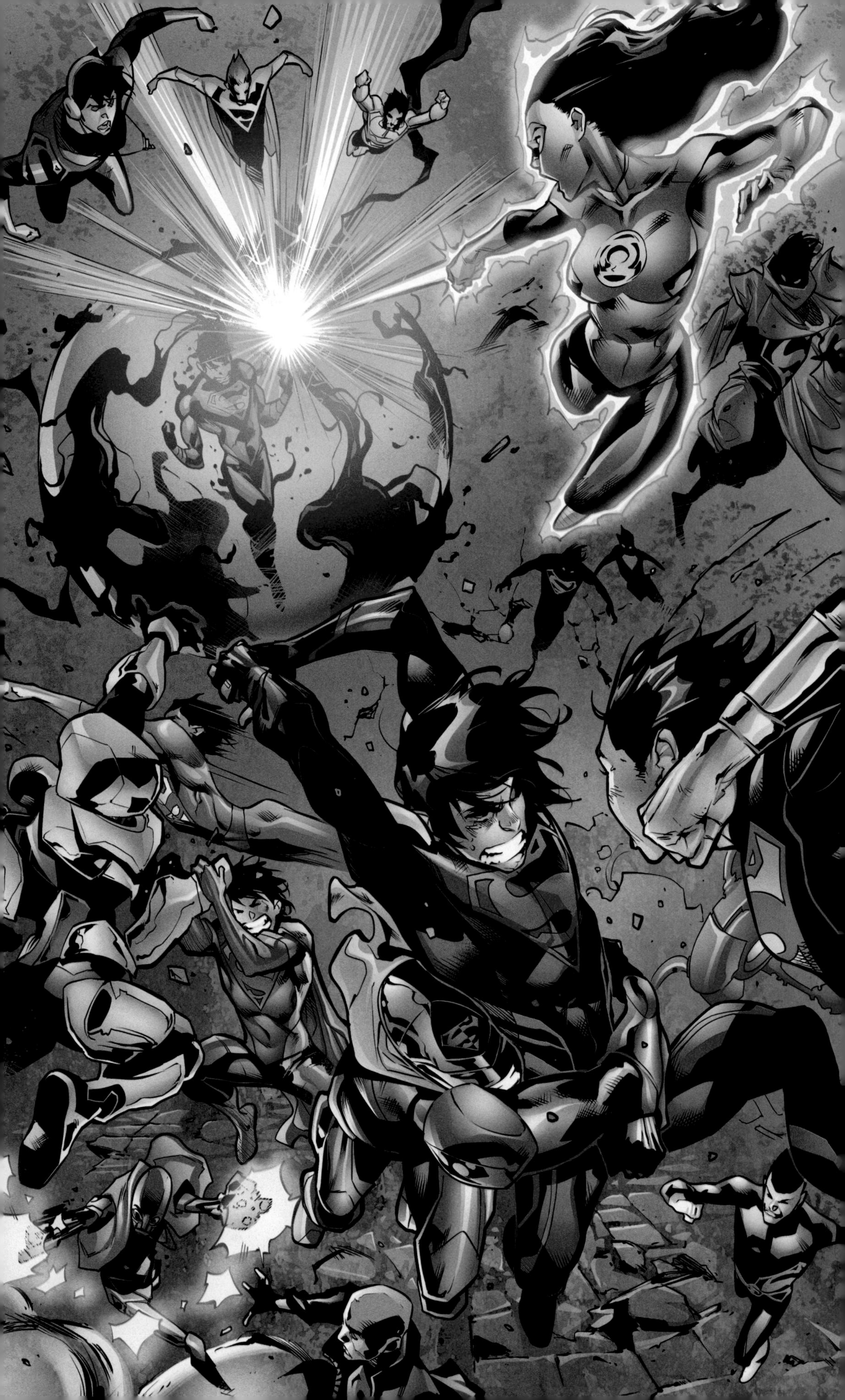

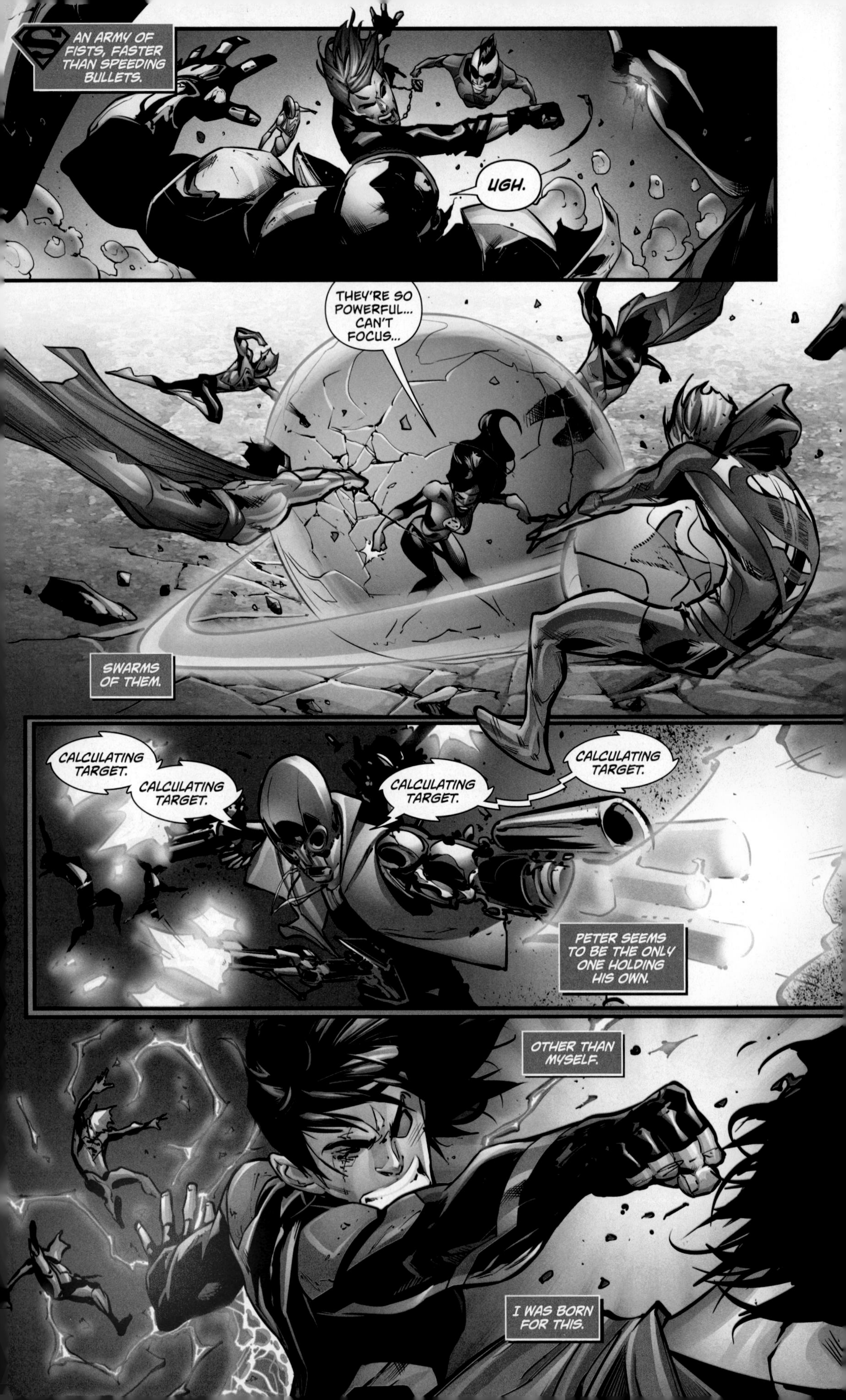
AN ARMY OF FISTS, FASTER THAN SPEEDING BULLETS.
UGH.
THEY'RE SO POWERFUL... CAN'T FOCUS...
SWARMS OF THEM.
CALCULATING TARGET.
CALCULATING TARGET.
CALCULATING TARGET.
CALCULATING TARGET.
PETER SEEMS TO BE THE ONLY ONE HOLDING HIS OWN.
OTHER THAN MYSELF.
I WAS BORN FOR THIS.

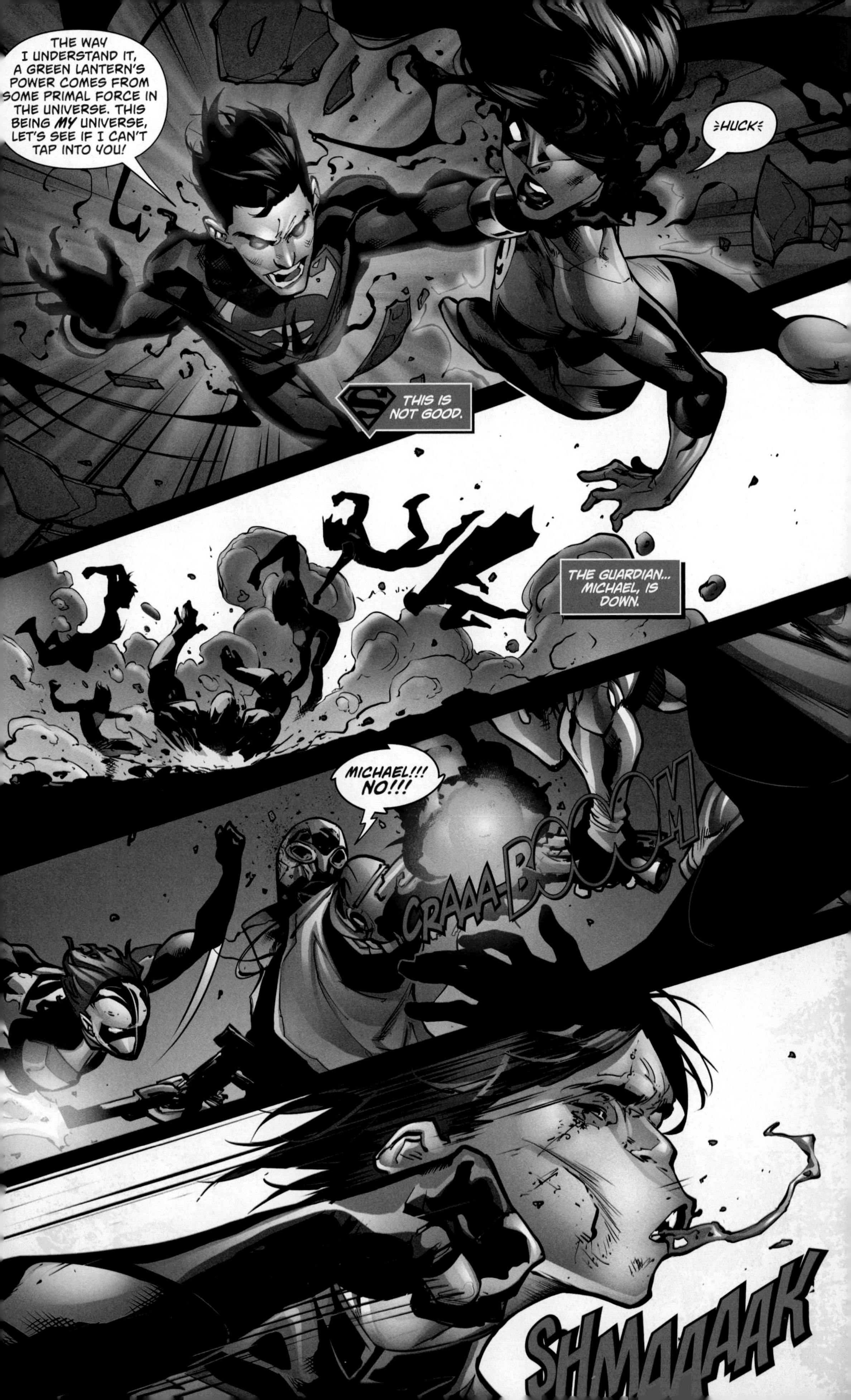
THE WAY I UNDERSTAND IT, A GREEN LANTERN'S POWER COMES FROM SOME PRIMAL FORCE IN THE UNIVERSE. THIS BEING MY UNIVERSE, LET'S SEE IF I CAN'T TAP INTO YOU!
HUCK
THIS IS NOT GOOD.
THE GUARDIAN... MICHAEL, IS DOWN.
MICHAEL!!! NO!!!
CRAAA-BOOOOM
SHMAAAK

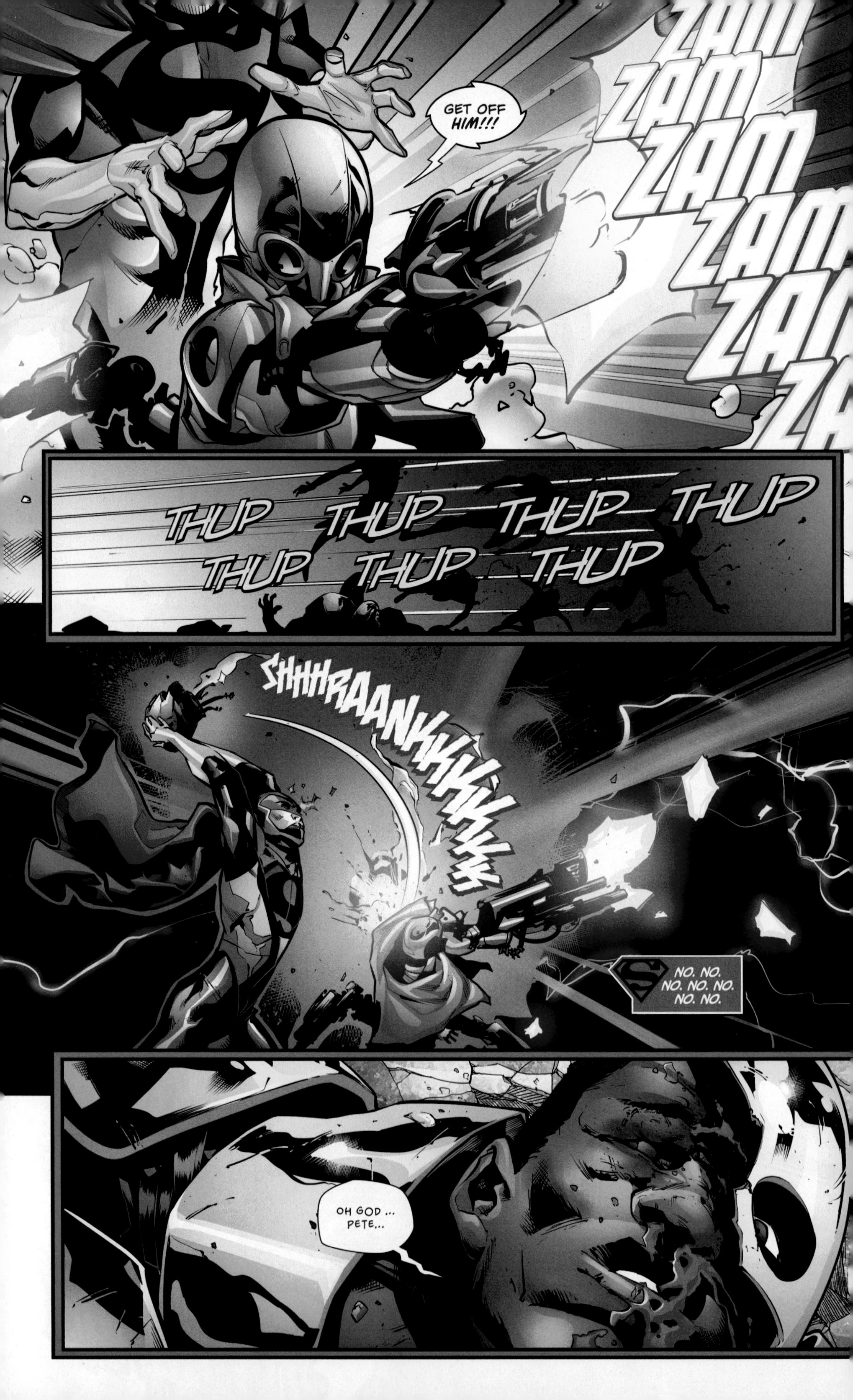

ZAM ZAM ZAM ZAM ZAM ZAM ZA ZA
GET OFF HIM!!!
THUP THUP THUP THUP
THUP THUP THUP
SHHHRAANKKKKKKK!!
NO. NO. NO. NO. NO. NO. NO.
OH GOD ... PETE...

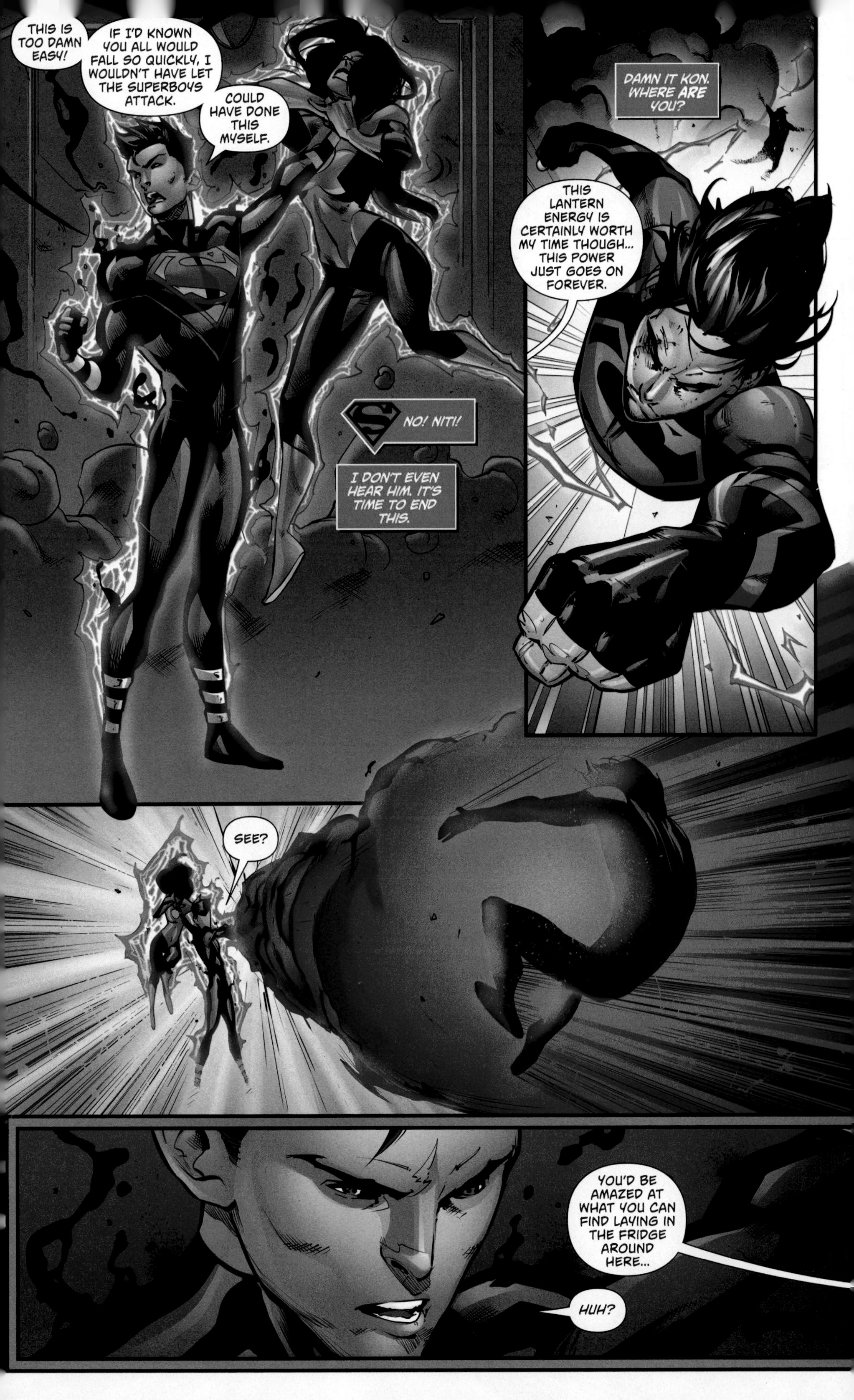
THIS IS TOO DAMN EASY!
IF I'D KNOWN YOU ALL WOULD FALL SO QUICKLY, I WOULDN'T HAVE LET THE SUPERBOYS ATTACK.
COULD HAVE DONE THIS MYSELF.
DAMN IT KON. WHERE *ARE* YOU?
THIS LANTERN ENERGY IS CERTAINLY WORTH MY TIME THOUGH... THIS POWER JUST GOES ON FOREVER.
NO! NITI!
I DON'T EVEN HEAR HIM. IT'S TIME TO END THIS.
SEE?
YOU'D BE AMAZED AT WHAT YOU CAN FIND LAYING IN THE FRIDGE AROUND HERE...
HUH?

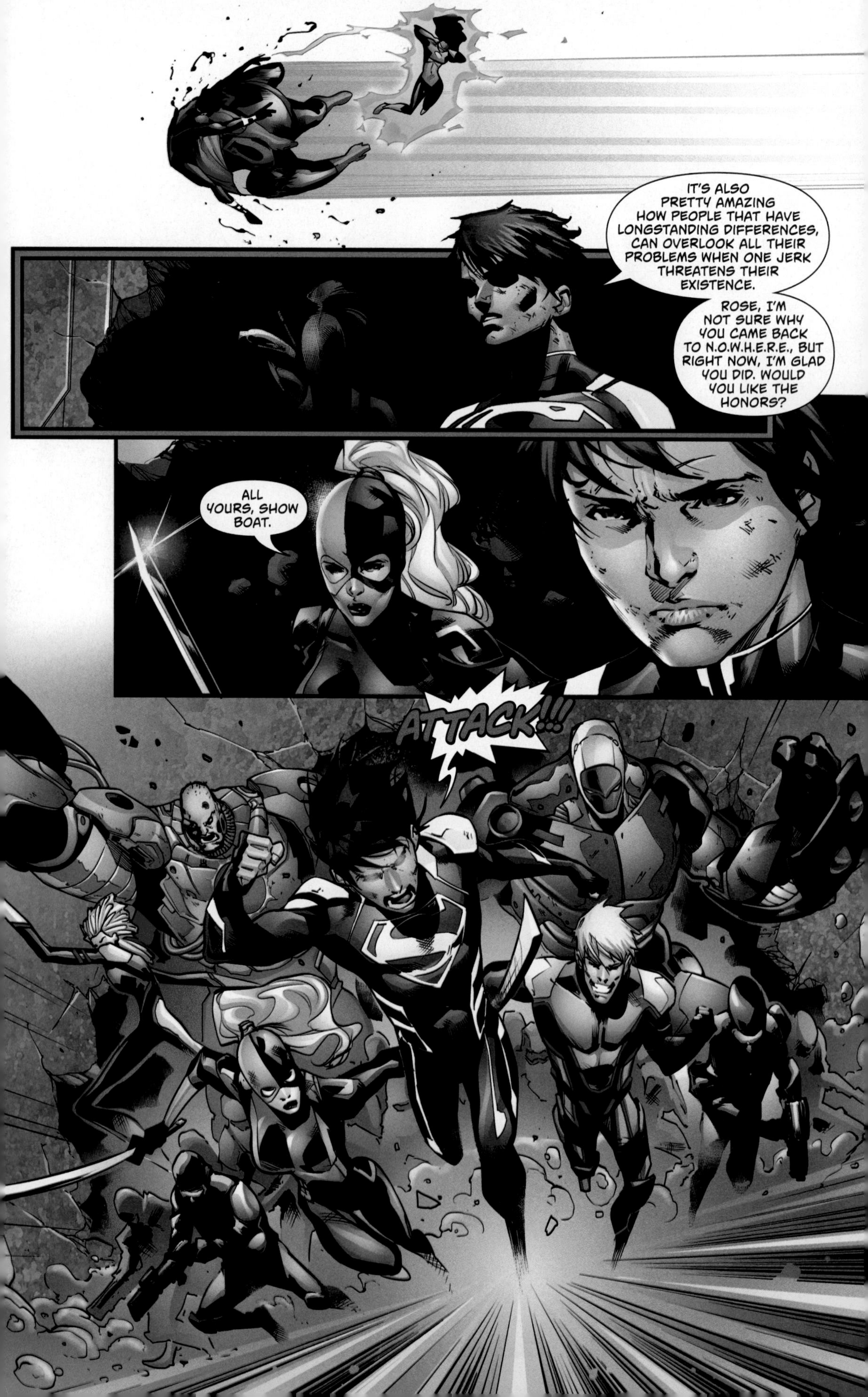
IT'S ALSO PRETTY AMAZING HOW PEOPLE THAT HAVE LONGSTANDING DIFFERENCES, CAN OVERLOOK ALL THEIR PROBLEMS WHEN ONE JERK THREATENS THEIR EXISTENCE.
ROSE, I'M NOT SURE WHY YOU CAME BACK TO N.O.W.H.E.R.E., BUT RIGHT NOW, I'M GLAD YOU DID. WOULD YOU LIKE THE HONORS?
ALL YOURS, SHOW BOAT.
ATTACK!!!

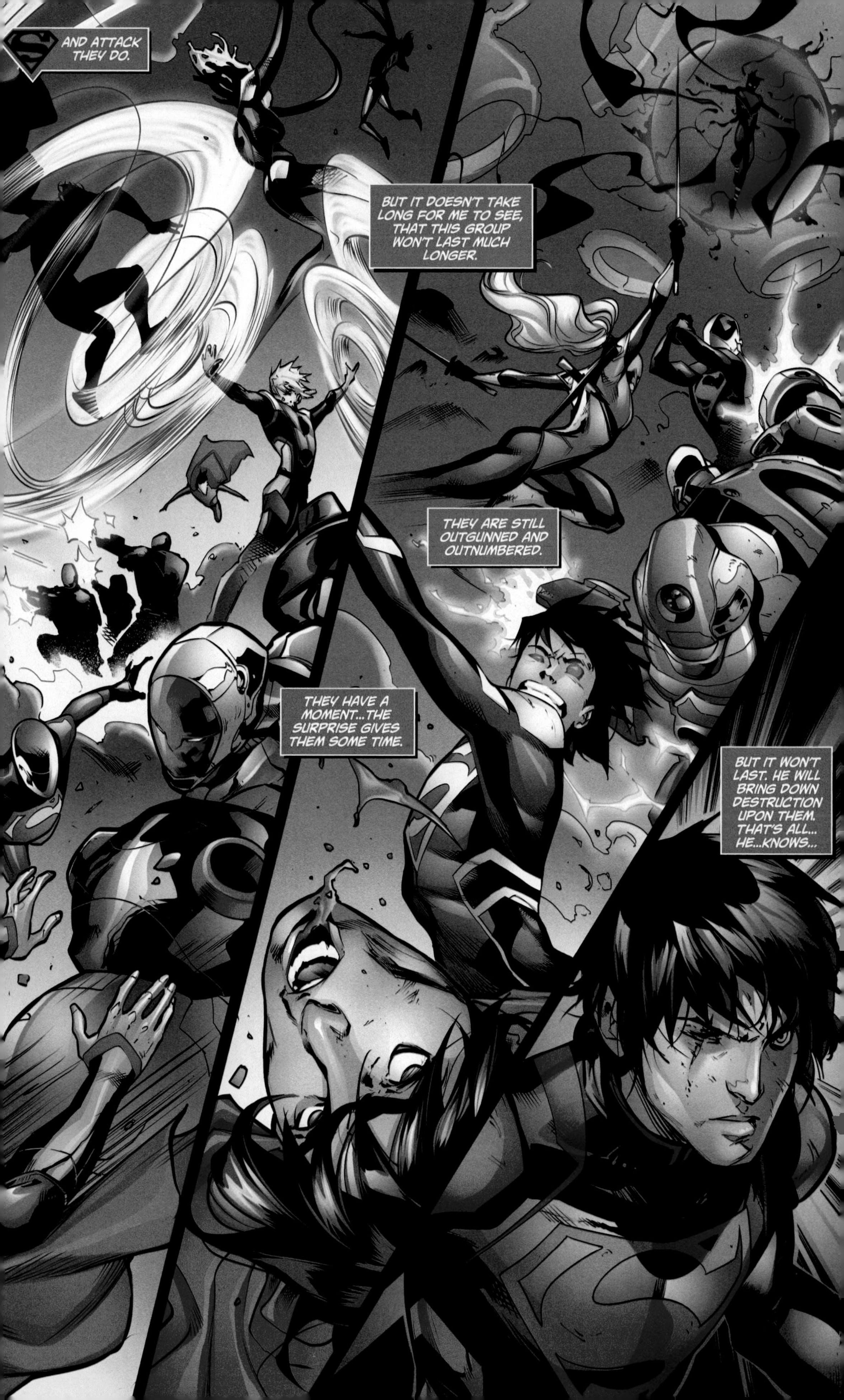
AND ATTACK THEY DO.
BUT IT DOESN'T TAKE LONG FOR ME TO SEE, THAT THIS GROUP WON'T LAST MUCH LONGER.
THEY ARE STILL OUTGUNNED AND OUTNUMBERED.
THEY HAVE A MOMENT...THE SURPRISE GIVES THEM SOME TIME.
BUT IT WON'T LAST. HE WILL BRING DOWN DESTRUCTION UPON THEM. THAT'S ALL... HE...KNOWS...

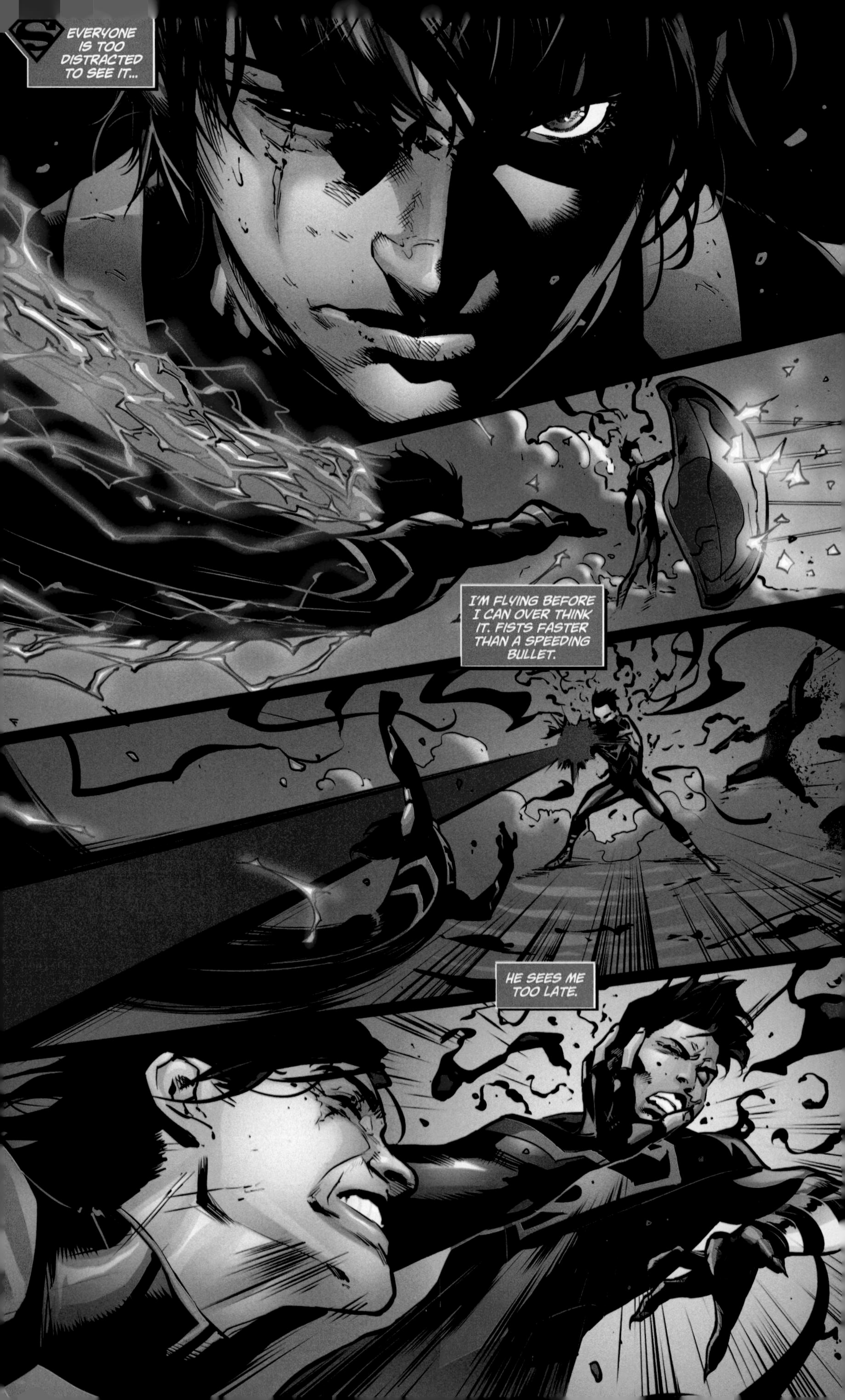
EVERYONE IS TOO DISTRACTED TO SEE IT...
I'M FLYING BEFORE I CAN OVER THINK IT. FISTS FASTER THAN A SPEEDING BULLET.
HE SEES ME TOO LATE.

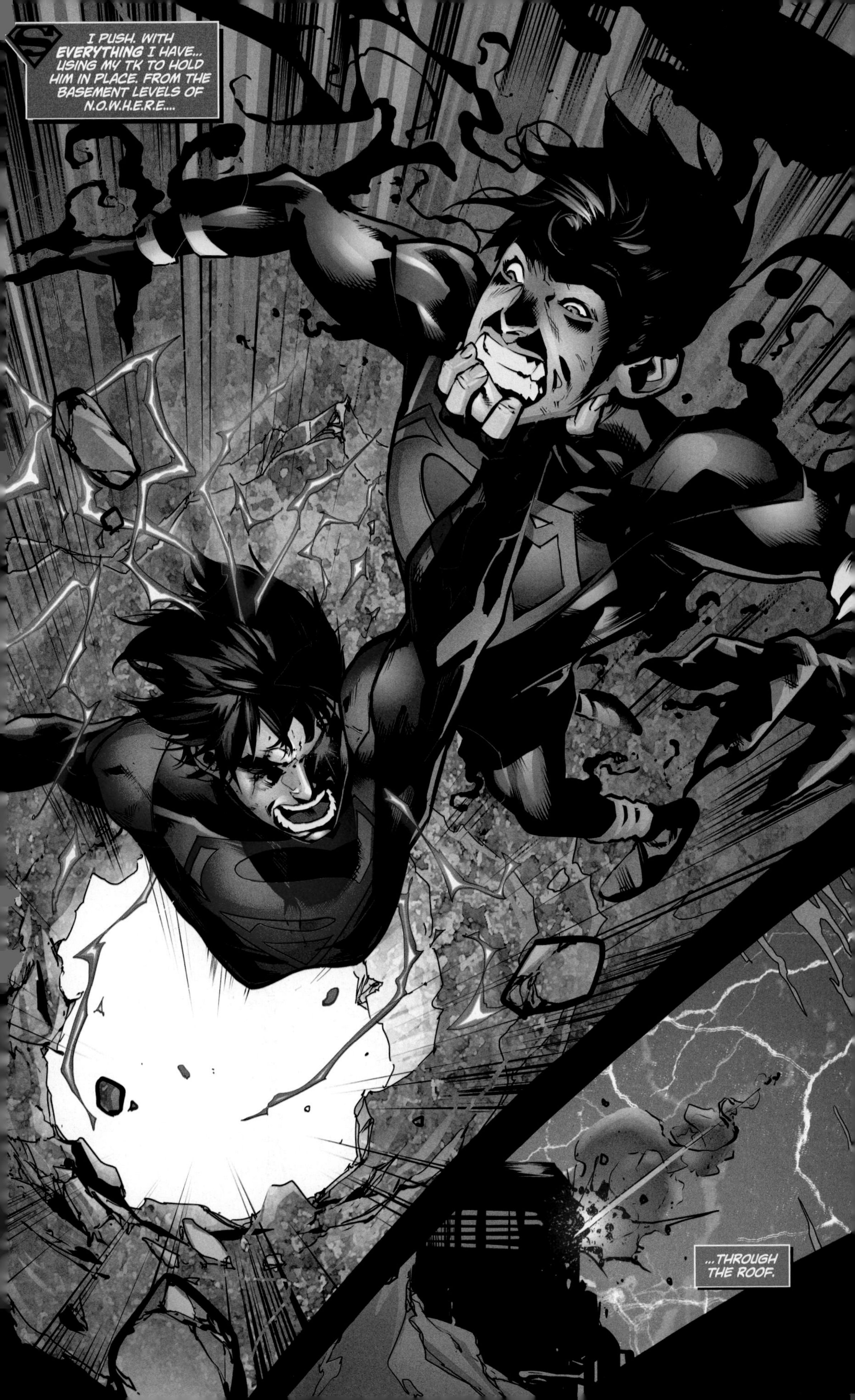
I PUSH. WITH EVERYTHING I HAVE... USING MY TK TO HOLD HIM IN PLACE. FROM THE BASEMENT LEVELS OF N.O.W.H.E.R.E....
...THROUGH THE ROOF.

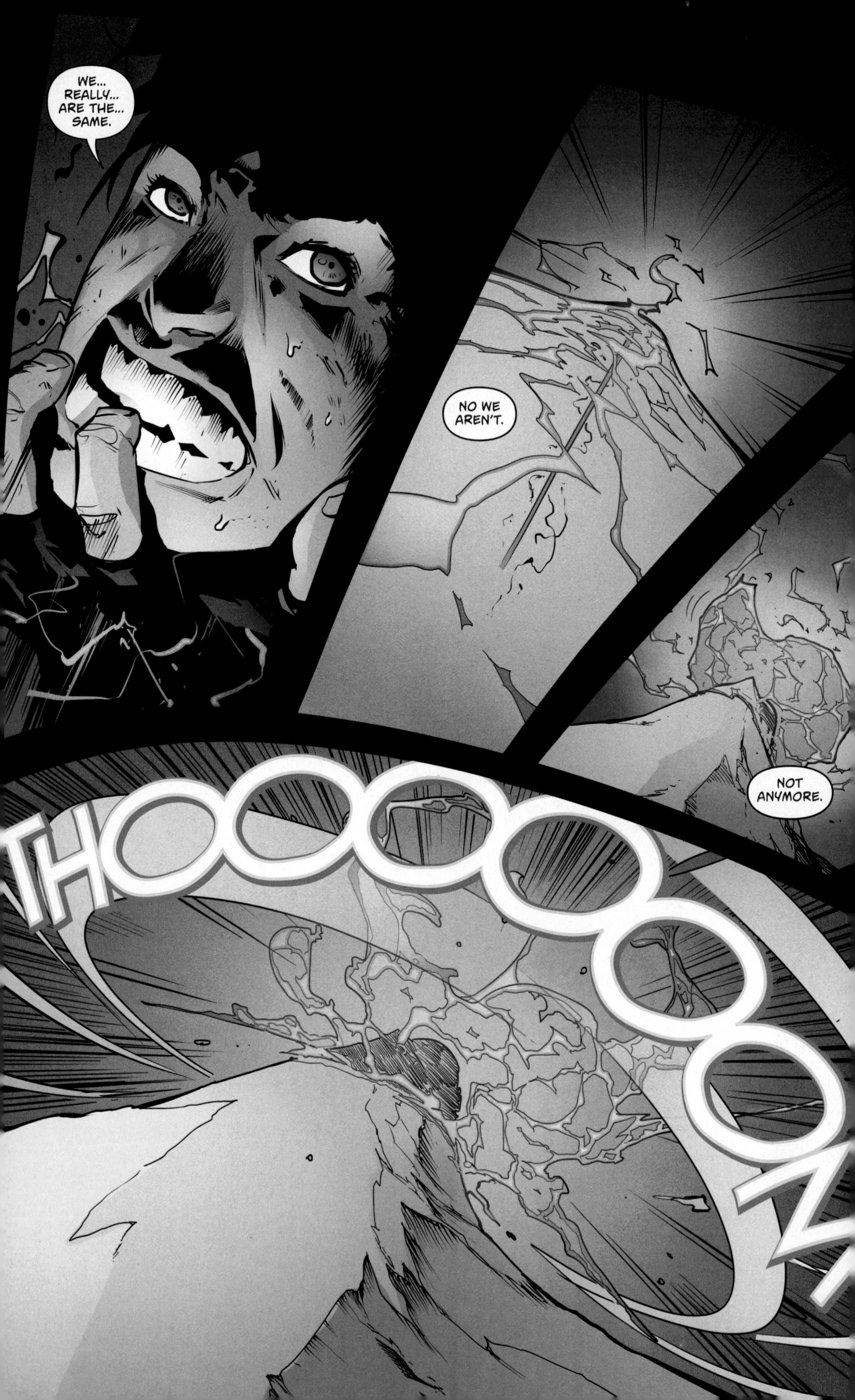
WE... REALLY... ARE THE... SAME.
NO WE AREN'T.
NOT ANYMORE.
THOOOOOOON

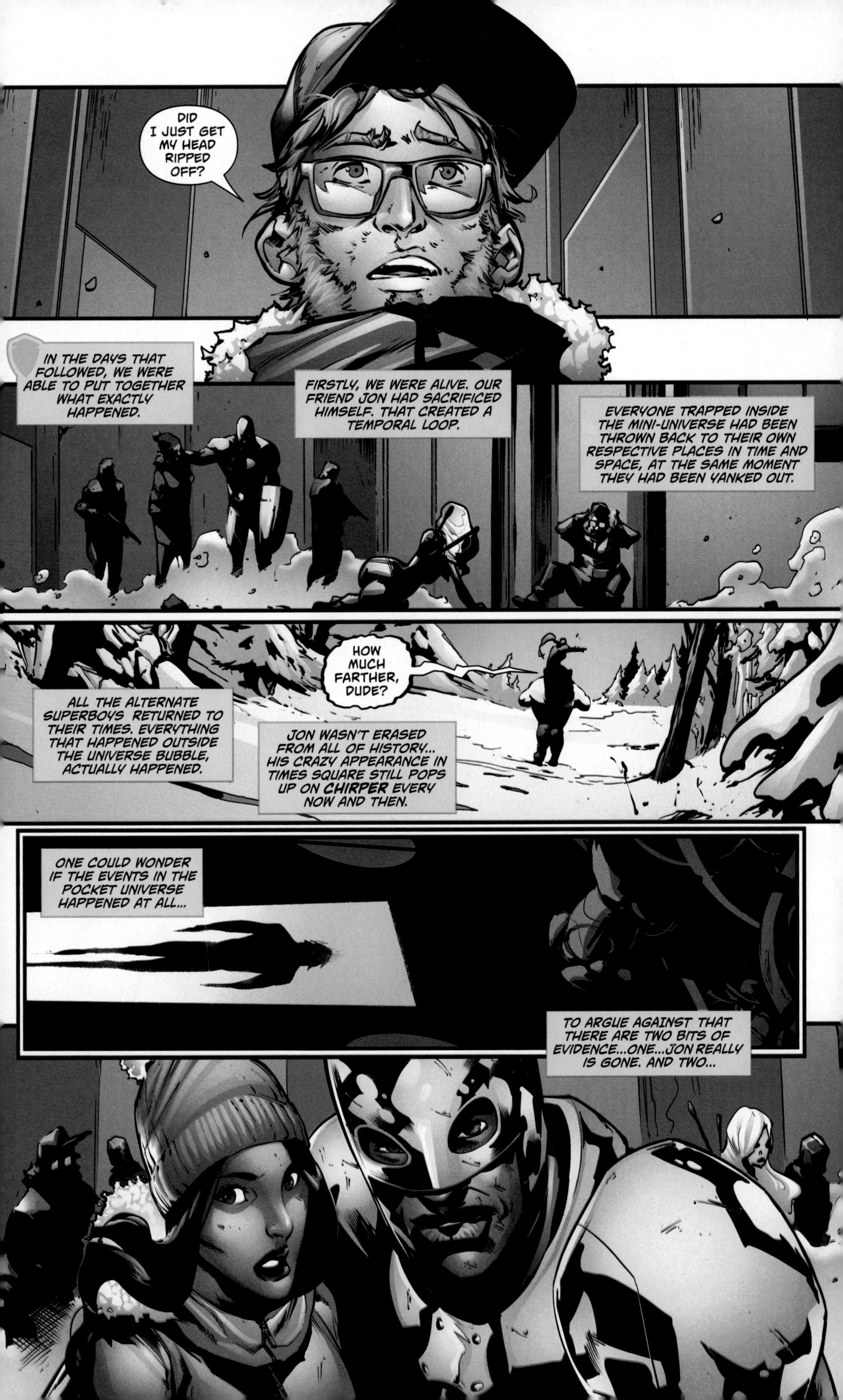
DID I JUST GET MY HEAD RIPPED OFF?
IN THE DAYS THAT FOLLOWED, WE WERE ABLE TO PUT TOGETHER WHAT EXACTLY HAPPENED.
FIRSTLY, WE WERE ALIVE. OUR FRIEND JON HAD SACRIFICED HIMSELF. THAT CREATED A TEMPORAL LOOP.
EVERYONE TRAPPED INSIDE THE MINI-UNIVERSE HAD BEEN THROWN BACK TO THEIR OWN RESPECTIVE PLACES IN TIME AND SPACE, AT THE SAME MOMENT THEY HAD BEEN YANKED OUT.
HOW MUCH FARTHER, DUDE?
ALL THE ALTERNATE SUPERBOYS RETURNED TO THEIR TIMES. EVERYTHING THAT HAPPENED OUTSIDE THE UNIVERSE BUBBLE, ACTUALLY HAPPENED.
JON WASN'T ERASED FROM ALL OF HISTORY... HIS CRAZY APPEARANCE IN TIMES SQUARE STILL POPS UP ON CHIRPER EVERY NOW AND THEN.
ONE COULD WONDER IF THE EVENTS IN THE POCKET UNIVERSE HAPPENED AT ALL...
TO ARGUE AGAINST THAT THERE ARE TWO BITS OF EVIDENCE...ONE...JON REALLY IS GONE. AND TWO...

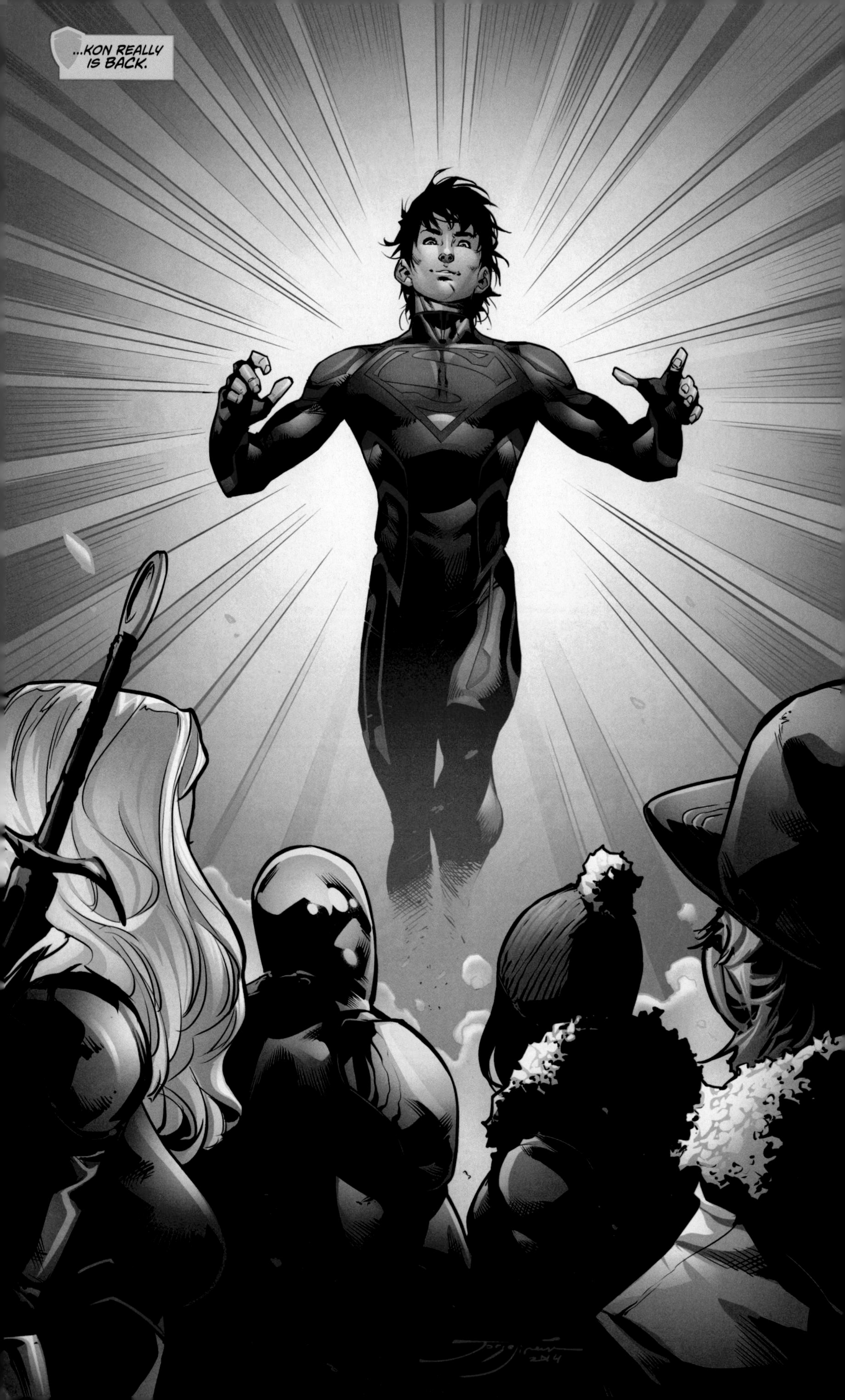
...KON REALLY IS BACK.

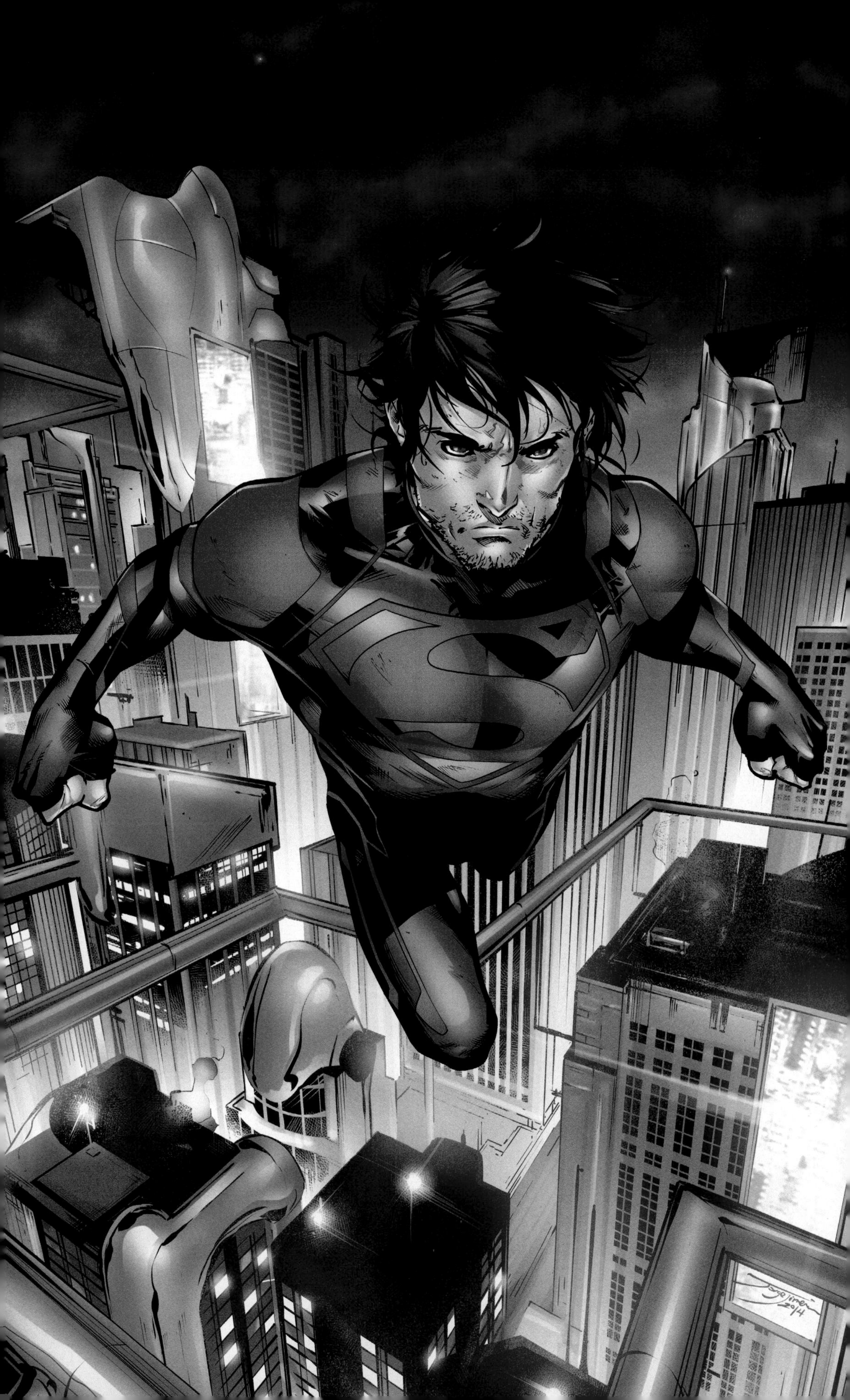

SUPER

FRANK J. BARBIERE writer BEN CALDWELL artist MIKE ATIYEH colorist
TRAVIS LANHAM letterer cover art by JORGE JIMÉNEZ and MIKE ATIYEH

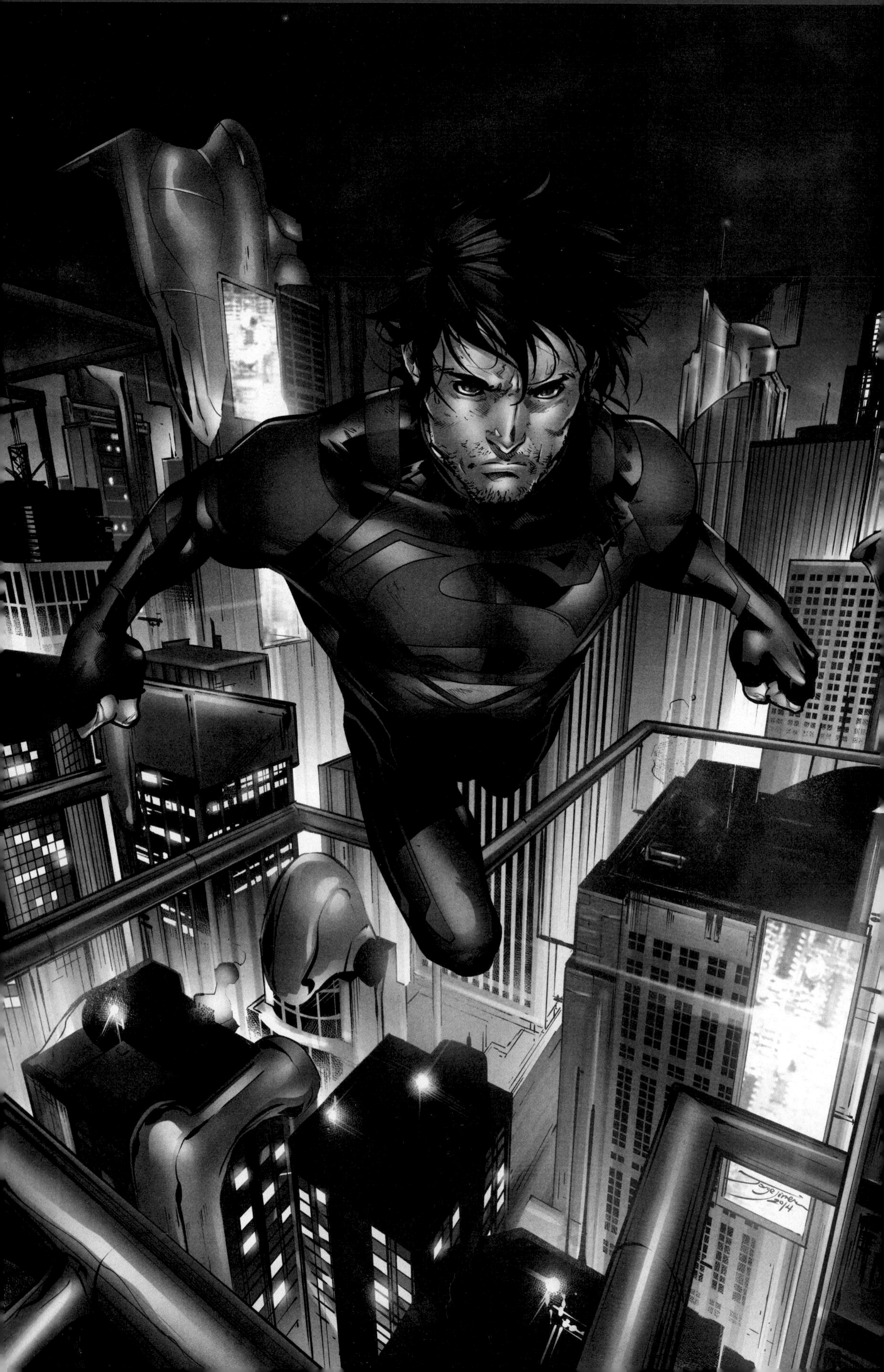

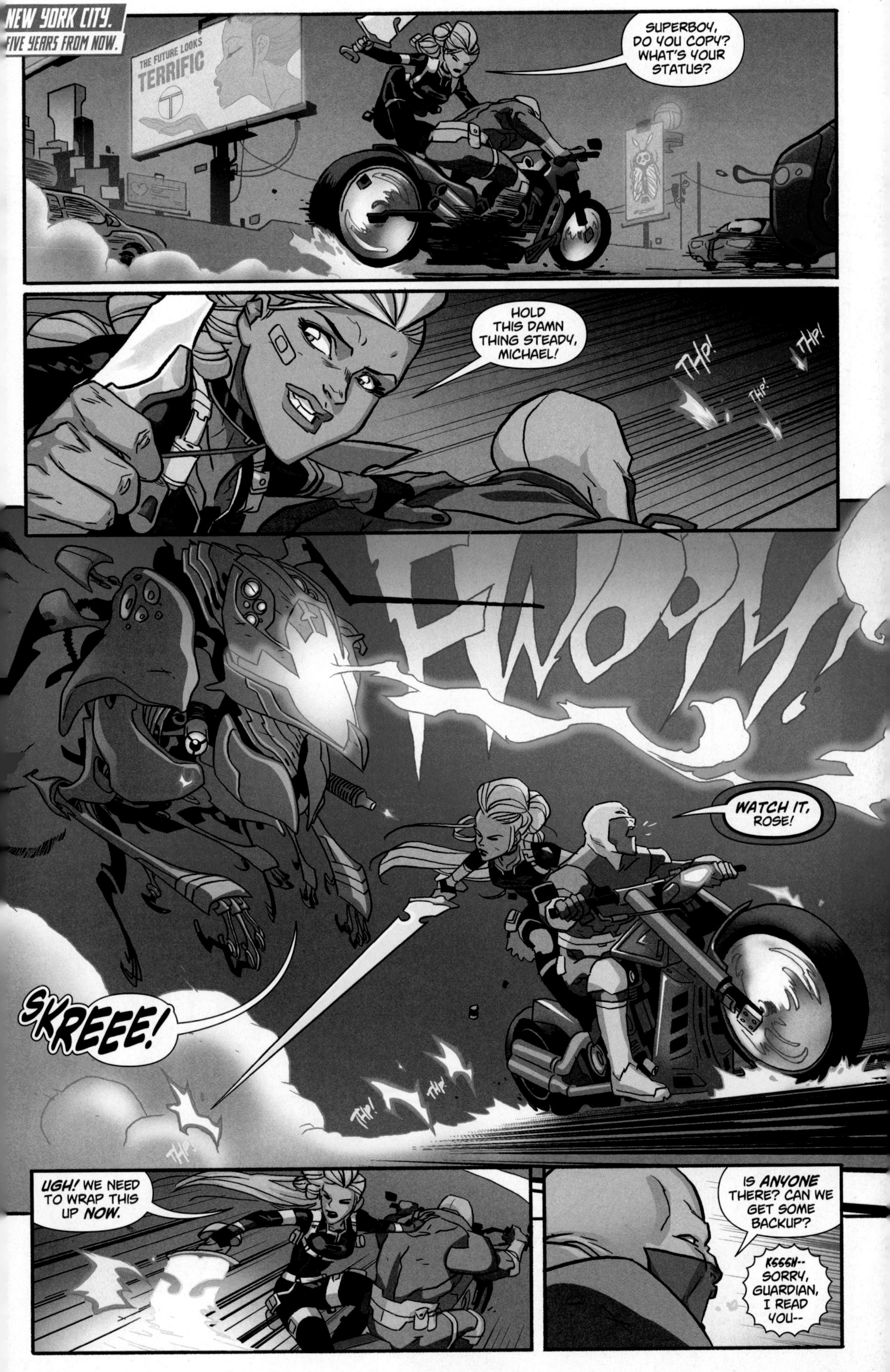
NEW YORK CITY.
FIVE YEARS FROM NOW.
THE FUTURE LOOKS TERRIFIC
SUPERBOY, DO YOU COPY? WHAT'S YOUR STATUS?
HOLD THIS DAMN THING STEADY, MICHAEL!
THP!
THP!
THP!
FWOOM!
WATCH IT, ROSE!
SKREEE!
THP!
THP!
THP!
UGH! WE NEED TO WRAP THIS UP NOW.
IS ANYONE THERE? CAN WE GET SOME BACKUP?
KSSSH-- SORRY, GUARDIAN, I READ YOU--

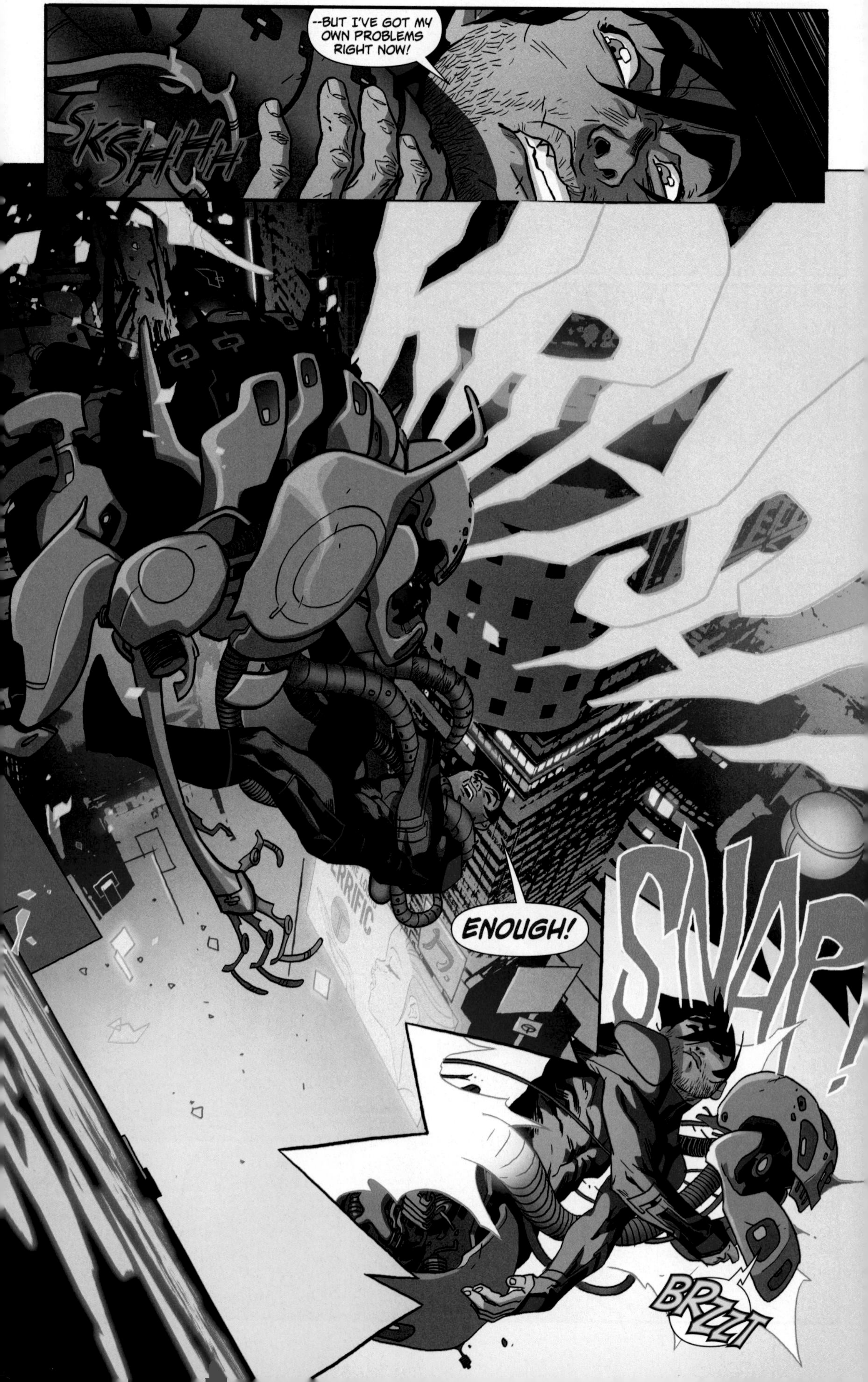
--BUT I'VE GOT MY OWN PROBLEMS RIGHT NOW!
SKSHHH
ENOUGH!
SNAP!
BRZZT

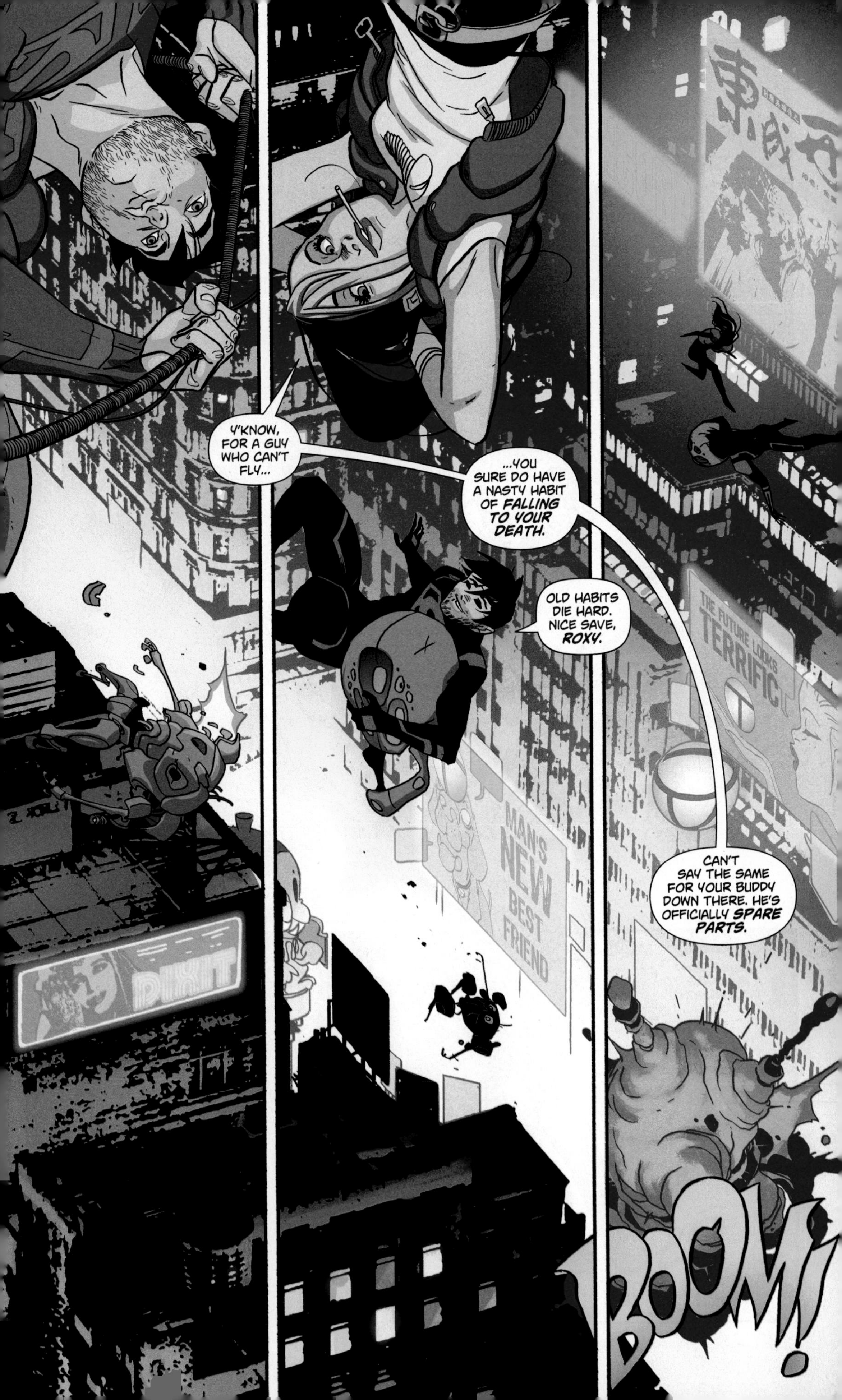
Y'KNOW, FOR A GUY WHO CAN'T FLY...
...YOU SURE DO HAVE A NASTY HABIT OF FALLING TO YOUR DEATH.
OLD HABITS DIE HARD. NICE SAVE, ROXY.
CAN'T SAY THE SAME FOR YOUR BUDDY DOWN THERE. HE'S OFFICIALLY SPARE PARTS.
THE FUTURE LOOKS TERRIFIC
MAN'S NEW BEST FRIEND
DIXIT
BOOM!

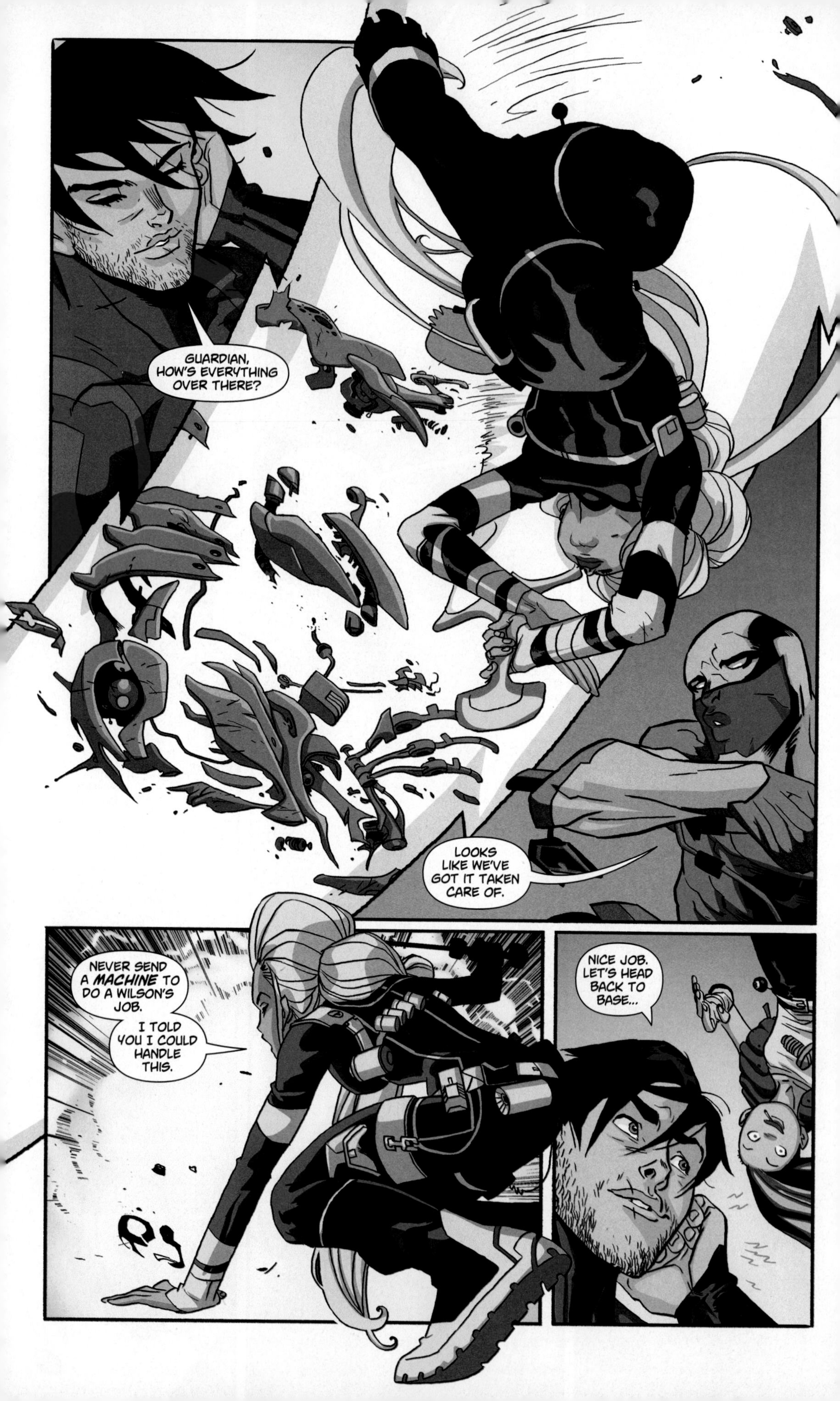
GUARDIAN, HOW'S EVERYTHING OVER THERE?
LOOKS LIKE WE'VE GOT IT TAKEN CARE OF.
NEVER SEND A *MACHINE* TO DO A WILSON'S JOB.
I TOLD YOU I COULD HANDLE THIS.
NICE JOB. LET'S HEAD BACK TO BASE...

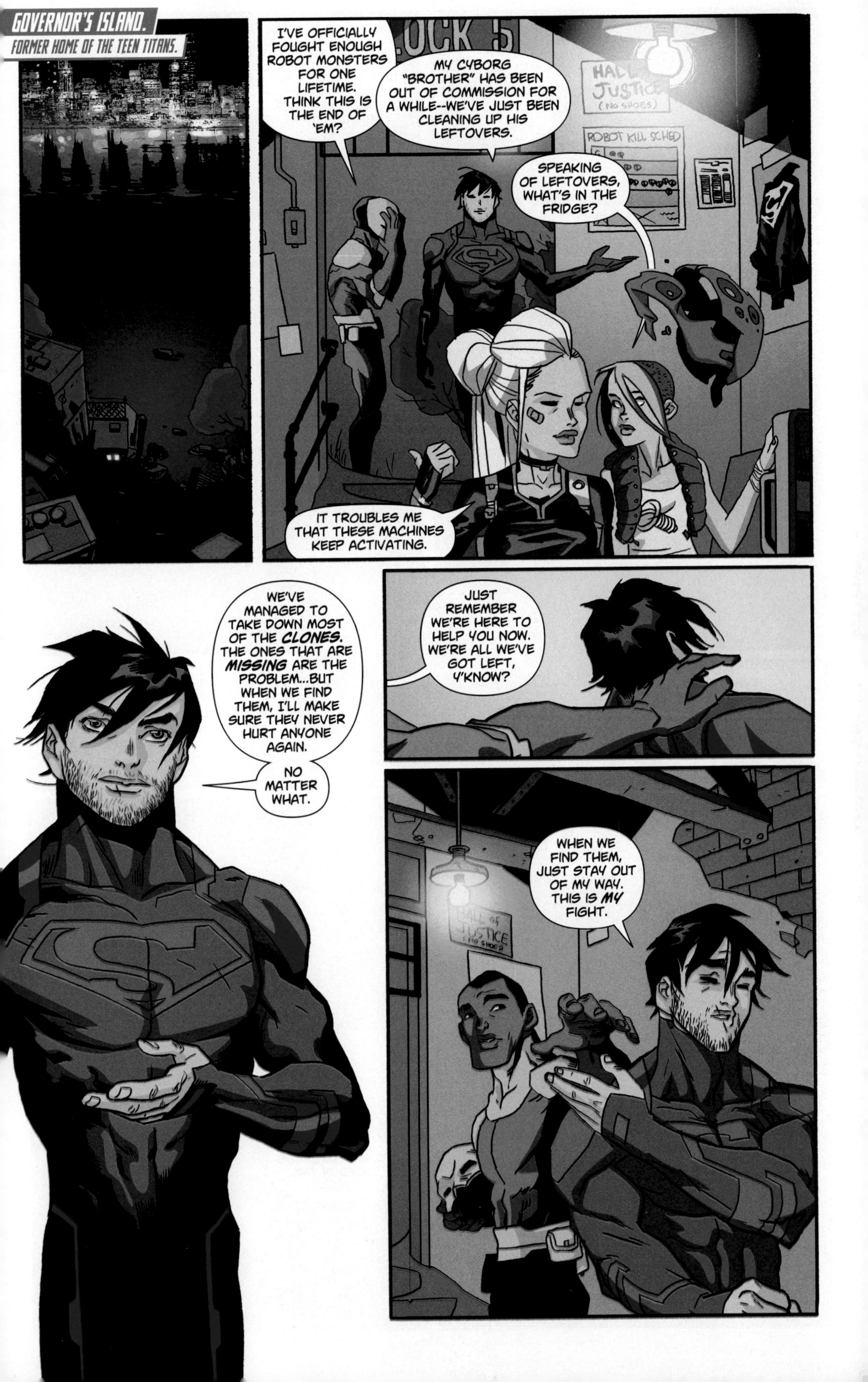
GOVERNOR'S ISLAND.
FORMER HOME OF THE TEEN TITANS.
I'VE OFFICIALLY FOUGHT ENOUGH ROBOT MONSTERS FOR ONE LIFETIME. THINK THIS IS THE END OF 'EM?
MY CYBORG "BROTHER" HAS BEEN OUT OF COMMISSION FOR A WHILE--WE'VE JUST BEEN CLEANING UP HIS LEFTOVERS.
SPEAKING OF LEFTOVERS, WHAT'S IN THE FRIDGE?
ROBOT KILL SCHED
IT TROUBLES ME THAT THESE MACHINES KEEP ACTIVATING.
WE'VE MANAGED TO TAKE DOWN MOST OF THE CLONES. THE ONES THAT ARE MISSING ARE THE PROBLEM...BUT WHEN WE FIND THEM, I'LL MAKE SURE THEY NEVER HURT ANYONE AGAIN.
NO MATTER WHAT.
JUST REMEMBER WE'RE HERE TO HELP YOU NOW. WE'RE ALL WE'VE GOT LEFT, Y'KNOW?
WHEN WE FIND THEM, JUST STAY OUT OF MY WAY. THIS IS MY FIGHT.
HALL OF JUSTICE (NO SHOES)

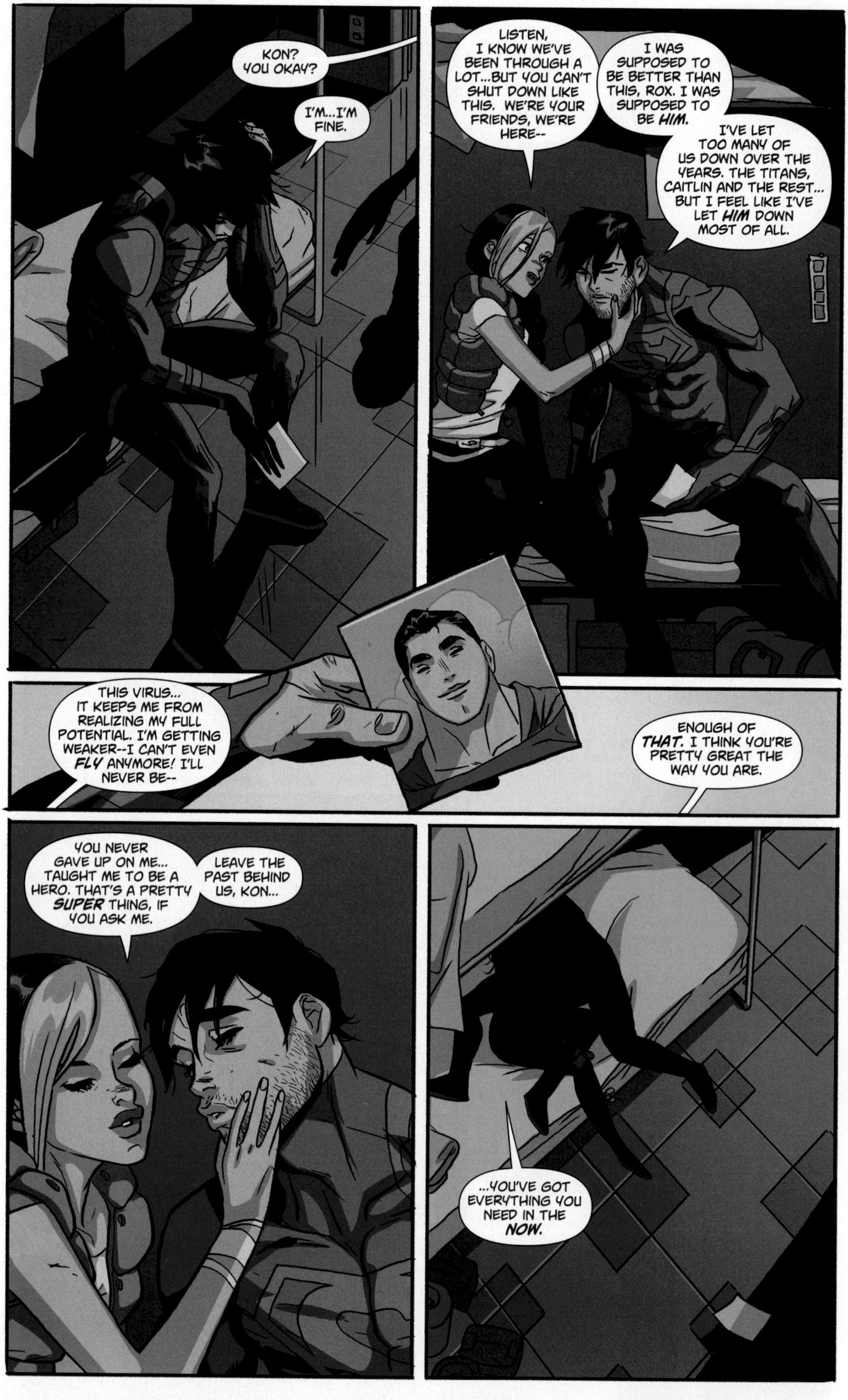
KON? YOU OKAY?
I'M...I'M FINE.
LISTEN, I KNOW WE'VE BEEN THROUGH A LOT...BUT YOU CAN'T SHUT DOWN LIKE THIS. WE'RE YOUR FRIENDS, WE'RE HERE--
I WAS SUPPOSED TO BE BETTER THAN THIS, ROX. I WAS SUPPOSED TO BE HIM.
I'VE LET TOO MANY OF US DOWN OVER THE YEARS. THE TITANS, CAITLIN AND THE REST... BUT I FEEL LIKE I'VE LET HIM DOWN MOST OF ALL.
THIS VIRUS... IT KEEPS ME FROM REALIZING MY FULL POTENTIAL. I'M GETTING WEAKER--I CAN'T EVEN FLY ANYMORE! I'LL NEVER BE--
ENOUGH OF THAT. I THINK YOU'RE PRETTY GREAT THE WAY YOU ARE.
YOU NEVER GAVE UP ON ME... TAUGHT ME TO BE A HERO. THAT'S A PRETTY SUPER THING, IF YOU ASK ME.
LEAVE THE PAST BEHIND US, KON...
...YOU'VE GOT EVERYTHING YOU NEED IN THE NOW.

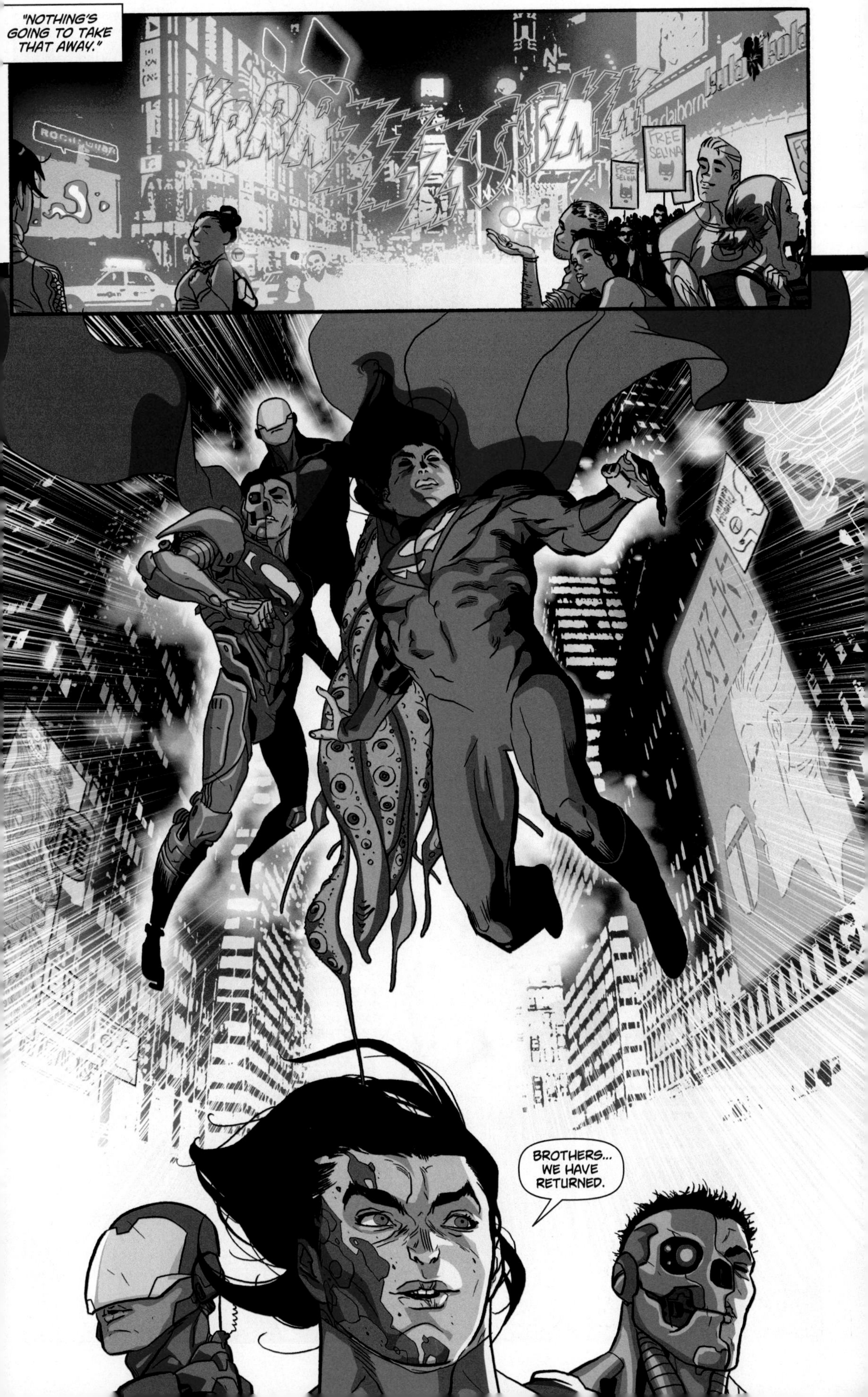
"NOTHING'S GOING TO TAKE THAT AWAY."
FREE SELINA
FREE SELINA
BROTHERS... WE HAVE RETURNED.

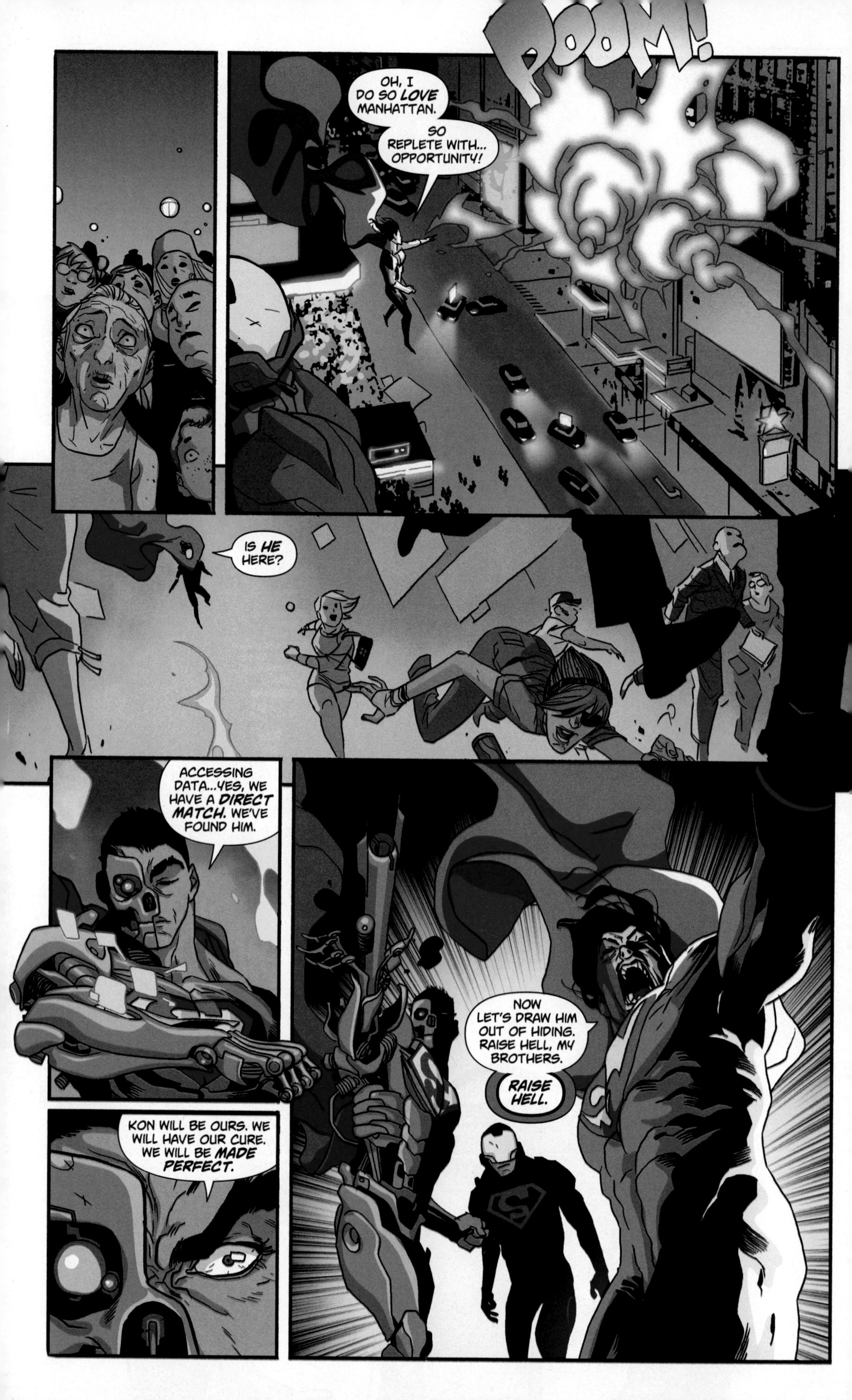
POOM!
OH, I DO SO LOVE MANHATTAN.
SO REPLETE WITH... OPPORTUNITY!
IS HE HERE?
ACCESSING DATA...YES, WE HAVE A DIRECT MATCH. WE'VE FOUND HIM.
KON WILL BE OURS. WE WILL HAVE OUR CURE. WE WILL BE MADE PERFECT.
NOW LET'S DRAW HIM OUT OF HIDING. RAISE HELL, MY BROTHERS.
RAISE HELL.

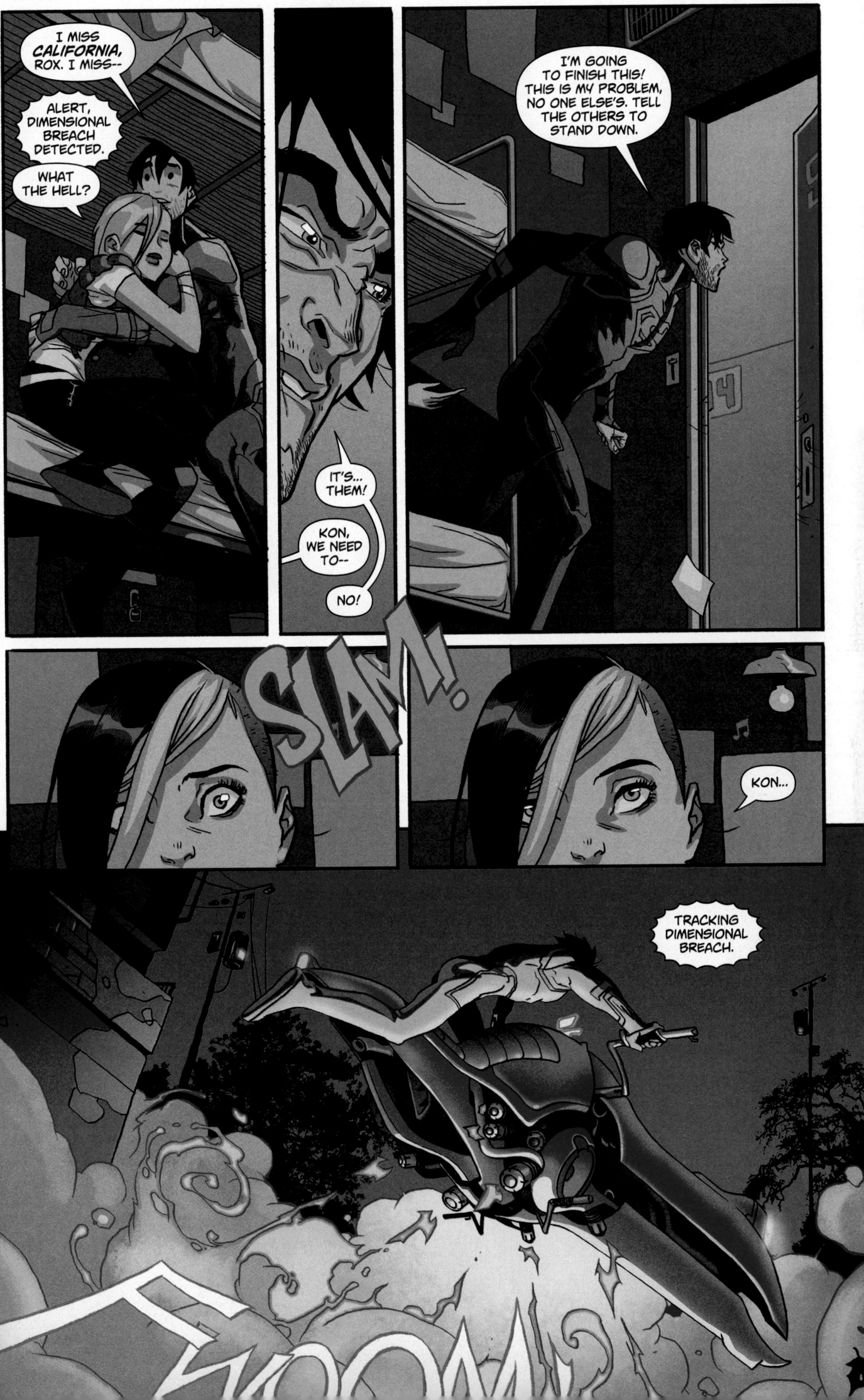
I MISS *CALIFORNIA*, ROX. I MISS--
ALERT, DIMENSIONAL BREACH DETECTED.
WHAT THE HELL?
IT'S... THEM!
KON, WE NEED TO--
NO!
I'M GOING TO FINISH THIS! THIS IS MY PROBLEM, NO ONE ELSE'S. TELL THE OTHERS TO STAND DOWN.
SLAM!
KON...
TRACKING DIMENSIONAL BREACH.

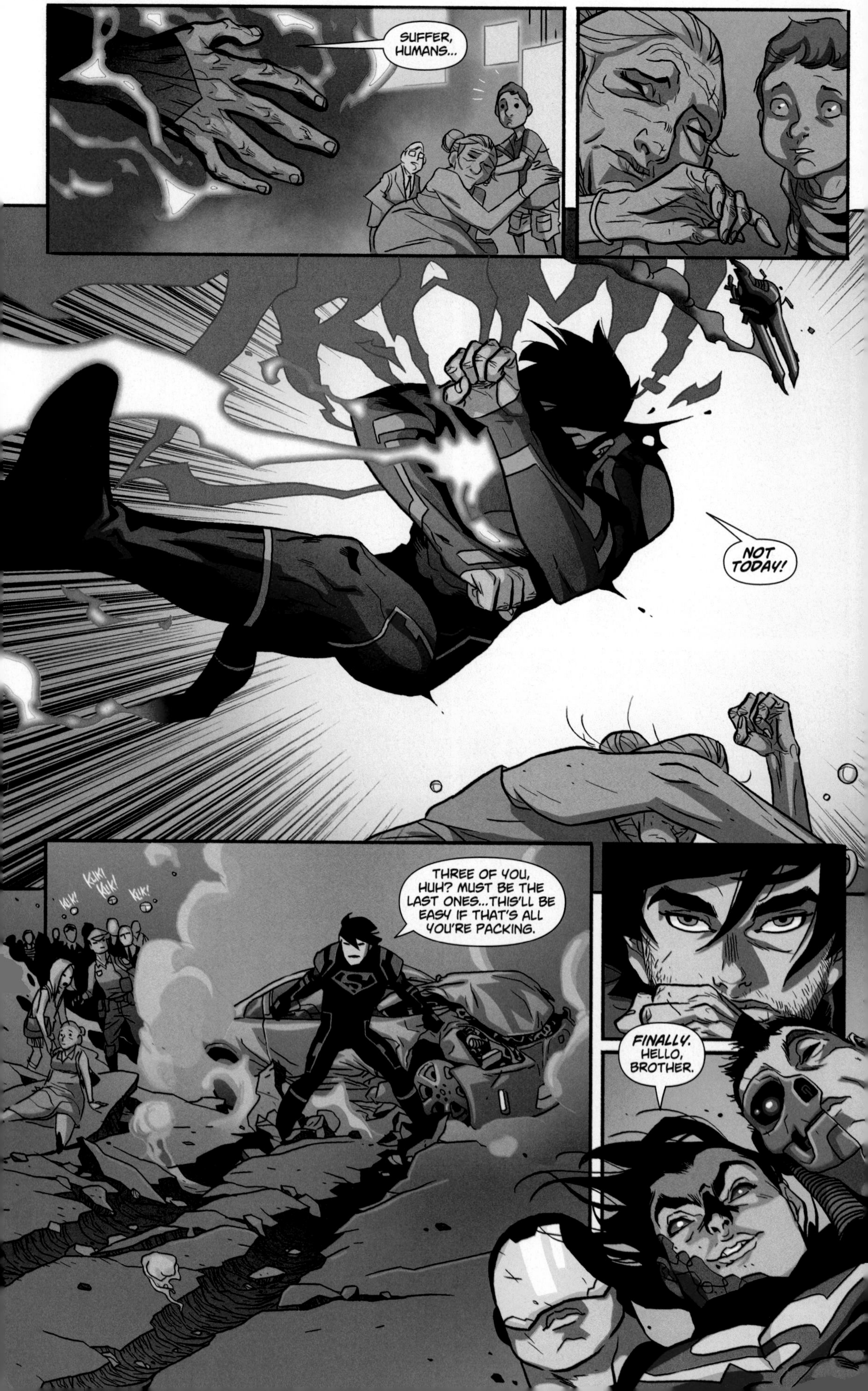
SUFFER, HUMANS...
NOT TODAY!
KLIK! KLIK! KLIK! KLIK!
THREE OF YOU, HUH? MUST BE THE LAST ONES...THIS'LL BE EASY IF THAT'S ALL YOU'RE PACKING.
FINALLY. HELLO, BROTHER.

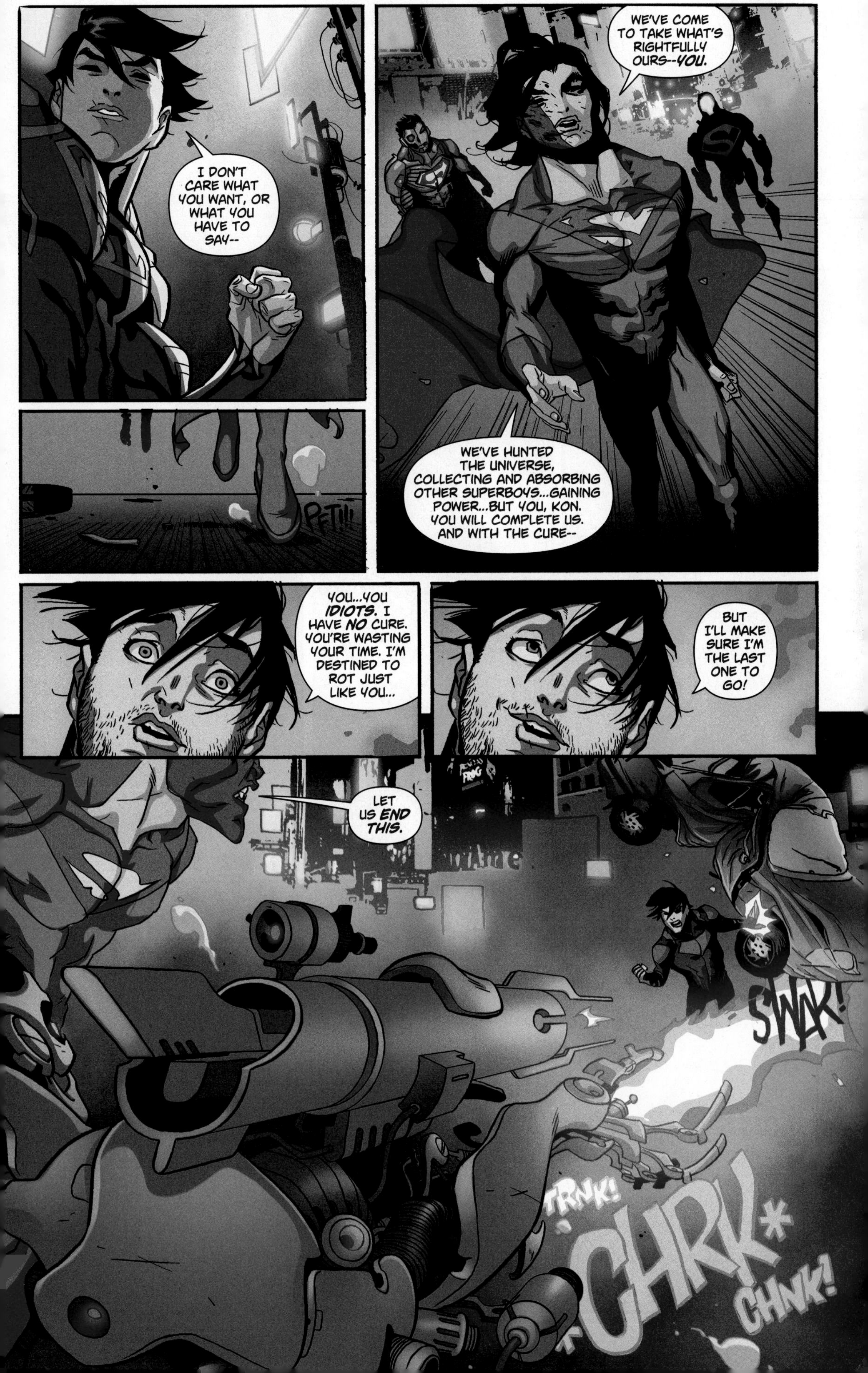
I DON'T CARE WHAT YOU WANT, OR WHAT YOU HAVE TO SAY--
WE'VE COME TO TAKE WHAT'S RIGHTFULLY OURS--YOU.
PFT!!!
WE'VE HUNTED THE UNIVERSE, COLLECTING AND ABSORBING OTHER SUPERBOYS...GAINING POWER...BUT YOU, KON. YOU WILL COMPLETE US. AND WITH THE CURE--
YOU...YOU IDIOTS. I HAVE NO CURE. YOU'RE WASTING YOUR TIME. I'M DESTINED TO ROT JUST LIKE YOU...
BUT I'LL MAKE SURE I'M THE LAST ONE TO GO!
LET US END THIS.
SWAK!
TRNK!
CHRK
CHNK!

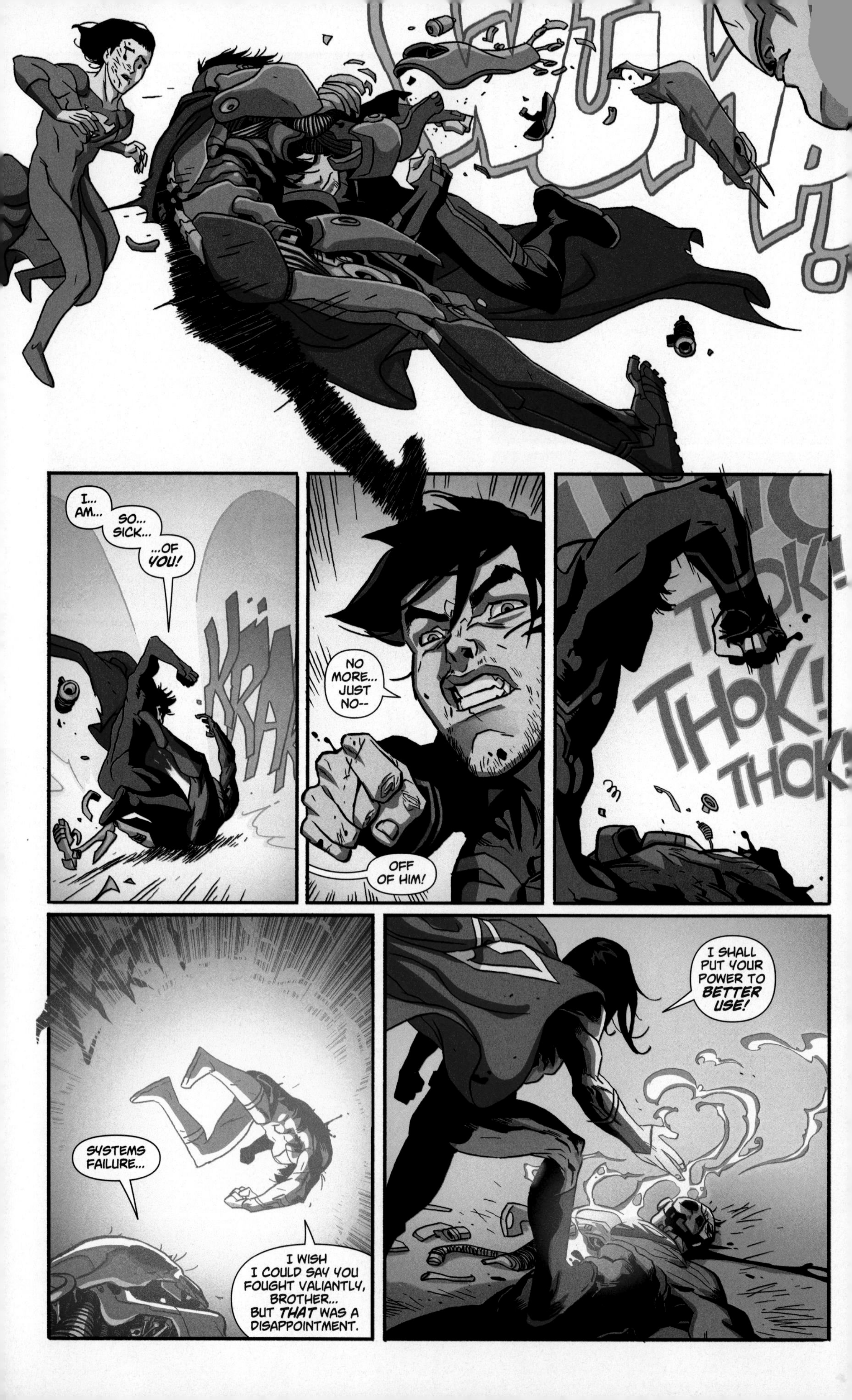
I... AM... SO... SICK... ...OF YOU!
NO MORE... JUST NO--
OFF OF HIM!
THOK! THOK! THOK!
SYSTEMS FAILURE...
I WISH I COULD SAY YOU FOUGHT VALIANTLY, BROTHER... BUT THAT WAS A DISAPPOINTMENT.
I SHALL PUT YOUR POWER TO BETTER USE!

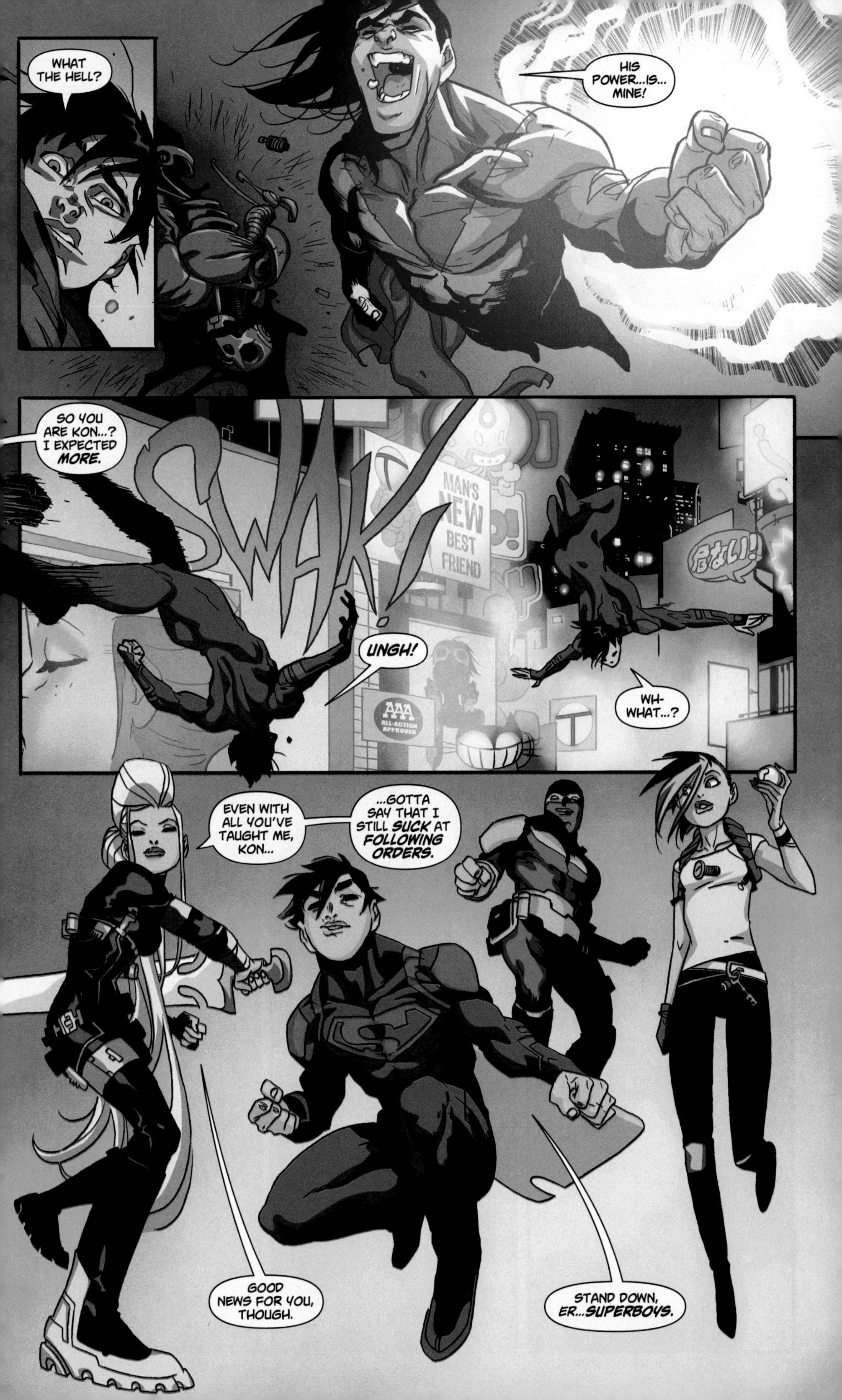
WHAT THE HELL?
HIS POWER...IS... MINE!
SO YOU ARE KON...? I EXPECTED MORE.
SWAK!
MAN'S NEW BEST FRIEND
危ない!
UNGH!
AAA ALL-ACTION APPROVED
WH-WHAT...?
EVEN WITH ALL YOU'VE TAUGHT ME, KON...
...GOTTA SAY THAT I STILL SUCK AT FOLLOWING ORDERS.
GOOD NEWS FOR YOU, THOUGH.
STAND DOWN, ER...SUPERBOYS.

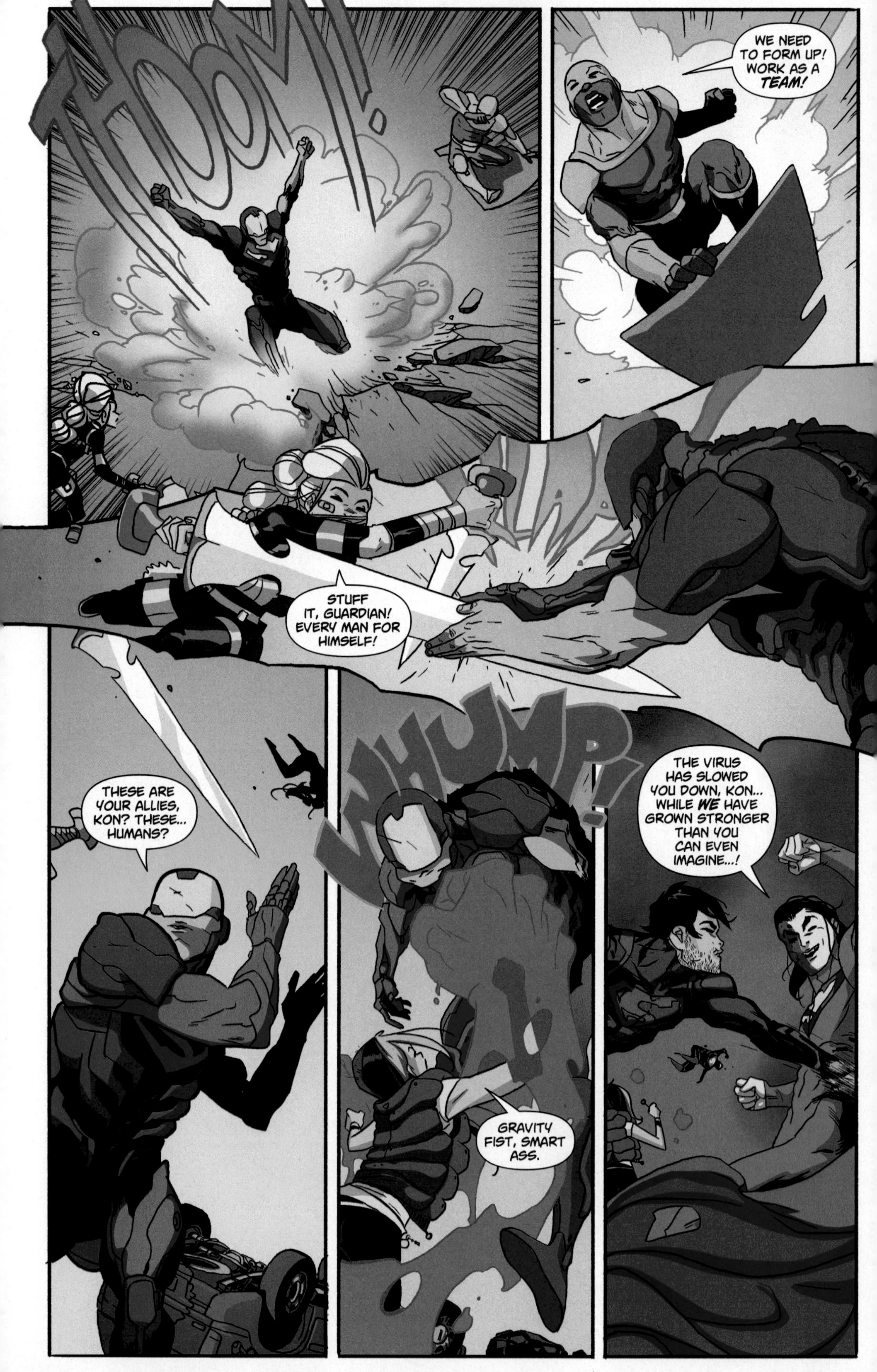
THOOM!
WE NEED TO FORM UP! WORK AS A *TEAM!*
STUFF IT, GUARDIAN! EVERY MAN FOR HIMSELF!
THESE ARE YOUR ALLIES, KON? THESE... HUMANS?
WHUMP!
GRAVITY FIST, SMART ASS.
THE VIRUS HAS SLOWED YOU DOWN, KON... WHILE *WE* HAVE GROWN STRONGER THAN YOU CAN EVEN IMAGINE...!

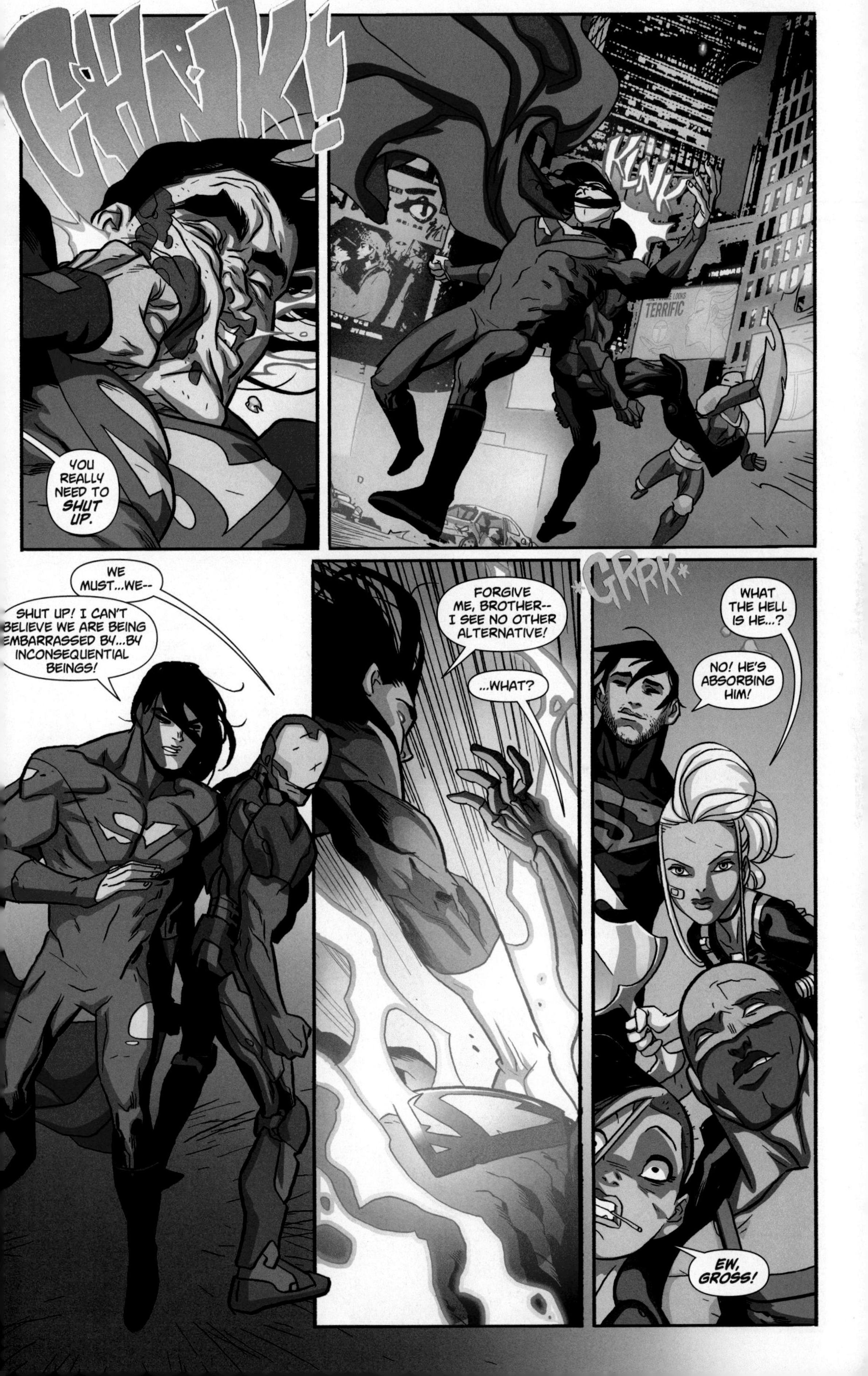
CHNK!
YOU REALLY NEED TO SHUT UP.
KLNK
THE FUTURE LOOKS TERRIFIC
WE MUST...WE--
SHUT UP! I CAN'T BELIEVE WE ARE BEING EMBARRASSED BY...BY INCONSEQUENTIAL BEINGS!
FORGIVE ME, BROTHER-- I SEE NO OTHER ALTERNATIVE!
...WHAT?
GRRK
WHAT THE HELL IS HE...?
NO! HE'S ABSORBING HIM!
EW, GROSS!

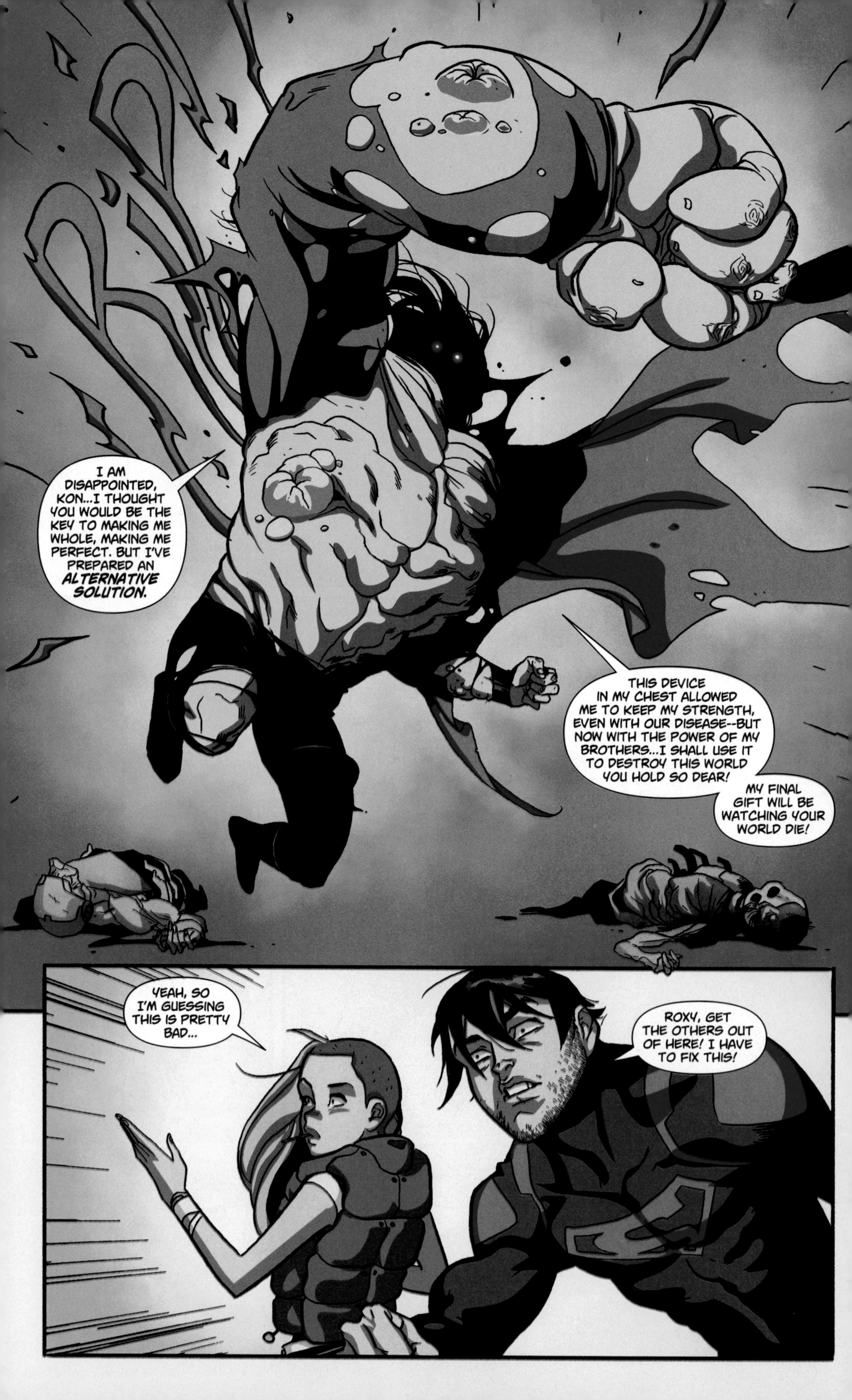

I AM DISAPPOINTED, KON...I THOUGHT YOU WOULD BE THE KEY TO MAKING ME WHOLE, MAKING ME PERFECT. BUT I'VE PREPARED AN *ALTERNATIVE SOLUTION.*
THIS DEVICE IN MY CHEST ALLOWED ME TO KEEP MY STRENGTH, EVEN WITH OUR DISEASE--BUT NOW WITH THE POWER OF MY BROTHERS...I SHALL USE IT TO DESTROY THIS WORLD YOU HOLD SO DEAR!
MY FINAL GIFT WILL BE WATCHING YOUR WORLD DIE!
YEAH, SO I'M GUESSING THIS IS PRETTY BAD...
ROXY, GET THE OTHERS OUT OF HERE! I HAVE TO FIX THIS!

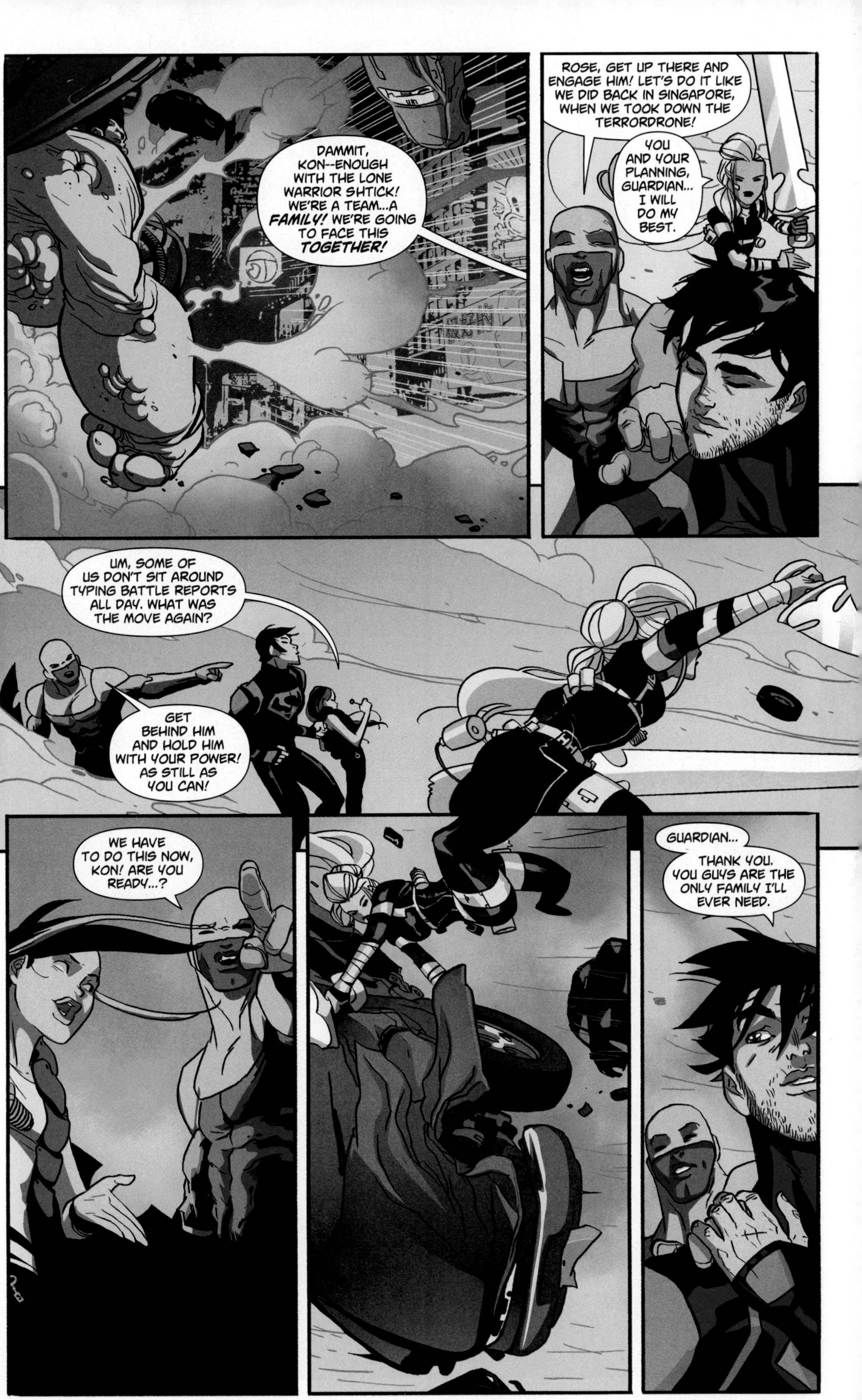
DAMMIT, KON--ENOUGH WITH THE LONE WARRIOR SHTICK! WE'RE A TEAM...A FAMILY! WE'RE GOING TO FACE THIS TOGETHER!
ROSE, GET UP THERE AND ENGAGE HIM! LET'S DO IT LIKE WE DID BACK IN SINGAPORE, WHEN WE TOOK DOWN THE TERRORDRONE!
YOU AND YOUR PLANNING, GUARDIAN... I WILL DO MY BEST.
UM, SOME OF US DON'T SIT AROUND TYPING BATTLE REPORTS ALL DAY. WHAT WAS THE MOVE AGAIN?
GET BEHIND HIM AND HOLD HIM WITH YOUR POWER! AS STILL AS YOU CAN!
WE HAVE TO DO THIS NOW, KON! ARE YOU READY...?
GUARDIAN...
THANK YOU. YOU GUYS ARE THE ONLY FAMILY I'LL EVER NEED.

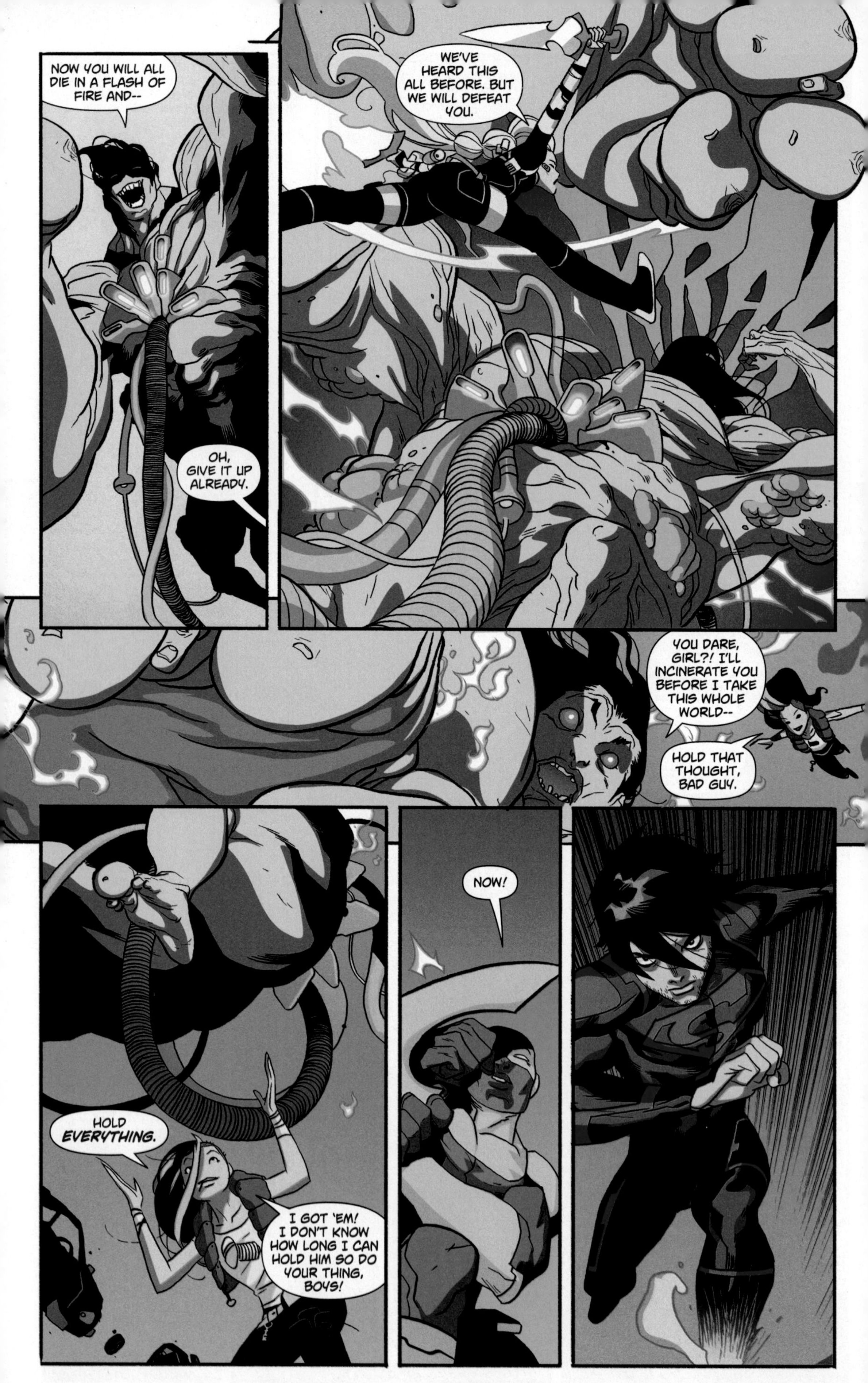
NOW YOU WILL ALL DIE IN A FLASH OF FIRE AND--
WE'VE HEARD THIS ALL BEFORE. BUT WE WILL DEFEAT YOU.
OH, GIVE IT UP ALREADY.
YOU DARE, GIRL?! I'LL INCINERATE YOU BEFORE I TAKE THIS WHOLE WORLD--
HOLD THAT THOUGHT, BAD GUY.
HOLD *EVERYTHING.*
I GOT 'EM! I DON'T KNOW HOW LONG I CAN HOLD HIM SO DO YOUR THING, BOYS!
NOW!

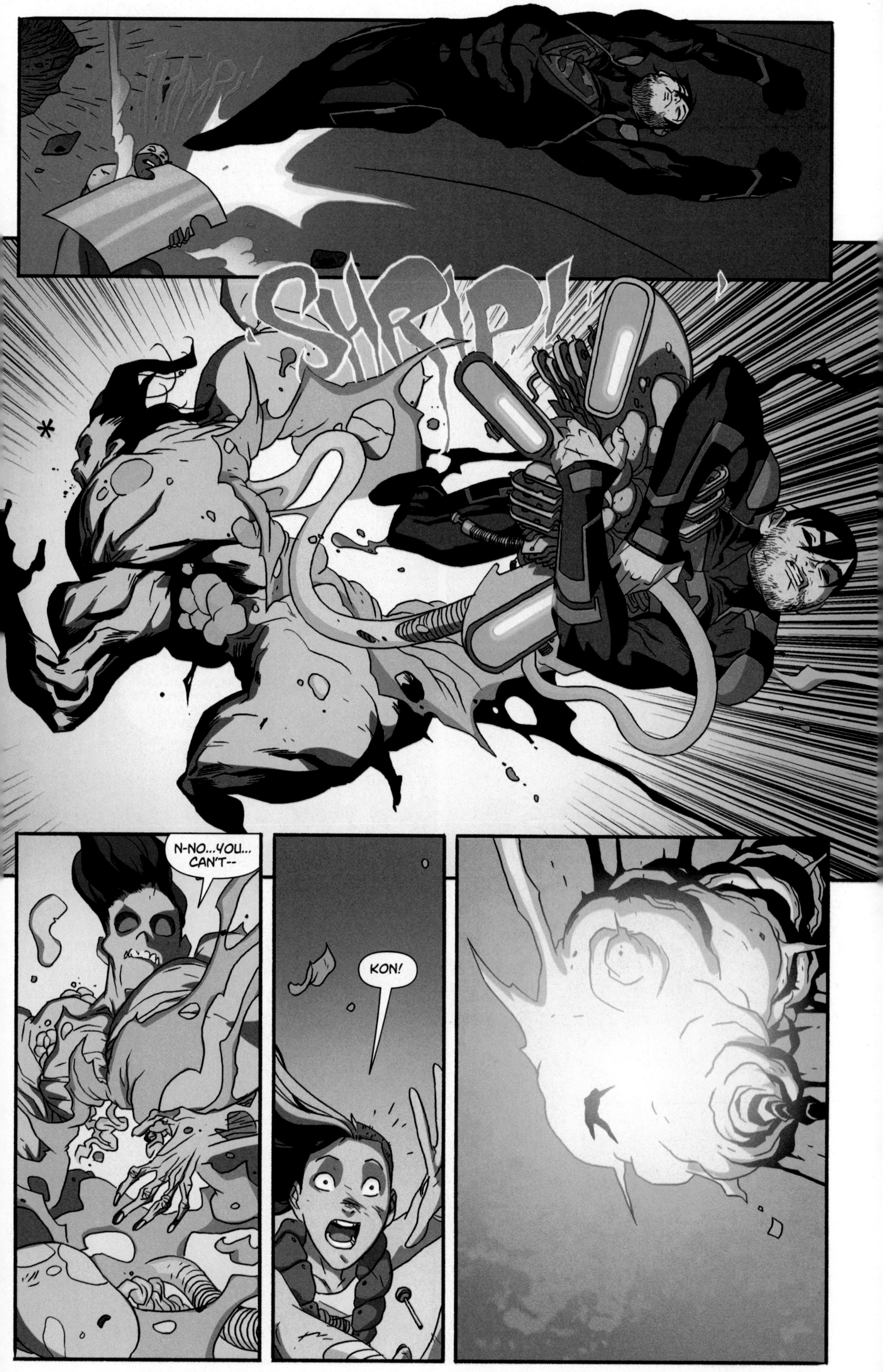
THMP!
SHRIP!
N-NO...YOU... CAN'T--
KON!

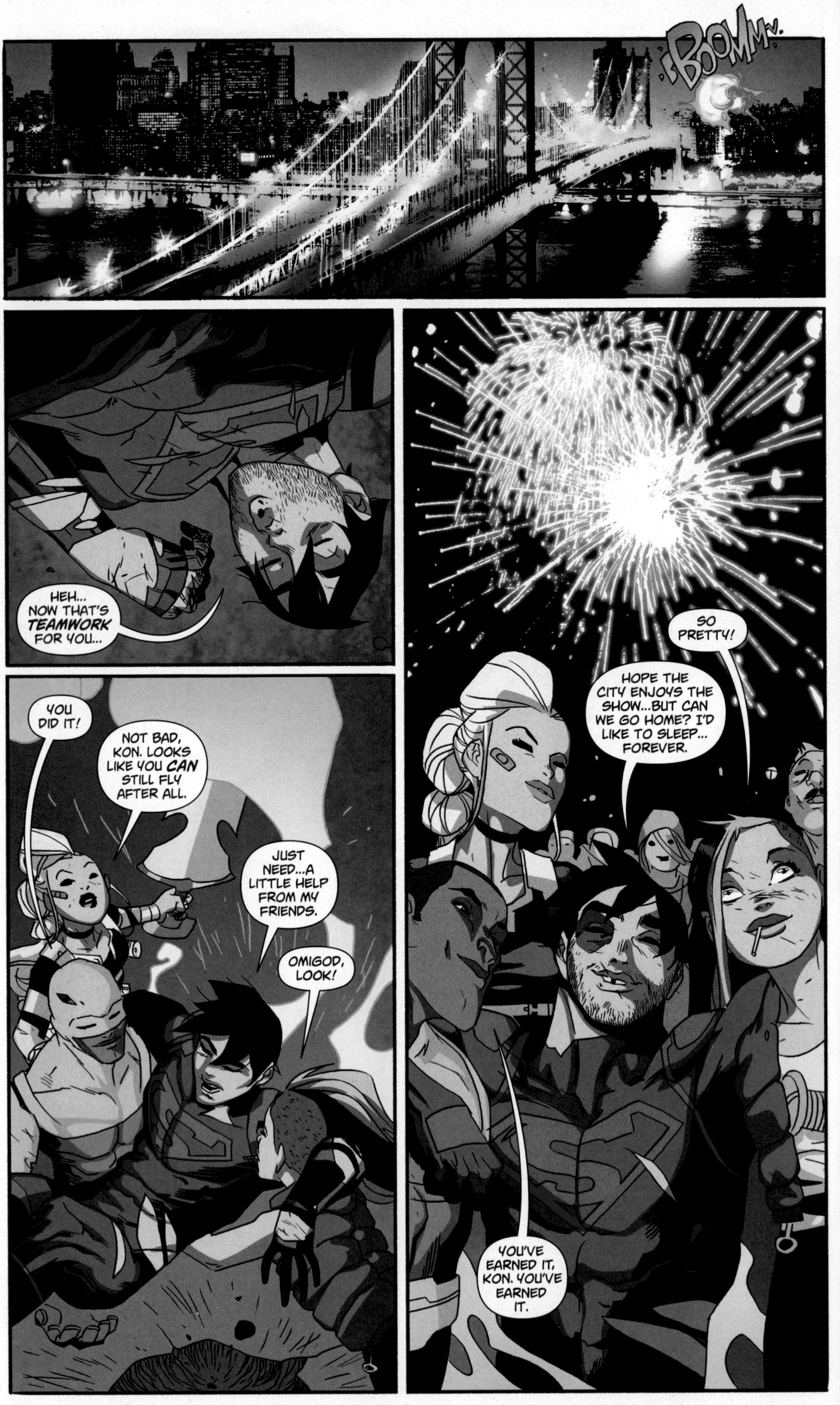
BOOMM
HEH... NOW THAT'S TEAMWORK FOR YOU...
YOU DID IT!
NOT BAD, KON. LOOKS LIKE YOU CAN STILL FLY AFTER ALL.
JUST NEED...A LITTLE HELP FROM MY FRIENDS.
OMIGOD, LOOK!
SO PRETTY!
HOPE THE CITY ENJOYS THE SHOW...BUT CAN WE GO HOME? I'D LIKE TO SLEEP... FOREVER.
YOU'VE EARNED IT, KON. YOU'VE EARNED IT.

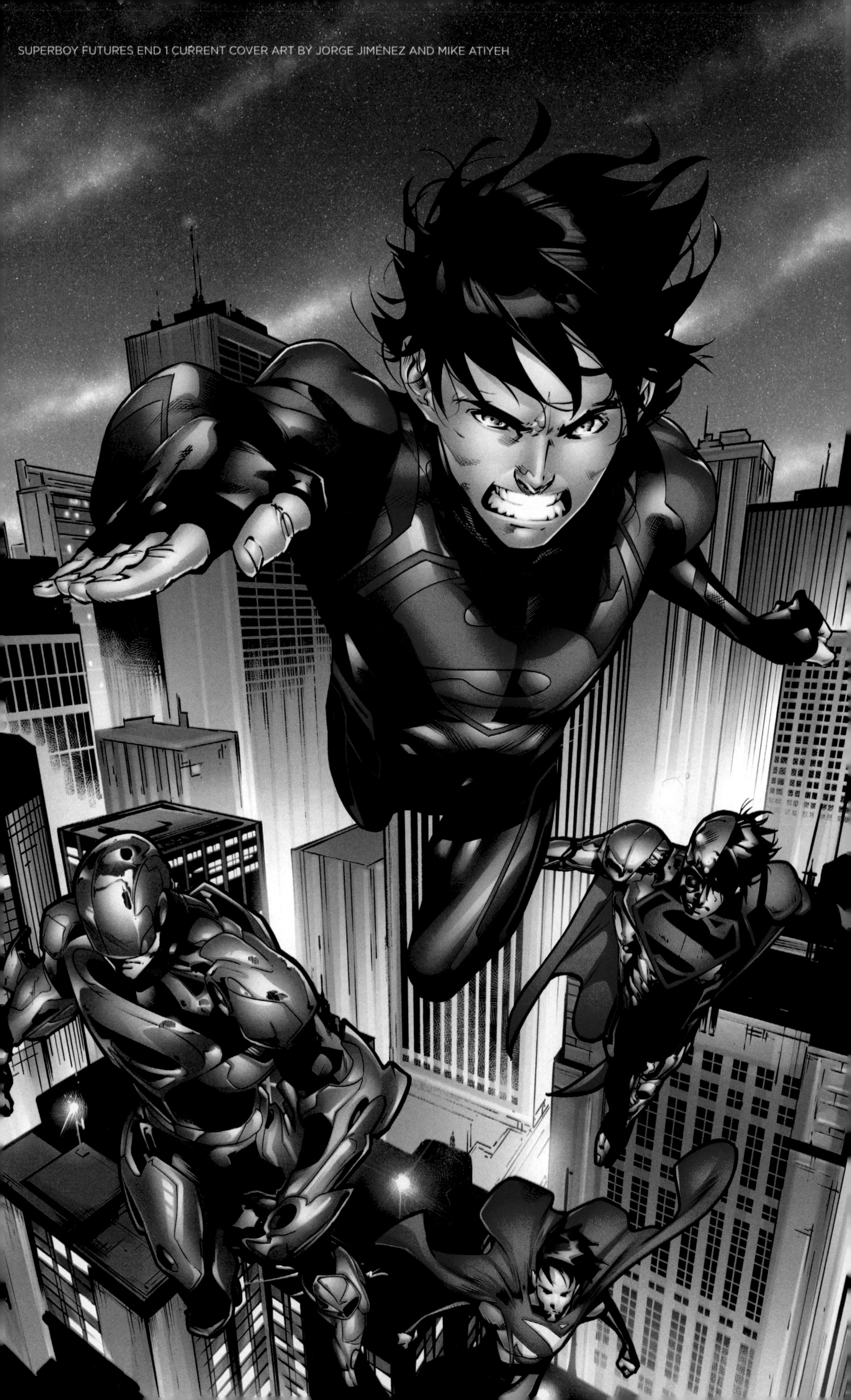

SUPERBOY FUTURES END 1 CURRENT COVER ART BY JORGE JIMÉNEZ AND MIKE ATIYEH

SUPERBOY #29 UNUSED COVER ART BY RAFA SANDOVAL, NORM RAPMUND AND MIKE ATIYEH

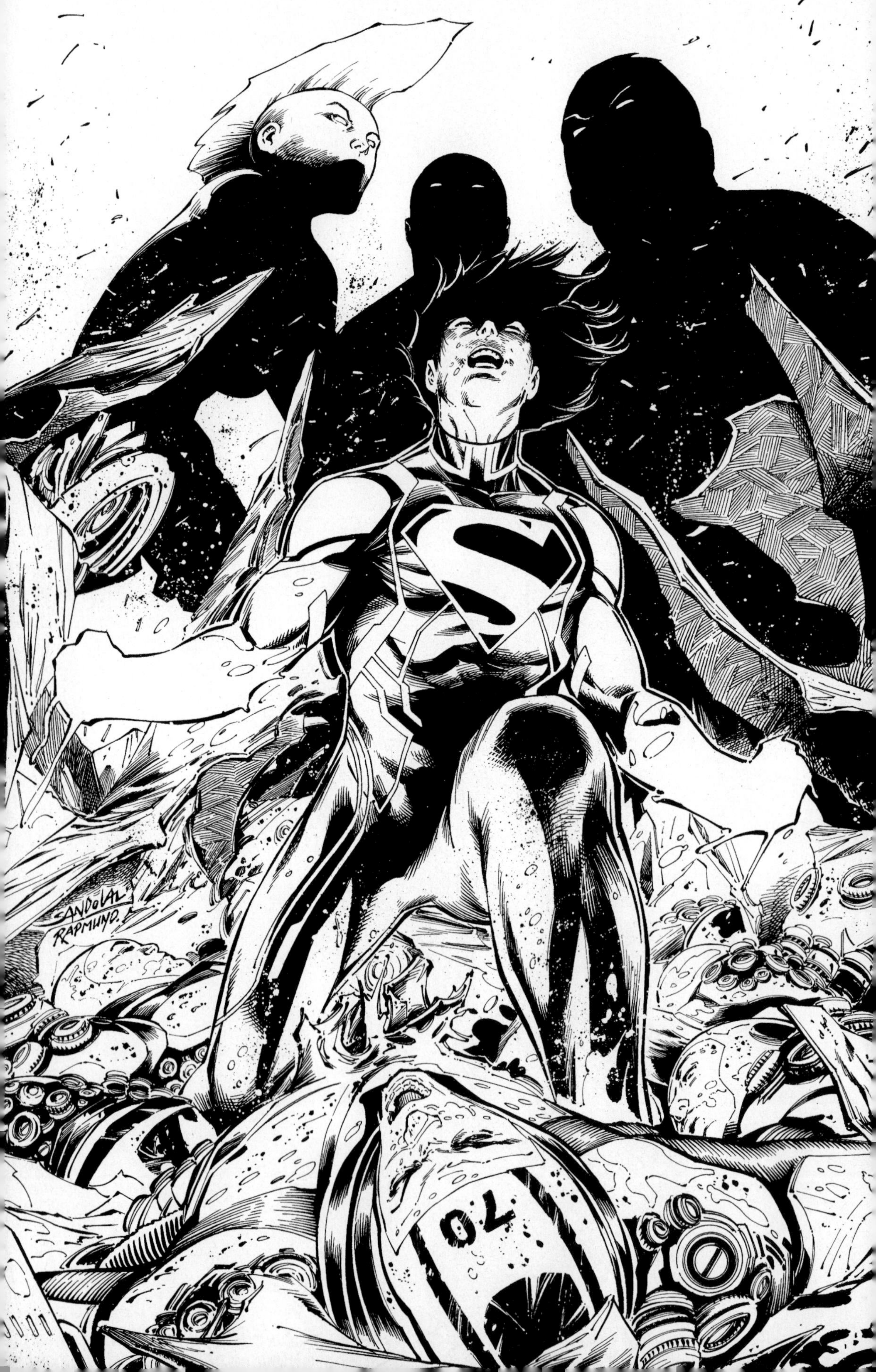
SANDOVAL
RAPMUND

START AT THE BEGINNING!

TEEN TITANS
VOLUME 1: IT'S OUR RIGHT TO FIGHT

TEEN TITANS VOL. 2: THE CULLING

TEEN TITANS VOL. 3: DEATH OF THE FAMILY

THE CULLING: RISE OF THE RAVAGERS

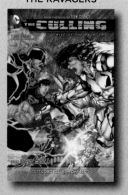

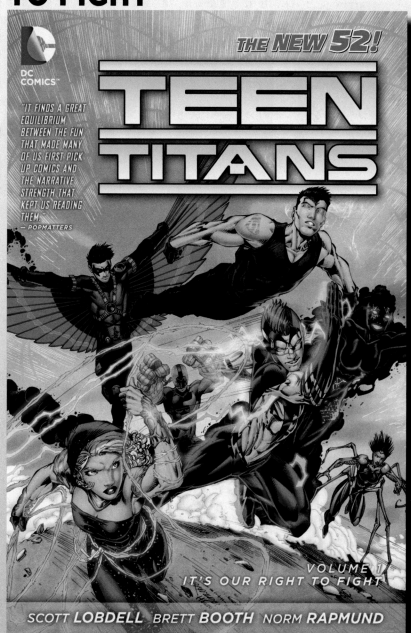

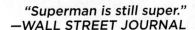

"Superman is still super."
—WALL STREET JOURNAL

"The SUPERMAN world is also one now where fans new and old, young and not-so-young, can come to a common ground to talk about the superhero that started it all."
—CRAVE ONLINE

START AT THE BEGINNING!

SUPERMAN VOLUME 1: WHAT PRICE TOMORROW?

SUPERMAN VOL. 2: SECRETS & LIES

SUPERMAN VOL. 3: FURY AT WORLD'S END

SUPERMAN: H'EL ON EARTH

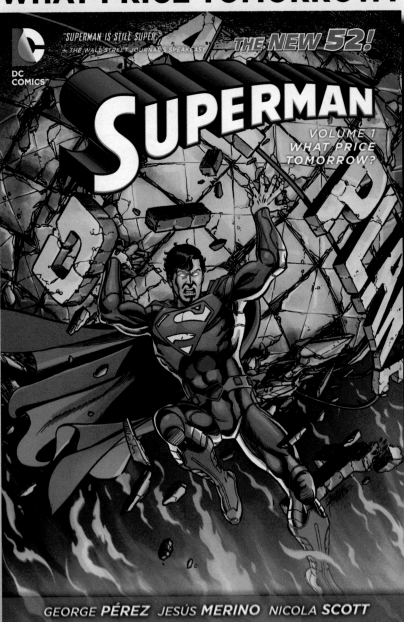

GEORGE **PÉREZ** JESÚS **MERINO** NICOLA **SCOTT**